Dale and Appelbe's
Pharmacy and Medicines Law

Dale and Appelbe's Pharmacy and Medicines Law

ELEVENTH EDITION

Edited by

Joy Wingfield   LL M, MPhil, BPharm, FRPharmS, Dip Ag Vet Pharm, FCPP

Honorary Professor of Pharmacy Law and Ethics, University of Nottingham, UK

Karen Pitchford   BSc (Hons), PGDip, MRPharmS, SFHEA

Senior Teaching Fellow in Pharmacy Law and Practice, Aston University, Birmingham, UK

Pharmaceutical Press

Published by the Pharmaceutical Press

66-68 East Smithfield, London E1W 1AW, UK

© Pharmaceutical Press 2017

(**P₁P**) is a trade mark of RPS Publishing

Pharmaceutical Press is the publishing division of the Royal Pharmaceutical Society

First published 1976
Second edition 1979
Third edition 1983
Fourth edition 1989
Fifth edition 1993
Sixth edition 1997
Seventh edition 2001
Eighth edition 2005
Ninth edition 2009
Tenth edition 2013
Eleventh edition 2017

i0078229032

Typeset by SPi Global, Chennai, India
Printed in Great Britain by TJ International, Padstow, Cornwall

Index provided by LNS Indexing

ISBN 978 0 85711 202 6 (print)
ISBN 978 0 85711 315 3 (ePDF)
ISBN 978 0 85711 316 0 (ePub)
ISBN 978 0 85711 317 7 (mobi)

Front cover images: © iStock.com/grinvalds; © Zadorozhnyi Viktor/Shutterstock.com

Contents

Preface to the Eleventh Edition

This book again seeks to provide in one volume an outline of the law that affects the practice of pharmacy in Great Britain. The editors hope that the book will prove useful not only to pharmacy undergraduates, pre-registration students and pharmacists in all branches of the profession, but also to others in Britain and overseas who may need some knowledge of contemporary British law relating to medicines and poisons and pharmacy professional regulation. The wide scope means that we have invited and incorporated new and revised material from well-known individuals in academia, professional and legal practice to bring the text up to date at the time of writing (November 2016). As ever, the period between the 10th and 11th editions has seen yet more changes in almost all of the areas of law and regulation addressed by this book. Although all the chapters needed some revision, we have tried to make the chapters on Controlled Drugs and poisons more accessible and user friendly through a complete re-write, added text on the Falsified Medicines Directive and pharmacovigilance to the relevant chapters, and included commentary on the latest standards and guidance from the General Pharmaceutical Council. Being some 7 years from the inception of the Council, the chapter on Fitness to Practise is now much enhanced with case law and revised procedural protocols. The NHS chapter continues to be challenging with many varying models of care developing across England but very little new national legislation to support consistency. The biggest change that we expect is, of course, 'Brexit', meaning that, at the time of going to press, a UK referendum had resulted in a decision to leave the EU. However, this process will take up to 2 years. Possible areas affected within the scope of this book include free movement and regulation of health professionals as well as all the legislation on medicines.

We have re-ordered and consolidated some chapters. Chapters 2–16 now cover all human medicines legislation, including Controlled Drugs;

chapter 17 covers legislation on animal medicines. A new chapter 18 consolidates the law on poisons, denatured alcohols and chemicals, few of which pass through the hands of pharmacists in modern times. Subsequent chapters are therefore re-numbered but their scope remains the same.

The law is that of Great Britain except where otherwise stated in the text. The aim has been to state the law as concisely as accuracy permits, but it should be borne in mind that only the courts can give a legally binding decision on any question of interpretation. The responsibility for the text and any views expressed therein lies with the editors and authors.

The original authors of this book have now passed away but we know that the name 'Dale and Appelbe' is recognised more widely than the title and we shall continue to retain this description. Both Joe Dale and Gordon Appelbe were staff members in the law department of the former Royal Pharmaceutical Society of Great Britain and they did the profession a great service by bringing together a law textbook to support the practice of pharmacists in Great Britain. With this edition, Joy Wingfield, also a former member of the same department, will relinquish further input and is pleased (and relieved) to have found an excellent successor in Karen Pitchford. The expansion of material means that no one person can sensibly update all the material and we are very grateful for the many specialists who have contributed to individual chapters. So please read our list of contributors – they represent a wealth of expertise and experience in the field of pharmacy law and regulation. Thanks also go to our publishers, in particular Heather Benson and Mark Pollard, for their forbearance in accommodating (again) an uncertain legislative programme that takes no account of publication dates!

Joy Wingfield
Karen Pitchford
November 2016

Foreword

In my Foreword to the 10th edition, written in February 2013, I highlighted what seemed to me at the time to be the increasingly fast pace of change affecting pharmacy practice. In hindsight I realise that I was grossly understating not only the pace but also the scope and scale of change affecting every aspect of pharmacy practice. Some of the debates we see going on reflect the uncertainty and indeed sometimes the frustration and concern that are so often a feature of significant change:

> "*What, if any, is the supposed distinction between a 'clinical pharmacist' working in general practice and a pharmacist who has always regarded themselves as a clinician in a community setting?*"

> "*What can a pharmacy technician do, and why won't the regulator – or someone else – just please tell me?*"

> "*How do we reconcile the professional ethos with the commercial imperative in times of pressure and austerity?*"

And fundamentally...

> "*Is there going to be a role for me and my skills in future?*"

What contribution can the professional regulator possibly make that might be helpful, at such a time?

Throughout 2016 we were working on, among many other important projects, the new standards for pharmacy professionals. Following extensive engagement, consultation and reflection, the text of these new standards has been agreed by the GPhC Council and they are coming into force in 2017.

The standards set out the attitudes and behaviours expected of pharmacy professionals, which in our view make the most significant contribution to the quality of care people receive. In many ways the principles they articulate are not new, and build on those which we have upheld since we came into existence in 2010. Yet there are three particular themes which are given a new prominence in the 2017 text which are strikingly relevant in times of uncertainty. The strengthened focus within our new standards on these three themes is timely:

- Candour: the duty to be open about mistakes and problems is now well-understood at the level of individual practitioners and patients or service-users; maybe we need to encourage greater candour at the macro level, about the challenges facing pharmacy professionals.
- Leadership: as the regulator we are explicitly calling upon all members of the pharmacy professions to step up to leadership. Within teams of all different sizes and shapes, leadership can and should be offered and welcomed at every level, regardless of hierarchies. If the most 'junior' team member points out an opportunity to improve patient safety for example, colleagues should welcome the leadership that their junior colleague has shown.
- Person-centredness: the new standards remind pharmacy professionals of the fundamental importance of devoting their energy and focus to the individual they are serving, appreciating them as an individual with unique priorities, values and sensibilities. An essential reminder of what professionalism is about, at a time when many aspects of professional self-identity may feel as if they are under threat.

Once again the writers and editors of *Dale and Appelbe* are to be congratulated and thanked for explaining so clearly and comprehensively the legal parameters within which pharmacy professionals are practising. I am sure it will prove a useful resource when pharmacy professionals are making their own unique contribution to the health and wellbeing of individual women, men, children, families and communities.

Duncan Rudkin
Chief Executive and Registrar
General Pharmaceutical Council
April 2017

About the contributors

Editors

Joy Wingfield, LL M, MPhil, BPharm, FRPharmS, DipAgVetPharm, FCPP, is Honorary Professor of Pharmacy Law and Ethics at the University of Nottingham and an independent pharmacy practice consultant. She qualified as a pharmacist in 1971 and then worked for 5 years in community pharmacy. She joined the staff of the Pharmaceutical Society in 1976 as an inspector under the Pharmacy Acts. From 1986 to 1991, she was the senior administrator in, and later head of, the Ethics Division in the Law Department, responsible for professional and registration matters. This was followed by 9 years as the assistant pharmacy superintendent for Boots before moving into academia.

Karen Pitchford, BSc(Hons), PGDip, MRPharmS, SFHEA, is a Senior Teaching Fellow in Pharmacy Law and Practice at Aston University. She qualified as a pharmacist in 1993 and then worked in community pharmacy for 9 years, as a pharmacy manager and then as a teacher/practitioner at Liverpool John Moores University. She joined the Leicester School of Pharmacy in 2002, where she held the role of Principal Lecturer in Pharmacy Law and Practice until early 2017, when she joined Aston University. She is a member of the Royal Pharmaceutical Society's Medicines, Ethics and Practice advisory panel and of the General Pharmaceutical Council's Board of Assessors and Accreditation and Recognition Panel.

Contributors

Sarah ME Cockbill, PhD, LL M, BPharm, MPharm, DipAgVetPharm, MIPharmM, FCPP, FRPharmS
Lecturer, Cardiff School of Pharmacy & Pharmaceutical Sciences

Ann Godsell, BSc(Hons)
Director, AGRegulatory Ltd

Michael Goodman, PhD, BSc, MRSC
Formerly Senior Lecturer, De Montfort University

Gordon Hockey, BSc(Hons), MRPharmS
Pharmacist and Barrister, Director of Operations and Support,
Pharmaceutical Services Negotiating Committee, formerly Registrar at
the Royal College of Veterinary Surgeons

Dai John, BPharm LL M, PhD, FHEA, FRPharmS
Professor of Pharmacy, Cardiff University

Thomas H John, BPharm(Lond.) LL B, MRPharmS (non-practising)
Barrister-at-Law (called 1997 by the Honourable Society of the
Middle Temple), Head, Goresbrook Chambers, Essex and self-employed
barrister in independent practice

Stephen Lutener, LL B, FRPharmS
Former Head of Regulation, Pharmaceutical Services Negotiating Committee

Edward Mallinson, LL M, MPharm, FRPharmS, Hon MFPH, FRSPH
Retired Consultant in Pharmaceutical Public Health

Susan Melvin, LL M, BSc, MRPharmS
Inspector of the General Pharmaceutical Council

David H Reissner, LL B(Hons)
Solicitor of the Senior Courts, Partner, Head of Healthcare at Charles
Russell Speechlys LLP

Helen Root, PGCertHE, MPharm(Hons), FHEA, MRPharmS
Senior Lecturer in Clinical Pharmacy and Pharmacy Practice, De Montfort University

Zoe Smith, BSc(Hons)
Manager, Medical Sales & Regulatory Affairs, Superintendent
Pharmacist, Weleda UK

Introduction

Development of the law in relation to pharmacy, medicines and poisons

Before the middle of the 19th century, there were no legal restrictions in England on the sale of poisons or drugs, and anyone could describe themselves as a pharmaceutical chemist. Statutory control over sales was first applied to arsenic because, as the preamble to the Arsenic Act 1851 stated, the unrestricted sale of arsenic facilitates the commission of crime. The first statute relating to pharmacy followed the next year. The Pharmacy Act 1852 confirmed the charter of incorporation of the Pharmaceutical Society of Great Britain, which had been granted in 1843. The 1852 Act established the framework of the Society and gave it power to hold examinations and to issue certificates. It also restricted the use of the title pharmaceutical chemist to members of the Society, although it did not restrict the use of the titles chemist or druggist. The Society received its Royal prefix in 1988. In 2010, the Society was wound up to be replaced by two bodies: the regulator, the General Pharmaceutical Council, and a new professional leadership body, the Royal Pharmaceutical Society. This book focuses only on the first of these bodies.

The Pharmacy Act 1868 brought new developments. It introduced a Poisons List (with 15 entries) and empowered the Society to add other substances to it, subject to the approval of the Privy Council. A poison was defined as any substance included in the Poisons List. Articles and preparations containing poisons could be sold by retail only by pharmaceutical chemists or by a new legal class of chemists and druggists. Both titles were protected by the Act. The class of chemists and druggists comprised (a) all those who before the passing of the Act had been engaged in the keeping of open shop for the compounding of the prescriptions of duly qualified medical practitioners, and (b) all those persons who had been registered as assistants under the provisions of the Pharmacy Act 1852.

The Registrar of the Society was thereafter required to keep registers of pharmaceutical chemists, of chemists and druggists, and of apprentices or students. The qualification of chemist and druggist (the Minor examination) became the statutory minimum for persons carrying on a business comprising the sale of poisons. Chemists and druggists were eligible to be elected members or associates of the Pharmaceutical Society but did not have all the privileges of a member who had qualified as a pharmaceutical chemist (by passing the Major examination). That state of affairs continued – slightly modified by a statute of 1898 – until the Pharmacy Act 1953 combined the two qualifications in one Register of Pharmaceutical Chemists. The profession of pharmacy was now regulated by the Pharmacy Act 1954, which absorbed the 1953 Act. The 1954 Act was subsequently repealed by a section 60 Order under the Health Act 1999, which paved the way for specific legislation establishing the General Pharmaceutical Council.

The 1868 Act not only introduced the first list of poisons but also regulated the manner in which they could be sold, specifying more stringent restrictions on sale for the more dangerous poisons. Fixed penalties, recoverable in the civil courts, were prescribed for breaches of the Act. The list of poisons was extended by the Poisons and Pharmacy Act 1908, which also stipulated that poisons for agricultural and horticultural purposes could be sold by licensed dealers as well as by pharmacists. This Act also prescribed conditions under which corporate bodies could carry on the business of a chemist and druggist. This had become necessary because it had been held in the High Court in 1880 that an incorporated company was not covered by the word person as used in the 1868 Act and was, therefore, not liable for penalties under the Act (*Pharmaceutical Society v London and Provincial Supply Association Ltd*, see earlier editions of this book).

Under the Pharmacy and Poisons Act 1933, a Poisons Board was established to advise the Secretary of State on what should be included in the Poisons List. Poisons in Part I of the list could be sold by retail only at pharmacies; poisons in Part II could be sold also by traders on a local authority list. Poisons were further classified by means of the Schedules to the Poisons Rules made under the Act. Schedule 4, for example, comprised a class of poisons which could be supplied to the public only on the authority of a prescription written by a practitioner. A Register of Premises was set up under the Act, and all registered pharmacists were required to be members of the Pharmaceutical Society.

One of the main features of the 1933 Act was the establishment of a disciplinary body (the Statutory Committee), which had authority not only over pharmacists who committed misconduct but also over pharmacists and corporate bodies convicted of offences under the Pharmacy Act. The Society was placed under a duty to enforce the Act and was authorised to appoint inspectors for the purpose. Proceedings under the Act were to be taken in courts of summary jurisdiction and not, as previously, in the civil courts. The Pharmacy and Poisons Act 1933 was repealed by the Medicines Act 1968. The Poisons Act 1972 dealt only with non-medicinal poisons. The Statutory Committee and its cases was replaced by a Disciplinary Committee in 2007 and then by the current Fitness to Practise processes of the General Pharmaceutical Council in 2010.

Pharmacy and poisons were firmly linked together by statute, but the sale and manufacture of medicines were not regulated in any way except for medicines containing poisons. Some control over quality was provided by a series of Food and Drugs Acts, culminating in the Food and Drugs Act 1955. Under those Acts, it was an offence to sell adulterated drugs, or to sell, to the prejudice of the purchaser, any drug not of the nature, substance or quality demanded. The effectiveness of those provisions was limited by the fact that most drugs were of vegetable origin and there were no precise standards for many of them. Furthermore, a manufacturer of a proprietary medicine did not have to disclose its composition, provided that s/he paid the appropriate duty by way of fixing the appropriate excise stamps to each bottle or packet as required by the Medicine Stamp Acts. That state of affairs was changed by the Pharmacy and Medicines Act 1941, which abolished medicines stamp duty and required, instead, a disclosure of composition of each container. It also restricted the sale of medicines to shops (as distinct from market stalls, etc.) and made it unlawful to advertise any article for the treatment of eight named diseases, including diabetes, epilepsy and tuberculosis. This was the first statute in which pharmacy and medicines were directly linked. The 1941 Act, however, did not apply to animal medicines.

The Therapeutic Substances Act 1925 controlled by licence the manufacture (but not the sale or supply) of a limited number of products the purity or potency of which could not be tested by chemical means, for example vaccines, sera, toxins, antitoxins and certain other substances. The list was greatly extended when antibiotics came into use. It had not been held necessary to restrict the retail sale or supply of vaccines, sera and antitoxins, but penicillin and most other antibiotics were found to be substances which were capable of causing danger to the health of the community if used without proper safeguards. Consequently, the Penicillin Act 1947 and the Therapeutic Substances (Prevention of Misuse) Act 1953 permitted the supply of antibiotics to the public only by practitioners, or from pharmacies on the authority of practitioners' prescriptions. The Therapeutic Substances Act 1956 replaced the earlier Acts, so bringing under the control of one statute both the manufacture and the supply of therapeutic substances. It could be regarded as the precursor to the Medicines Act 1968, which replaced it.

Legislation relating to medicines developed in a piecemeal manner, each problem being dealt with as it arose, and the law was scattered throughout a number of statutes. However, rapid developments in pharmaceutical research after the Second World War made available an increasing number of potent substances for use in medicine, and a working party was set up by the government in 1959 to examine the need for new controls. The thalidomide tragedy in 1961 almost certainly precipitated proposals for new legislation, which was published in 1967 in a White Paper entitled Forthcoming Legislation on the Safety, Quality and Description of Drugs and Medicines (Cmnd.3395). The Medicines Act 1968, which was designed to replace all earlier legislation relating to medicines, was based on the proposals in the White Paper.

European Community legislation has had, and still has, a large impact on UK law. The Treaty of Rome and the issue of regulations, directives, decisions and recommendations by the Council of Ministers in Brussels has led to amendments of pharmacy and medicines law in Great Britain, particularly with regard to the mutual recognition of pharmaceutical qualifications and the manufacture and distribution of medicines. In 2005, veterinary (animal) medicines were removed from the 1968 Medicines Act and consolidated under the European Communities Act 1972, with a view to annual updating. By 2012, the need to maintain compliance with European directives precipitated a consolidation and review of all the human medicines (but not pharmacy) regulations issued under the Medicines Act, to issue a single consolidated set of regulations, again under the European Communities Act 1972. The Medicines Act 1968 currently still contains the substantive provisions covering registered pharmacy businesses.

International agreement about the control of narcotics began with the International Opium Convention signed at The Hague in 1912, although the Convention was not implemented until after the First World War. A series of Dangerous Drugs Acts, beginning with the Dangerous Drugs Act 1920, brought the various international agreements into force in Great Britain. The Single Convention on Narcotic Drugs 1961 replaced all the earlier international agreements and was reflected in the Dangerous Drugs Act 1965.

The misuse of amphetamines and other psychotropic drugs widened the problems of abuse, and an International Convention on Psychotropic Substances was signed in 1971. In Great Britain, however, the Drugs (Prevention of Misuse) Act 1964 had provided a measure of control by making the unlawful possession of amphetamines, and certain other drugs, an offence. As problems of drug abuse continued to increase, the law was extended and recast in the Misuse of Drugs Act 1971, which repealed the various Dangerous Drugs Acts and the 1964 Act. The provisions of the 1971 Act and a series of regulations continue to apply to all aspects of dealings in Controlled Drugs.

The National Health Service Act 1946 and the National Health Service (Scotland) Act 1947 provided for a comprehensive health service across Great Britain, including the provision of pharmaceutical services. By 1999, both Scotland and Wales secured devolution of power in matters of health, and their legislation, organisation and practice within the NHS now differ considerably from those of England. Also in 1991, Crown immunity was removed from NHS services provided in hospitals and elsewhere such that medicines licensing legislation applies equally to services within the managed sector and the private sector (however, supply of medicines within hospitals remains exempted from the legislation).

List of legislation

European law

Reference	Title	Chapter
65/65/EEC	Directive on the approximation of provisions laid down by Law, Regulation or Administrative Action relating to proprietary medicinal products (now superseded), amended by Directive 87/21/EEC on the approximation of provisions laid down by law, regulation or administrative action relating to proprietary medicinal products	1, 2, 3
78/25/EEC	Directive on the colouring matters which may be added to medicinal products	1
85/432/EEC	Directive concerning the coordination of provisions laid down by Law, Regulation or Administrative Action in respect of certain activities in the field of pharmacy	1
85/433/EEC	Directive concerning the mutual recognition of diplomas, certificates and other evidence of formal qualifications in pharmacy, including measures to facilitate the effective exercise of the right of establishment relating to certain activities in the field of pharmacy	1
89/105/EEC	Directive relating to the transparency of measures regulating the pricing of medicinal products for human use and their inclusion in the scope of national health insurance systems	24
90/2377/EEC	Regulation laying down a Community procedure for the establishment of maximum residue limits of veterinary medicinal products in foodstuffs of animal origin	1
90/3677/EEC	Regulation laying down measures to be taken to discourage the diversion of certain substances to the illicit manufacture of narcotic drugs and psychotropic substances	1
91/412/EEC	Directive laying down the principles and guidelines of good manufacturing practice for veterinary medicinal products	1
92/29/EEC	Directive on the minimum safety and health requirements for improved medical treatment on board vessels	19

Reference	Title	Chapter
92/74/EEC	Directive laying down additional provisions on homoeopathic veterinary medicinal products	1
92/109/EEC	Directive on the manufacture and the placing on the market of certain substances used in the illicit manufacture of narcotic drugs and psychotropic substances	1
2309/93/EEC	Regulation laying down Community procedures for the authorisation and supervision of medicinal products for human and veterinary use and establishing a European Agency for the Evaluation of Medicinal Products	1
93/41/EEC	Directive on the approximation of national measures relating to the placing on the market of high-technology medicinal products, particularly those derived from biotechnology	1
95/46/EEC	Directive on the protection of individuals with regard to the processing of personal data and on the free movement of such data	1
EC/141/2000	Regulation on orphan medicinal products	14
2001/20/EC	Directive on the approximation of the laws, regulations and administrative provisions of the Member States relating to the implementation of good clinical practice in the conduct of clinical trials on medicinal products for human use	1, 3
2001/82/EC	Directive on the Community code relating to veterinary medicinal products	1, 3, 17
2001/83/EC	Directive on the Community code relating to medicinal products for human use	1, 3
2003/63/EC	Directive amending Directive 2001/83/EC on the Community code relating to medicinal products for human use	1
2003/94/EC	Directive laying down the principles and guidelines of good manufacturing practice in respect of medicinal products for human use and investigational medicinal products for human use (includes labelling and good manufacturing practice)	1, 3, 14
EC/727/2004	Directive amending Directive 2001/82/EC on the Community code relating to veterinary medicinal products	1, 17
2004/24/EC	Directive amending, as regards traditional herbal medicinal products, Directive 2001/83/EC on the Community code relating to medicinal products for human use	1, 12
2004/28/EC	Directive amending Directive 2001/82/EC on the Community code relating to veterinary medicinal products	1, 17

Reference	Title	Chapter
2004/27/EC	Directive amending Directive 2001/83/EC on the Community code relating to medicinal products for human use	1, 2, 3, 14
EC/273/2004	Regulation on drug precursors	16
EC/726/2004	Regulation laying down Community procedures for the authorisation and supervision of medicinal products for human and veterinary use and establishing a European Medicines Agency	1, 3, 12, 14, 17
2005/28/EC	Directive laying down principles and detailed guidelines for good clinical practice as regards investigational medicinal products for human use, as well as the requirements for authorisation of the manufacturing or importation of such products	3
2005/36/EC	Directive on the recognition of professional qualifications	1, 20
EC/111/2005	Regulation laying down rules for the monitoring of trade between the Community and third countries in drug precursors	16
EC/1277/2005	Regulation on drug precursors and for Council Regulation (EC) No. 111/2005 laying down rules for the monitoring of trade between the Community and third countries in drug precursors	16
EC/1901/2006	Regulation on medicinal products for paediatric use and amending regulation (EEC) No. 1768/92, Directive 2001/20/EC, Directive 2001/83/EC and Regulation (EC) No. 726/2004	14
EC/1907/2006	Regulation concerning the Registration, Evaluation, Authorisation and Restriction of Chemicals (REACH)	18
EU/1272/2008	Regulation on classification, labelling and packaging of substances and mixtures, amending and repealing Directives 67/548/EEC and 1999/45/EC, and amending Regulation (EC) 1907/2006	18
2010/32/EU	Directive implementing the Framework Agreement on prevention from sharp injuries in the hospital and healthcare sector concluded by HOSPEEM (European Hospital and Healthcare Employers Association) and EPSU (European Public Services Union)	19
2010/37/EU	Regulation on pharmacologically active substances and their classification regarding maximum residue limits in foodstuffs of animal origin	17
2010/84/EU	Directive amending, as regards pharmacovigilance, Directive 2001/83/EC on the Community code relating to medicinal products for human use	3, 14
2011/62/EU	Directive amending Directive 2001/83/EC on the Community code relating to medicinal products for human use, as regards the prevention of the entry into the legal supply chain of falsified medicinal products	2, 3

Reference	Title	Chapter
2014/536/EU	Regulation (EU) No. 536/2014 of the European Parliament and of the Council on clinical trials on medicinal products for human use, and repealing Directive 2001/20/EC	3
2016/161/EU	Commission delegated regulation (EU) supplementing Directive 2001/83/EC of the European parliament and of the Council by laying down detailed rules for the safety features appearing on the packaging of medicinal products for human use	3

UK law

Laws	Statutory Instruments	Chapter
Access to Health Records Act 1990		19, 24
Adults with Incapacity (Scotland) Act 2000		5
AIDS (Control) Act 1987 (repealed)		24
Alcoholic Liquor Duties Act 1979 and Customs and Excise Management Act 1979		18
	SI 2005 No. 1524 Denatured Alcohol Regulations 2005	18
Animal (Cruel Poisons) Act 1962		19
	SI 1963 No. 1278 Animal (Cruel Poisons) Regulations 1963	19
Animal (Scientific Procedures) Act 1986		19
Attendance of Witnesses Act 1854		16
Bribery Act 2010		19
Business Names Act 1985		19
Care Standards Act 2000		9
	SI 2008 No. 1976 Private Dentistry (Wales) Regulations 2008	9
Children Act 2004		24

Laws	Statutory Instruments	Chapter
Chiropractors Act 1994		3
Cities and Local Government Devolution Act 2016		24
Competition Act 1998		19
Computer Misuse Act 1990		24
Consumer Protection Act 1987		19
Corporate Manslaughter and Corporate Homicide Act 2007		24
Criminal Justice Act 2003		19
Criminal Justices and Courts Act 2015		19
Criminal Justice (International Co-operation) Act 1990		16
Criminal Law Act 1977		16
Data Protection Act 1998		19, 24
	SI 2000 No. 191 Data Protection (Subject Access) (Fees and Miscellaneous Provisions) Regulations 2000	19
	SI 2000 No. 413 Data Protection (Subject Access Modification) (Health) Order 2000	19
	SI 2000 No. 417 Data Protection (Processing of Sensitive Personal data) Order 2000	19
Dentists Act 1984		3, 8, 23
Deregulation Act 2015		18
	SI 2015 No. 968 Deregulation Act 2015 (Poisons and Explosives Precursors) (Consequential Amendments, Revocations and Transitional Provisions) Order 2015	18
Drug Trafficking Offences Act 1986		16

Laws	Statutory Instruments	Chapter
Environmental Protection Act 1990		19
	SI 2005 No. 894 Hazardous Waste (England and Wales) Regulations 2005 (also under EC Act 1972) as amended	19
	SI 2012 No. 811 Controlled Waste Regulations 2012 (also under EC Act 1972)	19
Equality Act 2010		19
European Communities Act 1972 (primarily)		
	SI 2004 No. 3144 Medicines for Human Use (Marketing Authorisations, Etc.) Regulations 1994 (repealed)	3
	SI 2000 No. 1059 Ionising Radiation (Medical Exposure) Regulations 2000	8
	SI 2002 No. 236 Medicines (Codification Amendments, Etc.) Regulations 2002 (repealed)	3
	SI 2002 No. 618 Medical Devices Regulations 2002	2
	SI 2002 No. 2013 Electronic Commerce (EC Directive) Regulations 2002	2
	SI 2002 No. 2677 Control of Substances Hazardous to Health Regulations 2002	18
	SI 2003 No. 1697 Medical Devices (Amendment) Regulations 2003	2
	SI 2003 No. 2426 Privacy and Electronic Communications (EC Directive) Regulations 2003	19
	SI 2003 No. 3148 European Qualifications (Health Care Professions) Regulations 2003	23
	SI 2004 No. 1031 Medicines for Human Use (Clinical Trials) Regulations 2004	3, 18
	SI 2005 No. 2754 Medicines (Advisory Bodies) (No.2) Regulations 2005 (partly consolidated in HMRs, remaining provisions amend SI 2004 No.1031	3

Laws	Statutory Instruments	Chapter
	SI 2005 No. 2759 Medicines (Marketing Authorisations, etc) (Amendments) Regulations 2005 (repealed)	3
	SI 2006 No. 1928 Medicines for Human Use (Clinical Trials) Amendment Regulations 2006	3
	SI 2007 No. 400 Medical Devices (Amendment) Regulations 2007	2
	SI 2008 No. 295 Controlled Drugs (Drug Precursors) (Community External Trade) Regulations 2008	16
	SI 2008 No. 2852 REACH Enforcement Regulations 2008	18
	SI 2008 No. 2936 Medical Devices (Amendment) Regulations 2008	2
	SI 2009 No. 716 Chemicals (Hazard Information and Packaging for Supply) Regulations 2009	18
	SI 2011 No. 2159 Veterinary Medicines Regulations 2011 (VMRs)	17
	SI 2012 No. 1426 Medical Devices (Amendment) Regulations 2012	2
	SI 2012 No. 1916 Human Medicines Regulations 2012 (HMRs)	2–18
	SI 2013 No. 2033 Veterinary Medicines Regulations 2013	17, 18
	SI 2013 No. 2327 Medical Devices (Amendment) Regulations 2013	2
	SI 2013 No. 2593 Human Medicines (Amendment) (No. 2) Regulations 2013	7, 9
	SI 2014 No. 490 Human Medicines (Amendment) Regulations 2014	8
	SI 2014 No. 599 Veterinary Medicines (Amendment) Regulations 2014	17

Laws	Statutory Instruments	Chapter
	SI 2014 No. 1878 Human Medicines (Amendment) (No. 2) Regulations	4, 9, 14
	SI 2015 No. 323 Human Medicines (Amendment) Regulations 2015	9
	SI 2015 No. 903 Human Medicines (Amendment) (No. 2) Regulations 2015	8
	SI 2015 No. 1503 Human Medicines (Amendment) (No.3) Regulations 2015	9
	SI 2016 No. 186 Human Medicines (Amendment) Regulations 2016	8, 9
Fair Trading Act 1973		17
	SI 2005 No. 2751 Supply of Relevant Medicinal Products Order 2005	17
Freedom of Information Act 2000		19, 24
Food Safety Act 1990		9
	SI 2003 No. 1387 Food Supplements (England) Regulations 2003	12
	SSI 2003 No. 278 Food Supplements(Scotland) Regulations 2003	12
	WSI 2003 No. 1719 (W186) Food Supplements (Wales) Regulations 2003	12
Food Safety (Northern Ireland) Order 1991	Statutory Rule 2003 No. 273 Food Supplements (Northern Ireland) Regulations 2003	12
Health Act 1999		
	SI 2002 No. 254 Health and Social Work Professions Order 2002	3

Laws	Statutory Instruments	Chapter
In conjunction with the European Communities Act 1972	SI 2010 No. 231 Pharmacy Order 2010	5, 20–23
	SI 2010 No. 299 Pharmacy Order (Commencement No. 1) Order of Council 2010	20, 22
	SI 2010 No. 300 General Pharmaceutical Council (Constitution) Order 2010	20
	SI 2010 No. 1367 General Pharmaceutical Council (Continuing Professional Development and Consequential Amendments) Order of Council 2010	20
	SI 2010 No. 1614 General Pharmaceutical Council (Appeals Committee Rules) Order of Council 2010	20, 22
	SI 2010 No. 1615 General Pharmaceutical Council (Fitness to Practise and Disqualification, Etc. Rules) Order of Council 2010	20, 22
	SI 2010 No. 1616 General Pharmaceutical Council (Statutory Committees and their Advisers Rules) Order of Council 2010	22
	SI 2010 No. 1618 General Pharmaceutical Council (Transfer of Property, Rights and Liabilities, Fees and Grants) Order of Council 2010	20
	SI 2010 No. 1619 Pharmacy Order (Registration – Transitional Provisions) Order of Council 2010	20
	SI 2010 No. 1620 Pharmacy Order 2010 (Approved European Pharmacy Qualifications) Order 2010 (also under EC Act 1972)	20
	SI 2010 No. 1621 Pharmacy Order (Commencement No. 2) Order of Council 2010	20
	SI 2010 No. 1617 General Pharmaceutical Council (Registration Rules) Order of Council 2010 (also made under Medicines Act powers)	5, 20
	SI 2011 No. 915 Medicinal Products (Herbal Remedies) (Amendment) Regulations 2011	12

Laws	Statutory Instruments	Chapter
Health and Social Care Act 2012		8, 24
	SI 2012 No. 1319 Health and Social Care Act (Commencement No. 1 and Transitory Provision) Order 2012	24
	SI 2012 No. 1631 NHS (Clinical Commissioning Groups) Regulations 2012 (and NHS Act 2006)	24
Health and Social Care Act 2015		24
Human Rights Act 1998		1, 24
Judicature (Northern Ireland) Act 1978		16
Legal Aid, Sentencing and Punishment of Offenders Act 2012		14
Legislative Reform Act 2006		24
	SI 2014 No. 2436 Legislative Reform (Clinical Commissioning Groups) Order 2014	24
Limited Liability Partnership Act 2000		19
Limited Partnerships Act 1907		19
Local Government and Public Involvement in Health Act 2007		24
Local Government etc. (Scotland) Act 1994		2
Medical Act 1983		
	SI 2009 No. 2739 General Medical Council (Licence to Practise) Regulations Order of Council 2009	8
	SI 2012 No. 2685 General Medical Council (Licence to Practise and Revalidation) Regulations Order of Council 2012	8

Laws	Statutory Instruments	Chapter
Medicines Act 1968		2, 5
	SI 1971 No. 1445 Medicines (Retail Pharmacists – Exemptions from Licensing Requirements) Order 1971 (repealed)	3
	SI 1977 No. 670 Medicines (Bal Jivan Chamcho Prohibition) (No. 2) Order 1977	13
	SI 1978 No. 1004 Medicines (Radioactive Substances) Order 1978	13
	SI 1978 No. 1006 Medicines (Administration of Radioactive Substances) Regulations 1978	8
	SI 1979 No. 382 Medicines (Chloroform Prohibition) Order 1979	13
	SI 1980 No. 1923 Medicines (Sale or Supply) (Miscellaneous Provisions) Regulations 1980 (repealed)	7, 10
	SI 1980 No. 1924 Medicines (Pharmacy and General Sale) (Exemptions) Order 1980	9
	SI 1984 No. 187 Medicines (Cyanogenetic Substances) Order 1984	13
	SI 1984 No. 769 Medicines (Products other than Veterinary Drugs) (General Sale List) Order 1984	7
	SI 1993 No. 832 Medicines (Applications for Manufacturer's and Wholesale Dealer's Licences) Amendment Regulations 1993 (repealed)	3
	SI 1997 No. 856 Medicines (Bal Jivan Chamcho Prohibition) (No. 2) Amendment Order 1997	13
	SI 1997 No. 1830 Prescription Only (Human Medicines) Order 1997 as amended up to 2006 and repealed in part by the HMRs 2012 (Arts. 5 and 10 and Schs. 1 and 2 remain)	8
	SI 2001 No. 1841 Medicines (Aristolochia and Mu Tong, Etc.) (Prohibition) Order 2001	12, 13
	SI 2002 No. 3170 Medicines for Human Use (Kava Kava) (Prohibition) Order 2002	12, 13

Laws	Statutory Instruments	Chapter
	SI 2005 No. 765 Medicines for Human Use (Prescribing) Order 2005 (repealed)	3
	SI 2005 No. 2791 Herbal Medicines Advisory Committee Order 2005	12
	SI 2008 No. 548 Medicines for Human Use (Prohibition) (Senecio and Miscellaneous Amendments) Order 2008	12, 13
	SI 2008 No. 2789 Medicines (Pharmacies) (Responsible Pharmacist) Regulations 2008	5
	SI 2011 No. 2647 Medicines Act (Pharmacy) Order 2011	5
Mental Capacity Act 2005		5
Mental Health Act 2007		24
Merchant Shipping Act 1979		19
	SI 1995 No. 1802 Merchant Shipping and Fishing Vessels (Medical Stores) Regulations 1995	19
Misuse of Drugs Act 1971		8, 16
	SI 1997 No. 1001 Misuse of Drugs (Supply to Addicts) Regulations 1997	16
	SI 2001 No. 3998 Misuse of Drugs Regulations 2001(as amended)	8, 9, 16, 17
	SR 2002 No. 1 Misuse of Drugs Regulations (Northern Ireland) 2002	8, 9
	SI 2003 No. 1432 Misuse of Drugs (Amendment) Regulations 2003	17
	SI 2005 No. 271 Misuse of Drugs (Amendment) Regulations 2005	16
	SI 2005 No. 1653 Misuse of Drugs (Amendment) (No. 2) Regulations 2005	17
	SI 2005 No. 2864 Misuse of Drugs and Misuse of Drugs (Supply to Addicts) (Amendment) Regulations 2005	16
	SI 2006 No. 1450 Misuse of Drugs (Amendment No. 2) Regulations 2006	16

Laws	Statutory Instruments	Chapter
	SI 2006 No. 3331 Misuse of Drugs Act 1971 (Amendment) Order 2006	16
	SI 2007 No. 2154 Misuse of Drugs and Misuse of Drugs (Safe Custody) (Amendment) Regulations 2007	16
	SI 2008 No. 3130 Misuse of Drugs Act 1971 (Amendment) Order 2008	16
	SI 2010 No. 2497 Misuse of Drugs (Licence Fees) Regulations 2010 (as amended)	16
	SI 2012 No. 973 Misuse of Drugs (Amendment No. 2) (England, Wales and Scotland) Regulations 2012	16
	SI 2014 No. 1106 Misuse of Drugs Act 1971 (Ketamine etc.) (Amendment) Order 2014	16
	SI 2014 No. 1352 Misuse of Drugs Act 1971 (Amendment) Order 2014	16
	SI 2014 No. 2081 Misuse of Drugs (Amendment No. 2) (England, Wales and Scotland) Regulations 2014	16
	SI 2015 No. 891 Misuse of Drugs (Amendment) (No. 2) (England, Wales and Scotland) Regulations 2015	16
NHS Act 1946		24
NHS (Scotland) Act 1947		24
NHS Reorganisation Act 1973		24
NHS Act 1977		24
With Health Act 1999	SI 2000 No. 617 NHS Bodies and Local Partnership Arrangements Regulations 2000	24
	SI 2004 No. 629 NHS (General Medical Services Contracts) (Prescription of Drugs) Regulations 2004	24

Laws	Statutory Instruments	Chapter
	SI 2005 No. 641 NHS (Pharmaceutical Services) Regulations 2005	24
NHS (Scotland) Act 1978		8, 24
	SI 2004 No. 38 NHS (Tribunal) (Scotland) Regulations 2004	24
	SSI 2004 No. 115 NHS (General Medical Services Contracts) (Scotland) Regulations 2004	8
	SI 2009 No. 183 NHS (Pharmaceutical Services) (Scotland) Regulations 2009	24
	SI 2009 No. 209 NHS (Pharmaceutical Services) (Scotland) Amendment Regulations 2009	24
	SI 2011 No. 32 NHS (Pharmaceutical Services) (Scotland) Amendment Regulations 2011	24
	SI 2014 No. 148 NHS (Pharmaceutical Services) (Scotland) Amendment Regulations 2014	24
	SI 2016 No. 372 Pharmacy (Premises Standards, Information Obligations, etc.) Order 2016	5
NHS and Community Care Act 1990		3, 24
	SI 1990 No. 2160 NHS Trusts (Membership and Procedures) Regulations 1990	24
NHS Reform and Health Care Professions Act 2002		24
NHS Reform (Scotland) Act 2004		24
NHS Act 2006		8, 22, 24
	SI 2007 No. 1320 Health Service Medicines (Information Relating to Sales of Branded Medicines, etc.) Regulations 2007	24
	SI 2008 No. 1938 Health Service Branded Medicines (Control of Prices and Supply of Information) Regulations 2008	24
	SI 2008 No. 3258 Health Service Branded Medicines (Control of Prices and Supply of Information) (No. 2) Regulations 2008	24

Laws	Statutory Instruments	Chapter
	SI 2010 No. 914 NHS (Pharmaceutical Services and Local Pharmaceutical Services) (Amendment) Regulations 2010	24
	SI 2011 No. 2237 NHS Commissioning Board Authority (Establishment and Constitution) Order 2011	24
	SI 2011 No. 2250 NHS Commissioning Board Authority Regulations 2011	24
	SI 2012 No. 1273 Health Education England (Establishment and Constitution) Order 2012	24
	SI 2012 No. 1399 NHS (Pharmaceutical Services) Amendment Regulations 2012	22
	SI 2012 No. 1631 NHS (Clinical Commissioning Groups) Regulations 2012	22
	SI 2012 No. 1909 NHS (Pharmaceutical Services) Regulations 2012	24
	SI 2013 No 235 National Treatment Agency (Abolition) and the Health and Social Care Act 2012 (Consequential, Transitional and Saving Provisions) Order 2013	9
	SI 2013 No. 349 NHS (Pharmaceutical Services) Regulations 2013	24
	SI 2015 No. 570 NHS (Charges for Drugs and Appliances) Regulations 2015	24
	SI 2015 No. 1940 NHS Bodies and Local Authorities Partnership Arrangements (Amendment) Regulations 2015	24
NHS (Wales) Act 2006		8, 24
	SI 2009 No. 778 (W66) Local Health Boards (Establishment and Dissolution) (Wales) Order 2009	24
	SI 2009 No. 779 (W67) Local Health Boards (Constitution, Membership and Procedures) (Wales) Regulations 2009	24
	SI 2009 No. 1511 (W147) Local Health Boards (Directed Functions) (Wales) Regulations 2009	24

Laws	Statutory Instruments	Chapter
	SI 2012 No. 1261 (W. 156) Velindre NHS Trust Shared Services Committee (Wales) Regulations 2012	24
	SI 2013 No. 898 (W.102) NHS (Pharmaceutical Services) (Wales) Regulations 2013	24
National Health Service Reform and Health Care Professions Act 2002		22, 23
Northern Ireland Act 1974	Mental Health (Northern Ireland) Order SI 1986 No. 595 (N.I. 4)	5
Northern Ireland	SI 1972 No. 1265 Health and Personal Services (Northern Ireland) Order 1972	8
Northern Ireland	SR 2004 No. 140 Health and Personal Social Services (General Medical Services Contracts) (Northern Ireland) Regulations 2004	8
Opticians Act 1989		9
Osteopaths Act 1993		3
Pollution Prevention and Control Act 1999		
	SI 2010 No. 675 Environmental Permitting (England and Wales) Regulations 2010	19
Poisons Act 1972		18
	SI 2015 No. 966 Control of Poisons and Explosives Precursors Regulations 2015	18
Police Reform and Social Responsibility Act 2011		16
Prevention of Damage by Rabbits Act 1939		19
Protection of Animals Act 1911		19
Protection of Animals (Amendment) Act 1927		19
Protection of Freedoms Act 2012		19
Psychoactive Substances Act 2016		16

Laws	Statutory Instruments	Chapter
Race Relations Act 1976		24
Rehabilitation of Offenders Act 1974		22
	SI 1975 No. 1023 Rehabilitation of Offenders Act 1974 (Exceptions) Order 1975	22
Road Traffic Act 1988		19
	SI 2014 No. 2868 Drug Driving (Specified Limits) (England and Wales) Regulations 2014	19
Safeguarding Vulnerable Groups Act 2006		22
	SI 2012 No. 2112 Safeguarding Vulnerable Groups Act 2006 (Miscellaneous Provisions) Regulations 2012	19
	SI 2012 No. 2113 Safeguarding Vulnerable Groups Act 2006 (Miscellaneous Provisions) Order 2012	19
Senior Courts Act 1981		16
Scotland Act 2012		16
Trades Descriptions Act 1985		19
Tribunals, Courts and Enforcement Act 2007		16, 24
	SI 2010 No. 22 Transfer of Tribunal Functions Order 2010	24
Weights and Measures Act 1985		19
Wildlife and Countryside Act 1981		19
Wireless Telegraphy Act 2006		16

Cases

Cases before the European Court of Justice

Case 322/01 *Deutscher Apothekerverband EV v 0800 DOCMORRIS NV and Jacques Waterval* (2003) ECJ 11/12/2003 (ch. 1)
Officier van Justitie v de Pejper [1976] ECR 613 (ch. 3)
R v Medicines Control Agency Ex p. Rhone Poulenc Rorer Ltd (C94/98) All ER (EC) 46 (ch. 3)
Upjohn 1989 C – 122/5 (ch. 2)

Cases before national courts and authorities, United Kingdom

Abdullah v General Medical Council [2012] EWHC 2506 (Admin) (ch. 22)
Abdul-Razzak v General Pharmaceutical Council [2016] EWHC 1204 (Admin) (ch. 5 and 22)
Abrahaem v General Medical Council [2008] EWHC 183 (Admin) (ch. 22)
Akodu v Solicitors Regulation Authority [2009] EWHC 3588 (Admin) (ch.22)
Ashraf v General Dental Council [2014] EWHC 2618 (Admin) (ch. 22)
Ashton v General Medical Council [2013] EWHC 943 (Admin) (ch. 22)
Bradshaw v General Medical Council [2010] Med L.R. 323 (ch. 22)
Burrows v General Pharmaceutical Council [2016] EWHC 1050 (Admin) (ch. 22)
Caelham v General Medical Council [2007] EWHC 2606 (Admin) (ch.22)
Cheatle v General Medical Council [2009] EWHC 645 (Admin) (ch. 22)
Cohen v General Medical Council [2008] EWHC 581 (Admin) (ch.22)
Davey v General Dental Council 2015 WL 6757832 (ch. 22)
Dhorajiwala v GPhC [2013] EWHC 3821 (Admin) (ch. 22)
Donoghue v Stevenson [1932] AC 562, 580 (ch. 21)
Dwyer v Roderick, Jackson and Cross Chemists (Banbury) Ltd (unreported 10 February 1982) (Box 21.4)
Eurovet VMD Annual review 2010/2011 (Box 17.1)

R v Bhatti and others [2015] EWCA Crim 1305 (ch. 1)

R v Department of Health, ex parte Source Informatics Ltd [1999] 4 All ER 185 (Box 19.1)

R v Dhorajiwala [2010] EWCA Crim 1237 (ch. 22)

R v Lee (Elizabeth) [2010] EWCA Crim 1404; [2011] 1 W.L.R. 418 (ch. 22)

R v Patel (Hitendra) [2010] 1 W.L.R. 1011 (ch. 22)

R (on the application of Alami) v Health and Care Professions Council [2013] EWHC 1895 (Admin) (ch. 22)

R (on the application of Rycroft) v Royal Pharmaceutical Society of Great Britain [2011] Med L R 23 (ch. 22)

R (on the application of Scholten v General Medical Council) [2013] EWHC 173 (Admin) (ch. 22)

R (on the application of Sheikh) v General Dental Council [2010] Med L.R. 323 (ch. 22)

R (on the application of Squier) v GMC [2015] EWHC 299 (Admin) (ch. 22)

R v Royal Pharmaceutical Society of Great Britain, ex parte Association of Parallel Importers and Others (1989) (unreported) (Box 3.3)

R (Redgrave) v Commissioner of Police for the Metropolis [2003] 1 W.L.R. 1136 (ch. 22)

R (on the application of Elizabeth Rose) v Thanet Clinical Commissioning Group [2014] EWHC 1182 (Admin) (ch. 24)

R v Statutory Committee of the Pharmaceutical Society of Great Britain and Martin and Shutt Ex p. Pharmaceutical Society of Great Britain [1981] 1 W.L.R. 886 (ch. 22)

Roberts v Coombs [1949] KB 221 (Box 8.1)

Roberts v Littlewoods Mail Order Stores Ltd [1943] All ER 1 271 (Box 6.1)

Shaikh v General Pharmaceutical Council [2013] EWHC 1844 (Admin) (ch. 22)

Summers v Congreve Horner & Co. [1992] 40 E G 144 (Box 6.2)

Susie MacLeod v The Royal College of Surgeons (Privy Council Appeal No. 88 of 2005) (Box 17.2)

Thilakawardhana v Office of the Independent Adjudicator and the University of Leicester [2015] EWHC 3285 (Admin) (ch. 22)

Vali v General Optical Council [2011] EWHC 310 (Admin) (ch. 22)

Wootton v J Docter Ltd [2008] EWCA Civ 1361 (ch. 21)

Yeong v General Medical Council [2009] EWHC 1923 (ch. 22)

Yusuf v Royal Pharmaceutical Society of Great Britain [2009] EWHC 867 (Admin) (ch. 22)

Abbreviations and acronyms

AHSN	academic health science network
AIS	Accessible Information Standard
All ER	All England (Law) Reports
ALL ER (EC)	All England Reports (European Community)
AUR	Appliance Use Review Service
AVM-GSL	Authorised Veterinary Medicine – General Sales List
BNF	*British National Formulary*
BP	*British Pharmacopoeia*
BPC	British Pharmacopoeia Commission
CCG	clinical commissioning group
CD	Controlled Drug
CE	*conformité Européene* (EC approval symbol for medical devices)
CFTP	continuing fitness to practise
CHIP	Chemicals (Hazard Information and Packaging for Supply) (legislation)
CHRE	Council for Healthcare Regulatory Excellence (superseded by PSAHSC)
CLP	Classification, Labelling and Packaging of Substances and Mixtures (legislation)
CMS	Concerned Member State
COSHH	Control of Substances Hazardous to Health (regulations)
CPD	continuing professional development
CPW	Community Pharmacy Wales
CQC	Care Quality Commission
CRB	Criminal Records Bureau
CSU	Commissioning Support Unit
DBS	Disclosure and Barring Service
DH	Department of Health
DEFRA	Department for Environment, Food and Rural Affairs
EAMS	Early Access to Medicines Scheme

EC	European Commission
ECR	European Court Reports
ECJ	European Court of Justice
EEA	European Economic Area
EEC	European Economic Community
EPS	Electronic Prescription Service
EU	European Union
EWCA	England and Wales, Court of Appeal: Civ. (civil division), Crim. (criminal division)
EWHC	England and Wales High Court: Admin (Administrative Court)
Ex	Exchequer Reports
FTP	Fitness to Practise Committee/Rules
GDC	General Dental Council
GDP	Good Distribution Practice
GMC	General Medical Council
GMP	Good Manufacturing Practice
GP	general practitioner
GPC	General Practitioners Committee
GPhC	General Pharmaceutical Council, also 'the Council'
GSL	General Sales List (medicines)
HMR	Human Medicines Regulation
HWB	health and wellbeing board
IRME	ionising radiation medical exposure
ISA	Independent Safeguarding Authority
JSNA	Joint Strategic Needs Assessment
LETB	local education and training boards
LLP	Limited Liability Partnership
LPC	local pharmaceutical committee
LPS	local pharmaceutical service
LS	*Law Medical* law reports published by Informa
Ltd	private limited company
MD	maximum dose
MDA	Misuse of Drugs Act
MDD	maximum daily dose
MHRA	Medicines and Healthcare products Regulatory Agency
MPharm	Master of Pharmacy (accredited degree)
MA	Marketing Authorisation
ML	Manufacturer's Licence
MPTS	Medical Practitioners Tribunal Service
MRL	maximum residue limit
MUR	Medication Use Review

NFA-VPS	non-food animal medicine prescribed by a veterinary, pharmacist or suitably qualified person only
NICE	National Institute for Health and Care Excellence
NHS	National Health Service
NHS England	the NHS Commissioning Board (NHSCB)
NHSCB	NHS Commissioning Board
NMS	New Medicines Service
NSAID	non-steroidal anti-inflammatory drug
OSPAP	Overseas Pharmacist Assessment Programme
P medicine	Pharmacy Medicine
PALS	patient advice and liaison service
PCT	primary care trust
PGD	Patient Group Direction
Pharm J	*Pharmaceutical Journal*
PHE	Public Health England
PI	Parallel Import
PLR	Product Licence of Right
plc	public limited company
PNA	pharmaceutical needs assessment
POM	Prescription Only Medicine
POM Order	Prescription Only Medicines Order (legislation)
POM-V	Prescription Only Medicine prescribed by a veterinary prescriber only
POM-VPS	Prescription Only Medicine prescribed by a veterinary, pharmacist or suitably qualified person only
PSA (HSC)	Professional Standards Authority (for Health and Social Care)
PSNC	Pharmaceutical Services Negotiating Committee
PSUR	Periodic Safety Update Report
QB	Queen's Bench
QC	Queen's Counsel
RP Reg.	Responsible Pharmacist Regulation
RPS	Royal Pharmaceutical Society
RPSGB	Royal Pharmaceutical Society of Great Britain (now wound up)
RCVS	Royal College of Veterinary Surgeons
SARSS	Suspected Adverse Reaction Surveillance Scheme
SCR	Summary Care Record
SI	Statutory Instrument
SPC/SmPC	Summary of Product Characteristics
SQP	suitably qualified person
STP	Sustainability and Transformation Plan
TDA	Trust Development Authority

UK	United Kingdom
UKPC	UK Privy Council
VAT	value added tax
VMD	Veterinary Medicines Directorate
VMR	Veterinary Medicines Regulation
W.L.R.	*Weekly Law Reports*
w/v	weight per volume
w/w	weight per weight

1

Sources of law

Thomas H John

Introduction

Since the accession of the United Kingdom (UK) (i.e. England, Scotland, Wales and Northern Ireland) to the European Treaty of Rome in 1973, almost all legislation relevant to pharmacy and medicines has derived from the European Union (EU) (formerly the European Economic Community (EEC)). Thus Europe is the highest legal authority for such law in the UK. Law emanating from the EU has then to be enacted into 'domestic' legislation to take effect in the UK. Domestic legislation in the UK operates at two levels: 'primary' legislation, that is, Acts of Parliament, and 'secondary' legislation, that is, the detailed provisions implementing the broad provisions of an Act. Public bodies are also subject to further 'Directions' made under the authority of primary and secondary legislation. This hierarchy is reflected in the processes by which law is made, how it is enforced and interpreted and how it may be challenged. This chapter provides an overview of aspects of UK law as they relate to pharmacy.

It is vital to remember that, strictly speaking, there is no such thing as 'Pharmacy Law'; rather, pharmacy as a profession and individual pharmacists are as much subject to the general law of the land as is any other individual or institution. Nevertheless, many legislative provisions are directed specifically to pharmacy and pharmacists and this is of course the central subject matter of this book.

This chapter explains how these laws are created; how they are implemented so as to apply them to our daily lives; how that implementation may be interpreted, policed and, if necessary, enforced; and, where applicable, whether any remedies may be available to individuals affected and society at large with regard to the interpretation of those laws, their policing and their enforcement.

One of the lynchpins to a democratic society such as the UK is the concept of the *separation of powers*. This concept was crystallised during and in the aftermath of the French Revolution in the late 18th century by philosophers such as Robespierre and Baron de Montesquieu. The concept holds that absolute power to regulate society should never be vested in the hands of one person or body of persons. Arguably, England was centuries ahead of these philosophers when, in 1215, King John signed the *Magna Carta* – the first time that the absolute monarch of this country ceded some of his powers to individuals besides himself.

Today, the structure of our democracy is designed to ensure that separate bodies make our laws (parliament), interpret our laws (the judiciary) and enforce our laws (the executive). These together ensure that the so-called 'rules of natural justice' are obeyed. The most important of these rules for our purposes is seen in the maxim 'no man may be a judge in his own cause'. This means that a person or body who creates a law (parliament) cannot then interpret it him- or itself (this is the function of the judiciary) and cannot then go on to enforce it him- or itself (that is the function of the executive, e.g. the civil service, the police and even the General Pharmaceutical Council (GPhC)). The benefits and safeguards of this arrangement for individual citizens are obvious.

European law

Following the Second World War, there was felt to be a need for trading agreements between the countries of Europe. In 1957, six states signed the Treaty of Rome, which established the EEC – now the EU. The UK acceded to the Treaty in 1973, along with Denmark and Ireland; Greece acceded in 1981 and Portugal and Spain followed in 1986. Sweden, Finland and Austria signed up to the Treaty in 1996, and Latvia, Lithuania, Estonia, Cyprus, the Czech Republic, Slovakia, Poland, Hungary, Malta and Slovenia joined in May 2004, followed by Romania and Bulgaria in 2007 and Croatia in July 2013, bringing the total number of Member States currently to 28.

The Single European Act 1987 was designed to expedite a single internal market and to remove all the remaining barriers that exist to the free movement of people, goods, services and capital. It is the object of the Community to ensure that there is no impediment to these 'four freedoms' and, if there is, to remove it. Harmonisation is one method by which such obstacles can be overcome and this is shown in many of the Directives that have affected the production and distribution of pharmaceuticals.

The legislation implementing the Treaty is formulated by the Council of Ministers in four basic forms.

Regulations. These have a direct effect and are binding on all Member States and on individuals in every respect.

Directives. These are binding as to their objectives but leave to Member States the method of implementation. Such implementation may be legislative or administrative. Most directives include 'derogations': a form of exception that Member States may claim if they feel that their particular circumstances require it.

Decisions. These are binding on those to whom they are addressed and are often of an administrative nature.

Recommendations. These are self-evident and are persuasive.

The European institutions

There are five main institutions of the EU.

The *Council of Ministers* is composed of politicians of each Member State and, in practice, the minister attending changes according to the item under discussion. The Council makes the ultimate decisions on European law. The Council is supported by working parties that include civil servants from each Member State and which study proposals put forward by the Council or the Commission. The working party reports are sent to the Committee of Permanent Representatives, which makes the decision whether or not to put the proposal forward to a Council meeting.

The *Commission* is made up of commissioners (civil servants), each with responsibilities for a particular area of interest, for example agriculture, internal affairs or environment. It has been called the Civil Service of the Community and proposes, executes and polices the policies of the Community as promulgated by the Council. Discussions between a commissioner's department and interested parties can lead to the formation of draft proposals. These are discussed by the Commission as a whole, which then decides on the form of any final proposal to be laid before the Council.

The *Assembly* (parliament) is a directly elected chamber of members from the 28 Member States (there will be 27 after Brexit) with representation related directly to population size. It has three main functions: control over the Community's budget, power of censure over the Commission and scrutiny of the legislative process. The last function has been of importance in the promulgation of directives affecting pharmacy upon which the Assembly must be consulted. The detailed work is done by standing committees who have a *rapporteur*, responsible for preparing the draft response of the Committee and presenting it to the plenary session of the Assembly.

The *Economic and Social Committee* comprises representatives of economic and social groups in the Member States. It is divided into three groups: employers, workers (trade unions) and a variety of interest groups, which includes the professions. The Economic and Social Committee has to be consulted before any final decision can be taken on proposed legislation. The work is mainly done in various specialist expertise sections (e.g. agriculture, transport). Within each section, there are study groups that deal with specific proposals. The section produces an 'opinion', which is presented to a plenary session of the Committee before being forwarded to the Council.

The *European Court of Justice* (ECJ) is covered below, under Courts. European law usually results from a request for action from an EU Member State. The Commission then drafts proposed legislation that passes through a lengthy debate, amendment and consultation process until the Council agrees the final form of the legislation.

British law

The scope of this book does not extend to Northern Ireland. Therefore, the law covered relates to England Scotland and Wales only, although the law in Northern Ireland often replicates British law. Law covering medicines and pharmacy practice generally applies across all of Britain but there is scope for differences. Law covering the administration of the National Health Service (NHS) differs significantly in the three component countries of Britain and may diverge further over time. There are two primary divisions in British law: statute law and common law (table 1.1). Common law itself is subdivided into criminal and civil law, but statutory law may encompass both and may or may not be accompanied by criminal, administrative or professional sanctions.

Table 1.1 Summary of UK law with relevance to pharmacy

	Statutory law			Civil law
	Criminal legislation	Administrative legislation	Professional legislation	Common law rights and duties, augmented by human rights
Examples of enforcement agencies	Police officers, GPhC inspectors	Representatives of administrative body	Professional regulator: GPhC	Direct action by claimant
Action for breach	Prosecution in the criminal courts	Appearance before relevant tribunal	Appearance before Fitness to Practise Committee	Being sued in the civil courts
Sanctions available to society at large	Fines, community orders, imprisonment	As set out in the law including loss of remuneration, withdrawal of contractual rights or position	Placing of conditions on registration, removal from professional register	Having to pay compensation; entry in the Register of County Court Judgments
Redress available to the unsuccessful party	Appeal to a higher court	Judicial review	Appeal to a higher tribunal	Appeal to a higher tribunal

The arrangements for the NHS and for professional discipline fall into these two categories. Legislation in Britain is made in the name of the Crown – the Queen. Properties owned by and activities carried out by the state on her behalf have in the past been subject to *Crown immunity*. Crown immunity means complete immunity from prosecution and the NHS, as a manifestation of the Crown, was immune from prosecution for offences committed within the NHS by its employees, including hospital pharmacists. This is no longer true as Crown immunity was formally removed from NHS hospital services in April 1991 and all the major pharmaceutical statutory legislation now applies, including the Medicines Act and the Misuse of Drugs Acts together with the subordinate legislation made under them. The prison health services and military health services are also expected to comply with UK legislation, other than in exceptional cases (chapter 24).

Statute law

A statute, strictly speaking, is an Act of Parliament. There are two kinds, public and private, but this book is only concerned with public acts such as the Medicines Act, the Misuse of Drugs Act and the Poisons Act (appearing principally in chapters 2 to 18). Acts are commonly referred to as *primary* legislation since they are the primary authority for legislation in the UK.

Statute law is also used to describe legislation that is subsidiary to an Act, normally in the form of Regulations or Orders in Council. These are collectively known as Statutory Instruments (SIs) or as *secondary* legislation. Once promulgated, secondary legislation has as much force in law as does primary legislation. Proposals to introduce new legislation come forward in the form of bills. Most are government bills but sometimes they are put forward by individual members of parliament (private member's bills). Before a bill is proposed, the government will normally signal its intentions in a 'white paper'. Often this is preceded by a discussion document, called a 'green paper'. The programme of primary legislation is usually outlined in the Queen's speech when parliament enters a new session every autumn.

Each bill is normally introduced into the House of Commons at a formal first reading and then passes through a series of 'readings'. After the second reading, the content and object of the bill is open to debate from members. If this stage is successfully passed, the bill goes to a committee stage, which examines the detail clause by clause. These stages are then repeated in the House of Lords. Once a bill successfully passes both Houses it is submitted to the monarch for Royal Assent. This stage is invariably a formality; under the UK constitutional law, a monarch who refuses assent to a bill that has successfully passed through both Houses of Parliament (and by doing so is thereby deemed to have the assent of the UK population at large) would inevitably precipitate a constitutional crisis of a magnitude not seen in modern times. This is because of the supremacy of the UK Parliament as a law-making body.

Statutes are most often 'enabling' instruments, that is, they give powers to the executive arm of the state, usually individual Secretaries of State, to do things. Major changes to an Act can normally only be made by another Act. An SI implements the detail of broad powers given by an Act. An SI does not go through parliamentary debate but is 'tabled' in parliament in the name of the minister and will be passed if no objections are raised.

Since the early 1980s there has been a huge annual increase in the number of SIs coming into force. For example, in 1980 a total of 178 SIs came into force. By 1990, this number had risen to 1630; there were 1744 in the year 2000 and during 2014 (the last full year for which figures are available) the number had rocketed to 3485.

Administrative law

Administrative law (appearing principally in chapter 24) is that body of law that regulates the activity of public bodies. Such bodies include: NHS authorities such as clinical commissioning groups (CCGs) in England, their predecessors and successors; local authorities; and education authorities. Every NHS body and CCG is set up by individual Regulation under an enabling Act of Parliament and any accompanying SIs, which confer statutory powers such as the power to manage budgets, hire and fire staff, and enter into contracts. These powers may not lawfully be exceeded by the public body in question. If they were to be exceeded, any party wronged may apply to the Administrative Court for *judicial review* of the action of the body in question on the ground that the decision was reached *ultra vires*, that is, in excess of its powers. Ambulance and mental healthcare trusts are also individually created by statute. Administrative law comprises statutes (Acts, Regulations, Orders) supplemented by a substantial body of Directions made by senior civil servants acting under the authority of the relevant minister. Policy statements and guidelines, all of which describe the standards to which the public sector is expected to work, supplement the legal framework further. Initially, the public authority itself usually enforces administrative law; a good example would be the enforcement of the NHS dispensing contract by NHS England. Enforcement is often also pursued through tribunals, appeal authorities and the courts. Sanctions are administrative such as a fine (withholding of reimbursement for dispensing NHS scripts), which reverts to the public body, or loss of contract.

As stated above, action by public bodies is susceptible to *judicial review*, a process whereby the Administrative Court (a branch of the High Court) determines whether the public body acted fairly, reasonably and within its statutory powers, rather than reviewing the factual basis on which the actual decision was reached. Three criteria are considered:

- Was a decision made by a public body lawful or not, that is, was it one that was within its powers?
- Was it a reasonable and rational one: had the body considered all the relevant facts and ignored those that were irrelevant?
- Was it based on the correct procedures laid down in a particular case, that is, did it comply with the rules of natural justice?

Decisions made in the Fitness to Practise (FTP) Committee of the GPhC and its predecessors, the Disciplinary and Statutory Committees, can be made subject to judicial review, particularly if there has been a breach of proper procedures or where the penalty imposed has been irrational or unreasonable (chapter 22).

Professional law

Professional law (appearing principally in chapters 20 to 23) comprises the law underpinning the powers to discipline health professionals such as pharmacists. The authority to discipline pharmacists lies in the Pharmacy Order 2010 and its associated Rules. The notion of an expected standard of care, which is also used in civil law cases (see below), is used by professional tribunals to judge whether a professional is guilty of professional misconduct. For pharmacists, these standards may principally be found in the GPhC Standards for Pharmacy Professionals (see chapter 21) and for registered pharmacies (see chapter 20).

Civil law

Civil law (referred to in chapter 21) derives from the notion of duties and responsibilities owed between individual citizens (Latin *civitas*, citizen). In its turn, civil law has developed through court judgments based on common law. Common law has developed from the middle ages since the King's courts gradually took the rule of law out into the shires to make judgments over the affairs of 'common' people. Action under civil law (called a *suit*) allows an aggrieved party to sue for compensation from another citizen who is alleged to have 'wronged' him. This concept of 'a civil wrong' is known in law as *tort* (an archaic term from mediaeval French). Some types of tort are now rarely seen in courts: breach of promise, for example. Libel, slander and trespass are all civil wrongs. In healthcare practice, the most likely actions are for negligence in the form of clinical negligence. Breach of confidentiality and defamation are other examples. In a case of clinical negligence, the complainant (claimant) makes an allegation that the actions of another person (the defendant or respondent) has caused them damage or injury. To succeed, the claimant would have to prove to a defined standard (the balance of probabilities) that the health professional firstly owed him a duty of care, secondly that the duty had been breached (i.e. was lower than the standard expected) and, thirdly, that that breach had caused the injury alleged. A civil action for battery is also a possible claim in tort if a patient is treated or physically touched without his or her consent.

Human rights in the UK

The Human Rights Act 1998 codified for the first time the rights enshrined in the European Convention on Human Rights. All UK courts and tribunals must now have regard to the principles of the European Convention of Human Rights when deciding cases which come before them.

The court system

Currently, the court with ultimate jurisdiction over EU law is the European Court of Justice (ECJ). This settles legal disputes involving Community legislation and its judgments are binding on each Member State. Much of its work now involves giving preliminary rulings on questions referred by the courts of the Member States.

In addition, under the auspices of the Council of Europe, there is the European Court of Human Rights, which developed separately, before the ECJ, to enforce the European Convention on Human Rights. This Convention was agreed in 1949 as a direct result of the human rights' atrocities of the Second World War. The UK was a founder member but was the last of the original signatories to enact the convention into domestic law. This was principally because the English common law conventions were held to embody adequate safeguards for human rights. Until 1998, any individual who wished to claim that their human rights had been violated had to complain for redress to the European Court of Human Rights. When the UK enacted the Convention in the Human Rights Act 1998, UK citizens then acquired the right to seek redress in the UK courts first, although the European Court of Human Rights remains an option if the complainant does not receive satisfaction in the UK.

A strict hierarchical system of UK courts means that the lowest possible tier of the court system will first make a judgment on the particular facts of a case. This judgment is binding on the parties to that case unless leave is given to appeal. On any such appeal, the higher court's decision may then set a precedent – or case law – for dealing with any similar future cases. The Appeal Court may dismiss the appeal (in which case the original judgment stands), allow the appeal (in which case the original judgment will be reversed) or grant leave to appeal to a still higher tribunal if there is one. The hierarchy of courts means that a decision on appeal that sets a precedent automatically binds all lower courts in future similar cases. More detail on the British legal system may be found in the Further reading given below.

The structure of the court system in England and Wales is shown in table 1.2.

A system of statutory tribunals also exists alongside that of the established court system. Examples include the employment tribunals, the VAT tribunals, and the social care and entitlement tribunals. As with the court system, there is a hierarchy within the tribunal system. Cases go firstly to the relevant *first tier* tribunal. Any appeal from the first tier tribunal (on points of law or procedure only) will go to the *second tier* tribunal. Any further appeal goes to the Court of Appeal (Civil Division). In very rare and exceptional cases the case may be further appealed to the Supreme Court provided that permission is given.

Always remember that the courts are themselves creatures of statute and only have the powers conferred on them by parliament under the doctrine of parliamentary supremacy. Courts do not *make* law, they can only *rule* on it by reason of the doctrine of separation of powers referred to above.

Scotland has a different system of courts to that in England and Wales based on its legal system's origins in Roman law (rather than the common law in England and Wales). In Scotland, the lowest tiers of Court include the

Table 1.2 Courts in England and Wales	
Criminal Division	**Civil Division**
Supreme Court (formerly the House of Lords)	Supreme Court
Hears appeals from the Court of Appeal and sometimes direct from the Divisional Court	Hears appeals from the Court of Appeal and sometimes direct from the High Court
Court of Appeal Criminal Division	Court of Appeal Civil Division
Hears appeals from the Crown Court on points of law or procedure relating to trial on indictment only	Hears appeals from the High Court or the County Court on points of law or procedure only
Crown Court	County Court
Hears cases committed to this court and appeals from the magistrates court and generally has greater powers of sentencing than the lower court	Deals with actions involving claims for small sums of money (£5–50 000) and negligence cases where the sum at stake is less than £50 000
Magistrates Court (bench of lay magistrates assisted by a professional legal adviser)	
May sometimes sit with a district judge (formerly known as a stipendiary magistrate) and hear the less serious criminal cases	

Sherriff's court, with the *Court of Session* undertaking most of the functions of the Crown and High Courts in England and Wales. However, the final domestic court of appeal for Scottish cases is still the Supreme Court, as it is for England and Wales.

How to find the law

Just as there are a vast number of statutes and secondary legislation (SIs, Orders in Council) governing our law so there is also an even larger body of case law. This is not surprising given that the original binding precedents date from the Middle Ages and will still hold as good law unless and until they are over-ruled by any subsequent precedents.

In order to discover exactly what the law is on any given subject matter, recourse must be had, firstly, to any statutory provision and the relevant secondary legislation covering the subject and, secondly to the case law, which will give an indication on how the courts interpret those statutory provisions. Each separate source of law has a unique and distinctive method of citation, whether searching in a law library, a volume of case reports or browsing online.

Statute law

An Act of Parliament always has a *long title* which appears at its head. Sometimes there is also a more succinct *short title*. The short title may also give a brief description of the purpose behind that Act and what it is designed to achieve. The *year* it was enacted is given in a specific way related to the name of the monarch at the time it was enacted and a *chapter number* chronologically designating the point during that year when it received Royal Assent. Thus, the full citation of the Medicines Act 1968 is The Medicines Act 1968 (16 Elizabeth II. Ch. 67). It was, therefore, passed in the 16th year of Queen Elizabeth II's reign (1968) and was the 67th Act of Parliament to be passed during that year. The Act of Parliament which replaced the House of Lords by bringing the Supreme Court into being is the Constitutional Reform Act 2005 (53 Eliz. II. Ch. 4) and so on. Acts are further subdivided into *Parts* setting out the broad subject areas the Act is legislating upon and, within those parts, *Sections* dealing with individual aspects of the relevant broad subject area.

An SI has a somewhat simpler method of citation involving just the year of its promulgation and a chronological number within that year. The subject matter of the SI is also generally easy to discern from a straightforward reading of its title. For example, the SI that sets out the precise structure of the GPhC is 'The General Pharmaceutical Council (Constitution) Order 2010 (SI 2010 No. 300)', meaning that it was the 300th Order in Council or SI to be promulgated in the year 2010.

Provided that the name of the Act or SI one is looking for is known (or even any one or more of the other citations) it is easy to find a copy by simply going to www.legislation.gov.uk and entering the known characters. This website has copies of all UK public Acts since 1842 and most are downloadable either as '.pdf' files or as 'Word' documents at no charge.

Case law

The method of citing precedents is evolving all the time and has changed significantly in recent years. Originally, approved accounts of cases (law reports) were produced by specialist journalists known as *law reporters*, who were invariably legal scholars or prominent practitioners. They were often then compiled into volumes of case reports at the end of each year. Over the years, those volumes would grow to form a *series*. Some series became obsolete or were eventually replaced by new series, often bearing the name of the new approved reporter or publisher. For example, the case of *Hadley v Baxendale* (which sets out the law on the limits to the amount of damages a Claimant can sue for in a claim for breach of contract) is cited as *Hadley v Baxendale* [1854] 9 Ex 341, which means that it was reported in the year 1854 in the 9th volume of the *Exchequer Reports* (ERs) beginning at page 341. Although now nearly 160 years old, it is still good law. Common series of law reports still in publication include the *Weekly Law Reports* (often abbreviated to W.L.R) and the All England Reports (All ER), which both deal with general common law cases, and the *Industrial Relations Law Reports*, a specialist series dealing with employment law. There is as yet no series dealing specifically with pharmacy law.

Recently, a new and simpler system of citing cases now passing through the higher courts has been established. They are known collectively as *Neutral Citation Numbers* and are designed to make for easy online searches for reports of cases. A recent example is the criminal case of *R v Bhatti and others* neutrally cited as *R v Bhatti and others* [2015] EWCA (Crim) 1305: 30th July 2015. This case dealt with an allegation by the prosecution that a college offering various courses to overseas students was, in fact, operated for the purpose of immigration fraud where documents were being dishonestly issued to non-EU nationals wishing to enter and remain in Britain. This means the case originated from a Crown Court situated in England or Wales; it was then appealed to the England or Wales Court of Appeal (EWCA) criminal division (Crim.), and judgment was given on 30th July and begins on page 1305 of the year's record of judgment.

The student may by now very well be thinking that all the above is fine provided that one knows the statute, case or citation one is looking for, but what if one only knows the subject matter? In this case, searching by the above methods is likely to be a long, not to mention tedious, process. Fortunately, there is a series of encyclopaedias and case digests available that are indexed by subject matter. A widely available (in most public libraries) encyclopaedia is *Halsbury's Laws of England* and its accompanying *Halsbury's Statutes*, which, although running to around 103 separate volumes, are set out in alphabetical order of subject matter. Volume 74 (medical professions) and volume 75 (medical products and drugs) include sections devoted to 'pharmacy and medicine'.

A timely word of warning is appropriate here, however: in addition to the vast body of law referred to above, there is also a huge body of procedural rules, guidelines and practice directions that accompany them. These rules, guidelines and practice directions govern the practical conduct of cases that come before courts and tribunals. Therefore, just as there is no substitute for taking professional advice from a competent pharmacist in matters relating to medicines, there is no substitute for taking professional legal advice if legal issues arise involving students and individual pharmacists in practice. There is a (rather 'tongue-in-cheek' but accurate nevertheless) maxim known to most practising lawyers which states simply 'he who represents himself has a fool for a client!'

Finding European law

Examples of European legislation affecting pharmacy, pharmacists and medicines are given below; further details may also be found in the reading list. Full details of the relevant British legislation appear in subsequent chapters of this book.

Most of the current UK law that applies to pharmacy practice derives from European legislation in the form of Directives, although Regulations have been made concerning, for example, the marketing authorisation of medicinal products (chapter 3). The first set of digits refers to the year of enactment; the second set refers to the number of this legal instrument within that year. All then retain either the EC (European Commission) or the EEC suffix.

European case law also has a relatively straightforward method of citation. Applications to the court are given a unique chronological reference numbers followed by 2 digits denoting the year. The name of the case is also commonly included but need not be, provided that there is a citation number. Thus, the 'Doc Morris' case, which dealt with limits to the free movement of pharmaceutical goods within the EU, is cited as *Case C-322/01- Deutscher Apothekerverband EV v 0800 DOCMORRIS NV & Jacques Waterval* (2003) ECJ 11/12/2003. This means that the case was the 322nd case to be referred to the ECJ for a preliminary opinion in the year 2001 and was finally decided by the full Court and reported in the official journal of the

European Communities on 11th December 2003. European legislation and case law can be consulted on the *euralex* website and copies downloaded free of charge.

Examples of European law

Free movement of pharmacists

The Pharmacy Directives concerned with the free movement of pharmacists, namely Directive 85/432/EEC, which dealt with the education and training of the pharmacist, and Directive 85/433/EEC, dealing with a pharmacist's right to establishment within the Member States, were revoked in 2005 and a consolidation directive embracing all the health professions was introduced, namely Council Directive 2005/36/EC. Each Member State is obliged to recognise, without impediment, the list of degrees (or equivalent) laid down in the Directives. Registration as a pharmacist in the UK is recognised. The competent authorities within the Member States deal with the procedure and those authorities in the UK are the GPhC and its equivalent in Northern Ireland. The new Directive 2005/36/EC also recognises a new category of registrant, namely a visiting practitioner who wants to provide services in the UK on a temporary or occasional basis.

In order for a pharmacist to move freely throughout the Community s/he must produce evidence from his/her own competent authority to the corresponding one in the host Member State that s/he:

1 is a national of a Member State of the Community or treated as such;
2a possesses a university degree (or equivalent) which was obtained following a course of study of not less than 5 years, at least 4 years of which comprised theoretical and practical training in a university, together with at least 6 months in-service training in a community or hospital pharmacy; or
2b has for at least 3 consecutive years during the previous 5 years been effectively and lawfully engaged in regulated pharmaceutical activity, e.g. a community pharmacy, hospital pharmacy, etc.; this is known as the acquired rights provision for those who cannot comply with point 2a above;
3 is in good physical and mental health; and
4 is of good character.

The pharmacy degrees in the UK together with the pre-registration year and the 'A'-level at university entrance are considered to be equivalent to the total 5-year requirement. Directive 2005/36/EC has been implemented in Great Britain by means of Regulations and Rules made under the Pharmacy Order 2010 (chapter 20). Pharmacists seeking free movement should contact the GPhC for advice.

Production and distribution of medicinal products for human use

Council Regulation 2309/93/EEC lays down Community procedures for the authorisation and supervision of medicinal products for human and veterinary use and established the European Agency for the Evaluation of Medicinal Products. Directive 2001/83/EC, which in 2001 consolidated all the earlier Council Directives, states that the primary purpose of controls on the production and distribution of medicinal products is to safeguard public health. This consolidation has also required consequential amendments to the Medicines Act and SIs in the UK, achieved by The Medicines (Codification Amendments Etc.) Regulations 2002 No. 236. The Directive defines a medicinal product and establishes that before a medicine can be put on the market it must possess a licence or marketing authorisation that has been granted on the basis of safety, quality and efficacy. In addition, the Directive covers the labelling of medicines. Commission Directive 2003/94/EC lays down the principles and guidelines of *Good Manufacturing Practice* that are applicable to all activities which require a licence under Council Directive 2001/83/EC. Good manufacturing practice means the part of quality assurance which ensures that products are consistently produced and controlled in accordance with the quality of standards appropriate to their intended use, the principles and guidelines of which are specified in Commission Directive 2003/94/EC. The Council Directive 65/65/EEC and its amending Directives were revoked by and consolidated in Council Directive 2001/83/EC. Council Regulation 2309/93/EEC, Council Directive 2001/83/EC and Commission Directive 2003/94 have been implemented in the UK under the provisions of the Medicines Act (chapters 2 and 3).

In 2004, the EU completed its review of legislation regulating medicinal products and in April 2004 published Council Directive 2004/27/EC, which amended Council Directive 2001/83/EC and Council Directive 2003/63/EC.

Council Regulation 2309/93/EC provides for marketing authorisations via the centralised procedures, the establishment of the European Agency for the Evaluation of Medicinal Products together with the setting up of a Committee for Veterinary Medicinal Products. The name of the European Agency for the Evaluation of Medicinal Products was changed to the European Medicines Agency by Council Regulation 2004/726/EC.

Analytical, toxicological and clinical standards for medicines
for human use

Council Directive 2001/83/EC set up standards and protocols for the analysis, and toxicological and pharmacological tests that have to be applied to medicinal products. Clinical trials are now controlled under Council Directive 2001/20/EC.

High-technology medicinal products for human and animal use

Directive 93/41/EEC set up procedures to deal with applications for marketing authorisations involving high-technology medicinal products, in particular those derived from biotechnology.

Homoeopathic medicinal products

Council Directive 2001/83/EC is concerned with the authorisation for marketing and the labelling of homoeopathic medicinal products for human use. It also provides for a special simplified registration procedure for those traditional homoeopathic medicinal products that are placed on the market without therapeutic indications in a pharmaceutical form and dosage which do not present a risk to the public. Directive 92/74/EEC relates to homoeopathic medicinal products for veterinary use. Chapter 3 discusses the UK legislation implementing both these Directives.

Herbal Medicinal Products

In March 2004, the EU issued the Directive on Traditional Herbal Medicinal Products (Council Directive 2004/24/EC) to regulate herbal products. Member States were required to have a simplified registration scheme in force by October 2005. Directive 2004/24/EC is based on long-standing use of the product and no clinical trial evidence will be required. All herbal products already on the market can remain so for 7 years (chapter 12).

Advertising, labelling and leaflets

Council Directive 2001/83/EC deals with the labelling of medicinal products and the availability of package leaflets aimed at the public. It requires that 'information supplied to users should provide a high degree of consumer protection in order that medicinal products may be used correctly on the basis of full and comprehensible information'. This was implemented in the UK on 1 January 1994 (chapter 14).

Council Directive 2001/83/EC deals with the advertising of medicinal products for human use both to the general public and to health professionals. It also deals with the question of hospitality related to sales promotion, advertising, samples, medical representatives, and so on (chapter 4).

Wholesale distribution

Council Directive 2001/83/EC covers the control of wholesale distribution of medicinal products for human use in the EC. It requires that such distribution should be subject to the possession of an authorisation to engage in the activity as a wholesaler in medicinal products and lays down the conditions for such an authorisation. Such activity is subject to licensing in the UK (chapter 3).

Colouring of medicinal products

Directive 78/25/EEC controls the colouring agents that can and cannot be added to medicinal products.

Production of medicinal products for animal use

Directive 2001/82/ECC as amended by 2004/28/EC provides that no veterinary medicinal product may be placed on the market of a Member State unless a marketing authorisation has been granted by the competent authorities of that Member State in accordance with these directives or in accordance with Regulation EC/726/2004 (UK requirements appear in chapter 17).

Directive 91/412/EEC introduced a legal requirement for a manufacturer of medicinal products for animal use to comply with the principles and guidelines of good manufacturing practice.

Regulation 90/2377/EEC lays down procedures to establish maximum residue limits (MRLs) for animal medicines in foodstuffs of animal origin.

Controlled Drugs

Council Directive 92/109/EEC applies to the manufacture and trade in scheduled substances within the EU and is implemented in the UK by the Controlled Drugs (Substances Useful for Manufacture) (Intra-Community Trade) Regulations 1993 as amended. It requires the person who manufactures or trades in these substances to be licensed and restricts the persons to whom supplies may be made. The 1993 UK Regulations treat the provisions of Council Directive 92/109/EEC as if they were requirements of Regulations by reason of the Misuse of Drug Act 1971 (Modification) Order 1990 (SI 1990 No. 2589).

Council Regulation 90/3677/EEC controls the import, export, recording and labelling of scheduled substances and the power to enter business premises to obtain evidence of irregularities. Records must be kept for two years. It also requires Member States to adopt measures to enable them to obtain information on any orders for, or activities in, scheduled substances. There is a list of scheduled substances (UK requirements appear in chapter 16).

Data protection

Council Directive 95/46/EEC extends data protection to all data maintained manually and affects the way in which patient medication records are stored. This Directive was implemented in the UK by way of the Data Protection Act 1998, which came into force on 1 March 2000. All data, both electronic and manual, are now controlled under the 1998 Act (chapter 19).

Human rights law

The Human Rights Act 1998 applies to public authorities such as the NHS or local authorities, but it also extends to 'private bodies which exercise public functions', so private contractors dispensing NHS prescriptions would be included. Since the Act came into force, all UK laws must be interpreted to respect and protect the human rights of all UK citizens. Human rights may go beyond the scope of our common law, for example they recognise a right to privacy that does not exist in the common law.

Human rights law departs from legal convention in the UK in three main ways.

- Precedent will not necessarily bind judgments in human rights cases. The courts are expected to reflect concepts of human rights at the time of consideration rather than at the time of the complaint and thus will reflect present-day attitudes and conditions.
- Statutes will be interpreted as to intention rather than 'as written'. This is a major departure from UK conventions on interpretation of statutes.
- The UK courts can issue a declaration of incompatibility so as to challenge the UK Parliament to amend the relevant statute to comply with European law.

Key human rights in relation to healthcare practice

Article numbers refer to those in the original European Convention and the text and schedules to the Human Rights Act 1998.

Article 2: The 'right to life'

The right to life is really a right not to be deprived of life except in very special circumstances. The judicial sanction of capital punishment is not a special circumstance. It should be noted that this 'right' does not equate to a right to unlimited healthcare in an effort to preserve life nor a right to death. Such rights may be cited in cases of assisted suicide or euthanasia and there are debates regarding issues such as assisted conception, contraception and abortion. Debate can also arise over resource allocation and equity in availability of treatment to all patients.

Article 3: The 'right to prohibition of torture or inhuman or degrading treatment or punishment'

At first sight, Article 3 may appear not to cover issues that have obvious relevance for healthcare but some commentators have asserted that aggressive treatment in terminal care or in some treatments of the mentally handicapped are close to being inhuman.

Article 5: The 'right to liberty'

The right to liberty is particularly relevant to the treatment of those with mental disorder, and the use of 'sectioning' and compulsory treatment is very relevant to the patient's ability to consent to treatment.

Article 6: The 'right to a fair trial'

The right to a fair trial is mostly relevant to disciplinary processes and such principles as the right to know what one is charged with, adequate time to prepare a response or defence, the right to an advocate of one's own choosing, and so on. In addition, any hearing has to be within a reasonable time and without delay, and there is a right not to incriminate oneself. The Fitness to Practise (FTP) processes within the GPhC should meet these criteria (chapter 22).

Article 8: The 'right for respect for private and family life'

Human rights issues may arise in the treatment of transsexuals and the right to practise particular forms of sexuality. This right has also been cited in relation to use of medical records in court. Article 8 is very relevant to issues of privacy in medical care, restrictions on disclosure of confidential information, and so on.

Article 9: The 'right to freedom of thought, conscience and religion'

Issues may arise where treatment is contrary to religious or cultural beliefs and practices. There also may be an issue for a 24-hour health service and religious restrictions on working at certain times or days.

Morals, ethics and law

Finally, a thought should be given to the twin concepts of 'morals' and 'ethics' as distinct from 'the law'. Detailed consideration is beyond the scope of this book and the reader is referred to the excellent volume by Professor Herbert Hart, *The Concept of Law*, which considers why and where the line is drawn between laws on the one hand and morals on the other. It is important to bear in mind that most people's ideas of morals or moral behaviour are not necessarily coterminous with the law. For example, many pharmacists were disgruntled over the recent decision by the Crown Prosecution Service to prosecute a practising pharmacist (Elizabeth Lee) for breach of section 68 of the Medicines Act 1968 after she inadvertently dispensed a product that was not what was ordered by the prescribing doctor. Many of those pharmacists no doubt believed it amoral (or even immoral) to have prosecuted in those circumstances (where the law does not require any degree of fault on the part of the dispensing pharmacist before criminal proceedings may be brought).

Yet other pharmacists may consider it an immoral act to assist someone to commit suicide. Assisting a suicide is currently also unlawful but, if the law is ever relaxed to make it lawful to assist a suicide in certain defined circumstances, it does not mean that those pharmacists should have to or indeed will change their view on the morality of assisting another person to die.

The concept of ethics and ethical codes as distinct from moral codes or legal codes is beyond the scope of this book.

Summary

- Introduction to the place and legal status of the UK in the EU:
  - the concept of the separation of powers within the state
  - the concept of natural justice.
- European law: the five European institutions are the Council of Ministers, the Commission, the Assembly, the Economic and Social Committee and the ECJ. The law is produced as directives, regulations, decisions and recommendations.
- British law and the scope of UK legislation:
  - statute law, the parliamentary process and parliamentary supremacy
  - administrative law, susceptibility of public bodies
  - professional law, codes of ethics and guidelines
  - civil law, civil wrongs or torts (including negligence), battery.
- The court system:
  - the ECJ
  - the court system in England & Wales and Scotland
  - hierarchy of courts
  - case law and binding precedents
  - statutory tribunals.
- How to find the law:
  - statute law
  - case law
  - European law.
- Examples of European law.
- The distinction between laws, morals and ethics.

Further reading

Beale HL, ed. (2015). *Chitty on Contracts*, 32nd edn. London: Sweet & Maxwell.

Bradley AW (2015). *Constitutional and Administrative Law*, 16th edn. Harlow: Pearson Education.

Jones, Michael *et al.*, eds (2014). *Clerk & Lindsell on Torts*, 21st edn. London: Sweet & Maxwell.

Hart HLA (2012). *The Concept of Law*, 3rd edn. Oxford: Oxford University Press.
Smith JC (2015). *Smith & Hogan Criminal Law*, 11th edn. Oxford: Oxford University Press.
Wingfield J, Badcott D (2007). *Pharmacy Ethics and Decision Making*. London: Pharmaceutical Press.
Zander M (2004). *The Law Making Process*, 7th edn. Oxford: Hart Publishing Ltd.

Websites

EU legislation: http://eur-lex.europa.eu
Legislation (can be searched on year and SI number or title): http://www.legislation.gov.uk

2

Human medicines: scope of regulation

Karen Pitchford

Consolidation of Medicines Legislation (2012)

Until August 2012, UK medicines legislation comprised the Medicines Act 1968 (the 1968 Act), around 60 principal SIs and around 130 amending SIs, which reflected developments in pharmaceuticals, wholesale trade, regulatory practice and European harmonisation. In 2012, a consolidation of medicines legislation was undertaken, leading to the production and enactment of the Human Medicines Regulations 2012.[1] These Human Medicines Regulations (HMRs) repealed, revoked or re-enacted most existing UK legislation regulating the authorisation, sale and supply of medicinal products for human use, and consolidated their effect in one place and in rationalised form. Since coming into force, the HMRs have been subject to more than a dozen other amending SIs.

The Human Medicines Regulations 2012 leave parts of the 1968 Act in place, principally Part IV of the Act, which deals with the registration and conduct of pharmacies (chapter 5). Also retained are certain powers to make secondary legislation in areas that fall outside the scope of Directive 2001/83/EC (the Directive).[2] The Human Medicines Regulations 2012 provide that medicines may be supplied to the public only from pharmacies, except those medicines which can with reasonable safety be sold without the supervision of a pharmacist. The Regulations also cover matters relating to the labelling of medicines, the containers in which they are supplied and the manner in which their sale is promoted, whether by advertisement or oral representation.

Certain pieces of medicines legislation have not been consolidated, including that concerned with clinical trials, the administration of radioactive

[1]Human Medicines Regulations SI 2012 No. 1916
[2]Directive 2001/83/EC of the European Parliament and of the Council on the Community Code Relating to Medicinal Products for Human Use

medicinal products and fees charged by the MHRA for the administration of procedures under the provisions. Various orders made under section 62 of the Act to prohibit the sale, supply and importation of products containing particular substances will also remain in force along with section 62, because prohibitions of this sort are outside the scope of the Directive.

Sections 104 and 105 of the 1968 Act provide for an Order to be made for the Human Medicines Regulations 2012 or the Clinical Trials Regulations to be applied for certain articles (chapter 13).

The Human Medicines Regulations 2012 repeal section 10(7) of the Medicines Act 1968 altogether. This section formerly exempted pharmacists from the need for a wholesale dealer's licence if wholesale dealing formed only an inconsiderable part of their business, but was not compatible with the Directive (chapter 10).

Since the Medicines Act 1968 remains partially in force, it should be read in conjunction with the Human Medicines Regulations 2012. References to Parts, Regulations and Schedules in this chapter relate to the Human Medicines Regulations 2012 and references to sections to the Medicines Act 1968, unless otherwise stated.

Neither the 1968 Act nor the Human Medicines Regulations 2012 apply to medical devices (see elsewhere in this chapter) or veterinary medicines (chapter 17).

The Human Medicines Regulations 2012

These Regulations comprise 18 Parts (with the addition of part 12a) and 35 Schedules. This book focuses on those Parts of greatest relevance to pharmacists and those involved in pharmacy. For full details, readers should consult the actual Regulations, the accompanying Explanatory Memorandum and the MHRA website. The contents of the Regulations are set out below, with where they are predominantly discussed within this book.

Part 1 General provisions: chapter 2
Part 2 Administration: chapter 2
Part 3 Manufacture and distribution of medicinal products and active substances: chapters 3 and 10
Part 4 Requirement for authorisation: chapter 3
Part 5 Marketing authorisations: chapter 3
Part 6 Certification of homoeopathic medicinal products: chapter 11
Part 7 Traditional herbal registrations: chapter 12
Part 8 Article 126a Authorisations: chapter 3
Part 9 Borderline products: chapter 3
Part 10 Exceptions to requirement for marketing authorisation, etc.: chapter 3

In addition, chapter 5 covers the provisions of the Medicines Act 1968 on pharmacies, chapter 13 the provisions in the Act for protection of the purchaser and chapter 17 the legislation on veterinary medicines.

Part 1 General provisions

Definition of medicinal product

The Regulations do not use the term 'medicine' but 'medicinal product', which is defined (HMRs Part 1, Reg.2) as:

a any substance or combination of substances presented as having properties of preventing or treating disease in human beings; or
b any substance or combination of substances that may be used by or administered to human beings with a view to:
  i restoring, correcting or modifying a physiological function by exerting a pharmacological, immunological or metabolic action, or
  ii making a medical diagnosis.

Whole human blood or any human blood components are specifically excluded from the above definition.

The above definition is transposed from Directive 2001/83/EC, as amended. The European Court of Justice (ECJ) has confirmed that falling under either (a) or (b) above is sufficient to classify a product as a medicinal product,[3] ruling that 'Directive 65/65 (now Directive 2001/83/EC) provides two definitions of the term *medicinal product*: one relating to presentation, the other to function. A product is medicinal if it falls within either of those definitions'. Directive 2004/27/EC adds a new provision to Article 2 of Directive 2001/83/EC as amended, which states: 'In cases of doubt, where, taking into account all its characteristics, a product may fall within the definition of a product covered by other Community legislation the provisions of this Directive shall apply.'

Taken together, these provisions are intended to ensure that where doubt exists over whether a product (those on the borderline between, for example,

[3] Upjohn 1989 C-122/5

medicines and medical devices, medicines and cosmetics, medicines and food supplements, etc.) should be regulated under medicines or other sectoral legislation, the stricter medicines regulatory regime should apply. This is a broader definition than that in the HMRs and can be defined as being a medicinal product (a) by presentation and (b) by function, as outlined by the ECJ, above.

Special provisions restricting scope

Where medicines are assembled in the course of the professional practice of a doctor, dentist, nurse, midwife or herbalist for the treatment of their patients, no manufacturing licences are required (HMRs Part 1, Reg.3). Similarly, where medicines are prepared under the supervision of a pharmacist and in accordance with exemptions in the retained section 10 of the 1968 Act (chapter 3), no licences are required, but see box 3.6 (HMRs Part 1, Reg.4).

Classification of medicines

Regulation 5 of the HMRs provides definitions of the three classifications governing the sale or supply of medicines; these are covered in chapter 6 (Pharmacy Medicines), chapter 7 (General Sale Medicines) and chapter 8 (Prescription Only Medicines).

Licensing authority and Ministers

The licensing authority is responsible for the grant, renewal, variation, suspension and revocation of licences, authorisations, certificates and registrations under the Human Medicines Regulations 2012 (Reg.6). The *licensing authority* means either or both the Secretary of State for Health (who must enforce or secure the enforcement of the Regulations and relevant EU provisions in England, Wales and Scotland) and the Minister for Health, Social Services and Public Safety (who is responsible for enforcement in Northern Ireland; note that Northern Ireland will not be considered further in this chapter). Note that the Regulations apply to the whole of the UK. Generally, any function that is conferred on the licensing authority by the Regulations is to be exercised by the Ministers acting jointly, although there are provisions for certain functions to be exercised by either of them acting alone or both of them acting jointly. While the Ministers comprise the licensing authority, these licensing functions are carried out by either the MHRA (which is an executive agency of the Department of Health) or the European Medicines Agency (chapter 3). The MHRA is also the licensing authority for all other licences required under the Regulations (e.g. manufacturers, wholesale dealers) and is also the enforcement authority for these matters in the UK.

Advertisements relating to medicinal products

Regulation 7 of the HMRs defines an advertisement as including anything to promote the prescription, supply or use of a medicinal product. Advertising and sales promotion is discussed in chapter 4.

General interpretation

Regulation 8 of the HMRs includes definitions that apply across the whole Regulations except where there are additional lists that refer to a particular Part only (e.g. there is a further list of definitions that apply only to Part 12, concerned with 'dealings' with medicinal products; Reg.213). Most have been defined in the relevant chapter but the following used in this chapter should be noted:

Administer means administer to a human being orally, by injection or by introduction into the body in any other way or by external application (whether or not by direct application to the body), either in its existing state or after it has been dissolved or dispersed in, or diluted or mixed with, a substance used as a vehicle

Hospital includes a clinic, nursing home or similar institution.

Part 2 Administration

Two advisory bodies are established under the Regulations, namely the Commission on Human Medicines (HMRs Reg.9) and the British Pharmacopoeia Commission (BPC) (HMRs Reg.11). Each advisory body must have at least eight members and may co-opt one or more additional members for the purposes of a meeting. An advisory body, or the advisory bodies acting jointly, may with the approval of the licensing authority appoint one or more subcommittees, known as expert advisory groups (see below). Each advisory body must give a report to the Ministers each year (HMRs Reg.12), at a time specified by the Ministers, about the performance of its functions and of those of any expert advisory group appointed by it. The Secretary of State must lay a copy of each report before parliament.

Commission on Human Medicines

The Commission on Human Medicines was established in 2005, under section 2 of the Medicines Act. The 2012 Regulations continue to provide for this body (Reg.9), the members and chair of which are appointed by the Ministers, who must consult the Scottish Ministers before making such appointments.

The Commission on Human Medicines must give advice to either or both of the ministers in relation to certain matters if the Minister (or Ministers) requests it or the Commission considers it appropriate to give it.

Those matters are any relating to the execution of any duty imposed by, or to the exercise of any power conferred by, the Human Medicines Regulations 2012 or the Clinical Trials Regulations, or otherwise relating to medicinal products.

The Commission on Human Medicines must:

a give advice with respect to the safety, quality and efficacy of medicinal products and promote the collection and investigation of information relating to adverse reactions, for the purposes of enabling such advice to be given; and

b advise the licensing authority if the licensing authority:

 i is required under Schedule 11 or the Clinical Trials Regulations, to consult the Commission about any matter arising under those provisions, or

 ii consults the Commission about any matter arising under those provisions.

British Pharmacopoeia Commission

The Medicines Act established the legal status of the BPC and of the *British Pharmacopoeia* (BP) as the UK standard for medicinal products. The 2012 Regulations continue to provide for this body, the members and chair of which are appointed by the Ministers, who must consult the Scottish Ministers before making such appointments. The BPC must prepare, or cause to be prepared editions of the BP and any other compendia (HMRs Reg.317) and lists of British Approved Names (HMRs Reg.319) (chapter 15).

Expert advisory groups

The licensing authority may direct that either of the above advisory bodies appoint one or more subcommittees (HMRs Part 2, Reg.14), known as expert advisory groups, to assist them in their work. An advisory body may delegate any of its functions other than those of providing advice to the licensing authority in any case where the licensing authority is required to consult the advisory body under Schedule 11 to the Regulations or the Clinical Trials Regulations. An advisory body may, however, arrange for an expert advisory group to provide advice to the advisory body in relation to the performance of those functions. Regulation 14 also stipulates who may be a member of an expert advisory group and further provisions about advisory bodies and expert advisory groups are found in Schedule 2 to the Regulations.

At the time of going to press, the following expert advisory groups have been established:

• Infection
• Cardiovascular, Diabetes, Renal, Respiratory and Allergy

- Chemistry, Pharmacy and Standards
- Clinical Trials, Biologicals and Vaccines
- Gastroenterology, Rheumatology, Immunology and Dermatology
- Medicines for Women's Health
- Neurology, Pain and Psychiatry
- Oncology and Haematology
- Paediatric Medicines
- Patient and Public Engagement
- Pharmacovigilance.

Part 11 Pharmacovigilance

Part 11 of the HMRs places general obligations on the licensing authority, with respect to pharmacovigilance, including an obligation to operate and audit a pharmacovigilance system. Further obligations are applied to the holders of marketing authorisations (chapter 3) but, for a detailed account of the pharmacovigilance regime, readers are directed to the HMRs themselves and to the relevant section of the MHRA website (see end of chapter).

Regulation 178 states that the licensing authority must:

a take all appropriate measures to encourage the reporting to it of suspected adverse reactions;

b facilitate reporting through the provision of alternative reporting formats in addition to web-based formats;

c take all appropriate measures to obtain accurate and verifiable data for the scientific evaluation of suspected adverse reaction reports;

d ensure that the public is given important information on pharmacovigilance concerns relating to the use of a medicinal product in a timely manner, through publication on the UK web portal, and through other means of publicly available information as necessary; and

e ensure that all appropriate measures are taken to identify any biological medicinal product (including name and batch number) prescribed, dispensed or sold in the UK which is the subject of a suspected adverse reaction report through the methods for collecting data and, where necessary, the follow up of suspected adverse reaction reports.

Falsified Medicines – Part 12A Sale of medicines to the public at a distance

Part 12A was inserted into the Regulations in 2013[4] in order to implement new provisions introduced by the Falsified Medicines Directive (2011/62/EU) on the sale and supply of medicinal products. The overall aim of the Directive

---

[4] Human Medicines (Amendment) Regulations SI 2013 No. 1855

is to assist in identifying and reporting counterfeit medicines found in the supply chain before they reach patients and so to strengthen the legal supply chain of medicines.

The amending SI that inserted Part 12A also introduced some new definitions to the HMRs (Reg.8) including that of a *falsified medicinal product*, which means any medicinal product with a false representation of:

- its identity, including its packaging and labelling, its name or its composition (other than any unintentional quality defect) as regards any of its ingredients including excipients and the strength of those ingredients;
- its source, including its manufacturer, its country of manufacturing, its country of origin or its marketing authorisation holder; or
- its history, including the records and documents relating to the distribution channels used.

Part 12A places requirements on persons who sell medicinal products to the public, at a distance (i.e. online retailers). In the UK, such a sale is not lawful unless the following conditions are satisfied:

a the person selling the products is included on the list of persons selling medicinal products at a distance that is published on the MHRA website;
b the product to be sold is covered by a marketing authorisation, an Article 126a authorisation, a certificate of registration or a traditional herbal registration;
c the person selling the medicinal product is authorised or entitled to sell medicinal products of that type or classification to the public;
d the sale takes place in accordance with regulations 214 (sale or supply of POMs), 220 (relating to the sale or supply of P medicines) and 221 (relating to the sale or supply of GSL medicines);
e the person selling the medicinal product has given a valid notification to the MHRA (i.e. they are included on and have not been suspended or removed from the MHRA list of sellers);
f the person selling medicinal products at a distance complies with the relevant provisions of the Electronic Commerce (EC Directive) Regulations 2002.[5]

The website used to sell medicinal products at a distance must contain:

- the contact details of the MHRA and a hyperlink to their website, where the list of sellers is maintained; and
- the EU common logo which is clearly displayed on every page of the listed person's website that relates to medicinal products offered for sale at a distance and contains a hyperlink to the entry of that person in the MHRA list.

[5] The Electronic Commerce (EC Directive) Regulations SI 2002 No. 2013

Part 16 Enforcement

Part 16 of the HMRs covers enforcement. The primary duty of enforcing the Regulations in England, Wales and Scotland rests with the Secretary of State (HMRs Reg.323). There are provisions for ministers to delegate many of their functions to other authorities, but licensing requirements and those provisions which affect hospitals (except so much of the hospital as is a registered pharmacy) or the premises of a doctor's or dentist's practice are solely the responsibility of the Ministers. In England, Wales and Scotland, arrangements can be made or directions given whereby local drugs authorities and/or the GPhC can have certain duties or exercise certain powers concurrently with the Ministers. In Scotland, these enforcement authorities cannot themselves institute proceedings. Under Reg.323(2), the Secretary of State may delegate (and has delegated) the duty of enforcement in connection with pharmacies and the retail distribution of medicines to the GPhC (chapters 20, 21 and 22). Other enforcement duties may be given to the GPhC and to local authorities (drugs authorities) as the appropriate Ministers may decide. In addition, Part IV of the Medicines Act 1968 (Pharmacies) is retained and, under that legislation, the GPhC is responsible for the maintenance of the Register of Pharmacy Premises (chapter 5) and for disciplinary control over bodies corporate and representatives of pharmacists carrying on retail pharmacy businesses (chapter 22).

The GPhC, concurrently with the Minister, is also required to enforce the provisions relating to sale and supply of medicines not subject to general sale (HMRs Reg.220) and sale or supply of a Prescription Only Medicine (POM; Reg.214). The provisions relating to sale or supply of medicinal products subject to general sale (Reg.221) and sale of medicinal products from automatic machines (Reg.222) are enforced, concurrently with the Minister, by the GPhC in relation to premises that are registered pharmacies and, in each area for which there is a drugs authority (see below), by that drugs authority in relation to premises that are not registered pharmacies. Here, *premises* includes any place and a ship, aircraft, hovercraft or vehicle (Reg.323(11)).

The Secretary of State may make arrangements for either or both the GPhC and, in respect of each area for which there is a drugs authority, the drugs authority for the area, concurrently with the Secretary of State, to enforce the following provisions:

1 compliance with standards specified in certain publications (Reg.251);
2 offences relating to dealings with medicinal products: compliance with standards specified in certain publications (Reg.255(1)(e));
3 packaging and leaflets (HMRs Part 13); and
4 requirements relating to advertising (HMRs Part 14).

Arrangements made with the GPhC in relation to HMRs Part 14, chapter 2 are to be limited to the enforcement of those provisions in respect of:

1 advertisements displayed or representations made on or in any premises where medicinal products are sold by retail or supplied in circumstances corresponding to retail sale;
2 advertisements displayed on any website associated with such premises; and
3 advertisements displayed on, or in close proximity to, a vending machine in which medicinal products are offered or exposed for sale.

Drugs authority (HMRs Reg.323(10)) means:

a in England:
  i in relation to a non-metropolitan county, metropolitan district or London borough, the council of that county, district or borough, and
  ii in relation to the City of London (including the Inner Temple and the Middle Temple), the Common Council of the City of London;
b in Wales, the council of a county or county borough; and
c in Scotland, a council constituted in relation to a local government area under section 2 of the Local Government etc. (Scotland) Act 1994.

Under the Act, the GPhC is also required to enforce the provisions relating to:

1 prohibition of sale or supply, or importation, of medicinal products of specified description (s.62) (chapter 13)
2 sale and supply and offer of sale or supply of adulterated medicinal products (s.63) (chapter 13)
3 sale of medicinal products not of the nature or quality demanded (s.64) (chapter 13)
4 annual return of premises to the Registrar (s.77) (chapter 5)
5 restrictions on use of titles, descriptions and emblems (s.78) (chapter 5)
6 regulations imposing further restrictions on titles (s.79(2)) (chapter 5)
7 regulations relating to requirements for containers (s.87(2)) (chapter 14)
8 regulations relating to distinctive colours, shapes and marking of medicinal products (s.88(3)) (chapter 14).

Inspection, sampling and seizure

A right of entry, and a right to inspect, take samples and seize goods and documents are given (HMRs Reg.325 and Reg.327) to an inspector in order to ascertain whether there has been a contravention of the Regulations. *Inspector* means a person authorised in writing by an enforcement authority for the purposes of Part 16 (enforcement) of the Human Medicines Regulations 2012 (HMRs Reg.8).

An inspector, having produced his/her identification if requested to do so, is empowered:

1 at any reasonable time, to enter premises (which includes any place and a ship, aircraft, hovercraft or vehicle) in order to determine whether there has been a contravention of any part of the Regulations which the enforcement authority is required or empowered to enforce;

2 to inspect any of the following to determine whether there has been a contravention of any provision of the Regulations which the enforcement authority must or may enforce:

   a a substance or article appearing to the inspector to be a medicinal product,

   b an article appearing to the inspector to be a container or package used or intended to be used to contain a medicinal product, or a label or leaflet used or intended to be used in connection with a medicinal product,

   c plant or equipment, including computer equipment, appearing to the inspector to be used or intended to be used in connection with the manufacture, assembly, importation, sale, supply or advertising of, or wholesale dealing in, medicinal products,

   d any process of manufacture or assembly of medicinal products,

   e the way in which medicinal products, or the materials used in the manufacture of medicinal products, are tested at any stage in the process of manufacture or assembly,

   f information and documents (including any that are stored electronically) relating to the manufacture, assembly, importation, sale, supply or advertising of, or wholesale dealing in, medicinal products, or

   g information and documents (including any that are stored electronically) relating to the safety of medicinal products, including information and documents relating to compliance with specified parts of the Regulations;

3 to take or purchase a sample of a substance or article which appears to the inspector to be a medicinal product which is, or is intended to be, sold or supplied or a substance or article used, or intended to be used, in the manufacture of a medicinal product;

4 to require a person carrying on a business which consists of or includes the manufacture, assembly, importation, sale, supply or advertising of, or wholesale dealing in, medicinal products, or a person employed in connection with such a business, to produce information or documents relating to the business which are in the person's possession or under the person's control;

5 to take copies of information or documents mentioned above;

6 to seize and retain a substance or article appearing to the inspector to be a medicinal product, or an active substance, if the inspector reasonably

believes that an offence under the Regulations is being or has been committed in relation to, or by means of, that substance or article;

7 to seize and retain any document (including any that are stored electronically) or anything inspected, or discovered in the course of an inspection, if the inspector reasonably believes that it may be required as evidence in proceedings; and

8 to require a person who has the authority to do so to open a container, package or vending machine or to allow the inspector to open a container, package or vending machine, for the purpose of enabling the inspector to seize a substance, article, document or other thing, as outlined above.

Where an inspector seizes a substance, article, document or other thing, s/he must, where practicable, inform the person, if any, from whom it was seized, and the occupier of the premises from which it was seized. If the seizure is from a vending machine, s/he must inform the person whose name and address are stated on the machine to be those of the machine's owner or, if no name and address are stated, the occupier of the premises on which the machine stands or to which it is affixed.

Twenty-four hours' notice must be given to the occupier if it is intended to enter any premises used only as a private dwelling. In cases where admission is refused, or such refusal is anticipated and notice of the intention to apply for a warrant has been given to the occupier, or where a request for admission, or the giving of notice, would defeat the object of the entry or where the case is one of urgency or the premises are unoccupied or the occupier is temporarily absent, a justice of the peace may issue a warrant authorising an inspector to enter premises, by force if necessary (Reg.326). Regulation 326 goes into further detail regarding who may issue a warrant and its period of validity.

An inspector entering any premises by virtue of a right of entry (Reg.325) or of a warrant under Regulation 326 may be accompanied by such persons, and take such equipment, as the inspector thinks appropriate. Where an inspector enters premises in pursuance of a warrant under Regulation 326, the inspector must, if the property is unoccupied or the occupier is temporarily absent, leave the premises as effectively secured against trespass as they were before the inspector entered.

It is an offence either to intentionally obstruct an inspector or to fail to comply with a requirement relating to inspection, sampling or seizure properly made by him or her. It is also an offence, without reasonable cause, to fail to give an inspector any other assistance or information which s/he may reasonably require in order to perform a function under the Regulations or to provide false information in relation to any such requirement (Reg.334). The Regulation goes on to say that 'Nothing in this regulation is to be read as requiring a person to answer a question or to give information if doing so might incriminate that person or the spouse or civil partner of that person' (HMRs Reg.334(8)). However, the Pharmacy Order 2010 Article 49 makes it clear that failure on the part of pharmacists or pharmacy technicians to supply information or produce any document required for a fitness to practise investigation may lead to a court order to comply (chapter 22).

An inspector who has exercised a right of entry and discloses to any other person, except in the performance of his/her duty, information about any manufacturing process or trade secret obtained by him/her in the premises commits an offence. It is similarly an offence for any person to disclose any information obtained by him/her in pursuance of the Regulations (Reg.332). An exception to this is if the inspector is or is acting on behalf of a public authority for the purposes of the Freedom of Information Act 2000.

Sampling

A detailed procedure is set out in Schedule 31 of the HMRs for dealing with samples taken by a *sampling officer* (i.e. a person authorised by an enforcement authority). A sample must be divided into three parts, two being retained by the sampling officer and the third given to the seller in the manner prescribed in the Schedule, according to the circumstances. One of the parts retained by the sampling officer may be submitted for analysis to a medicines control laboratory or to a laboratory available for the purpose in accordance with any arrangements made by the enforcing authority in question.

The laboratory to which a sample is submitted must analyse or examine the sample as soon as practicable and must issue and send to the sampling officer a certificate specifying the result of the analysis or examination. Such a certificate is to be sufficient evidence of the facts stated in the document in proceedings for an offence under the Regulations, unless another party to proceedings requires that the person who issued the certificate be called as a witness. In proceedings in Scotland, if the person who issued the certificate is called as a witness, that person's evidence is to be sufficient evidence of the facts stated in the certificate.

The second part of the sample retained by the sampling officer must be produced as evidence and, if required by either party, must be submitted for analysis to the government chemist or be sent for other examination to a laboratory specified by the court.

A sampling officer must pay the value of a sample if it is demanded by the person from whom it is taken; there is provision for arbitration about the value in case of a dispute. The taking of a sample by a sampling officer has effect as though it were a sale of a medicinal product and the provisions of section 64 of the Act relating to the protection of purchasers apply (see chapter 13). Any person, other than an inspector or person authorised by an enforcement authority, who has purchased a medicinal product may submit a sample of it for analysis to the public analyst for the area where it was purchased, subject to the analyst's right to demand payment of the prescribed fee in advance. The public analyst must analyse the sample as soon as is practicable and issue a certificate in the form prescribed (HMRs Reg.330).

Part 17 Legal proceedings

Where a contravention is by reason of the act or omission of another person, that other person may be charged and convicted whether or not proceedings are taken against the person committing the contravention. A person charged with an offence who proves to the satisfaction of the court (a) that s/he exercised all due diligence to prevent the contravention and (b) that the contravention was due to the act or omission another person shall, subject to certain procedural requirements, be acquitted of the offence (HMRs Reg.335).

When an offence is committed by a body corporate, any director, secretary or other similar officer of the body corporate may be proceeded against, as well as the body corporate, if it is proved that the offence was committed with his/her consent or connivance, or was attributable to his/her neglect (Reg.338). Section 124 of the Medicines Act specifically provides that the superintendent pharmacist of a retail pharmacy business (whether or not a member of the board), and any pharmacist manager or assistant acting under his/her direction, shall be regarded as officers for this purpose. Medicinal products proved to have been found on a vehicle from which those goods are sold are presumed to have been offered for sale unless the contrary is proved (HMRs Reg.340). This presumption applies when the offences concern the offering for sale of a medicinal product contrary to the restriction on retail sales (under HMRs Regs.220 and 221). There is also a presumption in respect of the possession of medicinal products (or leaflets referring to them) on premises at which the person charged carries on a business including the supply of those goods. When the offence concerns packaging and package leaflets (Regs.268 and 269) or requirements relating to child safety (Reg.276), a person is presumed, unless the contrary is proved, to have had medicinal products in his/her possession for the purpose of sale or supply.

Warranty can be pleaded (HMRs Reg.336) as a defence to a charge of contravening Regulations 251 (compliance with standards specified in certain publications), 268 and 269 (offences relating to packaging and package leaflets), 273 (child-resistant containers for regulated medicinal products) and 275 (colouring of aspirin and paracetamol products for children).

Subject to certain formalities, a defendant can rely on warranty if s/he proves that:

a   s/he purchased the substance or article in the UK as one which could lawfully be sold, supplied or offered for sale or supply or which could be lawfully sold, supplied or offered for sale or supply under the name or description or for the purpose under or for which it was sold;

b the relevant substance or article was sold with a written warranty certifying a matter specified in paragraph (a), and that if the warranty were true the alleged offence would not have been committed;

c at the time of the commission of the alleged offence the defendant had no reason to believe that the matter certified in the warranty was otherwise; and

d at the time of the commission of the alleged offence the relevant substance or article was in the same state as when the defendant purchased it.

A defendant who is an employee of the person who purchased the substance or article under warranty can rely on the same defence as his/her employer, and a name or description entered in an invoice is deemed to be written warranty that the article described can be sold under that description. It is an offence for a person to intentionally or recklessly give a purchaser a false warranty or intentionally to apply (a) a warranty or (b) a certificate of analysis (see above) given in relation to one substance or article to a different substance or article (Reg.337). The validity of licences and licensing decisions is considered under licensing (chapter 3), and certificates issued by the Registrar relating to the premises are dealt with under pharmacies (chapter 4).

Medical devices

The Medical Devices Regulations 2002[6] implement the EC Medical Devices Directives into UK law. They cover such items as intrauterine devices and diaphragms, dental fillings, contact lens care products, non-medicated dressings, sutures and ligatures. There are currently four sets of Medical Device Regulations implementing all of the Medical Devices Directives and amendments to date.

The Medical Devices Regulations 2002 define a *medical device* as any instrument, apparatus, appliance, software, material or other article, whether used alone or in combination, together with any accessories, including the software intended by its manufacturer to be used specifically for diagnosis or therapeutic purposes or both and necessary for its proper application, which:

a is intended by the manufacturer to be used for human beings for the purpose of:
  i diagnosis, prevention, monitoring, treatment or alleviation of disease,
  ii diagnosis, monitoring, treatment, alleviation of or compensation for an injury or handicap,

---

[6] SI 2002 No. 618

    iii investigation, replacement or modification of the anatomy or of a physiological process, or

    iv control of conception; and

b does not achieve its principal intended action in or on the human body by pharmacological, immunological or metabolic means, even if it is assisted in its function by such means, and includes devices intended to administer a medicinal product or which incorporate as an integral part a substance which, if used separately, would be a medicinal product and which is liable to act upon the body with action ancillary to that of the device.

The 2002 Regulations have been amended by Regulations in 2003[7] which cover, among other things, the re-classification of breast implants, in 2007[8] (which covers the re-classification of total hip, knee and shoulder joints) and in 2008,[9] 2012[10] and 2013[11] to meet EU obligations.

Conformity: CE marking

The Regulations place obligations on manufacturers to ensure that their devices are safe and fit for their intended purpose before they are CE marked and placed on the market in any EC Member State. The MHRA administers and enforces the legislation. *CE marking* is a mandatory conformity mark for products placed on the market in the European Economic Area (EEA). The letters *CE* are the abbreviation of the French phrase *conformité europeéne*, which literally means European conformity. The CE marking on a product indicates that the manufacturer is satisfied that the product conforms to all relevant essential requirements in the Directives and that it is fit for its intended purpose (Directive 93/68/EEC). In general, a medical device cannot be marketed in Europe without carrying a CE marking. A CE marking is applied by the manufacturer and means that the device meets the relevant regulatory requirements and, when used as intended, works properly and is acceptably safe.

For all but the very lowest-risk devices, this must be verified by an independent certification body, called a Notified Body, before the CE marking can be affixed. The MHRA is responsible for appointing UK Notified Bodies and regularly audits them to ensure that they perform to the required standards. Custom-made devices, devices undergoing a clinical investigation

[7]The Medical Devices (Amendment) Regulations SI 2003 No. 1697
[8]The Medical Devices (Amendment) Regulations SI 2007 No. 400
[9]The Medical Devices (Amendment) Regulations SI 2008 No. 2936
[10]The Medical Devices (Amendment) Regulations SI 2012 No. 1426
[11]The Medical Devices (Amendment) Regulations SI 2013 No. 2327

and *in vitro* diagnostic medical devices for performance evaluation are exempted from the requirement for CE marking. Unless there are grounds for suspecting that a device may pose a risk to public health, Member States must not 'create any obstacles to the placing on the market or the putting into service of any medical devices as defined under the Directive bearing a legitimate CE marking' (Directive 98/79/EC). This means that a CE-marked device may have access to the whole of the Community market and manufacturers are not required to comply with any national schemes when exporting their devices to other countries in the EU.

Summary

- European Directives and Regulations together with the Medicines Act 1968 and the Human Medicines Regulations 2012 regulate the manufacture, distribution and importation of medicines for human use.
- The advisory structure for the Ministers is principally the Commission on Human Medicines, which may delegate some of its functions to an expert advisory group.
- The definition of a medicinal product is set out in the Human Medicines Regulations 2012.
- There are obligations under the Human Medicines Regulations 2012 to operate a pharmacovigilance system.
- The Falsified Medicines Directive is implemented by part 12A of the Human Medicines Regulations 2012; this includes requirements placed on online retailers of medicines.
- The enforcement of parts of the Regulations falls upon the MHRA and the GPhC; some elements are enforced by 'drugs authorities'.
- The powers of the inspectors are laid down and stringent conditions relate to the taking of samples within a sampling procedure.
- Those liable to commit offences under the Regulations are listed together with any defences that can be raised.
- Medical devices are controlled under consumer protection legislation but are still administered by the MHRA; a CE mark means that a device is safe and fit for its intended purpose.

Further reading

Human Medicines Regulations (2012) SI 2012 No. 1916, *Explanatory memorandum*: http://www.legislation.gov.uk/uksi/2012/1916/pdfs/uksiem_20121916_en.pdf (accessed 14 November 2016).

Royal Pharmaceutical Society (published annually). *Medicines, Ethics and Practice: The Professional Guide for Pharmacists*. London: Royal Pharmaceutical Society (includes practice guidance on many of the topics in this chapter; free to members).

Websites

EU legislation: http://eur-lex.europa.eu

Legislation (can be searched on year and SI number or title): http://www.legislation.gov.uk

Medicines and Healthcare products Regulatory Agency: https://www.gov.uk/government/organisations/medicines-and-healthcare-products-regulatory-agency

Royal Pharmaceutical Society (member access only; lists legal classifications of medicines and further practice guidance): http://www.rpharms.com

3

Human medicines: the licensing system

Michael Goodman and Karen Pitchford

Box 3.1 *Commentary on the potential implications of the EU referendum on licensing for human medicines*

This edition is being prepared shortly after the June 2016 referendum on UK membership of the EU (known informally as 'Brexit'). Assuming that Article 50 of the Treaty on European Union is set in motion within 2 years, then the UK will cease to be a Member State of the EU, probably before the end of the present decade. This event is likely to bring about some change in the UK medicines licensing systems, although the extent of this is unclear presently; in practice, it is possible that much will remain largely unaltered, and fundamental change seems unlikely. No immediate changes are expected as it could take 2 years to negotiate a new relationship between the UK and the EU, and Article 50 itself will not be invoked until 2017.

Therefore, the authors have prepared this chapter based on the current legislative position, but have added commentary to some sections that could be affected by the UK ceasing to be a Member State of the EU. A short summary section on this topic is provided at the end of this chapter.

Modern medicines legislation in the UK was triggered by the thalidomide disaster. Thalidomide was a drug prescribed in the late 1950s and early 1960s to relieve morning sickness during pregnancy. Tragically, it later became apparent that the drug could cause serious birth defects, with around 10 000 cases worldwide. The realisation that drugs may come with risk led to the evolution of the current regulatory environment in the UK.

Present licensing requirements for human medicines and devices in the UK largely derive from EU Council Directives and Regulations. These directives were originally entered into UK law by the Medicines Act 1968 and subsequent revisions of this. This process enabled approximately 200 SIs to be created over the course of the next 44 years. These Regulations provided for marketing authorisations for individual medicinal products, manufacturer's licences involving production and assembly of such products, wholesale dealer's licences concerning the sale, supply and distribution of medicines, and clinical trial certificates.

In August 2012, to help simplify and coalesce legislation that was becoming fragmented, the Human Medicines Regulations 2012 (HMRs) came into force.[1] The aim was to bring the existing legislation into one set of Regulations and to make the legislation easier to use and understand. Although much of the 1968 Act and associated secondary legislation were repealed by the Human Medicines Regulations 2012, some sections/Regulations/Orders remain in force. In this chapter, the provisions of the Directives and the Act and its SIs are collated and summarised under appropriate headings. The SIs mentioned are those in force at the end of November 2016.

Without the appropriate marketing authorisation, licence or certificate, it is not lawful for any person, in the course of a business carried on by him/her, to manufacture, sell, supply, export or import into the UK any of these products unless some exemption is provided in the Act or the HMRs.

Marketing authorisations for human medicines

A marketing authorisation, formerly known as a Product Licence (PL), is the regulatory approval of a specific medicinal product, thus enabling it to be marketed. The approving authorities are national agencies or the European Medicines Agency, depending on the type of application procedure used. Unless a product falls under Part 10 (Exceptions to requirement for marketing authorisation) of the HMRs, each and every product must have a marketing authorisation (within the EU). These approvals are very specific and apply solely to that product; the marketing authorisation holder must comply with the terms of the authorisation. Only following approval may the product be potentially available for patient treatment.

The procedures that are used currently to apply for a marketing authorisation have evolved in Europe since the 1970s. In 1975, the Committee for Proprietary Medicinal Products (CPMP) was formed, comprising European expert scientific advisors. This committee has now become the Committee for Medicinal Products for Human Use (CHMP), and continues to play a

[1] Human Medicines Regulations SI 2012 No. 1916

central role in EU licensing procedures. In 1994, the EEC issued proposals for a two-tiered system for obtaining marketing authorisations, which was implemented in 1995, along with the establishment of the forerunner of the European Medicines Agency. The licensing system comprises a centralised system and a decentralised system based on national (Member State) regulatory bodies, such as the UK's MHRA. The centralised licensing system is administered by the European Medicines Agency. Assessment of applications is carried out by the CHMP, and their recommendation is sent for final decision to the European Commission (specifically, the Standing Committee on Medicinal Products for Human Use). The centralised procedure is set out in Regulation 2004/726/EC and is used for new active substances and certain high-technology and biotechnology products. A successful application results in the product being authorised for marketing in all Member States, without any separate implementation to the national regulatory authorities in those states.

The Member State system, which includes the mutual recognition and decentralised systems, is administered by national regulatory authorities, such as the MHRA in the UK. Council Directive 2001/83/EC, together with the other European Pharmaceutical Directives, implemented by UK Regulations,[2] established the procedures for the mutual recognition procedure, and Directive 2004/27/EC for the decentralised system. The Regulations implement the Pharmaceutical Directives concerned by cross-reference to the Directives themselves, rather than setting out the details in full.

The decentralised procedure is applicable where a marketing authorisation does not yet exist in any of the Member States. Under the rules of this procedure, identical applications are submitted in all Member States where a marketing authorisation is sought. A 'reference' Member State, selected by the applicant, prepares draft assessment documents within 120 days and sends them to the 'concerned' Member States. Concerned Member States (CMSs) either approve the assessment or the application continues into arbitration procedures.

Under the mutual recognition procedure, the assessment and marketing authorisation of one reference Member State are 'mutually recognised' by other concerned Member States. The implication of this is that if a product has a single national approval in any one Member State, then the regulatory authority in another State (CMS) does not need to carry out a full independent assessment, but accepts the judgement of the first Member State. However, CMSs can reject the application on the grounds of 'potential serious risk to public health'. There are arbitration procedures available

[2] The Medicines for Human Use (Marketing Authorisations etc.) Regulations SI 1994 No. 3144 as amended by SI 2002 No. 236 (both now repealed) and SI 2005 No. 2754

when disagreements arise. At the end of the mutual recognition procedure, a national marketing authorisation is issued by the CMS (e.g. by the MHRA). This mechanism is common for generic drugs.

Apart from the above European licensing procedures, it is possible to just apply for a single national authorisation if the intention of the applicant is to market in one Member State only. In this case, the application is assessed directly by the relevant national authority only.

Implications of marketing authorisations and definitions

One important outcome of any successful EU marketing authorisation application is the concurrent issue of the Summary of Product Characteristics (SPC or SmPC) document for that specific medicinal product. In brief, it is a description of a medicinal product's properties and the conditions attached to its use. They are the only part of a marketing authorisation to be 'public', and provide the fundamental information for healthcare professionals in terms of therapeutic indication, posology and safety. Summary of Product Characteristics is also the basis for the preparation of patient information leaflets, and it is a requirement that it is kept updated during the lifespan of the relevant product as new efficacy or safety data emerge.

Following regulatory approval, a person may not sell or supply, or offer to sell or supply, a medicinal product otherwise than in accordance with the terms of a marketing authorisation, a certificate of registration, a traditional herbal registration or an authorisation issued for justified public health reasons under Article 126a of Directive 2001/83/EC (HMRs Reg.46(2)).

Medicinal products may include immunological products, medicinal products based on human blood or blood constituents and medicinal products based on radioisotopes (radiopharmaceuticals). However, the Human Medicines Regulations 2012 do not apply to whole human blood or any human blood component other than plasma prepared by a method involving an industrial process (HMRs Reg.2). Homoeopathic medicinal products are dealt with separately (HMRs Part 6).

Proprietary medicinal product means any ready prepared medicinal product placed on the market in the UK under a special name and in a special pack (Council Directive 2001/83/EC, Art.1 and Art.2).

Radiopharmaceutical means a medicinal product which, when ready for use, contains one or more radionuclides included for a medicinal purpose (HMRs Reg.8).

Blood component means red cells, white cells, platelets or plasma (HMRs Reg.8).

The holder of a marketing authorisation for a medicinal product (HMRs Reg.58(4)) may:

a sell, supply or export the product;
b procure its sale, supply or exportation;

c procure its manufacture or assembly, in accordance with the marketing authorisation.

In dealing with an application for a marketing authorisation, the licensing authority must give particular consideration to the safety, quality and efficacy of the products.

If any of the medicinal products to which the application relates is liable to be imported from a country other than one in the EEA, the material or information accompanying the application (HMRs Reg.50(3)) may include an undertaking from the manufacturer of the product to comply with the matters set out in Schedule 9 of the Regulations (HMRs Reg.50(4)). An application for a marketing authorisation for a medicinal product for human use in either of the procedures must be accompanied by the particulars set out in Council Directive 2001/83/EC. Article 11 sets out the details of the Summary of Product Characteristics. Apart from the Summary of Product Characteristics, the particulars required to be given in a full application include: the kind of activity to be undertaken (e.g. selling, procuring manufacture, etc.); the pharmaceutical form of the product; its composition, physical characteristics and medicinal use; method of manufacture and assembly; quality control procedures; containers and labelling; reports of experimental and biological studies and of clinical trials and studies; any adverse reactions; and, where the product is made abroad, must include documentary evidence of authorisation relating to manufacture, assembly, and so on. Special additional conditions apply for applications concerning immunological products, radiopharmaceuticals and medicinal products derived from human blood or human plasma.

Abridged applications are permitted where the relevant data have been submitted in an earlier application, or data about the kind of product in question are well documented. A typical example would be for a generic product; the application does not need full pre-clinical and clinical efficacy studies, as would be the case for a new active drug. Renewal applications for licences and certificates are dealt with in HMRs Reg.66.

Standard conditions and obligations for marketing authorisations are prescribed in the relevant EC directives. These provisions are incorporated in the marketing authorisation unless the applicant desires that any of them shall be excluded or modified in respect of his/her product and his/her request is granted.

Revocation, variation or suspension

There is provision in the Regulations for the marketing authorisation to be revoked, varied or suspended (HMRs Reg.68). The licensing authority may impose an urgent safety restriction on the holder of a marketing authorisation (HMRs Reg.68(10)). Where this occurs, the authority must notify the suspension to the European Medicines Agency, the European Commission and all other Member States by the end of the next working day following the day on which the suspension comes into force (HMRs Reg.68(10)(b)). Provided that specific conditions are met, the licensing authority may suspend the use, sale, supply or offer for sale or supply within the UK of a product to which a UK marketing authorisation relates (HMRs Reg.69).

It is possible for the marketing authorisation holder to apply for a variation of licence. Marketing authorisations are very specific and it is quite common for a change to be sought at some point in the product lifecycle. Changes could involve the types of medicinal product in respect of which the licence was granted, an operation carried out under the licence, or an amendment to any premises, equipment or facilities in respect of which the licence was granted. Data justifying the variation may be needed, depending on the complexity. Application for variation is made to national regulators (e.g. if the original marketing authorisation was national) or to the European Medicines Agency (for centralised applications).

> **Box 3.2** *Possible impact of the EU referendum on licensing*
>
> Ultimately, any impact will follow on from the new relationship established between the UK and the EU. However, there could be differences with regard to the application procedures (assuming these will be the ones used in the future). The outcome of the mutual recognition and decentralised procedures are national licences. These procedures were established by an EU directive to harmonise the national laws across the EU, and the framework for these procedures is already part of UK legislation. However, for a product approved by the centralised procedure, a single EU licence is issued by the European Medicines Agency. Thus some legislative change may be required regarding the maintenance of a centralised licence, but this may not be protracted if the UK opts for 'observer' status on the European Medicines Agency's CHMP (akin to other non-EU European countries).

Post-authorisation requirements

After granting of a UK marketing authorisation, the licensing authority may impose obligations on the holder of the authorisation. Holders must operate a pharmacovigilance system and they may be required to conduct a post-authorisation safety study (if there are concerns about the risks of a medicinal product) or a post-authorisation efficacy study (if the understanding of the disease or the clinical methodology indicates that previous efficacy evaluations might have to be revised significantly) (HMRs Reg.61).

Generic products

Generic medicinal product (HMRs Reg.48(2)) means a medicinal product which:

1 has the same qualitative and quantitative composition in active substances and the same pharmaceutical form as the reference medicinal product; and
2 has demonstrated bioequivalence with the reference product in appropriate bioavailability studies.

There has to be a balance struck between allowing a person applying for a marketing authorisation for a follow-on product (e.g. a generic product) to be able to use the safety and efficacy data which has been used by the original innovator, against the need for such an applicant being forced to repeat that data for the product when that information is already with the licensing authority. This balance is achieved by allowing a follow-on competitor to rely on the data for the original product only after the passage of a 'data exclusivity period'. The procedure under which a generic product can rely on the innovator's data after the end of data exclusivity period is known as an 'abridged procedure'. An applicant for a UK marketing authorisation for a relevant medicinal product that is a generic medicinal product may provide abridged information in relation to the application in accordance with Articles 10(1), (5) and (6) of Directive 2001/83/EC (HMRs Reg.51(1)).

The existing 'data exclusivity periods' under Council Directive 2001/83/EC vary from 6 years to 10 years across the EU and continued to apply until November 2005, after which the amending Directive 2004/27/EC took effect. This harmonises the exclusivity period across the EU and is known as the 8 + 2 + 1 rule. The data can be used after 8 years but the product cannot be marketed for a further 2 years. An extra year's protection can be added if the original product had therapeutic indications which were of 'significant clinical benefit' over other remedies, under the terms of Article 10(1) of 2001/83/EC (HMRs Reg.51(2)).

Borderline products

Where the licensing authority is of the opinion that a product is a relevant medicinal product,[3] they may, by notice in writing, serve on any person who has placed the product on the market informing him/her that the product is a relevant medicinal product and needs to be licensed together with the reasons why they are so minded. Statutory provisions provide for initial

[3]Defined in HMRs Part 5, Reg.48 (not a registerable homoeopathic or traditional herbal medicinal product)

representations to be made to the licensing authority and, if necessary, for further representations to be made to an independent review body. Once a final determination has been made, the licensing authority may serve notice requiring the person not to put the product on the market or to stop marketing it from a date specified. A recent example of this related to products containing Cannabidiol.[4] Detailed procedures are set out in the legislation (HMRs Reg.159).

Immunity from liability for unauthorised medicinal products

In response to the suspected or confirmed spread of pathogenic agents, toxins, chemical agents or nuclear radiation which may cause harm to humans, the licensing authority may recommend or require the use of:

1 a medicinal product without an authorisation; or
2 a medicinal product with an authorisation, but for a therapeutic indication that is not permitted under the authorisation.

The holder of the marketing authorisation, a manufacturer of the product, an officer, servant or employee of the holder or manufacturer, or a healthcare professional shall not be subject to any civil liability for any loss or damage resulting from the use of the product in accordance with the recommendation or requirement (HMRs Reg.345). A 'healthcare professional' means a doctor, a dentist, a pharmacist, a registered pharmacy technician (HMRs Reg.8), a registered nurse, a registered midwife, a registered optometrist, a registered osteopath,[5] a registered chiropractor,[6] a relevant person (other than a social worker) registered with the Health and Care Professions Council[7] (chapter 23) or a person registered as a member of a profession complementary to dentistry.[8]

Early Access to Medicines Scheme

The aim of the Early Access to Medicines Scheme (EAMS) is to enable patients to access medicines which have not yet been authorised, in cases of life-threatening or seriously debilitating conditions, and where no suitable alternative may be available. The scheme is voluntary and consists of two parts. The first (promising innovative medicine) derives from early clinical data and an application approved by the MHRA could mean that the medicine is available several years ahead of a formal marketing authorisation approval. The second part of the scheme is based on scientific opinion

---

[4] MHRA statement on products containing Cannabidiol (CBD), October 2016
[5] As defined in s.41 of the Osteopaths Act 1993
[6] As defined in s.43 of the Chiropractors Act 1994
[7] Health Professions Order 2001 SI 2002 No. 254 (as amended)
[8] Under s.36B of the Dentists Act 1984, as amended

and considers the benefit/risk profile of the medicine. The opinion supports the prescribing decision with regard to the use of a medicine before licensing approval. Applications to the MHRA can be made via the dedicated EAMS webpage.

Parallel importing

The importation from an EU Member State of a medicinal product, which is a version of one already the subject of a UK marketing authorisation, is known as parallel importing. These products may be marketed in the UK, provided that certain conditions are met, enabling a parallel import licence to be granted by the MHRA. The reason for the trade is largely commercial, arising from the absence of price harmonisation of medicinal products in the EU – so the same product may be a different price in one or more Member States.

Legal basis for parallel imports

The legal basis for the trade in parallel imports arises from the Treaty of Rome 1957, Articles 30–34, which in general do not allow restrictions on imports. In effect, the Treaty allows neither direct restrictions, such as a complete ban, nor indirect restrictions, such as laws favouring the sale of home-produced products over those imported from other EU Member States. However, Article 36 permits import restrictions if they are justified on 'grounds of the protection of health and life of humans, animals or plants'.

This has led the matter to be considered by the European Court of Justice (ECJ), firstly in 1976[9] and then on further occasions. The outcome of this is that parallel imports into the UK are allowed, provided that they meet the following conditions:

- the imported product has no therapeutic difference from the equivalent UK product;
- it is produced and assembled in accordance with good manufacturing practice guidelines;
- the importer possesses a wholesale dealer's licence in accordance with Article 77 of Directive 2001/83/EC (as amended);
- the correct type of parallel import licence is held;
- the medicinal product must be labelled in English.

Marketing authorisations for parallel imports

In 1982, the European Commission produced a text outlining the basic principles for an abbreviated form of marketing authorisation for parallel-traded

[9] *Officier van Justitie v de Peijper* [1976] ECR 613

medicines.[10] On 22 December 1986, these recommendations were passed into EU law by Community Directive 87/21/EEC, which amended Article 4 of Directive 65/65/EEC. A modified form of licence application may be considered for such a product, subject to the following conditions:

1 the product to be imported must be a proprietary medicinal product (as defined in Art.1 of Council Directive 2001/83/EC) which is not a vaccine, toxin, serum or based on human blood; a blood constituent; a radioactive isotope; or homoeopathic product as specified in the Directive;
2 it must be covered by a currently valid marketing authorisation granted by the regulatory body of a Member State;
3 it must have no different therapeutic effect from the product covered by the UK licence; and
4 the correct type of parallel import licence is held.

If any of the above conditions is not met, the applicant will be invited to apply for a marketing authorisation in the normal way. The holder of a product licence (parallel import) does not require a separate marketing authorisation (HMRs Reg.172).

Regarding the correct type of parallel import licence, there are three categories: simple, standard and complex. With parallel import (simple), the holders of both the UK marketing authorisation and the marketing authorisation in the relevant Member State are from the same group of companies (and a licensing agreement exists between them). Parallel import (complex) is where the UK product and the product to be imported do not share a common origin, and:

- the product contains a new excipient, or the active ingredient is made by a different route;
- the product is a controlled release preparation, a metered dose inhaler, a powder for inhalation or an influenza vaccine;
- the product is a sterile product but is sterilised in a different way, or the container is made from a different material.

A parallel import (standard) applies when the UK and imported products do not share a common origin but the application is not considered to be complex. In all three cases, the MHRA needs to be satisfied that the imported product is bioequivalent to the UK product. Parallel distributors (in the UK) involved in repackaging or relabelling must employ at least one Qualified Person (see section on Manufacturer's licences) and hold a Manufacturing (assembly) Licence. A Wholesale Dealer's Licence is needed to distribute the product.

[10]Commission Communication on Parallel Imports of Proprietary Medicinal Products for which Marketing Authorisations Have Already Been Granted. C115/5. *Official Journal*, 6 May 1982

A product licence (parallel import) is granted for 5 years but normally continues in force only so long as *both* the UK marketing authorisation and the EU marketing authorisation to which it relates remain in force. If either marketing authorisation is revoked, the product licence (parallel import) will automatically be revoked also. If a marketing authorisation is withdrawn, it may be possible to continue to market the product in the UK, but only if the product licence (parallel import) satisfies the strict criteria that the ECJ have set for the survival of the product licence (parallel import) in these circumstances. These criteria follow from a referral to the ECJ in 1998.[11]

These requirements apply to the parallel importing of medicines for human use. Comparable requirements for veterinary medicines are controlled by the Veterinary Medicines Directorate (VMD – see chapter 17). Manufacturing authorisations for parallel imports apply to 'veterinary medicinal products' as defined in Directive 2001/82/EC (chapter 17).

A case in 1989 (box 3.3) has made it clear that the regulator (now the GPhC) may make additional rules concerning the use of licensed medicines on professional grounds for the protection of the public.

Box 3.3 *Importation of medicines from the EU*

R v Royal Pharmaceutical Society of Great Britain, ex parte Association of Pharmaceutical Importers and Others (1989)

In 1989, the then Royal Pharmaceutical Society of Great Britain (RPSGB) had adopted a provision in its Code of Ethics which, among other things, prohibited a pharmacist from substituting, except in an emergency, any other medicine for the medicine specifically ordered on a prescription, even if s/he believed that the quality and therapeutic effect were identical. In 1986, the RPSGB had published a statement to the effect that this rule applied to imported medicines as well as to medicines licensed in the UK. The Association of Parallel Importers, which represented companies which were involved in importing medicines from the European Community, maintained that the RPSGB rule infringed the provisions of the Treaty of Rome on the basis that its effect was to impose a quantitative restriction on their importing medicines – *parallel imports* – from the Community.

The ECJ held that, in the absence of any Community legislation regulating the doctor–pharmacist relationship, and in particular the doctor's freedom to prescribe any medicine s/he chose, it was for each EU Member State to decide, within the limits of the Treaty, the

---

[11] *R v Medicines Control Agency Ex p. Rhone Poulenc Rorer Ltd* (C94/98) [2000] All ER (EC) 46

degree to which they wish to protect the health of their people and how that was to be achieved. It was said that there was no evidence that the RPSGB rule went beyond what was necessary to achieve the objective, which was to leave the entire responsibility for the treatment of the patient in the hands of the doctor treating him/her. It followed, therefore, that the rule could also be justified under the Treaty on the grounds of the protection of public health.

Box 3.4 Possible impact of the EU referendum on parallel imports

Some legislative change regarding parallel imports could be more likely than other licensing areas. If the UK remains in the EEA, where EU exhaustion of rights applies, then parallel importing could remain possible. However, if the UK is not part of the EEA, then legislation for any form of exhaustion of rights outside the UK would be needed and it is not possible to predict the scope of such legislation prior to political debate. Some of the many points that would need to be addressed include whether testing would be needed on parallel imports, and whether certification by a non-UK-qualified person would be accepted.

Registration certificates for homoeopathic medicines for human use

The legislation relating to homoeopathic medicines is discussed more fully in chapter 11.

Homoeopathic medicinal product means a medicinal product prepared from homoeopathic stocks in accordance with a homoeopathic manufacturing procedure described by the *European Pharmacopoeia* or, in the absence of such a description in the *European Pharmacopoeia*, in any pharmacopoeia used officially in an EEA country (HMRs Reg.8).

Certificate of Registration means a certificate granted by the licensing authority under the HMRs (HMRs Reg.8). In the case of a registrable homoeopathic medicinal product, which meets the requirements laid out in HMRs Reg.102, a marketing authorisation is not required provided that a certificate of registration has been granted. Applications for a certificate of registration under the simplified procedure for a registrable homoeopathic medicinal product must be made in the manner prescribed in the Regulations (HMRs Reg.103). The application must be in writing, in English and include the particulars required by Council Directives 2001/83/EC and 2004/27/EC. Every holder of a certificate of registration must comply with all the obligations set in Council Directive 2001/83/EC, including record keeping, to facilitate withdrawal and recall (HMRs Reg.108).

A *national homoeopathic product* means a homoeopathic medicinal product which does not satisfy the conditions of HMRs Reg.102 and is indicated for the relief or treatment of minor symptoms or minor conditions in humans. Symptoms or conditions are minor 'if they ordinarily and with reasonable safety be relieved or treated without the supervision or intervention of a doctor'. The application for the grant of a UK marketing authorisation for a national homoeopathic product is required to be made in accordance with Schedule 10 of the Human Medicines Regulations 2012, including safety and efficacy data. The holder of the marketing authorisation must keep the data up to date and supply any information which entails amendment to the information.

Product Licences of Right for homoeopathic (and anthroposophic) medicines for human use

A *Product Licences of Right* means a product licence as defined in section 25(4) of the Medicines Act 1968, issued in relation to the requirements of section 7(2) of the 1968 Act and which was still in force immediately before the implementation of the HMRs.

Under transitional arrangements (HMRs Reg.347 – Sch. 32) these product licences, granted in the 1970s for medicinal products on the market at that time, are permitted to continue in force subject to certain specified provisions.

The majority of products granted Product Licences of Right in the 1970s have either been removed from the market or have gained a marketing authorisation, a certificate of registration, a traditional herbal registration or other suitable authorisation. However, there are some homoeopathic medicinal products that are not eligible for these schemes which continue to be on the market under these transitional arrangements with Product Licences of Right.

Registration of traditional herbal medicinal products

The legislation relating to herbal medicines, including definitions of key terms, is discussed more fully in chapter 12.

Applications for a traditional herbal registration under the simplified procedure for a traditional herbal medicinal product must be made in the manner prescribed in the Regulations (HMRs Reg.127). The application must be in writing, in English (HMRs Reg.127) and include the particulars required by Council Directives 2001/83/EC and 2004/27/EC so far as is applicable to traditional herbal medicinal products (HMRs Reg.128).

It is possible for herbal practitioners to be exempted from a traditional herbal registration licence, provided that the herbal medicines are manufactured or assembled and supplied to patients on their premises following one-to-one consultation.

If a herbal medicinal product can satisfy the criteria on quality, safety and efficacy as for (conventional) medicinal products, then an marketing authorisation may be applied for as outlined above (see Marketing authorisations for human medicines).

Article 126a authorisations

Where no UK marketing authorisation, certificate of registration or traditional herbal registration is in force for a product, nor is any registration application pending, the licensing authority may grant an Article 126a authorisation where it considers that the placing of the product on the market in the UK is justified for public health reasons (HMRs Reg.156). The product must be imported from another EU Member State in which the product is licensed in accordance with the 2001 Directive, and the Article 126a authorisation holder must be established in the EU. An Article 126a authorisation remains in force for the period specified in it unless revoked before the end of that period. That period may be specified by reference to the occurrence or non-occurrence of a particular event or events, such as an epidemic infection.

Falsified Medicines Directive

On 1 July 2011, the EU adopted a new directive on falsified medicines for human use (Directive 2011/62/EU). This directive aims to prevent falsified medicines entering the legal supply chain and reaching patients. It introduced harmonised safety and strengthened control measures across Europe by applying new measures, including:

- obligatory features on the packaging of medicines to demonstrate that they are authentic. These features are a unique identifier (a two-dimensional barcode that can be scanned along the supply chain) and tamper-evident features on the pack.[12] There is an implementation plan[13] for the introduction of these features, and marketing authorisation holders must place the new features on the packaging of most prescription medicines and certain non-prescription medicines no later than 9 February 2019;

[12] Commission Delegated Regulation (EU) 2016/161
[13] EMA/785582/2014 rev.1

- strengthened requirements for the inspection of the manufacturers of pharmaceutical ingredients;
- the obligation for manufacturers and distributors to report any suspicion of falsified medicines; and
- an obligatory logo that must be placed on the websites of legally operating online pharmacies, with a link to official national registers.

Manufacturer's and Wholesale Dealer's Licences

Issue of licences

In the UK, manufacturer's and wholesale dealer's licences are issued by the licensing authority, the MHRA. The MHRA may grant, refuse, review, suspend, revoke or vary them (HMRs Regs.23 and 26). A licence remains in force until it is revoked by the authority or surrendered by the holder (HMRs Reg.25). When an application for a licence is refused, the authority must state the reasons for refusal in a notice served on the applicant (HMRs Reg.23(6)). If the holder of a licence, subsequent to its issue, contravenes any provision of that authorisation, a notice suspending or revoking it may be served on the holder (HMRs Reg.26). Similarly, a licence may be suspended where it appears to the licensing authority that it is necessary in the interests of safety (HMRs Reg.28).

Manufacturer's licences

To manufacture or assemble human medicines or import them from a non-EEA country, a manufacturer's licence (ML) is required. This type of licence is needed before a company can apply for a marketing authorisation for a specific product. To attain an ML, it is a prerequisite that a company must comply with EU good manufacturing practice, and it will be inspected by the MHRA Inspectorate. Only when any issues raised during this inspection have been satisfactorily dealt with will an ML be granted. Following this initial inspection, the ML holder must pass regular inspections of their site. The holder of an ML must also comply with certain conditions regarding manufacture, assembly and importation (HMRs Regs.37–41). No licence is required for the importation of a medicinal product by a person who imports a medicinal product for administration to himself or herself or to any other person who is a member of that person's household (HMRs Reg.17(6)).

There are different types of MLs available, which can apply to the manufacture of authorised medicinal products, or 'specials' (named-patient medicine), or investigational medicinal products (for clinical trials). A licence is not required for the manufacture of chemicals and other substances used in the manufacture of ingredients of medicinal products.

Applications must be made in the manner prescribed in the Regulations (HMRs Reg.21 and Sch. 3) indicating whether the licence is to relate to manufacturing or assembly or to both. The applicant must describe the products to be manufactured or assembled and give details of any manufacturing operations to be carried out. The qualifications of the production manager and of the person in charge of quality control must be given, and the name and function of the person to whom they are responsible. Where relevant, the qualifications of the person in charge of animals, and of the person responsible for the culture of any living tissue, must also be given. At least one 'qualified person' is required to be nominated whose responsibilities are set out in the Regulations (HMRs Sch. 3, Reg.21(2)).

Manufacture includes any process carried out in the course of making the product but does not include dissolving or dispensing the product in, or diluting or mixing it with, some other substances used as a vehicle for administration to patients (HMRs Reg.8).

Assemble means the enclosing of the products (with or without other medicinal products of the same description) in a container which is labelled before the product is sold or supplied or, where the product (with or without medicinal products of the same description) is already enclosed in a container in which it is to be sold or supplied, labelling the container before the product is sold or supplied in it (HMRs Reg.8). Assembly has a corresponding meaning.

Good Manufacturing Practice means the part of quality assurance which ensures that products are consistently produced and controlled in accordance with the quality of standards appropriate to their intended use, the principles and guidelines of which are specified in Directive 2003/94/EC (The Good Manufacturing Practice Directive). The licence holder must comply with the principles and guidelines for good manufacturing practice set out in the Good Manufacturing Practice Directive, and use active substances as starting materials only if those substances have been manufactured or assembled in accordance with those principles and guidelines (insofar as those principles and guidelines relate to starting materials) (HMRs Reg.37).

A *qualified person* means a person who satisfies the provisions in Articles 49 and 50 of the 2001 Directive with respect to qualification and experience (HMRs Reg.8 and Sch. 7). The standard provisions for a manufacturer's licence are incorporated in every licence unless the applicant has successfully applied for any to be excluded or modified (HMRs Reg.24).

Wholesale dealer's licences

Wholesale dealing refers to selling, supplying, procuring, holding or exporting a medicinal product to a person for the purpose of selling or supplying the product, or administering it or causing it to be administered to one or more human beings, in the course of a business carried on by that person (HMRs Reg.18(8). In simple terms, it refers to the sale or supply of a medicinal product to a person who is not the end user of that product (i.e. for redistribution).

Council Directive 2001/83/EC requires a wholesale dealer's licence to be held by any person who, in the course of a business carried on by him/her (HMRs Reg.18 and VMRs Reg.13):

1 sells, or offers for sale, any medicinal products by way of wholesale dealing; or
2 distributes, otherwise than by way of sale, any medicinal product, ready-made veterinary drug or industrially produced medicinal product other than a veterinary drug which has been imported but was not consigned from a Member State of the EU.

No person may distribute, by way of wholesale, any medicinal product which is subject to Directive 2001/83/EC (proprietary and generic medicinal products) except in accordance with a wholesale dealer's licence and from premises specified in that licence (HMRs Reg.18(3)). A wholesale dealer's licence does not authorise the distribution of a medicinal product by way of wholesale dealing, or possession for the purpose of such distribution, unless a marketing authorisation, Article 126a authorisation, certificate of registration or traditional herbal registration is in force in respect of the product (HMRs Reg.18(9)). A wholesale dealer's licence is also required for exportation of any medicinal product which is subject to the 2001 Directive (proprietary and generic medicinal products) if it is to be exported to a Member State of the EEA (HMRs Reg.18(7)(b)).

There are some exemptions to the requirement for a wholesaler dealer's licence (HMRs Reg.19). The actual act of carrying out the selling of a medicinal product is exempt, provided that the person selling is the holder of a marketing authorisation, Article 126a authorisation, certificate of registration or traditional herbal registration, and the product has been kept on authorised premises (HMRs Reg.19(2)). A wholesaler dealer's licence is also not required by a person who has assembled the product to the order of the marketing authorisation holder and where the product has not left the premises of the manufacturer or assembler until the sale of the product (HMRs Reg.19(1)(b)). No wholesale dealer's licence is required by a person who provides facilities solely for the transport of the medicinal product, or who, in the course of his/her business as an import agent, imports a medicinal product solely to the order of another person who intends to distribute it (HMRs Reg.19(4)). However, the distribution itself must be in compliance with the EU guidelines on Good Distribution Practice of Medicinal Products for Human Use (2013/C 343/01). The requirement for a wholesale dealer's licence does not apply to the distribution of a medicinal product by way of wholesale dealing, or to the possession of a medicinal product for the purpose of such distribution, if the distribution or possession is solely for the purpose of exporting the product to states other than EEA countries (HMRs Reg.19(5)). The term *business* includes a professional practice and any activity carried on by a body of persons, whether corporate or unincorporated (HMRs Reg.8). Consequently, all sales that are made to practitioners (whether medical or dental) for use in their practices constitute sales by way of wholesale dealing.

Applications must be made in the manner prescribed in the Regulations (HMRs Reg.21 and Sch. 3) and state the classes of medicinal product which are the subject of the application and the uses for which they are intended, together with the particulars mentioned above. The applicant must also give the name and address and qualifications of the responsible person, details of an emergency plan for the recall of products and details for keeping records by way of invoices, on computer or in any other form relating to all products received or dispatched.[14]

There is no statutory requirement for the responsible person to be a pharmacist, although this is desirable. However, s/he should have access to pharmaceutical knowledge and advice when it is required and have personal knowledge of:

1 the relevant provisions of the Human Medicines Regulations 2012;
2 Articles 76–85 of Directive 2001/83/EC as amended on the Community Code relating to medicinal products for human use, as amended;
3 European Commission guidelines on good distribution practice of medicinal products for human use (94/C 63/03);
4 the conditions attached to the wholesale dealers licence for which s/he is nominated;
5 the products traded under the licence and the conditions necessary for their safe storage and distribution;
6 the categories of persons to whom products may be distributed; and
7 the quality system and standard operating procedures employed by the licence holder.[15]

The standard provisions for wholesale dealer's licences are incorporated in every licence unless the applicant has successfully applied for any to be excluded or modified (HMRs Reg.24). The holder of a wholesale dealer's licence must comply with the conditions set out in regulations 43–45 of the HMRs.

---

[14]The Medicines (Applications for Manufacturer's and Wholesale Dealer's Licences) Amendment Regulations SI 1993 No. 832 (now repealed)

[15]List adapted from *Notes for Applicants and Holders of a Wholesale Dealer's Licence*, MHRA Guidance Note No. 6, July 2014, available from MHRA website

Considerations common to manufacturer's and wholesale dealer's licences

In dealing with applications for manufacturer's or wholesale dealer's licences, the licensing authority must, in particular, take into consideration (HMRs Reg.22):

1 the operations proposed to be carried out in pursuance of the licence;
2 the premises in which those operations are to be carried out;
3 the equipment which is or will be available on those premises for carrying out those operations;
4 the qualifications of the persons under whose supervision those operations will be carried out; and
5 the arrangements made or to be made for ensuring the safe-keeping, and the maintenance, of adequate records in respect of medicinal products manufactured or assembled in pursuance of the licence.

Fees for licences

The fees for the various licences prescribed by the Human Medicines Regulations 2012 are made under the authority of the Medicines Act 1968 in respect of each licence period. These are amended from time to time to reflect increased charges and consistency with the relevant EU Directives.

Pharmacovigilance

Part 11 of the Human Medicines Regulations 2012 covers the obligations of the licensing authority (MHRA) and marketing authorisation holders with regard to pharmacovigilance; this implements Directive 2010/84/EU. A full account of these requirements is outside the scope of this book but both the licensing authority and holders of manufacturing authorisations must operate a pharmacovigilance system to capture and evaluate all information and take all appropriate measures to minimise and prevent risk, particularly concerning adverse drug reactions, presented by use of the medicinal product after the authorisation is granted. In brief:

- the authority/licence holder must operate a pharmacovigilance system;
- the pharmacovigilance system must enable the collection of information on the risks that medicinal products present to patients' health or public health;
- the licence holder must have permanently and continuously an appropriately qualified person responsible for the establishment and maintenance of the pharmacovigilance system;
- the licence holder must maintain and make available when requested a pharmacovigilance system master file;

- the licence holder must use its pharmacovigilance system to evaluate scientifically all information relevant to the product, consider options for minimising and preventing the risk presented by the use of the product, and take appropriate measures as soon as is reasonably practicable to investigate the potential risks of the product, communicate the risks, and implement actions for minimising and preventing the risks.

The licence holder is also required to submit regular Periodic Safety Update Reports (PSURs) (HMRs Regs.191–195). As of June 2016, marketing authorisation holders are required to submit all PSURs in the EU to the central PSUR repository. This applies whether they follow the EU single assessment or a purely national assessment procedure; marketing authorisation holders should no longer submit PSURs to national competent authorities directly.

Exemptions

Exemptions for clinical trials

A *clinical trial* is 'any investigation in human subjects intended to discover or verify the clinical, pharmacological and/or other pharmacodynamic effects of one or more investigational medicinal product(s), and/or to identify any adverse reactions to one or more investigational medicinal product(s), and/or to study absorption, distribution, metabolism and excretion of one or more investigational medicinal product(s) with the object of ascertaining its (their) safety and/or efficacy' (Clinical Trials Directive 2001/20/EC). For the manufacture or assembly of a medicinal product to be used only for the purpose of a clinical trial, a marketing authorisation is not required, but a clinical trial authorisation must be granted by the licensing authority for the purposes of clinical trials.[16] The manufacture of the product must be carried out according to Good Manufacturing Practice guidelines (Annex 13).

Details of the requirements for a clinical trial application are outlined in Part 6 and Schedule 6 of the 2004 Clinical Trials Regulations. Notification of the supplier's intention must be sent to the licensing authority. The notice must be accompanied by particulars of the trial and summaries of pharmaceutical data and of reports made and tests performed as specified in Schedule 1 to the Order. There is provision for termination of the exemption in certain circumstances, usually on the grounds of safety and for appeals to a person appointed (SI 2005 No. 2754). EC Council Directive 2005/28/EC (which is implemented by SI 2006 No. 1928) laid down the principles

---

[16]The Medicines for Human Use (Clinical Trials) Regulations SI 2004 No. 1031, as amended by SI 2005 No. 2754 and SI 2005 No. 2759 (now repealed) and SI 2006 No. 1928

and detailed guidelines for good clinical practice as regards investigational medicinal products for human use.

There is to be a new Clinical Trial Regulation EU No 536/2014, which aims to create an environment that is favourable for conducting clinical trials, and will streamline and harmonise the application procedure and assessment. Applications will be made under this new regulation via a single entry point, the EU portal. However, this is not yet fully developed and validated, and will probably be available in 2018.

Box 3.5 Possible impact of the EU referendum on application of the new Clinical Trial Regulation

This new regulation will not automatically apply to the UK, assuming exit from the EU beforehand. A new statutory instrument would be needed if a decision was taken to enact Regulation 536/2014.

Note that a certificate is not required if the product to be the subject of the clinical trial is covered by a marketing authorisation and the conditions set out in SI 2004 No. 1031 are met.

Exemptions for doctors and dentists

No licence is required where a medicinal product is manufactured or assembled by a doctor or dentist and is supplied to a patient in the course of their treatment. The medicinal product must not be manufactured or assembled on a large scale or by an industrial process (HMRs Reg.3).

Exemptions for pharmacists

The exemptions from licensing for pharmacists are contained in section 10 of the 1968 Act, to which a number of subsections were added by legislation.[17] Regulations relating to manufacturer's licences (HMRs Reg.17(1)) and marketing authorisations (HMRs Reg.46) do not apply where any provision of section 10 of the Medicines Act 1968 so provides. However, it is important to note that the HMRs repeal section 10(7) of the Medicines Act (HMRs Reg.349) has, since 1971, exempted retail pharmacies from the need to hold a wholesale dealer's licence for 'small-scale' wholesaling. See chapter 10 for more information.

Subject to the work being done by or under the supervision of a pharmacist and in a registered pharmacy, no licence of any kind is required for any of

---

[17]The Medicines (Retail Pharmacists – Exemptions from Licensing Requirements) Order SI 1971 No. 1445 and the Medicines for Human Use (Prescribing) Order SI 2005 No. 765 (both now repealed)

the following activities being carried out in a registered pharmacy (but see box 3.6):

1 Preparing or dispensing a medicinal product in accordance with a prescription given by a practitioner, or preparing a stock of medicinal products for this purpose (s.10(1)(a) and s.10(4)).[18]

2 Preparing or dispensing a medicinal product in accordance with a specification furnished by the person to whom the product is to be sold for administration to that person or to a person under his/her care (s.10(3)).

3 Preparing or dispensing a medicinal product for administration to a person when the pharmacist is requested to do so by or on behalf of that person in accordance with the pharmacist's own judgement as to the treatment required, and that person is present in the pharmacy at the time of the request (s.10(4)); a stock of medicinal products prepared in a registered pharmacy in accordance with 1 and 2 above and under this paragraph may be sold or supplied from any other registered pharmacy forming part of the same retail pharmacy business.

4 Preparing a medicinal product or a stock of medicinal products, not to the order of another person but with a view to retail sale or supply, provided that the sale or supply is made from the registered pharmacy where it was prepared and the product is not the subject of an advertisement (s.10(5)). In this connection, advertisement has the same meaning as in Reg.7 of the HMRs (chapter 4) (s.10(8)).

5 Assembling a medicinal product (s.10(1)). When medicinal products are assembled in a registered pharmacy for retail sale or supply, they may not be the subject of any advertisement and may only be sold or

---

Box 3.6 *Proposed changes to the Human Medicines Regulations to repeal section 10 of the Medicines Act*

In March 2016, the Department of Health and the MHRA launched a consultation regarding potential amendments to several aspects of the HMRs and the Medicines Act. These included a proposal to repeal section 10 of the Medicines Act (see also box 14.1).

In the consultation document it was stated that the draft amending regulations reproduced the substance of section 10. However, a specific question was asked about whether 'Chemist's Nostrums' have a place in the modern world of pharmacy.

At the time of going to press (November 2016), the final outcome of the consultation was not determined.

---

[18] All references in this paragraph refer to the Medicines Act 1968 (C. 67)

supplied at the registered pharmacy where they are assembled or at some other registered pharmacy forming part of the same retail pharmacy business.

The activities listed in (1) and (5) above may also take place in a hospital, a health centre or a care home service, without the requirement for a licence, subject to the work being done by or under the supervision of a pharmacist. *Care home service* has the meaning given in schedule 12 to the Public Services Reform (Scotland) Act 2010.

A retail pharmacist who is responsible for the composition of a medicinal product which s/he intends to sell or supply in the course of his/her business must hold a marketing authorisation if his/her activities fall outside the exemptions set out above. S/he must also have a manufacturer's licence or arrange for the product to be made by a manufacturer who has an appropriate licence.

Exemptions for nurses and midwives

No licence is required where a medicinal product is assembled by a registered nurse or a registered midwife if the nurse or midwife is acting in the course of his or her profession and the medicinal product is supplied to a patient in the course of the treatment of that patient, or to a patient of another doctor or dentist who is a member of the same medical or dental practice. The medicinal product must not be assembled on a large scale or by an industrial process (HMRs Reg.3).

'Specials'

An unlicensed medicinal product may be supplied in order to meet the special needs of an individual patient, provided that certain conditions are met. Medicinal products of this type are commonly referred to as 'specials'. Typical examples of such products would be for a patient who would have an allergy to a particular ingredient or lacks the ability to swallow a whole tablet.

A doctor, dentist, supplementary or independent prescriber does not require a licence of any kind in respect of such 'specials' products, prepared by him/her for administration to a particular patient. The exemption extends to the preparation of a medicinal product at the request of another practitioner for administration to one of his/her patients. No licence of any kind is required in relation to a 'special medicinal product' if:

1 the medicinal product is supplied in response to an unsolicited order;
2 the medicinal product is manufactured and assembled in accordance with the specification of a doctor, dentist, nurse independent prescriber, pharmacist independent prescriber or supplementary prescriber;

3 the medicinal product is for use by a patient for whose treatment that person is directly responsible in order to fulfil the special needs of that patient; and

4 the conditions outlined in HMRs Reg.167 are met.

These conditions include, but are not limited to that:

1 the medicinal product is supplied to a doctor, dentist, nurse independent prescriber, pharmacist independent prescriber or supplementary prescriber, or for use under the supervision of a pharmacist in a registered pharmacy, a hospital or a health centre;

2 no advertisement relating to the medicinal product is published by any person (but see chapter 14);

3 the manufacture and assembly of the medicinal product are carried out under such supervision, and such precautions are taken, as are adequate to ensure that the medicinal product meets the specification of the person who requires it; and

4 written records of the manufacture or assembly of the medicinal product in accordance with condition 3 are maintained and are available to the licensing authority or to the enforcement authority on request.

The manufacturer or assembler of 'specials' must hold a Manufacturer's 'Specials' Licence. A holder of such a licence may also be a registered pharmacy supplying unlicensed medicinal products prepared under the exemption provided by HMRs Reg.4.

Mixing of medicines

The Regulations affecting the manufacturing of medicinal products do not apply to the mixing of medicines by a nurse independent prescriber, a pharmacist independent prescriber, a supplementary prescriber (if the mixing of medicines forms part of the clinical management plan for an individual patient), a physiotherapist independent prescriber, a podiatrist independent prescriber or a therapeutic radiographer independent prescriber. Nor do they apply to a person acting in accordance with the written directions of a doctor, dentist, nurse independent prescriber, pharmacist independent prescriber, physiotherapist independent prescriber, podiatrist independent prescriber, therapeutic radiographer independent prescriber or supplementary prescriber if the mixing of medicines forms part of the clinical management plan for an individual patient (HMRs Reg.20).

Mixing of medicines means the combining of two or more medicinal products together for the purposes of administering them to meet the needs of an individual patient.

Hospitals

On 1 April 1991, by virtue of the National Health Service and Community Care Act 1990, all NHS hospitals lost their Crown immunity and became liable to licensing regulations. The type of activities relating to manufacture, assembly and wholesaling varies considerably from one hospital to another, and whether any particular licence is required depends on the individual activity. Certain exemptions exist where an activity takes place under the supervision of a pharmacist in a hospital (Medicines Act 1968, s.10, as amended). Hospital pharmacists requiring further details should contact the MHRA.

Summary

- All dealings in medicinal products are subject to licensing unless specifically exempted.
- Marketing authorisations or licences are needed to place a medicine on the market, to manufacture, wholesale or distribute medicinal products.
- Marketing authorisations relate to medicinal products.
- Registration certificates relate to homoeopathic remedies.
- Traditional herbal registration relates to traditional herbal medicinal products.
- Article 126a authorisations relate to unlicensed medicinal products imported from another EU Member State on public health grounds.
- A manufacturer's licence is required to manufacture, assemble or import a medicinal product from a state other than an EEA country.
- A wholesale dealer's licence is required to sell or supply a medicinal product to a person who is not the end user of that product.
- Applications for national (decentralised) marketing authorisations in the UK are administered by the MHRA; applications using the centralised system are administered by the EMA.
- A simplified system of licensing applies to parallel imports.
- Stringent requirements, set out in a Guide to Good Manufacturing Practice, apply to manufacturing licences and introduce the concept of a qualified person. Similar conditions apply to wholesale dealer's licences, which have a responsible person. Good distribution practice applies to the storage and transport of licensed products during distribution.
- Clinical trials are subject to certification by the licensing authority unless specifically exempted.
- Certain exemptions from licensing exist for doctors, nurses, pharmacists, other health professionals and hospitals.

- No licences are required for certain activities carried out in a pharmacy under the supervision of a pharmacist, although this is currently subject to consultation.
- Provisions are made for special dispensing or manufacturing services.
- There are possible impacts of the EU referendum on the licensing system; in the months following publication of this issue, any significant change is unlikely. It is anticipated that there will need to be some legislative change once the new relationship with the EU has been fully negotiated, but this may be relatively minor overall with regard to marketing authorisations. It is possible that parallel imports may be impacted more, but the extent and timing of any change are likely to be politically dependent.

Further reading

Human Medicines Regulations (2012) SI 2012 No. 1916, *Explanatory memorandum*: http://www.legislation.gov.uk/uksi/2012/1916/pdfs/uksiem_20121916_en.pdf (accessed 10 November 2016).

Pharmaceutical Press (2017). *Rules and Guidance for Pharmaceutical Manufacturers and Distributors* [The Orange Guide]. London: Pharmaceutical Press.

Royal Pharmaceutical Society (published annually). *Medicines, Ethics and Practice: The Professional Guide for Pharmacists*. London: Royal Pharmaceutical Society (includes practice guidance on many of the topics in this chapter; free to members).

Royal Society of Chemistry (2009, updated 2015). *Code of Practice for Qualified Persons*. London: Royal Society of Chemistry.

The following guides are available from the Medicines and Healthcare products Regulatory Agency (https://www.gov.uk/government/organisations/medicines-and-healthcare-products-regulatory-agency): *Good Manufacturing Practice (manufacturers), Good Pharmacovigilance Practice, Good Distribution Practice (wholesalers), Good Clinical Practice (clinical trials), Good Inspection Practice.*

Websites

EU legislation: http://eur-lex.europa.eu

Legislation (can be searched on year and SI number or title): http://www.legislation.gov.uk

Medicines and Healthcare products Regulatory Agency: https://www.gov.uk/government/organisations/medicines-and-healthcare-products-regulatory-agency

Royal Pharmaceutical Society (member access only; lists legal classifications of medicines and further practice guidance): http://www.rpharms.com

4

Human medicines: advertising

Helen Root

Advertising under Part 14 of the Human Medicines Regulations 2012

Control of medicines advertising in the UK is based on a system of self-regulation underpinned by statutory powers under EU and UK law. The Human Medicines Regulations 2012[1] Part 14 implements Council Directive 2001/83/EC and ensures that a relevant medicinal product is only promoted in accordance with its marketing authorisation.

Definitions

An *advertisement* is defined as (HMRs Reg.7) anything designed to promote the prescription, supply, sale or use of a medicinal product. This includes:

A door-to-door canvassing;
B visits by medical sales representatives to persons qualified to prescribe or supply medicinal products;
C the supply of samples;
D the provision of inducements to prescribe or supply medicinal products by the gift, offer or promise of any benefit or bonus, whether in money or in kind, except where the intrinsic value of such inducements is minimal;
E the sponsorship of promotional meetings attended by persons qualified to prescribe or supply medicinal products; and
F the sponsorship of scientific congresses attended by persons qualified to prescribe or supply medicinal products, including the payment of their travelling and accommodation expenses in that connection.

It does not include:

a a medicinal product's package or package leaflet;
b reference material and announcements of a factual and informative nature, including:

[1] Human Medicines Regulations SI 2012 No. 1916

    i material relating to changes to a medicinal product's package or package leaflet,

    ii adverse reaction warnings,

    iii trade catalogues, and

    iv price lists, provided that no product claim is made; and

c correspondence, which may be accompanied by material of a non-promotional nature, answering a specific question about a medicinal product.

In this Regulation, a 'person qualified to prescribe or supply medicinal products' includes persons who, in the course of their profession or in the course of a business, may lawfully prescribe medicinal products, or sell them by retail, or supply medicinal products in circumstances corresponding to retail sale, and the employees of such persons.

Publication in relation to an advertisement is defined in HMRs Reg.277 as the dissemination or issue of that advertisement orally, in writing or by means of an electronic communication network or in any other way, and includes causing or procuring that publication by or on behalf of another person.

Requirements related to advertising

Duties of holders of marketing authorisations (HMRs Reg.281)

Any person who holds a marketing authorisation, a certificate of registration, a traditional herbal registration or an Article 126a authorisation for a medicinal product must:

1 establish a scientific service to compile and collate all information relating to that product, whether received from medical sales representatives employed by him/her or from any other source;

2 ensure that any medical sales representative who promotes the product is given sufficient training, and has sufficient scientific knowledge, to enable the representative to provide information about the product that is as precise and complete as possible;

3 retain a sample of any advertisement for which s/he is responsible relating to that product, together with a statement indicating the persons to whom the advertisement is addressed, the method of publication and the date when it was first published; and

4 provide, if required and within the period specified in a notice served by the Ministers on him/her, a copy of the sample and statement mentioned in 3, above, and any other information and assistance requested by them in order to carry out their functions under Part 14 of the HMRs.

Scrutiny by Ministers

Ministers (chapter 2) may obtain copies of any advertisement relating to medicinal products by serving a notice on the person who issued it or caused it to be issued (HMRs Reg.304). The Ministers may apply to the court for an injunction against the person concerned, or likely to be concerned, with the publication of an advertisement which is incompatible with the prohibitions imposed by Part 14, Chapter 2 of the HMRs.

General principles

A person may not publish an advertisement for a medicinal product unless a marketing authorisation, a certificate of registration, a traditional herbal registration or an Article 126a authorisation is in force for the product (HMRs Reg.279). See later for advertising in relation to registered homoeopathic medicinal products.

The general requirements (HMRs Reg.280) are that a person may not publish an advertisement for a medicinal product:

1 with a marketing authorisation, a traditional herbal registration or an Article 126a authorisation unless it complies with the particulars listed in the Summary of Product Characteristics;
2 unless that advertisement encourages the rational use of that product by presenting it objectively and without exaggerating its properties;
3 which is misleading.

Advertisements directed to the public (HMRs Regs.282–292)

The Regulations dealing with advertisements that are directed to the public impose a range of prohibitions, restrictions and requirements, the most significant of which are set out below.

No advertisement may be published which is likely to lead to the use of a medicinal product:

1 for the purpose of inducing an abortion in women (Reg.283);
2 that is likely to lead to the use of a POM (Reg.284);
3 that contains a Controlled Drug or is listed in specified parts of the Psychotropic Substances Convention (Reg.285);
4 that states or implies that a medical consultation or surgical intervention is unnecessary, that offers to provide a diagnosis or suggest a treatment by post or by means of an electronic communications network or might, by a description or detailed representation of a case history, lead to an erroneous self-diagnosis (Reg.286);

5   that suggests a guaranteed effect or no adverse reactions, or that the effects of taking the medicinal product are better than or equivalent to those of another identifiable treatment or medicinal product (Reg.287);

6   that uses misleading or potentially alarming terms or pictures of changes in the human body caused by disease or injury or the action of the medicinal product on the human body (Reg.287);

7   that refers to claims of recovery in terms that are misleading or likely to cause alarm (Reg.287);

8   that suggests that the health of a person not suffering from any disease or illness could be enhanced by taking the medicinal product, or that (with the exception of approved vaccination campaigns) the health of a person could be affected by not taking the medicinal product (Reg.287);

9   that wrongly implies that the product is a foodstuff, cosmetic or other consumer product that is not a medicinal product or that its safety or efficacy is due to the fact that it is natural (Reg.288);

10   that the product is recommended by scientists, health professionals or persons who, because of their celebrity, could encourage use of the medicinal product (Reg.289); or

11   that contains any material that is directed principally at children (Reg.290).

Vaccination campaigns

Certain parts of the Regulations do not apply to an advertisement as part of a vaccination campaign which relates to a medicinal product that is a vaccine or serum and which has been approved by the Ministers. In essence, this allows for the advertising of a medicinal product that is a POM, or contains a narcotic or psychotropic substance, and also allows for claims that the health of a person who is not suffering from any disease or injury could be enhanced by taking the medicinal product or that the health of a person could be affected by not taking the medicinal product.

Form and content of advertisements

No person shall publish an advertisement relating to a medicinal product unless that advertisement (HMRs Reg.291) is presented so that it is clear that it is an advertisement and so that the product is clearly identified as a medicinal product, and includes:

a   the name of the medicinal product

b   the common name of the active ingredient when only one active ingredient is contained in the product

c   the information necessary for the correct use of the product, and

d   an express and clear invitation to read carefully the instructions on the package or on the package leaflet.

These provisions do not apply if the advertisement is intended solely as a reminder of a product (which states its name, international non-proprietary name or trademark) or relates to a registered homoeopathic medicinal product.

Prohibition of supply to the public for promotional purposes

No person who is the holder of a marketing authorisation, certificate of registration, traditional herbal registration or Article 126a authorisation, or who carries on a medicines business, may sell or supply a medicinal product for a promotional purpose to a person who is not qualified to prescribe medicinal products (HMRs Reg.293).

Advertising to persons qualified to prescribe or supply

No person may issue an advertisement relating to a medicinal product and aimed at persons qualified to prescribe or supply unless the advertisement contains the particulars set out in paragraphs 1 to 8 of Schedule 30 to the HMRs (HMRs Reg.294), as summarised below:

1   the number of the marketing authorisation, certificate of registration, traditional herbal registration or Article 126a authorisation for the medicinal product;

2   the name and address of the holder of the authorisation, certificate of registration, traditional herbal registration or Article 126a authorisation for the medicinal product or the business name and address of the part of the business responsible for its sale or supply;

3   the classification of the product, i.e. POM, Pharmacy or General Sale List (GSL);

4   the name of the medicinal product;

5   a list of the active ingredients of the medicinal product using their common names and placed immediately adjacent to the most prominent display of the name of the product;

6   one or more of the indications for the medicinal product consistent with the terms of the marketing authorisation, certificate of registration, traditional herbal registration or Article 126a authorisation for the product;

7   The entries or a succinct statement of the entries in the Summary of Product Characteristics relating to:

   a   adverse reactions, precautions and relevant contra-indications,

   b   dosage and method of use relevant to the indications shown in the advertisement, and

   c   where this is not obvious, method of administration so far as relevant to those indications;

8   the cost, excluding value added tax (VAT), of either a specified package of the product or a specified quantity or recommended daily dose, calculated by reference to any specified package of the product, except that the cost may be omitted in the case of an advertisement inserted in a publication which is printed in the UK but with a circulation outside the UK of more than 15% of its total circulation; and

9 the particulars in paragraph 7 above must be printed in a clear and legible manner and be placed in such a position in the advertisement that their relationship to the claims and indications for the product can readily be appreciated by the reader.

If the advertisement relates to a Pharmacy or GSL medicine, then only the particulars set out in paragraphs 2 to 6, above, must be included, together with the statement 'Information about this product, including adverse reactions, precautions, contra-indications and a method of use can be found at:' accompanied by a website address that corresponds to that statement. The website mentioned, here, must make available the particulars set out in paragraphs 1 to 8, above (i.e. those found in Schedule 30), or a copy of the Summary of Product Characteristics.[2]

Abbreviated advertisements

Abbreviated advertisement means an advertisement, other than a loose insert, which does not exceed in size an area of $420 \, cm^2$ in a publication sent or delivered wholly or mainly to persons qualified to prescribe or supply medicinal products (HMRs Reg.295). No person may issue such an advertisement unless it:

a contains the particulars set out in paragraphs 2 to 6 of Schedule 30 of the HMRs (as set out above) for advertising to persons qualified to prescribe or supply; and

b the statement 'Information about this product, including adverse reactions, precautions, contra-indications, and method of use can be found at'; accompanied by

c a website address which corresponds to that statement; and

d the name and address of the holder of the marketing authorisation, certificate of registration, traditional herbal registration or Article 126a authorisation for the medicinal product, or the business name and address of the part of the holder's business that is responsible for its sale or supply.

The website mentioned, here, must make available the particulars set out in Schedule 30 or a copy of the Summary of Product Characteristics.

Written material accompanying promotions

No person may send or deliver any written material to a person qualified to prescribe or supply medicinal products as part of a promotion (HMRs Reg.297) unless it:

[2] As amended by the Human Medicines (Amendment) (No. 2) Regulations SI 2014 No. 1878

a contains essential information compatible with Schedule 30 of the HMRs; and

b states the date on which it was drawn up or last revised.

Any such written material shall be accurate, up to date, verifiable and sufficiently complete to enable the recipient to form an opinion of the therapeutic value of the product to which it relates and not include any quotation, table or other illustrative matter taken from a medical journal or other scientific work unless it is accurately reproduced and the precise source indicated.

Medical sales representatives

All medical sales representatives promoting medicinal products to persons qualified to prescribe or supply such products must give to or have available for all persons they visit, for promotional purposes, a copy of the Summary of Product Characteristics for each product promoted. Such representatives must report all information which they receive from persons visited for promotional purposes, with particular reference to any adverse drug reactions, to the scientific service established under the Regulations (HMRs Reg.299).

Advertisements for registered homoeopathic products

An advertisement relating to homoeopathic medicinal products may not mention any specific therapeutic indications (HMRs Reg.301) and may contain only the details specified in Schedule 28 to the Regulations (which details the labelling requirements for a registerable homoeopathic medicinal product). Nothing in Reg.291(2) (form and contents of advertisement), Reg.294 (general requirements) or Reg.295 (abbreviated advertisements) requires an advertisement relating to a homoeopathic medicinal product to which a certificate of registration relates to contain any detail not specified in Schedule 28.

Advertisements for traditional herbal medicinal products

No person may issue an advertisement for products that are marketed in the UK under a traditional herbal registration unless it contains the words 'Traditional herbal medicinal product for use in', followed by a statement of one or more therapeutic indications for the product consistent with the terms of the traditional herbal registration for that product, followed by 'exclusively based on long standing use' (HMRs Reg.302).

Holders of 'specials manufacturer's licences'

Specials manufacturers may not publish any advertisement, catalogue or circular relating to a special medicinal product or make any representations in respect of that product (HMRs Reg.22). However, price lists may be sent at reasonable intervals or in response to an enquiry to healthcare professionals to whom the price of specials may be relevant. A *price list* would typically include the active ingredient, strength, dosage form, pack size and price for each product listed, and must make no product claims.[3]

Free samples for persons qualified to prescribe or supply medicinal products

A person may supply a sample of a medicinal product to another person only if the following conditions (A–F) are met (HMRs Reg.298):

A The recipient is qualified to prescribe medicinal products, and receives the sample for the purpose of acquiring experience in dealing with the product in question.

B The sample is supplied to the recipient on an exceptional basis, and in response to a request from, and signed and dated by, the recipient.

C Taking the year in which the sample is supplied as a whole, only a limited number of samples of the product in question are supplied to the recipient in that year.

D The sample is no larger than the smallest presentation of the product that is available for sale in the UK, is marked 'free medical sample – not for resale' or bears a similar description, and is accompanied by a copy of the Summary of Product Characteristics.

E The sample does not contain:

   i a substance which is listed in any of Schedules I, II or IV to the Narcotic Drugs Convention (where the product is not a preparation listed in Schedule III to that Convention), or

   ii a substance which is listed in any of Schedules I to IV to the Psychotropic Substances Convention (where the product is not a preparation which may be exempted from measures of control in accordance with paragraphs 2 and 3 of Article 3 of that Convention).

F The supplier maintains an adequate system of control and accountability in relation to the supply of free samples.

Note that supplying samples of medicinal products to the public is unlawful.

Inducements and hospitality

Hospitality includes sponsorship of a person's attendance at a meeting or event and the payment of travelling or accommodation expenses (HMRs Reg.300). When products are being promoted to persons qualified to

[3] MHRA (2014) *The Blue Guide: Advertising and Promotion of Medicines in the UK*. 3rd edn. First revision (available on the MHRA website)

prescribe or supply them, no person may supply, offer or promise any gift, pecuniary advantage or benefit in kind unless it is inexpensive and relevant to the practice of medicine or pharmacy.

Hospitality may be offered at events for purely professional or scientific purposes to persons qualified to prescribe or supply relevant medicinal products provided that:

- such hospitality is strictly limited to the main scientific objective of the event, and
- it is offered only to health professionals.

It is an offence for a person qualified to prescribe or supply medicinal products to solicit or accept any gift, pecuniary advantage, benefit in kind, hospitality or sponsorship prohibited by the Regulations.

Monitoring of advertising

Legal provisions covering the monitoring of advertising appear in the last section of Part 14 of the HMRs. However, the existing voluntary control under existing Codes of Advertising Practice administered by the Association of the British Pharmaceutical Industry (for POMs) and by the Proprietary Association of Great Britain (for over-the-counter medicines) continues. Complaints, in the first instance, will be referred to the appropriate self-regulatory body, but the minister has the power of civil injunction. A person holding a marketing authorisation will be required to issue corrective statements if their advertising is found to be in breach of the Regulations.

There are provisions which give the Ministers powers for determining whether or not certain advertisements, proposed or published, breach the advertising regulations. There is an opportunity for representations to be made to the Independent Regulator for Communications Industries (OFCOM) before the Ministers determine the case and breaches of notices issued by the Ministers create an offence.

The Advertising Standards Authority (ASA) acts as the UK's independent regulator of advertising, and it responds to complaints made about advertising in any medium, as well as proactively checking the media to take action against misleading, harmful or offensive advertisements. A recent healthcare case taken up by the ASA is explained in box 4.1.

Box 4.1 Advertising Standards Authority (ASA) Ruling on TV advert for Nurofen Joint and Back

Eighteen complaints were received about a TV advertisement, shown in the UK, which depicted a woman taking a product called Nurofen Joint and Back for her back pain. An anatomical image showed the drug moving through the body and to the site of the pain in the back, whilst onscreen text stated 'also indicated for other aches and pains'. The voice-over claimed that a single dose of the product would provide 'constant targeted pain relief for up to 8 hours'.

The complaint was that the advertisement misleadingly implied that the product specifically targeted joint and back pain.

In its ruling, the ASA said that, whilst they understood that the active ingredient in the product was scientifically proven to relieve pain (wherever that might be in the body), the advertisement had appeared to imply that the product had a special mechanism which meant it specifically targeted back and joint pain, and was especially effective at relieving those sources of pain, when that was not the case. The onscreen text, explaining that the product could treat other types of pain had been given insufficient prominence.

RB UK was found to be in breach of the BCAP code rules:

3.1 (Misleading advertising) – advertisements must not materially mislead or be likely to do so.

3.9 (Substantiation) – advertisements must not mislead by exaggerating the capability or performance of a product or service, and

3.12 (Exaggeration) – broadcasters must hold documentary evidence to prove claims that the audience is likely to regard as objective and that are capable of objective substantiation. The ASA may regard claims as misleading in the absence of adequate substantiation.

ASA Ruling on RB UK Commercial Ltd. 29th June 2016. https://www.asa.org.uk/Rulings/Adjudications/2016/6/RB-UK-Commercial-Ltd/SHP_ADJ_338459.aspx#.WBsLvk3cuUl

Summary

- The Regulations prohibit the advertising to the public of Controlled Drugs and POMs.
- Requirements as to the information on medicinal products which has to be given to persons qualified to prescribe or supply medicines include essential information compatible with the Summary of Product Characteristics. This may be given by way of written information accompanying promotions or by promotion by medical representatives.
- A limited number only of free samples may be supplied to a person qualified to prescribe relevant medicinal products. The samples may only be

supplied in response to a written request and suppliers must maintain an adequate system of control.

- No person who is the holder of a marketing authorisation or who carries on a business which consists of the manufacturing, selling or supplying of medicinal products shall, for promotional purposes, sell or supply medicinal products to any member of the public.
- Hospitality given to persons qualified to prescribe or supply medicines must be reasonable in level and subordinate to the main objective of meetings held solely for scientific or professional purposes. No person may supply or promise any gift, pecuniary advantage or benefit in kind unless it is inexpensive and relevant to the practice of medicine or pharmacy.
- Conditions are set out for the advertising of homoeopathic medicinal products and for traditional herbal medicinal products.
- Monitoring of advertising is undertaken by self-regulatory bodies but there are also legal provisions involving the Ministers.

Further reading

Human Medicines Regulations (2012) SI 2012 No. 1916, *Explanatory memorandum*: http://www.legislation.gov.uk/uksi/2012/1916/pdfs/uksiem_20121916_en.pdf (accessed 22 September 2016).

Medicines and Healthcare products Regulatory Agency (2014). *Advertising and Promotion of Medicines in the UK* [The Blue Guide]. London: The Stationery Office.

Prescription Medicines Code of Practice Authority (2012). *Association of the British Pharmaceutical Industry's (ABPI) Code of Practice*: http://www.pmcpa.org.uk/ Pages/default.aspx (accessed 22 September 2016).

Proprietary Association of Great Britain (no date). *Best Practice Guidelines*. London: Proprietary Association of Great Britain.

Royal Pharmaceutical Society (published annually). *Medicines, Ethics and Practice: The Professional Guide for Pharmacists*. London: Royal Pharmaceutical Society (includes practice guidance on many of the topics in this chapter; free to members).

Websites

Association of British Pharmaceutical Industry: http://www.abpi.org.uk

Legislation (can be searched on year and SI number or title): http://www.legislation.gov.uk Medicines and Healthcare products Regulatory Agency: https://www.gov.uk/government/ organisations/medicines-and-healthcare-products-regulatory-agency

Prescription Medicines Code of Practice Authority: http://www.pmcpa.org.uk

Proprietary Association of Great Britain: http://www.pagb.co.uk

Royal Pharmaceutical Society (member access only; lists legal classifications of medicines and further practice guidance): http://www.rpharms.com

5

Pharmacy businesses

Susan Melvin

Lawfully conducting a retail pharmacy business

Part IV of the Medicines Act 1968, which covers retail pharmacy businesses, has not been repealed by the Human Medicines Regulations 2012[1] but has been extensively amended by other legislation. The Health Act 2006 (ss.27–30) amended sections 70–72 of the Medicines Act and replaced *personal control* with a requirement that each registered pharmacy is to have a *Responsible Pharmacist* in charge of the business where this relates to the sale or supply of medicines and other conditions for registration. A new section (s.72A) placed a statutory duty on the Responsible Pharmacist to ensure the safe and effective running of a pharmacy. This is discussed in more detail under Responsible Pharmacist below.

A *retail pharmacy business* means[2] a business (not being a professional practice carried on by a practitioner) which consists of or includes the retail sale of medicinal products other than GSL products (whether such medicinal products are sold in the course of that business or not) (s.132(1)).[3] Such a business may, subject to certain conditions, lawfully be conducted by a person (s.69) who is:

1 a pharmacist, or a partnership where each partner is a pharmacist, or, in Scotland, a partnership where one or more partners are pharmacists; or
2 a body corporate where the business so far as concerns the keeping, preparing and dispensing of medicinal products, other than GSL medicinal products, is under the management of a superintendent who is a pharmacist and who does not act in a similar capacity for any other body corporate (s.71); or
3 a representative of a pharmacist who is deceased, bankrupt or becomes a person who lacks mental capacity[4] or who is judged, via some

[1] Human Medicines Regulations SI 2012 No. 1916
[2] A slightly different definition appears in the HMRs Reg.8
[3] Sections refer to the Medicines Act 1968
[4] Mental Capacity Act 2005 c. 9

legislative order,[5,6] to be mentally ill, whose name, together with the names and address of the representative, has been notified to the Registrar of the GPhC (s.72(2)).

With regard to item 3, the following apply:

1. In relation to a pharmacist who has died, 'representative' means his/her executor or administrator and, for a period of 3 months from the date of his/her death if s/he has died leaving no executor who is entitled and willing to carry on the business, includes any person beneficially interested in his/her estate. The representative of a deceased pharmacist may carry on the business for a period of up to 5 years from the date of his/her death. Should s/he cease to be a representative before the expiry of 5 years, on completing the distribution of the deceased pharmacist's estate, his/her authority lawfully to carry on the pharmacy business would also come to an end.

2. Where a pharmacist is adjudged bankrupt or, in Scotland, sequestration of his/her estate is awarded, the trustee in bankruptcy or in the sequestration is the pharmacist's representative. S/he may carry on the pharmacist's business for a period of 3 years from the date on which s/he is adjudged bankrupt or the date of the award of sequestration, as the case may be.

3. Where a pharmacist enters into a composition or scheme or deed of arrangement with his/her creditors, or in Scotland makes a trust deed for behoof of his/her creditors, or a composition contract, then the trustee appointed under any such arrangement is the pharmacist's representative. S/he may carry on the business for a period of 3 years from the date on which s/he became entitled to do so.

4. Where a deputy or donee is appointed for a pharmacist under the Mental Capacity Act 2005 or, in Scotland, a guardian or judicial factor is appointed for him/her on the grounds that s/he suffers from some mental disorder, or in Northern Ireland a controller is appointed in his case under the Mental Health (Northern Ireland) Order 1986, then that person is the pharmacist's representative. S/he may carry on the business for 3 years from the date of his/her appointment.

A person lawfully conducting a retail pharmacy business as the representative of a pharmacist may take or use in connection with that business any title, emblem or description which the pharmacist him/herself could have used (s.78(8)) (see below). The Health Ministers may, by Order, add to, revoke or vary any of these conditions relating to the carrying on of retail pharmacy business, or provide for alternative or modified conditions. Such an Order must receive the approval of each House of Parliament (s.73).

---

[5] Adults with Incapacity (Scotland) Act 2000
[6] Mental Health (Northern Ireland) Order SI 1986 No. 595 (N.I. 4)

Responsible Pharmacist

Under section 72A of the Medicines Act 1968, the Responsible Pharmacist must secure the safe and effective running of the pharmacy business at the premises in question so far as it concerns the sale or supply of medicinal products. A person may not be the Responsible Pharmacist for more than one set of premises at the same time[7] and the name of the Responsible Pharmacist for the time being with his/her registration name and number must be conspicuously displayed in the pharmacy. In addition, s/he must:

- establish, maintain and review pharmacy procedures that set out how activities are to be carried out in the pharmacy; and
- maintain a record at the pharmacy of the Responsible Pharmacist who is in charge of the pharmacy on any date and at any time; and
- comply with any other regulations made for Responsible Pharmacists.

In the 2016 case of *Abdul-Razzak v GPhC*,[8] it was ruled that the duty of the Responsible Pharmacist to ensure patient safety by supervising the supply and sale of POMs was 'a vital and pro-active responsibility which cannot be satisfied by relying on the experience of the counter-staff, who are not registered pharmacists'.

Where the business is carried on by a pharmacist or partners, the Responsible Pharmacist must be the person carrying on the business; in a partnership, one of the partners or another pharmacist must be the Responsible Pharmacist. Where the business is carried on by a body corporate, the Responsible Pharmacist must be the superintendent or a manager subject to the directions of the superintendent who is a pharmacist. Where the business is carried on by a representative, a pharmacist must be appointed as the Responsible Pharmacist.

Section 72A also provides that the person carrying on the business must ensure that the record of the Responsible Pharmacist is properly maintained and preserved for at least as long as is specified in Regulations (5 years, see below). This section also provides powers to specify the qualifications and experience which a pharmacist must have if s/he is to be a Responsible Pharmacist but this has not yet been implemented.

The Responsible Pharmacist Regulations

In the Responsible Pharmacist Regulations,[9] *pharmacy business* means the business in respect of which the Responsible Pharmacist has a duty under

---

[7] A long-standing provision that the Responsible Pharmacist (formerly the pharmacist in personal control) in a pharmacy, registered for less than 3 months, could not be from an EEA country was repealed by the Medicines Act (Pharmacy) Order SI 2011 No. 2647

[8] [2016] EWHC 1204 (Admin)

[9] The Medicines (Pharmacies) (Responsible Pharmacist) Regulations SI 2008 No. 2789

section 72A of the Medicines Act and *premises* means the premises from which the pharmacy business is carried on. *Pharmacy staff* means any pharmacist or any other person who is working at the premises in question in a role connected to the pharmacy business (Responsible Pharmacist (RP) Reg.2). *Business hours* means the period during which the pharmacy business is operational on any day and *day* means the 24-hour period beginning and ending at midnight (RP Reg.3).

Absence of the Responsible Pharmacist

The maximum period for which the Responsible Pharmacist may be absent from the premises is 2 hours during pharmacy business hours. If there is more than one Responsible Pharmacist during pharmacy hours, the maximum period applies to the total period of absence for all of them.

The Responsible Pharmacist must not be absent unless the following arrangements are in place:

- Where it is reasonably practical for the Responsible Pharmacist to be contactable during the period of absence, arrangements must ensure that s/he can be contactable by other pharmacy staff and return with reasonable promptness if in his/her opinion it is necessary to secure the safe and effective running of the business.
- Where it is not possible to put these arrangements into place, arrangements must be made to ensure another pharmacist is both available and contactable to advise other pharmacy staff.

The sale of GSL medicines may continue from the premises in the absence of the Responsible Pharmacist.

Pharmacy procedures

The matters which must be covered by pharmacy procedures are:

a the arrangements to secure that medicinal products are ordered, stored, prepared, sold or supplied by retail, delivered outside the pharmacy, and disposed in a safe and effective manner;
b the circumstances in which a pharmacy member of staff who is not a pharmacist may give advice on medicinal products;
c the identification of members of staff who are in the view of the Responsible Pharmacist competent to perform such tasks relating to the business;
d the keeping of records about the arrangements mentioned in (a) above;
e the arrangements which are to apply during the absence of the Responsible Pharmacist;
f the steps to be taken when there is a change of Responsible Pharmacist;
g the procedures to be taken when there is a complaint made against the pharmacy business;

h the procedures which should apply when an incident occurs which may indicate that the pharmacy business is not running in a safe and effective manner; and

i the manner in which changes to the pharmacy procedures are notified to the pharmacy staff.

Pharmacy procedures must be:

a recorded in writing, in electronic form or both;

b available for inspection by the person carrying out the business, the superintendent (if any), the Responsible Pharmacist and pharmacy staff; and

c reviewed regularly.

In this Regulation, *pharmacy procedures* means those procedures referred to in section 71A(3) of the Medicines Act.

Pharmacy records

The particulars to be kept are:

1 the name of the Responsible Pharmacist;

2 the registration number of the Responsible Pharmacist in the Register of Pharmacists;

3 the date and time at which the Responsible Pharmacist became the Responsible Pharmacist;

4 the date and time at which the Responsible Pharmacist ceased to be the Responsible Pharmacist;

5 in relation to any absence of the Responsible Pharmacist from the premises on a day on which they were a Responsible Pharmacist:

    a the date of the absence,

    b the time at which the absence commenced, and

    c the time at which s/he returned to the premises.

The pharmacy record must:

1 be kept in writing, in electronic form, or both;

2 be available for inspection by the person carrying on the business, the superintendent (if any), the Responsible Pharmacist and pharmacy staff;

3 be preserved by the owner of the business for a period of not less than 5 years commencing on:

    a in the case of record in electronic form, the date on which it was created, or

    b in the case of written record, the last day to which the record relates.

In this Regulation, *pharmacy record* means the record referred to in section 71A(4) of the Medicines Act.

Registration of pharmacy premises

Provision for the registration of pharmacies was originally under sections 74–77 of the Medicines Act but these sections have been significantly amended by Article 68 and Schedule 4 of the Pharmacy Order 2010[10] and will be subject to further amendment by the Pharmacy (Premises Standards, Information Obligations, etc.) Order 2016.[11] The registrar of premises is now the Registrar of the GPhC (Art.18) or, where appropriate, the Pharmaceutical Society of Northern Ireland. It is the Registrar's duty to keep the Register of Pharmacy Premises and, subject to the provisions described below, to enter in the Register, on payment of the prescribed fee, any premises in respect of which application is made (s.75(1)). A document purporting to be a certificate signed by the Registrar and stating that, on a specified date, specified premises were, or were not, entered in the Register shall be admissible in any proceedings as evidence (and, in Scotland, shall be sufficient evidence) that those premises were, or were not, entered in the Register on that date (s.74 L).

Registered pharmacy means premises entered for the time being in Part 3 of the GPhC Register (Art.3 and Art.19).[12] Where a business which concerns the retail sale or supply of medicinal products is carried on in one or more separate or distinct parts of a building, each part is taken to be separate premises (s.69(2)). A departmental store or supermarket, for example, might have a department or area which is a registered pharmacy and a separate department or area (which is not a pharmacy) where GSL medicines are sold.

Conditions for registration of pharmacy premises must be fulfilled in a prescribed manner (s.74B) and as in Part 5 of the Registration Rules[13] (chapter 20). An application must be in writing and be given or sent to the Registrar with the prescribed fee. It must be made and signed by or on behalf of the person carrying on, or who intends to carry on, a retail pharmacy business at the premises to which the application relates. A separate application must be made in respect of each premises. Each application has particular requirements with which the applicant must comply.

1 The applicant must specify:
   a the applicant's full name, address and contact details (including a telephone number and electronic mail address, where possible);
   b the full postal address of the premises to which the application relates;

[10] The Pharmacy Order 2010 SI 2010 No. 231
[11] SI 2016 No. 372
[12] A similar definition appears in HMRs Reg.3
[13] The GPhC (Registration Rules) Order of Council SI 2010 No. 1617

   c whether the applicant is aware that the premises to which the application relates have previously been entered in Part 3 of the Register;

   d the name under which the retail pharmacy business that is, or is to be, carried on at the premises trades or is to trade;

   e whether the applicant is, or will be, a person lawfully conducting a retail pharmacy business at the premises within the meaning of Part 4 of the (Medicines) Act;

   f the date, or intended date, of the commencement of the retail pharmacy business carried on, or to be carried on, at the premises;

   g where the retail pharmacy business is, or is to be, carried on at the premises by a representative, the name of the Responsible Pharmacist;

   h where the applicant is a partner in a partnership, the names of all the partners in the partnership;

   i where the applicant is a body corporate;

   j the names of all of the directors of the body corporate; and

   k the name of the superintendent pharmacist.

2 The applicant must pay the prescribed fee in respect of the application.

3 The applicant must provide:

   a a description of the premises to which the application relates;

   b details of the type of activities undertaken, or intended to be undertaken, at the premises;

   c a plan, drawn to scale, of the internal layout of the premises showing the areas in which medicinal products are intended to be sold or supplied, assembled, prepared, dispensed or stored;

   d a declaration:

      i confirming that the standards set in rules under Article 7(1) of the Order in connection with the carrying on of a retail pharmacy business at a registered pharmacy are met in connection with the retail pharmacy business carried on, or intended to be carried on, at the premises, and

      ii providing details of any relevant offence or relevant investigation within the meaning of Article 7(6)(a) and (b) of the Order.

4 The applicant must provide any other necessary supporting documents, information or evidence as mentioned in the application form.

5 The application procedure also informs the applicant that, if the declaration included in the application is not completed to the satisfaction of the Registrar, the Registrar may refuse to enter the premises in Part 3 of the Register because the conditions specified in section 74B of the Act are not met.

6 The applicant must sign and date the application.

The Registrar must refuse any application for the entry of premises in Part 3 of the Register if:

a it is not accompanied by the necessary supporting documents, information or evidence as mentioned in the application form or subsequently required by the Registrar; or

b the applicant has not paid, or has not made arrangements with the Registrar to pay by direct debit, the prescribed fee in respect of the application.

Change of ownership

Where a change occurs in the ownership of a registered pharmacy, the registration becomes void at the end of the period of 28 days from the date on which the change occurs. If it occurs on the death of the person carrying on the business (i.e. the death of a pharmacist owner or, in the case of a partnership, one of the partners), the period is 3 months from the date of the death (s.74H).

When the registration of pharmacy premises becomes void following a change of ownership, an application for restoration to the Register may be made by the new owner. The Registrar must restore the premises to the Register if s/he is reasonably satisfied that the new owner is a person lawfully conducting a retail pharmacy business or will be so at the time s/he commences business at the premises. A fee equal to a retention fee must be paid by the new owner, but only if the retention fee for the year has not already been paid (s.74H(5)). No description of the premises or sketch plan need be submitted.

Premises retention fees

A retention fee is payable annually in respect of any premises entered in the Register for each year subsequent to the year in which they were registered (Art.24). In this context, year means a rolling period of 12 months beginning on the date of registration of the premises. At least 3 months before the date of registration expiry, the Registrar will send to each person carrying on a retail pharmacy business, entered in Part 3 of the register, an application form, which must be returned by that person within 2 months of the renewal date.

The GPhC may direct the Registrar to remove any premises from the Register if the person carrying on the retail pharmacy business fails to pay a retention fee within 2 months from the date on which a demand for it has been made to him/her in the prescribed manner. If, before the end of the year, or whatever period is permitted by the GPhC in any particular case, the retention fee is paid, together with any prescribed sum by way of penalty, the Registrar must restore the premises to the Register. If the GPhC so directs, the restoration shall be deemed to have had effect as from the date on which the premises were removed from the Register. (For Northern Ireland, any reference to the GPhC in this section should be construed as a reference to the Minister of Health and Social Services for Northern Ireland.)

The GPhC is responsible for making any rules relating to the registration of pharmacies (Art.19(3)) and for setting the standards that are to be met in connection with the carrying on of a retail pharmacy business at a registered pharmacy (Art.7) (chapter 22).

Titles, descriptions and emblems

No person may, in connection with any business, use any title, description or emblem likely to suggest that s/he possesses any qualification with respect to the sale, manufacture or assembly of medicinal products which s/he does not in fact possess, or that any person employed in the business possesses any such qualification which that person does not in fact possess (s.78(6)).

Furthermore, the use of certain titles and descriptions is specifically restricted as follows:

1 The description *pharmacy* may only be used in respect of a registered pharmacy or the pharmaceutical department of a hospital or a health centre. It may not be used in connection with any business, other than a pharmacy, which consists of or includes the retail sale of any goods, or the supply of any goods in circumstances corresponding to retail sale (s.78(4)). Its use in connection with a business carried on at any premises shall be taken as likely to suggest that the person carrying on the business (where that person is not a body corporate) is a pharmacist, and that any other person under whose personal control the business is carried on at those premises (so far as concerns the retail sale of medicinal products or the supply of such products in circumstances corresponding to retail sale) is also a pharmacist.

2 The titles *Pharmaceutical Chemist, Pharmaceutist, Pharmacist (or* fferyllydd – its equivalent in the Welsh language) may only be taken or used by pharmacists (s.78(5)), that is, those on the Register held by the GPhC. These titles may not be used at any premises connected with a business which includes the retail sale or supply of any goods unless those premises are a registered pharmacy or a hospital or health centre (s.78(5)).

3 The titles *Chemist and Druggist, Druggist, Dispensing Chemist or Dispensing Druggist* may only be taken or used by a person lawfully conducting a retail pharmacy business (s.78(2)). The taking or using of the title

Chemist is also restricted to a person lawfully conducting a retail pharmacy business but only in connection with the sale of any goods by retail or the supply of any goods in circumstances corresponding to retail sale (s.78(2)) (see box 5.1).

Box 5.1 *Taking the title 'chemist'*

Norris v Weeks (1970)

The Pharmacy Act 1954 (s.19) read: 'it shall not be lawful for any person, unless he is a registered pharmaceutical chemist . . . (b) to take or use, in connection with the sale of goods by retail, the title of chemist.'

A notice, about 1 ft high by 2.5 ft wide (30 cm by 75 cm) was displayed at Mr Weeks' drug store over goods intended for retail sale. It bore the wording on three lines, *Wyn's/Chemist/Sundries*. The word 'chemist' was in larger script than the other words and in a different colour. The magistrate dismissed a summons under section 19(1)(b) on the grounds that, having regard to the articles displayed, the word *chemist* was merely descriptive of the type of goods sold.

The High Court dismissed an appeal against this decision. It was held that an offence is committed only if a person asserts that they are a chemist or takes to themself the title 'chemist'. It could not be said that an offence is committed whenever the word 'chemist' appears.

Pharm J, 14 March 1970, p. 268; *The Times*, 6 March 1970.

Where the person lawfully conducting the retail pharmacy business is a body corporate, these titles may only be used if the pharmacist who is superintendent is also a member of the board of the body corporate (s.78(3)). None of these titles may be used at any premises connected with a business which includes the retail sale or supply of any goods unless those premises are a registered pharmacy (s.78(3)). The Ministers may by Order, and after consultation with the GPhC, impose further restrictions or requirements with respect to the use of titles, descriptions and emblems. The Ministers may also provide that existing restrictions shall cease to have effect or be subject to specified exceptions. Regulations for these purposes must be approved by resolution of each House of Parliament (s.79).

Standards in pharmacies

Power to regulate standards in pharmacies originally lay in sections 66–68 of the Medicines Act 1968, but these sections were repealed by the HMRs

(Sch. 35). Power to set standards for pharmacies now lies with the GPhC and these are discussed more fully in chapter 20.

Summary

- Retail businesses which sell medicines not on a GSL must be registered as pharmacies. They may be owned by a pharmacist, a partnership, a body corporate or a representative of a deceased pharmacist. The concept of the Responsible Pharmacist was introduced as a new section in the Medicines Act 1968 (s.72A) with detailed Regulations.
- Detailed requirements relating to the premises, together with a fee, must be forwarded to the GPhC in order for registration to take place.
- Certain titles may only be used by pharmacists, for example pharmacist, pharmaceutical chemist.
- A body corporate may use the title dispensing chemist, chemist and druggist or chemist only if the superintendent is a member of the board, otherwise the body corporate may only use the title pharmacy in connection with its pharmacy premises.
- The GPhC, by way of rules, may impose a large range of conditions relating to premises from which medicines are sold.

Further reading

Websites

General Pharmaceutical Council (details of pharmacy standards):
   http://www.pharmacyregulation.org

6

Human medicines: Pharmacy Medicines

Karen Pitchford

Part 12 of the Human Medicines Regulations 2012[1] is concerned with the regulation of the sale and supply of medicines. The basic principle, set out in Reg.220, is that medicinal products may be sold or supplied by retail only from registered pharmacies, unless they are products classified as GSL (General Sale List: chapter 7) or subject to some other exemption under the Regulations.

Regulation 220 provides that medicinal products which are not subject to general sale (i.e. which are not GSL medicines) shall not be sold or supplied, or offered for sale or supply, in circumstances corresponding to retail sale by any person in the course of a business carried on by him/her unless:

1 that person is, in respect of that business, a person lawfully conducting a retail pharmacy business;
2 the product is sold, supplied or offered or offered for sale or supply on premises which are a registered pharmacy; and
3 that person or, if the transaction is carried out on his/her behalf by another person, then that other person is, or acts under the supervision of, a pharmacist.

The above does not apply to the supply of a medicinal product in the event or anticipation of pandemic disease (see pandemic exemption, chapter 8).

NB. A retail pharmacy business must be under the control of a Responsible Pharmacist so far as it concerns the sale of medicinal products including products classified as GSL (ss.27–29 Health Act 2006, chapter 5). The meaning of *supervision* has been considered by the High Court and the Statutory Committee (see box 6.1) and is the subject of guidance from the GPhC (see box 6.2) but is currently under review at the time of going to press.

[1]Human Medicines Regulations SI 2012 No. 1916

Box 6.1 *The meaning of 'supervision'*

Roberts v Littlewoods Mail Order Stores Ltd (1943)

The Pharmacy and Poisons Act 1933 (s.18) provided: '...it shall not be lawful for a person to sell any poison in Part I of the Poisons List unless...the sale is effected by, or under the supervision of, a registered pharmacist.' Similar wording (related to medicinal products not on a General Sale List) was included in section 52 of the Medicines Act and is now included in the Human Medicines Regulations 2012.

A sale of a Part I poison was made at a Littlewood's company pharmacy to one of the Society's inspectors while the sole pharmacist was in a stockroom upstairs and unaware that the sale was being made by an unqualified assistant. The magistrates found that the sale, though not effected by the pharmacist, was effected sufficiently under his supervision. His actual presence was not reasonably required.

The decision was reversed in the High Court, where it was held that the sale had not been supervised. Lord Caldecote said:

> ...the man who was upstairs might have been a person who was exercising personal control of a business, but I do not think that, while he was upstairs and therefore absent, he could be a person who was supervising a particular sale. It has been suggested that a man can supervise a sale without being bodily present. I do not accept that contention...each individual sale must be, not necessarily effected by the qualified person, but something which is shown by the evidence to be under his supervision in the sense that he must be aware of what is going on at the counter, and in a position to supervise or superintend the activities of the young woman by whom each individual sale is effected.

[1943] 1 All ER 271; *Pharm J*, 30 January 1943 p. 38.

Box 6.2 *The meaning of 'supervision'*

Summers v Congreve Horner & Co

In their *Guidance for Responsible Pharmacists* (2010), the General Pharmaceutical Council cites the case of *Summers v Congreve Horner & Co* in considering the meaning of supervision, as applied to the assembly of medicines. The case sets out that 'supervision' can exist, *even in the absence of physical presence.*

An assistant surveyor of less than 5 years' professional experience had received that degree of supervision required by good practice in the profession of surveying for the purposes of a particular professional indemnity policy, notwithstanding that the supervisor had not actually attended at the property being surveyed. D, a firm of surveyors, sent T, a graduate with 3.5 years' practical experience, to carry out a structural survey of the house in question. T was provided with a checklist by H, a partner, and his subsequent draft report was then submitted to, discussed with and eventually approved by H, who did not, however, visit the property. When P, the purchasers, subsequently brought proceedings claiming that the report was negligent, D sought to rely upon their professional indemnity policy. The policy was expressed not to cover any claim arising from the survey, inspection or valuation of real property unless the work had been carried out (a) by a fellow or associate of one of a number of professional bodies or (b) by anyone who had no less than 5 years' experience of such work or such other person nominated by the assured to carry out such work subject always to the supervision of such work by a person qualified in accordance with (a) above. The official referee held that, save in exceptional circumstances, some attendance at the property was required in order for there to be such supervision as to bring the claim within the insurance policy; and that, there having been no attendance by H, D could not claim under the policy.

Held, allowing D's appeal by a majority, that supervision is a matter of degree, and that there had in fact been that degree of supervision required by good practice in the profession of surveying for a person of T's training and experience.

[1992] 40 E.G. 144.

The current professional convention for facilitating supervision is by making sales by trained assistants and placing Pharmacy (P) Medicines behind a counter. There is case law on the meaning of the point of sale when it is effected by self-service (see box 6.3).

Selling by retail or retail sale includes all those sales which do not fall within the definition of selling by way of wholesale dealing, and supplying in circumstances corresponding to retail sale has a comparable meaning (HMRs Reg.8). Retail sale or supply, therefore, comprises all those sales or supplies of medicinal products made in the course of a business to a person who buys (or receives) them for the purpose other than that of (a) selling or supplying them or (b) administering them or causing them to be administered to one or more human beings in the course of a business carried on by him/her.

> ### Box 6.3 *The meaning of point of sale*
>
> Pharmaceutical Society of Great Britain v Boots Cash Chemists (Southern) Ltd (1953)
>
> This was a case arising under the Pharmacy and Poisons Act 1933 (s.18) (see also box 6.1). It was an appeal by the Pharmaceutical Society against a judgment of the Lord Chief Justice in the High Court.
>
> A Boots pharmacy was arranged on a 'self-service' system. A customer could select goods, including Part I poisons (roughly equivalent today to Pharmacy Medicines), from the shelves, place them in a wire basket and take them to the cash desk. Before the cashier accepted payment, a pharmacist at the cash desk could, if s/he thought fit, prevent a sale. It was suggested by the Society that a purchase was completed when a customer took an article and put it in the basket so that the pharmacist could not later intervene. That suggestion had not been accepted in the High Court by the Lord Chief Justice, who had said that self-service was no different from the normal transactions in a shop. He had continued:
>
> > . . . the mere fact that a customer picks up a bottle of medicine from the shelves in this case does not amount to an acceptance of an offer to sell. It is an offer by the customer to buy . . . By using the words the sale is effected by, or under the supervision of, a registered pharmacist, it seems to me the sale might be effected by somebody not a pharmacist. If it be under the supervision of a pharmacist, the pharmacist can say: 'You cannot have that. That contains poison'. In this case I decide . . . that there is no sale until the buyer's offer to buy is accepted by the acceptance of the money, and that takes place under the supervision of a pharmacist . . .
>
> The Court of Appeal upheld this decision and dismissed the appeal by the Society. This means that a sale is not complete until the price is agreed with the purchaser by the person selling, and that this point of sale remains the same whether or not goods have been handed over a counter or picked up by self-service.
>
> [1953] 1 All ER 482; *Pharm J*, 14 February 1953 p. 115.

Pharmacy Medicine defined

Prescription Only Medicines (POMs) may only be sold or supplied from pharmacies in accordance with a prescription given by an appropriate practitioner. Any medicinal product which is not a POM or a medicinal product classified as GSL is a *Pharmacy Medicine* (P Medicine) (HMRs Reg.5). There is no definitive list of Pharmacy Medicines as the total in the class cannot be determined. It comprises all those medicines which are covered by a marketing authorisation which specifies that the product is to be available only from a pharmacy, or which are covered by an EU marketing authorisation in which the product is not classified either as a GSL or a POM. It also includes all medicines made in a pharmacy for retail sale under the exemptions from licensing granted to pharmacists under section 10 of the Medicines Act 1968 (see exemptions for pharmacists, chapter 3), unless for some reason the product must be classified as a POM (see chapter 8). Schedule 1 of the HMRs also specifies certain classes of medicinal product which are to be available only from a pharmacy, that is, are not to be on general sale (chapter 7). Some GSL medicines, when presented in packs exceeding specified quantities, may only be sold or supplied from pharmacies (see retail pack sizes of certain products, chapter 7). Some POMs when presented in packs not exceeding specified quantities may only be sold or supplied from pharmacies (see Exemptions from prescription only control, chapter 8).

Exemptions in cases involving another's default

The restrictions imposed with regards to the sale of Pharmacy Medicines shall not apply to the sale or supply, or offer for sale or supply, of a medicinal product by a person if s/he, having exercised all due diligence, believes on reasonable grounds that the product is subject to general sale, that belief is due to the act or default of another person and the conditions applying to retail sale or supply of GSL medicinal products are met (HMRs Reg.244).

The conditions under which GSL medicines may be sold are described in chapter 7.

Exemption for collection and delivery arrangements

A *collection and delivery arrangement* means an arrangement whereby a person may take or send a prescription given by a doctor, dentist, nurse independent prescriber, pharmacist independent prescriber, physiotherapist independent prescriber, podiatrist independent prescriber, therapeutic radiographer independent prescriber or optometrist independent prescriber to premises other than a registered pharmacy, and which are capable of being closed by the occupier to exclude the public and collect or have collected on his/her behalf from such premises a medicinal product prepared or dispensed in accordance with such a prescription at a registered pharmacy by or under the supervision of a pharmacist. When an arrangement of this kind is used by a person lawfully conducting a retail pharmacy business, the supply of dispensed medicines at the non-pharmacy premises without the supervision of a pharmacist is rendered lawful by an exemption provided (HMRs Reg.248).

Summary

- Pharmacy Medicines comprise all medicinal products which are not classified as being subject to GSL or POM status or are exempt in some way from the latter.
- The legislation requires that retail sales or supplies of Pharmacy Medicines have to be made by a person conducting a retail pharmacy business, at a registered pharmacy and by, or under the supervision of, a pharmacist.
- The conditions under which Pharmacy Medicines must be sold do not apply where there is a collection and delivery arrangement in place, or where a pandemic situation exists.

Further reading

Human Medicines Regulations (2012) SI 2012 No. 1916, *Explanatory memorandum*: http://www.legislation.gov.uk/uksi/2012/1916/pdfs/uksiem_20121916_en.pdf (accessed 2 November 2016).

Royal Pharmaceutical Society (published annually). *Medicines, Ethics and Practice: The Professional Guide for Pharmacists*. London: Royal Pharmaceutical Society (includes practice guidance on many of the topics in this chapter; free to members).

Websites

Legislation (can be searched on year and SI number or title): http://www.legislation.gov.uk

Medicines and Healthcare products Regulatory Agency: https://www.gov.uk/government/organisations/medicines-and-healthcare-products-regulatory-agency

Royal Pharmaceutical Society (member access only; lists legal classifications of medicines and further practice guidance): http://www.rpharms.com

7

Human medicines: General Sale Medicines

Karen Pitchford

General Sale Medicines (commonly called GSL medicines) are those which may be sold or supplied at places other than pharmacy premises and without the supervision of a pharmacist.

In the Regulations (Reg.5), a medicinal product subject to general sale is defined as a product that is not a POM or a Pharmacy Medicine but is a product that is covered by an:

a authorisation of which it is a term that the product is to be available on general sale; or

b EU marketing authorisation, and is not classified in the authorisation as a POM and the licensing authority has determined should be available on general sale.

General Sale List Medicines defined

The classes of medicinal product on general sale for administration to human beings are set out in the Medicines (Products Other Than Veterinary Drugs) (General Sale List) Order 1984[1] (the GSL Order), as amended. They are defined, in the GSL Order, as medicinal products which, in the opinion of the Ministers, can with reasonable safety be sold or supplied otherwise than by or under the supervision of a pharmacist. They include medicinal products which are not POMs but which are medicinal products with a marketing authorisation, or a traditional herbal registration, in which the product is classified as being a General Sale List medicine. They also include products which are not POMs and do not have a marketing authorisation

[1]The Medicines (Products Other Than Veterinary Drugs) (General Sale List) Order SI 1984 No. 769

or traditional herbal registration, which fall within a class specified in Schedule 1, but not one specified in Schedule 3, of the GSL Order. The GSL Order also refers to 'product licences of right' which are licences which were in force immediately before the coming into force of the relevant legislation (the Act then the HMRs, as applicable). Reference to such licences was removed from the Act by the HMRs, although the HMRs still refer to this revoked part of the Act.

Schedule 1 to the GSL Order lists products which may be classified as being GSL, sometimes subject to a specified maximum dose, maximum daily dose, use, pharmaceutical form or route of administration, maximum strength or maximum amount released. Schedule 3 to the GSL Order lists those classes of medicinal products which are not to be on general sale (see below).

The GSL Order has not been updated for over 10 years. Where a product has a marketing authorisation, its classification for the purposes of the GSL Order is determined by that authorisation.

Conditions applying to retail sale or supply of General Sale List medicinal products

Regulation 221 of the HMRs sets out that a person may sell or supply, or offer for sale or supply, a medicinal product that is subject to general sale at a place elsewhere than at a registered pharmacy only if the following conditions are met:

1 The place at which the medicinal product is sold, supplied, or offered for sale or supply, consists of premises of which that person is the occupier and which s/he is able to close so as to exclude the public.
2 The medicinal product was made up for sale in its immediate and outer packaging elsewhere than at the place at which it is sold, supplied or offered for sale or supply and the immediate and outer packaging has not been opened since the product was made up for sale in it.
3 The medicinal product is of a kind specified in Schedule 15 to the HMRs (see below) and is presented for sale in accordance with the requirements specified in that Schedule for a product of that kind.

Note that it is now possible to sell GSL medicines from aircraft and trains (see below).

Schedule 15 to the HMRs relates to the retail pack sizes of certain products (see below).

The above does not apply to the supply of a medicinal product in the event or anticipation of pandemic disease (see chapter 8).

Sales on aircraft and trains

An amendment order to the Human Medicines Regulations[2] now permits the sale of GSL medicines from aircraft and trains, subject to certain conditions. The sale may be made by the operator or commander of an aircraft or the operator of a train provided that the medicinal product:

a has been made up for sale or supply in a container elsewhere than at the place at which it is sold or supplied; and

b is stored in a part of the aircraft or train which the operator is able to close so as to exclude the public.

Automatic machines

Medicinal products which are subject to general sale may be sold or offered for sale from automatic machines (HMRs Reg.222). Such machines must be located in premises which the occupier is able to close so as to exclude the public.

Retail pack sizes of certain products

Limits are imposed on the pack sizes of certain GSL products when they are sold or supplied by retail from businesses other than pharmacies. If sold outside the limits laid down, the medicinal products concerned are classed as *Pharmacy Medicines* or POMs. The limits for general sale are as follows.

Aloxiprin, aspirin and paracetamol

A medicinal product that contains aloxiprin, aspirin or paracetamol (or, where appropriate, any combination of those substances) and that is in the form specified in table 7.1 must be presented for sale in a separate and individual package containing not more than the amount of the product specified in the corresponding entry.

Effervescent, in relation to a tablet or capsule, means containing not less than 75%, by weight of the tablet or capsule, of ingredients included wholly or mainly for the purpose of releasing carbon dioxide when the tablet or capsule is dissolved or dispersed in water (HMRs Reg.8).

Ibuprofen

A medicinal product that contains ibuprofen and that is in the form specified in table 7.2 must be presented for sale in a separate and individual package

[2]Human Medicines (Amendment) (No. 2) Regulations SI 2013 No. 2593

Table 7.1 Retail pack sizes of aloxiprin, aspirin and paracetamol (Sch. 15 to Human Medicines Regulations 2012)

Form of product	Maximum amount
Effervescent tablets: (a) that do not contain aspirin, or (b) that do not contain more than 325 milligrams of aspirin per tablet	30 tablets
Effervescent tablets: (a) that contain more than 325 milligrams of aspirin per tablet, but (b) do not contain more than 500 milligrams of aspirin per tablet	20 tablets
Non-effervescent tablets: (a) that are enteric coated, (b) that contain aspirin only, and (c) that do not contain more than 75 milligrams of aspirin per tablet	28 tablets
Other non-effervescent tablets or capsules	16 tablets or capsules
Powder or granules	10 sachets
Liquid preparations of paracetamol intended for persons aged 12 years and over	160 mL
Liquid preparations of paracetamol intended for persons younger than 12 years	Individual unit doses of not more than 5 mL each, to a maximum of 20 unit doses

Table 7.2 Retail pack sizes of ibuprofen (Sch. 15 to Human Medicines Regulations 2012)

Form of product	Maximum amount
Tablets or capsules	16 tablets or capsules
Powder or granules	12 sachets
Liquid preparations of ibuprofen	Individual unit doses of not more than 5 mL each, to a maximum of 20 unit doses

containing not more than the amount of the product specified in the corresponding entry.

Other Regulations[3] also listed medicinal products where limits were imposed on the pack sizes of GSL products when they were to be sold or

[3]The Medicines (Sale or Supply) (Miscellaneous Provisions) Regulations SI 1980 No. 1923 (now revoked)

supplied by retail from businesses other than pharmacies. These Regulations were revoked by the Human Medicines Regulations 2012 since the powers in the Medicines Act 1968, under which they were made, were repealed by the HMRs (this revocation was made without the need to be listed in the repeals and revocations schedule of the HMRs 2012). The removal of these pack size restrictions was intentional since pack size limitations, other than for paracetamol, aspirin, aloxiprin, ibuprofen and pseudoephedrine, are covered by the relevant marketing authorisations. The MHRA website had included lists of substances, according to the legal classifications of the analogous products (lists A, B and C) but these are no longer published. Hence, any queries from marketing authorisation holders considering future reclassifications for their products must now be made directly to the MHRA.

Products not to be on general sale

The Human Medicines Regulations 2012 (Sch. 1) specify certain classes of medicinal product which are to be available only from a pharmacy: that is, which are not to be on general sale. They are:

a   a product comprising eye ointment;
b   a product that contains vitamin A, vitamin A acetate or vitamin A palmitate, in each case with a maximum daily dose equivalent to more than 7500 international units of vitamin A or 2250 micrograms of retinol; and
c   a product that contains vitamin D with a maximum daily dose of more than 400 units of antirachitic activity.

The following medicinal products shall be available only from a pharmacy unless they are the subject of a marketing authorisation or traditional herbal registration that classifies them as medicinal products subject to general sale:

a   a product that is for use as an anthelmintic;
b   a product that is for parenteral administration;
c   a product that is for use as an enema;
d   a product that is for use wholly or mainly for irrigation of wounds, or the bladder, vagina or rectum;
e   a product that is for administration wholly or mainly to children being a preparation of aloxiprin or aspirin;
f   if it is a medicinal product of a kind specified in Schedule 15 (see above) but is not presented for sale in accordance with the requirements specified in that Schedule for a product of that kind to be subject to general sale.

Summary

- Medicines which in the opinion of the Ministers can, with reasonable safety, be sold other than by or under the supervision of a pharmacist are classified as GSL medicines. They may only be sold from closable premises and in their original packs.

- Certain medicines may be sold other than by or under the supervision of a pharmacist subject to certain pack sizes. These include aspirin, aloxiprin, ibuprofen and paracetamol.
- Certain medicines cannot be on general sale. These include eye ointments, most anthelmintics, parenterals, those medicines promoted as enemas or for use as irrigations, and aspirin for children.

Further reading

Human Medicines Regulations (2012) SI 2012 No. 1916, *Explanatory memorandum*: http://www.legislation.gov.uk/uksi/2012/1916/pdfs/uksiem_20121916_en.pdf (accessed 21 November 2012).

Royal Pharmaceutical Society (published annually). *Medicines, Ethics and Practice: The Professional Guide for Pharmacists*. London: Royal Pharmaceutical Society (includes practice guidance on many of the topics in this chapter; free to members).

Websites

Legislation (can be searched on year and SI number or title): http://www.legislation.gov.uk

Medicines and Healthcare products Regulatory Agency: https://www.gov.uk/government/organisations/medicines-and-healthcare-products-regulatory-agency

Royal Pharmaceutical Society (member access only; lists legal classifications of medicines and further practice guidance): http://www.rpharms.com

8

Human medicines: Prescription Only Medicines

Karen Pitchford

Prescription Only Medicines defined

A *Prescription Only Medicine* (POM) means a medicinal product (HMRs Reg.5)[1] that is:

a covered by a UK marketing authorisation or an Article 126a authorisation of which it is a term that the product is to be available only on prescription;
b covered by an EU marketing authorisation and classified in the authorisation as a POM;
c a POM by virtue of Part 1 of Schedule 1 of the Prescription Only Medicines (Human Use) Order SI 1997 No. 1830 as amended;[2] 'the POM Order'; or
d the result of the assembly, or the reformulation (including the combining with other substances), of a medicinal product that is a POM by virtue of (a) or (b), above.

Schedule 1 to the Regulations describes the classes of medicinal product which are always to be available only on prescription. They are products that are:

a for parenteral administration;
b a Controlled Drug, unless it is covered by a marketing authorisation in which the product is classified as a Pharmacy Medicine or as a medicinal product subject to general sale;
c cyanogenic substances, other than preparations for external use;

---

[1] Unless otherwise stated all Regulations in this chapter refer to the Human Medicines Regulations SI 2012 No. 1916
[2] Much of this Order has been revoked, but Schedule 1 remains in force at the time of writing

d medicinal substances that on administration emit radiation, or contain or generate any substance which emits radiation, in order that radiation may be used;

e covered by a marketing authorisation in which the product is classified as a Pharmacy Medicine or as a medicinal product subject to general sale, and consists of or contains aloxiprin, aspirin or paracetamol in the form of non-effervescent tablets or capsules (see below for exemptions);

f covered by a marketing authorisation in which the product is clas-sified as a Pharmacy Medicine or as a medicinal product subject to general sale, and consists of or contains (in any pharmaceutical form) pseudoephedrine salts or ephedrine base or salts (see below for exemptions); or

g not covered by a marketing authorisation, and is a POM by virtue of Articles 5 and 10 of, and Schedules 1 and 2 to, the POM Order.[3]

Exemptions from Prescription Only control

Medicinal products exempt due to conditions specified in Schedule 1 of the POM Order

A medicinal product that is not the subject of a marketing authorisation is a POM for the purposes of the Human Medicines Regulations 2012 if it, or a substance in it, is listed in column 1 of Schedule 1 of the POM Order, unless there is:

a an entry in Columns 2, 3, 4 or 5 of that Schedule which contains a condi-tion and that condition is satisfied; or

b more than one such condition which applies where that substance is used in that product and each of those conditions is satisfied.

The conditions mentioned above differ for different products but may pertain to the maximum strength, a route of administration, use for a specified purpose or, in a specified class of persons, a particular pharmaceutical form or a maximum quantity that may be sold or supplied.

All these exempted medicinal products will be Pharmacy Medicines (chapter 6).

Preparations of aloxiprin, aspirin or paracetamol in the form of non-effervescent tablets or capsules exempt due to maximum strength or quantity sold or supplied

Products consisting of or containing aloxiprin, aspirin or paracetamol are exempt from POM control if the quantity of the product sold or supplied to a person at any one time does not exceed 100 tablets or capsules (HMRs Reg.236).

[3] Prescription Only Medicines (Human Use) Order SI 1997 No. 1830 (as amended)

In addition, these preparations may be exempt from POM control, if the strength of the preparation does not exceed stated maxima. These are as follows:

Aspirin. If the pack size for non-effervescent tablets or capsules does not exceed 32 and the maximum strength 500 mg then the product is a Pharmacy Medicine. The total quantity sold to a person at any one time must not exceed 100.

Aspirin. If the pack size for non-effervescent tablets or capsules does not exceed 100 and the maximum strength 75 mg then the product is a Pharmacy Medicine.

Paracetamol. If the pack size for non-effervescent tablets or capsules does not exceed 32 and the maximum strength 250 mg (wholly or mainly for children under 12) or maximum strength 500 mg (for adults or children over 12), then the product is a Pharmacy Medicine. The total quantity sold to a person at any one time must not exceed 100.

Aspirin and paracetamol in preparations other than non-effervescent tablets and capsules are also Pharmacy Medicines.

Maximum strength is defined in the POM Order as either:

a the maximum quantity of a substance by weight or volume contained in a dosage unit of a medicinal product; or

b the maximum percentage of a substance contained in a medicinal product calculated in terms of weight in weight (w/w), weight in volume (w/v), volume in weight (v/w) or volume in volume (v/v) and, if the maximum percentage calculated in those ways differs, the higher or highest percentage.

Maximum dose (MD) in relation to a product for internal use means the maximum quantity of the substance contained in the amount of the product that it is recommended should be taken or administered at any one time (HMRs Reg.213).

Maximum daily dose (MDD) in relation to a product for internal use means the maximum quantity of the substance contained in the amount of the product that it is recommended should be taken or administered in any period of 24 hours.

Preparations of pseudoephedrine salts or ephedrine base or salts exempt due to conditions

Products consisting of or containing pseudoephedrine salts or ephedrine base or salts that are POMs by virtue of point (f), above, are exempt from POM control, if the following conditions are met (HMRs Reg.237):

1 A product that contains pseudoephedrine salts is not sold or supplied at the same time as another medicinal product that consists of or contains ephedrine base or salts.

2 The medicinal products sold or supplied to a person at any one time do not in total contain more than:

   a in the case of pseudoephedrine salts, 720 mg pseudoephedrine salts; or

   b in the case of ephedrine base or salts, 180 mg ephedrine base or salts.

High dilution products

There is an exemption from POM control for high dilution products diluted to at least one part per million (6×).[4] This includes certain high diluted products which are not for parenteral administration and include aconite, arsenic trioxide, belladonna herb, ignatia bean and nux vomica seed.

Sale or supply of Prescription Only Medicines

A POM may only be sold or supplied by retail in accordance with a prescription given by an appropriate practitioner (HMRs Reg.214) (see box 8.1).

Box 8.1 The meaning of 'acting in accordance with the directions of a practitioner'

Roberts v Coombs (1949)

The Penicillin Act 1947 reads:

> ...no person shall sell or otherwise supply any substance to which this Act applies or any preparation of which any such substance is an ingredient or part unless (a) he is a duly qualified medical practitioner, a registered dental practitioner or a registered veterinary surgeon, or a person acting in accordance with the directions of any such practitioner or surgeon, and the substance or preparation is sold or supplied for the purposes of treatment by or in accordance with the directions of that practitioner or surgeon; or (b) he is a registered pharmacist or an authorised seller of poisons, and the substance or preparation is sold or supplied under the authority of a prescription signed and dated by any such practitioner or surgeon as aforesaid.

A shopkeeper (Coombs), who was not an authorised seller, sold penicillin ointment to customers who presented prescriptions signed and dated by a medical practitioner. The shopkeeper was charged with selling ointment containing penicillin contrary to section 1(1) of the Act, he not being one of the qualified persons mentioned in that subsection. The magistrates dismissed the summonses on the

---

[4]Prescription Only Medicines (Human Use) Order SI 1997 No. 1830 (as amended)

grounds that, although the shopkeeper was not a practitioner, he was a person acting in accordance with the directions of a duly qualified medical practitioner.

On appeal to the High Court it was held that a person acting in accordance with any such practitioner or surgeon was a person in the employment of a doctor or in some way actually under the direct orders of the doctor. A prescription signed and dated by a medical practitioner could be made up only by a registered pharmacist or an authorised seller of poisons.

Comment. The Penicillin Act 1947 was later replaced by the Therapeutic Substances Act 1956. The wording was subsequently retained in section 58(2)(b) of the Medicines Act 1968, which also repealed the 1956 Act. Section 58(2)(b) of the Medicines Act has subsequently been repealed by the Human Medicines Regulations 2012 and reference is made within those Regulations to 'acting in accordance with the directions of such an appropriate practitioner'.

[1949] KB 221; *Pharm J*, 14 May 1949 p. 356.

In the HMRs doctors, dentists, supplementary prescribers, nurse independent prescribers and pharmacist independent prescribers are designated as appropriate practitioners in relation to any POM.

Note that, in the HMRs, *doctor* means a registered medical practitioner and *dentist* means a person registered in the Dentists' Register under section 14 of the Dentists Act 1984 (as amended). Note that doctors wishing to practise medicine in the UK not only have to be registered with the General Medical Council (GMC), but are also required to hold a licence to practise issued by the GMC.[5]

Community practitioner nurse prescribers are appropriate practitioners in relation to POMs specified in Schedule 13 to the HMRs (see below). Optometrist independent prescribers are appropriate practitioners in relation to any POM other than Controlled Drugs or medicinal products that are for parenteral administration. Podiatrist independent prescribers are appropriate practitioners in relation to any POM excluding any Schedule 1, 2 or 3 Controlled Drug other than dihydrocodeine or temazepam.[6] Physiotherapist independent prescribers are appropriate practitioners in relation to any POM excluding any Schedule 1, 2 or 3 Controlled Drug

[5] The General Medical Council (Licence to Practise) Regulations Order of Council SI 2009 No. 2739, as amended by SI 2012/2685
[6] Human Medicines (Amendment) Regulations SI 2013 No. 1855

other than dihydrocodeine, fentanyl, morphine, oxycodone or temazepam.[7]
Therapeutic radiographer independent prescribers are appropriate practitioners in relation to any POM excluding any Schedule 1, 2 or 3 Controlled Drug other than codeine, fentanyl, midazolam, morphine, oxycodone, temazepam or tramadol.[8] Note that, whilst the HMRs (as amended) permit therapeutic radiographer independent prescribers to prescribe these specified Controlled Drugs, at the time of going to press corresponding changes had not yet been made to the Misuse of Drugs Regulations (see chapter 16) and so, in effect, such prescribing is not currently permitted.

An *EEA health professional* means a person in a relevant European State who is a doctor, a dentist, a nurse responsible for general care, a midwife or a pharmacist[9] who is lawfully engaged in healthcare practice in a relevant European country[10] and who is a person of equivalent professional status to a healthcare professional within the meaning of Regulation 8 of the HMRs. Essentially this means, in the case of pharmacists and nurses, that they must be prescribers in their own countries. An EEA health professional is an appropriate practitioner in relation to any POM other than a Controlled Drug specified in Schedule 1, 2 or 3 of the Misuse of Drugs Regulations 2001[11] or in Schedule 1, 2 or 3 of the Misuse of Drugs Regulations (Northern Ireland) 2002[12] or any POM which is not the subject of a marketing authorisation.

A *community practitioner nurse prescriber* means a registered nurse or a registered midwife against whose name is recorded in the professional register an annotation signifying that the person is qualified to order drugs, medicines and appliances from the *Nurse Prescribers' Formulary for Community Practitioners* in the current edition of the *British National Formulary* (HMRs Reg.8).

A *nurse independent prescriber* means a registered nurse or registered midwife noted in the professional register as qualified to order drugs, medicines and appliances as a nurse independent prescriber or a nurse independent/supplementary prescriber (HMRs Reg.8).

[7] Human Medicines (Amendment) Regulations SI 2013 No. 1855
[8] Human Medicines (Amendment) Regulations SI 2016 No. 186
[9] Human Medicines (Amendment) Regulations SI 2014 No. 490
[10] An EEA country other than the UK or Switzerland (although since 2008 the UK has recognised as legally valid for supply prescriptions written by a doctor or dentist registered in Switzerland). Relevant European States are Austria, Belgium, Bulgaria, Cyprus, Czech Republic, Denmark, Estonia, Finland, France, Germany, Greece, Hungary, Iceland, Ireland, Italy, Latvia, Liechtenstein, Lithuania, Luxembourg, Malta, the Netherlands, Norway, Poland, Portugal, Romania, Slovakia, Slovenia, Spain and Sweden
[11] The Misuse of Drugs Regulations SI 2001 No. 3998 (as amended)
[12] The Misuse of Drugs Regulations (Northern Ireland) SR 2002 No. 1 (as amended)

A *pharmacist independent prescriber* means a pharmacist who is noted in the relevant register as qualified to order drugs, medicines and appliances as a pharmacist independent prescriber (HMRs Reg.8).

An *optometrist independent prescriber* means a registered optometrist against whose name is recorded in the relevant register an annotation signifying that the person is qualified to order drugs, medicines and appliances as an optometrist independent prescriber (HMRs Reg.8).

A *supplementary prescriber* means a pharmacist, a registered nurse or midwife, chiropodist, podiatrist, physiotherapist, radiographer, registered optometrist or registered dietitian who is noted in the relevant register as qualified to order drugs, medicines and appliances as a supplementary prescriber (or, in the case of a registered nurse or registered midwife, as a nurse independent/supplementary prescriber) (HMRs Reg.8).

A *podiatrist independent prescriber* means a registered podiatrist against whose name is recorded in the relevant register an annotation signifying that the person is qualified to order drugs, medicines and appliances as a podiatrist independent prescriber.[13]

A *physiotherapist independent prescriber* means a registered physiotherapist against whose name is recorded in the relevant register an annotation signifying that the person is qualified to order drugs, medicines and appliances as a physiotherapist independent prescriber.[14]

A *therapeutic radiographer independent prescriber* means a registered radiographer, against whose name is recorded in the relevant register an entitlement to use the title 'therapeutic radiographer' and an annotation signifying that the person is qualified to order drugs, medicines and appliances as a therapeutic radiographer independent prescriber.[15]

The specified conditions for supplementary prescribers do not apply in relation to the prescribing and administration of medicines in accordance with the directions of another person who is an appropriate practitioner (other than a supplementary prescriber or an EEA health professional) in relation to the POM in question (Reg.216).

Administration of Prescription Only Medicines

Regulation 214 sets out that no person shall parenterally administer a POM, otherwise than to him/herself, unless the person is an appropriate practitioner (other than an EEA health professional) or is acting in accordance with the

[13] Human Medicines (Amendment) Regulations SI 2013 No. 1855
[14] Human Medicines (Amendment) Regulations SI 2013 No. 1855
[15] Human Medicines (Amendment) Regulations SI 2016 No. 186

directions of such an appropriate practitioner. However, this Regulation does not apply to the administration of:

1 certain medicines by way of parenteral injection for the purpose of saving life in an emergency (as listed in box 8.2);
2 smallpox vaccine, administered for the purpose of providing protection against smallpox virus:
   a in the event of a suspected or confirmed case of smallpox in the UK where the vaccine has been supplied by, on behalf of or under arrangements made by the Secretary of State, the Scottish ministers, the Welsh ministers, the Department of Health, Social Services and Public Safety, or an NHS body,
   b to members of Her Majesty's Forces or other persons employed or engaged by them where the vaccine has been supplied by, on behalf of, or under arrangements made by, Her Majesty's Forces;
3 a POM (other than a Schedule 1, 2 or 3 Controlled Drug) which is a radioactive medicinal product, administration of which results in a medical exposure or any other POM if it is being administered in connection with a medical exposure (see also below).

Box 8.2 *Medicinal products for parenteral administration in an emergency (HMRs Sch. 19) 2012)*

Adrenaline (epinephrine) 1:1000 up to 1 mg for intramuscular use in anaphylaxis
Atropine sulphate injection
Atropine sulphate and obidoxime chloride injection
Atropine sulphate and pralidoxime chloride injection
Atropine sulphate, pralidoxime mesilate and avizafone injection
Chlorphenamine injection
Dicobalt edetate injection
Glucagon injection
Glucose injection
Hydrocortisone injection
Naloxone hydrochloride
Pralidoxime chloride injection
Pralidoxime mesilate injection
Promethazine hydrochloride injection
Snake venom antiserum
Sodium nitrite injection
Sodium thiosulphate injection
Sterile pralidoxime

A *radioactive medicinal product*[16] means a medicinal product which consists of, contains or generates a radioactive substance so that, when the product is administered, the radiation it emits may be used.

Medical exposure[17] means any which involves an individual being exposed to ionising radiation:

a as part of their own medical diagnosis or treatment;
b as part of occupational health surveillance;
c as part of health screening programmes;
d to patients or other persons voluntarily participating in medical or biomedical, diagnostic or therapeutic research programmes; and
e to individuals as part of medicolegal procedures.

Other conditions apply to the administration of a radioactive medicinal product, namely that the medicine is not a Controlled Drug and that medical exposure has been authorised by an ionising radiation medical exposure (IRME) practitioner (a registered medical practitioner, dental practitioner or other health professional who is entitled in accordance with the employer's procedures to take responsibility for an individual medical exposure), or, where it is not practical for an IRME practitioner to authorise the exposure, by an operator acting in accordance with written guidelines issued by an IRME practitioner. The IRME practitioner must be the holder of an appropriate certificate[18] granted by the ministers.

Prescriptions

A POM may only be sold or supplied by retail in accordance with a prescription given by an appropriate practitioner (HMRs Reg.214). To meet that requirement, certain conditions must be satisfied, which are slightly different for EEA health professionals (HMRs Reg.218) and other appropriate practitioners (HMRs Reg.217).

The conditions are that the prescription:

1 is signed in ink by the appropriate practitioner or the EEA health professional giving it;
2 is written in ink or otherwise so as to be indelible or (in the case of a health prescription which is not for a Controlled Drug) is written in ink or otherwise so as to be indelible or by means of carbon paper or similar material [NB EEA health professionals cannot issue health prescriptions];

---

[16] Medicines (Administration of Radioactive Substances) Regulations SI 1978 No. 1006
[17] The Ionising Radiation (Medical Exposure) Regulations SI 2000 No. 1059
[18] In accordance with the Medicines (Administration of Radioactive Substances) Regulations SI 1978 No. 1006

3 is not dispensed after the end of the period of 6 months beginning with the appropriate date; or, in the case of a repeatable prescription, is not dispensed for the first time after the end of that period, and is dispensed in accordance with the directions contained in the prescription;

4 in the case of a repeatable prescription that does not specify the number of times it may be dispensed, it may be dispersed:

    a on more than two occasions, or

    b in the case of a prescription for an oral contraceptive, on more than six occasions or after the end of the period of 6 months beginning with the appropriate date;

5 for an appropriate prescriber, who is an EEA health professional, the prescription is issued in a relevant European State except the UK and the prescribing EEA health professional is legally entitled to issue a prescription of that kind in the country in which the prescription is issued;

6 contains the particulars set out in table 8.1.

An appropriate practitioner (other than an EEA health professional) may issue a prescription to be dispensed in an EEA State other than the UK. If the prescription is not a health prescription for a Schedule 1 Controlled Drug or, in the case of EEA prescriptions, for a Schedule 2 or 3 Controlled Drug, it may be issued as an electronic prescription (HMRs Reg.219 and 219A).[19] In this case, as an alternative to fulfilling conditions 1 and 2 specified above (for both non-EEA and EEA practitioners) the conditions are that the prescription is:

a created in an electronic form;

b signed with an advanced electronic signature;

c sent to the person by whom it is dispensed as an electronic communication (whether or not through one or more intermediaries); and

d sent via the Electronic Prescription Service if it is for a Schedule 2 or 3 Controlled Drug.[20]

Note that a health prescription for a Schedule 2 or 3 Controlled Drug may be issued via the Electronic Prescription Service by a UK prescriber who is entitled to prescribe that drug. Whilst such issue is lawful at the time of going to press, it was not a practical reality. In order for this function to be available, all Electronic Prescription Service-enabled pharmacies in England would be required to have Controlled Drug functionality. NHS Digital estimate that this may not be in place across all sites until the end of 2018.

---

[19]The Human Medicines (Amendment) (No. 2) Regulations SI 2015 No. 903
[20]The Human Medicines (Amendment) (No. 2) Regulations SI 2015 No. 903

Table 8.1 Particulars which must be included on a prescription for a POM

Description (the information in this column does not form part of the HMRs but is included to improve clarity)	Particulars to be included for prescriptions issued by a non-EEA appropriate practitioner (i.e. by a UK registered prescriber)	Particulars to be included for prescriptions issued by an EEA health professional for dispensing in the UK, or by a non-EEA appropriate practitioner for dispensing in an EEA State other than the UK
Date	The appropriate date	The issue date of the prescription
Patient details	The patient's name and address, and the patient's age if they are under 12 years	The patient's surname, first names written out in full and the patient's date of birth (whatever the age of the patient)
Prescriber details	The prescriber's address and an indication of the kind of appropriate practitioner issuing the prescription	The prescriber's: ● first names written out in full ● surname ● professional qualifications ● direct contact details including email address, telephone or fax number with the appropriate international prefix, work address, and name of the relevant Member State in which that EEA health professional works or confirmation that the prescriber works as a health professional in the UK
Details about the prescribed medicine	The HMRs do not specify that any particular information relating to the prescribed medicine is required by law	Details about the prescribed product, including where applicable: ● the common name of the product ● brand name (if the prescribed product is a biological medicinal product, or the prescriber deems it medically necessary for that product to be dispensed) and the prescriber's reasons justifying the use of the branded product ● pharmaceutical formulation (tablet, solution, etc.) ● quantity and strength of the medicinal product ● dosage regimen

Advanced electronic signature[21] means an electronic signature that is:

a uniquely linked to the person giving the prescription (the signatory);

b capable of identifying the signatory;

c created using means that the signatory can maintain under his/her sole control; and

d linked to the data to which it relates in such a manner that any subsequent change of the data is detectable.

[21] The Human Medicines (Amendment) (No. 2) Regulations SI 2015 No. 903

Electronic Prescription Service means the service of that name which is managed by the Health and Social Care Information Centre established under section 252 of the Health and Social Care Act 2012.

Electronic communication (HMRs Reg.8) means a communication transmitted (whether from one person to another, from one device to another or from a person to a device or vice versa):

a by means of an electronic communications network within the meaning of section 32(1) of the Communications Act 2003; or
b by other means but while in an electronic form.

Repeatable prescription (HMRs Reg.213) means a prescription which contains a direction that it may be dispensed more than once.

Health prescription (HMRs Reg.213) means a prescription issued by a doctor, dentist, supplementary prescriber, nurse independent prescriber, optometrist independent prescriber, pharmacist independent prescriber, physiotherapist independent prescriber, podiatrist independent prescriber, therapeutic radiographer independent prescriber or community practitioner nurse prescriber under:

a in England, the National Health Service Act 2006;
b in Wales, the National Health Service (Wales) Act 2006;
c in Scotland, the National Health Service (Scotland) Act 1978; or
d in Northern Ireland, the Health and Personal Social Services (Northern Ireland) Order 1972 No. 1265.

The *appropriate date* (HMRs Reg.217) is the date on which the prescription was signed by the appropriate practitioner giving it, or, in the case of a health prescription only, the date indicated by the appropriate practitioner as being the date before which it should not be dispensed. Where a health prescription bears both dates, the later of those dates is the appropriate one. EEA health professionals cannot issue health prescriptions, so, for an EEA prescription, the 'appropriate date' will always be the date on which it is signed by the EEA health professional.

Prescribing and administration by supplementary prescribers

A supplementary prescriber may give a prescription for a POM, parenterally administer a POM or give directions for the parenteral administration of a POM provided that s/he is acting in accordance with the terms of a clinical management plan that relates to the patient to whom the product is prescribed/administered, has effect when the prescription is given or when the product is administered or the direction to administer is given (HMRs Reg.215), and includes the particulars specified in Schedule 14 to the HMRs (see Appendix 1). In addition, the supplementary prescriber must have access to the health records of the patient to whom the plan relates and are used by any doctor or dentist who is a party to the plan. The above does not apply if the supplementary prescriber is a community practitioner nurse prescriber and the POM prescribed or administered, or in respect of which s/he gives directions for administration, is specified in Schedule 13 to the Regulations.

Due diligence clause

Where a prescription given by an appropriate practitioner does not fulfil a required condition, the sale or supply is not rendered unlawful if the person making the sale or supply, having exercised all due diligence, believes on reasonable grounds that that condition has been met (HMRs Reg.246). This due diligence clause also applies to the sale or supply made by a pharmacist in accordance with a prescription given by (HMRs Reg.228):

a another pharmacist, a registered nurse or a registered midwife, a person whose name is entered in the part of the Health and Care Professions Council Register relating to chiropodists and podiatrists, physiotherapists, radiographers (diagnostic or therapeutic) or a registered optometrist *who is not an appropriate practitioner* in relation to that POM but the pharmacist, having exercised all due diligence, believes on reasonable grounds that the person is such a practitioner; and

b a supplementary prescriber and the pharmacist, having exercised all due diligence, believes on reasonable grounds that the supplementary prescriber has complied with the requirements for prescribing by supplementary prescribers.

Forgeries

Similarly, the sale or supply by a pharmacist is not rendered unlawful if made against a forged prescription provided that the pharmacist has exercised all due diligence and believes on reasonable grounds that the prescription is genuine (HMRs Reg.245) (but see box 8.3).

Box 8.3 *Sale of Prescription Only Medicines: offence of strict liability*

Pharmaceutical Society of Great Britain v Storkwain Ltd (1986)

Section 58 of the Medicines Act 1968 provides for orders to be made specifying those medicinal products which may only be sold by retail in accordance with the prescription of an appropriate practitioner.

Storkwain Ltd supplied quantities of Physeptone ampoules, Ritalin tablets and Valium tablets, all of which are POMs, on the authority of two 'prescriptions' which were, in fact, forgeries. In 1984, the Royal Pharmaceutical Society of Great Britain prosecuted the company for unlawfully selling those medicines contrary to section 58(2)(a) of the Act. It was submitted for Storkwain Ltd that they were unaware that the 'prescriptions' were not genuine. In the absence of any guilty knowledge (*mens rea*) of the forgeries on the part of the company, the magistrates dismissed the charges. The Society successfully appealed to the Court of Appeal, who held that an offence under section 58(2)(a) was one of strict liability and directed the magistrates to convict.

On further appeal by Storkwain Ltd, the House of Lords confirmed the decision of the Court of Appeal. It was held that guilty knowledge (*mens rea*) was a required ingredient of offences under certain sections of the Act, but section 58 was not one of those sections. That view was supported by the construction of section 58(4) and (5) and by section 121. The wording of the Prescriptions Only Order also conformed with that construction of the statute. An offence under section 58(2)(a) is, therefore, one of strict liability.

Comment. Section 58(4) and 58(5b) of the Medicines Act remain in force. Regulation 214 of the Human Medicines Regulations 2012 states that 'a person may not sell or supply a POM except in accordance with a prescription given by an appropriate practitioner'.

[1986] 2 All ER 635; *Pharm J*, 28 June 1986 p. 829.

Pharmacy records

A person lawfully conducting a retail pharmacy business must, in respect of every sale or supply of a POM, make or cause to be made an entry in a written or computerised record kept for that purpose (HMRs Reg.253), unless:

1 it is a sale or supply in pursuance of a health prescription or a prescription for oral contraceptives;
2 a separate record of the sale or supply is made in accordance with Controlled Drugs legislation[22] (chapter 16);

[22]The Misuse of Drugs Regulations SI 2001 No. 3998 and the Misuse of Drugs Regulations (NI) SI 2002 No. 1

3 the sale is by way of wholesale dealing and the order or invoice relating to the sale (or a copy of it) is retained by the person lawfully conducting the retail pharmacy business who makes the sale;

4 in Scotland, the sale or supply is to a doctor of medicines and appliances for immediate treatment or personal administration which, under the NHS, the doctor is entitled or required to supply;[23] or

5 in Northern Ireland, the sale or supply is to a doctor of drugs, medicines and appliances for immediate treatment or personal administration which, under the NHS, the doctor is entitled or required to supply.[24]

An entry must be a written or computerised record kept for the purpose in respect of each sale or supply. The entry must be made on the day the sale or supply takes place or, if that is not reasonably practicable, on the following day.

Chapter 10 discusses records for wholesale transactions in POMs.

Particulars of prescriptions to be recorded

The particulars to be recorded in the case of a sale or supply of a POM in pursuance of a prescription given by a doctor or dentist, a supplementary prescriber, a community practitioner nurse prescriber, a nurse independent prescriber, an optometrist independent prescriber, a podiatrist independent prescriber, a physiotherapist independent prescriber, a therapeutic radiographer independent prescriber or a pharmacist independent prescriber are:

1 the date on which the POM was sold or supplied;

2 the name, quantity and, except where it is apparent from the name, the pharmaceutical form and strength of the POM sold or supplied;

3 the date on the prescription;

4 the name and address of the person giving the prescription; and

5 the name and address of the person for whom the POM was prescribed.

For second and subsequent supplies made on a repeat prescription it is sufficient to record the date of supply and a reference to the entry in the register relating to the first supply.

Additional particulars must be recorded in the case of emergency supplies to patients (see below).

[23] The NHS (General Medical Services Contracts) (Scotland) Regulations SSI 2004 No. 115 (provision of drugs, medicines and appliances for immediate treatment or personal administration)

[24] The Health and Personal Social Services (General Medical Services Contracts) (Northern Ireland) Regulations SR (NI) 2004 No. 140

Preservation of pharmacy records

The POM record must be preserved by the person lawfully conducting the retail pharmacy business for a period of 2 years from the date of the last entry in the record. Unless it is a health prescription or a prescription for a Schedule 1, 2 or 3 Controlled Drug, a prescription must be retained for 2 years from the date on which the POM was sold or supplied, or, for a repeat prescription, the date on which the medicine was supplied for the last time. Where a sale of a POM is by way of wholesale dealing, the order or invoice relating to the sale (or a copy of it) must be retained by the person lawfully conducting the retail pharmacy business who makes the sale for 2 years from the date on which the POM was sold or supplied.

Labelling of dispensed medicines

See chapter 14.

Exemptions from the need for a prescription

Exemptions for hospitals, clinics and similar settings

The requirement that a person may not sell or supply a POM except in accordance with a prescription given by an appropriate practitioner does not apply (HMRs Reg.227) when the sale or supply is made in the course of the business of a hospital, for the purpose of being administered (in the hospital or elsewhere) to a particular person in accordance with directions that:

a are in writing;
b relate to the particular person to whom the POM is to be administered; and
c are given by a person who is an appropriate practitioner in relation to that POM.

Such directions may be given by a supplementary prescriber *only* where s/he complies with any condition as to the cases or circumstances in which s/he may give a prescription for that medicine, as if the directions were a prescription. The exemption applies regardless of whether the directions satisfy the requirements for a prescription.

Exemptions for persons conducting retail pharmacy businesses

In Part 12, chapter 3 of the HMRs, there are specific exemptions for persons lawfully conducting retail pharmacy businesses from the conditions or restrictions on the retail sale and supply of POMs. Exemptions from control for other persons are to be found in chapter 9 of the HMRs.

In an emergency, a person lawfully conducting a retail pharmacy business can sell or supply a POM if and so long as certain conditions are satisfied. There are two kinds of emergency supply (those made at the request of a prescriber and those made at the request of a patient) and different conditions apply to them.

Exemption for emergency supply at the request of a prescriber

HMRs Reg.224 describe the conditions for an emergency sale at the request of a *relevant prescriber* which means any of the following:

- a doctor
- a dentist
- a supplementary prescriber
- a nurse independent prescriber
- a pharmacist independent prescriber
- a community practitioner nurse prescriber
- a physiotherapist independent prescriber
- a podiatrist independent prescriber
- a therapeutic radiographer independent prescriber
- an optometrist independent prescriber
- an EEA health professional.

The conditions that apply for emergency supply made at the request of a relevant prescriber are that:

1 the pharmacist by or under whose supervision the POM is to be sold or supplied is satisfied that the sale or supply has been requested by a relevant prescriber (see above) who by reason of an emergency is unable to provide a prescription immediately;
2 the relevant prescriber has undertaken to provide the person lawfully conducting the retail pharmacy business with a prescription within the period of 72 hours beginning with the sale or supply;
3 the POM is sold or supplied in accordance with the directions of the relevant prescriber;
4 the POM is not a Controlled Drug specified in Schedule 1, 2 or 3 of the relevant Regulations other than a POM that consists of or contains phenobarbital or phenobarbital sodium, and is sold or supplied for use in the treatment of epilepsy (note that, in the case of an EEA prescriber, no Schedule 1, 2 or 3 Controlled Drugs may be ordered, so such prescribers may not order phenobarbital or its salts);

5 an entry is made in the Prescription Only Register (see above) on the day of the sale or supply, or, if that is not reasonably practicable, on the day following that day, stating:

   a the date on which the POM was sold or supplied,

   b the name, quantity and, except where it is apparent from the name, the pharmaceutical form and strength of the POM sold or supplied,

   c the name and address of the person giving the prescription,

   d the name and address of the person for whom the POM was prescribed,

   e the date on the prescription (this may be entered on the day that the prescription is received), and

   f the date on which the prescription relating to that sale or supply is received (this may be entered on the day that the prescription is received).

Exemption for emergency supply at the request of a patient

The conditions that apply for an emergency supply made at the request of a patient set out in HMRs Reg.225 are:

1 that the pharmacist by or under whose supervision the POM is to be sold or supplied has interviewed the person requesting it and is satisfied:

   a that there is an immediate need for the POM to be sold or supplied and that it is impracticable in the circumstances to obtain a prescription without undue delay,

   b that treatment with the POM has on a previous occasion been pre-scribed by a relevant prescriber for the person requesting it, and

   c as to the dose which in the circumstances it would be appropriate for that person to take;

2 that the quantity of the product sold or supplied, for a POM shown in column A of table 8.2, does not exceed that shown in column B of the table for that POM;

3 that the POM:

   a does not consist of or contain a substance specified in box 8.4,

   b is not a Controlled Drug specified in Schedule 1, 2 or 3 of the relevant Regulations other than a POM that consists of or contains phenobar-bital or phenobarbital sodium, and is sold or supplied for use in the treatment of epilepsy [NB in the case of the patient of an EEA pre-scriber, no Schedule 1, 2 or 3 Controlled Drugs may be ordered, so the patients of such prescribers may not order phenobarbital or its salts];

4 that an entry is made in the Prescription Only Register (see above) on the day of the sale or supply, or, if that is not reasonably practicable, on the day following that day, stating:

   a the date on which the POM was sold or supplied,

   b the name, quantity and, except where it is apparent from the name, the pharmaceutical form and strength of the POM sold or supplied,

Table 8.2 Maximum quantities that may be sold or supplied for emergency supply at the request of a patient

Column A: description	Column B: maximum quantity
A POM that: (a) is a preparation of insulin, an aerosol (a product that is dispersed from its container by a propellant gas or liquid) for the relief of asthma, an ointment or cream, and (b) has been made up for sale in a package elsewhere than at the place of sale or supply	The smallest pack that the pharmacist has available for sale or supply
An oral contraceptive	A quantity sufficient for a full treatment cycle
An antibiotic for oral administration in liquid form	The smallest quantity that will provide a full course of treatment
A controlled drug within the meaning of Schedule 4 or 5 of the Misuse of Drugs Regulations 2001 or Schedule 4 or 5 of the Misuse of Drugs Regulations (Northern Ireland) 2002 or phenobarbital for the treatment of epilepsy	A quantity for 5 days of treatment
Any other POM	A quantity for 30 days of treatment

  c the name and address of the person requiring the POM, and
  d the nature of the emergency;
5 that the inner or outer packaging of the POM is labelled to show:
  a the date on which the POM is sold or supplied,
  b the name, quantity and (unless apparent from the name) the pharmaceutical strength of the POM,
  c the name of the person requesting the POM,
  d the name and address of the registered pharmacy from which the POM is sold or supplied, and
  e the words 'Emergency Supply'.

Box 8.4 Substances that may not be sold or supplied by a pharmacist without a prescription in response to a request for an emergency supply from a patient

Ammonium bromide
Calcium bromide
Calcium bromidolactobionate
Embutramide
Fencamfamin hydrochloride
Fluanisone

Hexobarbitone [hexobarbital]
Hexobarbitone sodium [hexobarbital sodium]
Hydrobromic acid
Meclofenoxate hydrochloride
Methohexital sodium
Pemoline
Piracetam
Potassium bromide
Prolintane hydrochloride
Sodium bromide
Strychnine hydrochloride
Tacrine hydrochloride
Thiopental sodium

Emergency supply by a pharmacist: pandemic diseases

The restrictions on the sale or supply of a POM do not apply in certain circumstances related to pandemic diseases (HMRs Reg.226). The conditions are that the sale or supply of the POM is made by a person lawfully conducting a retail pharmacy business and:

1 the supply is made while a disease is, or in anticipation of a disease being imminently, pandemic and a serious risk, or potentially a serious risk, to human health;
2 the pharmacist by or under whose supervision the POM is to be sold or supplied is satisfied:
   a that treatment with the POM has on a previous occasion been prescribed by a relevant prescriber for the person to be treated with it, and
   b as to the dose which in the circumstances it would be appropriate for that person to take.

Exemption for supply in the event or anticipation of pandemic disease

The restrictions on the sale or supply of a POM (or a Pharmacy Medicine or GSL medicine, chapters 6 and 7) do not apply in certain circumstances related to pandemic diseases (HMRs Reg.247). The conditions are that the supply:

1 is made while a disease is, or in anticipation of a disease being imminently, pandemic and a serious risk, or potentially a serious risk, to human health;

2 is in accordance with a protocol that:
   a is approved by the Ministers (chapter 2) or an NHS body,
   b specifies the symptoms of and treatment for the disease, and
   c contains requirements as to the recording of the name of the person who supplies the product to the person to be treated ('the patient') or to a person acting on the patient's behalf, and evidence that the product was supplied to the patient or to a person acting on the patient's behalf.

Exemptions from Prescription Only for certain persons, including persons who supply under Patient Group Directions

These exemptions are covered in chapter 9.

Mixing of medicines

Regulation 17 of the HMRs provides that no person may manufacture, assemble or import from a state, other than an EEA State, any medicinal product or possess a medicinal product for the purpose of any of these activities except in accordance with a manufacturer's licence. However, under HMRs Reg.20 these restrictions do not apply to the mixing of medicines by:

- a nurse independent prescriber;
- a pharmacist independent prescriber;
- a supplementary prescriber, if the mixing of medicines forms part of the clinical management plan for an individual patient;
- a physiotherapist independent prescriber;
- a podiatrist independent prescriber;
- a therapeutic radiographer independent prescriber;
- a person acting in accordance with the written directions of a doctor, dentist, nurse independent prescriber, pharmacist independent prescriber, physiotherapist independent prescriber, podiatrist independent prescriber or therapeutic radiographer independent prescriber; or
- a person acting in accordance with the written directions of a supplementary prescriber, if the mixing of medicines forms part of the clinical management plan for an individual patient.

Here, 'mixing of medicines' means the combining of two or more medicinal products together for the purposes of administering them to meet the needs of an individual patient.

Summary

- Certain medicines are POMs by description or class, including Controlled Drugs (unless exempted by virtue of a marketing authorisation), parenteral products and cyanogenic substances.

- In the HMRs doctors, dentists, supplementary prescribers, nurse independent prescribers and pharmacist independent prescribers are designated as appropriate practitioners in relation to any POM. Community practitioner nurse prescribers, optometrist independent prescribers, physiotherapist independent prescribers, podiatrist independent prescribers, therapeutic radiographer independent prescribers and EEA health professionals are appropriate practitioners in relation to a more restricted range of POMs.
- Certain POMs may be administered parenterally for the purpose of saving life in an emergency, for example adrenaline (epinephrine) injection.
- Detailed prescription requirements are laid down and these differ for prescriptions written by non-EEA and EEA practitioners. There are other provisions for prescriptions written by non-EEA practitioners for dispensing in an EEA State other than the UK.
- Detailed record keeping requirements are imposed for POMs, although there are some exemptions (e.g. for those on a health prescription or oral contraceptives).
- The HMRs allow for an emergency supply of a POM to be made at the request of a doctor, dentist, supplementary prescriber, nurse independent prescriber, pharmacist independent prescriber, community practitioner nurse prescriber, optometrist independent prescriber, physiotherapist independent prescriber, podiatrist independent prescriber, therapeutic radiographer independent prescriber or an EEA health professional. The HMRs describe the conditions for such a supply to be made, for example including the exclusion of many Controlled Drugs from these arrangements.
- The HMRs allow for an emergency supply of a POM to be made at the request of a patient. The HMRs describe the conditions for such a supply to be made, for example including the exclusion of many Controlled Drugs from these arrangements and the removal of certain conditions in the case of a declared pandemic. Detailed quantity, labelling and record conditions apply.
- The restrictions on the sale or supply of a POM (or Pharmacy Medicine or GSL, chapters 6 and 7) do not apply in certain circumstances related to pandemic diseases.
- Under certain conditions, POMs may be supplied under Patient Group Directions (see chapter 9).
- The Regulations allow for the mixing of medicines in certain circumstances.

Further reading

Human Medicines Regulations (2012) SI 2012 No. 1916, *Explanatory memorandum*: http://www.legislation.gov.uk/uksi/2012/1916/pdfs/uksiem_20121916_en.pdf (accessed 2 November 2016).

Royal Pharmaceutical Society (published annually). *Medicines, Ethics and Practice*: *The Professional Guide for Pharmacists*. London: Royal Pharmaceutical Society (includes practice guidance on many of the topics in this chapter; free to members).

Websites

Legislation (can be searched on year and SI number or title): http://www.legislation.gov.uk
Medicines and Healthcare products Regulatory Agency: https://www.gov.uk/government/organisations/medicines-and-healthcare-products-regulatory-agency
Royal Pharmaceutical Society (member access only; lists legal classifications of medicines and further practice guidance): http://www.rpharms.com

9

Human medicines: exemptions from controls

Karen Pitchford

Introduction

In the Human Medicines Regulations 2012, there are specified exemptions for certain classes of person from the conditions or restrictions on retail sale and/or supply[1] which apply to medicines subject to general sale (HMRs Reg.221), Pharmacy Medicines (HMRs Reg.220) and Prescription Only Medicines (POMs) (HMRs Reg.214). Exemption from the restriction on the administration of POMs for parenteral use is also conferred on certain persons (HMRs Reg.214). There are also some continuing exemptions that are defined in earlier legislation.[2] The classes of person and the body exempted, the medicinal products to which the exemptions apply and the conditions (if any) which attach to the retail sale, supply or administration by these exempted persons are described in this chapter.

The sale of a POM or a Pharmacy Medicine to any of these persons in accordance with the exemptions granted to them is a sale by way of wholesale dealing (HMRs Reg.18). Persons who may engage in wholesale dealing, the extent to which it may be carried on at retail pharmacy businesses and the records to be kept in respect of wholesale transactions are described in chapter 10.

Exemption for supplies by doctors, dentists or other healthcare professionals to their patients (HMRs Reg.223, as amended)

The restrictions on retail sale of medicinal products do not apply (HMRs Reg.223, as amended)[3,4] to the:

[1] Human Medicines Regulations SI 2012 No. 1916
[2] The Medicines (Pharmacy and General Sale – Exemption) Order SI 1980 No. 1924
[3] Human Medicines (Amendment) Regulations SI 2013 No. 1855
[4] Human Medicines (Amendment) Regulations SI 2016 No. 186

1 sale or supply of any medicine by a doctor or dentist to a patient of his/hers;

2 sale, offer for sale, or supply of General Sale List (GSL) and Pharmacy Medicines, to a person under the care of a doctor or dentist;

3 sale, offer for sale, or supply of GSL and Pharmacy Medicines in the course of the business of a hospital or health centre, where the product is sold, offered for sale or supplied for the purpose of being administered to a person in accordance with directions relating to that person and those directions are given by a doctor, a dentist, a supplementary prescriber, a pharmacist independent prescriber, an optometrist independent prescriber, a nurse independent prescriber, a podiatrist independent prescriber, a physiotherapist independent prescriber, a therapeutic radiographer independent prescriber or a community practitioner nurse prescriber.

The meaning of 'by a doctor or dentist to a patient of his' under the Medicines Act 1968 was tested in law in 1981 (box 9.1)

Box 9.1 The meaning of 'to a patient of his'

Pharmaceutical Society v Wright (1981)

The Medicines Act required that no person should sell a POM product except in accordance with a prescription given by an appropriate practitioner. However, the Act provided that this provision did not apply to the sale or supply of a medicinal product to a patient of his/hers by a doctor or dentist who is an appropriate practitioner.

Once a week, Dr Wright ran a slimming clinic and those attending were given a medicinal product which was on the POM list. Many of the persons attending the clinic were patients of other doctors in the town and only attended the clinic, which was supervised by a nurse, for slimming purposes. The issue turned upon whether or not there was a doctor–patient relationship between the attendees and Dr Wright.

Mr Justice Bingham said:

> ... if a doctor acting as such, treats or gives advice to a person and assumes responsibility for that treatment or advice, that person may very well be his patient ... in determining whether the relationship does exist it is not ... of primary importance whether the person is a patient of another doctor as well nor whether the treatment or advice is given by the doctor's staff under his supervision rather than the doctor himself. Nor ... whether the

relationship is a short-lived or long-lived. Nor . . . need it be of primary importance whether the doctor takes less care in giving the advice or treatment than he should . . .

Comment. In dismissing the appeal brought by the Pharmaceutical Society (which only became 'Royal' in 1988), Lord Donaldson, who sat with Mr Justice Bingham, said that it was for the Society to prove there was no doctor–patient relationship not for Dr Wright to prove there was.

1981, unreported.

Patient Group Directions

Patient Group Directions (PGDs) are written instructions which allow for the supply or administration of medicines to patients without having to meet the usual requirements for the sale or supply of medicines subject to General Sale, of P medicines or of POMs (as applicable for the medicine concerned). They are usually implemented in planned circumstances and MHRA guidance[5] states that they should be used only where there is an advantage for the patient without compromising patient safety. The MHRA further advises that PGDs should be constructed by a multidisciplinary group including a doctor, a pharmacist and a representative of any professional group expected to supply the medicines under the PGD.

There are different provisions for the supply under a PGD, according to who authorises the supply; these appear in HMRs Regs.229 to 234 together with Schedule 16 to the Regulations.

Box 9.2 shows the provisions that apply, for all PGDs. Note that different types of PGDs allow for sale, supply or administration, and the details in box 9.2 reflect these different arrangements.

Box 9.2 Provisions that must be in place for all PGDs

- The PGD must be in effect at the time at which the medicinal product is sold, supplied or administered (as the case may be for that particular PGD).
- The PGD must contain the particulars specified in Part 1 of Schedule 16 (see appendix 2).

---

[5] MHRA Guidance Patient group directions: who can use them, December 2014

- The product must be sold or supplied (as the case may be for that particular PGD) for the purpose of being supplied or administered (as the case may be) to a person in accordance with a PGD.
- The individual who sells or supplies or (as the case may be) administers the product is one of the classes of individual permitted to do so (as specified in Part 4 of Schedule 16 – see appendix 2).
- When the product is supplied or (as the case may be) administered, a marketing authorisation, Article 126a authorisation, certificate of registration or traditional herbal registration is in force in relation to it.

Supply under a Patient Group Direction by NHS bodies and local authorities

The usual restrictions on sale or supply of GSL, P medicines and POMs do not apply (HMRs Reg.229, as amended)[6,7,8] to the supply of any such medicine by any of the organisations listed in box 9.3, if the product is supplied for the purpose of being administered to a person in accordance with the written directions of a doctor, dentist, nurse independent prescriber, optometrist independent prescriber, physiotherapist independent prescriber, podiatrist independent prescriber, therapeutic radiographer independent prescriber or pharmacist independent prescriber relating to that person, regardless of whether the directions comply with HMRs Reg.217 (requirements for prescriptions).

Also, the usual restrictions on sale or supply of GSL, Pharmacy and POMs do not apply to the supply of any such medicine, by any of the organisations listed in box 9.3, subject to the following conditions:

1 the requirements set out in box 9.2 are met;
2 the PGD relates to the supply of a description or class of medicinal product by the person by whom the medicinal product is supplied and has effect at the time at which it is supplied;
3 the PGD is signed on behalf of the relevant body named above (the HMRs specify the classes of person who may act as signatory – see appendix 2 for details), and with whom an arrangement is made;
4 the individual who supplies the product is designated in writing, on behalf of the authorising person, for the purpose of the supply or administration of products under the PGD.

[6]The National Treatment Agency (Abolition) and the Health and Social Care Act 2012 (Consequential, Transitional and Saving Provisions) Order SI 2013 No 235
[7]The Human Medicines (Amendment) Regulations SI 2015 No. 323
[8]The Human Medicines (Amendment) Regulations SI 2016 No. 186

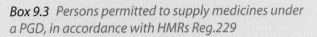

Box 9.3 Persons permitted to supply medicines under a PGD, in accordance with HMRs Reg.229

These include:

1 the Common Services Agency;
2 a health authority or special health authority;
3 an NHS trust;
4 an NHS foundation trust;
5 a local authority in the exercise of public health functions (within the meaning of the National Health Service Act 2006);
6 Public Health England;
7 Public Health Agency; or
8 a person who is not a doctor, a dentist or a person lawfully conducting a retail pharmacy business where the person supplies a product pursuant to an arrangement with a clinical commissioning group, the National Health Service Commissioning Board or one of the persons specified in paragraphs 1–7.

Supply under a Patient Group Direction to assist doctors or dentists

The restrictions on the sale, supply or administration of GSL, P medicines and POMs do not apply where an individual, acting in accordance with a PGD, supplies or (as the case may be) administers the product to assist a doctor in the provision of NHS primary medical services or a dentist in the provision of NHS primary dental services, subject to certain conditions (HMRs Reg.230, as amended):[9]

1 the requirements set out in box 9.2 are met;
2 the PGD relates to the supply or (as the case may be) administration of a description or class of medicinal product in order to assist the doctor or dentist in providing the services (whether or not it relates to such supply in order to assist any other doctor or dentist);
3 the PGD is signed by the doctor or dentist or, where it also relates to supply or administration to assist one or more other doctors or dentists, by one of those doctors or dentists;
4 that the PGD is signed:
   a in the case of NHS primary medical services, or NHS primary dental services in England or Wales, on behalf of the health authority, local authority or National Health Service Commissioning Board with

[9] Amended by the National Treatment Agency (Abolition) and the Health and Social Care Act 2012 (Consequential, Transitional and Saving Provisions) Order SI 2013 No 235

which a contract or agreement for the provision of those services has been made or which provides those services,

b in the case of dental services in Scotland under the National Health Service (Scotland) Act 1978, or general dental services in Northern Ireland, on behalf of the health authority with which an arrangement for the provision of those services has been made, and

c in the case of personal dental services provided under a pilot scheme in Scotland or Northern Ireland, on behalf of the health authority which is a party to the pilot scheme;

5 the individual supplying the product is designated in writing for the purpose of the supply or administration of medicinal products under the PGD by the doctor or dentist or, where it also relates to supply to assist one or more other doctors or dentists, by one of those doctors or dentists.

Supply under a Patient Group Direction by independent hospitals, etc. (HMRs Reg.231)

Regulation 231 relates to an independent hospital, an independent clinic, an independent medical agency or a nursing home (in Northern Ireland). It removes the restrictions on the sale, supply or administration of medicinal products, in accordance with the following conditions:

1 if, in England, the registered provider at the hospital, clinic or agency is registered in compliance with section 10 of the Health and Social Care Act 2008[10] in respect of one or more of the following regulated activities (as set out in section 8 of that Act):
  a treatment of disease, disorder or injury,
  b assessment or medical treatment of persons detained under the Mental Health Act 1983,
  c surgical procedures,
  d diagnostic and screening procedures,
  e maternity and midwifery services, and
  f family planning;
2 the requirements set out in box 9.2 are met;
3 that the PGD relates to the sale or supply or (as the case may be) administration of a description or class of medicinal product by the person by whom the medicinal product is sold or supplied or administered;
4 that the PGD is signed by or on behalf of the registered provider, and, if there is a relevant manager for the independent hospital, clinic or medical agency, or nursing home, by that manager;

[10]Registered with the Care Quality Commission (England) (see chapter 24)

5 that the individual who sells or supplies or (as the case may be) administers the product is designated in writing for the purpose of the sale or supply or (as the case may be) administration of products under the PGD by or on behalf of the registered provider, or, if there is a relevant manager for the independent hospital, clinic or medical agency, or nursing home, by that manager.

Supply under a Patient Group Direction by dental practices and clinics: England and Wales (HMRs Reg.232)

The restrictions on the sale or supply, or administration, of a medicinal product do not apply in a dental practice or dental clinic:

i in England, in respect of which the registered provider is registered in compliance with section 10 of the Health and Social Care Act 2008[11] in respect of the treatment of disease, disorder or injury, and/or diagnostic and screening procedures;

ii in Wales, in which dental services are provided by private dentists and those dentists are registered with Healthcare Inspectorate Wales in accordance with the Regulations,[12] in relation to the services provided by those dentists.

The following conditions must be met:

1 the requirements set out in box 9.2 are met;

2 the PGD relates to the sale or supply or (as the case may be) administration of a description or class of medicinal product by the person by whom the medicinal product is sold or supplied or administered;

3 that the PGD is signed:

    a in England by or on behalf of the registered provider, and, if there is a relevant manager for the practice or clinic, by that manager,

    b in Wales by the private dentist who is treating the person, and, if there is a manager for the practice or clinic, by that manager;

4 the individual who sells or supplies or (as the case may be) administers the product is designated in writing for the purpose of the sale or supply or (as the case may be) administration of products under the PGD:

    a in England, by or on behalf of the registered provider or, if there is a relevant manager for the practice or clinic, by that manager, or

    b in Wales, by the private dentist who is treating the person.

In relation to Wales, in this Regulation 'manager' means the person who carries on the dental practice or dental clinic, or, if there is no such person, a person who manages the practice or clinic.

[11] Registered with the Care Quality Commission (England) (see chapter 24)
[12] The Private Dentistry (Wales) Regulations SI 2008 No. 1976

Supply under a Patient Group Direction by a person conducting a retail pharmacy business

The restrictions on retail sale, supply or administration of POMs do not apply to the sale, supply or administration of any such medicine by a person lawfully conducting a retail pharmacy business where the person sells, supplies or (as the case may be) administers the POM in accordance with a PGD pursuant to an arrangement for the supply or administration of POMs with (HMRs Reg.233, as amended):[13],[14]

1 the Common Services Agency, a health authority or special health authority, an NHS trust, an NHS foundation trust, a clinical commissioning group, the NHS Commissioning Board, a local authority in the exercise of public health functions (within the meaning of the National Health Service Act 2006), Public Health England or Public Health Agency;
2 a police force in England, Wales or Scotland, the police service in Northern Ireland or a prison service;
3 Her Majesty's Forces; or
4 an authority or person carrying on the business of an independent hospital, an independent clinic, an independent medical agency or, in Northern Ireland, a nursing home.

The PGD must:

1 meet the requirements set out in box 9.2;
2 relate to the sale or supply or (as the case may be) administration of a description or class of medicinal product by the person lawfully conducting a retail pharmacy business who sells or supplies or (as the case may be) administers the POM;
3 be signed on behalf of the relevant body named above (the HMRs specify the classes of person who may act as signatory – see appendix 2 for details), and with whom an arrangement is made;
4 where the POM is administered by the person lawfully conducting a retail pharmacy business, that person is designated in writing for the purpose of the administration of medicinal products under the PGD on behalf of the body with which an arrangement has been made.

NB: As far as pharmacies are concerned, there is no provision to use PGDs to permit the supply or administration of P medicines and GSL medicines; however, such supplies are permitted in order to assist a doctor or dentist with the provision of NHS services (HMRs Reg.230).

[13]The National Treatment Agency (Abolition) and the Health and Social Care Act 2012 (Consequential, Transitional and Saving Provisions) Order SI 2013 No. 235
[14]The Human Medicines (Amendment) (No. 3) Regulations SI 2015 No. 1503

Supply under a Patient Group Direction to assist the police, etc. (HMRs Reg.234)

The restrictions on the supply, or administration, of a medicinal product do not apply if the following conditions are met:

1 the individual supplies or (as the case may be) administers the product to assist the provision of healthcare by, on behalf of, or under arrangements made by, one of the following bodies ('the relevant body'):
   a a police force in England and Wales or in Scotland,
   b the Police Service of Northern Ireland,
   c a prison service,
   d Her Majesty's Forces, or
   e a contractor carrying out helicopter search and rescue operations on behalf of the Maritime and Coastguard Agency;[15]
2 the requirements set out in box 9.2 are met;
3 that the PGD relates to the supply or (as the case may be) the administration of a description or class of medicinal product to assist the provision of healthcare by, on behalf of, or under arrangements made by, the relevant body;
4 the PGD is signed on behalf of the relevant body named above (the HMRs specify the classes of person who may act as signatory – see appendix 2 for details), and with whom an arrangement is made;
5 that the individual who supplies the product is designated in writing by or on behalf of the relevant body for the purpose of the supply or (as the case may be) the administration of medicinal products under the PGD.

Other exemptions for sale, supply or administration by certain persons (Sch. 17 to the HMRs)

Schedule 17 is divided into five parts, which cover many exemptions from restrictions:

Part 1: sale and supply of POMs
Part 2: supply of POMs
Part 3: administration of POMs
Part 4: for certain persons who sell, supply or offer for sale or supply certain P or GSL medicinal products
Part 5: for certain persons who supply certain P or GSL medicinal products.

Only some of these exemptions are discussed below.

[15] Human Medicines (Amendment) Regulations SI 2015 No. 323

Midwives

Sale or supply

The restrictions on the sale or supply of GSL or P medicinal products do not apply when the sale or supply is in the course of the registered midwife's professional practice, or is being delivered or administered by a registered midwife under arrangements made by the Secretary of State or Minister for Health, Social Services and Public Safety (HMRs Reg.223 and Sch. 17 Part 1(4)). These exemptions apply for:

1 all medicinal products that are not POMs;
2 POMs contained in Schedule 17 Part 1 for sale or supply, i.e. diclofenac, hydrocortisone acetate, miconazole, nystatin or phytomenadione.

Administration

Student or registered midwives may also parenterally administer, in the course of their professional practice, POMs containing any of the following substances (HMRs Sch. 17 Part 3(2)):

- adrenaline
- anti-D immunoglobulin
- carboprost
- cyclizine lactate
- diamorphine
- ergometrine maleate
- gelofusine
- Hartmann's solution
- hepatitis B vaccine
- hepatitis immunoglobulin
- lidocaine hydrochloride (only to be administered while attending on a woman in childbirth)
- morphine
- naloxone hydrochloride
- oxytocins, natural and synthetic
- pethidine hydrochloride
- phytomenadione
- prochlorperazine
- sodium chloride 0.9%.

Where administration is by a registered midwife, the medicinal product must be administered in the course of their professional practice. Where administration is by a student midwife it must be administered under the direct supervision of a registered midwife and not include diamorphine, morphine or pethidine hydrochloride.

Midwives may also supply or administer POMs, Pharmacy Medicines and GSL products under PGDs (see above).

Registered nurses

Community practitioner nurse prescribers may prescribe, but not sell or supply, a limited list of POMs (HMRs Sch. 13).

Registered nurses may also supply or administer POMs, Pharmacy Medicines and GSL products under PGDs (HMRs Sch. 16).

Registered optometrists

Registered optometrist means a person whose name is entered in the Register of Optometrists.[16]

The restrictions on retail supply or sale do not apply to the sale or supply (or offer for sale or supply) of certain medicinal products by registered optometrists provided that they are only in the course of their professional practice and, in the case of POMs, also only in an emergency (HMRs Sch. 17, Part 1(6)–(9)).

The medicinal products to which this exemption applies are:

1 all GSL medicinal products;
2 all Pharmacy Medicines;
3 POMs which are not for parenteral administration and which:
   a are eye drops and are POMs by reason only that they contain not more than 30% sulphacetamide sodium or 0.5% chloramphenicol, or
   b are eye ointments and are POMs by reason only that they contain not more than 30% sulphacetamide sodium, or 1% chloramphenicol, or
   c are POMs by reason only that they contain cyclopentolate hydrochloride, fusidic acid or tropicamide.

Supplies of these POMs may be obtained by registered optometrists for use in their practice from a retail pharmacy business subject to the presentation of an order signed by a registered optometrist. Registered optometrists may also *purchase* for use in their practice (but not for sale or supply) medicines which are POMs by reason only that they contain any one or more of the following substances (HMRs Reg.250):

- amethocaine hydrochloride
- lidocaine hydrochloride
- oxybuprocaine hydrochloride
- proxymetacaine hydrochloride.

---

[16] Maintained under Opticians Act 1989 (as amended) or the register of visiting optometrists from relevant European States maintained under that Act

Registered optometrists may also supply or administer POMs, Pharmacy Medicines and GSL products under PGDs (see above).

An *optometrist independent prescriber* is a registered optometrist whose name is annotated in the relevant register as qualified to order drugs, medicines and appliances as an optometrist independent prescriber.[17]

Additional supply optometrist means a person who is registered as an optometrist and against whose name particulars of the additional supply specialty has been entered in the register.[18] They may sell or supply the following POMs, not in a form for parenteral administration, in the course of their professional practice and in an emergency:

- acetylcysteine
- atropine sulphate
- azelastine hydrochloride
- diclofenac sodium
- emedastine
- homatropine hydrobromide
- ketotifen
- levocabastine
- lodoxamide
- nedocromil sodium
- olopatadine
- pilocarpine hydrochloride
- pilocarpine nitrate
- polymyxin B/bacitracin
- polymyxin B/trimethoprim
- sodium cromoglicate.

Persons lawfully conducting a retail pharmacy may sell these items on the presentation of a signed order from an additional supply optometrist.

Additional supply optometrists may also *purchase* for use in their practice (but not for sale or supply) a medicine which is a POM by reason only that it contains thymoxamine hydrochloride (HMRs Reg.250).

Registered dispensing opticians may *purchase* for them, or a doctor attending their practice, to use in their practice (but not for sale or supply) medicines which are POMs that contain any one or more of the following substances (HMRs Reg.250):

- amethocaine hydrochloride
- chloramphenicol
- cyclopentolate hydrochloride
- fusidic acid

[17] Defined in HMRs Reg.8
[18] Defined in HMRs Reg.250(10)

- lidocaine hydrochloride
- oxybuprocaine hydrochloride
- proxymetacaine hydrochloride
- tropicamide.

Registered dispensing opticians may *purchase*, for use in their practice as a contact lens specialist, medicines which are POMs that contain lidocaine hydrochloride, oxybuprocaine hydrochloride or proxymetacaine (HMRs Reg.250).

Registered chiropodists and podiatrists

Sale or supply (HMRs Sch. 17 Part 4(1))

The restrictions on retail sale or supply of certain medicinal products by registered chiropodists and podiatrists do not apply to:

1 medicinal products for external human use that are on a GSL; and
2 any of the following Pharmacy Medicines for external use only:
   a potassium permanganate crystals or solution,
   b ointment of heparinoid and hyaluronidase,
   c products containing, as their only active ingredients, any of the following substances, at a strength, in the case of each substance, not exceeding that specified in relation to that substance:
   - 9.0% borotannic complex
   - 10.0% buclosamide
   - 3.0% chlorquinaldol
   - 1.0% clotrimazole
   - 10.0% crotamiton
   - 5.0% diamthazole hydrochloride
   - 1.0% econazole nitrate
   - 1.0% fenticlor
   - 10.0% glutaraldehyde
   - 1.0% griseofulvin
   - 0.4% hydrargaphen
   - 2.0% mepyramine maleate
   - 2.0% miconazole nitrate
   - 2.0% phenoxypropan-2-ol
   - 20.0% podophyllum resin
   - 10.0% polynoxylin
   - 70.0% pyrogallol
   - 70.0% salicylic acid
   - 1.0% terbinafine
   - 0.1% thiomersal.

A registered chiropodist or podiatrist, against whose name is recorded in the relevant register an annotation signifying that they are qualified to use the following POMs, may sell or supply any of them in the course of their professional practice, as long as the product has been made up for sale or supply in a container elsewhere than at the place at which it is sold or supplied (HMRs Sch. 17 Part 1(11) and Part 4(2)):

- amorolfine hydrochloride cream: the maximum strength of amorolfine not to exceed 0.25% w/w
- amorolfine hydrochloride lacquer: the maximum strength of amorolfine not to exceed 5% w/v
- amoxicillin
- co-codamol
- co-dydramol 10/500 tablets
- codeine phosphate
- erythromycin
- flucloxacillin
- silver sulfadiazine
- tioconazole 28%
- topical hydrocortisone not exceeding 1% w/v.

Administration (HMRs Sch. 17 Part 3(1))

Registered chiropodists or podiatrists, against whose names are recorded in the relevant register annotations signifying that they are qualified to use the following medicines, may administer them in the course of their professional practice. Where the medicine includes a combination of substances, those substances shall not have been combined by the chiropodist or podiatrist. The medicinal products to which this exemption applies are parenteral formulations of:

- adrenaline
- bupivacaine hydrochloride
- bupivacaine hydrochloride with adrenaline where the maximum strength of adrenaline does not exceed 1 mg in 200 mL bupivacaine hydrochloride
- levobupivacaine hydrochloride
- lidocaine hydrochloride
- lidocaine hydrochloride with adrenaline where the maximum strength of adrenaline does not exceed 1 mg in 200 mL lidocaine hydrochloride
- mepivacaine hydrochloride
- methylprednisolone
- prilocaine hydrochloride
- ropivacaine hydrochloride.

Registered chiropodists may also supply or administer POMs, Pharmacy Medicines and GSL products under PGDs (see above).

Registered orthoptists

Registered orthoptist means a person who is registered in Part 7 of the Health and Care Professions Council register.

The restrictions on retail supply or sale do not apply to the sale or supply (or offer for sale or supply) of certain POMs by registered orthoptists provided that they are only in the course of their professional practice (HMRs Sch. 17, Part 1(13) and Part 4(13)).[19]

The POMs to which this exemption applies are:

- atropine
- chloramphenicol
- cyclopentolate
- fusidic acid
- lidocaine with fluorescein
- oxybuprocaine
- proxymetacaine
- tetracaine
- tropicamide.

Registered paramedics

Registered paramedic means a person who is registered in Part 8 of the Health and Care Professions Council's Register.

Registered paramedics may administer the following POMs for parenteral administration only for the immediate necessary treatment of sick or injured persons (HMRs Sch. 17 Part 3(8)):

- diazepam 5 mg/mL emulsion for injection;
- succinylated modified fluid gelatin 4% intravenous infusion;
- medicines containing ergometrine maleate 500 mcg/mL with oxytocin 5 IU/mL but no other active ingredient;
- POMs containing one or more of the following substances, but no other active ingredient:
  - adrenaline acid tartrate
  - adrenaline hydrochloride
  - amiodarone
  - anhydrous glucose
  - benzylpenicillin
  - compound sodium lactate intravenous infusion (Hartmann's solution)
  - ergometrine maleate
  - furosemide
  - glucose

[19]Human Medicines (Amendment) Regulations SI 2016 No. 1503

- heparin sodium (only for the purpose of cannula flushing)
- lidocaine hydrochloride
- metoclopramide
- morphine sulfate
- nalbuphine hydrochloride
- naloxone hydrochloride
- ondansetron
- paracetamol
- reteplase
- sodium chloride
- streptokinase
- tenecteplase.

Individuals who are state registered paramedics may also supply or administer POMs, Pharmacy Medicines and GSL products under PGDs (see above).

Public analysts, sampling officers and other such persons

The restrictions on retail sale or supply do not apply to persons who sell or supply any medicinal product (HMRs Sch. 17 Part 1(2) and Part 4(8)) to any of the following:

a a public analyst appointed under section 27 of the Food Safety Act 1990 or Article 27 of the Food (Northern Ireland) Order 1991;

b an authorised officer within the meaning of section 5(6) of the Food Safety Act 1990;

c or a sampling officer within the meaning of Article 38(1) of the Food (Northern Ireland) Order 1989;

d an inspector acting under Regulations 325 to 328 of the HMRs;

e a sampling officer within the meaning of HMRs Schedule 31.

The sale or supply must be only in connection with the statutory functions performed by these persons and is subject to the presentation of an order signed by or on behalf of the analyst, authorised officer, sampling officer or enforcement officer, as the case may be. It must state the status of the person signing it and the amount of the medicine required.

National Health Service drug testing

The restrictions on retail sale or supply of POMs do not apply to persons who sell or supply such medicinal products to any person employed or engaged in connection with the scheme for testing the quality and amount of the drugs and appliances supplied under the National Health Service Act 2006, the

National Health Service (Scotland) Act 1978, the National Health Service (Wales) Act 2006 and the Health and Personal Social Services (Northern Ireland) Order 1972 or any subordinate legislation made under those Acts or that Order (HMRs Sch. 17 Part 1(3)).

The sale or supply must be for the purpose of the relevant scheme and is subject to the presentation of an order signed on behalf of the person so employed or engaged stating the status of the person signing it, and the amount of the medicinal product required.

Owners and masters of ships

The restrictions on supply (but not sale) of any medicinal product do not apply when the supply is made by the owner or the master of a ship which does not carry a doctor on board as part of her complement (HMRs Sch. 17 Part 2(2) and Part 5(9)). An owner or master may also, in these circumstances, administer POMs that are for parenteral administration (HMRs Sch. 17 Part 3(4)). The supply or administration shall be only so far as is necessary for the treatment of persons on the ship.

Offshore installations

Persons employed as qualified first-aid personnel on offshore installations may, only so far as is necessary for the treatment of persons on the installation (HMRs Sch. 17 Part 2(8), Part 3(7) and Part 5(14)):

1 supply any medicinal product; and
2 administer all parenteral POMs.

Statutory requirements for medical treatment of employees

The restrictions on retail supply (but not sale) of medicinal products do not apply to supplies made by persons requiring medicinal products for the purpose of enabling them, in the course of any business carried on by them, to comply with any requirements made by or in pursuance of any enactment with respect to the medical treatment of employees (HMRs Sch. 17 Part 2(5) and Part 5(8)). The exemption extends to the POMs and the Pharmacy Medicines specified in the relevant enactment and to GSL products.

The supply shall be:

1 for the purpose of enabling them to comply with any requirements made by or in pursuance of any such enactment; and
2 subject to such conditions and in such circumstances as may be specified in the relevant enactments.

Persons employed or engaged in the lawful drug treatment services

Persons employed or engaged in the lawful provision of drug treatment services may, in the course of providing those services, supply ampoules of sterile water for injection containing not more than 2 mL of sterile water (HMRs Sch. 17 Part 5(7)). In addition, persons employed or engaged in the provision of drug treatment services provided by, on behalf of or under arrangements made by an NHS body, a local authority, Public Health England or the Public Health Agency, may supply naloxone hydrochloride for parenteral administration (but no other POM) in the course of providing lawful drug treatment services and only where required for the purpose of saving life in an emergency (HMRs Sch. 17 Part 5(7)(a)).[20]

Holders of Controlled Drugs authorities

The restrictions on the supply of POMs and some Pharmacy Medicines do not apply to persons authorised by licences granted under Regulation 5 of the Misuse of Drugs Regulations[21] to supply the Controlled Drugs specified in the licence (HMRs Sch. 17 Part 2(3) and 5(6)).

The supply shall be subject to such conditions and in such circumstances and to such an extent as may be specified in the licence. Similarly, the restrictions on the administration of POMs do not apply to persons who are authorised as members of a group by a group authority granted under Regulations 8(3) or 9(3) of the Misuse of Drugs Regulations (HMRs Sch. 17 Part 3(3)). The exemption is limited to the administration of Controlled Drugs that are specified in the group authority and is subject to such conditions and in such circumstances and to such an extent as may be specified in the group authority.

Royal National Lifeboat Institution

The restrictions on the retail supply of any medicinal product do not apply to supply by the Royal National Lifeboat Institution or certificated first-aiders of the Institution (HMRs Sch. 17 Part 2(1) and Part 5(1)). The supply of any medicine shall be only so far as it is necessary for the treatment of sick or injured persons in the exercise of the functions of the Institution.

British Red Cross Society and other such organisations

The restrictions on the retail supply of P and GSL medicines (but *not* POMs) do not apply to supply by the bodies specified below and their certificated

[20] Added by Human Medicines (Amendment) (No. 3) Regulations SI 2015 No. 354
[21] The Misuse of Drugs Regulations SI 2001 No. 3998 (as amended) and The Misuse of Drugs Regulations (Northern Ireland) SR 2002 No. 1 (as amended)

first-aid and certificated nursing members (HMRs Sch. 17 Part 5(2)–(5)). In all cases the supply shall be only so far as it is necessary for the treatment of sick or injured persons. The bodies concerned are:

- British Red Cross Society
- St John Ambulance Association and Brigade
- St Andrew's Ambulance Association
- Order of Malta Ambulance Corps.

School and pre-school dental schemes

Pharmacy Medicines that are for use in the prevention of dental caries and consist of or contain sodium fluoride may be supplied in the course of 'school dental schemes', by persons carrying on the business of a school providing full-time education and in the course of 'pre-school dental schemes', by health authorities or primary health trusts (HMRs Sch. 17 Part 5(11) and (12)).

A *school dental scheme*[22] means a scheme supervised by a doctor or dentist in which medicinal products are supplied at a school to pupils of that school for the purpose of preventing dental caries. A supply, under such a scheme, may be made to a child under 16 years of age only with the consent of the parent or guardian of that child.

A *pre-school dental scheme* means a scheme supervised by a doctor or dentist in which medicinal products are supplied to parents or guardians of children under 5 years of age for use by such children for the purpose of preventing dental caries. The supplies made under such a scheme must be made by a registered nurse.

Any medicinal products containing sodium fluoride which are POMs may not be sold, supplied or administered.

Sale of salbutamol inhalers to schools

Salbutamol inhalers may be sold or supplied to a school for the purpose of supplying the medicinal product to pupils at the school in an emergency, subject to the presentation of an order signed by the principal or head teacher at the school concerned (HMRs, Sch. 17 Part 1(12), as amended),[23] stating:

i the name of the school for which the medicinal product is required,

ii the purpose for which that product is required, and

iii the total quantity required.

A person, in the course of carrying on the business of a school who is trained to administer the relevant medicine may supply a salbutamol inhaler

[22]Defined in The Medicines (Pharmacy and General Sale – Exemption) Order SI 1980 No. 1924
[23]Amended by Human Medicines (Amendment) (No. 2) Regulations SI 2014 No. 1878

to a pupil of that school who is known to suffer from asthma, where the pupil requires the medicinal product in an emergency (HMRs, as amended, Sch. 17 Part 2(11)).

Mountain rescue teams

Pharmacy and GSL medicines and POMs may be sold or supplied to persons who hold a certificate in first aid from the Mountain Rescue Council of England and Wales or from the Northern Ireland Mountain Rescue Co-ordinating Committee, in response to an order in writing signed by a doctor. These persons may then supply these medicinal products as far as is necessary for the treatment of sick or injured persons in the course of mountain rescue services (HMRs Sch. 17 Part 2(9) and Part 5(16)).

Occupational health schemes

Pharmacy and GSL medicines and POMs may be supplied by a person operating an *occupational health scheme*,[24] that is, a scheme in which persons, in the course of a business carried on by them, provide facilities for their employees for the treatment or prevention of disease.

The supply/administration must be made in the course of the scheme. The medicinal products may be supplied to the person operating the scheme in response to a written order signed by a doctor or a registered nurse (HMRs Sch. 17 Part 5(10)).

The individual supplying or administering the medicines in the course of the scheme, if not a doctor, must be:

1 a registered nurse; and
2 where the medicinal product in question is a POM, acting in accordance with the written instructions of a doctor as to the circumstances in which POMs of the description in question are to be used in the course of the occupational health scheme.

Operators or commanders of aircraft

The commander or operator of an aircraft or the *operator*,[25] that is, the person for the time being having the management of the aircraft, may supply all P and GSL medicines, and such POMs which are not for parenteral administration and which have been sold or supplied to the operator or commander of an aircraft in response to an order in writing signed by a

[24] Defined in The Medicines (Pharmacy and General Sale – Exemption) Order SI 1980 No. 1924
[25] Defined in The Medicines (Pharmacy and General Sale – Exemption) Order SI 1980 No. 1924

doctor (HMRs Sch. 17 Part 5(13)). The supply shall be only so far as is necessary for the immediate treatment of sick or injured persons on the aircraft and, in the case of a POM, shall be in accordance with the written instructions of a doctor as to the circumstances in which the POMs of the description in question are to be used on the aircraft. The commander or operator of an aircraft may also administer POMs for parenteral use which have been sold or supplied to him/her in response to an order in writing signed by a doctor. The administration shall be only so far as is necessary for the immediate treatment of sick or injured persons on the aircraft and shall be in accordance with the written instructions of a doctor as to the circumstances in which POMs of the description in question are to be used on the aircraft.

In addition, an operator or commander of an aircraft may also sell, supply or offer for sale or supply any GSL medicine that has been made up for sale or supply in a container elsewhere than at the place at which it is sold or supplied. The GSL medicine must be stored in a part of the aircraft which the operator is able to close so as to exclude the public (HMRs, as amended, Sch. 17 Part 4(11)).

Operator of a train

An operator of a train may sell, supply or offer for sale or supply any GSL medicine that has been made up for sale or supply in a container elsewhere than at the place at which it is sold or supplied. The GSL medicine must be stored in a part of the train which the operator is able to close so as to exclude the public (HMRs, Sch. 17 Part 4(12), as amended).[26]

Universities, higher education institutions or institutions concerned with research

The restrictions on retail sale or supply of medicinal products do not apply to persons selling or supplying such products to a university, an institution concerned with higher education or an institution concerned with research, but only for the purposes of the education or research with which the institution is concerned (HMRs Sch. 17 Part 1(1)). The sale or supply is subject to the presentation of an order signed by the principal of the institution for education or research or the appropriate head of department in charge of a specified course of research. The order must state:

1 the name of the institution for which the medicinal product is required;
2 the purpose for which it is required; and
3 the total quantity required.

[26]Human Medicines (Amendment) (No. 2) Regulations SI 2013 No. 2593

Supplies by holders of marketing authorisations

The restrictions on sale or supply do not apply to holders of marketing authorisations and holders of manufacturer's licences who sell or supply medicinal products referred to in the licences to pharmacists so as to enable them to prepare an entry relating to the medicinal product in question in a tablet or capsule identification guide or similar publication. No greater quantity than is reasonably necessary for that purpose may be supplied (HMRs Sch. 17 Part 1(10)).

Summary

- Doctors and dentists may sell or supply all medicines to their own patients.
- Certain organisations and health professionals can supply medicines under PGDs. These are listed in appendix 2.
- For the purposes of their professional practice, midwives have a list of medicines which can be sold or supplied by them and another list of medicines which they may administer.
- Optometrists have a list of medicines which they may sell or supply to their patients in the course of their professional practice (for POMs, this is permitted only in an emergency). They may also purchase a limited list of POMs, for use in their practice, but not for sale or supply.
- Chiropodists may sell or supply to their patients, in the course of their professional practice, any GSL product for external use and a limited list of P Medicines. Chiropodists holding a certificate of competence in the use of certain medicines may administer, in their practice, those medicines (many of these are local anaesthetics).
- Registered orthoptists may sell or supply to their patients, in the course of their professional practice, a limited list of POMs.
- Registered ambulance paramedics may parenterally administer certain medicines for the immediate, necessary treatment of the sick or injured.
- Schools may supply salbutamol inhalers to pupils at the school in an emergency, subject to certain conditions.
- Other categories of activities also have limited lists of medicines which they may sell or supply. These include dental and occupational health schemes, owners and masters of ships, offshore installations, the Royal National Lifeboat Institution, public analysts, aircraft commanders, train operators, universities, mountain rescue teams and the British Red Cross.

Further reading

Human Medicines Regulations (2012) SI 2012 No. 1916, *Explanatory memorandum*: http://www.legislation.gov.uk/uksi/2012/1916/pdfs/uksiem_20121916_en.pdf (accessed 2 November 2016).

Royal Pharmaceutical Society (published annually). *Medicines, Ethics and Practice*: *The Professional Guide for Pharmacists*. London: Royal Pharmaceutical Society (includes practice guidance on many of the topics in this chapter; free to members).

Websites

Legislation (can be searched on year and SI number or title): http://www.legislation.gov.uk

Medicines and Healthcare products Regulatory Agency: https://www.gov.uk/government/organisations/medicines-and-healthcare-products-regulatory-agency

Royal Pharmaceutical Society (member access only; lists legal classifications of medicines and further practice guidance): http://www.rpharms.com

10

Human medicines: wholesale dealing

Susan Melvin

Regulations in Part 3 of the Human Medicines Regulations 2012[1] control the sale of medicinal products by way of wholesale dealing, that is, the sale or supply, or procuring, or holding or exporting it for the purposes of sale, or supply to a person for the purpose of (a) selling or supplying them or (b) administering them to, or causing them to be administered to, human beings in the course of a business (HMRs Reg.18).

Sales of medicinal products by way of wholesale dealing can be made as set out below by:

1 the holder of a marketing authorisation; or
2 a person carrying on a business which consists (wholly or partly) of manufacturing medicinal products or of selling them by way of wholesale dealing; the sales must be made in the course of the business (retail pharmacy owners who are not licensed as wholesalers may not sell by way of wholesale dealing; chapters 2 and 3).

> **Box 10.1** *The meaning of 'sale by way of wholesale dealing'*
>
> Oxford v Sanger (1964)
>
> The Pharmacy and Poisons Act 1933 (s.18) provided that poisons in Part I of the Poisons List could be lawfully sold only by authorised sellers of poisons. An exemption from this requirement was given in section 20(1) of the Act in respect of sales of poisons by way of wholesale dealing. Section 29 defined *sale by way of wholesale dealing* as 'sale to a person who buys for the purposes of selling again'.
>
> Sanger Ltd (wholesalers) had on five occasions sold Part I poisons to a retail shopkeeper who had subsequently sold the poisons (tablets)

[1] Human Medicines Regulations SI 2012 No. 1916

to the public by retail. The shopkeeper was not an authorised seller of poisons.

The wholesaler was charged with selling Part I poisons contrary to section 18 of the Act. It was contended for the prosecution that the company could not claim the benefit of the exemption for wholesale dealing as the poison had been sold to a shopkeeper who could not lawfully sell again. The magistrate dismissed the information, and an appeal to the High Court against that decision was also dismissed.

It was held in the High Court that the word *lawfully* could not be read into the definition of *wholesale dealing*. Section 20 did not lay any duty upon a wholesaler to ascertain that the retailer to whom he sold was lawfully entitled to resell. If it was desired to control wholesalers, it could and must be done by rule.

Comment. Rule 11 of the Poisons Rules made under the Poisons Act 1972 then required wholesalers who sold Part I poisons to be satisfied that their shopkeeper customers who order such poisons are authorised sellers of poisons, or that they do not intend to sell the poisons by way of retail trade. The Medicines Act 1968 (s.61) provided for similar Regulations to be made in respect of medicinal products (SI 1980 No. 1923) and HMRs Reg.44 enacts the same provisions.

[1965] 1 All ER 96; *Pharm J*, 12 December 1964 p. 599.

Conditions on sales by way of wholesale dealing

A person making sales by way of wholesale dealing must possess a wholesale dealer's licence (chapter 3). Such sales must be from a specified place and the licence holder must among other requirements (HMRs Reg.43):[2]

1 ensure, within the limits of the holder's responsibility, the continued supply of medicinal products to pharmacies, and others who may lawfully sell them, so that the needs of patients in the UK are met;
2 keep documents to facilitate withdrawal or recall of medicinal products and maintain an emergency plan for this purpose;
3 keep records in relation to the receipt and dispatch of medicinal products of:
   a the date of receipt and of dispatch,
   b the date of brokering,
   c the name of the products,
   d the quantity of the products received, dispatched or brokered, and the name and address of the person from whom, or to whom, the products are sold or supplied as appropriate,

[2] As amended by the Human Medicines (Amendment) Regulations SI 2013 No.1855

e the batch number of medicinal products bearing safety features referred to in point (o) of Article 54 of the 2001 Directive (the Falsified Medicines Directive);

4 adopt practices to ensure compliance with the Falsified Medicines Directive (see chapter 3);

5 distribute by wholesale dealing only to persons who may lawfully sell by retail or lawfully administer those products (HMRs Reg.44);

6 have at all times at his/her disposal the services of a person – a *responsible person* – who possesses in the opinion of the licensing authority (HMRs Reg.45):

    a knowledge of the activities to be carried out and of the procedures to be performed under the licence, and

    b experience in those activities and procedures which is adequate for those purposes.

The functions of the *responsible person* shall be to ensure that the conditions under which the licence has been granted have been, and are being, complied with and that the quality of the products is maintained in accordance with the requirements of the appropriate marketing authorisation.

Prescription Only and Pharmacy Medicines by wholesale dealing

Prescription Only Medicines (POMs) and Pharmacy Medicines (P medicines) may be sold by way of wholesale dealing (HMRs Reg.249 and Sch. 22) to:

1 doctors or dentists;

2 any person lawfully conducting a retail pharmacy business;

3 authorities or persons carrying on the business of an independent hospital, independent clinic, independent medical agency or a hospital or health centre which is not an independent hospital or clinic or, in Northern Ireland, a nursing home;

4 holders of wholesale dealer's licences, or persons to whom the requirements to hold a wholesale dealer's licence do not apply by virtue of an exemption conferred by the HMRs;

5 Ministers of the Crown and government departments: Scottish, Welsh or Northern Irish Ministers;

6 an NHS trust or foundation trust health authority, special health authority;

7 Public Health England, Public Health Agency, the Common Services Agency or a local authority in the exercise of public health functions (within the meaning of the National Health Service Act 2006);

8 any person other than an exempted person who carries on a business consisting (wholly or partly) of supplying medicinal products in circumstances corresponding to retail sale, or of administering such products, pursuant to an arrangement made with an NHS trust or NHS foundation trust, the Common Services Agency, a clinical commissioning group, the NHS Commissioning Board, a local authority, Public Health England, Public Health Agency, a health authority or a special health authority;

9 a person other than an exempted person who carries on a business consisting (wholly or partly) of the supply or administration of medicinal products for the purpose of assisting the provision of healthcare by or on behalf of, or under arrangements made by, the police force in the UK, a prison service, Her Majesty's Forces or a contractor carrying out helicopter search and rescue operations on behalf of the Maritime and Coastguard Agency;

10 any person who is the subject of an exemption in HMRs Schedule 17 but only in respect of the medicinal products covered by the exemption (chapter 9 and HMRs Reg.250);

11 registered optometrists in that there are certain POMs which optometrists are entitled to supply to their patients or use in their practice (chapter 9); and

12 any person selling or supplying by retail, or administering, unit preparations of POMs (other than Controlled Drugs) diluted to one part in a million (6×) having been requested by or on behalf of the particular person and in that person's presence to use their own judgement as to the treatment required (see also chapter 11).

Wholesale dealing from a pharmacy

In August 2012, when the Human Medicines Regulations 2012 came into force, the section 10(7) exemption in the Medicines Act 1968 was repealed in order to comply with EU legislation. This exemption previously allowed retail pharmacy businesses to wholesale medicines without a wholesale dealer's licence if this was an 'inconsiderable' part of their business. The MHRA has issued guidance, the relevant parts of which are reproduced in box 10.2[3] (see websites at end of chapter).

> **Box 10.2** *MHRA Guidance for pharmacists on the repeal of section 10(7) of the Medicines Act 1968*
>
> MHRA is concerned to ensure that the repeal of the section 10(7) exemption does not adversely impact on arrangements for supply of medicines in the UK. In determining how to address this issue, MHRA has taken careful account of the particular arrangements for delivery

[3]MHRA (2014) Guidance for pharmacists on the repeal of section 10(7) of the Medicines Act 1968

of healthcare in the UK which involve a wide range of individuals and in a diverse range of locations. In particular:

- Many healthcare professionals and others authorised or entitled to supply medicines to the public in the UK need to hold small quantities of medicines for local healthcare provision and look to a local community or hospital pharmacy to supply them as part of their professional practice.
- In contrast, some pharmacies engage in commercial trade in medicines, not solely as part of their professional practice within the UK healthcare system.
- Pharmacists may also occasionally need to obtain small quantities of a particular medicine or medicines from another pharmacist in order to meet the needs of individual patients.

MHRA enforcement

MHRA takes the view that the supply of medicines by community and hospital pharmacies to other healthcare professionals in the UK who need to hold small quantities of medicines for treatment of or onward supply to their patients represents an important and appropriate part of the professional practice of both community and hospital pharmacy. Also, community and hospital pharmacies may need to obtain small quantities of a medicine from other pharmacies to meet a patient's individual needs. Both these activities are considered by MHRA to fall within the definition of provision of healthcare services. In such circumstances, provided that the transaction meets all of the following criteria, MHRA will not deem such transactions as commercial dealing and pharmacies will not be required to hold a WDA(H):

- it takes place on an occasional basis;
- the quantity of medicines supplied is small;
- the supply is made on a not-for-profit basis;
- the supply is not for onward wholesale distribution.

Conversely, pharmacies who wish to engage in commercial trading in medicines are entitled to do so only if they hold a WDA(H) and comply with all the relevant requirements. As the authority responsible for enforcement, MHRA will take appropriate action to enforce the requirement of the legislation and will require any commercial trade in medicines to be undertaken only by holders of a WDA(H). These restrictions do not apply to the exchange of stock between pharmacies that are part of the same legal entity, although, where a legal entity holds a WDA(H) as one (or more) of its pharmacies is involved in the commercial trade of medicines, the supplying pharmacy must also be named on the WDA(H) if the stock supplied is for the purposes of wholesale.

Guidance on the need for a WDA(H), the application process and a downloadable application form are available on MHRA's website.

If the pharmacist does not possess a wholesale dealer's licence, then the only records required to be kept are a copy of the order or invoice relating to the supply or an entry made in the Prescription Only Register by the owner of the retail pharmacy business. Orders or invoices (and all orders required as a condition in connection with any exempted sale of a POM; chapter 9) must be kept for 2 years from the date of the sale or supply.

If the pharmacist does possess a wholesale dealer's licence, then all the provisions of such a possession apply (see above).

Wholesale dealing of veterinary products

See chapter 17.

Summary

- Normally, a person who sells medicines by way of wholesale dealing requires a wholesale dealer's licence, which requires special premises, records to be kept, and the appointment of a responsible person whose function is to ensure that the conditions of the licence are being complied with and that the quality of the products is maintained in accordance with the requirements of the appropriate marketing authorisation.
- A pharmacist may supply medicines by way of wholesale dealing (e.g. to a doctor) provided that the sales take place on an occasional basis and the quantity of medicines supplied is small and intended to meet the needs of an individual patient, and the supply is made on a not-for-profit basis.

Further reading

Human Medicines Regulations (2012) SI 2012 No. 1916, *Explanatory memorandum*: http://www.legislation.gov.uk/uksi/2012/1916/pdfs/uksiem_20121916_en.pdf (accessed 2 November 2016).

Royal Pharmaceutical Society (published annually). *Medicines, Ethics and Practice: The Professional Guide for Pharmacists*. London: Royal Pharmaceutical Society (includes practice guidance on many of the topics in this chapter; free to members).

Websites

Legislation (can be searched on year and SI number or title): http://www.legislation.gov.uk

Medicines and Healthcare products Regulatory Agency: https://www.gov.uk/government/organisations/medicines-and-healthcare-products-regulatory-agency

Royal Pharmaceutical Society (member access only; lists legal classifications of medicines and further practice guidance): http://www.rpharms.com

11

Human medicines: sale and supply of homoeopathic medicines

Zoe Smith

A *homoeopathic medicinal product* is defined (HMRs Reg.8) by its manufacturing method, prepared from a homoeopathic stock in accordance with a homoeopathic manufacturing procedure described by the *European Pharmacopoeia* or, in its absence, in any pharmacopoeia used officially in an EEA country.

Most 'homoeopathic medicinal products' for human use are subject to licensing procedures under the Human Medicines Regulations 2012.[1]

Provided that certain conditions are met, either a simplified system of certification is permitted (HR – homoeopathic registration[2]) or a simplified licence under national rules is granted (NR – national homoeopathic product[3]). Furthermore, Product Licences of Right (PLR), granted in the 1970s for homoeopathic (and anthroposophic) medicinal products on the market at that time, are currently permitted to continue in force under transitional arrangements.[4]

Whilst the MHRA have indicated that the PLR scheme will be the subject of a review, at the time of going to press no changes have been made.

Additionally, there are certain exemptions relating to the sale and supply of homoeopathic medicines referred to as 'medicinal products at high dilution'. These exemptions are the main subject of this chapter.

[1] Human Medicines Regulations SI 2012 No.1916 (HMRs)
[2] HMRs, Part 6, Regs.102–124
[3] HMRs Schedule 10
[4] HMRs Reg.347 – Sch. 32 (Transitional provisions and savings)

Homoeopathic medicines for human use: licensing

There are three main systems:

- Certificates of Registration (HRs);
- national homoeopathic products (NRs);
- Product Licences of Right (PLR) – under transitional arrangements.

See chapter 3.

Medicinal products at high dilutions (homoeopathic medicines)

Medicinal products at high dilutions are prepared from 'unit preparations'.

Unit preparation means 'a preparation, including a mother tincture, prepared by a process of solution, extraction or trituration with a view to being diluted tenfold or one hundredfold, either once or repeatedly, in an inert diluent, and then used either in this diluted form or, where applicable, by impregnating tablets, granules, powders or other inert substances' (HMRs Reg.213).

Exemptions for medicinal products at high dilution (homoeopathic medicines)

Homoeopathic medicines for treatment according to the judgement of the seller

Regulation 242 of the Human Medicines Regulations 2012 contains an exemption from the restrictions which apply to both the sale or supply of Pharmacy Medicines (HMRs Reg.220; see chapter 6) and GSL medicines (HMRs Reg.221; see chapter 7) subject to a number of conditions:

1 the medicinal product is neither for parenteral administration nor a Controlled Drug;
2 the person selling or supplying the product has been requested to do so by or on behalf of a particular person and in that person's presence and the seller has used his/her own judgement as to the treatment required; and
3 the medicinal product consists solely of one or more unit preparations of:
  a any substance where the unit preparation has been diluted to at least one part in a million (6×),
  b any substance that is listed in HMRs Part 1 of Schedule 21 where the unit preparation has been diluted to at least one part in a thousand (3×), or

c any substance that:
   i is the active substance of a medicine that is subject to general sale,
   ii is listed in HMRs Part 3 of Schedule 21, diluted to at least one part in ten $(1\times)$, or
   iii in the case of a medicinal product for external use only, is listed in HMRs Part 4 of Schedule 21, where the unit preparation has been diluted to at least one part in ten $(1\times)$.

This enables homoeopathic medicines at specified levels of dilution to be sold if the seller is requested by a customer to use the seller's own judgement as to the treatment required, without the restrictions that normally apply to General Sale or Pharmacy medicines.

Homoeopathic medicines for which General Sale is permitted

Regulation 242 also contains an exemption from the restrictions on sale or supply of Pharmacy Medicines (HMRs Reg.220) subject to a number of conditions:

1 the medicinal product is neither for parenteral administration nor a Controlled Drug;
2 the conditions regarding GSL (HMRs Reg.221) are met; and
3 the medicinal product is one that consists solely of one or more unit preparations of:
   a any substance where the unit preparation has been diluted to at least one part in a million million (6c or $12\times$),
   b any substance that is listed in HMRs Part 2 of Schedule 21 where the unit preparation has been diluted to at least one part in a million $(6\times)$, or
   c any substance that:
      i is the active substance of a medicine that is subject to general sale,
      ii is listed in HMRs Part 3 of Schedule 21, diluted to at least one part in ten $(1\times)$, or
      iii in the case of a medicinal product for external use only, is listed in HMRs Part 4 of Schedule 21, where the unit preparation has been diluted to at least one part in ten $(1\times)$.

This enables homoeopathic medicines at specified levels of dilution to be sold in accordance with the requirements of General Sale, but without the restrictions that normally apply to Pharmacy medicines.

Exemption for certain (registered) homoeopathic medicinal products (HMRs Reg.243)

The restrictions on neither sale nor supply of GSL or Pharmacy medicines apply where:

a   a certificate of registration is in force in relation to the product;
b   the product is not an *excluded product* (see below); and
c   the person selling or supplying the product has been requested to do so by or on behalf of a particular person and in that person's presence, and the seller has used his/her own judgement as to the treatment required.

In addition, the restrictions on sale or supply of Pharmacy Medicines do not apply where:

a   a certificate of registration is in force in relation to the product;
b   the conditions for GSL are met; and
c   the product is not an *excluded product* (see below).

An *excluded product* means a product that is promoted, recommended or marketed: for use as an anthelmintic; for parenteral administration; for use as eye drops; for use as an eye ointment; for use as an enema; for use wholly or mainly for irrigation of wounds or of the bladder, vagina or rectum; or for administration wholly or mainly to children being a preparation of aloxiprin or aspirin.

Specified medicinal products at high dilutions

Table 11.1 lists these products. Taken from HMRs Reg.242 Schedule 21.

Table 11.1 Medicinal products at high dilutions			
Part 1: unit preparations diluted to at least one part in a thousand (3x)	**Part 2: unit preparations diluted to at least one part in a million (6x)**	**Part 3: unit preparations diluted to at least one part in ten (1x)**	**Part 4: unit preparations diluted to at least one part in ten (1x) for external use**
Agaricus muscarius	Adonis vernalis	Abies excelsa	Adonis vernalis
Ailanthus glandulosa	Agaricus bulbosus	Abies nigra	Agricus bulbosus
Apocynum cannabinum	Agaricus muscarius	Abies nobilis	Agricus muscarius
Aurum Iodatum	Agnus castus	Acalpha indica	Agnus castus
Belladonna	Ailanthus glandulosa	Agate	Allanthus glandulosa
Bismuth subgallate	Alum	Alisma plantago aq.	Alum
Bryonia alba dioica	Amethyst	Alstonia scholaris	Amethyst
Calcium fluoride	Ammonium iodide	Aluminium	Ammonium iodide
Cantharis	Amygdalae amarae	Amber (Succinum)	Amygdalae amarae
	Apatite	Ambra grisea	Apatite

(continued overleaf)

Table 11.1 *(continued)*

Part 1: unit preparations diluted to at least one part in a thousand (3x)	Part 2: unit preparations diluted to at least one part in a million (6x)	Part 3: unit preparations diluted to at least one part in ten (1x)	Part 4: unit preparations diluted to at least one part in ten (1x) for external use
Cerium oxalicum	Apocynum androsaemifolium	Ammonium phosphate	Apocynum androsaemifolium
Chelidonium majus	Apocynum cannabinum	Angostura vera	Apocynum cannabinum
Chenopodium oil	Argentite	Anthoxanthum	Argentite
Cina	Argentum chloride	Apis mellifera	Argentum chloride
Colocynthis	Argentum iodide	Aqua marina	Argentum iodide
Convallaria majalis	Arnica	Aqua mellis	Artemisia cina
Gelsemium sempervirens	Artemisia cina	Aralia racemosa	Aspidium filix-mas
Hyoscyamus niger	Aspidium filix-mas	Aranea diadema	Aspidium anthelmintica
Lycopodium	Aspidium anthelmintica	Arum maculatum	Aurum sulphide
Manganese acetate	Aurum sulphide	Arum triphyllum	Balsamum copaivae
Ranunculus bulbosus	Balsamum copivae	Asarum	Balsamum peruvianum
Terebinthinae oleum	Balsamum peruvianum	Asperula odorata	Barium citrate
	Barium citrate	Astacus fluviatillis	Barium sulphate
	Barium sulphate	Auric chloride	Bismuth metal
	Bismuth metal	Badiaga	Bismuth subgallate
	Bismuth subgallate	Beech (*Fagus sylvestris*)	Bismuth subnitrate
	Bismuth subnitrate	Bellis perennis	Boletus laricis
	Boletus laricis	Berberis aquifolium	Bovista
	Bovista	Borago officinalis	Cade oil
	Cade oil	Butyric acid	Calcium fluoride
	Calcium fluoride	Calcium metal	Carduus marianus
	Cantharis	Calcium chloride	Cedar wood oil
	Carduus marianus	Calcium oxide	Cerium oxalicum
	Cedar wood oil	Calcium sulphate	Chalcocite
	Cerium oxalicum	Castoreum	Chalcopyrite
	Chalcocite	Ceanothus americanus	Chelidonium majus
	Chalcopyrite	Cedron	Chenopodium oil
	Chelidonium majus	Cerato (*Ceratostigma willmottiana*)	Colocynthis
	Chenopodium oil	Cherry Plum (*Prunus cerasifera*)	Convallaria majalis
	Colocynthis	Chestnut, red and sweet	Copper silicate, Nat
	Convallaria majalis	Cholesterinum	Crotalus horridus
	Copper silicate, Nat.	Chrysolite	Cucumis melo
	Crotalus horridus	Cistus canadensis	Cucurbita
	Cucurbita	Clematis erecta	Datura stramonium
	Cucumis melo	Conchae vera	Derris
	Datura stramonium	Conchiolinum	Diamond
		Corallium rubrum	Ephedra vulgaris
		Crab apple	Ferric acetate

(continued overleaf)

Table 11.1 *(continued)*

Part 1: unit preparations diluted to at least one part in a thousand (3x)	Part 2: unit preparations diluted to at least one part in a million (6x)	Part 3: unit preparations diluted to at least one part in ten (1x)	Part 4: unit preparations diluted to at least one part in ten (1x) for external use
	Derris	Crocus sativus	Ferrous iodide
	Diamond	Erbium	Ferrous oxalate
	Ephedra vulgaris	Erigeron canadense	Ferrous sulphide
	Ferric acetate	Fuligo	Formic acid
	Ferrous iodide	Genista tinctoria	Gall
	Ferrous oxalate	Geum urbanum	Gelsemium sempervirens
	Ferrous sulphide	Glycogen	Gneiss
	Formic acid	Gnaphalium	Hamamelis virginiana
	Gall	leontopodium	Hepar sulfuris
	Gelsemium	Gold	Hyoscyamus niger
	sempervirens	Gorse (*Ulex europaeus*)	Iris florentine
	Gneiss	Graphites	Jaborandi
	Granatum	Gratiola officinalis	Juniperus sabina
	(Pomegranate) bark	Gymnocladus (American	Kaolinite
	Hamamelis virginiana	coffee tree)	Lachmanthus tinctoria
	Hepar sulfuris	Haematoxylon	Lapis albus
	Hyoscyamus niger	campechianum	Lycopodium
	Iris florentine	Hecla lava (ash from	Magnesium
	Jaborandi	Mount Hecla)	Magnesium acetate
	Juniperus sabina	Hedeoma pulegioides	Magnesium chloride
	Kalinite	Hedra helix	Magnetite
	Lachmanthus	Heliotrope	Manganese acetate
	tinctoria	Heracleum spondylium	Nicotiana tabacum
	Lapis albus	Herniaria	Nicotiana tabacum oil
	Lycopodium	Hornbeam (*Carpinus	Oleander
	Magnesium	betulus*)	Opuntia vulgaris
	Magnesium acetate	Iberis amara	Oxalic acid
	Magnesium chloride	Impatiens	Petroleum
	Magnetite	Iris germanica	Phellandrium
	Manganese acetate	Iris pseudacorus	aquaticum
	Nicotiana tabacum	Jacaranda procera	Pix liquida
	Nicotiana tabacum oil	Jatropha curcas	Platinum
	Oleander	Juncus communis	Platinum chloride
	Opuntia vulgaris	Justica adhatoda	Potassium hydroxide
	Oxalic acid	Lamium album	Potassium silicate
	Petroleum	Laurus nobilis oil	Pyrethrum
	Phellandrum	Laurocerasus	Pyrolusite
	aquaticum	Ledum palustre	Ranunculus acris
	Pix liquida	Lilium tigrinum	

(continued overleaf)

Table 11.1 *(continued)*

Part 1: unit preparations diluted to at least one part in a thousand (3x)	Part 2: unit preparations diluted to at least one part in a million (6x)	Part 3: unit preparations diluted to at least one part in ten (1x)	Part 4: unit preparations diluted to at least one part in ten (1x) for external use
	Platinum	Lonicera caprifolium	Ranunculus bulbosus
	Platinum chloride	Lysimachia vulgaris	Ranunculus flammula
	Potassium hydroxide	Magnesium phosphate	Ranunculus repens
	Potassium silicate	Magnesite	Ranunculus scelerantus
	Pyrethrum	Magnolia	Rhodium oxynitrate
	Pyrolusite	Marum verum	Rhododendron chrysanthemum
	Ranunculus acris	Melilotus officinalis	Rhus toxicidendron
	Ranunculus bulbosus	Menispermum canadense	Salicylic acid
	Ranunculus flammula	Mephitis putorius	Scrophularia aquatica
	Ranunculus repens	Mercurialis perennis	Sodium aluminium chloride
	Ranunculus sceleratus	Mimulus (*Mimullis guttatus*)	Sodium auro-chloride
	Rhodium oxynitrate	Moschus	Sodium hypochlorite
	Rhododendron chrysanthemum	Myrica gale	Sodium nitrate
	Rhus toxicodendron	Myrtus communis	Squill
	Salicylic acid	Ocimum basilicum	Stannum metal
	Scrophularia aquatica	Olive	Sulphur iodide
	Sodium aluminium chloride	Oxalis acetosella	Tannic acid
	Sodium auro-chloride	Pangamic acid	Terebinthinae oleum
	Sodium hypochlorite	Paullinia cupana	Topaz
	Sodium nitrate	Penthorum sedoides	Uric acid
	Squill	Pollen (mixed)	Zinc hypophosphite
	Stannum metal	Polygonatum multiflorum	Zinc isovalerate
	Staphisagria	Polygonum aviculare	
	Sulphur iodide	Polypodium vulgare	
	Tamus communis	Primula vulgaris	
	Tannic acid	Prunella vulgaris	
	Terebinthinae oleum	Ptellea trifoliata	
	Theridion	Ratanhia	
	Thuja occidentalis	Robinia pseudoacacia	
	Topaz	Rubia tinctorum	
	Uric acid	Rumex acetosella	
	Zinc hypophosphite	Sal marina	
	Zinc isovalerate	Sarcolactic acid	
		Sarracenia purpurea	
		Scleranthus (*Scleranthus annuus*)	

(continued overleaf)

Table 11.1 *(continued)*			
Part 1: unit preparations diluted to at least one part in a thousand (3 x)	**Part 2: unit preparations diluted to at least one part in a million (6 x)**	**Part 3: unit preparations diluted to at least one part in ten (1 x)**	**Part 4: unit preparations diluted to at least one part in ten (1 x) for external use**
		Silica	
		Silphium laciniathum	
		Sodium benzoate	
		Spongia marina	
		Star of Bethlehem (*Ornithogalum umbellatum*)	
		Ulmus campestris	
		Vine	
		Walnut (*Juglerus regia*)	
		Water violet (*Hottonia palustris*)	
		Wild oat	
		Wild rose	

Summary

- Most homoeopathic medicines are GSL and may be sold from any retail shop which is closable to the public, particularly if diluted to at least 6c.
- Certain listed homoeopathic medicines may be sold if the seller is requested by a customer to use the seller's own judgement as to the treatment required, without General Sale or Pharmacy restrictions, particularly if diluted to at least 6c.
- Homoeopathic medicines with Certificates of Registration can be sold under similar circumstances as above. However, there are certain excluded categories.

Further reading

Human Medicines Regulations (2012) SI 2012 No. 1916, *Explanatory memorandum*: http://www.legislation.gov.uk/uksi/2012/1916/pdfs/uksiem_20121916_en.pdf (accessed 6 September 2016).

Royal Pharmaceutical Society (published annually). *Medicines, Ethics and Practice: The Professional Guide for Pharmacists*. London: Royal Pharmaceutical Society (includes practice guidance on many of the topics in this chapter; free to members).

Websites

Legislation (can be searched on year and SI number or title): http://www.legislation.gov.uk

Medicines and Healthcare products Regulatory Agency: https://www.gov.uk/government/organisations/medicines-and-healthcare-products-regulatory-agency

Royal Pharmaceutical Society (member access only; lists legal classifications of medicines and further practice guidance): http://www.rpharms.com

12

Human medicines: herbal medicines

Ann Godsell

Any product which makes a medicinal claim requires appropriate authorisation as a medicine. The Human Medicines Regulations 2012[1] (HMRs) Part 4 establishes that products must not be sold, supplied, or offered for sale or supply unless authorised, either by the United Kingdom licensing authority under the Regulations, or by the European Commission under Regulation (EC) No 726/2004. References to Parts, Regulations and Schedules in this chapter relate to the Human Medicines Regulations 2012 and those to sections to the Medicines Act 1968, unless otherwise stated.

Products with herbal active ingredient(s) may be authorised either with a marketing authorisation (also known as a 'product licence'), or with a traditional herbal registration (also known as a 'THR'). Details of the requirements for marketing authorisations to be granted are specified in the HMRs (see chapter 3). When authorised by the grant of a marketing authorisation, the labelling of an authorised herbal medicine will carry the authorisation number for clear identification, which consists of an authorisation number preceded by a 'PL'.

The licensing authority is the MHRA, and it is responsible for the grant, renewal, variation, suspension and revocation of licences, authorisations, certificates and registrations under these Regulations. Written applications for either a marketing authorisation or a traditional herbal registration must be made in the manner prescribed, which are then assessed and granted (see chapter 3).

An MHRA specialist committee, established formerly by the Act (as amended by the HMRs Sch. 11), known as the Herbal Medicines Advisory Committee,[2] advises:

---

[1] Human Medicines Regulations SI 2012 No. 1916
[2] The Herbal Medicines Advisory Committee Order SI 2005 No. 2791

1 with respect to safety, quality and efficacy in relation to human use of herbal medicinal products, other than any product:

   a in respect of which a marketing authorisation, product licence or certificate of registration has been granted, or

   b which is the subject of an application for such an authorisation, licence or certificate;

2 with respect to safety, quality and efficacy in relation to human use of any herbal medicinal product:

   a in respect of which a marketing authorisation, product licence or certificate of registration has been granted, or

   b which is the subject of an application for such an authorisation, licence or certificate, where ministers or the licensing authority requests such advice or provides the committee with information relating to that product, and

   c in relation to the sale, supply, manufacture or assembly of medicinal products under section 12 of the Act.

Definitions

The HMRs Reg.8 has the following definitions.

Herbal medicinal product means a medicinal product whose only active ingredients are herbal substances or herbal preparations (or both).

Herbal preparation means a preparation obtained by subjecting herbal substances to processes such as extraction, distillation, expression, fractionation, purification, concentration or fermentation, and includes a comminuted or powdered herbal substance, a tincture, an extract, an essential oil, an expressed juice or a processed exudate.

Herbal substance means a plant or part of a plant, alga, fungus or lichen, or an unprocessed exudate of a plant, defined by the plant part used and the botanical name of the plant, either fresh or dried, but otherwise unprocessed.

Traditional herbal registration means a registration granted by the licensing authority for a traditional herbal medicinal product under the Human Medicines Regulations 2012.

Registration of a traditional herbal medicinal product

In March 2004, the European Commission issued a Directive on Traditional Herbal Medicinal Products (2004/24/EC), amending Council Directive 2001/83/EC, which introduced the new category of registration as a traditional herbal medicinal product. The Human Medicines Regulations 2012 enacts these requirements for traditional herbal medicinal products in HMRs Part 7 and Schedule 29. Such products are referred to by the licensing authority as a traditional herbal registration.

Under the traditional herbal registration scheme, the pharmacological effects or efficacy of the medicinal product must be plausible on the basis of long-standing use and experience. Although it is not required to demonstrate efficacy as for a marketing authorisation, quality and safety must be demonstrated before a traditional herbal registration is granted.

Traditional herbal medicinal product means a herbal medicinal product to which HMRs Reg.125 applies. The conditions laid down are that a registration procedure is established for the product (chapter 3) which fulfils the following criteria. The product must also meet the following conditions:

A by virtue of its composition and indications the product is appropriate for use without the need for a medical practitioner to:
  a diagnose the condition to be treated by the product,
  b prescribe the product, or
  c monitor the product's use;
B the product is intended to be administered at a particular strength and in accordance with a particular posology;
C the product is intended to be administered externally, orally or by inhalation;
D the product:
  a has been in medicinal use for a continuous period of at least 30 years, and
  b has been in medicinal use in the EU for a continuous period of at least 15 years.
  It is immaterial for the purposes of condition D whether or not, during a period mentioned in that condition, the sale or supply of the product has been based on a specific authorisation, or the number or quantity of the ingredients (or any of them) has been reduced;
E there is sufficient information about the use of the product as mentioned in condition D (referred to in this Part as its 'traditional use'), so that (in particular):
  a it has been established that the traditional use of the product is not harmful, and
  b the pharmacological effects or efficacy of the product is plausible on the basis of long-standing use and experience.

Applications for a traditional herbal medicinal product registration must be made in the manner prescribed in the Regulations (HMRs Reg.127).

Labelling for traditional herbal medicinal products

HMRs Reg.265(1) and Schedule 29 set out additional requirements for labelling of traditional herbal medicinal products, as compared to medicinal products holding a marketing authorisation. These include the following requirements in Schedule 29 Part 1:

1   a statement to the effect that the product is a traditional herbal medicinal product, for use for specific purposes by reason of long-standing use; and
2   a statement that the user should consult a doctor or other healthcare practitioner if symptoms persist during use of the medicinal product, or if adverse effects not mentioned on the package or package leaflet occur.

HMRs Reg.265(2) specifies that no information need appear on:

a   a package containing a traditional herbal medicinal product where part of the package is transparent or open, provided that the information required by the HMRs is clearly visible through the transparent or open part of the package; or
b   a paper bag or similar wrapping, in which a package that contains a traditional herbal medicinal product and bears information required by the HMRs and Schedule 29 is placed at the time of sale or supply;
c   a package enclosing a package of a traditional herbal medicinal product for export;
d   an ampoule or other container of not more than 10 mL, which is enclosed in a package on which information appears in accordance with the requirements of the HMRs and Schedule 29; or
e   a blister pack or similar packaging, enclosed in a package labelled in accordance with the requirements of the HMRs and Schedule 29.

Subject to the above, HMRs Schedule 29 Part 2 states the conditions where, if the traditional herbal medicinal product is a P medicine, the outer and immediate packaging must be labelled to show the capital letter 'P' within a rectangle, within which there is no other matter of any kind.

The licensing authority have designed and launched an additional visible symbol, a THR Certification Mark (see figure 12.1), which is located on the packaging of all registered traditional herbal medicinal products. These products can also be identified by a nine-digit registration number starting with the letters 'THR' on the product container or packaging.

Figure 12.1   THR Certification Mark

Sale or supply by a licence holder

HMRs Reg.43(5) states that a licence holder must not sell or supply a medicinal product, or offer it for sale or supply, unless:

a there is a marketing authorisation or traditional herbal registration (an 'authorisation') in force in relation to the product; and
b the sale or supply, or offer for sale or supply, is in accordance with the authorisation.

It is also the responsibility of manufacturers, wholesale dealers, importers and anyone placing medicinal products on the market to ensure that they comply with the relevant legislation.

Herbal remedy

Under section 132(1) of the Act, a *herbal remedy* is defined as a medicinal product consisting of a substance produced by subjecting a plant or plants to drying, crushing or any other process, or of a mixture whose sole ingredients are two or more substances so produced, or of a mixture whose sole ingredients are one or more substances so produced and water or some other inert substance.

Exemptions on sale or supply of certain herbal remedies

There are certain special provisions that are specified in HMRs Reg.3(2), (6) and (9), which amend the scope of the HMRs 2012.

HMRs Reg.3(2) states that regulation 17(1) (manufacturing of medicinal products: requirement for licence) and 46 (requirement for authorisation) shall not apply in circumstances where paragraph (5) or (6) and paragraph (9), in both cases, of Reg.3 of the HMRs applies. Paragraph 5 relates to the manufacture or assembly of medicinal products by a doctor or dentist; it is further specified (paragraph 8) that the medicinal product is supplied to a patient in the course of the treatment of that patient or to a patient of another doctor or dentist who is a member of the same medical or dental practice. Paragraph 6 relates to the manufacture or assembly of herbal medicinal products where certain conditions are specified. Paragraph (9) specifies that the medicinal product is not manufactured or, as the case may be, assembled on a large scale or by an industrial process.

HMRs Part 12 (dealings with medicinal products) governs the circumstances in which medicinal products may be sold, supplied and administered. In HMRs Regs.220 and 221 it is specified that medicinal products classified as Pharmacy Medicines (known as P), may be sold or supplied by retail only from registered pharmacies (chapter 6), unless they are products classified as

General Sales List medicines (known as GSL) (chapter 7) or subject to some other exemption under the Regulations. The exemptions from the conditions on retail sale or supply that exist for herbal medicinal products are set out in Regulation 241, and apply to substances listed in HMRs Schedule 20.

There is a specific exemption for herbal remedies in Regulation 241 of the HMRs from the restrictions on sale or supply of herbal medicinal products.

1   Regs. 220 and 221 do not apply to the sale or supply, or offer for sale or supply by a person ('A') of a herbal medicinal product if:
   a   the product does not contain a substance listed in Part 1 of Schedule 20;
   b   the product does not contain a substance listed in column 1 of Part 2 of that Schedule, unless the product is sold or supplied:
      i   in the case of a product for which there is a corresponding entry in column 2 of that Part, in or from containers or packages labelled to show a dose not exceeding the maximum dose or maximum daily dose specified in that entry, and
      ii   in the case of a product for which there is a corresponding entry in column 3 of that Part, with the percentage of the substance in the product not exceeding that specified in that entry;
   c   the sale or supply, or offer for sale or supply, takes place on premises occupied by A and from which A can exclude the public; and
   d   the product is for administration to a person ('B') and A has been requested by or on behalf of B and in B's presence to use A's judgement as to the treatment required.
2   A reference in this regulation to a substance listed in either Part of Schedule 20 is a reference to a substance that is obtained from any botanical source listed in either Part.

HMRs Reg.3(9) states an additional condition applicable for all medicinal products to be exempt from the above requirements, which is where the medicinal product is not manufactured or, as the case may be, assembled, on a large scale, or by an industrial process.

Schedule 20 conditions on retail sale or supply

Schedule 20 to the HMRs is in two parts, reflecting the different degrees of control over the retail sale or supply of the listed plants in each part.

Part 1 sets out the plants that may only be sold by retail at registered pharmacies and by or under the supervision of a pharmacist. Plants listed in Part 2 can only be sold in herbal medicines following a one-to-one consultation with a practitioner, at the dosages in column 2 or percentage of the substance in the product not exceeding that specified in column 3 (HMRs Reg.3(6) (see above). If the dosage (or percentage of the substance in the product) specified is exceeded, the herbal medicines containing these plants can only be supplied in premises which are registered pharmacies and by or under the supervision of a pharmacist.

Banned or restricted herbal ingredients in medicines

Banned or restricted herbal ingredients for medicinal use are listed on the licensing authority website. This is an alphabetical list of herbal ingredients which are currently subject to various restrictions in the UK.

Some herbal ingredients are subject to more than one set of restrictions. In addition to Parts I and II of Schedule 20 to the HMRs, and HMRs Reg.241 as discussed above, the following legislation is in force:

- The Medicines (Aristolochia and Mu Tong etc.) (Prohibition) Order 2001:[3]
    - It is not permissible to manufacture, import, sell or supply any unlicensed medicine in the UK which contains the listed herbal ingredients.
- The Medicines for Human Use (Kava-kava) (Prohibition) Order 2002:[4]
    - prohibits the sale, supply or importation of any medicine for human use which consists of or contains a plant (or part of a plant) belonging to the species *Piper methysticum* or an extract from such a plant, except those for external use only.
- The Medicines for Human Use (Prohibition) (Senecio and Miscellaneous Amendments) Order 2008:[5]
    - prohibits the sale, supply or importation of any medicine for human use which consists of or contains a plant, or part of a plant, belonging to the species *Senecio* or an extract from such a plant.

Exemption of herbal remedies under the Medicines Act

Historically, the Act section 12.2 permitted the sale, supply, manufacture or assembly of a herbal remedy to be exempt from licensing if it contained plant(s) or processes only of drying, crushing or comminuting and had a designation which specified only the plant(s) and process. Section 12.2 of the Act is now repealed.[6] Furthermore, 30 April 2014 was the end of the sell-through period for all manufactured herbal medicines supplied by third parties which had hitherto been sanctioned via the Act.

[3] The Medicines (Aristolochia and Mu Tong etc.) (Prohibition) Order SI 2001 No. 1841
[4] The Medicines for Human Use (Prohibition) (Kava-kava) (Prohibition) Order SI 2002 No. 3170
[5] The Medicines for Human Use (Prohibition) (Senecio and Miscellaneous Amendments) Order SI 2008 No. 548
[6] The Medicinal Products (Herbal Remedies) (Amendment) Regulations 2011 SI 2011 No. 915

A herbal product that does not have a marketing authorisation (medicinal product) or a traditional herbal registration (traditional herbal medicinal product) is not permitted to make any medicinal claim.

Herbal products as food

Some herbal products may be legally sold under food legislation, commonly as food supplements.[7] No medicinal claims can be made for any food product. The MHRA can determine whether the claims that are made or the active substance(s) present would mean that a product is to be regarded a medicinal product.

Concerns over illegal herbal products

Herbal products can be legally sold under other legislation, for example as cosmetics, foods, medical devices or biocides, but are required to be compliant with the relevant legislation. The Inspection and Enforcement Division of the MHRA can be contacted directly with any concerns over potentially illegal herbal products.

Herbal practitioners

There is no definition in legislation of a herbal practitioner. There is ongoing discussion relating to the introduction of statutory regulation of herbal practitioners.

No licence to supply herbal medicines created on the premises to patients following one-to-one consultations is required. There is an exemption for supply or sale of herbal medicinal products in the HMRs Reg.241.

Summary

- Herbal medicines are authorised either by holding a marketing authorisation (medicinal product) or a traditional herbal registration (traditional herbal medicinal product).
- Authorised herbal traditional herbal medicinal products are required to meet the same quality and safety standards as all authorised medicinal products.

[7]Food Supplements (England) Regulations SI 2003 No. 1387; Food Supplements(Scotland) Regulations 2003 SSI 2003 No. 278; Food Supplements (Wales) Regulations 2003 WSI 2003 No. 1719 (W186); and Food Supplements (Northern Ireland) Regulations 2003 Statutory Rule 2003 No.273

- The labelling of an authorised herbal medicine will carry the authorisation number for clear identification, which consists of an authorisation number preceded by either 'PL' or 'THR'.
- The Herbal Medicines Advisory Committee advises as necessary on the quality, safety and efficacy of herbal products.
- Ordinary shopkeepers are permitted to sell authorised herbal medicines with 'GSL' status.
- Registered pharmacies are permitted, additionally, to sell authorised herbal medicines with 'P' status.
- Registered pharmacies are permitted to sell herbal ingredients as listed in Part 1 or Part 2 of the HMRs Schedule 20.
- The licensing authority provides a current list of restricted or banned herbal ingredients.
- A herbal product that does not have a marketing authorisation (medicinal product) or a traditional herbal registration (traditional herbal medicinal product) is not permitted to make any medicinal claim.
- Herbal practitioners are permitted to sell authorised traditional herbal medicinal products with 'GSL' status, and also those herbal ingredients subject to the requirements of Part 2 of Schedule 20 of the HMRs.

Further reading

Barnes J, Anderson, LA and Phillipson, JD (2013). *Herbal Medicines*, 4th edn. London: Pharmaceutical Press.

Websites

British Herbal Medicines Association: http://bhma.info
Legislation (searchable): http://www.legislation.gov.uk
MHRA (searchable): https://www.gov.uk/government/organisations/medicines-and-healthcare-products-regulatory-agency

13

Human medicines: prohibitions for protection of the purchaser

Karen Pitchford

Prohibition orders

The Medicines Act 1968 provides power (s.62) for the Ministers to make a prohibition, either total or limited in some way, on the sale, supply or importation of specified classes of medicinal product or of particular medicinal products if it appears to them necessary to do so in the interest of safety. Before making such an Order, the Ministers are required to consult the appropriate committee. These requirements may be waived if, in the opinion of the Ministers, it is essential to make the Order with immediate effect to avoid serious danger to health. An Order made without consultation is effective for 3 months only but may be renewed.

Any person who, otherwise than for performing or exercising a statutory duty or power, is in possession of such a medicinal product, knowing or having reasonable cause to suspect that it was sold, supplied or imported in contravention of the Order, is guilty of an offence (s.67).

Section 62 Orders

Bal Jivan Chamcho

The sale, supply or importation of Bal Jivan Chamcho is prohibited. This is a baby tonic in the form of a dark brown aromatic solid substance affixed to a spoon-shaped metal appliance. The prohibition[1] does not apply to importation from a Member State of the EU or if it originated in a state within the EEA. Neither does the prohibition apply to the sale or supply to a

[1] The Medicines (Bal Jivan Chamcho Prohibition) (No. 2) Order SI 1977 No. 670

public analyst, an authorised officer of a drugs authority, a sampling officer, a person duly authorised by an enforcement authority under the Act or a GPhC inspector.[2]

Herbal products

Four other section 62 banning orders have been made in relation to herbal medicines, namely for *Aristolochia*, Mu Tong or Fangji,[3] Kava-kava[4] and Senecio[5] (see also chapter 12).

Chloroform

The sale or supply of medicinal products for human use which consist of or contain chloroform is prohibited[6] subject to the following exceptions. A sale or supply made:

1. by a doctor or dentist to a patient of his/hers, where the medicinal product has been specially prepared by that doctor or dentist for administration to that particular patient;
2. by a doctor or dentist who has specially prepared the medicinal product at the request of another doctor or dentist for administration to a particular patient of that other doctor or dentist;
3. from a registered pharmacy or hospital or by a doctor or dentist where the medicinal product has been specially prepared in accordance with a prescription given by a doctor or dentist for a particular patient;
4. to a hospital, a doctor or a dentist for use as an anaesthetic;
5. to a person who buys it for the purpose of reselling it to a hospital, a doctor or a dentist for use as an anaesthetic;
6. where the medicinal product contains chloroform in a proportion of not more than 0.5% w/w or v/v;
7. where the medicinal product is solely for use in dental surgery;
8. where the medicinal product is solely for use by being applied to the external surface of the body which for the purpose of this Order does not include any part of the mouth, teeth or mucous membranes;
9. where the medicinal product is for export; or
10. where the medicinal product is sold for use as an ingredient in the preparation of a substance or article in a registered pharmacy, a hospital or by a doctor or dentist.

[2] Medicines (Bal Jivan Chamcho Prohibition) (No. 2) Amendment Order SI 1997 No. 856
[3] The Medicines (Aristolochia and Mu Tong etc.) (Prohibition) Order SI 2001 No. 1841
[4] The Medicines for Human Use (Kava-kava) (Prohibition) Order SI 2002 No. 3170
[5] The Medicines for Human Use (Prohibition) (Senecio and Miscellaneous Amendments) Order SI 2008 No. 548
[6] The Medicines (Chloroform Prohibition) Order SI 1979 No. 382

For the purposes of sale or supply (but not of importation) of medicines for human use, the exemption limits for chloroform given in the POM and GSL Orders are over-ridden by this Order. The practical effect is that only products falling within items 6 and 8 above may be sold by retail to the general public. But for the purposes of record keeping, the exemption levels in the POM Order still apply, so that records are required to be kept only of sales or supplies of products for internal use which contain more than 5% chloroform w/w or v/v as appropriate.

Section 104 and section 105 Orders

Orders made under section 104(1) of the 1968 Act can extend the application of specified provisions of the HMRs or Clinical Trials Regulations to articles and substances, which are not medicinal products as defined in the HMRs, but which are manufactured, sold, supplied, imported or exported for use wholly or partly for a medical purpose. In the past, Orders have been made in respect of surgical ligatures and sutures, dental filling substances, contact lenses and associated substances, and intrauterine contraceptive devices. However, since 1994, these substances have been considered to be medical devices rather than medicines and are now controlled under Medical Devices Regulations (see under Medical devices in chapter 2). Two Orders under this section are still extant, namely (a) the Medicines (Radioactive Substances) Order 1978,[7] which extends the application of the provisions relating to the holding of licences to certain articles and substances that are, contain or generate radioactive substances, and (b) the Medicines (Cyanogenetic Substances) Order 1984[8] which extends, to cyanogenetic substances, the application of those provisions of the HMRs or Clinical Trials Regulations relating to dealings with products (including sale, supply or importation), the packaging and promotion of products and miscellaneous and supplementary provisions. Licensing requirements are not applied.

Orders made under section 105(1)(a) of the Act extend the application of specified provisions of the HMRs or Clinical Trials Regulations to certain substances, which are not medicinal products, but which are used in the manufacture of medicinal products.

Orders made under section 105(1)(b) and 105(2) of the Act extend the application of specified provisions of the Act to substances which, if used without proper safeguards, are capable of causing damage to the health of the community, or of causing danger to the health of animals generally or of one or more species of animals. One Order has been made under this section, but has subsequently been repealed by the HMRs.

[7] SI 1978 No. 1004
[8] SI 1984 No. 187

Adulteration of medicinal products

The Medicines Act (s.63) makes it an offence:

1 to add any substance to, or abstract any substance from, a medicinal product so as to affect injuriously the composition of the product, with intent that the product shall be sold or supplied in that state; or
2 to sell or supply, or offer or expose for sale or supply, or have in possession for the purpose of sale or supply, any medicinal product whose composition has been injuriously affected by the addition or abstraction of any substance (s.63).

Protection for purchasers of medicinal products

It is also an offence to sell (or supply on a practitioner's prescription) to the prejudice of the purchaser (or patient) any medicinal product which is not of the nature or quality demanded by the purchaser (or specified in the prescription) (s.64).

There is no offence if the medicinal product contains some extraneous matter, the presence of which is proved to be an inevitable consequence of the process of manufacture, nor is it an offence where:

1 a substance has been added to, or abstracted from, the medicinal product which did not injuriously affect the composition of the product and was not carried out fraudulently; and
2 the product was sold having attached to it, or to a container or package in which it was sold, a conspicuous notice of adequate size and legibly printed specifying the substance added or abstracted.

Whilst this section of the Medicines Act remained unused for many years after the Act was passed, it has recently been used to prosecute pharmacists and other staff where an error has been made in dispensing a prescription (chapter 22). At the time of writing, these provisions were being reviewed by the Rebalancing Medicines Legislation and Pharmacy Regulation Programme Board.

Summary

- The sale or supply of some medicinal products is either prohibited (e.g. Bal Jivan Chamcho) or prohibited subject to exceptions (e.g. chloroform).
- It is an offence to adulterate, by way of addition or abstraction, a medicinal product or to sell, supply or possess an adulterated product.
- It is an offence to sell or supply to the prejudice of the purchaser (or patient) any medicinal product which is not of the nature or quality demanded by the purchaser (or specified on a prescription).

Further reading

Human Medicines Regulations (2012) SI 2012 No. 1916, *Explanatory memorandum*: http://www.legislation.gov.uk/uksi/2012/1916/pdfs/uksiem_20121916_en.pdf (accessed 2 November 2016).
Royal Pharmaceutical Society (published annually). *Medicines, Ethics and Practice: The Professional Guide for Pharmacists.* London: Royal Pharmaceutical Society (includes practice guidance on many of the topics in this chapter; free to members).

Websites

Legislation (can be searched on year and SI number or title): http://www.legislation.gov.uk
Medicines and Healthcare products Regulatory Agency: https://www.gov.uk/government/organisations/medicines-and-healthcare-products-regulatory-agency
Rebalancing Medicines Legislation and Pharmacy Regulation Programme Board: https://www.gov.uk/government/groups/pharmacy-regulation-programme-board
Royal Pharmaceutical Society (member access only; lists legal classifications of medicines and further practice guidance): http://www.rpharms.com

14

Human medicines: labelling, packaging, leaflets and identification

Karen Pitchford

Regulations and penalties

Provisions covering packaging and leaflets for medicinal products are largely found in Part 13 (Regs.257–276) and Schedules 24 to 29 of the Human Medicines Regulations (HMRs),[1] although there are still some residual sections of the Medicines Act 1968 that are relevant to this chapter, namely:

- section 88 of the Act, which relates to the colours, shapes or marking of particular medicinal products; and
- section 87 which allows for regulations to be made to specify the strength, materials, shapes or patterns of containers in order to preserve the quality of medicinal products, or to secure that medicinal products are correctly described, readily identifiable, contain appropriate and accurate warnings or information, and promote safety in relation to medicinal products.

It is an offence (HMRs Reg.269) for a person, other than the holder of a marketing authorisation, Article 126a authorisation, certificate of registration or traditional herbal registration for a medicinal product in the course of a business carried on by him/her, to sell, supply, offer to sell or supply, or have in his/her possession to sell or supply a product knowing or having reasonable cause to believe:

1 that a package or package leaflet supplied does not comply with Part 13 of the HMRs or Article 28 or 32 of the Paediatric Regulation;[2] or

---

[1]Human Medicines Regulations SI 2012 No. 1916 (HMRs)
[2]Regulation (EC) No 1901/2006 of the European Parliament and of the Council of 12 December 2006 on medicinal products for paediatric use and amending Regulation (EEC) No. 1768/92, Directive 2001/20/EC, Directive 2001/83/EC and Regulation (EC) No. 726/2004

2 that the product is not accompanied by a package leaflet when one is required.

Any person contravening the labelling regulations (see below) is liable on summary conviction to an unlimited fine[3] and, on conviction on indictment, to a fine or to imprisonment for a term not exceeding 2 years or to both (HMRs Reg.271).

Definitions

The terms defined here are those used in the HMRs in connection with labelling which are not explained elsewhere in the text (HMRs Reg.8 and Reg.213).

Common name in relation to a medicinal product, active substance or excipient means:

a its International Non-proprietary Name recommended by the World Health Organization; or
b if such a name does not exist, its usual common name (HMRs Reg.8).

Immediate packaging in relation to a medicinal product means the container or other form of packaging immediately in contact with the medicinal product (HMRs Reg.8).

A *container*, in relation to a medicinal product, means the bottle, jar, box, packet or other receptacle which contains or is to contain it, not being a capsule, cachet or other article in which the product is or is to be administered; and where any such receptacle is or is to be contained in another such receptacle, it includes the inner receptacle but not the outer (s.132 Medicines Act). It should be noted that a capsule, cachet or other article in which a medicinal product is to be administered is not normally a container, but, if the capsule, etc. is not to be administered, then it is a container.

A *package*, in relation to any medicinal products, means a container, any box, packet or other article in which one or more containers of the products are to be enclosed, and where any such box, package or other article is, or is to be itself, enclosed in one or more other boxes, packets or other articles, it includes each of the boxes, packets or other articles in question (HMRs Reg.8).

In effect, the inner receptacle which actually contains the medicinal products is a container; every outer receptacle is a package.

A *package leaflet* in relation to a medicinal product, means a leaflet that accompanies the product and contains information for the user of the product (HMRs Reg.8).

---

[3] Legal Aid, Sentencing and Punishment of Offenders Act 2012 c. 10

Labelling, in relation to a container or package of medicinal products, means affixing to or otherwise displaying on it a notice describing or otherwise relating to the contents (HMRs Reg.8).

External use in relation to a medicinal product means its use by application to the skin, teeth, mucosa of the mouth, throat, nose, ear, eye, vagina or anal canal in circumstances where local action only is necessary and systemic absorption is unlikely to occur, but it does not include its use by means of a throat spray, nasal spray, nasal inhalation or teething preparation or by means of throat pastilles, throat lozenges or nasal drops. (HMRs Reg.213).

Specified publication means the *European Pharmacopoeia, British Pharmacopoeia* (or other official compendia or list of names which may in the future be produced under the HMRs) and the Cumulative List of Recommended International Nonproprietary Names (HMR Reg.321).

Summary of Product Characteristics means the summary of the product characteristics as approved by the licensing authority (the UK or EU) in granting or varying the authorisation or registration for a medicinal product (HMRs Reg.8).

Labelling and packaging

The regulations apply at all stages of distribution, except where otherwise stated. Medicinal products which are Controlled Drugs must also be labelled in accordance with the Misuse of Drugs Regulations (see chapter 17).

General labelling provisions for medicinal products

All labelling of containers and packages must be:

1 legible, comprehensible and indelible (HMRs Reg.257(6)); and
2 given in English, except in the case of a medicinal product:
   a that has been designated as an orphan medicinal product[4] where any information specified is given in a language of an EEA state other than English and the licensing authority accedes to a reasoned request that the information need not be given in English, or
   b for which the licensing authority grants an Article 126a authorisation where the licensing authority decides that the information need not be given in English (HMRs Reg.266).

Where the holder of a marketing authorisation, Article 126a authorisation, certificate of registration or traditional herbal registration for a medicinal product wishes to make changes to the packaging or the package

[4]Regulation (EC) No. 141/2000 of the European Parliament and of the Council of 16 December 1999 on orphan medicinal products

leaflet (other than a change connected with the Summary of Product Characteristics), the proposed change must be submitted to the licensing authority and, unless the licensing authority has notified him/her that it does not approve the alterations, s/he may, after a period of 90 days from the date of notification by him/her, supply the product with the altered labelling (HMRs Reg.267).

Standard labelling particulars for medicinal products

The standard requirements for the labelling of containers and packages of medicinal products are set out in Council Directive 2001/83/EC[5] and HMRs Reg.257 and Schedule 24. There are modifications for small containers and blister packs (see below).

The standard labelling particulars are as follows (Sch. 24, Part 1):

1   the name of the medicinal product;
2   the strength and pharmaceutical form of the product;
3   where appropriate, whether the product is intended for babies, children or adults;
4   where the product contains up to three active substances, the common name of each active substance;
5   the product's expiry date (month and year), in clear terms;
6   the manufacturer's batch number;
7   the method of administration of the product and if necessary the route of administration;
8   a statement of the active substances in the product, expressed qualitatively and quantitatively per dosage unit or according to the form of administration for a given volume or weight, using their common names;
9   the pharmaceutical form and the contents by weight, by volume or by number of doses of the product;
10 a list of:
    a   all excipients when the product is injectable or is a topical or eye preparation, or
    b   in any other case, those excipients known to have a recognised action or effect and included in the guidance published pursuant to Article 65 of the 2001 Directive;
11 where appropriate, space for the prescribed dose to be indicated;
12 a warning that the product must be stored out of the reach and sight of children;

[5] As amended by Council Directive 2004/27/EC and Council Directive 2010/84/EU

13 any special warning applicable to the product;

14 any special storage precautions relating to the product;

15 any special precautions relating to the disposal of an unused product or part of a product, or waste derived from the product, and reference to any appropriate collection system in place;

16 the name and address of the holder of the marketing authorisation, Article 126a authorisation or traditional herbal registration relating to the product and, where applicable, the name of the holder's representative;

17 the number of the marketing authorisation, Article 126a authorisation or traditional herbal registration for placing the medicinal product on the market; and

18 in the case of a product that is not a Prescription Only Medicine (POM), instructions for use.

The outer packaging may be labelled to show symbols, diagrams or pictures designed to clarify certain information mentioned in 1 to 18 above and other information compatible with the Summary of Product Characteristics which is useful to the patient. Such symbols, diagrams, pictures or additional information must not include any element of a promotional nature (HMRs Reg.261).

The name of the medicinal product must also be expressed in Braille format on the outer packaging of the product. A holder of a marketing authorisation, Article 126a authorisation or traditional herbal registration must ensure that the package leaflet is available on request in formats suitable for blind and partially sighted persons (HMRs Reg.259).

In addition, EU Member States may require certain additional labelling, for example the price of the product, the reimbursement conditions and the classification, such as POM.

Blister packs for medicinal products

Where the container of a relevant medicinal product is a blister pack and is enclosed within a package which complies with the standard labelling (see above), the container must be labelled with (HMRs Reg.257 and Sch. 24 Part 2):

1 the information contained in points 1–6 of the standard labelling particulars, as shown above; and

2 the name of the holder of the marketing authorisation, Article 126a authorisation or traditional herbal registration relating to the product.

Small containers for medicinal products

Where the container of a medicinal product is *not* a blister pack but is too small to include all the standard particulars for medicinal products, it must be labelled with (HMRs Reg.257 and Sch. 24 Part 3):

1 the information contained in points 1–6 of the standard labelling particulars, as shown above;
2 the method of administration of the product and if necessary the route of administration; and
3 the contents of the packaging by weight, by volume or by unit.

Standard labelling requirements for containers and packages for radiopharmaceuticals (HMRs Reg.262)

Containers and packages for radiopharmaceuticals must be labelled with the standard particulars for relevant medicinal products together with the following additional particulars:

1 the carton and container must be labelled in accordance with regulations for the safe transport of radioactive materials laid down by the International Atomic Energy Agency and the labelling on the shielding and the vial must comply with the rest of the provisions of this legislation;
2 the label on the shielding must:
  a include the information specified in Part 1 of Schedule 24,
  b explain in full the codings used on the vial,
  c indicate, where necessary, for a given time and date, the amount of radioactivity per dose or per vial, and
  d indicate the number of capsules or, for liquids, the number of millilitres per container;
3 the label on the vial must include:
  a the name or code of the medicinal product, including the name or chemical symbol of the radionuclide,
  b the batch identification and expiry date of the product,
  c the international symbol for radioactivity,
  d the name and address of the manufacturer, and
  e the amount of radioactivity; as mentioned in paragraph 2(c).

Medicines on prescription

The packaging of medicines dispensed on prescription must be labelled to show the following particulars (HMRs Reg.258 and Sch. 25 Part 1):

1 where the product is to be administered to a particular individual, the name of that individual;

2 the name and address of the person who sells or supplies the product;

3 the date on which the product is sold or supplied;

4 unless para. 5 applies, such of the following particulars as the appropriate practitioner who prescribed the product may specify:

a the name of the product or its common name,

b directions for use of the product, and

c precautions relating to the use of the product.

A container need not be labelled if it is enclosed in a package which is labelled with the required particulars.

Medicines optimisation

Schedule 25 of the HMRs extends previous provisions to allow pharmacists to use their discretion when labelling dispensed medicines. If a pharmacist is of the professional opinion that the inclusion of any of the particulars in point 4 above is inappropriate, s/he may include other particulars of the same kind as the pharmacist thinks appropriate (HMRs Sch. 25 Part 1(5) and (6)).

Proposed changes to labelling provisions for medicinal products

In response to a government consultation, there may be changes to some labelling provisions. See box 14.1 for further details.

Box 14.1 *Proposed changes to the Human Medicines Regulations, as they relate to the labelling of medicinal products*

In March 2016, the Department of Health and MHRA launched a consultation regarding potential amendments to several aspects of the HMRs and the Medicines Act. These included provisions[6] relating to:

- 'hub and spoke' dispensing models;
- the inclusion of indicative pricing of medicines, and a statement about how that cost is met, on dispensing labels (for medicines prescribed on the NHS);
- labelling requirements for medicines packaged in monitored dosage systems;
- labelling requirements for medicines issued under Patient Group Directions;
- exemptions for pharmacists in section 10 of the Medicines Act 1968 in respect of the preparation and assembly of medicines (chapter 3).

---

[6]The Human Medicines (Amendment) (No. 2) Regulations 2016 (draft)

In June 2016, the Department of Health wrote to Pharmacy stakeholders' representative bodies, inviting them to further explore some of the issues (relating to 'hub and spoke' dispensing) that arose from the consultation. Because the labelling proposals were part of the same draft Statutory Instrument, this led to a pause in the process for all proposals in the consultation including the labelling proposals. The process remained paused at the time of writing (November 2016).

Packaging for transport, delivery and storage (HMRs Reg.258 and Sch. 25 Part 2)

An outer package, which contains a number of packages of medicinal products of the same description, must be labelled in accordance with the requirements of Part 2 of Schedule 25, for the purpose of transport, delivery or storage. The required particulars are:

1 any special requirements for the storage and handling of the product;
2 the expiry date of the product; and
3 the manufacturer's batch number.

These requirements do not apply to 'specials' (see chapter 3) or to any packing case, crate or other covering used solely for the purposes of transport or delivery of packages of medicinal products, so long as each of those individual packages is labelled in accordance with the Regulations.

Packaging of Pharmacy and Prescription Only Medicinal products

All Pharmacy and POM medicinal products when sold or supplied by retail, or held for such sale or distributed by wholesale must bear the capital letter 'P' or 'POM' (as applicable) within a rectangle containing no other matter on the packaging (HMRs Reg.258 and Sch. 25 Part 3).

Packaging requirements for medicines containing paracetamol (HMRs Sch. 25 Part 4)

The following must appear on the package if the product contains paracetamol:

1 except where the name of the product includes the word '*paracetamol*' and appears on the container or package, the words '*Contains paracetamol*';

2 the words '*Do not take more medicine than the label tells you to. If you do not get better, talk to your doctor*' (these words must appear adjacent to either the directions for use or the recommended dosage);

3 unless it is wholly or mainly intended for children who are 12 years old or younger (i.e. it is a product for children 12 and over), the words '*Do not take anything else containing paracetamol while taking this medicine*'; and:

  a if a package leaflet accompanying the product includes the words 'talk to a doctor at once if you take too much of this medicine even if you feel well. This is because too much paracetamol can cause delayed, serious liver damage', the package must contain the words '*Talk to a doctor at once if you take too much of this medicine, even if you feel well*', or

  b if no package leaflet accompanies the product or the package leaflet does not include those words, the words '*Talk to a doctor at once if you take too much of this medicine, even if you feel well. This is because too much paracetamol can cause delayed, serious liver damage*';

4 and is wholly or mainly intended for children who are 12 years old or younger, the words '*Do not give anything else containing paracetamol while giving this medicine*'; and:

  a if a package leaflet accompanying the product includes the words 'Talk to a doctor at once if your child takes too much of this medicine even if they seem well. This is because too much paracetamol can cause delayed, serious liver damage', the package must contain the words '*Talk to a doctor at once if your child takes too much of this medicine, even if they seem well*', or

  b if no package leaflet accompanies the product or the package leaflet does not include those words, the words '*Talk to a doctor at once if your child takes too much of this medicine, even if they seem well. This is because too much paracetamol can cause delayed, serious liver damage*'.

Those phrases must be in a prominent position.

Medicines manufactured by pharmacies under section 10 of the Medicines Act 1968

Pharmacies are permitted to manufacture medicines without the need for marketing authorisations or licences subject to conditions under section 10 of the Medicines Act 1968 (chapter 3). In these circumstances the medicines must bear packaging details as set out below (HMRs Sch. 26 Part 2):

1 where the product is to be administered to a particular individual, the name of that individual;

2 the name and address of the person who sells or supplies the product;

3 the date on which the product is sold or supplied;

4 where the product is prescribed by an appropriate practitioner, such of the following particulars as the appropriate practitioner who prescribed the product may specify, unless paragraph 5 applies:

    a the name of the product or its common name,

    b directions for use of the product, and

    c precautions relating to the use of the product;

5 this paragraph applies if a pharmacist, in the exercise of professional skill and judgement, is of the opinion that the inclusion of one or more of the particulars specified in paragraph 4, by the appropriate practitioner who prescribed the product, is inappropriate;

6 where paragraph 5 applies, the pharmacist may include such particulars, of the same kind as those mentioned in paragraph 4, as the pharmacist thinks appropriate; and

7 where the product is not prescribed by an appropriate practitioner, directions for use of the product. These may be omitted when a medicinal product is prepared or dispensed in a registered pharmacy, by or under the supervision of a pharmacist, in accordance with a specification furnished by the person to whom the product is or is to be sold or supplied, where the product is for administration to that person or to a person under his/her care.

See also boxes 3.6 and 14.1.

Labelling of investigational medicinal products for clinical trials

Investigational medicinal products intended for administration in a clinical trial (chapter 3) must be labelled in accordance with EU legislation[7] and should comply with the requirements of Directive 2003/94/EC.

The following information should be included on labels, unless its absence can be justified, for example, by use of a centralised electronic randomisation system:

a name, address and telephone number of the sponsor, contract research organisation or investigator (the main contact for information on the product, clinical trial and emergency unblinding – the address and telephone number may be omitted where the subject has been given a leaflet or card which provides these details and has been instructed to keep this in his/her possession at all times);

---

[7]EudraLex. The Rules Governing Medicinal Products in the European Union, Volume 4. EU Guidelines to Good Manufacturing Practice Medicinal Products for Human and Veterinary Use; Annex 13

b pharmaceutical dosage form, route of administration, quantity of dosage units and, in the case of open trials, the name/identifier and strength/potency;

c the batch and/or code number to identify the contents and packaging operation;

d a trial reference code allowing identification of the trial, site, investigator and sponsor if not given elsewhere;

e the trial subject identification number/treatment number and, where relevant, the visit number;

f the name of the investigator (if not included in (a) or (d));

g directions for use (reference may be made to a leaflet or other explanatory document intended for the trial subject or person administering the product);

h 'For clinical trial use only' or similar wording;

i the storage conditions;

j period of use (use-by date, expiry date or re-test date as applicable), in month/year format and in a manner that avoids any ambiguity;

k 'Keep out of reach of children' except when the product is for use in trials where the product is not taken home by subjects.

Particulars should appear in the official language(s) of the country in which the investigational medicinal product is to be used. There are variations on these rules, where the product is to be provided to the trial subject or the person administering the medication within a primary package, together with secondary packaging that is intended to remain together, or where the primary packaging takes the form of blister packs or small units such as ampoules.

Standard labelling requirements for containers and packages, and package leaflets, of homoeopathic medicinal products

The outer packaging and immediate packaging and, where a package leaflet (see next section) is included, the package leaflet of a homoeopathic medicinal product must clearly include the words '*homoeopathic medicinal product*'. In addition, they must carry the following particulars and no others (HMRs Reg.264 and Sch. 28):

1 the scientific name of the stock or stocks and the degree of dilution, making use of the symbols of the *European Pharmacopoeia* or, in the absence of an entry in the *European Pharmacopoeia*, of the *British Pharmacopoeia*;

2 the name and address of the holder of the certificate of registration and, where different, the name and address of the manufacturer;

3 the method and, if necessary, route of administration;

4 the expiry date of the product in clear terms, stating the month and year;
5 the pharmaceutical form;
6 the contents of the presentation, specified by weight, volume or number of doses;
7 any special storage precautions;
8 any special warning necessary for the product concerned;
9 the manufacturer's batch number;
10 the registration number allocated by the licensing authority;
11 the words '*Homoeopathic medicinal product without approved therapeutic indications*'; and
12 a warning advising the user to consult a doctor if the symptoms persist during the use of the product.

There are variations on these rules for blister packs and packaging that is too small to display the information required.

Package leaflets

General requirements

All leaflets included in the package or container of any medicinal product must comply with HMRs Reg.260 and Schedule 27.

A package leaflet for a medicinal product must:

1 be drawn up in accordance with the Summary of Product Characteristics; and
2 contain all the information specified and in the order specified in Schedule 27.

The leaflet must be legible, clear and easy to use, and the applicant for, or holder of, a marketing authorisation, Article 126a authorisation or traditional herbal registration relating to the product must ensure that target patient groups are consulted in order to achieve this.

The particulars which must be included are as follows:

1 the name of the medicinal product;
2 the strength and pharmaceutical form of the product;
3 where appropriate, whether the product is intended for babies, children or adults;
4 where the product contains up to three active substances, the common name of each active substance;
5 the pharmaco-therapeutic group or type of activity of the product, in terms easily comprehensible to the patient;

6 the product's therapeutic indications;

7 a list of:

a contra-indications,

b appropriate precautions for use,

c interactions with other medicinal products which may affect the action of the product,

d interactions with other substances, including alcohol, tobacco and foodstuffs, which may affect the action of the product, and

e special warnings, if any, relating to the product;

8 the list mentioned in paragraph 7 must:

a take into account the special requirements of particular categories of users (including, in particular, children, pregnant or breastfeeding women, the elderly and persons with specific pathological conditions),

b mention, if appropriate, possible effects on the ability to drive vehicles or to operate machinery, and

c list any excipients:

i if knowledge of the excipients is important for the safe and effective use of the product, and

ii the excipients are included in the guidance published pursuant to Article 65 of the 2001 Directive;

9 instructions for proper use of the product including, in particular:

a the dosage,

b the method and, if necessary, route of administration,

c the frequency of administration (including, if necessary, specifying times at which the product may or must be administered),

d the duration of treatment if this is to be limited,

e symptoms of an overdose and the action, if any, to be taken in case of an overdose,

f what to do if one or more doses have not been taken,

g an indication, if necessary, of the risk of withdrawal effects, and

h a specific recommendation to consult a doctor or pharmacist, as appropriate, for further explanation of the use of the product;

10 a description of the adverse reactions which may occur in normal use of the medicinal product and, if necessary, the action to be taken in such a case;

11 a reference to the expiry date printed on the packaging of the product with:

a a warning against using the product after that date,

b if appropriate, details of special storage precautions to be taken,

c if necessary, a warning concerning visible signs of deterioration,

d the full qualitative composition (in active substances and excipients), and the quantitative composition in active substances, using common names, of each presentation of the medicinal product,

e for each presentation of the product, the pharmaceutical form and content in weight, volume or units of dosage,

f the name and address of the holder of the marketing authorisation, Article 126a authorisation or traditional herbal registration relating to the product and, if applicable, the name of the holder's appointed representative, and

g the name and address of the manufacturer of the product;

12 where the product is authorised under different names in different EU Member States in accordance with Articles 28 to 39 of the 2001 Directive, a list of the names authorised in each Member State;

13 for medicinal products included in the list referred to in Article 23 of Regulation (EC) No. 726/2004, the statement: '*This medicinal product is subject to additional[8] monitoring*';

14 a standardised text relating to adverse event reporting in accordance with the third sub-paragraph of Article 59(1) of the 2001 Directive; and

15 the date on which the package leaflet was last revised.

The outer packaging and the package leaflet of a medicinal product may include (HMRs Reg.261) symbols, diagrams or pictures designed to clarify information mentioned on the outer and immediate packaging or on the leaflet, and other information, compatible with the Summary of Product Characteristics, which is useful to the patient. Such symbols, diagrams, pictures or additional information included in accordance with this regulation must not include any element of a promotional nature.

Leaflets for medicines containing paracetamol (HMRs Sch. 27 Part 2)

If a medicinal product contains paracetamol, unless the product is wholly or mainly intended for children 12 years old or younger, the words '*Talk to a doctor at once if you take too much of this medicine even if you feel well. This is because too much paracetamol can cause delayed, serious liver damage*' must be used.

If a medicinal product contains paracetamol and is wholly or mainly intended for children 12 years old or younger, the words '*Talk to a doctor at once if your child takes too much of this medicine even if they seem well. This is because too much paracetamol can cause delayed, serious liver damage*' must be used.

---

[8]The word 'safety' removed by the Human Medicines (Amendment) (No. 2) Regulations SI 2014 No. 1878

Leaflets relating to radionuclides (HMRs Reg.263)

A leaflet enclosed with a radiopharmaceutical or radionuclide generator, kit or precursor must, in addition to the general requirements (see above), include:

1 details of any precautions to be taken by the user and the patient during the preparation and administration of the product; and
2 special precautions for the disposal of the packaging and its unused contents.

Requirements relating to child safety (HMRs Regs.272–276)

Regulated medicinal products means (HMRs Reg.272) medicinal products containing, aspirin, paracetamol or more than 24 mg of elemental iron, which are in the form of tablets, capsules, pills, lozenges, pastilles, suppositories or oral liquids, except for:

1 effervescent tablets containing not more than 25% of aspirin or paracetamol by weight;
2 medicinal products in sachets or other sealed containers which hold only one unit of dose;
3 medicinal products that are not intended for retail sale or for supply in circumstances corresponding to retail sale; or
4 for export.

Regulated medicinal products may only be sold or supplied in containers which are opaque or dark tinted and child resistant (HMRs Reg.273), except where the sale or supply of such products is carried out (HMRs Reg.274):

a by or under the supervision of a pharmacist, on premises which are a registered pharmacy and either:
  i in accordance with a prescription given by an appropriate practitioner where it is not reasonably practicable to provide the regulated medicinal products in containers that are both opaque or dark tinted and child resistant, or
  ii at the request of a person who is aged 16 years or over and specifically requests that the regulated medicinal products not be contained in a child-resistant container;
b by a doctor or dentist to a patient, or the patient's carer, for the patient's use;
c by a doctor or dentist to a person who is an appropriate practitioner, at the request of that person, for administration to a patient of that person; or

d in the course of the business of a hospital or health centre, where the sale or supply is for the purposes of administration, whether in the hospital or health centre or elsewhere, in accordance with the directions of an appropriate practitioner.

The term 'child resistant' is defined in the Regulations in terms of the relevant British Standard or equivalent technical specification recognised for use in the EEA.

The sale or supply of a medicinal product containing aspirin or paracetamol of any colour other than white is prohibited if it is a product for children aged 12 years or under, and, in the case of paracetamol, it is in a solid form (including tablets, capsules, pills, lozenges, pastilles or suppositories) (HMRs Reg.275).

Summary

- There are detailed labelling requirements for medicinal products for human use.
- There are additional warning labels for paracetamol containing products.
- There are modified labelling provisions for medicinal products which are in small containers, blister packs and homoeopathic products, and for radio-pharmaceuticals.
- There are specific labelling provisions for medicines supplied on a prescription, but some of these may be amended by the dispensing pharmacist if, in his/her professional opinion, it is appropriate to do so.
- There are packaging requirements for the transport, delivery or storage of medicinal products.
- There are separate labelling requirements for medicines produced extemporaneously by pharmacists (under s.10 of the Medicines Act) and for investigational medicinal products for use in clinical trials.
- Every container or package of medicinal products must contain a patient leaflet. Detailed requirements exist for the contents of these leaflets.
- Special leaflet provisions exist for homoeopathic medicinal products.
- Special requirements apply to the sale of medicinal products which contain aspirin or paracetamol. These products must (with certain exceptions) be packed in containers which are opaque or dark tinted and child resistant.

Further reading

Human Medicines Regulations (2012) SI 2012 No. 1916, *Explanatory memorandum*: http://www.legislation.gov.uk/uksi/2012/1916/pdfs/uksiem_20121916_en.pdf (accessed 7 November 2016).

Royal Pharmaceutical Society (published annually). *Medicines, Ethics and Practice: The Professional Guide for Pharmacists*. London: Royal Pharmaceutical Society (includes practice guidance on many of the topics in this chapter; free to members).

Websites

Legislation (can be searched on year and SI number or title): http://www.legislation.gov.uk

Medicines and Healthcare products Regulatory Agency: https://www.gov.uk/government/organisations/medicines-and-healthcare-products-regulatory-agency

Royal Pharmaceutical Society (member access only; lists legal classifications of medicines and further practice guidance): http://www.rpharms.com

15

Human medicines: pharmacopoeias and compendia

Susan Melvin

Part 15 of the HMRs[1] covers pharmacopoeias and compendia which contain the standards for 'official' (British or European) medicinal products and pharmaceutical substances.

British Pharmacopoeia and compendia

Until 1970, the *British Pharmacopoeia* (BP) was compiled by the GMC under the Medical Act 1956 when the copyright was assigned to Her Majesty (Medicines Act, s.98). A committee now established under Regulation 11 of the HMRs, known as the British Pharmacopoeia Commission (BPC), prepares new editions[2] of the BP and any amendments to such editions.

The BPC must prepare editions of the BP containing such relevant information relating to substances, combinations of substances and articles as detailed below (HMRs Reg.317(1 and 2)):

1 substances, combinations of substances and articles (whether medicinal products or not) which are or may be used in the practice of medicine or surgery (other than veterinary medicine or veterinary surgery), dentistry and midwifery; and
2 substances, combinations of substances and articles used in the manufacture of substances and articles listed under 1 above.

The BPC may also publish a compendium other than the BP if it thinks this appropriate (HMRs Reg.317(3)). Information relating to substances and

[1] Human Medicines Regulations SI 2012 No. 1916
[2] The next BP at the time of writing comes into force from 1 January 2017

articles used in veterinary medicine and surgery (whether veterinary drugs or not) is published in a separate compendium, the *British Pharmacopoeia (Veterinary)*.

Lists of names

The BPC is authorised to prepare lists of suitable names for substances and articles for placing at the head of monographs in the BP or in the compendia (HMRs Reg.318). The publication of any such lists supersedes any previously published list.

Publication

If the Commission on Human Medicines so recommends, the BP, the compendia and the lists of names must be published and made available for sale to the public by the appropriate ministers. Every copy must specify the date from which it is to take effect, and notice must be given in the *London*, *Edinburgh* and *Belfast Gazettes* not less than 21 days before that date (HMRs Reg.320(1) and (2)). Apart from the BP and the compendia, other publications containing relevant information may be prepared at the discretion of the Commission on Human Medicines (HMRs Reg.319).

European Pharmacopoeia

The *European Pharmacopoeia* is published under the direction of the Council of Europe (Partial Agreement) in accordance with the Convention on the Elaboration of a European Pharmacopoeia held in 1964. In 1973, the standards in the *European Pharmacopoeia*, together with any amendments or alterations published in the *Gazette*, took precedence over the standards in other publications. The Health Ministers may publish amendments to the BP when necessary to give effect to the Convention but, should a difference exist at any time between the two pharmacopoeias, the standard of the *European Pharmacopoeia* would prevail (HMRs Reg.320(3)).

Compliance with official standards

It is unlawful for any person, in the course of a business carried on by him/her:

a   to sell a medicinal product which has been demanded by the purchaser by, or by express reference to, a particular name; or

b   to sell or supply a medicinal product in pursuance of a prescription given by a practitioner in which the product required is described by, or by express reference to, a particular name; or c to sell or supply a medicinal product which, in the course of the business, has been offered or exposed for sale by, or by express reference to, a particular name;

If, in any of the above, that name is at the head of the *relevant monograph* in a specified publication, or is an approved synonym for such a name, and the product does not comply with the standard specified in that monograph (HMRs Regs.251 and 255).

It is also an offence if the name in question is the name of an active ingredient of the product and, in so far as the product consists of that ingredient, it does not comply with the standard specified (HMRs Reg.251(4)). A name is taken to be an approved synonym for a name at the head of a monograph in the *European Pharmacopoeia* if, by a notice published in the *Gazette* and not subsequently withdrawn, it is declared to be approved by the Commission on Human Medicines as a synonym for that name (HMRs Reg.251).

The publications to which these requirements extend are the *European Pharmacopoeia*, the BP and any compendium published under Part 15 of the HMRs. For the purpose of complying with official standards, the *relevant monograph* is ascertained as follows (HMRs Reg.252):

1 If a particular edition of a particular publication is specified together with the name of the medicinal product, then the relevant monograph is (a) the monograph (if any) headed by that name in that edition of the publication or (b) if there is no such monograph in that edition, the *appropriate current monograph* (if any) headed by that name.

2 If a particular publication, but not a particular edition, is specified, together with the name of the medicinal product, then the relevant monograph is (a) the monograph (if any) headed by that name in the current edition of the specified publication or (b) if there is no such monograph in the current edition of the publication, the *appropriate current monograph* headed by that name, or (c) if there is no *appropriate current monograph*, then the monograph headed by that name in the latest edition of the specified publication which contained a monograph so headed.

3 If no publication is specified together with the name of the medicinal product, the relevant monograph is *the appropriate current monograph*, if any.

Appropriate current monograph, in relation to a particular name, means the monograph (if any) headed by that name, or by a name for which it is an approved synonym, in the current edition of the BP, or a compendium published under Part 15 of the HMRs.

Current means current at the time when the medicinal product in question is demanded, described in a prescription, or offered or exposed for sale; and the current edition of a publication is the one in force at that time, together with any amendments, alterations or deletions. Any monograph shall be construed in accordance with any general monograph, notice, appendix, note or other explanatory material applicable to the monograph which is contained in the relevant edition of the publication (HMRs Reg.252(5–7)).

Specified publications

The HMRs use the term *specified publication* to mean (HMRs Reg.321):

a *European Pharmacopoeia*
b *British Pharmacopoeia*
c the Cumulative List of Recommended International Nonproprietary Names
d any other compendium or list prepared under HMRs Regs.317 or 318.

When reference is made in a marketing authorisation, manufacturer's or wholesale dealer's licence, an Article 126a authorisation, a certificate of registration or a traditional herbal registration (chapters 3, 11 and 12) to a specified publication, but no particular edition is mentioned, then it is to be construed as the current edition.

The *British National Formulary* and other formularies under the *British National Formulary* are published jointly by the British Medical Association and the Pharmaceutical Press and are not 'official' publications under the HMRs.

Summary

- The BP comprises information consisting of descriptions and standards for substances and articles which may be used in medicine other than veterinary medicine together with substances and articles used in the manufacture of medicinal products.
- The *European Pharmacopoeia*, where appropriate, takes precedence over the standards in other publications.
- It is an offence to sell, supply or dispense a medicinal product of a particular name if that name is at the head of a monograph in a pharmacopoeia, and the product does not comply with the standard specified in that monograph.

Further reading

Human Medicines Regulations (2012) SI 2012 No. 1916, *Explanatory memorandum*: http://www.legislation.gov.uk/uksi/2012/1916/pdfs/uksiem_20121916_en.pdf (accessed 2 November 2016).

Royal Pharmaceutical Society (published annually). *Medicines, Ethics and Practice: The Professional Guide for Pharmacists*. London: Royal Pharmaceutical Society (includes practice guidance on many of the topics in this chapter; free to members).

Websites

Legislation (can be searched on year and SI number or title): http://www.legislation.gov.uk

Medicines and Healthcare products Regulatory Agency: https://www.gov.uk/government/organisations/medicines-and-healthcare-products-regulatory-agency

Royal Pharmaceutical Society (member access only; lists legal classifications of medicines and further practice guidance): http://www.rpharms.com

16

Controlled Drugs

Karen Pitchford

The aim of the Misuse of Drugs Act 1971 is to control 'dangerous or otherwise harmful drugs'. This control is exercised since the Act renders unlawful all activities associated with the drugs controlled under it, other than some limited provisions for licences for importation and exportation (s.3). Other than these provisions, any other activity associated with Controlled Drugs is rendered unlawful by the Act, except as permitted in Regulations made under the Act. The extent to which these Regulations relax the restrictions is dealt with in this chapter.

In this chapter, references to 'the Act', and to sections, are to the Misuse of Drugs Act 1971 and those to 'the Regulations' are to the Misuse of Drugs Regulations 2001,[1] unless otherwise stated. Both the Act and the Regulations have been variously amended by over 80 Statutory Instruments and other Acts of Parliament so any reference to the Act or Regulations is to the amended versions now in force. References to the Secretary of State are to the Home Secretary or, for some (but not all) parts of the Act, to the Scottish Ministers if in Scotland.[2]

The Act and Regulations extend to Northern Ireland (s.38). There are some small differences between the law of England, Wales and Scotland and that of Northern Ireland, so far as Controlled Drugs are concerned, but the latter is not covered here since the scope of this book does not extend to Northern Ireland.

Advisory Council on Misuse of Drugs

The Act requires that there is an Advisory Council (s.1), called The Advisory Council on Misuse of Drugs. The Council advises the 'ministers' who, for the purposes of this part of the Act, are the Home Secretary, the Minister of Home Affairs for Northern Ireland, and the ministers responsible for health and education in England, Wales, Scotland and Northern Ireland.

[1] The Misuse of Drugs Regulations SI 2001 No. 3998, as amended
[2] Added by Scotland Act 2012

The Advisory Council is required to keep under review the situation in the UK with respect to drugs which are being, or appear to them likely to be, misused and which are having or could cause harmful effects, which might constitute a social problem. It has a duty to advise the ministers on the action to be taken. In particular, it must advise on measures:

1 to restrict the availability of such drugs or to supervise the arrangements for their supply;
2 to enable persons affected by the misuse of such drugs to obtain proper advice, and to secure the provision of proper facilities and services for the treatment, rehabilitation and aftercare of such persons;
3 to promote co-operation between the various professional and community services which, in the opinion of the Council, have a part to play in dealing with social problems connected with the misuse of such drugs;
4 to educate the public (particularly the young) in the dangers of abusing such drugs, and to give publicity to those dangers; and
5 to promote research into, or otherwise to obtain information about, any matter which in the opinion of the Council is of relevance for the purpose of preventing the misuse of such drugs or dealing with any social problem connected with their misuse. The Secretary of State has authority to conduct or assist in conducting such research (s.32).

The Advisory Council consists of not fewer than 20 members appointed by the Secretary of State after consultation with such organisations as s/he considers appropriate.[3] The Home Secretary appoints one of the members of the Advisory Council to be chairman, and the Council may appoint committees and include on them persons who are not members of the Council.

The Advisory Council also has a duty to consider, and advise on, any matter relating to drug dependence or misuse of drugs which any of the ministers may refer to it. In particular, the Advisory Council is required to advise the Home Secretary on communications relating to the control of any dangerous or otherwise harmful drug received from any authority established under a treaty, convention or other agreement to which HM Government is a party. The ministers – ordinarily the Home Secretary – are obliged to consult the Advisory Council before laying orders before Parliament or before making regulations (or any changes to the same) under the Act.

Class A, B and C drugs

The drugs subject to control are listed in Schedule 2 to the Act and the term *Controlled Drug* means any substance or product either listed in Schedule 2 or in a temporary class drug order as a drug subject to temporary control.[4]

[3] Amended by Police Reform and Social Responsibility Act 2011
[4] Added by Police Reform and Social Responsibility Act 2011

The Schedule is divided into three parts or classes largely on the basis of decreasing order of harmfulness: Part I (class A), Part II (class B) and Part III (class C). This division into three classes is solely for the purpose of determining penalties for offences under the Act (s.25); the relevant penalties are set out in Schedule 4 to the Act. Some examples of drugs in each class are given in table 16.1. A full list is not given here, but is available on the Home Office website or by reference to the legislation.

Table 16.1 Some commonly encountered Controlled Drugs, according to their classification under the Act		
Class A	Class B	Class C
Cocaine	Amphetamine	Anabolic steroids
Diamorphine	Cannabis and cannabis	Benzodiazepines, including
Lysergic acid diethylamide (LSD)	resin[6]	diazepam, midazolam and
Methylamphetamine[5]	Codeine	temazepam (among others)
3,4-Methylenedioxymethamphetamine	Dihydrocodeine	Buprenorphine
(MDMA)	Ketamine[7]	Khat[8]
Methadone	Methylphenidate	Tramadol[9]
		Zopiclone[10]

Changes may be made to the list of Controlled Drugs subject to consultation with the Advisory Council. Amendment is made by an Order in Council which must be approved by an affirmative resolution of each House of Parliament (s.2).

It should be noted that the classification of Controlled Drugs for purposes of control when these drugs are used for lawful purposes appears in the Schedules to the Misuse of Drugs Regulations 2001,[11] rather than in Schedules to the Act, itself. This classification is of importance to practitioners and pharmacists in their daily work (see section on Regimes of control).

Restrictions and exemptions

The importation or exportation of Controlled Drugs is prohibited, except in accordance with a licence issued by the Secretary of State (s.7) or when

---

[5] Added by Misuse of Drugs Act 1971 (Amendment) Order SI 2006 No. 3331
[6] Amended by Misuse of Drugs Act 1971 (Amendment) Order SI 2008 No. 3130
[7] Added by Misuse of Drugs Act 1971 (Ketamine etc.) (Amendment) Order SI 2014 No. 1106
[8] Added by Misuse of Drugs Act 1971 (Amendment) Order SI 2014 No.1352
[9] Added by Misuse of Drugs Act 1971 (Ketamine etc.) (Amendment) Order SI 2014 No. 1106
[10] Added by Misuse of Drugs Act 1971 (Ketamine etc.) (Amendment) Order SI 2014 No. 1106
[11] The Misuse of Drugs Regulations SI 2001 No. 3998

permitted by Regulations (s.3). Certain activities are specifically declared to be unlawful, unless permitted by regulations:

1 producing a Controlled Drug (s.4);
2 supplying or offering to supply a Controlled Drug to another person (s.4);
3 possessing a Controlled Drug (s.5); and
4 cultivating any plant of the genus *Cannabis* (s.6).

Producing a Controlled Drug means producing it by manufacture, cultivation or any other method, and supplying includes distribution (s.37). For the purposes of the Act, the things which a person has in his/her possession are taken to include anything subject to his/her control which is in the custody of another (s.37). Cannabis (except in the expression cannabis resin) means any plant of the genus *Cannabis* or any part of any such plant (by whatever name designated) except that it does not include cannabis resin or any of the following products after separation from the rest of the plant, namely:

- mature stalk of any such plant;
- fibre produced from mature stalk of any such plant; and
- seed of any such plant.[12]

Exemptions from these controls may be authorised by the Secretary of State, who may:

1 by regulations, exempt any specified Controlled Drug from any of the restrictions on import, export, production, supply or possession (s.7);
2 by regulations, make it lawful for persons to produce, supply or possess Controlled Drugs to the extent which s/he thinks fit (s.7); and
3 permit, by licence or other authority, any of the activities in 2 and prescribe any conditions to be complied with (s.7).

The Home Secretary must exercise his/her powers to make regulations which make it lawful for practitioners, pharmacists and persons lawfully conducting retail pharmacy businesses (when acting in their professional capacity) to possess, supply, manufacture or compound Controlled Drugs, and for practitioners (when acting in their professional capacity) to prescribe and administer such drugs (s.7). The term *practitioner* (except in the specific expression 'veterinary practitioner') means a doctor, dentist, veterinary practitioner or veterinary surgeon (s.37).

If the Home Secretary (or the Ministry of Home Affairs for Northern Ireland) considers that it is in the public interest for a drug to be used only for the purposes of research or other special purposes, s/he may make an order to that effect. It is then unlawful for a practitioner, pharmacist or a person lawfully conducting a retail pharmacy business to possess or do anything in

---

[12]Definition of Cannabis, substituted by Criminal Law Act 1977

relation to that drug except under licence. When making an order of this kind, the Home Secretary must act on the recommendation of the Advisory Council or after consulting that Council (s.7). Licence fees are prescribed in regularly updated SIs.[13]

The 2001 Regulations list 'exempted' products (Reg.2), which means a preparation or other product consisting of one or more component parts, any of which contains a Controlled Drug, where:

1 the preparation or other product is not designed for administration of the Controlled Drug to a human being or animal;
2 the Controlled Drug in any component part is packaged in such a form or in combination with other active or inert substances in such a manner that it cannot be recovered by readily applicable means or in a yield which constitutes a risk to health; or
3 no one component part of the product or combination contains more than 1 mg of the Controlled Drug or 1 microgram in the case of lysergide or any other N-alkyl derivative of lysergamide.

Other exemptions apply, for example to *in vitro* diagnostic devices or kits used by laboratories for the detection of drugs of misuse or for clinical diagnosis or other products containing very small quantities of Controlled Drugs (e.g. radioactive research compounds). The provisions of the Act apply to the possession of a stock of Controlled Drugs for the purpose of producing kits and other exempted products. The safe custody regulations also apply to any stock of Schedule 1 and 2 Controlled Drugs and stocks of buprenorphine, diethylpropion, flunitrazepam and temazepam held for the propose of manufacture of the exempted products.

Prohibitions on possession, prescribing and supply

Directions following convictions

Where a pharmacist or practitioner has been guilty of any offence under the Act or of any offence under the Customs and Excise Act 1952 or the Customs and Excise Management Act 1979 relating to the unlawful importation or exportation of Controlled Drugs, or of an offence under section 12 or 13 of the Criminal Justice (International Co-operation) Act 1990, the Secretary of State may make a direction in respect of him/her. If s/he is a practitioner, the direction will prohibit him/her from having in his/her possession, prescribing, administering, manufacturing, compounding and supplying, and from authorising the administration and supply of the Controlled Drugs specified in the direction. If s/he is a pharmacist, the direction will prohibit him/her from having in his/her possession, manufacturing, compounding and

[13]The Misuse of Drugs (Licence Fees) Regulations SI 2010 No.2497 (as amended)

supplying and from supervising and controlling the manufacture, compounding and supply of the Controlled Drugs specified in the direction (s.12).

A copy of any such direction given by the Secretary of State must be served on the person to whom it applies and notice of it must be published in the *London, Edinburgh* and *Belfast Gazettes*. A direction takes effect when a copy has been served on the person concerned and it is then an offence for him/her to contravene it. The Secretary of State may cancel or suspend any direction which s/he has given. S/he may also bring a suspended direction into force again by cancelling its suspension (ss.12, 13 and 16).

Conviction for an offence under the Act committed by a pharmacist or other person who is a director, officer or employee of a body corporate carrying on a retail pharmacy business renders that body liable to disqualification under Part 4 of the Pharmacy Order 2010 and consequent removal of its premises from the Register (chapter 22).

Prohibitions affecting doctors

If a doctor contravenes the Regulations relating to notification of addicted persons or the prescribing of certain Controlled Drugs for addiction, s/he does not commit any offence under the Act. The Secretary of State may, however, make a direction prohibiting him/her from prescribing, administering or supplying, or authorising the administration or supply of, the Controlled Drugs specified in the direction. The doctor commits an offence if s/he contravenes that direction (s.13).

Irresponsible prescribing

If the Secretary of State is of the opinion that a practitioner has been prescribing, administering or supplying, or authorising the administration or supply of, any Controlled Drugs in an irresponsible manner, s/he may give a direction in respect of the practitioner concerned prohibiting him/her from prescribing, administering and supplying or authorising the administration and supply of the Controlled Drugs specified in the direction (s.13).

Tribunals, advisory bodies and professional panels

The Act sets out that if the Secretary of State considers that there are grounds for giving a direction, prohibiting a doctor or other practitioner from prescribing, administering or supplying Controlled Drugs, s/he must follow the procedure set out in the Act (ss.14, 15 and 16). S/he must refer the case to a *tribunal* consisting of four members of the practitioner's profession and with a legally qualified person as chairman (Sch. 3[14] sets out the criteria

---

[14] As amended by Tribunals, Courts and Enforcement Act 2007

for this latter role). Legislation[15] prescribes certain procedures to be followed before tribunals. If, as a result of the tribunal's finding that the practitioner has been found to be responsible for the contravention or conduct alleged, the Secretary of State then proposes to make a direction, the practitioner must be informed and given the opportunity to make representations in writing within 28 days. If the practitioner does so, then the case must be referred to an *advisory body* of three appointed persons, one being a member of the practitioner's profession. After receiving the advice of that body, the Secretary of State may (a) advise that no further proceedings be taken; (b) refer the case back to the same, or another, tribunal; or (c) give a direction under section 13 as described above (s.14). Although the legal underpinning for such tribunals is still in place, in practice the Misuse of Drugs Tribunal is now in abeyance and the Home Office has no oversight of this process. Instead, medical practitioners and interim order tribunal hearings are now run by the Medical Practitioners Tribunal Service.

In a case of irresponsible prescribing, if the Secretary of State considers circumstances require that a direction be given with the minimum of delay, s/he may refer the matter to a *professional panel* consisting of three members of the practitioner's profession appointed by the Secretary of State. The panel must afford the practitioner an opportunity to appear before it and, after considering the circumstances of the case, must report to the Secretary of State whether or not it believes there are reasonable grounds for thinking that there has been conduct as alleged. If the panel considers there are such grounds, the Secretary of State may give a direction at once which is effective for a period of 6 weeks. S/he must also refer the case at once to a tribunal, in accordance with the procedures outlined above. The period of operation of the temporary direction may be extended from time to time by a further 28 days if the tribunal consents. After the tribunal, or the advisory body as appropriate, has considered the case, the Secretary of State may, if s/he thinks fit, make a permanent direction, if that is the advice given to him/her. If no such direction is given, the temporary prohibition will cease (s.15).

Offences, penalties and enforcement

Schedule 4 to the Act is a tabulated summary of offences under the Act and the penalties applicable to them. The level of penalty for offences which concern a Controlled Drug varies according to the class (A, B or C) into which the drug falls, the generally more harmful drugs attracting greater penalties.

---

[15] The Senior Courts Act 1981, the Judicature (Northern Ireland) Act 1978 and the Attendance of Witnesses Act 1854

The occupier or manager of any premises commits an offence (s.8) if s/he knowingly permits or suffers any of the following to take place on the premises:

- producing or supplying, or attempting to produce or supply, or offering to supply any Controlled Drug in contravention of the Act;
- preparing opium for smoking; and
- smoking cannabis, cannabis resin or prepared opium.

It is an offence (s.9) for any person to:

1 smoke or otherwise use prepared opium; or
2 frequent a place used for the purpose of opium smoking; or
3 have in his/her possession:
   a any pipes or other utensils made or adapted for use in connection with the smoking of opium, being pipes or utensils which have been used by him/her or with his/her knowledge and permission in that connection or which s/he intends to use or permit others to use in that connection, or
   b any utensils which have been used by him/her or with his/her knowledge and permission in connection with the preparation of opium for smoking.

Other offences are described in some detail in Schedule 4. Those relating to contravention of the Regulations or of conditions of any licence, or of directions relating to safe custody of Controlled Drugs, are of special concern to practising pharmacists (ss.11 and 18). A person commits an offence if, in the UK, s/he assists in or induces the commission in any place outside the UK of an offence punishable under the provisions of a corresponding law in force in that place (s.20).

Corresponding law means a law stated, in a certificate purporting to be issued by or on behalf of the government of a country outside the UK, to be a law providing for the control and regulation in that country of the production, supply, use, export and import of (ss.20 and 36):

1 drugs and other substances in accordance with the provisions of the Single Convention on Narcotic Drugs signed at New York on 30 March 1961; or
2 dangerous or otherwise harmful drugs in pursuance of any treaty, convention or other agreement or arrangement to which the government of that country and of the UK are parties.

Attempting to commit an offence under any provision of the Act and inciting or attempting to incite another to commit such an offence are also offences (s.19).

Where any offence under the Act committed by a body corporate is proved to have been committed with the consent or connivance of, or to be attributable to any neglect on the part of, any director, manager, secretary or other similar officer of the body corporate, or any person purporting to act in any such capacity, s/he, as well as the body corporate, is guilty of the offence and is liable to be proceeded against accordingly (s.21).

For some offences, the accused may be acquitted if s/he can prove that s/he did not believe, suspect or have reason to suspect that the substance or product in question was a Controlled Drug. The offences in question are producing, supplying, offering to supply or possessing Controlled Drugs, cultivating cannabis, smoking or preparing opium, frequenting a place used for the purpose of opium smoking or possessing opium pipes and utensils. When it is necessary, in connection with any offence, to prove that a substance or product is a Controlled Drug, the accused may prove that s/he believed it to be a different Controlled Drug. This in itself will not constitute a defence unless there could have been no offence had the drug been of that description (s.28).

It is also a defence for a person accused of unlawful possession of a Controlled Drug to prove that s/he took possession of it to prevent another person committing an offence, and that s/he took steps to destroy it as soon as possible, or that s/he took possession of the drug to hand it over to some authorised person as soon as possible (s.5).

An inspector of the GPhC is authorised by the Secretary of State to inspect books and documents. It is an offence to conceal any such books, documents or stock.

A constable, or other person authorised by the Secretary of State, has power to enter any premises of a person carrying on a business as a producer or supplier of any Controlled Drugs and inspect books and documents and any stocks of drugs. A constable may also, on the authority of a warrant, enter any premises named in the warrant, by force if necessary, and search them and any person found therein, seizing any Controlled Drug or any document relevant to the transaction if s/he has reasonable grounds to consider that an offence under the Act has been committed (s.23). S/he may detain for the purposes of search any person whom s/he has reasonable grounds to suspect is in unlawful possession of a Controlled Drug. S/he may also stop and search any vehicle or vessel for the same reason and may seize anything which appears to be evidence of an offence under the Act (s.23).

In Scotland, a constable may arrest, without warrant, a person who has committed an offence under the Act, or whom s/he suspects has committed an offence, if that person's name and address are unknown to him/her or cannot be ascertained, if s/he suspects the name and address are false or if s/he has reasonable cause to think that the person may abscond unless arrested (s.24).

It is an offence intentionally to obstruct a person exercising his/her powers of examination or search. Failure to produce any book, documents, stocks or drugs without reasonable excuse is also an offence, and proof of the reasonableness of the excuse rests with the person offering it as a defence (s.23).

Upon a conviction, anything relating to the offence may be forfeited and destroyed or otherwise dealt with by order of the court, subject to any person claiming to be the owner showing cause why the order should not be made (s.27). The Proceeds of Crime Act 2002 provides for the confiscation of the proceeds of drug trafficking received by convicted persons.

Scheduled substances: substances used in the manufacture of narcotic drugs or psychotropic substances

Article 12 of the United Nations Convention against Illicit Traffic in Narcotic Drugs and Psychotropic Substances (adopted in 1988) relates to 'substances frequently used in the illicit manufacture of narcotic drugs and psychotropic substances'. EU legislation[16] defines these as 'scheduled substances' and establishes harmonised measures within the EU for controlling and monitoring certain chemical substances that are frequently used in the illicit manufacture of narcotic drugs. Some substances, including medicinal products and pharmaceutical preparations, are specifically excluded from the definition of 'scheduled substances'. Other EU legislation regulates trade in these substances within the EU[17] and between the EU and other countries.[18] These EU Regulations are enacted in the UK via two statutory instruments.[19,20] Between them, these two SIs allow for a competitive internal market for legitimate trade in drug precursors (which can be used in the manufacture of other substances, such as perfumes or flavourings) whilst preventing their diversion for illicit manufacture. There is a licensing system for UK-based operators who trade in these chemicals.

Powers of the Secretary of State

The power of the Secretary of State to make Regulations is exercised by statutory instruments (ss.7, 10, 22 and 31). Regulations may make different provisions for different cases and circumstances and for different Controlled

[16] Commission Regulation (EC) No. 1277/2005
[17] (EC) No. 273/2004
[18] (EC) No. 111/2005
[19] Controlled Drugs (Drug Precursors) (Intra-Community Trade) Regulations 2008 SI 2008 No. 295
[20] Controlled Drugs (Drug Precursors) (Community External Trade) Regulations 2008 SI 2008 No. 296

Drugs and different classes of person. The opinion, consent or approval of a prescribed authority or of any person may also be made material to a regulation, for example the approval of a chief officer of police is required in connection with certain safekeeping requirements for drugs (s.31). Any licence or other authority issued by the Secretary of State for the purposes of the Act may be made subject to such conditions as s/he thinks proper and may be modified or revoked at any time (s.30).

The application of any provision of the Act which creates an offence and those provisions of the Customs and Excise Management Act 1979 that apply to the importation and exportation of Controlled Drugs may, in prescribed cases, be excluded by regulation. Similarly, any provision of the Act or any regulation or order made under it may, by regulation, be made applicable to servants and agents of the Crown (s.22).

Most of the Regulations are designed to render lawful various activities in connection with Controlled Drugs which would otherwise be unlawful under the Act. For example, they are necessary to enable doctors, pharmacists and others to prescribe, administer, manufacture, compound or supply Controlled Drugs as appropriate to their particular capacities. They also govern such matters as the safekeeping of Controlled Drugs and their destruction, the notification of addicts and the supply of Controlled Drugs to addicts.

Regimes of control

The drugs controlled under the Act are classified in the Misuse of Drugs Regulations 2001[21] into five schedules in descending order of control, the most stringent controls applying to drugs in Schedule 1. Full lists of the drugs included in each schedule are not included here. The *British National Formulary* includes information regarding classification under the Regulations. Pharmacists may also refer to the individual Summaries of Product Characteristics for medicinal products, to information on the Home Office website or by reference to the legislation.

Schedule 1

Schedule 1 lists Controlled Drugs which may not be used for medicinal purposes, their production and possession being limited, in the public interest, to purposes of research or other special purposes. Certain limited classes of person have a general authority to possess these drugs in the course of their duties, for example constables or carriers (Reg.6). Other persons may only produce, supply or possess the drugs within the authority of a licence issued by the Secretary of State. The requirements of the Misuse of Drugs

[21]The Misuse of Drugs Regulations SI 2001 No. 3998 (as amended)

Regulations relating to documentation, the keeping and preservation of records, supply on prescription, marking of containers and procedure for destruction apply in full to these drugs in Schedule 1.

Examples of drugs in Schedule 1 include cannabis (except for certain products licensed by the MHRA), cannabis resin, khat, LSD (lysergic acid diethylamide) and MDMA (3,4-methylenedioxymethamphetamine).

Schedule 2

Schedule 2 includes the opiates (such as diamorphine, morphine and methadone) and the major stimulants (such as the amphetamines). A licence is needed to import or export drugs in this schedule but they may be manufactured or compounded, when acting in a professional capacity, by a practitioner, a pharmacist, a person lawfully conducting a retail pharmacy, a nurse independent prescriber, a supplementary prescriber (acting under and in accordance with the terms of a clinical management plan) or a person acting in accordance with the written directions of any of these prescribers, for the purposes of administration. A pharmacist may supply a Schedule 2 drug to a patient (or the owner of an animal) only on the authority of a prescription in the required form issued by an appropriate practitioner (Regs.15 and 16). See section on Prescription requirements for Schedule 2 and 3 Controlled Drugs.

The drugs may only be administered to a patient by (Reg.7, as amended):

- a doctor or dentist or by any person acting in accordance with the directions of a doctor or dentist;
- a nurse or pharmacist independent prescriber or by any person acting in accordance with the directions of a nurse or pharmacist independent prescriber (for those drugs, and in such circumstances that such independent prescribers may prescribe);
- a supplementary prescriber acting under and in accordance with the terms of a clinical management plan, or any person acting in accordance with the directions of a supplementary prescriber, acting under such a plan;
- a registered physiotherapist or registered chiropodist independent prescriber or by any person acting in accordance with the directions of a registered physiotherapist or registered chiropodist independent prescriber (for those drugs, and in such circumstances that such independent prescribers may respectively prescribe).

Requirements as to safe custody in pharmacies and control over destruction apply to these drugs, and the provisions relating to the marking of containers and the keeping of records must also be observed (Regs.18 and 19).

Schedule 3

Schedule 3 includes the barbiturates (except quinalbarbitone (secobarbital), which is a Schedule 2 Controlled Drug), buprenorphine, diethylpropion, meprobamate, pentazocine and tramadol, as well as three benzodiazepines: flunitrazepam, midazolam and temazepam.

These drugs are not thought likely to be so harmful, when misused, as the drugs in Schedule 2.

The controls which apply to Schedule 2 also apply to drugs in Schedule 3, except that:

1 they may also be manufactured by persons authorised in writing by the Secretary of State;
2 there is a difference in the classes of person who may possess and supply them; and
3 entries in a Controlled Drugs register need not be made in respect of these drugs but invoices or like records must be kept for a period of 2 years (see below).

Schedule 4, Part I

Part I of Schedule 4 contains many of the benzodiazepines, ketamine and zaleplon, zolpidem and zopiclone. The restrictions applicable to Schedule 3 drugs apply to these drugs with the relaxations 1 to 5 as given for Schedule 4 Part II drugs below.

Schedule 4, Part II

Part II of Schedule 4 contains the anabolic and androgenic steroids and derivatives, together with an adrenoceptor stimulant and polypeptide hormones. The restrictions applicable to Schedule 3 drugs apply to them with the following relaxations:

1 there is no restriction on the possession of any Schedule 4, Part II drug when contained in a medicinal product;
2 prescription and labelling requirements under the Misuse of Drugs Act do not apply, but the provisions of medicines law do apply;
3 records need not be kept by retailers;
4 destruction requirements apply only to importers, exporters and manufacturers;
5 there are no safe custody requirements; and
6 there is no restriction on imports or exports provided that they are imported or exported by a person for self-administration.

A previous requirement (under 6 above) that the drugs specified in Part II of Schedule 4 must be in the form of a medicinal product was removed in 2012.[22]

Schedule 5

Schedule 5 specifies those preparations of certain Controlled Drugs for which there is only negligible risk of abuse. There is no restriction on the import, export, possession or administration of these preparations, and safe custody requirements do not apply to them. A practitioner or pharmacist, acting in his/her capacity as such, may manufacture or compound any of them.

No record in the register of Controlled Drugs need be made in respect of Schedule 3, 4 or 5 drugs obtained by a retail dealer, but the invoice, or a copy of it, must be kept for 2 years. Producers and wholesale dealers must retain invoices of quantities obtained and supplied (Reg.24(1)). No authority is required to destroy these drugs, and there are no special labelling requirements, although medicines law labelling requirements apply.

A retail dealer is defined as a person lawfully conducting a retail pharmacy business or a pharmacist engaged in supplying drugs to the public at an NHS health centre.

Poppy-straw

Poppy-straw (which means all parts of the opium poppy, except the seeds, after mowing), and concentrate of poppy-straw (which means the material produced when poppy-straw has entered into a process for the concentration of its alkaloids) are listed as Class A Controlled Drugs under the Act. Poppy-straw is not included in any of the schedules to the regulations. Although a licence is required to import or export poppy-straw, its production, possession and supply are free from control (Reg.4). Concentrate of poppy-straw is designated as a Schedule 1 Controlled Drug under the Regulations, and so all of the stringent controls, described above, for this Schedule apply to this substance.

Import and export

Controlled Drugs may only be imported or exported in accordance with the terms and conditions of a licence issued by the Secretary of State (s.3 of the Act) but drugs in Schedule 5 are exempted from this requirement (Reg.4).

[22]The Misuse of Drugs (Amendment No.2) (England, Wales & Scotland) Regulations SI 2012 No.973

Drugs in Schedule 4 Part II are also exempted, in the case of importation or exportation which is carried out in person for administration to that person. Unlawful import or export is an offence under the Customs and Excise Management Act 1979 (see below).

Possession and supply

It is unlawful for any person to be in possession of a Controlled Drug unless the Regulations allow it. Possession of poppy-straw or of any drug specified in Part II of Schedule 4 or in Schedule 5 is not controlled.

Table 16.2 shows those classes of person who may possess and supply specified Controlled Drugs. In each case, where the Regulations permit certain activities in relation to a person because s/he is a member of a class of people, s/he may only lawfully undertake those activities, whilst acting in his/her capacity as a member of that class. In addition, those authorised to supply specified Controlled Drugs may only supply them to those who are authorised to possess such drugs. Where a supply is made in accordance with medicines law, for example by a supplementary, or nurse or pharmacist independent prescriber, then the supply must be made in accordance with that law (i.e. under a clinical management plan, in the case of supplementary prescribing, or of those drugs and for those purposes permitted for nurse or pharmacist independent prescribing).

	Class of person	Possession and supply
Table 16.2 Possession and supply of Controlled Drugs (Regs.4–10 and Sch. 8)		
1	A practitioner	May possess, manufacture, compound, administer, supply or offer to supply any Schedule 2, 3, 4 or 5 drug
2	A pharmacist	May possess, manufacture, compound, supply or offer to supply any Schedule 2, 3, 4 or 5 drug
3	A person lawfully conducting a retail pharmacy business	May possess, manufacture, compound, supply or offer to supply any Schedule 2, 3, 4 or 5 drug The manufacture or compounding of the drug must take place at the registered pharmacy at which that person carries on that business
4	A nurse or pharmacist independent prescriber or a supplementary prescriber	May compound any Schedule 2, 3, 4 or 5 drug, for the purposes of administration, and may possess, administer, supply or offer to supply any Schedule 2, 3, 4 or 5 drug

(continued overleaf)

Table 16.2 *(continued)*

	Class of person	Possession and supply
5	Any person acting in accordance with the written directions of a doctor, a dentist, a nurse or pharmacist independent prescriber, or a supplementary prescriber acting under and in accordance with the terms of a clinical management plan	May compound any Schedule 2, 3, 4 or 5 drug for the purposes of administration
6	A registered midwife	See the section on 'Midwives and Controlled Drugs'
7	A registered nurse or a pharmacist	May possess, supply or offer to supply, under and in accordance with the terms of a Patient Group Direction (PGD), diamorphine or morphine where administration of such drugs is required for the immediate, necessary treatment of sick or injured persons
8	Any of the following: ● a registered nurse ● a person holding a certificate of proficiency in ambulance paramedic skills issued by, or with the approval of, the Secretary of State ● a registered paramedic ● a registered midwife ● a registered optometrist ● a registered chiropodist ● a registered orthoptist ● a registered physiotherapist ● a registered radiographer ● a registered occupational therapist ● a registered orthotist and prosthetist	May possess, supply or offer to supply, under and in accordance with the terms of a PGD: ● any drug specified in Schedule 4 or 5 ● ketamine ● midazolam The following may not be supplied: ● anabolic steroid drugs specified in Part II of Schedule 4 ● any drug or preparation which is designed for administration by injection and which is to be used for the purpose of treating a person who is addicted to a drug
9	A person who is authorised as a member of a group, under and in accordance with the terms of his/her group authority and in compliance with any attached conditions	May possess, supply or offer to supply any Schedule 2, 3, 4 or 5 drug
10	The senior or acting senior registered nurse, or registered midwife, for the time being in charge of a ward, theatre or other department in the hospital, care home or prison, where the drug was supplied to him/her by a person responsible for the dispensing and supply of medicines at a hospital, care home or prison	May possess, supply or offer to supply any Schedule 2, 3, 4 or 5 drug. The supply must be for administration to a patient in that ward, theatre or department in accordance with the directions of a doctor, dentist or a supplementary prescriber or nurse or a pharmacist independent prescriber lawfully prescribing that drug

(continued overleaf)

Table 16.2 *(continued)*

	Class of person	Possession and supply
11	The person in charge or acting person in charge of a hospital or care home which is wholly or mainly maintained by a public authority out of public funds or by a charity or by voluntary subscriptions	May possess, supply or offer to supply any Schedule 2, 3, 4 or 5 drug, but not if there is a pharmacist responsible for the dispensing and supply of medicines
12	The person in charge or acting person in charge of a hospital or care home	May possess, supply or offer to supply any drug specified in Schedule 3, 4 or 5, but not if there is a pharmacist responsible for the dispensing and supply of medicines
13	The person in charge or acting person in charge of an organisation providing ambulance services	May possess, supply or offer to supply any Schedule 2, 3, 4 or 5 drug, but not if there is a pharmacist responsible for the dispensing and supply of medicines. Such supplies may only be made directly to employees of the organisation for the immediate treatment of sick or injured persons
14	An operating department practitioner practising in a hospital, where the drug was supplied to them by a person responsible for the dispensing and supply of medicines at that hospital	May possess, supply or offer to supply any Schedule 2, 3, 4 or 5 drug The supply must be for administration to a patient in that ward, theatre or department in accordance with the directions of a doctor, dentist or a supplementary prescriber or nurse or a pharmacist independent prescriber lawfully prescribing that drug
15	The installation manager of an offshore installation or the owner of a ship, or the master of a ship which does not carry a doctor among the seamen employed in it Master of a ship includes any other person (except a pilot) who has command or charge of the ship[23]	May supply or offer to supply any Schedule 2, 3, 4 or 5 drug to any person on that installation or ship in order to comply with provisions as a result of: (a) the Mineral Workings (Offshore Installations) Act 1971 (b) the Health and Safety at Work etc. Act 1974 or (c) the Merchant Shipping Act 1995 They may also supply or offer to supply any Schedule 2, 3, 4 or 5 drug to any person who may lawfully supply that drug to him or (for Schedule 2 or 5 drugs) to any constable for the purpose of the destruction of that drug
16	The master of a foreign ship which is in a port in Great Britain	May possess any Schedule 2, 3, 4 or 5 drug, so far as necessary for the equipment of the ship (as authorised by the proper officer of the port health authority, or equivalent)
17	A person engaged in conveying the drug to a person who may lawfully have that drug in his/her possession	May possess any Controlled Drug or supply any Controlled Drug to any person who may lawfully have that drug in his/her possession

(continued overleaf)

[23]Wireless Telegraphy Act 2006

	Table 16.2 *(continued)*	
	Class of person	**Possession and supply**
18	A person who is in charge of a laboratory, the recognised activities of which consist in, or include, the conduct of scientific education or research and which is attached to a university, university college or such a hospital as aforesaid, or to any other institution approved for the purpose under this sub-paragraph by the Secretary of State	May supply or offer to supply any Schedule 2, 3, 4 or 5 drug to any person who may lawfully have that drug in his/her possession
19	A person in charge of a laboratory, the recognised activities of which consist in, or include, the conduct of scientific education or research	May possess, supply or offer to supply any drug specified in Schedule 3, 4 or 5 to any person who may lawfully have that drug in his/her possession
20	A person in charge of a laboratory	May possess, supply or offer to supply any drug specified in Schedule 3 which is required for use as a buffering agent in chemical analysis to any person who may lawfully have that drug in his/her possession
21	A public analyst appointed under section 27 of the Food Safety Act 1990	May possess, supply or offer to supply any Schedule 2, 3, 4 or 5 drug
22	A sampling officer within the meaning of Schedule 3 to the Medicines Act 1968	May possess, supply or offer to supply any Schedule 2, 3, 4 or 5 drug
23	A person employed or engaged in connection with a scheme for testing the quality or amount of the drugs, preparations and appliances supplied under the National Health Service Act 1977 or the National Health Service (Scotland) Act 1978 and the regulations made thereunder	May possess, supply or offer to supply any Schedule 2, 3, 4 or 5 drug
24	A person authorised by the General Pharmaceutical Council for the purposes of section 108 or 109 of the Medicines Act 1968	May possess, supply or offer to supply any Schedule 2, 3, 4 or 5 drug
25	A constable when acting in the course of his/her duty as such	May possess any Controlled Drug or supply any Controlled Drug to any person who may lawfully have that drug in his/her possession
26	A person engaged in the business of a carrier when acting in the course of that business	May possess any Controlled Drug or supply any Controlled Drug to any person who may lawfully have that drug in his/her possession

(continued overleaf)

	Class of person	Possession and supply
	Table 16.2 *(continued)*	
	Class of person	**Possession and supply**
27	A person engaged in the business of a postal operator (within the meaning of Part 3 of the Postal Services Act 2011) when acting in the course of that business	May possess any Controlled Drug or supply any Controlled Drug to any person who may lawfully have that drug in his/her possession
28	An officer of customs and excise when acting in the course of his/her duty as such	May possess any Controlled Drug or supply any Controlled Drug to any person who may lawfully have that drug in his/her possession
29	A person engaged in the work of any laboratory to which the drug has been sent for forensic examination when acting in the course of his/her duty as a person so engaged	May possess any Controlled Drug or supply any Controlled Drug to any person who may lawfully have that drug in his/her possession
30	Any person licensed under the Wildlife and Countryside Act 1981	May supply, offer to supply or have in his/her possession any drug specified in Schedule 2 or 3 for the purposes for which that licence was granted
31	A person with the written authority of the Secretary of State, at the premises specified in that authority and in compliance with any specified conditions	May possess, produce, supply or offer to supply any drug specified in Schedule 3, 4 or 5
32	A person holding an appropriate licence from the Home Office	May produce, possess, supply or offer to supply any Controlled Drug, in accordance with the terms of the licence and in compliance with any conditions attached to the licence

Other general authorities to possess and supply include:

1 any person who is lawfully in possession of a Controlled Drug may supply that drug to the person from whom s/he obtained it;
2 any person who is in possession of a Schedule 2, 3, 4 or 5 drug which has been supplied for him/her by, or on the prescription of, somebody authorised to prescribe that item, or under a Patient Group Direction (PGD), may supply that drug to any doctor, dentist or pharmacist for the purpose of destruction;
3 any person who is in lawful possession of a Schedule 2, 3, 4 or 5 drug which has been supplied by, or on the prescription of, a veterinary surgeon or veterinary practitioner for the treatment of animals may supply that drug to any veterinary surgeon, veterinary practitioner or pharmacist for the purpose of destruction;
4 any person may possess a Schedule 2, 3, 4 or 5 drug for administration for medical, dental or veterinary purposes in accordance with the directions of a practitioner, a supplementary prescriber or a nurse or pharmacist

independent prescriber. Such possession will not be lawful if the person prescribed the drug (or supplied that drug under a PGD):

a was then being supplied with any Controlled Drug by or on the prescription of another prescriber, or under a PGD, and failed to disclose that fact to the person prescribing or making the supply, or

b made a declaration or statement, or had such a statement made on his/her behalf, which was false in any particular, for the purpose of obtaining the supply or prescription.

Prescriptions for Controlled Drugs

Prescribing permissions

Doctors, dentists and supplementary prescribers (under the terms of a clinical management plan) may prescribe any Controlled Drug specified in Schedules 2–5.

EEA health professionals may not prescribe drugs specified in Schedule 2 or 3, but may prescribe those in Schedule 4 or 5.

Nurse and pharmacist independent prescribers may prescribe any Controlled Drug specified in Schedule 2, 3, 4 or 5, except cocaine, diamorphine or dipipanone for the treatment of addiction.

A registered physiotherapist independent prescriber may prescribe any of the following Controlled Drugs for the treatment of organic disease or injury, provided that the drug is prescribed to be administered by the specified method:

- diazepam by oral administration
- dihydrocodeine by oral administration
- fentanyl by transdermal administration
- lorazepam by oral administration
- morphine by oral administration or by injection
- oxycodone by oral administration
- temazepam by oral administration.

A registered chiropodist independent prescriber may prescribe diazepam, dihydrocodeine, lorazepam and temazepam, for oral administration, for the treatment of organic disease or injury.

The HMRs were amended in 2016, to permit therapeutic radiographer independent prescribers to prescribe certain Controlled Drugs[24] (see chapter 8) but, at the time of going to press, corresponding changes had not yet been made to the Misuse of Drugs Regulations and so, in effect, such prescribing is not currently permitted.

Schedule 1 Controlled Drugs

Since Schedule 1 drugs will rarely (if ever) be prescribed, they are not mentioned in this section. However, should a Schedule 1 drug ever be

---

[24] Human Medicines (Amendment) Regulations SI 2016 No. 186

prescribed, it should be noted that all of the requirements in this section that apply to Schedule 2 Controlled Drugs, apply equally to Schedule 1 drugs.

Prescription requirements for Schedule 2 and 3 Controlled Drugs

A prescription for a Schedule 2 or 3 Controlled Drug for human use (veterinary prescriptions are considered in chapter 17) must not be issued unless it complies with the following requirements:

1 it must be written so as to be indelible, be dated and be signed by the person issuing it with his/her usual signature or be prescribed on an electronic prescription form[25] (it is unlikely that a carbon copy, even one bearing an original signature, would be sufficient to satisfy the indelibility requirement);[26]
2 except in the case of a health prescription, or unless prescribed on an electronic prescription form, it must be written on a prescription form provided by an NHS Commissioning Board or an equivalent body for the purposes of private prescribing (this is the 'standardised private Controlled Drug prescription form': FP10PCD in England, PPCD(1) in Scotland and WP10PCD or WP10PCDSS in Wales);
3 except in the case of a health prescription, specify the prescriber identification number and address of the person issuing it;
4 if issued by a dentist, have the words 'for dental treatment only' written on it;
5 it must specify the name and address of the person for whose treatment it is issued;
6 it must specify the dose to be taken;
7 in the case of a prescription containing a Controlled Drug which is a preparation, it must specify the form and, where appropriate, the strength of the preparation, and either the total quantity (in both words and figures) of the preparation or the number (in both words and figures) of dosage units, as appropriate, to be supplied; in any other case, it must specify the total quantity (in both words and figures) of the Controlled Drug to be supplied;
8 in the case of a prescription for a total quantity intended to be dispensed by instalments, it must contain a direction specifying the amount of the instalments of the total amount which must be dispensed and the intervals to be observed when dispensing (Reg.15(1)).

A Schedule 2 or 3 Controlled Drug must not be supplied by any person on a prescription (Reg.16):

● unless the prescription complies with the prescription requirements, set out above;

---

[25] Misuse of Drugs (Amendment) (No. 2) (England, Wales and Scotland) Regulations SI 2015 No. 891

[26] The Misuse of Drugs and the Misuse of Drugs (Supply to Addicts) (Amendment) Regulations SI 2006 No. 2864

- unless the prescriber's address on the prescription is within the UK;
- unless the supplier is either acquainted with the prescriber's signature, and has no reason to suppose that it is not genuine, or has taken reasonably sufficient steps to satisfy him/herself that it is genuine;
- before the date specified on the prescription; and
- later than 28 days after the date specified on the prescription unless it is an instalment prescription (see below).[27]

No prescription requirements are laid down for any Controlled Drug in Schedule 4 or 5 to the Regulations.

Note that, whilst the above requirements do not apply to prescriptions for Schedule 4 and 5 drugs, a prescription for a Schedule 4 Controlled Drug is valid for only 28 days from the date specified on the prescription.

Endorsing the prescription

A person supplying a Schedule 2 or 3 Controlled Drug on prescription shall, at the time of the supply, mark on the prescription the date on which the drug was supplied. A copy of every prescription, other than a veterinary prescription, must be sent to the relevant NHS service agency. A person supplying temazepam in accordance with an electronic prescription shall at the time of supply enter on the form by electronic means the date on which the drug was supplied.[28]

Instalment prescriptions

Prescriptions for Schedule 2 or 3 Controlled Drugs, which contain a direction that specified instalments of the total amount may be supplied at stated intervals must not be supplied otherwise than in accordance with the directions (Regs.16(4) and 23(3)), and:

1 the first instalment must be supplied not later than 28 days after the date specified on the prescription;
2 the prescription must be marked with the date when each instalment is supplied;
3 a copy of the prescription must be sent to the relevant NHS service agency; and
4 repeat prescriptions as such are not provided for, in that the total quantity of drug prescribed must be stated on the prescription.

Technical errors on prescriptions

A pharmacist may supply a Schedule 2 or 3 Controlled Drug if the prescription contains minor typographical errors or spelling mistakes or if it

---

[27] The Misuse of Drugs (Amendment No.2) Regulations SI 2006 No. 1450
[28] The Misuse of Drugs Regulations SI 2001 No. 3998, as amended

specifies the total quantity of the preparation, or of the Controlled Drug, or the number of dosage units (as the case may be) in either words or figures but not both, provided that:[29]

1 having exercised all due diligence, s/he is satisfied on reasonable grounds that the prescription is genuine;
2 having exercised all due diligence, s/he is satisfied on reasonable grounds that the supply of the drug is in accordance with the intention of the person issuing the prescription;
3 s/he amends the prescription in ink or otherwise indelibly to correct the minor errors or mistakes or to add either the total quantity in words or figures, as necessary;
4 s/he marks the prescription so that the amendment s/he has made is attributable to her/him.

Procedures for when the drug is collected

A person who is asked to supply a Schedule 2 Controlled Drug must first ascertain whether the person collecting the drug is the patient, the patient's representative or a healthcare professional acting in his/her professional capacity on behalf of the patient, and:[30]

1 where the person is the patient or the patient's representative, s/he may request evidence of identity, and refuse to supply the drug if s/he is not satisfied as to the identity of that person;
2 where the person is a healthcare professional acting in his/her professional capacity on behalf of the patient, s/he must obtain that person's name and address and must, unless s/he is acquainted with that person, request evidence of the identity of the person but may supply the drug even if not satisfied as to the identity of that person.

Prescribing in hospitals, etc.

A pharmacist may supply a Schedule 2 or 3 Controlled Drug other than on a health prescription in a hospital if it does not comply with the usual requirements for private prescriptions for such drugs, i.e. to be written on the standardised private prescription form and to specify the prescriber identification number of the person issuing it.

A prescription issued for the treatment of a patient in a hospital, care home or prison and written on the patient's bed card or case sheet need not specify the name and address of the patient (Reg.15(3)). When a drug is administered from stock held in the ward, the prescription requirements do not apply.

[29] The Misuse of Drugs (Amendment No.2) Regulations SI 2006 No. 1450
[30] The Misuse of Drugs (Amendment No. 2) Regulations SI 2006 No. 1450

Exemption for certain prescriptions and other provisions

Nothing in the Regulations relating to prescriptions (Regs.15 and 16) has effect in relation to prescriptions issued for the purposes of a scheme for testing the quality and amount of the drugs, preparations and appliances supplied under the NHS or to any prescriptions issued for the purposes of the Medicines Act 1968 to sampling officers within the meaning of that Act (Reg.17).

A person is not in lawful possession of a drug if s/he obtained it on a prescription, or via a PGD, which s/he obtained from the prescriber, or person supplying, either by making a false statement or declaration or by not disclosing to the prescriber, or person supplying, that s/he was being supplied with a Controlled Drug by or on the prescription of another prescriber, or under a PGD (Reg.10(2)).

EEA prescribers, who are appropriate practitioners within the meaning of the relevant regulations, may give prescriptions for Controlled Drugs in Schedule 4 or 5 only.[31]

Emergency supplies

It is not lawful to make an emergency supply (chapter 8) at the request of a patient or prescriber of any Schedule 2 or 3 Controlled Drug, with the exception of medicines containing phenobarbital or phenobarbital sodium, for use in the treatment of epilepsy. Such supplies of Schedule 4 and 5 drugs are permitted. In all cases, supplies must be made in accordance with the HMRs. When the supply is made at the request of a patient, for phenobarbital (for epilepsy), or a Schedule 4 or 5 drug, a maximum of 5 days' supply may be given.

Marking of containers

The container in which a Controlled Drug, other than a preparation, is supplied must be plainly marked with the amount of drug contained in it. If the drug is a preparation made up into tablets, capsules or other dosage units, the container must be marked with the amount of Controlled Drug(s) in each dosage unit and the number of dosage units in the package. For any other kind of preparation, the container must be marked with the total amount of the preparation in it and the percentage of Controlled Drug(s) in the preparation (Reg.18(1)). These requirements do not apply to:

- any exempt product;
- poppy-straw;

[31] The Human Medicines Regulations 2012 SI 2012 No. 1916

- Schedule 4 or 5 Controlled Drugs;
- any Schedule 3 drug contained in or comprising a preparation used as a buffering agent in chemical analysis, which has present in it both a substance in that Schedule and a salt of that substance or is pre-mixed in a kit;
- Controlled Drugs supplied on the prescription of a practitioner, a supplementary prescriber, a nurse independent prescriber or a pharmacist independent prescriber; or
- the supply of a Controlled Drug for administration in a clinical trial or a medicinal test on animals (Reg.18(2), as amended).

Registers and records

Register means either a bound book, which does not include any form of loose-leaf register or card index (Reg.2, as amended),[32] or a computerised system which is in accordance with best practice guidelines endorsed by the Secretary of State for Health.

There is no statutory format for the register provided that the following information is recorded. However, the National Pharmacy Association does produce a register which complies with the requirements. An entry in a Controlled Drugs register must be made in respect of every quantity of any drug in Schedule 1 or 2 which is obtained or supplied (whether by way of administration or otherwise), except for:

- drugs returned to a practitioner or a pharmacist for the purposes of destruction;
- the supply of a drug by a person who holds a Home Office licence, within the terms of that licence, if the licence does not require a register to be kept;
- the receipt or supply of a drug by the senior or acting senior registered nurse or registered midwife, for the time being in charge of a ward, theatre or other department in a hospital, care home or prison.

Note that there are different provisions for drugs obtained and supplied by midwives – see section on Midwives and Controlled Drugs.

General provisions relating to the keeping of records in the Controlled Drugs register

The class of drug recorded, together with its strength and form, must be specified at the head of each page of the register. Entries in the register must be made in chronological sequence. A separate register or separate part of

[32] Misuse of Drugs (Amendment No.2) (England, Wales and Scotland) Regulations SI 2012 No. 973

the register must be used in respect of each class of drugs and a separate page should be used in respect of each strength and form of that drug.[33]

Entries must be made on the day of the transaction or, if that is not reasonably practicable, on the following day. No cancellation, obliteration or alteration of any entry may be made, and corrections must be by way of marginal notes or footnotes, which must be dated. Every entry and every correction of such an entry must be in ink or be otherwise indelible or shall be in a computerised form in which every entry is attributable and capable of being audited, and which is in accordance with best practice guidelines endorsed by the Secretary of State.[34]

A separate register must be kept in respect of each set of premises of the business. There may only be one such register for each premises unless the Secretary of State has approved the keeping of separate registers in different departments (Reg.20). The register must be kept at the premises to which it relates and, where the register is in a computerised form, it must be accessible from those premises.

Nothing prevents the use of the register to record additional information to that required or allowed under these provisions, but the register must not be used for any purpose other than for purposes related to these regulations.

Minimum information to be recorded regarding Controlled Drugs obtained

The headings in respect of entries made for drugs obtained are:

1 date supply received
2 name and address from whom received
3 quantity received.

Minimum information to be recorded regarding Controlled Drugs supplied

The following information must be recorded, in respect of drugs supplied:

- date supplied;
- name and address of person or firm supplied;
- details of authority to possess – prescriber or licence holder's details;
- quantity of drug supplied;
- person collecting Schedule 2 drug (i.e. patient/patient's representative/ healthcare professional and, if a healthcare professional, his/her name and address (see section on 'Procedures for when the drug is collected');

[33] The Misuse of Drugs and Misuse of Drugs (Safe Custody) (Amendment) Regulations SI 2007 No. 2154

[34] Misuse of Drugs and the Misuse of Drugs (Supply to Addicts) (Amendment) Regulations SI 2006 No. 2864

- was proof of identity requested of patient/patient's representative (Yes/No); and
- was proof of identity of person collecting provided (Yes/No)?

Where a supply of a Schedule 2 drug is made to a member of the crew of a ship or a person on an off-shore installation, an entry, specifying the drug, in the official log book or installation log book is a sufficient record. These books are required to be kept under the Merchant Shipping Act 1995 or the Offshore Installations (Logbooks and Registration of Death) Regulations 1972. In the case of a ship which is not required to carry an official log book, a report signed by the master of the ship is sufficient if it is delivered as soon as possible to the superintendent of a mercantile marine office.

Return of Controlled Drugs from patients

A pharmacist or practitioner need not legally record any prescribed drug returned to him/her for destruction, but it is suggested[35] that the destruction and disposal of such drugs are recorded in a separate book, kept for this purpose, with the record including the dates of receipt and destruction and the signatures of any witness and of the person destroying the Controlled Drugs. It would seem sensible to also record the quantity, strength and name of the Controlled Drug returned.

Note that standard operating procedures set out under Welsh legislation are required to detail arrangements for the disposal and destruction of Controlled Drugs and standard operating procedures set out by Accountable Officers in England and Scotland may include specific details as to such arrangements.

Running balances

At present there is no legal requirement to keep running balances. However, it is recommended[36] that they be kept in accordance with a standard operating procedure.

Furnishing of information with respect to Controlled Drugs (Reg.26)

The persons listed below must, in response to a request made by the Secretary of State or by a person authorised in writing by him/her, provide any particulars requested in respect of producing, obtaining, supplying or

[35] NICE (2016) Controlled drugs: safe use and management; NICE guideline [NG46]
[36] NICE (2016) Controlled drugs: safe use and management; NICE guideline [NG46]

stocking any Controlled Drug.[37] The register, the stocks of drugs and other relevant books and documents must also be produced if requested. If records are held in a computerised form, a copy of the computerised form must be supplied if requested.

Those required to furnish information are:

- practitioners;
- wholesale dealers;
- retail dealers;
- persons or acting persons in charge of hospitals, organisations providing ambulance services or care homes;
- persons in charge of a laboratory;
- persons authorised under the Act or regulations to produce, import or export any Controlled Drug;
- persons authorised under Regulation 9(4)(a) to supply drugs in Schedules 3 and 4 (Reg.26(2));
- supplementary prescribers;[38] and
- nurse independent prescribers.[39]

Professional personal records relating to the physical or mental health of an individual are exempt.

Preservation of records

All registers and midwives' record books must be preserved for 2 years from the date on which the last entry was made therein. Every prescription on which a Schedule 2 or 3 Controlled Drug is supplied must be sent to the relevant NHS agency in accordance with arrangements specified by that agency (Reg.23).

For Controlled Drugs in Schedules 3 and 5 to the Regulations, it is sufficient if every invoice is preserved for 2 years from the date on which it is issued. Producers and wholesalers must keep invoices in respect of Schedule 3 and 5 drugs obtained or supplied by them, and retail dealers must keep invoices in respect of the drugs they obtain. Copies of invoices (e.g. in a computerised form) may be retained in place of the original document (Reg.24).

Record-keeping requirements for Schedule 3 and 4 drugs

There are specific record-keeping requirements for those licensed to produce Schedule 3 or 4 drugs, those authorised to import or export Schedule 3

---

[37] Added by the Misuse of Drugs (Amendment No.2) (England, Wales and Scotland) Regulations SI 2012 No. 973 and amended by the Misuse of Drugs (Amendment) (No. 2) (England, Wales and Scotland) Regulations SI 2015 No. 891

[38] The Misuse of Drugs (Amendment) Regulations SI 2005 No. 271

[39] The Misuse of Drugs (Amendment No.2) (England, Wales and Scotland) Regulations SI 2012 No. 973

or 4 drugs and for specified persons (not, for example, patients, constables or carriers) who are authorised to possess or destroy, or cause to be destroyed, specified Schedule 4 cannabis-containing products, which possess a marketing authorisation issued by the MHRA.

Destruction of Controlled Drugs

Persons who are required to keep records in respect of Controlled Drugs in Schedule 1, 2, 3 or 4 may only destroy them in the presence of a person authorised (an 'authorised person'), either personally or as a member of a class, by the Secretary of State or an Accountable Officer. Authorised persons include police constables and GPhC inspectors and anyone appointed by an Accountable Officer (see below). An Accountable Officer cannot be an authorised person.

Particulars of the date of destruction and the quantity destroyed must be entered in the register of Controlled Drugs and signed by the authorised person in whose presence the drug was destroyed. The authorised person may, for the purposes of analysis, take a sample of the drug which is to be destroyed, and destruction must be carried out according to his/her directions.

A pharmacist or practitioner may destroy prescribed drugs returned by a patient or the patient's representative without legally being required to make any record and without the presence of an authorised person (but see 'Registers and records' above). However, it is suggested[40] that a second member of staff (preferably a registered health professional) should witness the destruction and disposal of these drugs.

The master of a ship or installation manager of an off-shore installation may not destroy any surplus drugs but may dispose of them to a constable or to a person who is lawfully entitled to supply them (i.e. to any pharmacist or licensed dealer who could have supplied them to him/her) (Reg.26).

Midwives and Controlled Drugs

A registered midwife who has, in accordance with the Nursing and Midwifery Order 2001, notified to the local supervising authority his/her intention to practise may, as far as is necessary for his/her professional practice, possess and administer or supply any Controlled Drug which medicines law permits him/her to administer. Supplies may only be made to him/her, or be possessed by him/her, on the authority of a midwife's supply order, that is, an order in writing specifying:

- the name and occupation of the midwife obtaining the Controlled Drug;
- the name of the person to whom it is to be administered or supplied;

[40]NICE (2016) Controlled drugs: safe use and management; NICE guideline [NG46]

- the purpose for which it is required and the total quantity to be obtained (Reg.11, as amended).[41]

It must be signed by the appropriate medical officer, which means:

1 a doctor who is for the time being authorised in writing for the purposes of Regulation 11 by the local supervising authority for the region or area in which the Controlled Drug was, or is to be, obtained; or

2 a person appointed under, and in accordance with, the Nursing and Midwifery Order 2001 by that authority to exercise supervision over registered midwives within his/her area.

A midwife may surrender any stocks of Controlled Drugs in his/her possession which are no longer required by him/her to the appropriate medical officer (Reg.11) or to the person from whom s/he obtained them (Reg.6).

The midwife must, on each occasion on which s/he obtains a supply of a Schedule 2 Controlled Drug, enter in a book kept by him/her solely for this purpose, the date, the name and address of the person from whom the drug was obtained, the name of the person to whom it is to be administered or supplied, the amount obtained and the form in which it was obtained. When administering or supplying such a drug to a patient, s/he must enter in the same book as soon as practicable the name and address of the patient, the name of the person to whom it was administered or supplied, the amount administered and the form in which it was administered (Reg.21). A midwife's supply order must be retained for 2 years by the pharmacist who supplies the Controlled Drug (not submitted to the relevant NHS service agency) and s/he must make an appropriate entry in his/her register of Controlled Drugs (Regs.19 and 22).

Requisitions

When a person (the supplier) other than a practitioner supplies a Schedule 1, 2 or 3 Controlled Drug otherwise than on a prescription or by way of administration, to a person authorised to possess that drug, s/he may do so only on receipt of a requisition in writing. The requisition must be signed by the recipient, stating his/her name, address and profession or occupation, and must specify the total quantity of the drug to be supplied and the purpose for which it is required. The supplier must be reasonably satisfied that the signature is that of the person purporting to have signed the requisition and that s/he is engaged in the profession or occupation stated (Reg.14(2)).

---

[41] Misuse of Drugs (Amendment) (No. 2) (England, Wales and Scotland) Regulations SI 2015 No. 891

The following persons are authorised to requisition a Controlled Drug via this mechanism:

- a practitioner;
- the person in charge or acting person in charge of a hospital, organisation providing ambulance services or care home;
- a person who is in charge of a laboratory;
- the owner of a ship or the master of a ship which does not carry a doctor among the seamen employed on it;
- the master of a foreign ship in a port in Great Britain;
- the installation manager of an off-shore installation;
- a supplementary prescriber;
- a nurse independent prescriber;
- a pharmacist independent prescriber; and
- a person who holds a certificate of proficiency in ambulance paramedic skills issued by, or with the approval of, the Secretary of State, or a person who is a registered paramedic.

Standard requisition forms are produced by the NHS. From 20 November 2015, it has been a legal requirement (in most cases) for these to be used for the requisitioning of Schedule 2 and 3 Controlled Drugs. Some transactions are exempt for the requirement to use a standardised requisition form, including where supplies are made to a hospital ward from a dispensary within the same hospital. Some hospital wards source their Controlled Drugs from other trusts or wards which do not form part of the same legal entity. In these cases, the standard form is required, although the Home Office has issued guidance[42] on the use of a 'bulk' or 'global' requisition.

A requisition is not required for the supply of:

- Schedule 4 or 5 drugs or poppy-straw;
- Schedule 3 drugs contained in or comprising a preparation which is required for use as a buffering agent in chemical analysis, has present in it both a substance specified in paragraph 1 or 2 of that Schedule and a salt of that substance and which is pre-mixed in a kit;
- any exempt product;
- any drug which is required for use in a prison or hospice;
- any drug, when supplied by a wholesale dealer to a registered pharmacy.

Other than in the case of a veterinary requisition, the supplier must mark the requisition (in ink or otherwise indelibly) with his/her name and address and send the original document to the relevant NHS agency. The Royal Pharmaceutical Society advise that it is good practice for pharmacies

[42]The Home Office (2015) Additional Guidance issued by the Home Office on the use of the mandatory requisition form for Schedule 2 and 3 controlled drugs.

to retain a copy of the requisition for 2 years from the date of supply. These requirements, as to marking the requisition and sending it to the relevant NHS agency, do not apply where the supplier is a wholesale dealer or a person responsible for the dispensing and supply of medicines at a hospital, organisation providing ambulance services, care home or prison.

Note that the Home Office have advised that a midwife's supply order should not be treated as a requisition for the purposes of these Regulations (see 'Midwives and Controlled Drugs' above).

Where a recipient is a practitioner who represents that s/he urgently requires a Controlled Drug for the purpose of his/her profession, the supplier, if s/he is reasonably satisfied that the practitioner requires the drug and is by reason of some emergency unable to furnish a written requisition, may deliver the drug on an undertaking by the practitioner to furnish a written requisition within the next 24 hours. Failure to do so is an offence on the part of the practitioner (Reg.14(2)).

A requisition furnished by the person in charge or acting person in charge of a hospital, organisation providing ambulance services or care home must be signed by a doctor or a dentist employed or engaged in that hospital, organisation or care home (Reg.14(5)).

A requisition furnished by the master of a foreign ship must contain a statement that the quantity of drug to be supplied is the quantity necessary for the equipment of the ship (Reg.14(5)) signed by the proper officer of the port health authority or, in Scotland, a health board competent person designated under section 3 of the Public Health etc. (Scotland) Act 2008 by the health board within whose jurisdiction the ship is.

An operating department practitioner, senior or acting senior registered nurse or registered midwife for the time being in charge of any ward, theatre or other department of a hospital, care home or prison who obtains a supply of a Controlled Drug from the person responsible for dispensing and supplying medicines at that hospital, care home or prison must furnish a requisition in writing signed by him/her which specifies the total quantity of the drug required. S/he must retain a copy or note of the requisition. The person responsible for the dispensing and supply of medicines must mark the requisition in such a manner as to show that it has been complied with and must retain the requisition in the dispensary (Reg.14(6)).

On occasion, a third party who is not, him/herself, authorised to possess the drug will be sent by the recipient (i.e. the person who is lawfully permitted to order the drug via a requisition) to collect the drug on his/her behalf. This third party is sometimes called a 'messenger', although this term is not found in the Regulations. Where such a messenger purports to have been sent on behalf of the recipient, then the drug may not be supplied to him/her until s/he furnish, to the supplier, a statement in writing signed by the recipient to the effect that s/he is empowered by the recipient to receive that drug on behalf of the recipient. The supplier must be reasonably satisfied that the document is genuine.

Accountable Officers

Regulations applicable in England and Scotland[43] and in Wales[44] provide for the appointment of Accountable Officers. The regulations across all three nations are broadly similar.

The Regulations provide that providers or designated bodies (i.e. bodies providing healthcare services) must nominate or appoint an Accountable Officer who is a fit, proper and suitable experienced person, to ensure the safe, appropriate and effective management and use of Controlled Drugs within organisations subject to their oversight. The Accountable Officer must not routinely supply or handle Controlled Drugs him/herself as part of his/her duties within his/her organisation.

The Regulations set out how Accountable Officers should be appointed, together with their responsibilities. The Accountable Officer must establish and operate appropriate arrangements for securing the safe management and use of Controlled Drugs, and review those arrangements as appropriate. His/her role extends either to his/her employing organisation or to those contracted to provide services on behalf of that organisation (e.g. community pharmacies contracted to provide services by a commissioning body) and includes duties to secure:

- the safe and effective use and management of Controlled Drugs within his/her own organisation and by any body or person providing services to his/her organisation;
- systems for assessing, investigating and recording concerns (including complaints) relating to the safe management or use of Controlled Drugs, and take action on well-founded concerns;
- incident reporting systems for untoward incidents relating to the safe management or use of Controlled Drugs;
- the implementation of up-to-date standard operating procedures in relation to the management and use of Controlled Drugs (see section on Standard operating procedures, below);
- that appropriate information, education or training is delivered to relevant individuals within the organisation, in relation to the required standard operating procedures;
- appropriate arrangements for monitoring and auditing the designated/provider body's management and use of Controlled Drugs;

---

[43] The Controlled Drugs (Supervision of Management and Use) Regulations SI 2013 No. 373
[44] The Controlled Drugs (Supervision of Management and Use) (Wales) Regulations SI 2008 No. 3239

- appropriate arrangements for the safe destruction and disposal of Controlled Drugs by his/her designated body;
- appropriate arrangements for ensuring the proper sharing of information, with relevant persons/bodies.

Accountable Officers have the right of access, to carry out periodic inspections of premises, to investigate concerns and to take action if there are well-founded concerns. Accountable Officers must always act to protect the safety of patients and the general public and are immune from civil action when sharing information if disclosure is made in good faith.

Standard operating procedures

One role of the Accountable Officer is to ensure that up-to-date standard operating procedures are in place, in relation to the management and use of Controlled Drugs. In Wales,[45] these must cover the following matters:

- who has access to the Controlled Drugs;
- where the Controlled Drugs are stored;
- security in relation to the storage and transportation Controlled Drugs as required by the misuse of drugs legislation;
- disposal and destruction of Controlled Drugs;
- who is to be alerted if complications arise;
- maintaining relevant Controlled Drugs registers under the misuse of drugs legislation;
- maintaining a record of Schedule 2 Controlled Drugs that have been returned by patients.

In England and Scotland[46] the Regulations state only that the standard operating procedures must cover (among other matters) best practice relating to:

- the prescribing, supply and administration of Controlled Drugs; and
- clinical monitoring of patients who have been prescribed Controlled Drugs.

Earlier Regulations,[47] which were repealed by the 2013 Regulations applicable in England and Scotland had contained a list similar to that currently found in the Regulations in force in Wales. This minimum list of standard operating procedures was removed in the new English/Scottish Regulations in order to reduce regulatory burdens. Instead, the development

---

[45] The Controlled Drugs (Supervision of Management and Use) (Wales) Regulations SI 2008 No. 3239

[46] The Controlled Drugs (Supervision of Management and Use) Regulations SI 2013 No. 373

[47] Controlled Drugs (Supervision of Management and Use) Regulations SI 2006 No. 3148

and dissemination of standard operating procedures lies with each organisation or group of organisations and at the discretion of the Accountable Officer.

Substance misusers

A person is regarded as being addicted to a drug 'if, and only if, s/he has, as a result of repeated administration, become so dependent upon that drug that s/he has an overpowering desire for the administration of it to be continued'.[48] The expression drug in this context means those specified in the Misuse of Drugs (Supply to Addicts) Regulations 1997 (as amended), namely:

1 cocaine, dextromoramide, diamorphine, dipipanone, hydrocodone, hydromorphone, levorphanol, methadone, morphine, opium, oxycodone, pethidine, phenazocine and piritramide;
2 any stereoisomeric form of a substance specified in item 1 above, except dextrorphan;
3 any ester or ether of a substance specified in item 1 or 2 above not being a substance for the time being specified in Part II of Schedule 2 to the Misuse of Drugs Act 1971;
4 any salt of a substance specified in any of item 1 to 3 above; and
5 any preparation or other product containing a substance or product specified in any of items 1 to 4 above.

Provisions for preventing misuse

The Secretary of State may make such regulations as appear to him/her necessary or expedient for preventing the misuse of Controlled Drugs (s.10). In particular s/he may make provisions that:

- require precautions to be taken for the safe custody of Controlled Drugs;
- impose requirements as to the documentation of transactions involving Controlled Drugs, and require copies of documents relating to such transactions to be furnished to the prescribed authority;
- require the keeping of records and the furnishing of information with respect to Controlled Drugs and in such circumstances and in such manner as may be prescribed;
- provide for the inspection of any precautions taken or records kept in pursuance of regulations under this section;
- relate to the packaging and labelling of Controlled Drugs;
- regulate the transport of Controlled Drugs and the methods used for destroying or otherwise disposing of such drugs when no longer required;

[48]The Misuse of Drugs (Supply to Addicts) Regulations SI 1997 No. 1001

- regulate the issue of prescriptions containing Controlled Drugs and the supply of Controlled Drugs on prescriptions, and require persons issuing or dispensing prescriptions containing such drugs to furnish to the prescribed authority such information relating to those prescriptions as may be prescribed;
- require any doctor who attends a person who s/he considers, or has reasonable grounds to suspect, is addicted (within the meaning of the Regulations) to Controlled Drugs of any description to furnish to the prescribed authority such particulars with respect to that person as may be prescribed; and
- prohibit any doctor from administering, supplying and authorising the administration and supply to persons so addicted, and from prescribing for such persons such Controlled Drugs as may be prescribed, except and in accordance with the terms of a licence issued by the appropriate authority in pursuance of the Regulations.

In addition to making regulations about safe custody, the Secretary of State may also, by notice in writing, require the occupier of any premises where Controlled Drugs are kept to take further precautions as specified in a written notice (s.11).

Information concerning misuse

Doctors, pharmacists and persons lawfully conducting retail pharmacy businesses in any area may be called upon to give particulars of the quantities of any dangerous or otherwise harmful drugs (not necessarily controlled under the Act) which have been prescribed, administered or supplied over a particular period of time. The Home Secretary may call for this information if it appears to him/her that a social problem, caused by such drugs, exists in that area.

A notice in writing may be served on the persons concerned specifying the period and requiring particulars of the drug to be furnished in such a manner and within such time as set out in the notice. Pharmacists may be required to give the names and addresses of the prescribing doctors but may not be required to identify the patients concerned. It is an offence to fail, without reasonable excuse, to give the information required or to give false information (s.17).

Prescribing for addicted persons

When prescribing for an addicted person, anyone who may prescribe Schedule 2 Controlled Drugs may administer or authorise the supply of cocaine, diamorphine or dipipanone, or the salts of any of these, for the purpose of treating organic disease or injury. However, only doctors may also prescribe these drugs to treat addiction and only if licensed to do so by the Secretary of State.[49]

There is provision for addicted persons to receive instalment prescriptions. In England, instalments can be dispensed on form FP10MDA. Schedule 2 Drugs, buprenorphine, buprenorphine/naloxone (Suboxone) and diazepam may be ordered on this form. In Wales, instalments of any Schedule 2, 3, 4 or 5 Controlled Drug may be ordered on form WP10MDA. Both FP10MDA and WP10MDA forms are limited to a maximum period of treatment of 14 days. The above are administrative arrangements made under the NHS and do not form part of the Misuse of Drugs Regulations. The prescriber must specify the instalment amount and the interval between each instalment. In Scotland, there is no specific form for instalments; they can be written on any prescription type. GPs can order instalments on the standard GP10 form, whilst hospital-based prescribers prescribing for substance misuse patients use form HBP(A). When using these forms to order instalments, prescribers indicate that such instalments are required by including instructions to that effect in the prescribing instructions. There are no legal limitations on the number of days' treatment that may be ordered (although good practice dictates that no more than 28 days should be supplied) and no limitations on the drugs that may be ordered, other than restrictions related to the prescribing of drugs as determined by the Scottish Drug Tariff.

Supply of articles for administering or preparing Controlled Drugs

In general, it is unlawful for a person to supply, or offer to supply, any article which may be used or adapted to be used in the unlawful preparation or administration of a Controlled Drug (s.9A).[50] It is not an offence to supply or offer to supply a hypodermic syringe, or any part of one.

Certain persons may, when acting in a professional capacity, supply or offer to supply the specified articles for administering or preparing Controlled Drugs (Reg.6A).[51] Those persons are:

- a practitioner
- a pharmacist

[49] Misuse of Drugs (Amendment No.2) (England, Wales and Scotland) Regulations SI 2012 No. 973
[50] Inserted by Drug Trafficking Offences Act 1986 (c.32)
[51] Added by Misuse of Drugs (Amendment No.2) (England, Wales and Scotland) Regulations SI 2012 No. 973

- a person employed or engaged in the lawful provision of drug treatment services
- a supplementary prescriber acting under and in accordance with the terms of a clinical management plan
- a nurse independent prescriber.

The articles that may be supplied or offered to supply are:

- a swab
- utensils for the preparation of a Controlled Drug
- citric acid or ascorbic acid
- a filter
- ampoules of water for injection, only when supplied, or offered for supply, in accordance with the Medicines Act and its Regulations.

In addition, a person employed or engaged in the lawful provision of drug treatment services may, when acting in that capacity, supply or offer to supply aluminium foil in the context of structured steps to engage a patient in a drug treatment plan, or which form part of a patient's drug treatment plan. Here, a 'drug treatment plan' means a written plan, relating to the treatment of an individual patient, and agreed by the patient and the person employed in the lawful provision of drug treatment services (Reg.6A).[52]

Safe custody of Controlled Drugs

The Regulations relating to safe custody apply to all Controlled Drugs, except for:

1 any drug in Schedule 4 or 5;
2 any liquid preparations, apart from injections, which contain any of the following:
   a amphetamine
   b benzphetamine
   c chlorphentermine
   d fenethylline
   e mephentermine
   f methaqualone
   g methylamphetamine
   h methylphenidate;

[52] Added by Misuse of Drugs (Amendment No. 2) (England, Wales and Scotland) Regulations SI 2014 No. 2081

    i phendimetrazine
    j phenmetrazine
    k pipradrol
    l any stereoisomeric form of a substance specified in any of paragraphs (a) to (k) above
   m any salt of a substance specified in any of paragraphs (a) to (l) above.

3 any of the following:

    a any 5,5-disubstituted barbituric acid
    b cathine
    c ethchlorvynol
    d ethinamate
    e mazindol
    f meprobamate
    g methylphenobarbitone (methylphenobarbital)
    h methyprylone
    i midazolam
    j pentazocine
    k phentermine
    l tramadol
   m any stereoisomeric form of a substance specified in (a) to (l) above
    n any salt of a substance specified in (a) to (m) above
    o any preparation or other product containing a substance or product specified in (a) to (n) above.

The premises to which the safe custody requirements apply are:

1 any premises occupied by a retail dealer for the purposes of his/her business; and

2 any care home within the meaning of the relevant legislation.

Retail dealer means a person lawfully conducting a retail pharmacy business or a pharmacist engaged in supplying drugs to the public at a health centre within the meaning of the Medicines Act 1968.

The occupier and every person concerned in the management of any of these premises must ensure that all Controlled Drugs (except those exempted, as mentioned above) are, so far as circumstances permit, kept in a locked safe, cabinet or room which is so constructed and maintained as to prevent unauthorised access to the drugs. This requirement does not apply in respect of any Controlled Drug which is for the time being constantly under the direct personal supervision of:

1 a pharmacist in the premises of a retail dealer (e.g. when dispensing prescriptions); or

2 in the case of a care home, the person in charge of the premises, or any member of his/her staff designated by him/her for the purpose.

Schedule 2 to the Regulations sets out detailed requirements as to the specifications (such as materials, construction, fixing, etc.) which apply to safes, cabinets and rooms in which Controlled Drugs are kept. The owner of a pharmacy may, as an alternative, elect to apply to the police for a certificate that his/her safes, cabinets or rooms provide an adequate degree of security. Applications must be made in writing. After inspection by the police, and if the degree of security is found to be adequate, a certificate, renewable annually, may be issued. The certificate may specify conditions to be observed and may be cancelled if there is a breach of any condition, if the occupier has refused entry to a police officer or if there has been any change of circumstances lowering the degree of security.

Apart from these special requirements, which affect only certain classes of premises, a person having possession of any Controlled Drug to which the safe custody regulations apply must ensure that, as far as circumstances permit, it is kept in a locked receptacle which can be opened only by him/her or by a person authorised by him/her. This requirement does not apply to a carrier in the course of his/her business or to a person engaged in the business of a postal operator when acting in the course of that business, or to a person to whom the drug has been supplied on the prescription of a practitioner for his/her own treatment or that of another person or an animal.

Psychoactive substances

The Psychoactive Substances Act 2016 creates a blanket ban on the production, distribution, sale and supply of psychoactive substances in the UK. Essentially, this Act makes substances which were formerly often referred to as 'legal highs' illegal. Under the Act, a *psychoactive substance* means any substance which is capable of producing a psychoactive effect in a person who consumes it, and is not an exempted substance. Exempted substances include Controlled Drugs, medicinal products, alcohol or alcoholic products, nicotine, tobacco products, caffeine or caffeine products and any substance which is ordinarily consumed as food or drink, and which does not contain a prohibited ingredient.

Summary

Table 16.3 summarises Controlled Drugs legislation.

Table 16.3 Summary of the Misuse of Drugs Regulations

	Schedule 1	Schedule 2	Schedule 3	Schedule 4, Part I	Schedule 4, Part II	Schedule 5
Administration	By licence only	To a patient by a doctor, dentist, nurse independent prescriber, pharmacist independent prescriber, supplementary prescriber (acting in accordance with a clinical management plan) or by any person acting in accordance with the directions of a person who is entitled to prescribe Controlled Drugs	To a patient by a doctor, dentist, nurse independent prescriber, pharmacist independent prescriber, supplementary prescriber (acting in accordance with a clinical management plan) or by any person acting in accordance with the directions of a person who is entitled to prescribe Controlled Drugs	To a patient by a doctor, dentist, nurse independent prescriber, pharmacist independent prescriber, supplementary prescriber (acting in accordance with a clinical management plan) or by any person acting in accordance with the directions of a person who is entitled to prescribe Controlled Drugs	To a patient by a doctor, dentist, nurse independent prescriber, pharmacist independent prescriber, supplementary prescriber (acting in accordance with a clinical management plan) or by any person acting in accordance with the directions of a person who is entitled to prescribe Controlled Drugs	No restriction
Import and export	By licence only	By licence only	By licence only	By licence only	By licence only, except if imported or exported by a person for self-administration	No restriction
Possession	By licence only	See section on Possession and supply	See section on Possession and supply	See section on Possession and supply	No restriction	No restriction
Supply	By licence only	See section on Possession and supply	See section on Possession and supply	See section on Possession and supply	See section on Possession and supply	See section on Possession and supply
Emergency supply	No	No	No, except phenobarbital for epilepsy	Yes	Yes	Yes

(Continued overleaf)

Table 16.3 *(continued)*

	Schedule 1	Schedule 2	Schedule 3	Schedule 4, Part I	Schedule 4, Part II	Schedule 5
Production	By licence only	Licence holders, pharmacists, practitioners and persons lawfully conducting a retail pharmacy business	Licence holders, pharmacists, practitioners and persons lawfully conducting a retail pharmacy business	Licence holders, pharmacists, practitioners and persons lawfully conducting a retail pharmacy business	Licence holders, pharmacists, practitioners and persons lawfully conducting a retail pharmacy business	Licence holders, pharmacists, practitioners and persons lawfully conducting a retail pharmacy business
Prescription requirements	Yes – by licensed persons only	Yes	Yes	Do not apply	Do not apply	Do not apply
Register	Yes	Yes	No register, but some classes of persons are required to keep records or invoices	No register, but some classes of persons are required to keep records or invoices	No register, but some classes of persons are required to keep records or invoices	No register, but some classes of persons are required to keep records or invoices

(Continued overleaf)

Table 16.3 *(continued)*

	Schedule 1	Schedule 2	Schedule 3	Schedule 4, Part I	Schedule 4, Part II	Schedule 5
Marking of containers	Yes	Yes	Yes (with the exception of some pre-mixed kits used for chemical analysis)	No	No	No
Destruction – requirement for an authorised witness and an entry in the Controlled Drugs register when destroyed in the pharmacy	Yes	Yes, but do not apply to drugs returned by patients	No, except if the pharmacy is engaged in manufacturing, compounding, importing or exporting such drugs	No, except if the pharmacy is engaged in manufacturing, compounding, importing or exporting such drugs	No, except if the pharmacy is engaged in manufacturing, compounding, importing or exporting such drugs	No
Safe custody requirements	Yes	Yes (except certain liquids, quinalbarbital [secobarbital]) (see section on Safe custody)	No (except buprenorphine, diethylpropion, flunitrazepam and temazepam) (see section on Safe custody)	No	No	No
Requisition requirements	Yes	Yes	No	No	No	No

Further reading

Department of Health (2013). Controlled Drugs (Supervision of management and use) Regulations 2013 Information about the Regulations.

NICE (2016). Controlled drugs: safe use and management; NICE guideline [NG46].

Royal Pharmaceutical Society (published annually). *Medicines Ethics and Practice: The Professional Guide for Pharmacists*. London: Royal Pharmaceutical Society (includes practice guidance on many of the topics in this chapter; free to members).

The Home Office (2015). Additional Guidance issued by the Home Office on the use of the mandatory requisition form for Schedule 2 and 3 Controlled Drugs.

Websites

Legislation (can be searched on year and SI number or title): http://www.legislation.gov.uk

Royal Pharmaceutical Society: http://www.rpharms.com (member access only; lists legal classifications of medicines and further practice guidance are included).

17

Veterinary medicines

Gordon Hockey

The Veterinary Medicines Regulations (VMRs)[1] set out the legal framework in the UK for the authorisation, marketing and supply of veterinary medicines. The Veterinary Medicines Directorate (VMD), an executive agency of DEFRA, licenses veterinary medicines and many of those involved in the supply chain, including manufacturers and wholesale dealers. The VMRs are issued under the European Communities Act 1972 and until recently have been annual. Unless otherwise stated, references relate to the current VMRs, which came into force on 1 October 2013.

A Veterinary Products Committee (VPC) provides scientific advice on any aspect of veterinary medicines requested by the VMD, on behalf of the Secretary of State. The Committee's main role is to provide advice on applications for marketing authorisations and animal test certificates (for clinical trials of veterinary medicines), and to monitor veterinary pharmacovigilance. The Veterinary Residues Committee provides advice on the residue surveillance programmes.

The VMD provides Veterinary Medicine Guidance notes on aspects of the VMRs as well as links to the relevant UK and EU legislation on its website (see the end of this chapter).

The European Medicines Agency (EMA) established by Regulation (EC) No. 726/2004 includes a veterinary medicines division, which carries out similar activities to the VMD, but on a European level, liaising with the VMD and other national authorities. The majority of current veterinary medicines are authorised at national level because they were authorised before the EMA was established or because they are not within its scope.

The regulations concerning the retail supply of veterinary medicines (Schedule 3 of the VMRs) are complicated by provision for two types of Prescription Only Medicine – those that may be prescribed by pharmacists and suitably qualified persons (SQPs) (as well as veterinary surgeons) and those that may be prescribed only by veterinary surgeons. This was

---

[1] The Veterinary Medicines Regulations SI 2013 No. 2033, as amended by SI 2014 No. 599

introduced to maintain a category of medicines that may be supplied by agricultural merchants and pharmacists without veterinary direction, while at the same time satisfying an EU requirement that all veterinary medicines for food-producing animals must be prescribed by a professional person.[2]

Scope of the Veterinary Medicines Regulations

The scope of the VMRs is broad, applying to all products considered to be veterinary medicines and most animals. Substances may be medicinal by presentation or function, even if they have not been authorised as veterinary medicines by the VMD or EMA.

A *veterinary medicinal product* (veterinary medicine) means (VMRs Reg.2):[3]

1 any substance or combination of substances presented as having properties for treating or preventing disease in animals; or
2 any substances or combination of substances which may be used in, or administered to, animals with a view to restoring, correcting or modifying physiological functions by exerting a pharmacological, immunological or metabolic action or by making a medical diagnosis.

In addition:

1 'animal' means all animals, other than man, and includes birds, reptiles, fish, molluscs, crustacea and bees'; and
2 'horse' means all species of Equidae and a horse is a food-producing animal unless it has been declared not intended for slaughter for human consumption in accordance with various 'passport' regulations.

The VMRs do not apply or do not apply fully to (VMRs Regs.3 and 15):

1 veterinary medicines based on radioactive isotopes;
2 a product intended for administration in the course of a procedure licensed under the Animal (Scientific Procedures) Act 1968, but if animals are to be put into the human food chain, the only products that may be administered are those within their marketing authorisation and those administered in accordance with an animal test certificate; and
3 inactivated autogenous vaccines, blood or blood products from an authorised blood bank and equine stem cell products from an authorised centre (subject to certain conditions).

---

[2] Articles 1 and 66 of Directive 2001/82/EC as amended by Directive 2004/28/EC of 31 March 2004; this was introduced into UK legislation with the first VMRs in 2005. (Prior to this date the relevant veterinary medicines legislation was primarily linked to the Medicines Act 1968.)
[3] VMRs Reg.2, originally from consolidated Directive 2001/82/EC, as amended by Directive 2004/28/EC

Offences

Offences under the VMRs include those relating to the manufacture, authorisation, marketing, prescription, retail supply and administration of veterinary medicines, as well those relating to the advertising and use of authorised
human medicines. There are also offences for unlawful importation or possession of veterinary medicines, which were strengthened with changes to the
2013 Regulations to tackle those persons not directly involved in unlawful
imports but who were profiting from them, and to distinguish between those
possessing products unlawfully for use only (such as animal owners) and
those possessing them for supply to others. The offences are set out at the
end of the regulations (VMRs, Reg.43) and the end of each Schedule of
the VMRs.

Particular offences include:

1 to place a veterinary medicine on the market unless that product has
a marketing authorisation granted by the Secretary of State (VMRs
Regs.43(a) and 4);

2 to administer a veterinary medicine to an animal unless;

a the product has a marketing authorisation for administration of the
product in the UK, or

b it is administered in accordance with Schedule 4 (cascade) or Schedule
6 (exemptions for small pet animals) (VMRs Regs.43(d) and 8);

3 to supply a veterinary medicine that has passed its expiry date (VMRs
Regs.43(c) and 7(2));

4 to open a package (including the outer package) before it has been
supplied to the final user, other than as permitted by Schedule 3 (VMRs
Regs.43(c) and 7(3)) (a pharmacist may break open any package
containing a veterinary medicine for the purposes of supply other than the
immediate packaging of an injectable product (VMRs Sch. 3 para. 10(5));

5 to supply a medicinal product authorised for human use for administration to an animal other than in accordance with a prescription given
by a veterinary surgeon for administration under the cascade (VMRs
Regs.43(c) and 7(4));[4]

6 to possess a veterinary medicine not supplied in accordance with Schedule
3 (VMRs Regs.43(c) and 7(5)), and to possess an unauthorised medicine
or possess it with the intention of supplying it to others, subject to various
exemptions including medicines supplied as part of the cascade (VMRs
Regs.43(r) and 26);

[4]This is a problem for pharmacists asked to sell P medicines (see chapter 6) for administration to animals, but the VMD has indicated it would not take issue with a pet owner using a
medicine commonly found in the home in an emergency and if advised by a veterinary surgeon;
VMD Guidance note on Cascade: Prescribing unauthorised medicines.

7 to import an authorised veterinary medicine contrary to the VMRs, but a pharmacist or a veterinary surgeon may import these and there are no restrictions on the importation of Authorised Veterinary Medicines on the General Sale List (AVM-GSL) (VMRs Regs.43(e) and 9); to import or be concerned with the importation of an unauthorised veterinary medicine (VMRs Regs.43(q) and 25); and

8 to advertise an authorised human medicine for administration to animals (VMRs Regs.43(f) and 10(2)); however, there is a limited exemption for wholesale dealers (see section on advertising of veterinary products).

Improvement notices (VMRs Reg.38) and seizure notices (VMRs Reg.41) must usually be made public (VMRs Reg.42) and prosecutions are reported in the VMD's Marketing Authorisations Veterinary Information Service (MAVIS), which is available on the VMD's website (see the end of this chapter). The most significant prosecution in recent years was reported in the VMD's Annual Review 2010/2011 (see box 17.1).

Box 17.1 The Eurovet case and illegal import

Eurovet convictions for the illegal importation and supply of veterinary medicines were reported in *VMD Annual Review 2010/2011*.

In July 2011, 13 people were convicted in Europe's largest illegal veterinary medicines business to date, which smuggled more than £6 million of veterinary medicines into the UK. The two ring-leaders were sentenced to 28 months' and 20 months' imprisonment. Other sentences varied from 13 months' imprisonment to suspended sentences and unpaid work. Investigations by the DEFRA Investigation Services began in 2006 and identified approximately 4000 customers of the company Eurovet; more than 20 tonnes of medicines were seized from the company's premises in Picardy. The VMD have stated that:

> The company in this case had no connection or involvement whatsoever with the bona-fide veterinary medicines company Eurovet Animal Health BV or its UK branch Eurovet Animal Health Limited, based in Cambridge.

Marketing authorisations (VMRs Part 2 and Sch. 1)

There are four types of marketing authorisation system: centralised, decentralised, multi-recognition and national. Applications for a European marketing authorisation through the centralised system are made to the EMA and the procedure is compulsory for veterinary medicines for use as growth or yield enhancers. Applications for veterinary medicines are evaluated through the Committee for Veterinary Medicines[5] and the decision to grant a marketing authorisation is made by the European Commission.

The decentralised scheme is available where the applicant wishes to license a product for more than one EU Member State, and the multi-recognition procedure applies where the medicine is authorised in one EU Member State already. The national scheme applies where registration is only required in one state. An application for a marketing authorisation for a medicinal product for animal use in any of the procedures must be accompanied by the appropriate particulars.[6]

A nationally approved veterinary medicine is approved for use in one Member State only. In the UK, the Secretary of State gives approval following a successful application assessed by the VMD and the VPC.

A product authorised by the VMD will have the letters or symbol 'Vm' followed by the authorisation number. A product authorised by the EMA will have an identifier in the form e.g. 'EU/2/01/011/001'.

Homoeopathic veterinary medicines (VMRs Sch. 1, Part 9 and Sch. 3, para. 10(4))

The VMRs set out a simplified marketing authorisation procedure for veterinary homoeopathic products and provide that a homoeopathic remedy may be prepared extemporaneously and supplied directly to the end user by a pharmacist in a registered pharmacy, provided that it is prepared in accordance with paragraph 63 of Schedule 1 of the VMRs. This states that the route of administration must be as described in the official *European Pharmacopoeia* or in a pharmacopoeia currently used officially in any Member State, and there must be a sufficient degree of dilution to guarantee the safety of the product and, in any event, it must not contain more than one part in 10 000 of the mother tincture.

Exemptions for small pet animals (VMRs Sch. 6)

These exemptions apply solely to aquarium animals (including fish kept in closed water systems), cage birds, ferrets, homing pigeons, rabbits, small rodents and terrarium animals. A veterinary product intended solely for one of these categories of pets may be placed on the market, imported, sold by retail or administered without a marketing authorisation provided that it complies with certain conditions, including the following:

[5] Established by EU Regulation 726/2004
[6] See, in particular, VMRs Schedule 1, Part 1, Reg.2(2), which refers to requirements set out in Council Directive 2001/82/EEC

1 the Secretary of State must approve the active substance in a veterinary medicine manufactured in accordance with the Schedule (approval is not given if the active substance requires veterinary control);

2 the product must not be an antibiotic;

3 the product must not contain any narcotic or psychotropic drug;

4 the product is not for treatments or pathological processes that require precise prior diagnosis, or the use of which may cause effects that impede or interfere with subsequent or therapeutic measures;

5 the product must comply with detailed labelling requirements set down in the Schedule; and

6 the method of administration must be oral or topical or (in the case of a product for fish) by addition to the water.

The manufacturer, importer or retailer must notify DEFRA within 15 days of learning of any serious adverse reaction to such a product and keep an appropriate record for 3 years; failure to comply is an offence.

Pharmacovigilance (VMRs Sch. 1, Part 8)

A marketing authorisation holder must have an appropriately qualified person for pharmacovigilance who resides in a EU Member State and whose responsibilities include establishing a system that ensures information about adverse events, for example adverse reactions, is collected and collated by the manufacturer. These are reported to the Secretary of State at least every 3 years or more frequently as appropriate, for example for newer veterinary medicines or serious adverse events.

The VMD manages the reporting of adverse events, relating to animals, humans or the environment associated with the use or misuse of products, as well as incidents following the implant of a microchip in an animal.

Classification of veterinary medicines (VMRs Sch. 3, para. 1): two types of Prescription Only Medicines

There are four main classes of veterinary medicine, two of which are classes of Prescription Only Medicines (POMs), the names of which indicate what they are and who can prescribe the medicine. They are:

1 POM-V: Prescription Only Medicines prescribed by a veterinary surgeon (or veterinary practitioner);

2 POM-VPS: Prescription Only Medicines prescribed by a veterinary surgeon, pharmacist or SQP;

3 NFA-VPS: non-food animal medicine (e.g. for pets) prescribed by a veterinary surgeon, pharmacist or SQP;

4 AVM-GSL: Authorised Veterinary Medicines on the General Sale List.

The Secretary of State must specify the classification of the veterinary medicine when granting a marketing authorisation but may vary it by compulsory variation or at the request of the holder of the authorisation. The classification rules are briefly:

1 products must be classified as POM-V:
   a if containing narcotic or psychotropic substances, or
   b for administration following a diagnosis or clinical assessment by a veterinary surgeon;
2 products must be classified as POM-V or POM-VPS:
   a for food-producing animals, subject to certain exceptions, for example where there is no risk to human or animal health as regards residues or the development of resistance to antimicrobial or anthelmintic substances even when the products are used incorrectly,
   b to avoid unnecessary risk for the target species, the person administering the product or the environment,
   c if the product may impede or interfere with subsequent diagnosis or therapeutic measures, or
   d if the product contains a new active substance that has not been included in an authorised veterinary medicine for 5 years.

A list of authorised veterinary medicines is available on the VMD website. The details of the classification and supply of veterinary medicines, wholesale dealers and sheep dip are set out in Schedule 3.

Wholesale supply of veterinary medicines (VMRs Sch. 3, Part 1, para. 2 and Part 2)

A wholesale dealer's authorisation is granted only if premises fulfil certain criteria and wholesale supplies are regulated as follows:

1 only a holder of a marketing authorisation, the holder of a manufacturing authorisation or the holder of a wholesale dealer's authorisation may supply veterinary medicine by wholesale or be in possession of it for that purpose;
2 a person described above may only supply to a person who may supply veterinary medicines either by wholesale or by retail;
3 if supply by wholesale supply is made to an SQP, the supply must be made to the SQP's approved premises;
4 a wholesale dealer may break open any package (other than the immediate package of a veterinary product);
5 it is irrelevant whether or not the supply is for profit; and
6 a retailer, such as a pharmacy, may supply another retailer with such products as necessary for the purpose of alleviating a temporary shortage that could be detrimental to animal welfare.

Retail supply of veterinary medicines (VMRs Sch. 3)

Retail supply means any supply other than to or from the holder of a wholesale dealer's authorisation, whether or not for payment, and, therefore, essentially is the supply of veterinary medicines to those who will administer them to animals (supplies to veterinary practices remain wholesale transactions). In this chapter, in context, retail supply and supply are used interchangeably. The four classes of products may be supplied by the following:

1 POM-V products may only be supplied by a veterinary surgeon or a pharmacist and must be supplied in accordance with a prescription from a veterinary surgeon.
2 POM-VPS products may only be supplied by a veterinary surgeon, pharmacist or a SQP and must be in accordance with a prescription from one of those persons.
3 NFA-VPS products may be supplied without a prescription but may only be supplied by a veterinary surgeon, a pharmacist or a SQP.
4 AVM-GSL products have no such supply restrictions (VMRs Sch. 3, para. 3).

Veterinary medicines that are also Controlled Drugs are subject to the Misuse of Drugs Act 1971 and associated Regulations.

Prescription and supply requirements (VMRs Sch. 3)

Prescription Only Medicine (POM-V) prescribed by a veterinary surgeon

A veterinary surgeon who prescribes a veterinary medicine classified as POM-V must first carry out a clinical assessment of the animal and the animal must be under his/her care; failure to do so is an offence. This seeks to ensure a degree of proximity between the prescribing veterinary surgeon and the animal treated. This does not apply in relation to the administration of such a product to a wild animal where the administration is authorised by the Secretary of State (VMRs Sch. 3, para. 4).

The Royal College of Veterinary Surgeons (RCVS) provides an interpretation of 'under his/her care' (or under their care) that is endorsed by the VMD as meaning:[7]

a the veterinary surgeon must have been given the responsibility for the health of the animal or herd by the owner or the owner's agent;
b that responsibility must be real and not nominal;

[7]RCVS supporting guidance to the Code of Conduct for veterinary surgeons on 'veterinary medicines' (no. 4), available on the RCVS website at the end of this chapter. VMD guidance called the 'Retail of veterinary medicines' implies acceptance of the RCVS interpretations of 'under their care' and clinical assessment'.

c the animal or herd must have been seen immediately before prescription or recently enough or often enough for the veterinary surgeon to have personal knowledge of the condition of the animal or current health status of the herd or flock to make a diagnosis and prescribe;

d the veterinary surgeon must maintain clinical records of that herd/flock/individual.

The RCVS interpretation was subject to judicial scrutiny in an appeal from the RCVS Disciplinary Committee to the Privy Council (box 17.2).

Box 17.2 The meaning of 'under the care of a veterinary surgeon'

Susie Macleod v The Royal College of Veterinary Surgeons (Appeal No. 88 of 2005)

The appeal concerned Mrs Macleod's vaccination clinic that was staffed by veterinary nurses and had no resident veterinary surgeon. The RCVS Disciplinary Committee found on the facts that veterinary medicines were prescribed and supplied to animals that were not under the care of a veterinary surgeon, as interpreted by the RCVS Guide (now Code) to Professional Conduct, and directed that her name be suspended from the register of veterinary surgeons. At the appeal, their Lordships said that the RCVS interpretation was clear and provided an accurate and helpful interpretation; and that 'the detailed findings made by (the RCVS Disciplinary Committee) and the expression of opinion contained in its judgment that (Mrs Macleod's) actions were capable of jeopardising animal welfare give sustainable grounds for reaching its ultimate decision...'. However, Mrs Macleod's appeal was successful for other reasons and the Privy Council reduced the direction that her name be suspended from the register to a reprimand.

Prescription Only Medicine (POM-VPS) prescribed by a pharmacist, suitably qualified person or veterinary surgeon

Any person who prescribes a POM-V or POM-VPS product (a pharmacist who supplies POM-VPS medicines is likely to have prescribed them) or supplies an NFA-VPS product must (VMRs Sch. 3, para. 7):

a before doing so, be satisfied that the person who will use the product is competent to do so safely, and intends to use it for a purpose for which it is authorised;

b when doing so, advise on its safe administration and any warnings or contra-indications on the label or package leaflet; and c not prescribe (or, in the case of a NFA-VPS product, supply) more than the minimum amount required for the treatment. (It is a defence to show the manufacturer does not supply a smaller container under its marketing authorisation and that the person prescribing or supplying is not authorised to break open the package before supply.)

In each case, a veterinary surgeon, pharmacist or SQP supplies veterinary medicines from registered premises which, if appropriate, can be removed from the relevant register (for pharmacists, the register of pharmacy premises is held by the GPhC).

Written prescriptions

A veterinary medicine classified as POM-V or POM-VPS must be prescribed, but a prescription may be oral or written. A written prescription is required if the medicine is supplied by a person other than the prescriber – the prescriber could be a veterinary surgeon, pharmacist or SQP, as appropriate and subject to the class of POM (VMRs Sch. 3, para. 5(1)). It is difficult to envisage what an oral prescription is, but it is suggested this is a term for the completeness of the legislation rather than any practical effect.

A written prescription must be in ink or other indelible format and must include (VMRs Sch. 3, para. 6):

a the name, address, and telephone number of the person prescribing the product;
b the qualifications enabling the person to prescribe the product;
c the name and address of the owner or keeper;
d the identity (including the species) of the animal or group of animals to be treated;
e the premises at which the animals are kept if this is different from the address of the owner or keeper;
f the date of the prescription;
g the signature or other authentication of the person prescribing the product;
h the name and amount of the product prescribed;
i the dosage and administration instructions;
j any necessary warnings;
k the withdrawal period if relevant; and
l if it is prescribed under the cascade, a statement to that effect.

A prescription for a POM-V or POM-VPS is valid for 6 months or such shorter period as may be specified in the prescription. If the medicine is also a Controlled Drug of Schedules 2, 3 or 4 of the Misuse of Drugs Regulations 2001[8] it is valid for only 28 days. If the prescription is a repeatable, it must

---

[8]The Misuse of Drugs Regulations 2001(as amended) SI 2001 No. 3998; relevant amending instruments are SI 2003 No. 1432 and 2005 No. 1653.

specify the number of times the product may be supplied (VMRs Sch. 3, para. 6(3) and (4)).

The person supplying the veterinary medicine may only supply the product specified on the prescription, must take all reasonable steps to be satisfied that the prescription has been written and signed by a person entitled to prescribe the product, and must take all reasonable steps to ensure that it is supplied to the person named on the prescription. It is an offence to alter a written prescription unless authorised to do so by the person who signed it (VMRs Sch. 3, para. 5(2) and (3)).

The practical reality of two categories of POM medicine

The two classes of POMs produce a mass of legislation, but the practical reality is simpler than the legislation suggests.

POM-V medicines are often prescribed and supplied by veterinary surgeons for the convenience of the animal owner. This does not involve a written prescription. Increasingly, pharmacists are competing for the retail supply business of POM-V medicines through, for example, internet pharmacies. This requires a veterinary surgeon's prescription which, in most cases, they have a professional responsibility to provide, usually charging a fee. The VMRs also provide that veterinary surgeons may also make retail supplies of POM-V medicines against the prescription of another veterinary surgeon in competition with pharmacists and other veterinary surgeons.

POM-VPS medicines are likely to be prescribed and supplied for retail by the same pharmacist or SQP, again without any written prescription. This is essentially a responsible supply function rather than true prescribing, which is evident when considering prescribing by veterinary surgeons. POM-VPS medicines may also be prescribed and supplied by veterinary surgeons who do not have the relevant animals under their care and have not made a clinical assessment of the animals before prescribing, which is what is required prior to prescribing a POM-V medicine. This is essentially a responsible supply function as well. However, in many cases a veterinary surgeon will have the animals under his/her care and will have made a clinical assessment as part of his/her professional practice and associated liabilities, and so will have prescribed in the true sense of the word even though the VMRs do not require this.

Prescriptions for Controlled Drugs

Prescriptions for Controlled Drugs (by veterinary surgeons) are subject to all the same requirements as those for other veterinary medicines, subject to the following:

1. a prescription for a Schedule 2 or 3 Controlled Drug must include a declaration by the veterinary surgeon that the drugs are prescribed for the

treatment of an animal or herd under his/her care (Reg. 6(3) of the Misuse of Drugs Regulations 2001, as amended);

2   a prescription for a Schedule 2 or 3 Controlled Drug must include the prescribing veterinary surgeon's RCVS registration number;

3   a prescription for a Schedule 2, 3 or 4 Controlled Drug is valid for only 28 days (from the date on the veterinary surgeon's prescription) (VMRs, Sch. 3, para 6(2)); for Schedule 2 and 3 drugs, the prescription must include the quantity of the drug in words and figures;

4   repeatable prescriptions are permitted only for Schedule 4 and 5 Controlled Drugs (VMD guidance suggests that the prescription may be repeat dispensed only within the 28 days that the prescription is valid for dispensing, although there does not appear to be any legal basis for this assertion);

5   in addition to the formal Controlled Drugs register, the VMD suggests that an informal running balance is kept for schedule 2 Controlled Drugs;

6   prescription and requisitions (which do not need to be in standard form as for human health prescriptions and requisitions) must be retained for 5 years on the premises from which they were supplied.

Whilst not legally required, it is suggested that pharmacists should follow similar practices and procedures for the collection of Controlled Drugs dispensed for human patients.

The cascade (VMRs Sch. 4)

Generally, the VMRs provide that only authorised veterinary medicines may be prescribed and administered to animals. The cascade system is the exception to this rule and provides a series of options for veterinary surgeons until there is an appropriate veterinary or human medicine to treat the animal. Thus, if there is no veterinary medicine (in the UK) for a condition, the veterinary surgeon responsible for the animal may, in particular to avoid unacceptable suffering, treat the animal concerned under the following cascade in the following order (VMRs Sch. 4, para. 1):

1   a veterinary product authorised in the UK for use with another animal species or for another condition in the same species; or

2   if and only if there is no such product that is suitable, either;
    a   a medicinal product authorised in the UK for human use, or
    b   a veterinary product not authorised in the UK but authorised in another Member State of the EC for use with any animal species (if for a food-producing animal, it must be a food-producing species); or

3   if there is no such product that is suitable, a veterinary product prepared extemporaneously by a pharmacist, a veterinary surgeon or a person holding a manufacturing authorisation authorising the manufacture of that type of product.

A veterinary medicine that is administered outside its marketing author-isation or has no marketing authorisation must be prescribed by a veterinary surgeon under the cascade (VMRs Part 1, Reg.8(b)). This includes medicinal products authorised for human use.

Unless the prescribing veterinary surgeon supplies or administers the veterinary medicine to the animal, the person supplying it, for example a pharmacist or another veterinary surgeon, must label the product with the following information (VMRs Sch. 3, para. 13):

1   the name and address of the pharmacy or veterinary surgery or approved premises supplying the product;
2   the name of the veterinary surgeon who prescribed it;
3   the name and address of the animal owner;
4   the identification (including the species) of the animal or group of animals;
5   the date of supply;
6   the expiry date of the product, if applicable;
7   the name or description of the product, which should include at least the name and quantity of the active ingredients;
8   the dosage and administration instructions;
9   any special storage precautions;
10 any necessary warnings for the user, target species, administration or disposal of the product;
11 the withdrawal period, if relevant; and
12 the words '*Keep out of reach of children*' and '*For animal treatment only*'.

A veterinary surgeon prescribing or administering a veterinary medicine to a food-producing animal must specify an appropriate withdrawal period (VMRs Sch. 4, para. 2(1)).

Supply by veterinary surgeons and pharmacists (VMRs Sch. 3, paras. 8, 9 and 10)

A veterinary surgeon supplying veterinary products must do so from a 'veterinary practice premises' registered with the RCVS under the VMRs (VMRs Reg.8); however, the premises is more of a base and supplies may be made, for example, while on domiciliary visits. A pharmacist may supply a veterinary product which is classified POM-V, POM-VPS or NFA-VPS from premises registered as a pharmacy or a veterinary practice and an SQP may supply those classified as POM-VPS or NFA-VPS from premises approved as SQP retailers' premises.

A veterinary surgeon or pharmacist supplying veterinary products (other than AVM-GSL) must be present when the product is handed over unless s/he authorises each transaction individually before the product is supplied and s/he is satisfied that the person handing it over is competent to do so.

A pharmacist may:

a supply veterinary products prepared extemporaneously in a pharmacy in accordance with the prescription of a veterinary surgeon;

b supply certain homoeopathic remedies prepared extemporaneously in a pharmacy provided they are supplied to the end-user; and

c may break open any package containing a veterinary medicine other than the immediate packaging of an injectable product.

The VMD runs a voluntary Accredited Internet Retailer (AIRS) Scheme to facilitate self-regulation of UK-based internet retailers selling veterinary medicines. The aim of the scheme is to ensure that animal owners buying veterinary medicines over the internet have appropriate advice from a veterinary surgeon, pharmacist or SQP and buy medicines authorised for use in the UK. Those registered with the VMD may display the AIRS logo. Details of the scheme are available on the VMD website (see the end of this chapter).

Any pharmacist involved in the retail supply of veterinary medicines, particularly if supplied via the internet, should be clear whether s/he is making the supply and, if so, from which type of premises.

Supply by suitably qualified persons (VMRs Sch. 3, para. 14)

A *suitably qualified person* is a person who is trained and registered to be able to sell a limited range of veterinary medicines and often works from a pet shop, saddler or agricultural merchant's premises. SQPs prescribe and supply veterinary medicines classified as POM-VPS and NFA-VPS.

The Secretary of State may recognise bodies that are suitable to maintain a register, for example the Animal Medicines Training Regulatory Authority.

The Secretary of State must be satisfied that the body:

1 has in place a system for ensuring that the person applying for registration has had adequate training to act as an SQP;

2 has adequate standards in deciding whether to register an SQP;

3 maintains a programme of continuing professional development (CPD) for persons registered with it; and

4 operates an adequate appeal system if it intends to refuse to register anyone with appropriate qualifications or to remove anyone from the register.

The supply of veterinary medicines by an SQP must take place from premises approved by the Secretary of State as being suitable for the storage and supply of such products. An SQP may also make supplies from a registered pharmacy or a registered veterinary practice premises. An SQP may break open any package (other than an immediate package) containing a veterinary product.

An SQP who supplies POM-VPS or NFA-VPS products must:

a hand over or dispatch the product personally;
b ensure that when the product is handed over or dispatched s/he is in a position to intervene if necessary; or
c check that the product allocated for supply is in conformity with a prescription and satisfy him/herself that the person handing over the product or dispatching it is competent so to do.

The list of registered SQPs and the premises approved for sales by the Secretary of State is available on the VMD website (see end of this chapter).

The Secretary of State has the power to remove the approval of SQP premises if they are no longer suitable for the storage and supply of veterinary medicines. An SQP who considers that his/her registered premises no longer complies with its approval conditions must notify the Secretary of State and failure to do so is an offence.

The Secretary of State has issued a *Code of Practice for SQPs* (VMRs Sch. 3, para. 14(7)) and the Animal Medicines Training Regulatory Authority, as a recognised body, must take appropriate action in accordance with its disciplinary code if an SQP registered with it does not comply with the Code. The Code of Practice sets out the standards which SQPs are expected to meet and supplements the legal requirements with other provisions relating to personnel, sale and storage arrangements, and standards of premises. The Code is available on the VMD website (see end of this chapter).

Records of receipt and supply for Prescription Only Medicines

Any person permitted to supply veterinary medicines, who sells or receives veterinary medicines classified as POM-V and POM-VPS, must keep all documents and/or the relevant information relating to the transaction that show (VMRs Part 3, Reg.23(1)):

1 the date;
2 the name of the product;
3 the batch number (except that, in the case of a product for a non-food-producing animal, this need only be recorded on the date s/he receives the batch or the date s/he starts to use it);
4 the quantity;
5 the name and address of supplier or recipient; and
6 if there is a written prescription, the name and address of the person who wrote the prescription and a copy of the prescription.

If the documents do not include this information, the person must make a record of the missing information as soon as reasonably practicable following the transaction, or make a record of the missing information as soon as reasonably practicable. The records must be kept for at least 5 years (VMRs Reg.23(3) and (4)).

There are strict record-keeping provisions relating to those who keep food-producing animals and veterinary surgeons who prescribe for them (VMRs Part 3).

Records and storage by wholesalers

An authorised wholesaler must keep detailed records of all incoming and outgoing sales including disposal for at least 3 years. These must include the (VMRs Reg.22):

1 date and nature of the transaction;
2 name of the product;
3 manufacturer's batch number;
4 expiry date;
5 quantity; and
6 name and address of supplier or recipient.

The wholesale premises must be weatherproof, secure and lockable, clean and free from contaminants. The wholesaler must have the services of technically competent staff and an effective recall system. The authorisation, which may cover more than one site, must list the type of products dealt with, where they are stored, the name and address of the person holding the authorisation, the address of the premises and the name of the qualified person under the relevant provisions (VMRs Sch. 3, Part 2).

Annual audit (VMRs Sch. 3, para. 15)

At least once a year, every person entitled to supply veterinary products on prescription must carry out a detailed audit, and incoming and outgoing products must be reconciled with products currently held in stock, and any discrepancies recorded.

Exemptions for horses (VMRs Sch. 4 para. 3)

Horses in the UK must have a passport that indicates whether the horse is intended for human consumption (food producing) or not intended for human consumption. All horses should be treated with veterinary medicines which have a UK marketing authorisation for use in horses as the first choice. If there is no suitable authorised medicine available, for animals under their care, a veterinary surgeon may prescribe an alternative medicine under the cascade. However, a food-producing horse may only be treated with:

a a veterinary medicine that contains an active substance in the legally permitted essential substances list for such horses;

b a veterinary medicine that contains an active substance listed in table 1 of Commission Regulation 37/2010 on pharmacologically active substances and their classification regarding medicine residue limits in foodstuffs of animal origin.

If a food-producing horse is treated with a veterinary medicine that is not on one of these lists, it must be permanently excluded from the food chain and the relevant declaration signed in the passport. VMD guidance on horse medicines and record-keeping requirements provides further information.

Advertising of veterinary products (VMRs Reg.10)

It is an offence to advertise a veterinary medicine if the advertisement is misleading or carries a claim not in the Summary of Product Characteristics. It is also an offence to advertise a human medicine for administration to animals, including sending a price list of human medicines or the medicines to a veterinary surgeon or veterinary practice. There is a defence for publishers (VMRs Reg.12). However, a wholesaler may send a list of human medicines with prices to a veterinary surgeon provided that the list has been requested by the veterinary surgeon and the list states clearly that the products do not have a marketing authorisation as a veterinary product, and may only be prescribed and administered under the cascade.

Advertising of Prescription Only Medicines (VMRs Reg.11)

Regulation 11 of the VMRs covers both products classified as POM-V and those classified as POM-VPS. It is an offence to advertise veterinary medicines that are available on a veterinary prescription only or contain psychotropic drugs or narcotics.

In the case of POM-V medicines, the prohibition does not apply to price lists or to advertisements aimed at veterinary surgeons, veterinary nurses, pharmacists or (except antimicrobials) professional keepers of animals.

In the case of POM-VPS medicines, the prohibition does not apply to price lists or to advertisements aimed at veterinary surgeons, pharmacists, registered SQPs, other veterinary healthcare professionals or professional keepers of animals.

Importation of veterinary medicines (VMRs Reg.9)

Authorised veterinary medicines may be imported into the UK only by:

1 the holder of the marketing authorisation for the veterinary medicine;
2 the holder of a relevant manufacturing authorisation;
3 an authorised wholesale dealer provided that the authorisation covers the product and the holder of the marketing authorisation has been notified in writing in advance of the importation;
4 a veterinary surgeon or pharmacist; and
5 a SQP appropriately registered, but only for veterinary medicines that s/he may supply.

There are no restrictions on the importation of AVM-GSL products.

Unauthorised veterinary medicines may be imported into the UK in limited circumstances (VMRs Reg.25) This includes importation by a veterinary surgeon of such products, in accordance with an appropriate certificate granted by the Secretary of State, for the purpose of administration under the cascade to animals that are the responsibility of the veterinary surgeon. The product may be imported by the veterinary surgeon personally or by using a wholesale dealer or pharmacist acting as his agent.

Labelling requirements for veterinary medicines (VMRs Sch. 1, Part 7)

All labels and leaflets must be in English but may contain other languages provided that they give identical information in all languages. The regulations require the following information to appear in legible characters on the manufacturer's immediate packaging:

1 the name, strength and pharmaceutical form of the veterinary medicine;
2 the name and strength of each active substance, and of any excipient, if this is required under the Summary of Product Characteristics;
3 the route of administration (if not immediately apparent);
4 the batch number;
5 the expiry date;
6 the words 'for animal treatment only' and if appropriate 'to be supplied only on a veterinary prescription';
7 the contents by weight, volume or number of dose units;
8 the marketing authorisation number;
9 the name and address of the marketing authorisation holder or, if there is a distributor authorised in the marketing authorisation, the distributor;
10 suitably labelled space to record a discard date (if relevant);
11 the target species;
12 the distribution category;

13 the words '*keep out of reach of children*';

14 storage instructions;

15 the in-use shelf-life (if appropriate);

16 for food-producing species, the withdrawal period for each species or animal product concerned;

17 any warning specified in the marketing authorisation;

18 disposal advice;

19 full indications;

20 dosage instructions;

21 contra-indications;

22 further information required by the marketing authorisation; and

23 if the product is one where the dose needs to be specified for the animal being treated, a space for this.

If all these are on the immediate package, there is no necessity for any out-packaging or a package leaflet (VMRs Sch. 1, Part 7, para. 48(2)).

In the case of reduced labelling, the full information must be on the outer packaging and if this is not practicable then in a leaflet accompanying the product (VMRs Sch. 1, Part 7, para. 49(4)). If it is not reasonably practicable to have all the required information on the immediate or outer packaging, the leaflet must contain all the information in 1–23 as above except the expiry date and the batch number (VMRs Sch. 1, Part 7, para. 50(1)).

Labelling of ampoules (VMRs Sch. 1, Part 7, para. 51)

For containers such as ampoules or other unit dose forms, where the container cannot bear legibly the required information, the following information must be shown on the immediate package:

1 the name of the veterinary medicine;

2 the name and strength of the active ingredient;

3 the route of administration, if not immediately apparent;

4 the batch number;

5 the expiry date; and

6 the words '*for animal treatment only*' or, if appropriate, '*to be supplied only on a veterinary prescription*'.

The outer packaging must contain all the required information and if this is not reasonably practicable, a package leaflet may be required, but the ampoule need not refer to it.

Small containers other than ampoules (VMRs Sch. 1, Part 7, para. 52)

For small immediate packaging containing a single dose, other than ampoules, on which it is impossible to give the required information the immediate package must be labelled with the batch number and the expiry date.

Dispensed medicines (VMRs Sch. 3, para. 12)

If a veterinary medicine is prescribed (and supplied) in accordance with the marketing authorisation, no additional labelling is required by the VMRs, and it is an offence if any of the relevant information is not clearly visible at the time of supply. There is no offence if a veterinary surgeon amends the product label or a pharmacist amends the label in accordance with a prescription from a veterinary surgeon, for example by adding a dispensing label, provided that the manufacturer's information remains clearly visible.

If a veterinary medicine is supplied in a container other than that specified in the marketing authorisation, the container must be suitably labelled by the veterinary surgeon or pharmacist and additional information supplied (which may include a copy of the Summary of Product Characteristics or the package leaflet) to enable the product to be used safely.

If a veterinary medicine is supplied under the cascade, a dispensing label is required (see The cascade above).

Sale of sheep dips (VMRs Sch. 3, Part 2)

Any veterinary medicine that is a sheep dip must be used by, or under the supervision and in the presence of, a person qualified to use sheep dip, a person who holds either:

- a Certificate of Competence in the Safe Use of Sheep Dips showing that Parts 1 and 2 of the assessment referred to in the certificate have been satisfactorily completed; or
- National Proficiency Tests Council Level 2 Award in the Safe Use of Sheep Dip (Qualification and Credit Framework).

The certificate must be issued by a specified authority (VMRs Sch. 3, Part 3, para. 23). The sale of sheep dip must be to a person (or to a person acting on his/her behalf) who is qualified to use it. The supplier must keep a record of that person's certificate number as soon as is reasonably practicable and retain it for 3 years from the date of the sale.

If the active ingredient is an organophosphorus compound, the supplier must give to the buyer:

- a double-sided laminated notice meeting the specification set out in the regulations as to advice on sheep dipping (unless the notice has been provided to the buyer within the previous 12 months and the supplier knows or has reasonable cause to believe the buyer still has it available for use); and

- two pairs of gloves, either as described in the notice or providing demonstrably superior protection to the user against exposure to the dip than would be provided by the gloves described.

The notice must be at least A4 size with laminated cover and must tell the reader:

1 to read and act in accordance with instructions, including instructions on measuring and diluting concentrate;
2 that sheep dip is absorbed through the skin and always to wear the recommended protective clothing including gloves and have a spare set of clothing;
3 always to wash protective clothing before taking it off; and
4 to direct any questions to the supplier or manufacturer.

The notice must also contain a diagram showing recommended protective clothing.

Medicated feeding stuffs and specified feed additives (VMRs Sch. 5)

The rules relate to the use of veterinary medicines and specified feed additives (products used in animal nutrition for the purposes of improving the quality of the feed, the quality of food from animal origin or to improve the animals' performance and health).

The rules cover the incorporation of a veterinary medicine or a specified feed additive into a premixture, the incorporation of a veterinary medicine or a premixture into a feeding stuff, and top dressing with a veterinary medicine. There are different approvals for feed businesses depending on the activity covered. The details are set out in the VMRs, Schedule 5.

Fair trading

A set of Fair Trading regulations (FT Regs.) concerning supply and prescribing of veterinary medicines was issued by the Department of Trade and Industry under competition law,[9] which for 3 years between 31 October 2005 and 30 October 2008 prohibited a veterinary surgeon from charging a client a fee for a prescription (FT Reg.3(2)). Whilst this is no longer in force, the regulations continue to provide that:

1 a veterinary surgeon may not discriminate between a client to whom s/he provides a prescription and a client to whom s/he does not as far as the price s/he charges for any relevant veterinary medicine (broadly veterinary

[9]The Supply of Relevant Veterinary Medicinal Products Order 2005 SI 2005 No. 2751

medicines classified as POM-V) and fees for supplying services other than the giving of a prescription (FT Reg.6); and

2 a manufacturer or wholesaler may not discriminate unreasonably between veterinary surgeons and pharmacists (FT Reg.4) in:

   a the price that they charge for the supply of a relevant veterinary medicine,

   b any discount or rebate in connection with such a supply, or

   c any other terms or conditions upon which they supply.

In addition, a manufacturer must, at intervals of not more than 3 months, notify in writing the relevant veterinary surgeon and pharmacist of the net price at which s/he supplies veterinary medicines. Net price means the list price less any discount and should state whether it includes VAT (FT Reg.4). It is unlawful for a veterinary manufacturer or veterinary wholesaler to discriminate unreasonably between veterinary surgeons and pharmacists in the price they charge for relevant veterinary medicinal products, any discount or rebate given in connection with the supply or other terms and conditions of the supply (FT Reg.6). The Competition and Markets Authority may request any relevant information from the main classes of persons involved in the supply of veterinary medicines (FT Reg.7) and monitors the market to ensure that it is working properly.

Summary

- Veterinary surgeons may administer or supply by retail any veterinary medicine.
- There are four classes of veterinary medicines, two of which are prescription only:

  1 POM-V medicines:

     a may be prescribed by a veterinary surgeon provided that the relevant animal or herd is under his/her care and s/he first carries out a clinical examination of the animals; these terms are interpreted by the RCVS,

     b may be supplied by the prescribing veterinary surgeon or, in accordance with a written prescription, by another veterinary surgeon or a pharmacist;

  2 POM-VPS products:

     a may be prescribed by a veterinary surgeon, pharmacist or SQP,

     b may be supplied by the prescriber or, in accordance with a written prescription, by another prescriber – veterinary surgeon, pharmacist or SQP.

- There are detailed rules governing supply, administration and advertising of authorised human medicines, which may in particular circumstances be used to treat animals.
- Generally, the authorised veterinary medicine (species and condition) must be used, and if there is none, the cascade system provides for the prescription and administration of medicines (including human medicines) for a species and/or condition for which they are not authorised.
- Details are laid down for the registration and training of SQPs and the premises from which they may supply veterinary medicines.
- Pharmacists and veterinary surgeons must supply veterinary medicines from registered premises.
- Fair trading rules exist to allow pharmacists and veterinary surgeons to compete for the retail supply of prescribed POM-V and POM-VPS medicines.

Further reading

Kayne S (2011). *An Introduction to Veterinary Medicines*. Glasgow: Saltire Books.

Veterinary Medicines Directorate (2011) *Veterinary Medicines Guidance Notes*. London: Veterinary Medicines Directorate: https://www.gov.uk/government/collections/veterinary-medicines-guidance-notes-vmgns (accessed 4 September 2016).

Veterinary Medicines Directorate (2012) *Veterinary Medicines Advice for Pharmacists*. London: Veterinary Medicines Directorate: https://www.gov.uk/government/publications/veterinary-medicines-advice-for-pharmacists (accessed 4 September 2016).

Veterinary Medicines Regulations (2011) SI 2011 No. 2159: http://www.legislation.gov.uk/uksi/2013/2033/contents/made (accessed 4 September 2016).

Websites

Animal Medicines Training and Regulatory Authority: http://www.amtra.org.uk

Department for Environment, Food and Rural Affairs: https://www.gov.uk/government/organisations/department-for-environment-food-rural-affairs

Legislation (can be searched on year and SI number or title): http://www.legislation.gov.uk

Royal College of Veterinary Surgeons: http://www.rcvs.org.uk

Veterinary Medicines Directorate: https://www.gov.uk/government/organisations/veterinary-medicines-directorate

18

Poisons, denatured alcohols and chemicals

Karen Pitchford

Non-medicinal poisons: legal framework

The Poisons Act 1972 was substantially amended by the Deregulation Act 2015,[1] the relevant parts of which were brought into force by the Deregulation Act 2015 (Poisons and Explosives Precursors) (Consequential Amendments, Revocations and Transitional Provisions) Order 2015).[2] Rather than being concerned solely with Poisons, the Act is now concerned with the sale of 'regulated' and 'reportable' substances. The Poisons Act does not extend to Northern Ireland. The previously existing Poisons Board was abolished under this new legislation and the previous Poisons Rules and Poisons List Order were revoked.

A *regulated substance* means a regulated explosives precursor or a regulated poison and a *reportable substance* means a reportable explosives precursor or a reportable poison.

Schedule 1A to the Act (see Appendix 3) lists the regulated and reportable substances, which are defined as follows:

- A 'regulated poison' is a substance listed in Part 2 of Schedule 1A in a concentration higher than the limit (if any) set out for that substance in that Part.
- A 'reportable poison' is a substance listed in Part 4 of Schedule 1A in a concentration higher than the limit (if any) set out for that substance in that Part.
- A 'regulated explosives precursor' is a substance listed in Part 1 of Schedule 1A in a concentration higher than the limit set out for that substance in that Part.
- A 'reportable explosives precursor' is a substance listed in Part 3 of Schedule 1A.

[1] The Deregulation Act 2015
[2] SI 2015 No. 968

Each of the above definitions includes a mixture, or another substance in which a substance listed in the relevant Part is present in a concentration higher than the relevant limit (if such a limit is specified).

Exemptions from control under the Poisons Act

Some substances or mixtures are excluded from the above definitions; namely if they are:

a a medicinal product as defined by Regulation 2 of the Human Medicines Regulations 2012;[3]

b an investigational medicinal product as defined by Regulation 2 of the Medicines for Human Use (Clinical Trials) Regulations 2004;[4]

c a substance to which Part 12 of the Human Medicines Regulations 2012 or Part 6 of the Medicines for Human Use (Clinical Trials) Regulations 2004 applies by virtue of an order under section 104 or 105 of the Medicines Act 1968 (whether applying subject to exceptions and modifications or not and, in the case of an order under section 104, whether the substance is referred to in the order as a substance or an article);

d a veterinary medicinal product as defined by Regulation 2 of the Veterinary Medicines Regulations 2013;[5]

e contained in a 'specific object', which means:

  i an object that, during production, is given a special shape, surface or design that determines its function to a greater degree than does its chemical composition, or

  ii an article that contains explosive substances or an explosive mixture of substances designed to produce heat, light, sound, gas or smoke, or a combination of such effects through self-sustained exothermic chemical reactions, including pyrotechnic equipment falling within the scope of Council Directive 96/98/EC on marine equipment, and percussion caps intended specifically for toys falling within the scope of Council Directive 88/378/EEC concerning the safety of toys;

f listed as being exempt in the Schedule to the Control of Poisons and Explosives Precursors Regulations 2015.[6] This includes substances or articles subject to general exemptions (such as adhesives, builders' materials or cosmetic products) and those subject to special exemptions (such as barium chloride when contained in a fire extinguisher). See tables 18.1 and 18.2 for a full list.

[3] Human Medicines Regulations SI 2012 No. 1916
[4] Medicines for Human Use (Clinical Trials) Regulations SI 2004 No. 1031
[5] Veterinary Medicines Regulations SI 2013 No. 2033
[6] SI 2015 No. 966

Table 18.1 Items exempt from control under the Poisons Act 1972: general exemptions

Adhesives; anti-fouling compositions; builders' materials; ceramics; cosmetic products; distempers; electrical valves; enamels; explosives; fillers; fireworks; fluorescent lamps; flux in any form for use in soldering; glazes; glue; inks; lacquer solvents; loading materials; matches; medicated animal feeding stuffs; motor fuels and lubricants; paints; photographic paper; pigments; plastics; propellants; rubber; varnishes; vascular plants and their seeds

Table 18.2 Items exempt from control under the Poisons Act 1972: specific exemptions for poisons contained in specified substances or articles

Poison	Substance or article in which exempted
Ammonia	Substances not being solutions of ammonia or preparations containing solutions of ammonia; substances containing less than 10%, weight in weight, of ammonia; refrigerators
Arsenic; its compounds	Pyrites ores or sulfuric acid containing arsenic or compounds of arsenic as natural impurities; in reagent kits or reagent devices, supplied for medical or veterinary purposes, substances containing less than 0.1%, weight in weight, of arsanilic acid
Barium, salts of	Witherite other than finely ground witherite; barium carbonate bonded to charcoal for case hardening; fire extinguishers containing barium chloride; sealed smoke generators containing not more than 25%, weight in weight, of barium carbonate
Bromomethane	Fire extinguishers
Formaldehyde	Substances containing less than 5%, weight in weight, of formaldehyde; photographic glazing or hardening solutions
Formic acid	Substances containing less than 25%, weight in weight, of formic acid
Hydrochloric acid	Substances containing less than 10%, weight in weight, of hydrochloric acid
Hydrogen cyanide	Preparations of wild cherry; in reagent kits supplied for medical or veterinary purposes, substances containing less than the equivalent of 0.1%, weight in weight, of hydrogen cyanide
Methomyl	Solid substances containing not more than 1%, weight in weight, of methomyl
Nicotine; its salts; its quaternary compounds	Tobacco; in cigarettes, the paper of a cigarette (excluding any part of that paper forming part of or surrounding a filter), where that paper in each cigarette does not have more than the equivalent of 10 milligrams of nicotine; preparations in aerosol dispensers containing not more than 0.2% of nicotine, weight in weight; other liquid preparations, and solid preparations with a soap base, containing not more than 7.5% of nicotine, weight in weight

(continued overleaf)

Table 18.2 *(continued)*	
Poison	**Substance or article in which exempted**
Oxamyl	Granular preparations
Oxydemeton-methyl	Aerosol dispensers containing not more than 0.25%, weight in weight, of oxydemeton-methyl
Phenols	Liquid disinfectants and antiseptics containing less than 0.5% phenol and containing less than 5% of other phenols Motor fuel treatments not containing phenol and containing less than 2.5% of other phenols; in reagent kits supplied for medical or veterinary purposes Solid substances containing less than 60% of phenols; In tar oil distillation fractions containing not more than 5% of phenols
Phosphoric acid	Substances containing phosphoric acid, not being descaling preparations containing more than 50%, weight in weight, of ortho-phosphoric acid
Potassium hydroxide	Substances containing the equivalent of less than 17% of total caustic alkalinity expressed as potassium hydroxide; accumulators; batteries
Sodium fluoride	Substances containing less than 3% of sodium fluoride as a preservative
Sodium hydroxide	Substances containing the equivalent of less than 12% of total caustic alkalinity expressed as sodium hydroxide
Sodium silicofluoride	Substances containing less than 3% of sodium silicofluoride as a preservative

The Act follows the definitions of the Medicines Act for 'persons lawfully conducting a retail pharmacy business' and a 'registered pharmacy' (chapter 5).

Powers of the Secretary of State

The Secretary of State has powers to make regulations to amend parts of the Poisons Act, including powers to make different provision for different purposes, to make consequential, incidental or supplemental provision, and to make transitional, transitory or saving provision. These include powers to amend Schedule 1A, whether to add, vary or remove a substance or concentration limit or make any other change. It is intended that, in determining the distribution of substances between the various Parts of Schedule 1A, substances should be allocated to Parts 3 and 4 (and so be 'reportable' rather than 'regulated') if they are in common use, or are likely to come into common use, for purposes other than the treatment of human ailments, and it is reasonably necessary to include them in one of those Parts if members of the general public are to have adequate facilities for obtaining them.

The Secretary of State is, further, empowered to make regulations to disapply some or all of the requirements of the Poisons Act or to apply exclusions in specified circumstances.

Inspection and enforcement

It is the duty of the GPhC to secure compliance with the provisions of the Poisons Act 1972 by registered pharmacists and persons carrying on a retail pharmacy business. This is achieved by the GPhC inspectorate (chapter 20).

An inspector appointed by the GPhC may at all reasonable times:

a enter any registered pharmacy to ascertain whether an offence relating to the Poisons Act has been committed by a pharmacist or a person carrying on a retail pharmacy business;

b enter any premises in which the inspector has reasonable cause to suspect that a breach of the law has been committed in respect of any regulated poison; whether in a retail pharmacy business or any other premises, an inspector has power to make such examination and inquiry and to do such other things (including the taking, on payment, of samples) as may be necessary to ascertain that the Act is being complied with.

It is an offence for any person wilfully to delay or obstruct an inspector, to refuse to allow a sample to be taken, or to fail, without reasonable excuse, to give any information which the Poisons Act requires him/her to give to an inspector. It is specifically provided that nothing in the Poisons Act authorises an inspector to enter or inspect the premises of a doctor, a dentist, a veterinary surgeon or a veterinary practitioner unless those premises are a shop.

Penalties and legal proceedings

Section 8 of the Act sets out the various penalties that apply in the case of a breach of the Act. These include terms of imprisonment and/or fines, which vary according to the nature of the offence and the country (England and Wales or Scotland) in which it is tried. In the case of proceedings against a person under the Poisons Act in connection with the supply of a regulated or reportable substance, where the act in question was done by an employee, it is not a defence that the employee acted without the authority of the employer and any material fact known to the employee is deemed to have been known to the employer.

Information in respect of any offence under the Poisons Act must be laid within 12 months of the commission of the offence. There is an additional provision that the Secretary of State may institute proceedings within a period of 3 months after the date on which evidence sufficient in his/her opinion to justify a prosecution for an offence comes to his/her knowledge.

For England and Wales, sections 8, 17 and 18 of the Police and Criminal Evidence Act 1984 (powers of entry and search) apply in relation to certain offences under the Poisons Act.

For certain offences under the Act it is a defence for the accused to prove that s/he did not know, did not suspect or had no reason to suspect the existence of some fact (alleged by the prosecution) that the prosecution relies on to prove that s/he committed the offence. This defence operates where the accused proves (on a balance of probabilities) that s/he lacked the necessary knowledge.

Sale and supply of regulated substances

Requirement for a licence

Members of the general public require a licence, or a recognised non-GB licence (called 'licences' from hereon), in order to lawfully import, acquire, possess or use a regulated substance (i.e. a substance included in Part 1 or Part 2). 'Use' in this context includes processing, formulating, storing, treating or mixing a regulated substance or including one in the production of an article. The licence may permit, and will specify, which of these activities is or are permitted with respect to one or more of the regulated substances.

A 'member of the general public' means an individual who is acting (alone or with others) for purposes not connected with his/her trade, business or profession or the performance by him/her of a public function. Business-to-business transactions are exempt from the requirement to hold a licence.

Licences issued in Great Britain are granted by the Secretary of State and each licence is valid for a maximum of 3 years, although individuals may apply to renew their licence and the Secretary of State has powers to vary, suspend or revoke the licence before it expires. In deciding whether to grant or amend a licence with respect to a substance, the Secretary of State must have regard to all the circumstances of the case, including in particular:

a the use intended to be made of the substance;
b the availability of alternative substances that would achieve the same purpose;
c the proposed arrangements to ensure that the substance is kept securely;
d any danger to public safety or public order that may be caused by possession of the substance; and
e whether the applicant is a fit and proper person to possess the substance.

If there are reasonable grounds for doubting the legitimacy of the use intended to be made of the substance or the intentions of the user to use the substance for a legitimate purpose, the Secretary of State must in any event refuse the application so far as it relates to that substance.

A licence may be granted or amended subject to such terms and conditions as may be specified in the licence. Such terms and conditions may relate to the storage, use, maximum quantities or maximum levels of concentration that may be purchased and the reporting of disappearances or thefts.

The Secretary of State may, by regulations, make provision about the procedure for applying for and determining applications for the grant or amendment of licences under this section, including provision as to:

a who may make an application;
b the form and manner in which an application is to be made and any documents or evidence that must accompany it;
c the amount and payment of any fees;
d the supply of any further information or document required to determine an application;
e notice and publication of any decision about an application; and
f the procedure for an internal review of any such decision.

The Secretary of State may charge applicants a fee for processing applications for the grant or amendment of a licence or for the replacement of any lost, damaged or stolen licence. The amount of any such fees must be specified in regulations and must not exceed the reasonable cost of processing such applications.

As well as the licences described, above, there may also be recognised non-GB licences. These are licences issued in a Member State which is 'recognised' for these purposes in accordance with Article 7(6) of the Precursors Regulation or a licence granted under relevant Northern Ireland legislation. The Secretary of State must publish a list from time to time of recognised Member States (if there are any). At the time of going to press, no such licences had been recognised by the Home Office.

The Secretary of State has powers to make regulations to amend the operation of this part of the Poisons Act, for example by amending the circumstances in which the requirement for a licence applies or amending the control of any substance under this legislation.

Supply of regulated substances

It is an offence to supply a regulated substance (i.e. a regulated explosives precursor or regulated poison) to a member of the general public without first verifying that the member of the general public has a licence. Such a licence is also required by a member of the public for him/her to possess and use such a substance.

The Home Office[7] advise that, when a member of the public requests to purchase a regulated substance, the seller should:

- ask the purchaser for his/her licence and the associated photographic ID – the licence states which form of ID is associated with the licence (including a note of the ID reference number). The associated ID will be a current UK or EEA passport, biometric residence permit or UK driver's licence only (no other forms of photographic ID are permitted);
- check that both the licence and the photographic ID match the purchaser – this includes comparing the photograph to the customer and verifying the photographic ID reference number against the ID reference on the front page of the licence;
- check whether the customer is permitted to use, store or possess the substance s/he is attempting to obtain – the licence will specify which substances s/he is licensed to purchase;
- check whether the customer has exceeded the volume of the substance s/he is licensed to purchase – a record of previous transactions should be listed on the reverse of the licence certificate;
- only when satisfied that the above steps have been taken, record the details of the sale on the licence, before the regulated substance is supplied to a member of the general public.

There are additional record-keeping requirements when selling a Regulated Poison (see next section).

Supply of regulated poisons

A regulated poison may only be supplied to a member of the general public if:

a the person making the supply is lawfully conducting a retail pharmacy business;
b the supply is made on premises that are a registered pharmacy; and
c the supply is made by or under the supervision of a pharmacist.

The person making the supply must make (or cause to be made) a record of the supply, which must be signed by the member of the general public purchasing the item. The record must state:

a the date of the supply;
b the name and address of the member of the general public;
c the name and quantity of the regulated poison supplied; and
d the purposes for which it is stated by the member of the general public to be required.

[7]The Home Office (May 2015). Guidance for Pharmacies selling non-medicinal poisons to the general public

These record-keeping requirements are in addition to those required for all regulated substances (i.e. that the details of the transaction are entered on to the licence) before the regulated substance is supplied to a member of the general public.

Storage of poisons in retail premises

A regulated poison or reportable poison may be stored in a retail shop, or in premises used in connection with a retail shop, only if:[8]

a it is stored in a cupboard or drawer reserved solely for the storage of poisons;

b it is stored in a part of the premises that is partitioned off, or is otherwise separated from, the remainder of the premises and to which customers are not permitted to have access; or

c it is stored on a shelf reserved solely for the storage of poisons and no food or drink is kept directly under the shelf.

In the case of a poison to be used in agriculture, horticulture or forestry, the poison may be stored in a cupboard or drawer only if that is reserved solely for the storage of poisons to be used in agriculture, horticulture or forestry. Such a poison may not be stored in any part of premises in which food or drink is kept or on any shelf.

Labelling and packaging of regulated and reportable substances

These substances are subject to the CLP Regulations (see section on Labelling of chemicals, below). Regulated substances must bear the warning label, 'acquisition, possession or use by the general public is restricted', before such substances are supplied to a member of the general public. This phrase should be placed in the section for supplemental information within the CLP label on products that fall within the scope of the CLP.

Reporting of suspicious transactions, disappearances and thefts

A supplier must report any transaction involving the supply, or proposed supply, of a regulated or reportable substance to a customer if the supplier has reasonable grounds for believing the transaction to be suspicious. This applies to all such supplies, or proposed supplies, whether they be to an

[8] The Control of Poisons and Explosives Precursors Regulations SI 2015 No. 966

end-user or a customer higher up the supply chain and whether to a business or to a private customer.

A transaction involving one of these substances is 'suspicious' if there are reasonable grounds for suspecting that the substance in question is intended for:

a the illicit manufacture of explosives (in the case of a regulated or reportable explosives precursor); or

b any illicit use (in the case of a regulated or reportable poison).

In deciding whether there are reasonable grounds for suspicion, in these transactions, regard must be had to all the circumstances of the case, including in particular where the prospective customer:

a appears unclear about the intended use of the substance;

b appears unfamiliar with the intended use of the substance or cannot explain it plausibly;

c intends to buy substances in quantities, combinations or concentrations uncommon for private use;

d is unwilling to provide proof of identity or place of residence; or

e insists on using unusual methods of payment, including large amounts of cash.

A person carrying on a trade, business or profession that involves regulated or reportable substances must report the disappearance or theft of any such substances if the disappearance or theft is significant and is from stocks in the person's possession, custody or control in Great Britain. In deciding whether a disappearance or theft is significant, regard must be had to whether the amount involved is unusual in all the circumstances of the case.

A duty under this section to 'report' something is a duty to give notice of it to the Secretary of State in accordance with such requirements as may be specified by the Secretary of State by regulations made under this subsection.

As with any part of the Poisons Act, the Secretary of State has powers to make regulations to disapply the legal requirements to report described in this section.

Denatured alcohols

The law relating to alcohol and denatured alcohol is contained mainly in the Customs and Excise Management Act 1979, the Alcoholic Liquor Duties Act 1979 and the Denatured Alcohol Regulations 2005,[9] as amended.

Alcohol means spirits, beer, wine, made-wine or cider as defined in section 1 of the Alcoholic Liquor Duties Act 1979.

---

[9]The Denatured Alcohol Regulations SI 2005 No. 1524

Retail sales of 'intoxicating liquor' and alcohol duty

Businesses, organisations and individuals who want to sell or supply alcohol must have a licence or other authorisation from a licensing authority; this is usually a local council. The licensing system relates both to premises and to personal licences. Legislation also make provisions for such things as permitted opening hours and so on. In addition, 'dutiable alcoholic liquors'[10] are liable to a customs duty, and all alcohol made in the UK by a licensed distiller is liable to an excise duty (Customs and Excise Management Act 1979). Exemption from Customs and Excise duty exists for alcohol used in making denatured alcohol (see below).

Since pharmacists will rarely be involved in the sale or supply of 'intoxicating liquors', this chapter will not consider these matters further but will focus, instead, on the production, sale and supply of denatured alcohols.

Classes of denatured alcohols

Denatured alcohol is alcohol which has been made unsuitable for drinking by the addition of denaturants in accordance with Regulations made by the Commissioners under the Alcoholic Liquor Duties Act 1979.

There are three classes of denatured alcohol:

a completely denatured alcohol (CDA);
b industrial denatured alcohol (IDA); and
c trade specific denatured alcohol (TSDA).

The pharmacist is generally concerned only with the first two classes – completely denatured alcohol and industrial denatured alcohol.

The Denatured Alcohol Regulations[11] set out the particulars for the supply, receipt, sale, storage, and so on, of all types of denatured alcohol, although the provisions for licensing and inspection are to be found in the Act itself. The Schedule to the Regulations sets out the formulae to which each of these classes of alcohol must be prepared.

Production and distribution of denatured alcohol

A licence or authorisation, issued in writing by HM Revenue and Customs (HMRC), is required before any person may denature alcohol. In addition, unless the premises at which the denatured alcohol is made are approved as an Excise warehouse, the producer must 'make entry' of each set of premises with HMRC; this essentially means to register the premises with them. Producers of denatured alcohols are responsible for the security of the

---

[10] Alcoholic Liquor Duties Act 1979
[11] The Denatured Alcohol Regulations SI 2005 No. 1524

alcohol and HMRC will check to make sure that any security systems are sufficient.

A licence issued by HMRC is also required by persons who wish to distribute denatured alcohol. Distributors who hold stocks of denatured alcohol must also 'make entry' of their premises with HMRC, before beginning to hold any stocks of denatured alcohol.

Supply of denatured alcohol by producers or distributors

A producer or distributor can supply CDA to anyone, including the general public, and can supply IDA to authorised persons on receipt of a copy of their authorisation.

Wholesale quantities of denatured alcohols may only be supplied by licensed or authorised producers and distributors. Wholesale quantities are those greater than 20 litres.

HMRC sets out rules and procedures for the receipt or supply of denatured alcohols outside of the UK.

Completely denatured alcohol (CDA)

As the name suggests, this is the most heavily denatured alcohol. When produced in the UK, the standard formulation is for every 100 parts by volume of alcohol to mix 3 parts by volume of isopropyl alcohol, 3 parts by volume of methyl ethyl ketone and 1 g of denatonium benzoate. Prior to 1 July 2013 the formulation also included methyl violet dye, although such inclusion is no longer mandatory. Some formulations still include the purple dye; this is permitted and the resultant mixture is still treated as CDA.

CDA can be used for heating, lighting, cleaning and general domestic use, and can be obtained, by members of the public from a variety of retailers, including DIY shops. CDA must not be purified, re-distilled or made drinkable. No licence or authorisation is required for a member of the public to purchase or use CDA, there are no restrictions on the amount that may be purchased and there are no conditions on its use.

Industrial denatured alcohol (IDA)

This class of denatured alcohol is designed for industrial use. It usually consists of 95 parts by volume of alcohol and 5 parts by volume of wood naphtha, or a substitute for wood naphtha. IDA can be used for a wide range of industrial, scientific and external medical applications. It must not be used for heating, lighting or the preparation of beverages, nor may it be purified, recovered or re-distilled without the written agreement of HMRC.

Authorisation to receive and use IDA

Any person, including persons lawfully conducting a retail pharmacy business, wishing to receive IDA must be authorised by HMRC to do so. The authorisation sets out the conditions of use of the IDA, and these must be adhered to.

Those who wish to hold stocks of denatured alcohol must also 'make entry' of their premises with HMRC, before beginning to hold any stocks of denatured alcohol.

All stocks of IDA and TSDA must be kept under lock and key, and under the control of the pharmacist or of a responsible person appointed by him/her.

Supply of IDA by a pharmacist

A pharmacist, who is an authorised user of IDA, may supply IDA:

- in quantities of less than 20 litres at any one time to another authorised user; the pharmacist must hold a copy of that user's authorisation to receive IDA;
- for medical use in response to the prescription or order of a medical or veterinary practitioner. There is no limit on the amount of IDA which can be supplied on an order.

An order is not defined in the regulations but is a request to be supplied with a specific quantity of IDA. There is no set format for an order, but it should include the quantity and class of denatured alcohol required.

Medical use means any medical, veterinary, surgical or dental purpose other than administration internally, and *medical or veterinary practitioner* means any person entitled by law to provide medical or veterinary services in the UK. HMRC have confirmed that this includes dentists, nurses and chiropodists.

Schools, colleges or universities wishing to use up to 5 litres of IDA per annum do not need to be authorised and so a copy of an authorisation to receive and use denatured alcohol is not needed in the case of such sales.

Records

Producers and distributors must keep records which show:

- purchases of materials used in the production of denatured alcohol;
- imports of denatured alcohol, including details of the country of origin;
- the class of denatured alcohol held in containers, that is whether it is CDA, IDA or TSDA;
- quantities of alcohols, denaturants, markers, dyes and denatured alcohol held and used on their premises;

- the results of stocktakes and action taken to investigate deficiencies and surpluses identified by those stocktakes;
- exports and sales of denatured alcohol;
- copy authorisations received in support of orders for denatured alcohols.

Users (this will include pharmacists) must keep records which show:

- purchases of IDA or TSDA;
- imports of IDA or TSDA, including details of the country of origin;
- the class of denatured alcohol held in containers, that is whether it is IDA or TSDA;
- quantities of IDA or TSDA held and used on their premises;
- the results of stocktakes and action taken to investigate deficiencies and surpluses identified by those stocktakes;
- sales of IDA or TSDA to other authorised users;
- copy authorisations received in support of supplies of IDA or TSDA.

HMRC will, from time to time, visit those who use, produce or distribute denatured alcohols in order to inspect their records and premises and to examine any denatured alcohol held on the premises. If HMRC uncovers any errors then they may require the user, producer or distributor to pay the duty on any alcohol lost as the result of those errors. Errors can include:

- unexplained losses of undenatured or denatured alcohol;
- as a producer, a failure to carry out denaturing to the required standards;
- as a producer or distributor, the making of supplies to persons who are not authorised users or without receiving copy authorisations; or
- as a user, using the denatured alcohol for an unauthorised use.

Further penalties may also be applied and HMRC may withdraw the person's authorisation.

Chemicals

This section contains public sector information published by the Health and Safety Executive and licensed under the Open Government Licence.

> *Box 18.1 Possible impact of the EU referendum on chemicals legislation*
>
> Most legislation relating to chemicals, in the UK and other Member States, is derived from the EU. Two important pieces of legislation relating to chemicals (CLP and REACH) are EU Regulations and so both have direct effects in the UK. Whilst the outcome of any negotiations regarding the UK's relationship with the EU is not known at the time of going to press, it is evident that the decision to withdraw from the EU may have implications for this area of law.

The CLP Regulations

CLP relates to the Classification, Labelling and Packaging of chemicals.

The aim of the CLP Regulations[12] is to 'ensure a high level of protection of human health and the environment as well as the free movement of chemical substances, mixtures and certain specific articles, while enhancing competitiveness and innovation'. This is achieved by providing an obligation for (Art.1):

a manufacturers, importers and downstream users to classify substances and mixtures placed on the market;
b suppliers to label and package substances and mixtures placed on the market;
c manufacturers, producers of articles and importers to classify those substances not placed on the market that are subject to registration or notification under Regulation (EC) No. 1907/2006.

The Regulations were made in 2008 and there was a transition period for their implementation, up to June 2015. At that point, the previous legislation (CHIP)[13] was revoked.

Retailers (including pharmacists), who store and sell chemicals to consumers without altering them in any way, can rely on the classification and labelling information that has been provided to them by those further up the supply chain (e.g. from the manufacturer). If they alter the chemical in any way (e.g. by reformulating it) before placing it on the market, they then adopt the role of a downstream user and become responsible for classifying, labelling and packaging that chemical.

Definitions

The following definitions are included in CLP (Art.2):

Substance means a chemical element and its compounds in the natural state or obtained by any manufacturing process, including any additive necessary to preserve its stability and any impurity deriving from the process used, but excluding any solvent which may be separated without affecting the stability of the substance or changing its composition.

Mixture means a mixture or solution composed of two or more substances.

Manufacturer means any natural or legal person established within the Community who manufactures a substance within the Community.

Importer means any natural or legal person established within the Community who is responsible for import.

[12] Classification, Labelling and Packaging EC Regulation No. 1272/2008
[13] The Chemicals (Hazard Information and Packaging for Supply) Regulations SI 2009 No. 716

Supplier means any manufacturer, importer, downstream user or distributor placing on the market a substance, on its own or in a mixture, or a mixture.

Distributor means any natural or legal person established within the Community, including a retailer, who only stores and places on the market a substance, on its own or in a mixture, for third parties.

Downstream user means any natural or legal person established within the Community, other than the manufacturer or the importer, who uses a substance, either on its own or in a mixture, in the course of his/her industrial or professional activities. A distributor or a consumer is not a downstream user.

Downstream users include those who formulate mixtures, transfer substances or mixtures from one container or packaging into another or who re-import chemicals. Hence, pharmacists who stock and sell chemicals to consumers in their original packaging are defined as distributors under CLP.

The Globally Harmonised System of Classification and Labelling of Chemicals ('the GHS')

CLP sets out that, in order to facilitate worldwide trade in chemicals, whilst also protecting human health and the environment, it is necessary for there to be an internationally agreed system of chemicals classification and labelling. Such a system has been developed within the United Nations (UN) structure, resulting in the Globally Harmonised System of Classification and Labelling of Chemicals (or GHS).

The UN GHS is not a formal treaty, but is, instead, a non-legally binding international agreement. This means that countries (or trading blocks) must create local or national legislation to implement the GHS. CLP adopts the GHS throughout the Member States of the EU.

Application of the Regulations and exceptions

The CLP Regulation applies to the classification, packaging and labelling of any substance or mixture which has been classified as hazardous. It also applies where a mixture, which has not been classified as hazardous, contains any substance which has been classified as hazardous.

CLP does not apply to the following chemicals:

a radioactive substances and mixtures;
b substances and mixtures which are subject to customs supervision (with certain provisos);
c non-isolated intermediates;
d substances and mixtures for scientific research and development, which are not placed on the market, provided that they are used under

controlled conditions in accordance with community workplace and environmental legislation;

e waste.

It also does not apply to substances and mixtures in the following forms, which are in the finished state, intended for the final user:

a medicinal products
b veterinary medicinal products
c cosmetic products
d medical devices
e food or feeding stuffs, including when they are used as a food additive, a flavouring, an additive in feeding stuffs or in animal nutrition.

Except where Article 33 applies (specific rules for labelling of outer packaging, inner packaging and single packaging), CLP does not apply to the transport of dangerous goods by air, sea, road, rail or inland waterways.

Classification

Classification is the process by which the hazards which chemicals may pose are identified. CLP places an obligation on manufacturers, importers and downstream users to classify substances or mixtures, in accordance with the Regulation, before placing them on the market. When classifying a chemical, there are criteria for:

a physical hazards (e.g. being corrosive);
b health hazards (e.g. carcinogenicity, skin irritation, etc.); and
c environmental hazards (e.g. harmful to the aquatic environment, etc.).

Labelling of chemicals

A substance or mixture classified as hazardous and contained in packaging must bear a label including the following elements (references to Articles are to CLP):

a the name, address and telephone number of the supplier(s);
b the nominal quantity of the substance or mixture in the package made available to the general public, unless this quantity is specified elsewhere on the package;
c product identifiers as specified in Article 18;
d where applicable, hazard pictograms in accordance with Article 19;
e where applicable, signal words in accordance with Article 20;
f where applicable, hazard statements in accordance with Article 21;
g where applicable, the appropriate precautionary statements in accordance with Article 22;
h where applicable, a section for supplemental information in accordance with Article 25.

Product identifiers

For a substance, these are usually the substance name and an identification number, as included in Annex VI of CLP, or the 'CAS number'. Product identifiers for a mixture are usually the trade name or the designation of the mixture and the identity of all substances in the mixture that contribute to the classification of the mixture as regards acute toxicity, skin corrosion or serious eye damage, germ cell mutagenicity, carcinogenicity, reproductive toxicity, respiratory or skin sensitisation, specific target organ toxicity or aspiration hazard.

Hazard pictograms

These are intended to alert users to the presence of a hazardous chemical. They consist of a black symbol on a white background with a red frame (and must always adhere to this colour scheme); they must be sufficiently wide to be clearly visible (and not smaller than $1\,cm^2$). The hazard pictograms are shown in figure 18.1. The colour and presentation of any label must be such that the hazard pictogram stands out clearly.

The CLP hazard pictograms are very similar to those used in the old labelling system (which were black on an orange background). A package may bear one or more pictograms.

Signal words

A signal word, either 'Danger' or 'Warning' (but not both) is assigned to hazardous chemicals, in accordance with their classification. This signal word must appear on the label. For those with less severe hazards, the signal word is 'Warning' and for those with a more severe hazard, the signal word is 'Danger'. The signal word relevant for each specific classification is set out in Annex I of the CLP Regulation.

Hazard statements

These are statements that describe the nature of the hazard associated with the substance or mixture. The hazard statements to be applied are determined by the classification of the chemical and are set out in Parts 2 to 5 of Annex I of the CLP Regulation. Examples include statements such as:

- Extremely flammable gas
- May be corrosive to metals
- Toxic if swallowed.

Precautionary statements

These are statements that set out the precautions that should be taken to minimise or prevent the potential hazards that might arise when using

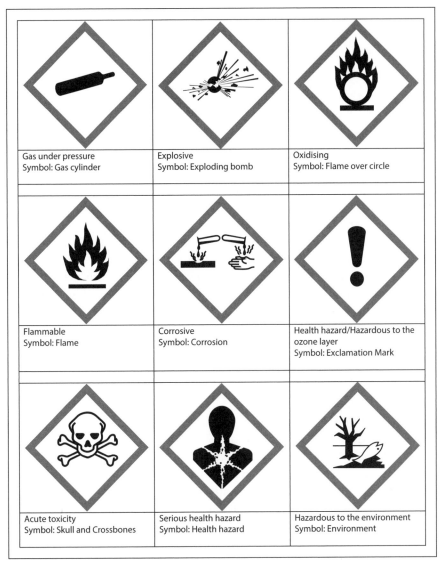

Gas under pressure Symbol: Gas cylinder	Explosive Symbol: Exploding bomb	Oxidising Symbol: Flame over circle
Flammable Symbol: Flame	Corrosive Symbol: Corrosion	Health hazard/Hazardous to the ozone layer Symbol: Exclamation Mark
Acute toxicity Symbol: Skull and Crossbones	Serious health hazard Symbol: Health hazard	Hazardous to the environment Symbol: Environment

Figure 18.1 CLP hazard pictograms

or disposing of hazardous chemicals. The precautionary statements to be applied are set out in Parts 2 to 5 of Annex I of the CLP Regulation, taking into account the hazard statements and the intended or identified use or uses of the substance or the mixture. Examples include statements such as:

- If medical advice is needed, have product container or label at hand
- Keep container tightly closed
- Do not eat, drink or smoke when using this product.

Supplemental information

Supplemental information may be obligatory or non-obligatory. Obligatory information is required where a hazardous chemical has particular physical or health properties and includes phrases such as:

- Explosive when dry (this is a physical property)
- Repeated exposure may cause skin dryness or cracking (this is a health property).

Other obligatory information includes (but is not limited to) required labelling elements arising from other legislation, such as REACH.[14]

Non-obligatory supplemental information includes elements that are not required by legislation but which are necessary for the safe handling and use of the product, such as usage instructions.

Statements such as 'non-toxic', 'non-harmful', 'non-polluting', 'ecological' or any other statements indicating that the substance or mixture is not hazardous or any other statements that are inconsistent with the classification of that substance or mixture must not appear on the label or packaging of any substance or mixture.

Substances restricted to professional users

REACH specifies that certain substances must be marked legibly and indelibly with the phrase 'restricted to professional users'. These include:

- 2-naphthylamine and its salts;
- benzidine and its salts;
- 4-nitrobiphenyl;
- 4-aminobiphenyl xenylamine and its salts;
- substances which appear in Annex I to Directive 67/548/EEC classified as mutagen category 1 or mutagen category 2;
- substances meeting the criteria of flammability in Directive 67/548/EEC and classified as flammable, highly flammable or extremely flammable regardless of whether they appear in Annex I to that Directive or not.

General rules for labels

The label on the package must be written in the official language(s) of the Member State(s) where the substance or mixture is placed on the market, unless the Member State(s) concerned provide(s) otherwise. Suppliers may use more languages on their labels than those required by the Member States, provided that the same details appear in all languages used.

Labels must be firmly affixed to one or more surfaces of the packaging immediately containing the substance or mixture and must be able to be

[14]Regulation concerning the Registration, Evaluation, Authorisation and Restriction of Chemicals (REACH) EC/1907/2006

read horizontally when the package is set down normally. The label elements must be clearly and indelibly marked and must stand out clearly from the background and be of such size and spacing as to be easily read.

The hazard pictograms, signal word, hazard statements and precautionary statements must be located together on the label, although the supplier may decide the order of the hazard statements and precautionary statements on the label. Groups of hazard statements and groups of precautionary statements should be located together on the label by language, where more than one language is used. Supplemental information, including that arising from other legislation, should be placed in the supplemental information section of the label.

In addition to its use in hazard pictograms, colour may be used on other areas of the label to implement special labelling requirements. The dimensions of the label must be as shown in table 18.3.

Table 18.3 Label dimensions for supply	
Capacity of package	**Dimensions of label (in mm)**
3 litres or less	If possible at least 52 × 74
Exceeding 3 litres but not exceeding 50 litres	At least 74 × 105
Exceeding 50 litres but not exceeding 500 litres	At least 105 × 148
Exceeding 500 litres	At least 148 × 210

Exemptions from labelling requirements

The following are exempt from the labelling requirements:

a   transportable gas cylinders;
b   gas containers intended for propane, butane or liquefied petroleum gas;
c   aerosols and containers fitted with a sealed spray attachment and containing substances or mixtures classified as presenting an aspiration hazard;
d   metals in massive form, alloys, mixtures containing polymers, mixtures containing elastomers;
e   explosives, as referred to in section 2.1 of Annex I, placed on the market with a view to obtaining an explosive or pyrotechnic effect.

In addition, if the size, shape or form of the packaging means that the full labelling requirements cannot be applied, CLP allows for the use of fold-out labels, tie-on tags or for the outer packaging to be used to include all of the necessary label elements. If it is impossible to meet the labelling requirements (because of the small size, shape or form of the package) and the full label information cannot be provided in fold-out labels, on tie-on tags or on an outer packaging, CLP allows for the use of reduced label information, subject to conditions specified in Annex I to the Regulation.

Packaging of chemicals

CLP requires that packaging containing hazardous substances or mixtures must satisfy the following requirements:

a the packaging must be designed and constructed so that its contents cannot escape, except in cases where other more specific safety devices are prescribed;

b the materials constituting the packaging and fastenings must not be susceptible to damage by the contents, or liable to form hazardous compounds with the contents;

c the packaging and fastenings must be strong and solid throughout to ensure that they will not loosen and will safely meet the normal stresses and strains of handling;

d packaging fitted with replaceable fastening devices must be designed so that it can be refastened repeatedly without the contents escaping;

e if the product is supplied to the general public, the packaging must not have either a shape or design likely to attract or arouse the active curiosity of children or to mislead consumers, or have a similar presentation or a design used for foodstuff or animal feeding stuff or medicinal or cosmetic products, which would mislead consumers.

Child-resistant fastenings and tactile warning devices

CLP requires that some substances or mixtures must, when supplied to the general public, be packaged with a child-resistant fastening and/or a tactile warning device. A tactile warning device is a raised triangle that can be felt by touch; it is designed to be understood by those with impaired vision.

The requirements to include a child-resistant fastening and/or a tactile warning device as part of packaging is determined either by the classification of the substance or the mixture under a certain hazard class or category or because the substance meets a specified concentration. Annex II of CLP sets out the details of this.

Examples of classifications that would require the substance or mixture to be packaged with a child-resistant fastening include those classified for acute toxicity (categories 1–3), specific target organ toxicity (single exposure category 1 or repeated exposure category 1) and skin corrosion (category 1).

Examples of classifications that would require the substance or mixture to be packaged with a tactile warning include those classified for acute toxicity, skin corrosion, germ cell mutagenicity (category 2), carcinogenicity (category 2), reproductive toxicity (category 2), respiratory sensitisation, or specific target organ toxicity (categories 1 and 2), aspiration hazard, or flammable gases, liquids and solids (categories 1 and 2).

REACH and Safety Data Sheets

Distributors (as defined under CLP), such as pharmacies, have duties under REACH (Registration, Evaluation, Authorisation and Restriction of Chemicals) Regulations[15,16] to pass information to their customers. REACH also imposes further duties on manufacturers, importers and downstream users.

One important element of REACH is the duty to provide purchasers of chemicals with a Safety Data Sheet (SDS) pertaining to that chemical.

An SDS must be provided when a substance or mixture, which is subject to REACH (this will include all chemicals controlled under CLP), is supplied for the first time in connection with work, for example a supply to a doctor for use in his/her practice, to a health centre or to factories. This is to ensure that the recipient can take any necessary precautions relating to the protection of health and safety at work and relating to the protection of the environment. The SDS should be provided to the recipient free of charge, on paper or electronically. The supplier does not need to re-supply the SDS, for subsequent orders from the same recipient, unless the sheet's contents have changed. If there are any updates to the SDS the new version of the SDS must be supplied to all customers (who received an SDS in connection with the receipt of the substance/mixture in question) from the preceding 12 months.

SDSs do not have to be given when supplies are made to the general public for private use, so long as the supplier provides sufficient information to enable users to take the necessary measures as regards safety and the protection of human health and the environment.

Control of substances hazardous to health

The COSHH Regulations[17] impose duties on employers to protect employees and other persons who may be exposed to substances hazardous to health and impose certain duties on employees concerning their own protection in the workplace. The Regulations apply to any place of work including hospital or community pharmacies, pharmaceutical laboratories or administrative offices. They cover virtually any substance (except those subject to specific legislation such as lead, asbestos and radioactive substances) but, in a pharmacy context, are particularly relevant to chemicals and harmful microorganisms.

The COSHH Regulations require that a risk assessment is made of substances used and procedures operated in the workplace.

[15]Regulation concerning the Registration, Evaluation, Authorisation and Restriction of Chemicals (REACH) EC/1907/2006
[16]The REACH (Registration, Evaluation, Authorisation and Restriction of Chemicals) Enforcement Regulations SI 2008 No. 2852
[17]The Control of Substances Hazardous to Health Regulations SI 2002 No. 2677

Risk, in relation to the exposure of an employee to a substance hazardous to health, means the likelihood that the potential for harm to the health of a person will be attained under the conditions of use and exposure and also the extent of that harm.

Every employer must ensure that the exposure of his/her employees to substances hazardous to health is either prevented or, where this is not reasonably practicable, adequately controlled.

Substances hazardous to health (which includes mixtures) means any:

a   which meets the criteria for classification as hazardous within any health hazard class laid down in the CLP Regulation;
b   for which the Health and Safety Executive has approved a workplace exposure limit;
c   which is a biological agent;
d   which is dust (with some exceptions);
e   which, because of its chemical or toxicological properties and the way it is used or is present at the workplace, creates a risk to health.

An employer must not carry out work which is liable to expose his/her employees to any hazardous substance unless s/he has made a suitable and sufficient assessment of the risks created by that work and the steps needed to avoid risk as set out in the Regulations. Where employees are exposed to risk, the employer must ensure that they are under suitable health surveillance. Manufacturers of substances which may be hazardous to health must provide full details (e.g. labels, leaflets, data sheets, instruction manuals) of the precautions to be taken when handling the substance. Employers must take measures to train and inform staff of the dangers associated with substances hazardous to health, to prevent or minimise exposure where possible and, if necessary, to monitor exposure and implement a health surveillance programme for all those exposed. Risk can be reduced by avoiding the substance altogether, using a safer substance or the same substance in a safer form, by enclosing the process and extracting the by-products, by improving ventilation or hygiene facilities, by instituting safer handling procedures or by introducing personal protective equipment such as gloves, masks and respirators. In cases of difficulty, advice should be sought from the local area office of the Health and Safety Executive or from the local authority environmental health officer.

Summary

- The Poisons Act 1972 was substantially amended by the Deregulation Act 2015 and now applies to 'regulated' and 'reportable' substances.
- Schedule 1A to the Act (see Appendix 3) lists the regulated and reportable substances.

- The Act includes provisions as to the possession of a licence by members of the general public who wish to import, acquire, possess or use a regulated substance; the seller must enter details of the sale on to the licence.
- There are provisions relating to the application of a warning label to the packaging of a regulated substance before it is supplied to a member of the general public.
- Regulated poisons may only be supplied to a member of the general public from a registered pharmacy, by or under the supervision of a pharmacist, and records of the sale must be made.
- Sellers of regulated or reportable substances have a legal duty to report suspicious transactions, disappearances and thefts of these substances.
- There are three types of denatured alcohol but the pharmacist is generally concerned with two types: completely denatured alcohol and industrial denatured alcohol. There are specific Regulations governing the supply, receipt, sale, storage, and so on, of all types of denatured alcohol.
- The CLP Regulation applies to the Classification, Labelling and Packaging of chemicals
- CLP places an obligation on manufacturers, importers and downstream users to classify substances or mixtures, in accordance with the Regulation, before placing them on the market.
- There are detailed labelling and packaging requirements for substances or mixtures controlled under CLP.
- The REACH Regulations include a duty to provide purchasers of chemicals with a Safety Data Sheet pertaining to that chemical.
- The COSHH Regulations impose duties on employers to protect employees and other persons who may be exposed to substances hazardous to health and impose certain duties on employees concerning their own protection in the workplace.
- Employers must take measures to train and inform staff of the dangers, to prevent or minimise exposure where possible and, if necessary, to monitor exposure and implement a health surveillance programme for all those exposed.

Further reading

Control of Substances Hazardous to Health Regulations SI 2002 No. 2677.
European Chemicals Agency (2016). Guidance on labelling and packaging in accordance with Regulation (EC) No. 1272/2008 Version 2.0.
European Regulation (EC) No. 1272/2008 on classification, labelling and packaging of substances and mixtures.
Home Office (2014). Guidance: Refusing a sale.
Home Office (2016). Guidance for pharmacies selling non-medicinal poisons to the general public.
Home Office (2016). Guidance: Licensing for home users of poisons and explosive precursors.
Home Office (2016). Guidance: Supplying explosives precursors and poisons.

Regulation (EC) No. 1907/2006 of the European Parliament and of the Council on the Registration, Evaluation, Authorisation and Restriction of Chemicals (REACH) (accessible at https://echa.europa.eu/web/guest/regulations/reach/legislation).

Royal Pharmaceutical Society (2015). Quick reference guide: Poisons and chemicals from pharmacy.

UK REACH Competent Authority (2016). Information Leaflet Number 10 – Guidance for Distributors – available on the Health and Safety Executive website.

Websites

HM Revenue and Customs: http://www.hmrc.gov.uk

Home Office: https://www.gov.uk/government/organisations/home-office

Royal Pharmaceutical Society: www.rpharms.com

European Chemicals Agency: https://echa.europa.eu/

Health and Safety Executive: http://www.hse.gov.uk/chemical-classification/index.htm; http://www.hse.gov.uk/reach/index.htm; http://www.hse.gov.uk/coshh/index.htm

19

Miscellaneous legislation affecting pharmacy

Joy Wingfield

The principal statutes concerning medicines, Controlled Drugs, poisons, alcohol and chemicals have been explained in chapters 2 to 18. There remain several enactments, and other measures, which are relevant to pharmacy. Some are of general application; others may apply only to one of the branches of pharmacy practice. This chapter comprises notes on some relevant statutes and regulations. The law outlined is that applying in England and Wales, but similar provisions apply in Scotland. The notes are grouped under appropriate subject headings, as follows:

- data protection and freedom of information
- pharmacy ownership
- workplace law
- consumer protection law
- health and safety law
- environmental law
- merchant shipping: medical scales
- jury service.

Data protection and freedom of information

Data Protection Act 1998

The Data Protection Act 1998 regulates the 'processing' of 'personal data'.

Personal data means any information whereby a living individual can be identified.

Processing means virtually any activity such as: obtaining, recording or holding the data; carrying out operations or sets of operations on the data; organisation, adaptation or alteration of the data; retrieval; consultation or use of the data; and alignment, combination, blocking, erasure or destruction of the data.

Unlike the earlier Act of 1984, which applied only to 'computerised' data, the 1998 Act additionally covers paper records and filing systems and, indeed, any storage system structured so that data relating to a living individual can be retrieved.

The person to whom the data relates is called the *data subject*. The person who determines how and for what purposes the personal data is processed is called the *data controller*; anyone else who actually processes the data is called a *data processor* (s.1). The 1998 Act also imposes additional controls on *sensitive personal data*, which includes any information, including opinion, relating to the physical or mental health or condition of the data subject (s.2).

The Act is administered by the Information Commissioner (formerly Data Protection Registrar, then Commissioner) who maintains a Register of *Registrable Particulars* notified by data controllers, who pay an annual fee (s.18). Data controllers must comply with the eight *data protection principles* set out in the Act (Sch. 1). These principles have the force of law. Briefly, the principles require that personal data shall be:

1 obtained and processed fairly and lawfully and shall not be processed at all unless certain conditions are met (see below);
2 obtained and processed for, or in ways compatible with, one or more lawful purposes;
3 adequate, relevant and not excessive in relation to that purpose or purposes;
4 accurate and kept up to date;
5 kept for no longer than necessary;
6 processed in accordance with the rights of data subjects under the Act (see below);
7 protected against unauthorised or unlawful processing and against accidental loss, destruction or damage; and
8 not transferred (with certain exceptions) outside the EEA unless the recipient country operates the same controls on data protection as applies within the EEA.

The Information Commissioner may refuse to register notification if s/he considers that these principles will be contravened (s.22). Processing personal data without notification is a criminal offence (s.21).

The Act imposes conditions which must be met even before processing of personal data can be contemplated (see principle 1 above). Generally, no personal data may be processed at all unless either the data subject has given consent or one of a series of other conditions has been met. These include 'the need to pursue the legitimate interests of the controller' *provided* that these are not prejudicial to the interests of the data subject (Sch. 2). This condition should be applicable to all uses of personal data in pharmacy practice. In addition, where the data are also *sensitive* personal data, either *explicit consent* must be obtained from the data subject or such consent may not be needed if the processing is 'necessary for medical purposes' and is undertaken by:

1 a health professional; or
2 a person who in the circumstances owes a duty of confidentiality which is equivalent to that which would arise if that person were a health professional.

Medical purposes includes the purposes of preventative medicine, medical diagnosis, medical research, the provision of care and treatment, and the management of healthcare services (Sch. 3).

Therefore, virtually all personal data used in pharmacy practice are 'sensitive' but 'explicit consent' (which implies a written explanation, a consent form and a decision freely made in appreciation of all its consequences) is not deemed necessary for patient medication records at least, provided that all personnel who may process such data are bound by the health professional's duty of confidentiality.

In October 2015, prompted by a report in the *Daily Mail*, an investigation into online company Pharmacy 2U by the Information Commissioner[1] led to a fine of £130 000 for selling details of patients to marketing companies without their consent. These were advertised for sale at a cost of £130 per 1000 records. The database included patients with conditions such as asthma, Parkinson's disease and erectile dysfunction, together with a breakdown of the data if required. The information had already been sold to a health supplements company and to an Australian lottery company before the investigation took place. The GPhC suspended the company's pharmacist commercial director, Julian Harrison, from the register for 3 months and gave a warning to the pharmacist Chief Operating Officer, Daniel Lee, at its enquiry in May 2016 (see also chapter 22).

The definition of *health professional* in the Act includes pharmacists (s.69).

The Act sets out explicit rights of data subjects and others (s.7; see principle 6 above). Data controllers must, on receipt of a written request accompanied by a fee:

1 inform the data subject if personal data are being processed;
2 give data subjects a description of the data which are being processed, for what purposes and to whom the data will be disclosed; and
3 provide data subjects with that information in an intelligible form within 40 days of the request.

---

[1] https://ico.org.uk/action-weve-taken/enforcement/pharmacy2u-ltd/ Pharmacy 2U Ltd Monetary penalty notice 14 October 2015

Data subjects also have a right to prevent processing of their data for marketing purposes (s.11) and to be notified if 'automated' decisions are taken in relation to, for example, work performance, creditworthiness, reliability or conduct (s.12). Rights are also conferred to allow data subjects to claim compensation from the data controller for failure to comply with any of the requirements of the Act or to fail to rectify, block, erase or destroy any inaccurate data (s.14).

There are exemptions allowing the data controller to exclude information relating to an individual other than the data subject, to allow some latitude where provision of copy records is very difficult or impossible to achieve, to protect trade secrets (s.8) and to withhold data if it is likely to cause substantial damage or distress to the data subject or any other person (s.10). Regulations made under section 7 also allow data controllers to decline to disclose data if this would be likely to cause serious harm to the physical or mental health or condition of the data subject or any other person. Information should not normally be disclosed without data subject consent unless it has been established that the data subject is incapable of managing his/her own affairs and the person requesting disclosure has been appointed by a court to manage those affairs.[2]

Parents, guardians or carers may seek disclosure of information about data subjects other than themselves for whom they undertake parental or carer responsibility. If the data subject is a child or anyone else who is likely to understand fully his/her rights to confidentiality, then consent should be established if at all possible. The maximum fee for arranging access to automated health records is £10, although £50 is the maximum if paper records are included.[3]

A further condition for the processing (which includes disclosure) of sensitive personal data is in accordance with circumstances specified by the Secretary of State (para. 10, Sch. 3 of the Act). This could, therefore, include disclosure where it is necessary for the prevention or detection of crime or for protecting the public against dishonesty, malpractice, incompetence or mismanagement where seeking the consent of the data subject would prejudice those purposes.[4]

Additional controls[5] over the processing of personal data electronically introduced two new rules for email marketing: all marketing messages must disclose the sender's identity and provide a valid address for opt-out requests

[2]The Data Protection (Subject Access Modification) (Health) Order SI 2000 No. 413

[3]The Data Protection (Subject Access) (Fees and Miscellaneous Provisions) Regulations SI 2000 No. 191

[4]The Data Protection (Processing of Sensitive Personal Data) Order SI 2000 No. 417

[5]The Privacy and Electronic Communications (EC Directive) Regulations SI 2003 No. 2426

and unsolicited messages, and, in most circumstances, require prior consent from the recipient.

In 2007, a detailed Code of Practice on information security management was introduced for NHS providers of healthcare, as part of their *information governance* arrangements. This Code applies to both managed NHS services and contractors who provide services for the NHS and covers all forms of patient health records, administrative information, radiographs ('X-rays'), photographs, digital media such as DVDs and removable memory sticks, networked computer records, and email, text and other message types.

Access to health records

Most of the provisions of the Access to Health Records Act 1990 are now within the Data Protection Act 1998, but the 1990 Act continues to provide that a personal representative of a deceased person or anyone who has a claim arising out of a patient's death can also claim access to 'sensitive personal data' maintained in health records.

Generally speaking, the requirements of data protection legislation do not apply to any information which relates to a data subject who has died (but see above) or to data which have been 'anonymised' (i.e. have been detached from any details or any links whatsoever which could identify a living individual). A legal case has been brought to clarify the limits on the use of anonymised data when derived from patient medication records held by community pharmacists (see box 19.1).

Box 19.1 Sale of prescription data

R v Department of Health, ex parte Source Informatics Ltd (2000)

Source Informatics Ltd proposed a scheme whereby after they, Source Informatics, had obtained the prescribers' consent, pharmacists, for a fee, would supply anonymised information contained on NHS prescriptions for the purposes of market research. The Department of Health in a policy document entitled *The Protection and Use of Patient Information* had made clear that under common law and the Data Protection Act principles the general rule was that information given in confidence may not be disclosed without the consent of the provider of the information (i.e. doctor or pharmacist). It also stated that anonymisation, with or without aggregation, did not remove the duty of confidence towards patients who are the subject of the data, namely details on their prescriptions written by the doctor and dispensed by the pharmacist. The High Court ([1999] 4 All ER 185) agreed with the Department of Health. The Court of Appeal on judicial review reversed the decision and Mr Justice Simon Brown said:

> the patient has no proprietorial claim to the prescription form or to the information it contains ... [he has] no right to control its use provided only and always that his privacy is not put at risk...

He concluded by saying:

> Participation in Source's scheme by doctors and the pharmacists would not in my judgment expose them to any serious risk of successful breach of confidence proceedings by a patient.

Comment. This case was not appealed and it would seem that the Data Protection Act does not normally cover data which have been anonymised, that is, detached from any details which could identify a living individual.

The Times, 18 January 2000.

Freedom of Information Act 2000

The Freedom of Information Act 2000 seeks to promote the openness and accountability of public authorities. Whereas the Data Protection Act is concerned to protect the privacy of individuals and their personal data, the Freedom of Information Act gives people the right to seek information from public authorities about how they carry out their duties, why they make the decisions they do and how they spend public money. Public authorities would include NHS trusts and CCGs. Such bodies must adopt and maintain a publication scheme, setting out details of information it will routinely make available, how the information can be obtained and whether there is any charge for it. Each body must comply, normally within 28 days, with requests for the information that it holds unless an exemption from disclosure applies. Exemptions include personal data covered by the Data Protection Act (see above), information provided to the public authority in confidence and some limited protection from disclosure which may jeopardise commercial interests. However, where services provided from community pharmacies are funded by the NHS, such as medicines use reviews or new medicines checks (see chapter 24), under the Freedom of Information Act contractors must respond to requests for information about their delivery. From 1 January 2009, pharmacies providing NHS services were required to adopt a model publication scheme approved by the Information Commissioner.

Defamation Act 2013

In an attempt to limit inappropriate libel claims ('libel tourism'), this Act requires claimants under libel law to show actual or probable serious harm before suing for libel in England and Wales. Among a number of enhanced defences against a libel action, the Act provides a defence for peer-reviewed publications to claim to be privileged publications.

Pharmacy ownership

A full explanation has been given in chapter 5 of the controls applied by the Medicines Act 1968 to the conduct of 'retail pharmacy businesses'. As such, a business can be owned by an individual pharmacist, a partnership of pharmacists or a body corporate (i.e. a company); it is desirable that the legal status of partnerships and companies should be understood. Only a brief explanation can be given here and any pharmacist contemplating ownership should seek advice from a suitably specialised lawyer or from the business law pages on the website of the Department for Business, Innovation and Skills (formerly the Department for Business, Enterprise and Regulatory Reform, formerly the Department of Trade and Industry).

Partnerships

A partnership is defined in the Partnership Act 1890 as the relationship which exists between persons carrying on a business in common with a view of profit. In contrast to a company (see below), a partnership, or *firm*, is simply a number of individuals each of whom has a responsibility for the affairs and the liabilities of the firm as a whole.

In England and Wales, a partnership (firm) does not have a legal status of its own as does a company. This means that the private assets of each partner can be called upon to satisfy any of the firm's debts. All the partners are liable for any debts incurred by one partner acting on behalf of the firm.

In Scotland, a partnership has a status similar to that of a body corporate (i.e. it *is a legal person distinct from the partners of whom it is composed*). It is for this reason that in a partnership owning a retail pharmacy in England and Wales, all the partners must be pharmacists, whereas in a Scottish partnership only one partner need be a pharmacist (chapter 5).

A partnership can arise in either of two ways: by express agreement or by implied agreement between two or more persons. A partnership can be implied if two or more persons work together in such a way as to fall within the definition as set out in the Act. Generally, if they share in the management of the business and share the profits, then the law will recognise them as partners.

When a partnership is formed to run a retail pharmacy, it is invariably a partnership of express agreement, and the conditions of the partnership are set out in a partnership contract or articles. The articles can be altered at any time with the consent of all the partners, whether this is express or implied. The only exception is where the articles restrict the right to vary (e.g. that no change may be made for 2 years).

A partnership can be formed where one of the partners may limit his/her responsibility for the firm's debts, leaving the other partners to share the unlimited liability. This partner is often referred to as a *sleeping partner*, as s/he takes no part in the management of the firm. Partnerships of this type are not common and are governed by the Limited Partnerships Act 1907. If a person wishes to limit his/her liability in this way today, s/he is more likely to invest in a limited company. Once again, it is stressed that, before contemplating forming a partnership, pharmacists should take legal advice and have any partnership contract drawn up by a solicitor.

The Limited Liability Partnership Act 2000 allowed the creation of limited liability partnerships within England, Scotland and Wales to retain the organisational flexibility and tax treatment of a partnership but also to derive benefit from the separate legal personality of a company with limited liability. Limited liability partnerships must register and submit annual accounts to Companies House.

Companies

A company (or corporation aggregate or *body corporate*) is a body of persons combined or incorporated for some common purpose having in law an existence and rights and duties distinct from those of the individual persons who from time to time form it. The most common form is a limited liability company (Ltd); other forms include Limited Liability Company (LLP) and public limited company (plc). The notes given here can only outline the general principles of company law, with some special reference to certain aspects which particularly affect pharmacy businesses. Incorporation as a company enables a group of people to act and to trade in the same way as an individual owner. It also enables them to trade with limited liability to the individual shareholder. Once incorporated, a company is *a legal person* and quite distinct from its members. It can own property, employ persons and be a creditor or debtor just like a human being, and can be liable criminally for acts of omission and for the acts of its employees committed in the course of their employment. This is a fundamental principle of company law.

The promoters of a company must file (electronic submission became permitted in 2006) the following documents with the Register of Companies:

1 memorandum of association;
2 articles of association;

3 list of directors and name of secretary;

4 statement of the nominal share capital;

5 notice of the address of the registered office; and

6 declarations by a solicitor or a person named in the articles as a director or secretary that all the requirements of the Companies Acts in respect of registration have been complied with.

If all the documents are in order, the Registrar will issue a certificate of incorporation, which is conclusive evidence that the company has been registered and that the requirements of the Act have been complied with.

There are at least three types of company: a public company, a private limited company and a private unlimited company. Most pharmacists will be concerned with the private company, whether limited or not.

A *private company* needs only one director but, if there is a sole director, s/he cannot also be the company secretary. Shares and debentures in a private company cannot be offered to the public.

An *unlimited company* is one where there is no limit on the members' liability to contribute to the assets in order to satisfy the company's debts.

Memorandum of association

The memorandum of association regulates the external affairs of the company and must include five clauses, namely those relating to the name, registered office, objects, liability and capital of the company. It must be signed by each subscriber.

The name of a private limited company must end with the word *limited*. For a public limited company, the last words must be *public limited company* or *plc*.

There is a general freedom of choice of the company name, but a company cannot be registered under the Act by a name which includes, otherwise than at the end of its name, the word *limited, unlimited* or *public limited company* or the Welsh equivalents (e.g. *cfyngedig*). Where *cfyngedig* is used, the fact that the company is a limited company must be stated in English and in legible characters on all official company stationery and publications, and in a notice conspicuously displayed in every place where the company's business is carried on.

No name may be used which the Registrar considers offensive or which, if used, would constitute a criminal offence. In the latter category would fall a retail company which is not conducting a retail pharmacy business and which wished to use the title *chemist*.

Certain words and expressions may only be used in company or business names with the approval of the Secretary of State or other relevant body specified in Regulations. For the word *chemist* the GPhC is the relevant body, but, when *chemist* or *chemistry* is used in an industrial sense, it is the Royal Society of Chemistry. Similarly, for the word *apothecary* the relevant body in England and Wales is the Worshipful Society of Apothecaries and, in Scotland, the GPhC.

Articles of association

The articles regulate the internal affairs of the company (i.e. the rights of shareholders and the manner in which the business of the company is conducted). A model set of articles is set out in Regulations made under the Act. It may be used by a company as it is or adapted as required. If no articles are submitted with the application for registration, the statutory ones will apply. The articles of a company are freely alterable by special resolution, subject to certain safeguards.

The legal effect of the memorandum and articles is that they bind the company and its members as if they had been signed and sealed by each individual member and contained covenants on the part of each member to observe all the provisions of the memorandum and articles.

Directors

The first directors of a company are usually appointed in accordance with the articles; if not they are appointed by the original subscribers to the company. Subsequent appointments are usually governed by a procedure laid down in the articles. It must be stressed that a pharmacist becoming a director should be fully aware of the contents of the memorandum and articles of association of the company s/he joins. Directors must exercise their powers as directors for the benefit of the company. A director has a duty to the company to exercise such skill and care as s/he possesses. If appointed in a specific capacity calling for a particular skill (e.g. a pharmacist who is a director of a body corporate), s/he must exercise that skill in a reasonable manner for the benefit of the company. Directors are not bound to give continuing and unremitting attention to the company's affairs and are justified in trusting the officers of the company to perform their duties honestly.

A pharmacist who becomes superintendent chemist (pharmacist) of a company will almost invariably be appointed a director, and a knowledge of the powers and duties of directors is essential. For example, if a company fails to make its annual return then the company and/or any of its officers or directors is liable to a default fine. A pharmacist who resigns as a superintendent chemist should ensure that s/he also resigns as a director. Instances have occurred where a pharmacist, some years after having resigned as a superintendent chemist, has been prosecuted for failing to make an annual return as s/he had remained a director of the company.

Business Names Act 1985

A *business name* is a name used by a business which is other than: (a) for a sole trader, his/her surname; (b) for a partnership, the surnames or corporate names of all members of the partnership; or (c) for a corporate business, the names of the company concerned. Certain additions are permitted (e.g. forenames or initials). Where a business name is used, the true name(s) and address(es) of the owner(s) must appear on all business stationery and that information must be prominently displayed at the business premises. The use of certain types of business name require the written approval of the Secretary of State and regulations may specify certain words or expressions which may only be used with the approval of a government department or some other relevant body.

Workplace law

Workplace law covers both *employment law* and a range of *antidiscrimination and public protection law* and these can affect pharmacists and sometimes their staff in the workplace. Knowledge of employment law is important to pharmacists in their capacity both as employer and as an employee. Employment rights derive from two main areas: those created by Acts of Parliament (statutory employment rights) and those created by decisions of courts over time (common law rights; chapter 1).

Statutory employment rights

Employment rights cover rights such as: equal pay; sick pay; the right not to be unlawfully discriminated against on the grounds of sex or marital status, sexual orientation, race, disability, religion or belief, age, trade union membership, or part-time or fixed term status; not to suffer a detriment for making a protected disclosure in the public interest ('whistle blowing'); and not to be dismissed unfairly. Employees have also been granted rights to a written statement of the terms of employment, of the reasons for dismissal, to minimum disciplinary procedures, to be accompanied at a disciplinary hearing, to an itemised pay statement, for time off for public duties, for time off for antenatal care, for time off for care of dependants, to a minimum wage, to a minimum period of notice for termination of employment, to maternity leave and pay, to paternity leave and pay, to request flexible working, and to entitlement to rest breaks and restrictions on weekly working time. This list is not exhaustive.

The rights are enforceable by employees through the Employment Tribunal. Some rights require the employee to have a qualifying period of service before the rights can be enforced in the Employment Tribunal. The compensation that can be awarded by the tribunal is sometimes subject to a statutory minimum or a statutory cap depending on the nature of the claim. However, in other claims, the tribunal considers what is just and equitable in all the circumstances having regard to the loss sustained by the employee.

In the context of employment law, *disability* means 'a physical or mental impairment which has a substantial and long-term adverse effect on a person's ability to carry out normal day-to-day activities'. *Day-to-day activities* involve: mobility; manual dexterity; physical co-ordination; ability to lift, carry or move ordinary objects; speech, hearing or eyesight; memory; or ability to concentrate, learn, understand or perceive physical danger. Therefore, the definition includes those with hearing or visual impairment, those with learning disabilities or mental illness, and those with long-term illnesses such as severe arthritis, human immunodeficiency virus infection, multiple sclerosis and muscular dystrophy. Certain conditions are excluded, notably addiction to alcohol, nicotine or non-therapeutic drugs.

Common law rights

In the employment context, the principal common law claim is where an employee claims that the employer has acted in breach of the contract of employment. Employment Tribunals can deal with breach of contract claims where the breach has arisen or is outstanding on the termination of the employment. There is a limit of £25 000 on the awards a tribunal can make in these circumstances. Alternatively, employees can make claims in either the County Court or the High Court (chapter 1), depending on the amount of damages claimed and other certain criteria applied by the courts.

European law

Sometimes, UK national law is in conflict with EU legislation. In these instances, the case may be referred to the ECJ (chapter 1), the decisions of which will be binding on UK courts and tribunals. Decisions of the ECJ may also result in amendments to national law. However, the referendum decision in June 2016 to take the UK out of the EU, when implemented, may change this position.

Further information on this complex and fast-changing area of law can be obtained at the websites at the end of this chapter.

Vicarious liability

The term *vicarious liability* in this context signifies the liability which an employer may incur to a customer for damage caused by an employee in the course of his/her employment. This, in legal terms, is the relationship between *master* and *servant* and means that the 'master' cannot only order or require *what* must be done but also *how* it shall be done.

All employee pharmacists should have a contract of employment, but in many areas pharmacists themselves will decide *how* a task should be performed and this will often be a matter for the pharmacist's own professional judgement. Therefore, if an employee pharmacist makes a mistake or is so careless as to cause *damage* (e.g. injury, fear, anxiety, etc.) to a patient or customer, the employer would probably be liable. However, if the act or omission fell into the realm of professional judgement, the pharmacist may also incur additional personal liability and might be accountable to the GPhC and/or to his/her employer to justify his/her actions. This is why pharmacists are advised to carry their own professional indemnity insurance or ensure that they practise only in an establishment which is covered by such insurance.

Access to goods, facilities and services

The Equality Act 2010 has replaced previous anti-discrimination laws with a single Act which bans unfair treatment and helps to achieve equal opportunities in the workplace and in wider society. The Act covers nine 'protected characteristics' which may not be used as a reason to treat people unfairly. They are:

- age
- disability
- gender reassignment
- marriage and civil partnership
- pregnancy and maternity
- race
- religion or belief
- sex
- sexual orientation.

The Equality Act sets out the different ways in which it is unlawful to treat someone, such as direct and indirect discrimination, harassment, victimisation and failing to make a reasonable adjustment for a disabled person. The Act prohibits unfair treatment in the workplace: when providing goods, facilities and services; when exercising public functions; in the disposal and management of premises; in education; and by associations (such as private clubs). The Act has been brought into force gradually; for example, from October 2010 breastfeeding mothers gained protection from harassment if they wish to feed in public places, pay secrecy clauses were made unenforceable and the definition of gender reassignment was changed by removing the requirement for medical supervision. In April 2011, the public sector (which includes the NHS, NHS contractors and regulators such as the GPhC) gained a duty positively to promote equality in their recruitment and promotion policies and in all other public activities. From October 2012, it will be unlawful to discriminate on the basis of age unless the practice is covered by an exception from the ban, or good reason can be shown for the differential treatment ('objective justification'). The health and social care services do not have any such general exceptions.

From July 2016, all providers of NHS health and adult social care must comply with the Accessible Information Standard (AIS).[6] The aim of the AIS is to establish a framework and set a clear direction such that patients and service users (and where appropriate carers and parents) who have information or communication needs relating to a disability, impairment or sensory loss (such as impaired hearing or sight) receive accessible information which is capable of being read or received and understood by the individual or group for which it is intended, and communication support to enable effective, accurate dialogue between a professional and a service user.

The AIS requires that 'service providers' such as community pharmacies or hospital pharmacy departments must:

- ask as a matter of routine whether patients have any information support needs relating to a disability, sensory loss or other impairment (for example, a stroke);
- record clearly and consistently those needs and possible solutions in the patient's records;
- flag that information in the records so that it can be seen and acted upon whenever the individual's records are accessed;
- share the information where lawful and appropriate, and particularly at referral and handover, with other health professionals;
- make reasonable adjustments to ensure that people receive information in a format they can understand.

The AIS enables individuals to make decisions about their health and wellbeing and their care and treatment, to self-manage conditions, to access services appropriately and independently, and to make choices about treatments and procedures, including giving or withholding consent. The provider may not always have to make the adjustments themselves (using British Sign Language, for example), but should be prepared to direct the patient to an appropriate source of support if not.

Safeguarding users of health services

Persons working in either health or social care are now subject to several areas of legislation. Before employment, employers of health professionals are required to check with the Disclosure and Barring Service (DBS) to establish their identity, ascertain whether they have a criminal record and whether they are barred from carrying out certain work, usually involving

[6]NHS England 2016 Accessible Information Standard specification and implementation guidance

children or vulnerable adults. The DBS was formed in 2012 by merging the functions of the Criminal Records Bureau (CRB) and the Independent Safeguarding Authority (ISA) under the Protection of Freedoms Act 2012. It covers England and Wales but similar processes apply in Scotland and Northern Ireland.

Employers are legally required to report safeguarding concerns to the DBS and it is illegal for anyone barred by the DBS to work, or apply to work, within the sector from which they are barred. It is also illegal for an employer to knowingly employ a barred person in the sector from which they are barred. Pharmacists and pharmacy technicians are subject to DBS checks but 'other staff' such as sales assistants and delivery drivers are not, provided that their activities are supervised by a pharmacist or pharmacy technician.[7] Further, certain activities such as using a private taxi (as opposed to a hospital ambulance) to convey a patient to hospital have been exempted in regulations.[8]

All health professionals are now required by law to have indemnity arrangements and professional liability insurance[9] as a condition of registration. Amendments to the Pharmacy Order 2010 and to the GPhC registration rules require pharmacists and pharmacy technicians to inform the registrar if their cover provided under an indemnity arrangement ceases to be in force, and to inform the registrar if appropriate cover under an indemnity arrangement is provided by an employer. The provisions do not apply to visiting pharmacists from relevant European states who are providing services on a temporary and occasional basis. This law ensures that patients who suffer harm from the actions of a pharmacist or pharmacy technician may be able to secure damages (payments or restitution) in an action for negligence (see chapter 21).

From April 2015, it is a criminal offence[10] for an individual who has the care of another individual by virtue of being a care worker (this includes a healthcare worker) or care provider (includes provider of healthcare) to ill-treat or wilfully to neglect that individual. The offence focuses on the conduct of the individual, not the outcome – in other words, what the healthcare worker actually did (or failed to do) rather than any harm that resulted. For organisations, the offence focuses on the way their activities are managed and organised and whether an incident amounts to a gross breach of the relevant duty of care to the patient.

[7]The Safeguarding Vulnerable Groups Act 2006 (Miscellaneous Provisions) Order SI 2012 No. 2113
[8]The Safeguarding Vulnerable Groups Act 2006 (Miscellaneous Provisions) Regulations SI 2012 No. 2112
[9]The Healthcare and Associated Professions (Indemnity Arrangements) Order SI 2014 No. 1887
[10]Criminal Justices and Courts Act 2015, s.20

Further legislation[11] gives statutory force to a 'duty of candour' where healthcare is provided within hospitals or from any care provider registered with the Care Quality Commission. This is in addition to the ethical duty of candour within the GPhC's guidance (chapters 22 and 23) and within the NHS contract (chapter 24). Briefly this means that pharmacists and pharmacy technicians are legally required to tell patients when things go wrong, to apologise and to try to put things right. The same legislation also requires that directors of care provider organisations meet a 'fit and proper person' test. This aims to assess the person's honesty, integrity, suitability and fitness for the post, for example, that they have the right level of qualifications, skills and experience for the role.

Pharmacies and their staff have been asked to help patients to understand how their medication may bring them under the provisions of drug driving legislation.[12] From March 2015, it is an offence to drive with certain specified drugs in excess of specified levels in England and Wales. There is a statutory 'medical defence' for patients taking their medicines as prescribed or in accordance with product information.

Consumer protection law

Detailed information on consumer protection law may be found on the Department for Business, Innovation and Skills' website (given at the end of this chapter). All retailers are subject to controls on price, description and the safety of the goods they sell. The majority of the law in this area is enforced by the local authority, usually the trading standards departments. In some cities, those duties may be shared with the local environmental health officer. The general principle of most of this law is that it makes it a criminal offence to mislead consumers as to the description, price or safety of goods and services. The majority of the criminal offences in this area are strict liability offences, coupled to a defence of due diligence. It is, therefore, vitally important that processes and procedures are in place so that a pharmacist can show that s/he took reasonable steps and precautions to check that descriptions of goods and services were accurate or that the goods s/he sold were safe. The following topics may be of interest.

Trades Descriptions Act 1968

The Trades Descriptions Act makes it an offence to falsely describe goods or services in the course of a trade or business. The law is wide enough

[11] The Health and Social Care Act 2008 (Regulated Activities) Regulations SI 2014 No. 2936
[12] The Drug Driving (Specified Limits) (England and Wales) Regulations SI 2014 No. 2868 made under the Road Traffic Act 1988

to cover all forms of description and it should be noted that the retailer is to some extent in double jeopardy as there is an offence for supplying goods to which a false description has been applied as well as an offence of applying a false description to goods. Particular care needs to be taken where verbal descriptions are being applied to goods, as the individual becomes personally liable for those descriptions should they subsequently prove to be inaccurate. With regard to services, it is an offence to knowingly make a false statement.

Product liability

The Consumer Protection Act 1987 creates liability without fault on the part of the producer for damage caused by a defect in their product. Four classes of person may face liability for a defective product: the manufacturer, the importer, the person who holds him/herself out as the manufacturer or, in the event of none of the former being identified, the person supplying the product to the victim. The first three groups have a primary liability; the supplier has a secondary liability based upon his/her inability to identify a primary producer. When medicines might be the subject of an action in the courts (there have been very few cases under the Act), the primary producer will normally be the product licence holder. The supplying pharmacist should, therefore, ensure that s/he has adequate systems and records to ensure that the licence holder or manufacturer can always be identified with some certainty. Liability probably does not arise from repackaging licensed medicines or from supplying them against a prescription, provided that the source is known.

The supplying pharmacist will carry full liability for 'own branded' goods in which the pharmacy's name and address are affixed to containers of medicines made up elsewhere and not so identified. The supplying pharmacist also carries full liability when s/he prepares his/her own remedies for a patient under section 10 of the Medicines Act (chapter 3). In these circumstances, it is advisable to maintain full manufacturing records so that the producer of the ingredients can always be identified. Claims may be made for up to 3 years after the 'relevant date' – when the victim became aware of the facts – subject to a maximum of 10 years from the date of putting the product into circulation.

Price control

Customers' rights on pricing are protected in two areas of consumer protection law: controls on misleading price indications and requirements to display price, and in certain circumstances unit price, in close proximity to the goods. It is an offence to give a misleading price indication and it is, therefore, important for any pharmacist involved in retailing to be aware of the Code of Practice for Traders on Price Indications. This code provides guidance to retailers on what constitutes 'misleading' and how 'offer' prices can be constructed. A second obligation is simply a requirement to display a price in such a way that customers see it without having to ask in close proximity to all goods available for sale. If those goods are required to be sold by weight or measure, then there is an obligation to give a unit price (cost per kilogram or litre) as well as the actual selling price. Unit price controls do not apply to medicines. Within pharmacies, cosmetics, toiletries and food supplements are the items most likely to be affected. Unit price controls apply only in larger stores (over $280\,m^2$). Details of the controls are complicated and subject to change. Advice on price indications should, therefore, be sought from the local trading standards department.

Safety of goods

Consumer protection law also creates an obligation to provide customers with goods that are safe. Any reasonably foreseeable risks arising out of the goods should have been dealt with by the manufacturer and addressed either by changing the design of the goods to make them safer or by issuing warnings or instructions that deal with the issue. Where local authorities find unsafe goods, as well as prosecuting they can also serve enforcement notices requiring that the products are removed from the marketplace.

Weights and Measures Act 1985

The Weights and Measures Act 1985 and the Regulations made under it control the manner in which goods should be weighed, measured and retailed. They also control the way quality indications should be given on the packaging. The legislation lays down specific construction criteria for equipment and measures and sets down the accuracy tests that the equipment must pass if it is to be used for selling goods. The Regulations also set out a detailed regime for the packaging of goods, and those pharmacists involved in packing bulk goods should consult the BIS website (see end of chapter) as well as seeking guidance from the local trading standards department. The selling of goods deficient in weight or volume is a strict liability offence but defences are available.

Competition Act 1998

The Competition Act 1998 reflects a worldwide trend to open up markets, stimulate competition and establish transparent and fair marketing arrangements. It seeks to do this by outlawing agreements between businesses and decisions taken by businesses on concerted practices that affect trade in the UK or Europe. Those decisions are not allowed to have as their object or effect the prevention, distortion or restriction of competition within the UK. An example of such a practice would be people acting together directly or indirectly to fix the purchase or selling process. The rules not only affect retailers but also trade associations or any other group of persons acting together in such a way as to distort competition. The fines under the Competition Act can be very high, as the maximum ceiling on the fine is 10% of company turnover.

In pharmacy, the advent of the Competition Act led to the abolition of *resale price maintenance* on the price at which medicines available over the counter could be supplied.[13] At that time, this Act also affected the profession's Code of Ethics. The rules of trade associations and professional bodies are covered by the anti-competitive prohibitions in the Act unless they are specifically exempted in Schedule 4. For historical reasons, pharmacy was not included in Schedule 4 (although some other health professions were) and the Code of Ethics for pharmacy had to comply with the provisions of the Act. Prior to 2002, the Codes of Ethics contained several restraints, in the public interest, on the promotion and supply of medicines but there are none in subsequent codes (former RPSGB) or standards (GPhC). In August 2012, the Office of Fair Trading[14] announced that it had obtained assurances from eight NHS trusts that they would cease sharing commercially sensitive information about their private patient unit prices.[15] This was held to have the 'potential to facilitate collusion' and create an illegal cartel to maintain prices.

Bribery Act 2010

Bribery is broadly defined in the Act as giving someone a financial or other advantage to encourage that person to perform his/her functions or activities improperly or to reward that person for having done so. An organisation (company, trust, etc.) could be liable under the Bribery Act if a very senior person (e.g. a managing director) commits a bribery offence. It could also be liable where someone who performs services for it (e.g. an employee or an agent) pays a bribe specifically to get business, keep business or gain a business advantage for the organisation. A defence is provided if the organisation can show that it had adequate processes in place to prevent bribery.

Websites providing detailed information on trading and other retail law are given at the end of this chapter.

---

[13] *Pharm J*, 16 August 1997 p. 236; 25 October 1997 p. 676

[14] Now closed down; responsibilities passed to a variety of other bodies

[15] *OFT Welcomes Action by NHS Trusts to Ensure Compliance with Competition Law*, Press release, Office of Fair Trading 12 August 2012

Health and safety law

Health and Safety at Work Act 1974

The Health and Safety at Work Act 1974 is extremely broad and basically sets out the requirements for a 'duty of care' for everyone in the workplace, including the protection of the health and safety of the public against the risks to health arising from work activities. It, therefore, applies to employers, employees, owners/occupiers of premises, suppliers and the self-employed. The Act provides a framework for other health and safety legislation. Detailed requirements are set out in specific Regulations. These Regulations are themselves supported by an Approved Code of Practice that expands the requirements contained within individual Regulations by providing detailed interpretation and guidance. Approved Codes of Practice are the main working documents for those with health and safety responsibilities.

Employers have a duty of care under the Health and Safety at Work Etc. Act 1974, together with its associated Regulations, to ensure, so far as is reasonably practicable, the health, safety and welfare of employees while they are at work. The main areas covered are:

- safe plant and machinery (work equipment) and safe operating procedures;
- safe use, handling and storage and transport of articles and substances;
- provision of information, instruction, training and supervision;
- provision and maintenance of a safe place of work with safe means of access and egress; and
- for an employer with more than four employees, provision of a written policy for health and safety and details of the arrangements for carrying out the requirements of the policy.

Employers, including the self-employed (e.g. a locum pharmacist), and owners/occupiers have a similar duty to safeguard the health and safety of others who are not employees but who may be affected by his/her business activities. 'Others' include customers, visitors and the general public. Employees themselves also have a duty under the Act to take reasonable care for their own health and safety and for that of anyone else who may be affected by what they (employees) do or fail to do. There is also a duty to co-operate with their employer on health and safety issues.

Enforcement of health and safety requirements is undertaken by inspectors from the Health and Safety Executive for 'industrial premises' or by officers from the local authorities for 'retail premises'. Both regulatory groups have the powers to inspect, investigate cases of non-compliance, warn and issue 'improvement notices' or 'prohibition notices' as well as prosecute offenders.

It is beyond the scope of this book to provide much detail about health and safety legislation. However, it is important to raise the awareness of *risk assessment* as the basic 'tool' for identifying and managing risk. Areas where risks might arise in pharmacy practice include:

- work equipment (Provision and Use of Work Equipment Regulations);
- substances (COSHH Regulations, ch. 18); and
- manual handling (Manual Handling Operations Regulations).

To manage health and safety risks, it is necessary to identify the risks. The risk-assessment process achieves this by examining the workplace itself and work activities (tasks). Hazards (things with the potential to cause harm) are noted and the associated consequences (severity) of each hazard ranked should the harm be inflicted. For each hazardous situation, the types of person at risk are also identified. An assessment is also made of the likelihood of the harm actually occurring, again ranked according to likelihood. An assessment of the risk is then made for each situation based on the equation:

Risk = Consequence × Likelihood for each category of persons at risk

The basic principles of risk assessment are detailed in a Health and Safety Executive Approved Code of Practice *Management of Health and Safety at Work Regulations 1999*, to which reference should be made. Persons compiling risk assessments must be trained and have sufficient knowledge and experience of the process such that they are able to demonstrate their competence to the persons at risk depending upon the assessment and any regulatory inspector. Consideration should always be given to engaging suitable experts to do this work for anything other than situations where there are low consequences from workplace hazards. A key outcome of risk assessment is to require the identification and implementation of control measures to reduce risks to as low a level as is reasonably practicable. Control measures may range from hardware (e.g. guards for machinery) to procedural matters (e.g. operating procedures) to personal protective equipment (e.g. gloves/goggles). Risk can be eliminated only if a hazard is eliminated. Substituting something less hazardous (e.g. less-toxic cleaning materials) can reduce risk.

Regulatory inspectors would expect to see 'suitable and sufficient' risk assessments during any visit. It is important to review risk assessments and other health and safety arrangements periodically, or in the event of an accident or even a 'near miss', to see if the assessment and control measures are still valid and whether they can be improved to reduce risks to health and safety further. All such assessments should be discussed with employees who are 'at risk'.

Websites providing detailed information on health and safety law are given at the end of this chapter.

Environmental law

DEFRA is the government department responsible for a vast range of public services and controls such as air quality, noise pollution, litter, energy and chemicals. This section provides an overview of two areas that are relevant to pharmacy practice: controls on waste and the protection of animals and birds. Controls on poisons are covered in chapter 18.

Controls on waste

The Environmental Protection Act 1990 introduced a *duty of care* which applies to all persons who import, produce, carry, keep, treat or dispose of controlled waste. This, therefore, applies to pharmacists, who necessarily handle waste or unwanted medicines in the course of their practice. The duty of care lies on all holders of waste at every stage in its history, such that a pharmacist having held controlled waste may only pass it on to an *authorised person*, such as registered carriers, permit/licence holders or someone who is exempt from either being a registered carrier or operating under a permit/licence. Further, s/he must transfer with the waste such a written description of the waste – a transfer note, setting out the type and quantity of the waste – as will enable others to dispose of the waste appropriately and avoid committing an offence under the Act.

Controlled waste includes household, industrial and commercial waste of any kind, whether conventionally thought of as polluting or not. The Controlled Waste Regulations[16] define *clinical waste* as, among other things,

> waste from a healthcare activity (including veterinary healthcare) that
> (a) contains viable micro-organisms or their toxins which are known or reliably believed to cause disease in humans or other living organisms or
> (b) contains or is contaminated with a medicine that contains a biologically active pharmaceutical agent . . .

The Regulations also define the type of waste (household, industrial or commercial) based on its source. This is significant, because while a local authority has a duty to collect household waste, the Regulations allow a charge to be made for collection and sometimes disposal of some household wastes specified in Schedule 1 of the Regulations. Clinical waste produced in a domestic property, for example, may incur a collection charge, but its disposal attracts no charge. Producers of commercial or industrial wastes are more likely to have to use private contractors for this purpose. Under the Environmental Protection Act 1990, permits or licences are required for the storage, transfer, treatment and disposal of waste. A permit or

---

[16] The Controlled Waste Regulations SI 2012 No. 811

licence is not generally required to store waste on the premises at which it was produced.

Further Regulations set out arrangements that may be made[17] and which, if they comply with the conditions specified, will be exempt from section 33(1)(a) of the Environmental Protection Act 1990 (the restriction on knowingly permitting the deposit of controlled waste on any land without an environmental permit). One such exemption is for the 'temporary storage at a collection point'. This exemption allows a community pharmacy to temporarily store waste in a secure container where returned medicines have been received from domestic premises. This exemption does not require registration, but waste disposal companies collecting waste from pharmacies will need to be satisfied that the pharmacy is complying with the conditions specified.

Under this exemption, wastes of different types should not be mixed. Where practicable, for example, blisters of unused or unwanted medicines should be removed from the cardboard cartons so that they can be sent for incineration, whereas the cardboard cartons (and any patient information leaflets) can be sent for recycling. Discharge of pharmaceutical waste to sewer must have the prior agreement of the water authorities. Non-pharmaceutically active products (such as saline bags) may be discharged but, at the other extreme, cytotoxic or ecotoxic products would not be permitted. The agreement of the water authorities may depend on the amounts and types of discharge upstream and downstream of the pharmacy.

Hazardous Waste Regulations[18] essentially replaced the 1996 Special Waste Regulations. Hazardous waste is classified as hazardous waste by the Hazardous Waste Regulations 2005 and the List of Wastes Regulations 2005 if it has hazardous properties. In pharmacy, the main hazardous properties seen in medicinal waste are cytotoxic or cytostatic products. The Regulations require the producer of the hazardous waste to keep hazardous waste separate from non-hazardous waste, and to segregate hazardous from non-hazardous waste if mixed wastes are received. This poses a challenge to a pharmacy that accepts unwanted medicines from patients, as the pharmacy would need to be able to identify whether any waste received is hazardous in order to carry out this segregation.

In England and Wales, producers of hazardous waste must notify the Environment Agency that it is a producer, but if a pharmacy produces less than 500 kg per year (taking into account not only medicines, but all other hazardous waste such as fluorescent tubes, computer monitors, etc.), then it is exempt from notification. Movement of hazardous waste is tightly

---

[17]Schedule 15 of the Environmental Permitting (England and Wales) Regulations SI 2010 No. 675
[18]The Hazardous Waste (England and Wales) Regulations SI 2005 No. 894 (as amended)

controlled, and must be accompanied by a detailed consignment note which describes the waste sufficiently to allow safe ultimate disposal.

Controlled Drugs

The special restrictions on the destruction of Controlled Drugs under the Misuse of Drugs Act 1971 were considered in chapter 16. Controlled Drugs, whether stock or returned by patients, are subject to the same considerations described above for other returned medicines and advice, so disposal via the sewage system would not generally be permitted. Further, the Misuse of Drugs Act requires that Controlled Drugs be denatured in such a way as to render the drug irretrievable, such as use of specially designed Controlled Drug denaturing kits. The denaturing of Controlled Drugs would be classified as 'treatment' of waste, which would require a permit, but the 2010 Regulations (see above) set out an exemption for sorting and denaturing Controlled Drugs for disposal. This exemption must be registered with the Environment Agency.

Sharps

Sharps can be returned to a pharmacy, but the health and safety of staff and persons using the pharmacy is paramount, and procedures must protect from risk of injury. The European Directive 2010/32/EU sets out requirements to prevent sharps injuries in the healthcare sector and was implemented through domestic legislation in May 2013.[19] This focuses on risk assessment, and then elimination, prevention and protection. Under this directive, the practice of recapping of needles will be prohibited (this is aimed at healthcare workers and is designed to minimise the number of needlestick injuries).

Controls to protect animals and birds

Animals in research

The Animal (Scientific Procedures) Act 1986 makes provision for the protection of animals used for experimental or scientific procedures.

A *protected animal* for the purposes of the Act means *any living vertebrate other than a human.*

A *regulated procedure* is any experimental or other scientific procedure applied to a protected animal which may have the effect of causing that animal pain, suffering, distress or lasting harm.

The Act provides for a system of (a) personal licences, (b) project licences and (c) scientific establishment licences. Before issuing any licence, the Secretary of State must consult one of the inspectors appointed under the Act (s.9). The breeding and sale of animals for experimental purposes is also controlled.

---

[19]The Health and Safety (Sharp Instruments in Healthcare) Regulations SI 2013 No. 645

The Act specifies the type of programmes for which project licences may be issued, including, among other things: the prevention, diagnosis or treatment of disease; certain educational purposes; and forensic enquiries. Projects may only be carried out by licensed persons on licensed scientific establishments. The Act deals specifically with humane methods of killing experimental animals. The Animals Procedures Committee has the duty of advising the Secretary of State on matters concerned with the Act. S/he may consult the Committee on the question of licences and on the preparation of codes of practice. Regulations[20] implementing European Directive 2010/63/EC came into force in December 2012.

Wild animals and farm livestock

Where under the Animal (Cruel Poisons) Act 1962, the Secretary of State has specified that a poison cannot be used for destroying animals without causing undue suffering and that other suitable methods of destroying them exist, s/he may, by regulations, prohibit or restrict the use of that poison for destroying animals or animals of a particular description.

Regulations have been made which prohibit the use of yellow phosphorus and red squill for the destruction of animals.[21] The Regulations also prohibit the use of strychnine for killing any animals including moles. The supply of these substances for prohibited purposes could constitute aiding and abetting an offence under the Act.

NB. Where the minister believes or suspects that rabies exists in any area, s/he may by an Order made under the Rabies Act 1974 declare that area to be an *infected area* for purposes connected with the control and eradication of that disease. S/he may also take steps to secure destruction of foxes in an *infected area* and an officer of DEFRA and any person authorised in writing by the minister may enter any land for the purpose of carrying out such destruction. Where the minister exercises this power, methods of destruction may be used (e.g. the use of strychnine) which would apart from these provisions be unlawful.[22] The Protection of Animals Act 1911 provides that it is unlawful wilfully to administer, or cause or procure to be administered, to any animal a poisonous or injurious drug or substance. Similarly, it is unlawful to sell or offer or expose for sale any grain or seed which has been rendered poisonous except for *bona fide* use in agriculture. It is also an offence to place upon any land or in any building any poison or any fluid or edible matter (not being seed or grain) which has been rendered poisonous. It is a defence to prove that the poison was placed for the purpose of destroying insects and other invertebrates where it is found necessary in the interest of public health or agriculture, or to preserve other animals, and that adequate

[20]The Animals (Scientific Procedures) Act 1986 Amendment Regulations SI 2012 No. 3039
[21]The Animals (Cruel Poisons) Regulations SI 1963 No. 1278
[22]Rabies (Control) Order SI 1974 No. 2212

precautions have been taken to prevent injury to dogs, cats, other domestic animals and wild birds.[23]

A defence also exists where a person uses poisonous gas in a rabbit hole or places in a rabbit hole a substance which by evaporation or any contact with moisture generates poisonous gas (e.g. Cymag).[24] These defences are not valid where the poison concerned is prohibited by the Animal (Cruel Poisons) Act 1962 (see above). It is also a defence under the Wildlife and Countryside Act 1981 to prove that what was done was performed in accordance with a licence granted under that Act.

In relation to wildlife, the Wildlife and Countryside Act 1981 prohibits certain methods of killing or taking of wild birds and wild animals, including the laying of 'any poisonous, poisoned or stupefying substance'. The prohibition does not apply to anything done under or in accordance with the terms of a licence granted by the appropriate authority. The appropriate authority varies according to the purpose of the licence (e.g. if the licence is issued for the purpose of preventing the spread of disease, then the appropriate authority is the Agriculture Minister). Such a licence may be issued by the Agriculture Minister for the killing or taking of certain wild birds (e.g. feral pigeons, house sparrows, etc.) using the chemical alpha-chloralose. Alpha-chloralose can be sold to local authorities and to *bona fide* pest control companies who have had issued to them by the Agriculture Minister a licence which allows them to compound and use their own bait. Farmers have been known to make approaches to pharmacists for supplies of alpha-chloralose; although the pharmacist may lawfully supply this chemical under poison legislation, a supply made for the purpose of stupefying birds could be an offence under the Wildlife and Countryside Act 1981. Pharmacists receiving requests for alpha-chloralose or stupefying bait should, before supplying, contact the RPS for further details.

Merchant shipping: medical scales

Regulations implement Council Directive 92/29/EEC and make for the minimum safety and health requirements for improved medical treatment so far as the Directive relates to the carriage of medicines and other medical stores at sea.[25] They cover the carrying of appropriate medical stores on board ships, including fishing vessels.

A *ship* in this context means a UK ship other than pleasure vessels used for non-commercial purposes and not manned by professional crews and ships employed in inland navigation.

[23] Protection of Animals (Amendment) Act 1927

[24] Prevention of Damage by Rabbits Act 1939

[25] The Merchant Shipping and Fishing Vessels (Medical Stores) Regulations SI 1995 No. 1802 (as amended)

The master of any ship which does not carry a doctor is required to make arrangements for securing medical attention on board ship to be given by him/herself or by some other person appointed by him/her for the purpose. There are minimum requirements for the medicines and medical stores to be carried before a ship may put to sea and the *scale of medicines* to be carried depends upon whether or not there is a duly qualified medical practitioner in the ship's complement.

The various scales are provided for in the 1995 Regulations and in Merchant Shipping Notices M.1607 and M.1608. The Regulations also specify requirements for the packaging, labelling and storage of medicines and other medical items (e.g. disinfectants). The containers must be labelled among other things, with:

1 the name of the medicine, in English, as indicated in the respective scale;
2 the expiry date, where appropriate;
3 any storage requirements;
4 name and address of supplier, product licence number and batch number; and
5 any further information required by the notices.

The containers of capsules and tablets must be capable of reclosure so as to prevent the ingress of moisture.

A ship in the UK may be detained if a person empowered under the Act to inspect the medical stores is not satisfied that the required stores are being carried.

Orders made under the Misuse of Drugs Act 1971 and the Medicines Act 1968 permit the owner or master of a ship which does not carry a doctor as part of its complement to obtain certain Controlled Drugs and any other POMs which are necessary for the treatment of persons on the ship. The medical scales issued under the Merchant Shipping Act are minimum requirements only.

Jury service

All persons normally resident in the UK and aged between 18 and 70 years who are registered as parliamentary or local government electors are, with very few exceptions, liable for jury service. Schedule 33 (under s.321 of the Criminal Justice Act 2003) sets out the exemptions, which are broadly: persons who are mentally disordered; persons who are or have been subject to certain detention, custody, prison or court martial sentences; and, as a discretionary exemption, persons who are needed for military service at the material time. Pharmacists have no occupational exemption. Details of what jury service entails and the payment and expenses arrangements can be found on the Court Service website at the end of this chapter.

In Scotland, pharmacists may be eligible for exemption from jury service. Exemption is not automatic and the pharmacist who wishes to be excused must give written notice to the clerk of the court from whom the citation is received, indicating his/her right and desire to be so excused. Details can be found on the Scottish Courts' website at the end of the chapter.

Summary

- This chapter outlines enactments and other measures which can be relevant to pharmacy. Some are of general application and others may apply only to one of the branches of pharmacy practice.
- Data protection and freedom of information legislation covers virtually all personal data used in pharmacy practice. Under the legislation, health professionals, including pharmacists, have a duty of confidentiality.
- The law covering being an owner, an employer or an employee is outlined as is the law relating to running a retail business and health and safety issues.
- There are controls on disposal of waste, on supply of pesticides and to protect animals and birds.
- The carriage of appropriate medical stores on board ships to fulfil minimum safety and health requirements for medical treatment where a ship does not carry a doctor is covered by scales that specify the medicines to be included.

Further reading

Fradgley S, Smith J (2012) Purple waste: how a hospital trust deals with hazardous waste medicines. *Pharm J*, 288: 417–418.

Ministry of Justice (2012) Bribery Act 2010: Guidance to help commercial organisations prevent bribery. London: Ministry of Justice: https://www.gov.uk/government/publications/bribery-act-2010-guidance (accessed 27 July 2016).

Pate R, Anderson M (2011) Good relationships must come first (about the Bribery Act). *Pharm J*, 287: 572.

Santillo M (2012) What you need to know about the new EU legislation on needlestick injuries. *Pharm J*, 288: 760–761.

Weinbren, E (2012) Pharmacy wins three-year battle against disproportionate staff vetting plans. *Chemist and Druggist*, 8 May (online).

Wilkinson E (2012) How to be disability friendly. *Chemist and Druggist*, 7 July, p. 23.

Websites

Advisory, Conciliation and Arbitration Service: http://www.acas. org.uk (accessed 27 July 2016)

Chemist and Druggist: http://www.chemistanddruggist.co.uk (accessed 27 June 2016)

Department for Business, Innovation and Skills: https://www.gov.uk/government/organisations/department-for-business-innovation-skills (accessed 27 July 2016)

Department for Environment, Food and Rural Affairs: https://www.gov.uk/government/organisations/department-for-environment-food-rural-affairs (accessed 27 July 2016)

Environment Agency (waste disposal): https://www.gov.uk/government/organisations/
environment-agency (accessed 27 July 2016)

Equality Act: https://www.gov.uk/guidance/equality-act-2010-guidance (accessed 27 July
2016)

Health and Safety Executive: http://www.hse.gov.uk (accessed 27 July 2016)

Home Office https://www.gov.uk/guidance/research-and-testing-using-animals (accessed 27
July 2016)

Home Office (disclosure and barring): https://www.gov.uk/government/organisations/
disclosure-and-barring-service

Jury service: https://www.gov.uk/jury-service/overview (accessed 27 July 2016)

Jury service in Scotland: http://www.scotcourts.gov.uk (accessed 27 July 2016)

Ministry of Justice: http://www.justice.gov.uk or
https://www.gov.uk/government/organisations/ministry-of-justice (accessed 27 July 2016)

National Pharmacy Association (leaflets and guidance on disposal of hazardous waste):
http://www.npa. co.uk (accessed 27 July 2016)

Office of the Information Commissioner: https://ico.org.uk/ (accessed 27 July 2016)

Pharmaceutical Journal: http://www.pharmaceutical-journal.com/ (accessed 27 July 2016)

Trading Standards Departments: https://www.citizensadvice.org.uk/consumer/get-more-
help/report-to-trading-standards/ (accessed 27 July 2016)

20

Pharmacy regulation

Dai John

The GPhC became the independent regulator for pharmacists, pharmacy technicians and pharmacy premises in Great Britain on 27 September 2010. Prior to this date, the RPSGB had dual regulatory and professional leadership roles. Pharmacy was the last of the healthcare professions to have an independent regulator in Great Britain. The GPhC has appointed a director in each of Scotland and Wales, recognising the divergence in Great Britain health policy and delivery.

The General Pharmaceutical Council

The role of the GPhC (also referred to as the Council) is to protect, promote and maintain the health, safety and wellbeing of members of the public by upholding standards and public trust in pharmacy. Article 4(3) of the Pharmacy Order 2010[1] identifies the principal functions of the GPhC:

a   to establish and maintain a register of pharmacists, pharmacy technicians and premises at which a retail pharmacy business is, or is to be, carried on;

b   to set and promote standards for the safe and effective practice of pharmacy at registered pharmacies;

c   to set requirements by reference to which registrants must demonstrate that their fitness to practise is not impaired;

d   to promote the safe and effective practice of pharmacy by registrants (including, for example, by reference to any code of conduct for, and ethics relating to, pharmacy);

e   to set standards and requirements in respect of the education, training, acquisition of experience and CPD that it is necessary for pharmacists and

[1] The Pharmacy Order SI 2010 No. 231; all references in this chapter are to the Pharmacy Order unless otherwise stated

pharmacy technicians to achieve in order to be entered in the Register or to receive an annotation in the Register and to maintain competence; and

f to ensure the continued fitness to practise of registrants.

The GPhC is a 'body corporate' (defined in chapter 19) which became a legal entity on 10 February 2010, with the chair and the other 13 members of the Council appointed by the Appointments Commission as designate appointments in 2009. This was formalised by the Pharmacy Order 2010 and the General Pharmaceutical Council (Constitution) Order 2010[2] and other 'commencement' orders.[3] The Pharmacy Order 2010 was enacted under powers conferred by sections 60, 62(4) and 62(4A) of, and Schedule 3 to, the Health Act 1999, as read with paragraph 1A of Schedule 2 to the European Communities Act 1972. The Council has a Great Britain rather than a UK jurisdiction, that is, it has regulatory powers in England, Scotland and Wales. The Pharmaceutical Society of Northern Ireland is the pharmacy regulator for Northern Ireland, although the two organisations work collaboratively via a Memorandum of Understanding (see websites at the end of this chapter). The GPhC has adopted the principle that, in the conduct of public business in Wales, it will treat the English and Welsh languages on a basis of equality to fulfil its obligations under the Welsh Language Act 1993 (see website at the end of this chapter).

The main powers and responsibilities of the GPhC derive from the Pharmacy Order 2010 and the Rules made under the Order. The GPhC has powers and responsibilities for the registration of pharmacy premises and for enforcing certain provisions under the Medicines Act 1968 and the Poisons Act 1972. To carry out its functions effectively the GPhC works in close collaboration with a number of other individuals and organisations. These include other regulators, other organisations such as those representing patients and the public, professional bodies such as the RPS, educators and employers. The GPhC works with a number of government agencies to avoid duplication of effort and to improve patient safety; these include the police, Care Commission in Scotland, Care Quality Commission (CQC), Health Inspectorate Wales, NHS Protect, a part of the NHS Business Services Agency (formerly the Counter Fraud and Security Management Services of the NHS), the Crown Prosecution Service, Her Majesty's Inspectorate of Prisons, the patient safety division of NHS Improvement since April 2016 (formerly the National Patient Safety Agency),[4] and the National Treatment Agency for Substance Misuse, together with the Medicines and Healthcare products Regulatory Agency (MHRA) and the Veterinary Medicines Directorate (VMD).

[2]SI 2010 No. 300
[3]SI 2010 Nos. 299, 1618, 1619 and 1621
[4]https://www.england.nhs.uk/patientsafety/

The Professional Standards Authority for Health and Social Care

The Professional Standards Authority for Health and Social Care (PSAHSC or PSA), formerly the Council for Healthcare Regulatory Excellence, oversees the work of the GPhC and eight other healthcare regulators, and promotes the health and wellbeing of patients and the public in the regulation of health professionals. The PSAHSC is also empowered to receive details of all the decisions of the GPhC's fitness to practise cases and, subject to certain conditions, to refer cases to the High Court or to the Court of Session in Scotland. (The PSAHSC is more fully discussed in chapters 21, 22 and 23.)

The Pharmacy Order 2010

This Pharmacy Order 2010 makes provision for establishing the GPhC and sets out the arrangements for regulating pharmacists and pharmacy technicians in Great Britain. It also amends and supplements various provisions in Part 4 of the Medicines Act 1968 (C. 67), and in section 9 of the Poisons Act 1972 in respect of the regulation and inspection of registered pharmacies in Great Britain. The Order also implements in part the European Council Directive 2005/36/EC, as amended by Council Directive 2006/100/EC, on pharmacy professional qualification recognition.

The Order comprises eight parts with an associated six schedules:

Part 1 Preliminary matters
Part 2 The Council and its Committees
Part 3 Registered Pharmacies: Standards in retail pharmacies
Part 4 Registration
Part 5 Education, training and acquisition of experience and continuing professional development
Part 6 Fitness to practise
Part 7 Proceedings
Part 8 Miscellaneous:

    Schedule 1 Constitution of the General Pharmaceutical Council
    Schedule 2 Visiting Practitioners from relevant European States
    Schedule 3 The Directive: Designation of competent authority etc.
    Schedule 4 Amendments, repeals and revocations
    Schedule 5 Transitional Provisions
    Schedule 6 Savings (primary and secondary legislation).

The term registrant is used in the Order and refers to a pharmacist and/or pharmacy technician, as appropriate. Article 3(2) defines what is meant by 'practice', that is, 'a person practises as a pharmacist or a pharmacy technician if, while acting in the capacity of or purporting to be a pharmacist or a pharmacy technician, that person undertakes any work or gives any advice in relation to the preparation, assembly, dispensing, sale, supply or use of medicines, the science of medicines, the practice of pharmacy or the provision of healthcare'. A registrant must have appropriate indemnity cover in respect of liabilities which may be incurred as a result of practising as a pharmacist or pharmacy technician (Art.32(1)).

Restricted titles

It is an offence for anyone, including a pharmacy student or pre-registration trainee, to use the title/practise as a 'pharmacist' or 'pharmacy technician' unless s/he is registered.

A person commits an offence (Art.38(2)) who:

a uses the title 'pharmacist' or *'fferyllydd'* (its equivalent in the Welsh language) without being entered as a pharmacist in Part 1 or 4 of the Register;

b uses the title 'pharmacy technician' or *'technegydd fferylliaeth'* (its equivalent in the Welsh language) without being entered as a pharmacy technician in Part 2 or 5 of the Register; or

c uses a title in respect of a particular annotation, which is a prescribed specialist title, where that person does not have an entry in any part of the Register with that particular annotation.

During 2014/15, the GPhC brought three criminal prosecutions under the Pharmacy Order, which each resulted in a conviction.[5]

Other restricted titles under the Medicines Act 1968 are chemist in connection with the sale of goods by retail or the supply of goods corresponding to retail sale, chemist and druggist, druggist, dispensing chemist, and dispensing druggist.[6]

Constitution Order

The Constitution Order[7] made under Article 4(2) of the Pharmacy Order requires that the Council consists of seven registrant members who are registered as pharmacists or pharmacy technicians and seven lay[8] members. There are limitations on the period for which members may serve on the Council (Art.3). The GPhC is to make provision with regard to the

---

[5]Details can be found on the GPhC website in its e-publication Regulate (12 May 2015)

[6]s.78

[7]The General Pharmaceutical Council (Constitution) Order SI 2010 No. 300

[8]Lay members are defined in Schedule 1 to the principal Order as 'members who are not and never have been entered in the register of any regulatory body and do not hold qualifications which would entitle them to apply for registration under this Order'

education and training of the Council members in standing orders (Art.4). Certain categories of people, for example people who have been convicted of certain types of offences, are disqualified from being members of the Council (Art.5) and, once members have been appointed, there are certain circumstances in which they may be removed (Art.6) or suspended from office (Art.7). Provisions relating to the chair (including powers to appoint a deputy chair) of the Council can be found in Articles 8, 9 and 10. There are also provisions relating to the proceedings of the Council including its quorum, which is eight members (Arts.11 and 12). Members of Council are appointed by the appointments commission to ensure a balance of qualities, skills and experience, and to reflect the diversity of the public and of the pharmacy profession.

Functions of the General Pharmaceutical Council

The GPhC's functions may best be grouped as the setting and enforcement of standards for pharmacy premises, education and training for entry on to the GPhC registers of registrants, registration and maintenance of their fitness to practise. The requirements for pharmacy registration are largely set out in chapter 5, but standards and enforcement are covered below. Details of these functions are set out in the Order and its schedules and in Registration Rules made under the Pharmacy Order 2010,[9] supplemented by standards and guidance formulated by the GPhC under the authority of the Order and Registration Rules. The requirements are very detailed and the standards are under regular review so reference should be made to the GPhC website for the current requirements at any time. The following is an overview of the legal underpinning for the first three of the GPhC's functions; chapter 21 looks at the range of measures which affect the professional conduct of pharmacy professionals and a full account of the fitness to practise arrangements and their application is given in chapter 22.

Standards for pharmacy premises and their enforcement

The standards for registered pharmacies set out the requirements for the provision of pharmacy services at or from a registered pharmacy (Art.7).[10] The standards for registered pharmacies are designed to create and maintain the right environment for the safe and effective practice of pharmacy, and to improve the quality and safety of services provided to patients and the public. The GPhC has also published guidance (see below).

[9] The GPhC (Registration Rules) Order of Council SI 2010 No. 1617 'Registration Rules'
[10] Art. 7 amended by the Pharmacy (Premises Standards, Information Obligations, etc.) Order SI 2016 No. 372 (Premises Standards Order)

Guidance on standards for registered pharmacies

The standards have been categorised under five principles and are of equal importance. They are as follows (with the number of components of each principle in parentheses):

- *Principle 1.* The governance arrangements safeguard the health, safety and wellbeing of patients and the public (8).
- *Principle 2.* Staff are empowered and competent to safeguard the health, safety and wellbeing of patients and the public (6).
- *Principle 3.* The environment and condition of the premises from which pharmacy services are provided, and any associated premises, safeguard the health, safety and wellbeing of patients and the public (5).
- *Principle 4.* The way in which pharmacy services, including the management of medicines and medical devices, are delivered safeguards the health, safety and wellbeing of patients and the public (4).
- *Principle 5.* The equipment and facilities used in the provision of pharmacy services safeguard the health, safety and wellbeing of patients and the public (3).

In 2013, the GPhC started to inspect registered pharmacies against these standards. As a result of moving away from a prescriptive or rules-based approach and developing standards that focus on achievement of results for patients, the GPhC has operated a prototype inspection model.

Following an inspection, the inspection decision framework is a guide to help assess how well a pharmacy is achieving the standards. The outcome of an inspection of a pharmacy premises currently results in one of four overall judgements:

1 The pharmacy is poor.
2 The pharmacy is satisfactory.
3 The pharmacy is good.
4 The pharmacy is excellent.

Where a pharmacy has not met one or more of the five GPhC premises standards, it can only be either satisfactory or poor. Further information is available on the GPhC website.[11]

The Premises Standards Order 2016 also gives the GPhC a number of new powers including the application of sanctions to owners of registered pharmacies. This Order also gives the GPhC the power to publish reports and ratings for registered pharmacies. The rating and format of reports are likely to change (see the GPhC website).

[11] http://www.pharmacyregulation.org/pharmacystandardsguide/inspections

Responding to complaints and concerns

The guidance document covers dealing with complaints and concerns raised by patients, the public and other healthcare professionals. Dispensing errors are frequently the basis for complaints to the GPhC and so it has published guidance on how to minimise the risk of a dispensing error occurring, what to do if a dispensing error occurs, and what to do afterwards (error review or root cause analysis). It supports the standards for registered pharmacies.

Guidance for registered pharmacies providing pharmacy services at a distance, including on the internet

This guidance sets out what pharmacy owners and superintendents of a body corporate should consider in providing pharmacy services at a distance. It supports the standards for registered pharmacies.

Guidance for registered pharmacies preparing unlicensed medicines

This guidance sets out what pharmacy owners and superintendents of a body corporate should consider when a registered pharmacy prepares medicines, including the preparation of extemporaneously prepared methadone. It supports the standards for registered pharmacies.

The GPhC must establish an inspectorate (Art.8) and must make provision in Rules about the intervals at which inspectors may conduct routine inspections of registered pharmacies and the circumstances in which inspectors may conduct special inspections of, and visits to, registered pharmacies (Art.9). The powers of a Council inspector are set out in Article 11 and to intentionally obstruct them in exercising their powers is an offence (Art.12). The inspector may serve an improvement notice on the person conducting a retail pharmacy business (Art.13) subject to certain conditions; further Articles detail offences committed by partnerships, appeals against improvement notices and the powers of the courts on appeal.

The GPhC reached agreement with the Care Quality Commission, the MHRA, NHS England and NHS Protect (formerly NHS Counterfraud Service) that it would be the principal regulator for inspections of registered pharmacies. Memoranda of agreement/understanding also exist with the GPhC and Health Inspectorate Wales, NHS Scotland Counter Fraud Services.

In addition to the general standards, the GPhC has issued *guidance* to owners and superintendent pharmacists on their responsibilities in ensuring compliance with the Responsible Pharmacist Regulations (chapter 5).

The Schedule to the Registration Rules makes detailed provision in respect of applications relating to Part 3 of the Register (registered pharmacies). These applications relate to entries of premises and their renewal and restoration. Applications must be made on the relevant application form and have to be accompanied by a fee determined by GPhC. Applications for the voluntary removal of an entry will usually be refused where there is an ongoing investigation or there are outstanding proceedings relating to the retail pharmacy business carried on at the registered pharmacy. The Registration Rules also set out the procedure to be followed if an entry relating to a pharmacy premises has been fraudulently procured or incorrectly made.

Education and training

Parts 4 and 5 of the Order set out the obligations of the GPhC to appoint a Registrar (Art.18), to establish, maintain and ensure access to the Register and to maintain the Register in the appropriate form and content (Art.19). The Register is in five parts:

Part 1 relating to pharmacists other than visiting practitioners
Part 2 relating to pharmacy technicians other than visiting practitioners
Part 3 relating to premises
Part 4 relating to pharmacists who are visiting practitioners
Part 5 relating to pharmacy technicians who are visiting practitioners.

Parts 4 and 5 also provide for entitlement to entry in Part 1 or Part 2 of the Register, in particular the requirements and standards for education and training of all registrants, both before and after registration. The GPhC does not register pharmacy support staff such as dispensing assistants and medicine counter assistants, but it does accredit courses for them. Part 5 requires the GPhC to set the requirements for appropriate qualifications, to hold assessments and to appoint examiners (Art.44). In connection with all aspects of education and training, the GPhC may appoint visitors to inspect any site at which relevant education or training is provided and to examine the associated assessments or tests of competence (Art.45). Education and training providers must provide the Council with relevant information when required (Art.46) and the GPhC may refuse or withdraw approval of a course, qualifications and institutions as a result of any visitor's report (Art.47).

Parts 3, 4 and 5 of the Order should be read in conjunction with the Registration Rules, which provide the detail in relation to registration issues. Part 2 of the Registration Rules requires the Register to be kept in writing and securely, although certain information is also available online in a searchable format. Part 2 also contains provisions relating to the recording of fitness to practise matters in the Register, for example if conditions have been imposed by the FTP Committee (chapter 22). Registrants are required to notify the Registrar in writing of any changes to their name or contact details. Part 3 of the Registration Rules makes detailed provision in respect of the form and manner of various applications in relation to entries in the Register and include annotations in respect of specialisations (so far the only annotations are as a pharmacist independent prescriber or a pharmacist supplementary prescriber). Applications must be made on the relevant application form (available on the GPhC website) and must be accompanied by the fee prescribed in Rules made under Article 36 of the Pharmacy Order 2010, which are reviewed annually by Council.[12] Pharmacists who have completed the relevant approved education and training as a supplementary prescriber and/or independent prescriber apply to the GPhC with evidence so that the appropriate annotation to their entry is made in the Register (chapter 8 and the GPhC website). Applications, including those regarding annotations, must generally be refused if they are not made within the prescribed time limit and if the prescribed fee is not paid (Part 3). Provision is made for the voluntary removal of entries (including annotations) in the Register for pharmacists and pharmacy technicians. Applications for the voluntary removal of an entry from the Register will generally be refused where there is an ongoing investigation or there are outstanding proceedings relating to a registrant's fitness to practise.

Part 4 of the Registration Rules contains a procedure to be followed by the Registrar for dealing with Register entries relating to registrants that may have been fraudulently procured or incorrectly made, or where the fitness to practise of a registrant was impaired at the time of the registrant's entry in the Register but was not declared.

Registration as a pharmacist

Registration in the UK can be achieved through one of two routes:

a   UK accredited 4-year Master of Pharmacy (MPharm) degree, successful completion of 52 weeks of pre-registration training in England, Scotland or Wales and having passed the GPhC's registration assessment; or

b   a UK-accredited 4-year MPharm degree, successful completion of 52 weeks of pre-registration training in Northern Ireland[13] and having passed the Pharmaceutical Society of Northern Ireland's registration examination.

Accreditation of UK pharmacist training

If a UK MPharm degree or an Overseas Pharmacist Assessment Programme (OSPAP) (see below) is not accredited (or is not provisionally accredited)

---

[12]For example, the fees for 2016 appear in the General Pharmaceutical Council (Registration and Renewal Fees) Rules 2015

[13]Formerly referred to as 'reciprocity' arrangements

by the GPhC, then this means that the graduates will not be eligible to be registered as a pharmacist. The GPhC accreditation process involves peer review, site visits, provider self-assessment and public reports. Course providers are required to periodically submit for re-accreditation. Article 42 of the Order requires the GPhC to produce standards for the initial education and training of pharmacists for MPharm and OSPAPs; these are summarised in box 20.1. The GPhC is reviewing its suite of education standards for publication some time in 2017/2018.

Box 20.1 Summary of standards for initial education and training of pharmacists

These standards provide universities with the standards for the initial education and training of pharmacists. There are requirements for submitting a degree for accreditation, which are published in the GPhC's *Accreditation and Recognition Manual*, published separately. The time between starting an MPharm degree and registration normally must be no more than 8 years.

Standard 1 Patient and public safety. There must be clear procedures to address concerns about patient safety arising from initial pharmacy education and training. Concerns must be addressed immediately.

Standard 2 Monitoring, review and evaluation of initial education and training. The quality of pharmacy education and training must be monitored, reviewed and evaluated in a systematic and developmental way.

Standard 3 Equality, diversity and fairness. Initial pharmacy education and training must be based on principles of equality, diversity and fairness. It must meet the requirements of all relevant legislation.

Standard 4 Selection of students and trainees. Selection processes must be open and fair and comply with relevant legislation. Processes must ensure that students and trainees are fit to practise as students or trainees at the point of selection. Selection includes recruitment and admissions.

Standard 5 Curriculum delivery and the student experience. The curriculum for MPharm degrees and the pre-registration scheme must deliver the outcomes in Standard 10. Most importantly, curricula must ensure that students and trainees practise safely and effectively. To ensure this, pass criteria must describe safe and effective practice.

Standard 6 Support and development for students and trainees. Students and trainees must be supported to develop as learners and professionals during their initial education and training.

Standard 7 Support and development for academic staff and pre-registration tutors. Anyone delivering initial education and training should be supported to develop in their professional role.

Standard 8 Management of initial education and training. Initial pharmacist education and training must be planned and maintained through transparent processes which must show who is responsible for what at each stage.

Standard 9 Resources and capacity. Resources and capacity are sufficient to deliver outcomes.

Standard 10 Outcomes. The outcomes for the initial education and training of pharmacists are listed in this standard.

In addition to the standards themselves, the document also lists criteria that need to be met for each standard, the evidence required in support of meeting the standards and guidance on meeting the standard. There are also prerequisites for meeting particular standards.

The standards document also contains a number of appendices and some further information:

Appendix 1 Indicative syllabus

Appendix 2 European requirements for the initial education training of pharmacists

Appendix 3 National and European requirements for master's level qualifications

Appendix 4 Sites for pharmacist pre-registration training.

Students are required to comply with the Council code of conduct for student pharmacists. The code is based on the GPhC's document *Standards of Conduct, Ethics and Performance*. Indeed, the wording of the seven principles is identical but the sub-elements sometimes differ so as to be of relevance to, and in the appropriate context for, pharmacy students. For example, Article 3.1 reads 'recognise diversity and respect the cultural differences, values and beliefs of others, including students and staff', whereas the standards for conduct, ethics and performance for registrants state at Article 3.1, 'Recognise diversity and respect people's cultural differences and their right to hold their personal values and beliefs' (chapter 21). There is a current GPhC consultation on the need or otherwise for a separate code of conduct for students or whether a single document applying to registrants and students would be more appropriate.

In addition, the GPhC has issued guidance to schools of pharmacy on developing and applying consistently fitness to practise procedures for students. Pharmacy students, as student health professionals, have certain privileges and responsibilities, for example through dealing with patients, some of whom would be classed as vulnerable. Schools of pharmacy are responsible for ensuring that students have opportunities to learn and practise to the high standards expected of them, and that they are required to be fit to practise (in terms of health and good character). It may well be, in the public interest, that an individual's conduct, for example, is not compatible with registration with the GPhC. The GPhC guidance on fitness to practise procedures states that the schools should make students aware of the requirements for registration as a pharmacist, including those relating to health and good character. In part, this is to contextualise the requirement for student fitness to practise procedures (see website references at the end of the chapter).

A number of UK universities have GPhC-accredited MPharm degrees, and a number of schools of pharmacy offer an accredited MPharm degree that is taught, in part, overseas at a partner university, currently with partner universities in Malaysia. Students enrolled on the latter, commonly referred to as 2 + 2 programmes, study the first 2 years of the MPharm at the partner university and join the university's UK MPharm course for years three and four. Students who graduate from a GPhC-accredited 2 + 2 MPharm course are eligible to enter pre-registration training in the UK and, as such, may follow the UK route to registration allowing them to practise as a pharmacist in the UK (subject to finding employment and UK Border Agency requirements). Institutions offering both types of programmes are listed on the GPhC website.

Pharmacists qualified in Northern Ireland

Reciprocity continues to exist between the Pharmaceutical Society of Northern Ireland and the GPhC (Art.20(4)). Details of additional documentation and supporting evidence that must be submitted to the GPhC can be found on the GPhC website.

Pharmacists qualified from European Economic Area countries

Regulations provide for the registration of those who are a national of an EEA country and have qualified as a pharmacist in an EEA country other than the UK.[14] Details of additional documentation and supporting evidence that must be submitted to the GPhC can be found on the GPhC website.

Pharmacists qualified from outside the European Economic Area

For those who qualified as a pharmacist outside of the EEA or for those who have an EEA pharmacist qualification (other than a UK-recognised pharmacist qualification) but are not a national of an EEA country, they must have successfully completed (a) an OSPAP, (b) 52 weeks of pre-registration training approved by the GPhC and (c) the GPhC registration assessment. Further information, including details of those universities offering the OSPAP programme, is available from the GPhC website.

Pre-registration pharmacist training

In addition to approval of qualifications, the GPhC is required to set out the conditions for a period of training, together with successful completion of a registration assessment, to be undertaken prior to registration. An integrated course combining 4 years of academic study with the equivalent of 12 months of training in practice is an alternative approach. In future years, this integrated programme (co-terminous graduation and registration) may become the norm.[15] Pre-registration training must be managed by an approved pre-registration tutor at an accredited training site. All trainees are required to achieve competence in a defined set of performance standards during their training, namely personal effectiveness, interpersonal skills and knowledge and understanding relating to medicines and health. The pre-registration period currently assesses competence in practice and establishes the individual's ability to apply knowledge, to develop and demonstrate new knowledge and skills, and to demonstrate appropriate attitudes and behaviours in practice. Individuals have a maximum of three attempts to pass the Registration Assessment. Further details of the conditions for pre-registration training and the registration assessment may be found on the GPhC website.

Registration as a pharmacy technician

Pharmacy technician training involves completing both a knowledge and a competency-based qualification. This can be achieved by undertaking either GPhC-accredited courses or qualifications recognised by the GPhC. A summary of the current standards for the initial education and training of

[14]The Pharmacy Order 2010 (Approved European Pharmacy Qualifications) Order SI 2010 No. 1620

[15]Under the Modernising Pharmacy Careers Programme, hosted by Health Education England

pharmacy technicians is set out in box 20.2. These standards are currently being reviewed.

Box 20.2 *Standards for initial training of pharmacy technicians*

The 14 standards set out the criteria against which the GPhC reviews (and approves or otherwise) pharmacy technician qualifications and training programmes.

1 There must be clear procedures to address immediately any concerns about patient safety arising from pharmacy technician education and training involving patients and the public.

2 All selection procedures must be open, fair and designed to identify those applicants who will practise safely and effectively and uphold the standards of the profession.

3 All aspects of pharmacy technician education and training must be based on principles of equality, diversity and fairness and meet the requirements of all relevant legislation.

4 The quality of pharmacy technician education and training must be monitored, reviewed and evaluated in a systematic way.

5 Trainees must be supported to acquire the necessary skills and experience through induction, effective supervision, an appropriate and realistic workload, personal support and time to learn.

6 Those involved in providing the teaching and learning must be supported to acquire the necessary skills and experience through induction, effective mentoring, continuing professional development and personal support.

7 Education and training must be planned and maintained through transparent processes which show who is responsible at each stage.

8 The education and training facilities, infrastructure, leadership and other staffing must be sufficient to deliver outcomes.

9 The programme must develop the required skills, knowledge and understanding.

10 The programme must be delivered at Qualifications and Credit Framework level 3, Scottish Credit and Qualifications Framework level 6 or equivalent.

11 The curriculum must remain relevant to current practice and national standards.

12 The assessment strategy must assure appropriate standards of assessment.

13 The assessment strategy must ensure that trainees can demonstrate the required outcomes and practise safely and effectively according to the standards of proficiency and other relevant standards and guidance when they register.

14 There must be effective monitoring and evaluation mechanisms in place to ensure appropriate standards in the assessment.

Student pharmacy technicians must abide by the GPhC Code of Conduct for pre-registration trainee pharmacy technicians. Once they are registered, they must abide by the standards for conduct, ethics and performance (see below). Applications for registration with the GPhC as a pharmacy technician can be made if the person has GPhC-approved qualifications and meets the work experience requirements, or s/he is an EEA national with an EEA pharmacy technician qualification (see website references at end of the chapter).

Other conditions for registration as a pharmacy professional

As well as completing the appropriate qualification, training and assessment requirements and paying the appropriate fee, the applicant must provide evidence of his/her identity, that his/her fitness to practise is not impaired by reason of physical or mental health and, in certain cases, evidence as to his/her good character and good repute (Arts.20–23 of the Order). A registrant must have in force an adequate and appropriate arrangement that provides cover in relation to that registrant in respect of liabilities which may be incurred by that registrant when practising (Art.32).[16] Registrants and applicants must also have the necessary knowledge of English for safe and effective practice.[17] From November 2016, the GPhC may require evidence of English language skills and has issued guidance on how this requirement is interpreted.[18] Other articles in Part 4 make provision for visiting registrants (Art.33) and temporary registrations in the case of emergencies (Art.34).

Registration appeals

Certain registration decisions are appealable and these are set out in Article 39. The GPhC must operate an Appeals Committee to deal with these

[16] The Health Care and Associated Professions (Indemnity Arrangements) Order SI 2014 No. 1887
[17] The Health Care and Associated Professions (Knowledge of English) Order SI 2015 No. 806
[18] New Rule 8A in registration rules as amended by the GPhC (Amendment of Miscellaneous Provisions) Rules Order of Council SI 2016 No. 1008

appeals (Art.40) and further appeal is permitted to the courts (Art.41). Further details of these processes are set out in GPhC Rules[19] and on the GPhC website. The Appeals Committee must, as soon as is reasonably practicable, send the person bringing the appeal the Committee's decision and the reasons for it and of any right of appeal. Rule 10 provides that the burden of proof is on the appellant and that the civil standard of proof applies (chapter 1). An example of an Appeals Committee case is provided in box 20.3.

Box 20.3 *Registration Appeal case: pharmacy technician Tuesday, 18th October 2011*

The appellant appealed against a decision of the Registrar on 11 July 2011 not to enter her as a pharmacy technician in Part 2 of the Register maintained by the Council. By virtue of Article 39(1)(b) of the Order, a decision by the Registrar not to enter a person in Part 2 of the Register is an appealable decision. This was a meeting of the Appeals Committee and not a hearing and so it did not hear oral evidence.

On 5 December 2005, the appellant had pleaded guilty at Croydon Magistrates' Court to four offences of making a false representation with a view to obtaining a benefit under the social security legislation for herself. The offences were committed in the period 2001 to 2004. She was sentenced to a community punishment order for 100 hours in respect of each offence and was also sentenced to a fine. The appellant applied to the RPSGB for voluntary registration as a pharmacy technician in 2008. In her application dated 24 May 2008 she declared that she had been convicted of a criminal offence which related to the overpayment of benefit. On receipt of this information, the then RPSGB Registrar investigated the circumstances of the conviction and following that investigation decided on 2 October 2008 to refuse the appellant's application to be entered in the Register.

In February 2011, the appellant then made an application to be entered in the Council's Register. In that application at paragraph 3.1 she was asked 'Have you ever applied previously for registration with the Royal Pharmaceutical Society of Great Britain (RPSGB) or the General Pharmaceutical Council (GPhC), either as a pharmacy technician ... ?' The appellant ticked the 'No' box.

She was also asked: 'Have you previously been convicted or cautioned for a criminal offence in the British Islands or elsewhere ... ?'

---

[19]The General Pharmaceutical Council (Appeals Committee Rules) Order of Council SI 2010 No. 1614 'Appeals Rules'

The appellant ticked the 'No' box. Further on in the application the appellant made a number of declarations as follows

7.2 The information that I have provided in this application for registration is complete, true and accurate...

I understand that [7.6] If I am found to have given false or misleading information in connection with my application for registration in the Register, this may be treated as misconduct, which may result in my removal from the Register.

The Registrar wrote to the appellant on 11 July 2011 to notify her of his decision to refuse her application for registration as a pharmacy technician. In giving his reasons, he referred to the appellant's failure to declare her conviction and a previous application for registration with the Society; her declarations on the application form and to her understanding of the consequences of giving false or misleading information at 7.6 of the application form.

He also referred to the conviction in the following terms:

In your application of 24 May 2008 you disclosed your conviction at Croydon Magistrates' [sic] in December 2005 for making dishonest representations to obtain benefit. Following careful consideration by the Registrar of the former pharmacy regulator [the Society], your application for registration was refused. You were notified of the Registrar's decision by letter dated 2 October 2008. Reasons for the decision to refuse included not only the serious nature of the offences and that they were committed whilst you were practising as a pharmacy technician but also:

i your failure to provide evidence of your insight into the offences,

ii your lack of understanding of the offences' relevance to the practice of pharmacy, and

iii your decision not to provide supporting testimonials despite being given the opportunity to do so.

In concluding his reasons for refusing to register the Registrar wrote:

The GPhC's standards of conduct, ethics and performance require registrants to act with honesty and integrity to maintain public trust and confidence in the profession. In all the circumstances, I consider that you have demonstrated a failure to meet this standard and that granting your application would undermine public confidence in the regulation of the pharmacy profession and may bring the profession into disrepute.

Rule 10 of the Appeal Rules establishes that the Appellant bears the burden of establishing that the appealable decision should be overturned and Rule 10(2) sets out that:

> If the appeal is against a decision to refuse to enter the appellant . . . in the Register, the Committee may only decide to enter, or direct the Registrar to enter, the appellant . . . in the Register if the appellant has proved that the appellant is . . . entitled to be so entered.

Article 20(1)(a)(ii) of the Pharmacy Order states that a person is entitled to be entered in Part 2 of the register as a pharmacy technician if, among other matters, the Registrar is satisfied that the person's fitness to practise is not impaired. Article 51(1) of the same order states that 'A person's fitness to practise is to be regarded as "impaired" for the purposes of this Order only by reason of' and then sets out 14 criteria, including misconduct and a conviction in the British Islands for a criminal offence.

The representations of the appellant included statements relating to remorse and regret of her actions and 'mistakes'. She stated that she believed that her conviction had no bearing on her ability to carry out a role as a pharmacy technician to the highest possible standard.

Written submissions on behalf of the Council argued that the appellant 'deliberately told untruths to her regulatory body by positively asserting that she had no previous convictions and that she does not in her notice of appeal address the issue why she did not mention her previous application for registration'.

> Having carefully considered all the evidence submitted together with the submissions made by both the appellant and the respondent the decision of the committee is to dismiss the appeal. The committee noted that the Council had argued that both misconduct and a conviction, in fact four convictions, were present here triggering consideration of impairment of fitness to practise. The committee recognised that the convictions were in respect of behaviour several years ago and also noted that the offences did not, on the information supplied to it, require proof of dishonesty to establish a conviction. The committee therefore

regarded the convictions as not establishing dishonest behaviour by the appellant in 2001, 2002 and 2004. The committee did however regard the appellant's behaviour in knowingly submitting an application for registration in 2011 that was wrong in a number of respects as dishonest, which the appellant accepts. The committee also noted that the appellant's behaviour both in relation to the matters for which she was convicted and in relation to her application in 2011 all involved her over a period of ten years in making false representations in order to secure an advantage to herself; benefits to which she was not entitled in the case of the convictions and to improve her chances of being registered in the case of the application this year.

The committee concluded that it was 'not satisfied that the appellant has proved that her fitness to practice is not impaired' and informed the appellant of her right of appeal, under Article 41(1) of the Pharmacy Order, against its decision.

See chapter 22 for information relating to impaired fitness to practise.

Continuing fitness to practise

Part 5 of the Order contains powers to regulate training both before and after registration (Arts.42 and 43) through continuing professional development (CPD) and, in due course, through processes to ensure continuing fitness to practise (often called revalidation). In September 2014, the GPhC published its timetable for developing and implementing a continuing fitness to practise (CFTP) framework, which pharmacists and pharmacy technicians will use in 2018. A pilot is currently under way. Until then, the standards for CPD in box 20.4 apply to all registrants. There is a current consultation on the sampling of CPD records for review by the GPhC.

Box 20.4 *Standards for continuing professional development*

The CPD requirements apply to all pharmacy professionals and the CPD record is expected to cover the full scope of practice and roles. The CPD standards are as follows:

1.1 Keep a record of your CPD that is legible, either electronically online at the website www.uptodate.org.uk, on another computer, or as hard copy on paper and in a format published or approved by us and carrying the CPD-approved logo.

1.2 Make a minimum of nine CPD entries per year which reflect the context and scope of your practice as a pharmacist or pharmacy technician.

1.3 Keep a record of your CPD that complies with the good practice criteria for CPD recording published in Plan and Record by us (www.uptodate.co.uk).

1.4 Record how your CPD has contributed to the quality or development of your practice using our CPD framework.

1.5 Submit your CPD record to us on request.

Rules made under Article 43 of the Pharmacy Order[20] mean that an appearance before the FTP Committee is possible (subject to the following of procedures as laid out in rules) for failing to submit appropriate CPD records in response to a request by the Council.

English language competency

As stated above under conditions for registration, legislation has strengthened the GPhC's powers to require all applicants to provide evidence of their knowledge of the English language before registration. Once registered, however, all registrants are required to practise pharmacy in Great Britain in accordance with the GPhC's Standards for Pharmacy Professionals (see chapter 21), which cover effective communication to enable users to make informed decisions and choices. Practising pharmacy in breach of these standards could result in fitness to practise proceedings (chapter 22). Entry requirements to UK MPharm and OSPAP programmes generally require evidence of English language proficiency.

Remaining parts of the Pharmacy Order 2010

Parts 6 and 7 of the Pharmacy Order are concerned with standards of conduct ethics and performance (Art.48; see chapter 21) and powers and processes to deal with allegations of impaired fitness to practise (chapter 22). Part 8 of the Order provides powers for the GPhC to charge reasonable fees in connection with its functions (Art.65) and to make Rules in connection

[20]The General Pharmaceutical Committee (CPD and Consequential Amendments) Order of Council SI 2011 No. 1367

with its functions (Art.66). Article 67 designates the GPhC as the competent authority in respect of Directive 2005/36/EC.

Other standards and guidance

Much of the GPhC standards and guidance relates to the behaviour and conduct of registrants – pharmacists and pharmacy technicians – and these are covered in greater detail in chapter 21. Some set out obligations on registrants and require the owner and pharmacist superintendent to support registrants in achieving them (the legal requirements for Responsible Pharmacists are covered in chapter 5). Standards and guidance are available on the GPhC website as is a glossary of terms used within them.

Summary

- The primary role of the GPhC is to protect, promote and maintain the health, safety and wellbeing of members of the public by upholding standards and public trust in pharmacy. It achieves this in a number of ways such as:
  - approving qualifications for registrants,
  - accrediting education and training providers,
  - maintaining a register of pharmacists, pharmacy technicians and pharmacy premises,
  - establishing and promoting standards for registered pharmacies,
  - monitoring pharmacy professionals' fitness to practise and dealing in a proportionate and fair way with complaints and concerns, and
  - setting standards and providing guidance.
- The GPhC derives its powers from the Pharmacy Order 2010 and Rules made under the Order.

Further reading

Websites

Association of Pharmacy Technicians UK: http://www.aptuk.org
General Pharmaceutical Council (details of pharmacy standards): http://www.pharmacy regulation.org

> The GPhC is a public body and all its activities are mostly available to the public and professionals alike (some exceptions are hearings on fitness to practise that are held in private). The material appearing on its website is expanding rapidly at the time of going to press and it may not be helpful to give precise locations as these may change. However, the following guide may help readers to locate many of the documents referred to in the chapter text:
>
> - Memorandum of Understanding with Pharmaceutical Society of Northern Ireland: see under about us
> - Organisations which Council works with: see under about us

- Welsh language scheme: see under pharmacy regulation
- UK and overseas registration: see under registration
- All standards and guidance: see under standards
- Student registrant code of conduct: see under education
- Accredited institutions and courses: see under education
- Pre-registration training: see under education

Guild of Healthcare Pharmacists: http://www.ghp.org.uk

Legislation (can be searched on year and SI number or title): http://www.legislation.gov.uk

National Pharmacy Association (for pharmacy owners and their employees): http://www.npa.org.uk

Pharmacists Defence Association (for individual pharmacists): http://www.the-pda.org

Professional Standards Authority for Health and Social Care (formerly Council for Healthcare Regulatory Excellence): http://www.professionalstandards.org.uk

Royal Pharmaceutical Society: http://www.rpharms.com

21

Professional conduct

Dai John and David H Reissner

This chapter deals with the professional conduct of pharmacists, pharmacy technicians and pharmacy students. The concept of professional conduct also includes professional ethics. It will be seen that professional conduct is not limited to behaviour in a professional setting. A wider exposition of pharmacy ethics, its underpinning moral philosophy and how it interfaces with healthcare law is beyond the scope of this book. However, interested readers are referred to the Further reading at the end of the chapter. The concept of good professional conduct and misconduct is now embodied in the wider disciplinary term 'impaired fitness to practise', which is the basis for all disciplinary referrals within the pharmacy profession (chapter 22) and indeed all other health professions.

The term 'profession' was formerly applied only to the church, the law and medicine – the three 'learned' professions. The meaning of the term is now broader, as is apparent from the definition in the *Oxford English Dictionary*: 'a vocation in which a professed knowledge of some department of learning is used in its application to the affairs of others, or in the practice of an art founded upon it'. In modern usage, it seems that almost all occupations that require some measure of intellectual training can be described as professions. However, an organised profession requires more than the mere existence of an intellectual discipline. The essence of professionalism is the relationship of trust which exists between the practitioner and the person who receives his/her advice or services. The recipient, relying entirely on the knowledge of the practitioner, must be able to have complete trust in his/her services and the impartiality of his/her advice. It follows that there must be an established minimum standard of knowledge for practitioners, and that there must be agreement amongst them about standards of behaviour in their professional work. This means that there must be a body – a regulator – which determines the standard of education and establishes the code of conduct. In the past, this regulator has been representative of practitioners and subject to their control but since the various scandals of the late 1990s, and reports such as those following the Bristol Royal Infirmary Inquiry and the Shipman Inquiry, healthcare professional regulators who maintain registers of practitioners are required to put the public interest first; they set standards and oversee the fitness to practise of registrants (chapters 22 and 23). Further change remains possible. For example, in 2014, the Law Commission recommended[1] among other things that the law should set out that the main objective of each regulator and of the Professional Standards Authority should be to protect, promote and maintain the health, safety and wellbeing of the public, and that there should be a general objective to promote and maintain public confidence in the profession and to promote and maintain proper standards and conduct for individual registrants. Although some of the Law Commission's recommendations are modelled on the Pharmacy Order 2010 and the regulations made under it, other recommendations have not yet been given legal effect.

The profession of pharmacy

If the characteristics described are accepted as the elements of a profession, then pharmacy meets the essential requirements, which are four in number (box 21.1).

> **Box 21.1** *Elements of a profession*
>
> *An intellectual discipline and a standard of knowledge.* Pharmacy is of ancient origin. In Great Britain, it was never clearly separated from medicine until the formation of the Pharmaceutical Society of Great Britain in 1841. Membership of the Society was, from the first, by examination, but it was not until the Pharmacy Act 1868 that all newcomers to the profession who wished to practise were required to pass a qualifying examination, whether or not they intended to become members of the Society. Today, a university degree in pharmacy together with 12 months of practical training is required before registration as a pharmacist (see chapter 20).
>
> *A representative body of practitioners.* The GPhC is the regulatory body for pharmacists and pharmacy technicians. The standards of conduct, ethics and performance for pharmacists and pharmacy technicians reflect not just of the views of pharmacists and pharmacy technicians, but also of those who support, regulate and use pharmacy services.
>
> *Standards of conduct.* There are accepted standards of conduct, ethics and performance known throughout the profession. They are

---

[1] Regulation of Health Care Professionals, Law Com No. 345

enforceable by virtue of the Pharmacy Order 2010 via the GPhC's fitness to practise procedures. The GPhC's FTP Committee takes into account the standards of conduct, ethics and performance when considering professional conduct but is not bound by it (chapter 22).

Service and advice. Pharmacists have traditionally been mainly concerned with the supply to the public of medicines, either in response to a prescription or other authority or sold over the counter. In these supplies, the pharmacist should give whatever advice is necessary in the interest of the patient or customer. Increasingly, pharmacists are also concerned with the provision of services specifically to improve health and the management and use of medicines, usually accompanied by advice or recommendations, intervention and support for patients and fellow health professionals. Some pharmacists have prescribing rights.

Trade and profession

There is a deep-rooted feeling that trading and professional activities are incompatible. Yet what is the difference between making a living from selling one's professional services and making a living from the buying and selling of goods? The professional person might have some difficulty in explaining his/her objections to commerce without casting doubts on the integrity of the tradesperson. Although there is an element of snobbery in it, there is undoubtedly a difference between the trading outlook and the professional outlook. The tradesperson, however honest, is principally concerned with the profitability of his/her business. His/her main object is to achieve as large a financial return as possible. S/he holds his/her customers to be the best judges of what they want and s/he seeks to satisfy their demands. The old common law maxim applicable to *trade* (contracts of sale) was 'let the buyer beware'.

Professional people working in their special field of knowledge where their advice is crucial must often be the judges of what is best for their clients or customers, although patients are increasingly encouraged to take part in and exercise choice over healthcare decisions. Indeed this principle is now accepted in the 2010–2012 NHS reforms, which promote the policy of 'no decision about me without me'[2] and principle 4 of the NHS Constitution ('The patient will be at the heart of everything the NHS does').[3] If professionals act according to the standards of their profession, then

[2] Available on the Department of Health website: www.dh.gov.uk
[3] 2015 – the Constitution applies to England, but similar principles are expected elsewhere in the UK

the advice they give must, at times, be to the practitioners' own financial disadvantage. It is recognition of this essential trust by the public which confers any special status the professional person may have.

Some pharmacists do not engage in trade, although within the context of the NHS (chapter 24) they are increasingly involved in marketing their services and operating within budgets and business constraints similar to those applied in retailing. However, the majority of pharmacists in community pharmacy practise pharmacy in a trading environment. In addition to the supply of medicines and the provision of other professional services, they often sell other goods. Those working in retail pharmacy businesses were referred to as working in a trading profession by Lord Wilberforce in the Dickson case of the 1960s (box 21.2).

Box 21.2 *The Dickson case*

Pharmaceutical Society of Great Britain v Dickson (1968)

Arising out of a recommendation of the Report on the General Practice of Pharmacy (*Pharm J*, 20 April 1963), a motion was put to the Annual General Meeting of the Pharmaceutical Society in 1965 (then both the regulator of the profession and a members' organisation) in the following terms:

New pharmacies should be situated only in premises which are physically distinct, and should be devoted solely to:

 i Professional services, as defined
 ii Non-professional services, as defined, and
 iii such other services as may be approved by the Council, and
 iv the range of services as may be approved by the Council; and the range of services in existing pharmacies, or in pharmacy departments of larger establishments should not be extended beyond the present limits except as approved by the Council.

RCM Dickson (a director of Boots Pure Drug Co. Ltd) sought an injunction to restrain the holding of a meeting to consider the recommendation, claiming that the motion was outside the scope of the Society's powers and was a restraint of trade.

The case went to the House of Lords, where it was held that:

The proposed restriction, although intended to be binding in honour only, might be a basis for disciplinary action.

It was not within the powers or purposes of the Society to control selling activities which did not interfere with the proper performance of professional pharmaceutical duties.

This decision did not affect the Society's powers to regulate professional conduct in pharmacy – a function now of the GPhC.

NB The Pharmaceutical Society became 'Royal' in 1988

[1968] 2 All ER 686 *Pharm J*, 1 June 1968 p. 651. This was an appeal by the Society to the House of Lords against an Order of the Court of Appeal ([1967] All ER 558; *Pharm J*, 4 February 1967 p. 113), which upheld a judgment of the High Court (Chancery Division) ([1966] 3 All ER 404; *Pharm J*, 2 July 1966 p. 22).

Professional ethics and law

Ethics is the science of morals, or moral philosophy. The principles, written or unwritten, that are accepted in any profession as the basis for proper behaviour are the ethics of the profession. Rules of law and rules of ethics are commonly held to differ because law is enforced by the state whilst ethical rules are only morally binding. However, law and ethics are not opposites. The law itself has a basis in ethics; in general, it reflects the moral standards of the community. Criminal law comprises those rules of conduct which the community (through the common law and through parliament) has decided must be observed on pain of a penalty, such as a fine or imprisonment. Criminal law, therefore, includes the Medicines, Poisons and Misuse of Drugs Acts and the Human Medicines Regulations,[4] where transgression may result in prosecution. Other parliamentary legislation creates administrative law, which gives power to public bodies to regulate certain activities carried out on behalf of the public. The NHS Terms of Service is an example. A breach may result in an administrative sanction following investigation under the NHS complaints procedures (chapter 24).

Moral obligations are also recognised by the state through common law, which essentially enshrines certain duties which individuals owe to one another. Breach of these duties may result in action through the civil law courts to seek compensation for a 'civil wrong'. The most familiar of these is probably an action alleging negligence on the part of a health practitioner. Negligence is just one of a range of torts, or civil wrongs, and is discussed in more detail later in this chapter. Another tort which might arise in pharmacy practice is breach of confidentiality. Pharmacists, as they become integrated into the healthcare team, will increasingly come into possession of sensitive information and will be expected to observe strict confidentiality over the use and disclosure of such information. The

[4]Many offences formerly in the Medicines Act 1968 are now to be found in the Human Medicines Regulations 2012

Information Commissioner has brought a prosecution[5] where a pharmacist accessed patient records of friends and family out of curiosity rather than for professional purposes, and the FTP Committee[6] has imposed sanctions on the pharmacist and, in another case (see chapter 22), a pharmacy technician who did something similar. In the case of Pharmacy2U,[7] an online pharmacy business that sold patient data, the Information Commissioner imposed a fine of £130 000, and the FTP Committee[8] suspended one of its directors from practice.

However, the state does not attempt to enforce every rule of social behaviour, nor does it interfere in those matters which are by common consent left to the consciences of individuals (e.g. religious observance) so long as they do not affect compliance with professional standards, or in those standards which are agreed among a profession provided that they can be seen to be necessary for the further protection of the public. In the fitness to practise case of Piotr Majchrowicz (see chapter 22), the registrant had told a patient seeking emergency hormonal contraception that she was ending a life. The FTP Committee said that the GPhC recognises and makes allowance for the inability of pharmacists with certain religious beliefs to supply certain medicines or provide certain services as to do so would be in conflict with their religious beliefs. The proper course in these situations is to refer the patient to another pharmacy or pharmacist. What a pharmacist must not do is endeavour to impose his/her own beliefs and moral code upon the patient.

Former codes of ethics

Ever since the foundation of the then Pharmaceutical Society of Great Britain in 1841, there has been concern about the need to maintain and improve standards of conduct in pharmacy. The advantage of having a written code was recognised, but nothing positive emerged until the changes made by the Pharmacy and Poisons Act 1933 gave the Society wider authority, including the power to take disciplinary action and to remove names from the Register. A proposal for a code of ethics made by the Teesside branch of the Society in 1937 was widely discussed, but it was found difficult to strike the right balance between a general description of good behaviour and the expression of specified principles in clear-cut terms. The document which was finally

[5] https://ico.org.uk/about-the-ico/news-and-events/news-and-blogs/2014/11/pharmacist-who-unlawfully-spied-on-family-and-friends-medical-records-prosecuted/
[6] https://www.pharmacyregulation.org/search/search_decisions/dhanju
[7] https://ico.org.uk/action-weve-taken/enforcement/pharmacy2u-ltd/
[8] https://www.pharmacyregulation.org/search/search_decisions/pharmacy2u

accepted by the profession was the first attempt at a written code. An amended version of this *Statement upon Matters of Professional Conduct* was later published in the *Pharmaceutical Journal* (17 June 1944). Other amendments led to the publication of revised versions in 1953, 1964, 1970, 1984, 1992 and 2007. Since October 2010, the setting of standards and guidance for pharmacists and pharmacy technicians became the responsibility of the GPhC and this chapter looks first at the professional control exercised by the regulator. The GPhC also publishes a Code of Conduct for Pharmacy Students. In addition, it should be noted that, in July 2014, the GPhC and the Royal Pharmaceutical Society (RPS) published a joint statement 'Using standards and guidance to ensure patient centred professionalism in the delivery of care'. The statement outlines the importance of using standards and guidance from both bodies (where relevant) to ensure patient-centred professionalism in the delivery of care. The principal functions of the GPhC[9] include setting and promoting standards for the safe and effective practice of pharmacy. The prime purpose of GPhC standards is the protection of the public; the RPS publishes professional standards to describe good practice and systems of care or working.

Standards for pharmacy professionals

As outlined in chapter 20, the GPhC has the duty to set standards as the basis by which a registrant's fitness to practise may be assessed.[10] The GPhC must also make Rules setting out the criteria to which the FTP Committee (chapter 2) is to have regard when considering whether a registrant (pharmacist or pharmacy technician) is fit to practise.[11] The legislation makes it clear that failure to comply with such standards is not, of itself, evidence of misconduct (one of the grounds for alleging impaired fitness to practise) but is to be taken into account in any fitness to practise proceedings against a registrant. At its inception in 2010, the GPhC largely adopted the wording of the Code of Ethics developed by the former RPSGB in its standards of conduct, ethics and performance. Since these were still in force at the time of writing, a summary of these standards appears in Appendix 4. However, from 1 May 2017, registrants must comply with the standards for pharmacy professionals, a summary of which is given in box 21.3 below. The full and current text with accompanying guidance is available on the GPhC website.

[9] Article 4 of the Pharmacy Order 2010
[10] Article 48 of the Pharmacy Order SI 2010 No. 231
[11] The GPhC (Fitness to Practise and Disqualification, Etc. Rules) Order SI 2010 No. 1615 (FTP Rules)

> **Box 21.3** *Summary of standards for pharmacy professionals*
>
> Standards for pharmacy professionals
>
> All pharmacy professionals contribute to delivering and improving the health, safety and wellbeing of patients and the public. Professionalism and safe and effective practice are central to that role.
>   Pharmacy professionals must:
>
> 1 provide patient-centred care;
> 2 work in partnership with others;
> 3 communicate effectively;
> 4 maintain, develop and use their professional knowledge and skills;
> 5 exercise professional judgement;
> 6 behave in a professional manner;
> 7 respect and maintain the person's privacy and confidentiality;
> 8 speak up when they have concerns or when things go wrong;
> 9 demonstrate leadership.

Each standard is underpinned by examples of attitudes and behaviour which are expected in meeting the standards. However, the application of ethical standards can be challenging, particularly when two competing ethical principles may be present in a given situation. A significant understanding is needed of the moral theory underpinning professional behaviour coupled with possession of skills in resolving professional dilemmas and taking decisions, and an appreciation of competing accountabilities both in law and through professional regulation (for more information see the Further reading list at the end of this chapter).

The standards for registered pharmacies are covered in chapter 20.

Guidance

The GPhC has seen fit to publish additional guidance in certain areas of practice where the application of the Standards may not be sufficient to support practice. The guidance that has been published at the time of going to press is given below; however, the Council is committed to a regular review of all its standards and guidance so readers should check on the GPhC website for the latest versions, which are also available in the Welsh language.

Guidance on standards for pharmacy professionals

Responsible Pharmacists

The legislation on Responsible Pharmacists is covered in chapter 5. This guidance is intended to complement guidance for owners and superintendent pharmacists who employ Responsible Pharmacists.

Consent

The guidance describes what is meant by consent, the two types of consent (explicit and implied), ways in which consent can be obtained, and capacity or otherwise to give consent (including assessment of capacity).

Maintaining clear sexual boundaries

The guidance outlines the importance of maintaining clear sexual boundaries. It describes the power imbalance which normally exists between a patient and a pharmacy professional, identifies that cultural and other reasons can lead to differences in what individuals see as appropriate or inappropriate and also provides guidance on the use of a chaperone, which is defined within the guidance (at 5.1):

> A chaperone is a person (usually the same sex as the patient) who is present as a safeguard for the patient and the healthcare professional. They are also a witness to the patient's continuing consent for the procedure. Their role may vary depending on the needs of the patient, the pharmacy professional and the examination or procedure being carried out.

Patient confidentiality

The guidance contains information on the duty of confidentiality, protecting confidential information and disclosing information (with consent and under circumstances where there has not been consent).

The provision of pharmacy services affected by religious and moral beliefs

The guidance document includes guidance for pharmacy professionals and for those who employ them. It includes guidance for those who hold such beliefs on what they should do before (or if) they accept employment as well as what to do when circumstances arise.

Raising concerns

The guidance outlines the importance of raising concerns, how to raise a concern and the legal aspects, including an outline of the Public Interest Disclosure Act 1998, which protects employees who raise genuine concerns in the workplace. Furthermore, it provides additional guidance for employers.

Demonstrating professionalism online

This guidance sets out what should be considered by pharmacy professionals when using social media.

Female genital mutilation: mandatory duty for pharmacy professionals to report

This guidance explains when a mandatory duty applies, when to follow existing local safeguarding procedures and how these obligations align with GPhC standards.

Duty of candour

Following the Francis report into very poor care received by patients at Mid Staffordshire Hospital Trust (see chapter 23), a legal duty of candour was added to the standards required of sites and activities regulated by the Care Quality Commission. In October 2014, the chief executives of statutory regulators of healthcare professionals (including the GPhC) adopted guidance in the form of a joint statement about openness and honesty with patients when things go wrong. The statement says that healthcare professionals must:

- tell the patient (or, where appropriate, the patient's advocate, carer or family) when something has gone wrong;
- apologise to the patient (or, where appropriate, the patient's advocate, carer or family);
- offer an appropriate remedy or support to put matters right (if possible); and
- explain fully to the patient (or, where appropriate, the patient's advocate, carer or family) the short- and long-term effects of what has happened.

Moreover, health professionals must be open and honest with their colleagues, employers and relevant organisations, and take part in reviews and investigations when requested. They must be open and honest with their regulators, raising concerns where appropriate, supporting and encouraging each other to be open and honest, and not stop someone from raising concerns. The guidance has the title 'Joint statement on the professional duty of candour'.

Negligence

Taken together, the standards and associated guidance from the GPhC set the 'standard of care' and hence the 'duty of care' expected of practising pharmacists and pharmacy technicians. These terms are also used widely in the civil law, which is concerned with duties owed between one citizen and another, particularly in matters of *negligence*. The extent to which a healthcare professional did, or did not, discharge his/her duty of care towards a patient, or other recipient of his/her services is the key consideration in negligence cases and the award of compensation if a failure of duty of care is found. Readers should also note that the two processes, a fitness to practise inquiry by the GPhC and an action in negligence in the civil courts, are not mutually exclusive. The same failure of duty of care may lead to both. If a failure in care leads to a death then allegations may also be heard in the criminal courts as charges of 'gross negligence manslaughter' and/or 'corporate manslaughter'. These are discussed at the end of this chapter and a discussion of types of law can also be found in chapter 1. Furthermore, errors that result in a death may lead to a prosecution under section 64 of the Medicines Act 1968 (see chapters 13 and 22) and any errors could lead to a performance tribunal under the NHS law governing the community pharmacy contract (chapter 24).

Professional or clinical negligence

A pharmacy owner, pharmacist and/or any member of the pharmacy staff may be faced with an action for negligence in the civil courts. The essence of the tort of negligence is that there is on the part of the defendant a legal duty of care which s/he has failed to meet, as a result of which the plaintiff has suffered damage. The duty to take care was described in the case of *Donoghue v Stevenson*[12] thus:

> You must take reasonable care to avoid acts or omissions which you can reasonably foresee would be likely to injure your neighbour. Who, then, in law is my neighbour? The answer seems to be...persons who are so closely and directly affected by my act that I ought reasonably to have them in contemplation as being so affected when I am directing my mind to the acts or omissions which are called in question.

The law imposes a duty to take care in a variety of circumstances. As sellers of goods, community pharmacists have a duty to take reasonable care to warn customers of any potential dangers arising from them.[13] Quite apart from this general duty on all sellers of goods, there is a special relationship between pharmacists and their customers in respect of transactions involving pharmaceutical knowledge. Reliance is placed upon the special skill and knowledge of the pharmacist when selling, dispensing or prescribing medicinal products. The law would expect him/her to exercise that degree of competence which the average member of the profession is required to possess. This is known as the 'duty of care'. A pharmacist occupying a special position in any branch of pharmacy would be expected to have a degree of ability commensurate with that position. Pharmacists are with good reason recognised as experts on medicines, and their role in the provision of health services continues to widen.[14] Every right has its correlative duty, and pharmacists, as they achieve greater recognition, must expect the law to require from them a higher degree of skill. It is probable that they will, as a consequence, be increasingly liable to actions for professional negligence.

[12] [1932] Appeal Cases 562, 580
[13] This is in addition to the strict liability imposed by the Sale of Goods Act 1979 on the sellers of goods that are not fit for purpose or which are not of satisfactory quality
[14] http://www.nhs.uk/NHSEngland/AboutNHSservices/pharmacists/Pages/pharmacistsand chemists.aspx

Four High Court decisions illustrate this point well (box 21.4). The apportioning of liability is now an accepted principle in dispensing negligence cases, as demonstrated in the more recent cases in box 21.4, the 'Epilim case' and the 'dexamethasone case'.

Box 21.4 Four High Court decisions illustrating issues of liability to actions for professional negligence

The 'Migril case'

A woman who suffered gangrene in both feet, requiring extensive surgery, as a result of receiving an overdose of Migril (ergotamine tartrate, cyclizine hydrochloride and caffeine citrate) prescribed for migraine was awarded over £130 000 damages.

The owner of the pharmacy, who admitted negligence, was held liable for 45% of the damages awarded. The judge, Mr Justice Stuart-Smith, in making the award said that the pharmacist owed a duty to the patient to ensure that drugs were correctly prescribed and that the pharmacist should have spotted the doctor's error and queried the prescription with the prescriber. He said:

> Pharmacists . . . have to exercise an independent judgment to ensure that the drug is apt for the patient as well as that it conforms to the physician's requirements. It is an active duty and . . . it is what the chemist writes on the label that is the critical thing so far as the patient is concerned. The patient will often forget, or not pay attention to what the doctor may say at the time of prescribing, but he or she relies on the written instructions on the bottle given by the chemist.

It is clear from the judgment that a pharmacist must not be deterred in querying prescriptions with the prescriber by any adverse response on the part of the prescriber, who may resent his/her decisions being questioned. The legal and professional responsibility of the pharmacist to verify and question prescriptions has been highlighted and established by this case.

Dwyer v Roderick, Jackson and Cross Chemists (Banbury) Limited (unreported, 10 February 1982); *Pharm J*, 20 February 1982 p. 205

The 'Daonil case'

In another case in 1988, a patient visited his doctor for his regular prescription for inhalers and tablets. At the same time, he was prescribed Amoxil (amoxicillin) for a chest infection. When he took the handwritten prescription to the pharmacy, the pharmacist misread amoxil (with the first letter written as a lower case 'a') as Daonil (glibenclamide) and the patient suffered irreversible brain damage.

Mr Justice Auld in awarding a total of £100 000 damages (apportioned according to perceived responsibility for negligence as to 75% against the pharmacist and 25% against the doctor) said that, even assuming that the prescription was unclear, the pharmacist should have been alerted to the fact that Daonil was being recommended in an inappropriate dosage and quantity. He should also have noticed that the man who collected the drugs did not claim exemption from paying an NHS prescription charge for the Daonil, although diabetics were entitled to exemption from prescription charges. It was not enough for pharmacists to blindly dispense drugs without giving thought to what they were doing. Giving the decision in the High Court, Mr Justice Auld held that a doctor had a duty to his/her patient to write a prescription sufficiently legibly so as to reduce the likelihood of it being misread by a busy or careless pharmacist. But the pharmacist, in turn, was under a duty to give some thought to the prescriptions s/he was dispensing. If there was an ambiguity in the prescription, s/he should not dispense a drug without first satisfying him/herself that it was the correct one.

Lord Justice Auld said:

> The GP should have taken account of the possibility that a poorly written prescription might be misinterpreted by the pharmacist: Every now and then the competent or tired and/or flustered and/or distracted pharmacist might very well mechanically dispense a prescription which in more alert and quieter moments he would question...

> It is accepted that a prescription which is so written as to invite or reasonably permit mis-reading by a pharmacist under ordinary working conditions (which it is accepted may be less than ideal) falls below the necessary standard...

> ...it is well-established that the pharmacist, if in any doubt at all, should contact the doctor before [dispensing]...

> ...Looking at the case as a whole...the chain of causation from Dr Miller's bad handwriting was not broken and the consequence of his writing a word which could reasonably be read as 'Daonil', even with the other factors [which should have caused the pharmacist to realise the prescription was not for Daonil] is not

enough to make it beyond reasonable forseeability that Daonil would be prescribed.

Prendergast v Sam & Dee Ltd (1989) 1 Med LR 36, *Pharm J*, 26 March 1988 p. 404

The 'Epilim case'

In a settlement in the High Court in Manchester on 28 February 2000, the claim arose from a negligently written prescription, in November 1999, for Epilim (sodium valproate) 500 mg tablets where the strength, and hence the dosage and administration instructions, were incorrect. The pharmacy's professional indemnity insurer agreed to pay 25% of the settlement (£225 000 plus costs) for the pharmacist's failure to detect and correct the error. The prescribing doctor was held liable for the remaining 75% of the compensation paid to the patient.

Shipman v Mayfair Chemists (Hyde) Limited; *Chemist and Druggist*, 4 March 2000 p. 5

The 'dexamethasone case'

In 2006, despite patient medication records showing a series of previous supplies of dexamethasone 0.5 mg, a pharmacist dispensed a prescription that had incorrectly been written by a prescriber in England for dexamethasone 4 mg. The pharmacist checked that the prescribed strength was within the therapeutic range for dexamethasone, but did not query with the prescriber a strength that was much greater than the patient had previously been prescribed, according to the pharmacy's records. The consequences of this omission were compounded when the patient went to the USA and her physician there continued to prescribe 4 mg tablets for her, based on the label on her supply made in the UK. She suffered severely from Cushing's syndrome which led to the loss of her business and personal difficulties. The trial judge said:

> ... the dramatic increase in strength should have alerted [the pharmacist] to the need to go behind the guidance in the BNF [*British National Formulary*] and to question the correctness of the prescription with [the English prescriber] or [the patient] ... the prescription did not have to be dispensed urgently ... The accepted wisdom is that whenever pharmacists dispense a prescription, they should consider whether the medication being prescribed is suitable for the patient ... If the prescription ... had been for a patient who had not had previous

prescriptions dispensed by the branch, it may have been sufficient for [the pharmacist] to check in the BNF ... a significant increase raised at the very least the possibility that the prescription might be inaccurate. The question was no longer whether the strength of the dexamethasone being prescribed came within its usual therapeutic range.

In this case, nearly £1.5 million compensation was awarded and was apportioned between the UK doctor and the employer of the pharmacist.

Horton v Evans and Lloyds Pharmacy Limited [2006] EWHC 2808 (QB); [2007] LS Law Medical 212; (2007) 94 B.M.L.R. 60; [2007] P.N.L.R. 17

Pharm J, 18 November 2006 p. 595; 17 March 2007 p. 302

The 'dexamethasone case' in box 21.4 also provides an indication of meaning for the term *professional assessment* in relation to the dispensing of a prescription (box 21.5). The case is also important in terms of the access pharmacists are increasingly being given to patients' summary care records (see below).

Box 21.5 Meaning of professional assessment

In the 'dexamethasone case' described in box 21.4, comment was made by the judge on what is meant by the term 'professional assessment' (in the service specifications accompanying the former RPSGB's Code of Ethics) in relation to the dispensing of prescriptions. He said:

The accepted wisdom is that whenever pharmacists dispense a prescription they should consider whether the medication prescribed is suitable for the patient. That is what the Royal Pharmaceutical Society of Great Britain's Code of Medicines, Ethics and Practice[15] requires pharmacists to do – namely 'Every prescription must be professionally assessed by a pharmacist to determine the suitability for the patient'. That is recognised by Lloyds because its branch procedures manual is to the same effect. These requirements mirror pharmacists' obligations under common law. As Stuart-Smith J said in *Dwyer v Roderick*

[15] Reproduced in the RPSGB *Medicines, Ethics and Practice* guide until July 2010.

(10 February 1982)[16] 'pharmacists . . . have to exercise an independent judgement to ensure that the drug is apt for the patient as well as that it conforms to the physicians requirements'.

The defence raised the issue that the pharmacist had noted the strength on the prescription was large, had checked in the BNF, found that a 4 mg dosage was within the usual therapeutic range and had, therefore, dispensed the prescription without referring to the doctor. The judge dealt with this defence thus:

> It was true that the prescription was for a strength of dexamethasone which could be properly prescribed, but the dramatic increase in strength should have alerted the pharmacist to the need to go behind the guidance in the BNF and to question the correctness of the prescription with Dr Evans or Mrs Horton . . . It was no longer whether the strength came within its usual therapeutic range and could for that reason be said to be suitable for Mrs Horton.

> If the patient already has a patient medication record on the computer, previous prescription medication details on the PMR should be studied in order to check that there has been no change to the strength or dose of the patient's medication. Any changes should be queried with the patient or the prescriber.

> In these circumstances I have no doubt that what the pharmacist should have done was to follow the instruction in the branch procedure manual and question the correctness of the prescription with Dr Evans or Mrs Horton. Had he done that, Dr Evans' mistake would have been discovered. In failing to do that the pharmacist fell below the standards which could reasonably have been expected of a reasonably careful and competent pharmacist.

A patient may hold a pharmacy owner vicariously liable for the acts or omissions of a pharmacist, but individual pharmacists owe patients an independent duty of care. As such, if a pharmacy owner is sued by a patient, the pharmacy owner is entitled to claim an indemnity from a pharmacist (whether an employee or a self-employed locum) responsible for an error, or a contribution to any damages payable to the patient.[17]

[16] The 'Migril case', described above in box 21.4.

[17] See, for example, *Wootton v J Docter Ltd* [2008] EWCA Civ. 1361; [2009] *LS Law Medical* 63; this was a case in which no actual indemnity or contribution was ordered because the court held that, although a dispensing error had been made, it had not caused the patient any injury or loss

Now that pharmacies are gaining access to patients' NHS summary care records, a failure to view them and to take account of these records may expose a pharmacy owner or pharmacist to a claim if a patient suffers injury that may have been avoided if the records had been taken into account. The RPS has published guidance[18] that there is no need to refer back to the record every time a repeat prescription is dispensed. Instead, it recommends that the record should be checked:

- for drug allergies;
- when the patient is new;
- if there are any queries or concerns.[19]

Criminal negligence

Although negligence is most likely to be considered in the civil courts in an action for compensation for harm caused by a pharmacist's duty of care, if the failure is associated with the death of a patient, a pharmacist may be charged with the serious criminal offence of manslaughter if the error is considered to be gross negligence. The 'leading case' in relation to health professionals is that involving a hospital doctor, an anaesthetist, in 1995.[20] The case was considered by the House of Lords, which held:

> The question is whether it (the defendant's conduct) should be characterised as gross negligence and therefore a crime; and whether, having regard to the risk of death involved, the defendant's conduct was so bad in all the circumstances as to amount to a criminal act or omission.

Put colloquially, the question was whether the defendant was 'criminally negligent'. Until 2000, there had been no modern case in which a pharmacist had been prosecuted following a dispensing error linked to the death of a patient. However, this position changed following charges of manslaughter brought in that year (the Peppermint Water case) against a pharmacist and a pre-registration graduate who failed to prevent a fatal dispensing error when preparing a mixture for an infant. The mixture was erroneously compounded using concentrated instead of double-strength chloroform water. When the case came to court, the Crown Prosecution Service agreed to drop the charges of manslaughter and to substitute prosecutions under section 64 of the Medicines Act (chapter 13) for supplying a medicine not of the nature

---

[18]'Electronic Health Records (EHR): Guidance for Community Pharmacists and Pharmacy Technicians' (March 2016) available on the Royal Pharmaceutical Society's website

[19]Reissner D (2016) The risks of ignoring summary care records, *Chemist & Druggist*, 26 April http://www.chemistanddruggist.co.uk/opinion/david-reissner-risks-ignoring-summary-care-records

[20]*R v Adomako* [1995] 1 A.C. 171

and quality demanded.[21] Since that time, it has become increasingly common for pharmacists and their staff to be involved in Coroner's inquests following deaths associated with medication and to be at risk of charges of criminal negligence if their failings may have led directly to the death.

Following a patient's death in 2005, a pharmacist Phillip Dean was accused of criminal negligence manslaughter associated with the supply of an unintended dose of 100 mg Oramorph (morphine sulphate) rather than 10 mg. The prosecution asserted that because Mr Dean did not check that what he was dispensing was intended by the doctor he was grossly negligent. Mr Dean said that he knew such a high dose of morphine could cause serious harm but that he had dispensed that strength since: two general practitioners (GPs), a nurse and even medical experts all concluded that what appeared to have been written on the prescription was indeed '100 mg'. Mr Dean was acquitted.[22]

Corporate manslaughter

The Corporate Manslaughter and Corporate Homicide Act 2007 came into force in 2008 and may mean that manslaughter charges will be laid against managers, directors and superintendents of companies or NHS bodies, such as hospital trusts and primary care organisations, if death occurs through major failures in management arrangements, such as staffing, training or resources. In May 2015, Maidstone and Tunbridge Wells Trust became the first NHS Trust to be charged with corporate manslaughter following the death of a 30-year-old patient. In the event, the Trust was found not to have a case to answer, but the case illustrates the possibility of corporate manslaughter cases being brought against trusts or companies that provide health services.[23]

Summary

- Pharmacists and pharmacy technicians are regarded as professionals; they are bound by regulated standards.
- Pharmacists' activities are subject to criminal law, administrative law, civil law and fitness to practise arrangements based on the GPhC's standards and supporting guidance.
- Several legal cases now demonstrate the duty of care owed by pharmacists to their patients.

[21] *Pharm J*, 4 March 2000 p. 356; 11 March 2000 pp. 389–392; 18 March 2000 p. 427
[22] *Chemist and Druggist*, 3 January 2008, available online
[23] *Health Service Journal*, 1 May 2015 p. 15

Further reading

Buerki RA, Vottero LD (2013). *Pharmacy Ethics: A Foundation for Professional Practice.* American Pharmacists Association. [Written for a North American audience.]

Elvey R, Hassell K, Lewis P, Schafheutle E, Willis S, Harrison S (2015). Patient-centred professionalism in pharmacy: values and behaviours. *J Health Organ Manag* 29: 413–430.

General Pharmaceutical Council (2015). *Patient-centred Professionalism in Pharmacy.* London: General Pharmaceutical Council.

Rapport F, Doel MA, Hutchings HA, John DN, Wainwright P, Jerzembek GS, Dobbs C, Newbury S, Trower CS (2010). Through the looking glass: public and professional perspectives on patient-centred professionalism in modern-day community pharmacy. *Forum Qualitative Social Research* 11(1), Art 7 (http://www.qualitative-research.net/index.php/fqs/article/view/1301/2892).

Rapport F, Doel MA, Hutchings HA, Wright S, Wainwright P, Jerzembek GS, John DN (2010). Eleven themes of patient-centred professionalism in community pharmacy: Innovative approaches to consultation about the concept 'patient-centred professionalism' in community pharmacy. *Int J Pharm Pract* 18: 260–268.

Reissner D (2008). Fatal distraction. *Chemist and Druggist* 29 March, p. 15 (http://www.chemistanddruggist.co.uk).

Reissner D (2016). The risks of ignoring summary care records, *Chemist & Druggist*, 26 April (www.chemistanddruggist.co.uk/opinion/david-reissner-risks-ignoring-summary-care-records).

Rodgers R, John D (2006). Paternalism to professional judgement: the history of the Code of Ethics. *Pharm J* 276: 721.

Schafheutle EI, Hassell K, Ashcroft DM, Hall J, Harrison S (2012). How do pharmacy students learn professionalism? *Int J Pharm Pract* 20: 118–128.

Veatch RM, Haddad A (2008). *Case Studies in Pharmacy Ethics*, 2nd edn. New York: Oxford University Press. [Written for a North American audience.]

Wingfield J (2007). Consent: the heart of patient respect. *Pharm J* 279: 411–414.

Wingfield J (2007). When confidences should be kept and what constitutes an exception. *Pharm J* 279: 533–536.

Wingfield J, Badcott D (2007). *Pharmacy Ethics and Decision Making.* London: Pharmaceutical Press.

Websites

Chemist and Druggist (a weekly publication mostly concerned with community pharmacy): http://www.chemistanddruggist.co.uk

General Pharmaceutical Council (details of pharmacy standards): http://www.pharmacyregulation.org

The GPhC is a public body and all its activities are mostly available to the public and professionals alike (some exceptions are hearings on fitness to practise that are held in private). The material appearing on its website is expanding rapidly at the time of going to press and it may not be helpful to give precise locations as these may change. However, standards and guidance may be found under 'standards'

Royal Pharmaceutical Society: http://www.rpharms.org

The RPS is a membership organisation for pharmacists and the *Pharmaceutical Journal* (*http://www.pharmaceutical-journal.com*) is provided free to its members. The RPS also issues annually the Medicines, Ethics and Practice Guide which is intended to assist members in interpretation of the law and standards of practice in real-life situations.

22

Fitness to practise

David H Reissner

The role of the General Pharmaceutical Council

The role of the GPhC[1] (chapter 20) is to protect the health, safety and wellbeing of patients and people who use pharmacy services. Its principal functions (Art.4)[2] include:

a establishing and maintaining a register of pharmacists, pharmacy technicians and premises at which a retail pharmacy business is, or is to be, carried on;

b setting and promoting standards (chapters 20 and 21) for the safe and effective practice of pharmacy;

c setting requirements by reference to which registrants must demonstrate that their fitness to practise is not impaired;

d promoting the safe and effective practice of pharmacy by registrants (including, for example, by reference to any code of conduct for, and ethics relating to, pharmacy); and

e ensuring the continued fitness to practise of registrants.

Fitness to practise

Although not a legal definition, the GPhC defines 'fitness to practise'[3] as 'a person's suitability to be on [its] register without restrictions'.

In practical terms, this means:[4]

● maintaining appropriate standards of proficiency;

● being of good health and good character; and

[1] The law applicable to fitness to practise is the same across Great Britain, but some other statutory provisions referred to in this chapter apply specifically to England and Wales

[2] Article 4 of the Pharmacy Order 2010 (all Articles are from the Pharmacy Order 2010 unless otherwise stated)

[3] The GPhC *Annual Fitness to Practise Report 2014–2015*

[4] These words are taken from the GPhC's annual fitness to practise report for 2013–14; they were not repeated in the reports for 2014–15 or 2015–16

- following principles of good practice as set out in [its] standards and guidance, and other relevant best practice advice.

Decisions of the Fitness to Practise (FTP) Committee are included in this chapter. The dates of decisions are given in footnotes, and transcripts of decisions may be accessed via the GPhC's website, but not all decisions are available there indefinitely.

Specific occasions when fitness to practise falls should be considered

The Council will consider the fitness to practise of a registrant specifically:

a   when a registrant first applies for registration (Art.23(1)(5));
b   if it is shown to the satisfaction of the Registrar that a registrant's
    fitness to practise is impaired as a result of prescribed circumstances
    (see below) or because of a problem with the registrant's physical or
    mental health (Art.30) at the time of entry or renewal of an entry in the
    Register;
c   where an allegation is made to the Council that a registrant's fitness to
    practise is impaired (Art.52); or
d   the GPhC has information that calls into question a registrant's fitness to
    practise, even though no allegation has been made to that effect (Art.52).

Under the FTP Rules,[5] a registrant must notify the GPhC's Registrar in writing within 7 days if (Rule 4), among other things, s/he

a   is convicted of any criminal offence;
b   accepts a caution;
c   becomes subject to an investigation into his/her fitness to practise by
    another regulatory body;
d   becomes the subject of any fraud investigation in relation to the Health
    Service; or
e   is the subject of a ruling that renders him/her unable to practise within the
    NHS on fitness to practise grounds.

When renewing registration annually, registrants are also required to answer questions about, among other things, whether they have previously been convicted or cautioned for a criminal offence, or if a determination has been made by a health or social care regulator that fitness to practise is impaired, or if they have any physical or mental health problems that may impair their ability to carry out their duties in a safe and effective manner. The GPhC informs registrants that they are not covered by the Rehabilitation of Offenders Act. In most cases, cautions will be protected from the need to

[5] The General Pharmaceutical Council (Fitness to Practise and Disqualification etc. Rules) SI 2010 No. 1615

disclose them after 6 years, and most convictions will be protected from the need to disclose them after 11 years.[6]

Failure to give disclosure may itself be considered misconduct, and the courts have upheld the serious view taken by regulators of such failure because it strikes at the heart of the registration process and the reliability of the Register; the failure to disclose is highly relevant to whether an applicant is fit to practise.[7]

Grounds for finding impairment

A person's fitness to practise may only be regarded as 'impaired' by reason of (Art.51):

a misconduct;

b deficient professional performance (which includes competence);

c adverse physical or mental health which impairs his/her ability to practise safely and effectively or which otherwise impairs his/her ability to carry out the duties of a pharmacist or a pharmacy technician in a safe and effective manner;

d not having the necessary knowledge of English;

e failure to comply with a reasonable requirement imposed by an individual assessor or an assessment team in connection with carrying out a professional performance assessment;

f a conviction or police caution for a criminal offence,[8] or being bound over to keep the peace; or

g a determination of impairment of unfitness to practise by another regulatory body or inclusion in a barred list maintained by the Disclosure and Barring Service.[9]

Misconduct

Misconduct may relate to professional practice, including dispensing errors (see below), but the meaning of 'misconduct' is much wider. Specifically in relation to pharmacy practice, in a case in which a pharmacist failed to query an ambiguous prescription for a mixture that contained a fatal overdose of pethidine, the High Court held that misconduct is simply to be defined as 'incorrect or erroneous conduct of any kind provided that it is of a serious

[6]The Rehabilitation of Offenders Act 1974 and the Rehabilitation of Offenders Act 1974 (Exceptions) Order SI 1975 No. 1023

[7]*Harris v Registrar of Approved Driving Instructors* [2010] EWCA Civ 808

[8]The conviction may occur anywhere in the world but, in the case of a conviction outside the British Islands, must be for something that would be a criminal offence in the British Islands

[9]Under the Safeguarding Vulnerable Groups Act 2006

nature judged according to the rules written or unwritten governing the profession'.[10]

Since this decision, the term 'misconduct' has found its way into pharmacy legislation, and the courts have considered the meaning of misconduct on numerous occasions. If misconduct is alleged to have occurred at a pharmacy, the fact of being superintendent pharmacist[11] of a body corporate that owns a pharmacy, or ownership of a pharmacy,[12] is not sufficient on its own to justify referring an allegation of misconduct against either. In a 2009 case[13] against the superintendent pharmacist of a company at one of whose branches dispensing errors had been made, the former Disciplinary Committee said 'before finding misconduct, there must be consent, connivance or neglect by [the superintendent] and it must be of a serious nature – that is to say there must be evidence on which we could find serious fault by the superintendent'.

In 2016, the GPhC's FTP Committee held a pharmacist[14] guilty of misconduct in relation to the conduct of an online pharmacy business because she was a director, even though she was not the superintendent or a responsible pharmacist. She had noticed orders for medicines such as codeine linctus and did not take action to stop supplies. The FTP Committee said she 'ought to have done more' but was 'content to let the business proceed without raising any questions'. This failure to make patients her first concern – described as an abdication of responsibility as a registered pharmacist – had the potential to cause harm to patients and brought the profession into disrepute.

The concept of misconduct is not confined to pharmacy practice. This is usefully encapsulated in a sentence in the GPhC's draft standards which were under consultation at the time of going to press: 'The privilege of being a pharmacist or pharmacy technician calls for appropriate behaviour at all times.'

Misconduct in pharmacy legislation

There are express statutory references to misconduct in the legislation governing the practice of pharmacy. Specifically, if a registrant fails to comply with standards of conduct, ethics or performance set by the GPhC (see chapters 20 and 21, any such failure is not, of itself, to be taken to constitute misconduct. However, it is to be taken into account in any fitness to practise proceedings (Art.48(3)).

[10] Mr Justice Webster in *The Queen v Statutory Committee of the Pharmaceutical Society, ex parte Sokoh, The Times*, 4 December 1986

[11] *The Queen v The Statutory Committee of the Pharmaceutical Society of Great Britain, Ex parte Lewis and Jeffreys Limited, Berg and Brandon* (unreported, Mr Justice Woolf, 20 December 1982)

[12] *Akodu v Solicitors Regulation Authority* [2009] EWHC 3588 (Admin)

[13] Case of Martin Hardy, 26 January 2009

[14] Mrs Elizabeth Nickels, 29 June 2016

Responsible Pharmacists at registered premises have a legal duty to secure the safe and effective running of the pharmacy business, so far as the sale or supply of all medicines at those premises are concerned, and to keep certain records. The Responsible Pharmacist must also maintain and keep under review procedures designed to secure the safe and effective running of the business at the relevant premises.[15] Failure to comply with any such requirements will not automatically be regarded as misconduct, but it may constitute misconduct for the purpose of any fitness to practise proceedings.[16]

Before the introduction of the legal requirement for Responsible Pharmacists,[17] it was common practice to bring disciplinary proceedings against companies that owned a pharmacy where something untoward had occurred and against the superintendent pharmacist of that company. Fitness to practise proceedings are now brought less often against companies or superintendents. Since then, the principal focus has been on Responsible Pharmacists.

Dispensing errors as misconduct or as deficient professional performance

The question of whether a single dispensing error can be misconduct has been considered by the High Court, which ruled that a single error is capable of constituting misconduct if it is sufficiently serious, although whether it crosses the threshold of seriousness depends on the facts of individual cases.[18] The modern approach may be summarised in the words of Lord Cooke[19] in a dental appeal:

> It is settled that serious professional misconduct does not require moral turpitude. Gross professional negligence can fall within it. Something more is required than a degree of negligence enough to give rise to civil liability but not calling for the opprobrium that inevitably attaches to the disciplinary offence.

The GPhC does not express a view whether single dispensing errors are misconduct, but is not likely to refer single errors to its FTP Committee, because the GPhC considers that single dispensing errors do not raise fitness to practise concerns unless there are significant other factors.[20] Such other factors may include the seriousness of harm to a patient.

The case of Aukse Austinskaite[21] may be thought to represent the modern approach to dealing with dispensing errors. Ms Austinskaite was

---

[15] Section 72A Medicines Act 1968
[16] Section 72B Medicines Act 1968
[17] Introduced by amending the Medicines Act 1968 with effect from 1 October 2009
[18] See end of chapter for finding cases cited in this chapter
[19] *Preiss v General Dental Council* [2001] 1 W.L.R 26
[20] General Pharmaceutical Council's *Annual Report 2011–2012*
[21] 16 April 2012 (*Pharm J*, 15 September 2012 p. 307)

a pharmacist who admitted a series of dispensing errors. The Council contended that her fitness to practise was impaired on the alternative grounds of deficient professional performance or misconduct. The FTP Committee followed a ruling of the High Court[22] that, where charges of misconduct and deficient professional performance are founded on the same facts, then the Committee can only find impairment on one of those grounds, not on both.

The Committee noted that deficient professional performance has been defined in these terms[23] in a GMC case involving a medical practitioner:

> It connotes a standard of professional performance which is unacceptably low and which (save in exceptional circumstances) has been demonstrated by reference to a fair sample of the [registrant's] work.

The Committee went on to rule that 'not every instance of deficient professional performance...will necessarily give rise to impairment'. The Committee had regard to the fitness to practise criteria (see below) and concluded that, on the facts of the case, the registrant presented an actual risk to patients and the frequency and gravity of the dispensing errors were such that she might well bring the profession of pharmacy into disrepute. The case was thus dealt with as deficient professional performance, rather than as misconduct.

Convictions and other misconduct

The 'double jeopardy' rule does not apply to fitness to practise proceedings.[24] The FTP Committee may find facts proved on the balance of probabilities even though a registrant may have been acquitted of an offence in a criminal court where the burden of proof – beyond reasonable doubt – was higher. In the case of Ahmed Abdulla,[25] the registrant had been acquitted of rape following a Crown Court trial. Having considered the evidence put forward in the Crown Court and having heard from witnesses, the FTP Committee found the sexual misconduct allegation proved, and directed the removal of Mr Abdulla's name from the Register. The High Court has ruled[26] that the test in deciding whether to bring fitness to practise proceedings after an acquittal is not 'whether a second bite at the cherry might secure a "better" outcome, but rather what is in the public interest, viewing the case through the lens of the obligations placed on the regulator'. There may be cases where further investigation by a regulator would be unfair after a registrant has

[22] *Vali v General Optical Council* [2011] EWHC 310 (Admin)
[23] *Caelham v General Medical Council* [2007] EWHC 2606, [2008] *LS Law Medical* 96
[24] *R (Redgrave) v Commissioner of Police for the Metropolis* [2003] 1 W.L.R. 1136
[25] 14 December 2012 (*Pharm J*, 9 February 2013, p.154)
[26] *Ashraf v General Dental Council* [2014] EWHC 2618

been acquitted, for example, if the allegations do not touch on professional responsibilities to patients or to the NHS, but each case must be considered on its merits.

Mrs Bhavna Dhorajiwala had been convicted of stealing thousands of pounds from her employer's till. Her conviction was quashed by the Court of Appeal[27] because an alleged confession was wrongly allowed into evidence. The same evidence was put before the FTP Committee, and the allegation of theft was found proved on the balance of probabilities. The High Court[28] dismissed an appeal against the decision to remove Mrs Dhorajiwala's name from the Register.

Convictions and misconduct need not be related to the practice of pharmacy, so there are no limitations on the scope of allegations, including convictions of students,[29] that may lead to consideration of whether fitness to practise is impaired. Examples of modern cases that have led to fitness to practise proceedings include:

- failure to disclose to the GPhC convictions for theft,[30] for motoring offences[31] or for drug misuse;[32]
- sexual activity with a 14-year-old girl;[33]
- sexually touching a patient during acupuncture treatment;[34]
- touching a patient in a consulting room[35] (not with a sexual motive, but because the pharmacist lacked appropriate expertise);
- convictions for drink driving or for doing an act to pervert the course of justice;[36]
- theft from an employer;[37] and
- shoplifting.[38]

[27] R v Dhorajiwala [2010] EWCA Crim 1237

[28] Dhorajiwala v GPhC [2013] EWHC 3821 (Admin)

[29] Pharmacy students had been involved in a fracas at the London School of Pharmacy. They were found guilty of unlawful wounding and each given a conditional discharge (which is not classed as a conviction). The High Court held that it was open to the Pharmaceutical Society to bring a case alleging misconduct in disciplinary proceedings, relying on the same facts as were before the criminal court; R v Statutory Committee of the Pharmaceutical Society of Great Britain and Martin and Shutt Ex p. Pharmaceutical Society of Great Britain [1981] 1 W.L.R. 886

[30] Maria Del Rosario Ferrero Alvarez-Rementaria (Pharm J, 3 March 2012 p. 284)

[31] Jasmeet Kaur Brar (Pharm J, 3 March 2012 p. 283)

[32] Patrick O'Sullivan (Pharm J, 24 March 2012 p. 395)

[33] Hailmarim Lakew (Pharm J, 7 January 2012 p. 14)

[34] Jasbinder Singh Bansal (Pharm J, 7 January 2012 p. 14)

[35] Asif Ghafoor (Pharm J, 28 January 2012 p. 122)

[36] Vijay Ratilal Mistry (Pharm J, 5 May 2012 p. 570)

[37] Monji v General Pharmaceutical Council [2014] EWHC 3128 (Admin) (theft of fragrance testers, resulting in a decision to remove the pharmacist's name from the Register)

[38] Jyoti Patel (Pharm J, 27 June 2012) – repeated shoplifting leading to striking off; Juliya Kondrasova (Chemist & Druggist, 25 January 2012) – resulting in suspension

Students

University schools of pharmacy are required to have fitness to practise procedures that can be used to deal with allegations concerning students, for example if they breach the GPhC's Code of Conduct for Pharmacy Students. Similar arrangements are in place for medical students. Raliku Thilakawardhana was a medical student who posted on a fellow student's Facebook page a message with the words in capital letters: 'I will look for you, I will find you. And I will kill you'. These words were viewable by the fellow student's Facebook friends. There was also a private message to the fellow student which was offensive and could be considered threatening. Allegations of misconduct were investigated by a university panel which had guidance that expulsion should be applied if a student's behaviour is considered to be fundamentally incompatible with continuing on a medical course or eventually practising as a doctor. The panel decided that Mr Thilakawardhana was not fit to practise medicine because his fundamental unsuitability for the medical profession could not be corrected. An appeal was unsuccessful, as was a complaint to the Office of the Independent Adjudicator. An application to the High Court for Judicial Review of the decision[39] of the Adjudicator was dismissed.

First registration and good character

Before being registered with the GPhC, an applicant must satisfy registration requirements to establish that s/he is fit to practise the profession (Art.23(1)(d)). The same obligation is placed both on applicants who have never been on the Register of the RPSGB or the GPhC and on those formerly on the Register of the RPSGB but who were not on the Register at the date its regulatory functions were taken over by the GPhC;[40] for example, in the case of the latter because they had been removed at the direction of the Statutory Committee or the Disciplinary Committee following a finding of misconduct that rendered them unfit to be on the Register.

Healthcare regulators are overseen by the Professional Standards Authority for Health and Social Care (PSA). The PSA has published guidance[41] that there are four key elements which form the basis of assessing good character. These are whether an applicant has acted, or there is reason to believe s/he is liable in future to act:

a in such a way that puts at risk the health, safety or wellbeing of a patient or other member of the public;

---

[39] *Thilakawardhana v Office of the Independent Adjudicator and the University of Leicester* [2015] EWHC 3285 (Admin)

[40] This was on 27 September 2010

[41] *A Common Approach to Good Character Across the Health Professions Regulators*, December 2008, available on PSA website (published when the PSA was known as the Council for Healthcare Regulatory Excellence)

b in such a way that his/her registration would undermine public confidence in the profession;

c in such a way that indicates an unwillingness to act in accordance with the standards of the profession; or

d in a dishonest manner.

The same principles for assessing fitness to practise in the case of someone already registered apply to the case of an applicant for registration.[42] However, in contrast to the position of an existing registrant, the burden is on the applicant to satisfy the Registrar that s/he is fit to practise.

If the Registrar of the GPhC refuses registration on fitness to practise grounds, the reasons for refusal must be given (Art.24(3)(b)). The applicant has a right of appeal (Art.40) to the Appeals Committee provided that the appeal is brought within 28 days of the date on which the written statement of the reasons for the decision was sent. The procedure governing appeals is set out in separate Rules.[43]

Interim orders

Where the Registrar[44] or the Investigating Committee considers that the FTP Committee should consider making an interim order (Art.53(3)(c)) suspending the registrant from practice pending a full ('principal') fitness to practise hearing, the allegation must be referred to the FTP Committee. The FTP Committee must hold a hearing and give the registrant reasonable notice. The notice period is nevertheless usually very short. The registrant is entitled to attend and be represented at the hearing.

The FTP Committee will approach applications for interim orders on the basis of the evidence available so far and the nature of the allegations, and it will make a decision on the basis that the allegation is true, without deciding the facts of the case. It is not the responsibility of the Committee to make findings of fact or to resolve factual disputes, even if the registrant contends that the evidence is weak.[45] Out of fairness to registrants who have not been found guilty of any offence or misconduct, hearings are held in private, so usually the only reported cases are those where there has been an appeal to the High Court.

[42] *Jideofo v The Law Society* [2007] EW Misc 3 (31 July 2007)

[43] The General Pharmaceutical Council (Appeals Committee) Rules (SI 2010 No. 1614)

[44] Rule 6(4) of FTP Rules

[45] *Abdullah v General Medical Council* [2012] EWHC 2506; the High Court (Mr Justice Lindblom) held that Parliament had entrusted to the GMC's Interim Orders Panel the power to make decisions on a doctor's freedom to practise while his fitness to do so was investigated, using its own experience and expertise and its own knowledge of the public's expectations of the medical profession. The allegations against the doctor were very serious. There was a need to maintain public confidence in the medical profession or the medical regulator, and action would sometimes have to be taken to protect public confidence even where there was no immediate risk to patients

If it is satisfied that it is necessary for the protection of members of the public or is otherwise in the public interest, or is in the interests of the registrant, the Committee may make an immediate order suspending the registrant from practice for up to 18 months, or may impose conditions of practice pending a full fitness to practise hearing (Art.56). While 18 months is the maximum length of interim suspension, it should not be regarded as the default period.[46] In deciding whether to impose an interim suspension, the Committee must balance the protection of patients and the public interest against the impact of suspension on registrants who may lose income, home, family, and be on the verge of bankruptcy, and whose health may be affected.[47] No member of the FTP Committee that has made an interim order may sit as a member of the Committee at a final hearing of the allegation.[48]

If an interim order is made, the GPhC will be expected to prepare its case for a final hearing during the lifetime of the order. If the Council has not been able to bring the case to a final hearing within that time and if it is unable to do so within the 18-month maximum period of suspension, the Council may apply to the High Court for an interim order to be extended. The High Court has power to extend an interim order by up to a further 12 months (Art.56(5)). The High Court has generally been willing to grant extensions while the regulator completes the preparation of its case for a final hearing, although not always for the period sought by the regulator. In one of the leading cases,[49] in which an extension was granted, the High Court held that the court could take into account the gravity of the allegations, the nature of the evidence, the seriousness of the risk of harm to patients, the reasons why the case had not been concluded and the prejudice to the practitioner if an interim order were continued. However, there are examples of refusal, such as in a case in which, by the time a previous 3-month extension granted by the court had expired, the regulator had still not even decided whether to formulate charges against the registrant. The judge took into account that the order had been considered necessary to protect the public from harm but much of the delay was unexplained, and he held that this could not be decisive for all time.[50]

---

[46] R (on the application of Scholten v General Medical Council [2013] EWHC 173 (Admin)

[47] R (Scholten) v GMC (see above reference)

[48] Paragraph 5 of Schedule 1 of the Pharmacy Order 2010; but where the chair at the hearing of an interim order application heard matters relating to another registrant (Mr Hussain Rasool), the same chair was not required to stand down when Mr Rasool's case later came before him at a principal hearing, and an allegation of bias was rejected by the High Court – Rasool v GPhC [2015] EWHC 217 (Admin)

[49] General Medical Council v Hiew [2007] 1 W.L.R. 2007

[50] Nursing and Midwifery Council v Maceda [2011] EWHC 3004 (Admin)

Examples of cases in which registrants have been suspended under interim orders include:

- a pharmacist about to stand trial for putting counterfeit Viagra on the market, presumably because of concern about public confidence in the profession when the trial was reported in the press if it became known that the defendant was a practising pharmacist;[51]
- a pharmacist who had made a single but fatal dispensing error, after the case had been reported in a local newspaper;[52]
- a pharmacist accused of taking financial advantage of a vulnerable adult;
- a number of pharmacists were filmed in a BBC television Inside Out programme, selling Prescription Only Medicines without prescriptions. The FTP Committee imposed interim suspensions, stating that a reasonable onlooker with knowledge of the facts would be appalled if no interim suspension were imposed, and the allegations against the registrant were eventually proved. The High Court[53] rejected an appeal in one case. The judge emphasised that the FTP Committee must scrutinise the unproven allegations with great care to test their cogency. He drew a distinction between cases involving a lack of training, or an honest mistake, or theft, where it might be appropriate to impose conditions of practice pending a final hearing, and a case involving 'the very important role played by pharmacists in ensuring that drugs for which prescriptions are required are not supplied to those who do not have prescriptions for them'.

An interim order was refused in a case where the registrant had been arrested and bailed following an allegation of domestic violence but not yet charged at the time of the application for an interim order. The Committee was at pains to emphasise that it was not engaged in a fact-finding exercise, and that the allegations were vehemently denied by the registrant. The Committee ruled that, in considering an allegation of domestic violence in the context of whether an order is necessary for the protection of members of the public, the existence of a threat to the safety of members of the family cannot be regarded as the existence of a threat to the public at large; suspension from practice as a pharmacist would not protect family members.

As to whether suspension would be necessary in the public interest, the High Court has held in the case of a dental practitioner convicted of

---

[51]In the event, the pharmacist's conviction in the Crown Court was quashed by the Court of Appeal: *R v Patel (Hitendra)* [2010] 1 W.L.R. 1011

[52]*Cambridge News*, 21 June 2008 (http://www.cambridge-news.co.uk/Cambridge/Pharmacy-to-blame-for-death-coroner.htm)

[53]*Gulamhusein v General Pharmaceutical Council* [2014] EWHC 2591 (Admin)

conspiracy to defraud[54] that 'it is . . . likely to be a relatively rare case where a suspension order will be made on an interim basis on the ground that it is in the public interest' because of the impact on a registrant's ability to earn a living. The Court held that, in the absence of necessity for suspension at an interim stage, 'the question of public perception and public confidence could be reflected by an appropriate decision by the Panel, if so minded, at the final hearing when all the facts had been fully explored, all the mitigation fully advanced and the position finally assessed at [the final hearing]'. Indeed, in a case of non-clinical allegations, it has been held that only something that would impinge more directly on members of the public, such as murder, rape or abuse of children, would justify interim suspension for the purpose of public protection.[55]

The FTP Committee has similar powers of interim suspension in relation to pharmacy premises.[56]

Registrants have a right of appeal (Art.58) to the High Court against interim orders. Any such appeal must be brought within 28 days of the date on which written notice of the reasons for the decision was sent to the registrant, or such longer period as the court may allow. In the event of an appeal, the interim order will not take effect until the expiry of the date for appealing or, in the event of an appeal, its final disposal (Art.59). However, the FTP Committee may order a suspension until its interim order comes into effect if it is satisfied that it is necessary to do so for the protection of members of the public or is otherwise in the public interest or in the interests of the registrant.

The FTP Committee must review interim orders within 6 months and must keep orders under review. Registrants may request an earlier review once 3 months have passed (Art.56). On a review, the Committee may continue, vary or revoke the interim order.

Initial action in respect of allegations

A schematic plan of the FTP process appears as Figure 22.1. If the GPhC has information or receives information or an allegation that a registrant's fitness to practise is or might be impaired, the Registrar must normally refer the information or allegation to the Council's Investigating Committee (Art.52) unless the allegation falls within the Council's threshold criteria[57] (Art.52

---

[54] R (on the application of Sheikh) v General Dental Council [2010] Med. L.R. 323
[55] Bradshaw v General Medical Council [2010] Med L.R 323
[56] Section 82A of the Medicines Act 1968
[57] The criteria reflect the Standards of conduct, ethics and performance which were under review at the time of going to press.

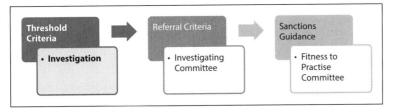

Figure 22.1 The fitness to practise decision-making process. Taken from GPhC's Guidance on Threshold Criteria Policy.

and Rule 6 of FTP Rules) for not making a referral (box 22.1)[58] or unless more than 5 years have elapsed since the most recent events referred to in the allegation. If more than 5 years have elapsed, the Registrar may only refer the case if s/he considers that it is necessary for the protection of the public, or otherwise in the public interest for the allegation to be referred.

Box 22.1 GPhC threshold criteria in fitness to practise allegations

The threshold criteria are that cases are not to be referred to the Investigating Committee unless one of the following statements is true:

Principle 1, make patients your first concern:
- there is evidence that the registrant's conduct or performance caused moderate or severe harm or death, which could and should have been avoided;
- there is evidence that the registrant deliberately attempted to cause harm to patients and the public or others;
- there is evidence that the registrant was reckless with the safety and wellbeing of others.

Principle 2, use your professional judgement in the interests of patients and the public:
- there is evidence that the registrant put his/her own interests, or those of a third party, before those of his/her patients;
- there is evidence that the registrant culpably failed to act when necessary in order to protect the safety of patients.

Principle 3, show respect for others:
- there is evidence that the registrant failed to respect the human rights of patients, or demonstrated in his/her behaviour attitudes which are incompatible with registration as a pharmacy professional;

---

[58] Additional guidance is available on the GPhC's website https://www.pharmacyregulation.org/raising-concerns/registrants/what-happens-if-complaint-made-against-me/investigation-procedure

- there is evidence that the registrant failed to maintain appropriate professional boundaries in his/her relationship with patients and/or others.

Principle 4, encourage patients and the public to participate in decisions about their care:

- there is evidence that the registrant damaged or put at significant risk the best interests of patients by failing to communicate appropriately with patients or others.

Principle 5, develop your professional knowledge and competence:

- there is evidence that the registrant practised outside of his/her current competence;
- there is evidence that the registrant failed to maintain his/her knowledge and skills in a field relevant to his/her practice;
- there is evidence of a course of conduct, which is likely to undermine public confidence in the profession generally or put patient safety at risk, if not challenged by the regulatory body.

Principle 6, be honest and trustworthy:

- there is evidence that the registrant behaved dishonestly;
- there is evidence of behaviour on the part of the registrant which is likely to undermine public confidence in the profession generally, if not challenged by the regulatory body.

Principle 7, take responsibility for your working practices:

- there is evidence that the registrant has practised in a way that was systemically unsafe or has allowed or encouraged others to do so, where s/he has responsibilities for ensuring a safe system of working;
- there is evidence of adverse physical or mental health which impairs the registrant's ability to practise safely or effectively.

If the Registrar is in doubt as to whether the above criteria have been met, s/he shall refer the case to the Investigating Committee.

When making a referral to the Investigating Committee, the Registrar is under an obligation to make any referral to the Investigating Committee within a reasonable time, but failure to do so would not invalidate the referral or provide grounds to set it aside unless a fair disciplinary process is no longer possible.[59]

---

[59] *R (on the application of Rycroft) v Royal Pharmaceutical Society of Great Britain* [2011] Med. L.R. 23

The Investigating Committee

The Investigating Committee consists of a lay member who is the chair, two lay members who are deputy chairs, two other lay members, and between three and eleven others who may be lay members or registrants.[60] They have a 4-year term of office. The quorum comprises three members and must include a chair or deputy chair, a registrant and a lay member. A legal adviser may be asked to attend any meeting.[61] The legal adviser's function is to ensure that the committee's proceedings are conducted fairly.

The Investigating Committee meets in private. Its primary function is to decide whether an allegation ought to be considered by the FTP Committee (Art.53). The Committee may not hear oral evidence. Instead, registrants will be given at least 21 days in which to make written representations. In relation to a heath allegation, the Committee may require the registrant to agree to be examined by a nominated medical practitioner.

The Investigating Committee will not investigate or determine the facts of a case. In deciding whether to refer an allegation to the FTP Committee, the Investigating Committee will decide whether it considers that there is a real prospect of an allegation being proved at an FTP hearing, and whether the facts, if proved, could demonstrate that the registrant's fitness to practise is impaired. In deciding whether an allegation ought to be referred to the FTP Committee, it will also consider whether referral to the FTP Committee is a proportionate outcome. In making a decision, the Investigating Committee will follow outcomes guidance published by the GPhC. This will involve considering a number of factors including:

- the public interest;
- any aggravating or mitigating factors;
- the circumstances and whether there is any ongoing risk to members of the public;
- the registrant's behaviour, attitude and actions;
- the Registrar's recommendation (which is not binding on the Investigating Committee);
- any written representations from the registrant;
- any relevant fitness to practise history.

Where the Committee determines that the allegation ought to be considered by the FTP Committee or a registrant has requested a referral, the

---

[60] A 'lay member' is defined in rule 1 of the General Pharmaceutical Council (Statutory Committees and their Advisers) Rules (SI 2010 No. 1616) as a member who is not, and has never been, entered in the Register of any regulatory body and does not hold qualifications which would entitle them to apply for entry in the Council's Register

[61] Rule 21 of the Statutory Committee Rules

Committee must refer the case to the FTP Committee. In the event of such a referral, the Registrar must inform the person who made the allegation.[62]

If the Investigating Committee decides that an allegation need not be considered by the FTP Committee, then it may give a warning or give advice (including advice to a person against whom an allegation has not been made, such as a pharmacist's employer). The Register (including the online version) will say that the registrant has received a warning to ensure public confidence in the profession and the regulatory process, and to protect the public by reminding the registrant concerned to adhere to all legal and professional obligations in their practice in future. This statement will be removed after 2 years. The background circumstances will not be disclosed.

If the Investigating Committee concludes that the Council should consider exercising any of its powers to bring criminal proceedings, it must notify the Registrar accordingly (Art.53(4)).

Prosecutions

Many breaches of the Human Medicines Regulations 2012 are criminal offences (for example, Reg.255). The GPhC has the power to enforce many of the relevant provisions of the Regulations (Reg.323). The Council has published a prosecution policy (see the list of further reading at the end of this chapter). Its view is that taking a proportionate and cost-effective approach means using alternatives to prosecution, including seeking voluntary compliance and non-criminal regulatory interventions, for example fitness to practise proceedings, where appropriate. In view of this policy, it is rare for the GPhC to prosecute pharmacists and pharmacy technicians. However, the GPhC's annual report for 2015–16[63] states that the GPhC considered it was proportionate to bring four criminal prosecutions in that year against people practising as a pharmacist or pharmacy technician while not on the Register. Three of those cases resulted in convictions and the fourth case was pending at the end of the year.

When offences are committed by pharmacists and pharmacy employees, these usually involve strict liability,[64] meaning that offences may be committed unintentionally. The Council's powers to prosecute are not exclusive. Prosecutions have also been brought by the Crown Prosecution Service. In the case of dispensing errors, prosecutions have typically alleged that a pharmacist has supplied a product to the prejudice of the patient that is not

---

[62]Further information can be found in the GPhC's publication 'Good decision making: investigating committee meetings and outcomes guidance' (January 2016)

[63]Available on the GPhC website

[64]See, for example, *Pharmaceutical Society of Great Britain v Storkwain Limited* (although after the House of Lords upheld a conviction for unwittingly dispensing a forged prescription, a due diligence defence was introduced, which is now in Regulation 245 of the Human Medicines Regulations 2012)

of the nature or quality demanded[65] (and chapter 13). It is not only pharmacists who may be prosecuted. Where a dispenser had selected an incorrect drug and passed it to a pharmacist, who then authorised an incorrect prescription, both the dispenser and the pharmacist have been convicted of an offence.[66] The High Court held that the dispenser could not avoid conviction by arguing that the pharmacist was more in control of the supply, had higher qualifications and a more important position, nor did the pharmacist's failure to carry out the necessary checks break the chain of supply.

In another case, that of Elizabeth Lee,[67] who made a non-fatal dispensing error for which she initially received a suspended prison sentence[68] in respect of labelling offences, such had been the concern in pharmacy circles about the fairness of this sentence that the Crown Prosecution Service was forced to review its policy on prosecution and publish guidance to prosecutors.[69] In future, while dispensing errors continue to be criminal offences, the Crown Prosecution Service will apply a detailed analysis before deciding whether to prosecute, taking into account such factors as whether a simple error was made, whether there was recklessness and whether remedial action was taken.

Ordinarily, police cautions and convictions have to be declared to the GPhC, except when fitness to practise falls should be considered (see above). The issue of whether pharmacists and pharmacy employees should be at risk of conviction for dispensing errors has been the subject of considerable debate. The Government published draft regulations[70] in 2015 with a view to affording a defence in the case of a pharmacist who is prosecuted for the inadvertent incorrect supply of a prescription medicine.

Disqualification

If a body corporate is convicted of a pharmacy-related offence, or if a director, officer or employee of a body corporate is convicted of an offence, or has been guilty of misconduct, then the FTP Committee may disqualify the body corporate and direct the removal from the Register of some or all of its

---

[65] Section 64 of the Medicines Act 1968

[66] *Mahoney v Prestatyn Magistrates' Court* [2009] EWHC 3237 (Admin)

[67] *R v Lee (Elizabeth)* [2010] EWCA Crim 1404. Mrs Lee was charged under s.64 (chapter 13) and under s.85 of the Medicines Act 1968 (chapter 14) but only the second charge was heard. Mrs Lee resigned from the Register of the former RPSGB and was not the subject of further enquiry

[68] The sentence was overturned on appeal and replaced by a fine of £300, *R v Lee (Elizabeth)* [2010] EWCA Crim 1404

[69] Available on the Crown Prosecution Service website (see end of chapter)

[70] The Pharmacy (Preparation and Dispensing Errors) Order 2015 – not in force at the time of going to press

premises.[71] The powers of disqualification and removal of premises from the Register have been extended to cases where there has been a failure to meet premises standards (instead of treating failings as criminal offences).[72] These powers are not limited to registered pharmacy premises, but also extend to associated premises.

The powers to disqualify and remove premises from the Register are only exercisable if the owner of the premises is found unfit to carry on a retail pharmacy business safely and effectively, so far as concerns the sale or supply of medicines (including GSL medicines). Disqualification proceedings are rare and are only likely to be brought in the case of a business conducted in wholesale disregard of the rules governing the profession or in flagrant disregard of the need to protect patients and the public.

Disposal of allegations without hearings

Following a decision of the Investigating Committee to refer an allegation to the FTP Committee, the person responsible for presenting the Council's case may conclude that the case should not proceed to a hearing, for example because there is insufficient evidence to justify a finding that a registrant's fitness to practise is impaired, or because the decision to refer was legally flawed because the Investigating Committee failed to take into account a relevant consideration, such as delay. In that event, the Investigating Committee must be informed and the Committee may rescind the referral,[73] after giving any complainant an opportunity to comment. The Investigating Committee is not bound to rescind the referral and on occasions has declined to do so. Where a case has been referred by the GPhC Registrar to the FTP Committee, for example where the registrant has been convicted of a criminal offence, the Registrar considers that s/he has power to rescind that referral, though there are no words to this effect in the FTP Rules.

The Fitness to Practise Committee

The FTP Committee is to consist of:

- a lay member who is the chair;
- between three and eight lay members who are deputy chairs;
- between eight and fifty other members who may be lay members or registrants.

The quorum for the FTP Committee comprises the chair or a deputy chair and at least two other members, one of whom must be a lay member and

---

[71] Section 80(1) of the Medicines Act 1968

[72] Section 80(1A) of the Medicines Act 1968

[73] Rule 38 of the FTP Rules

one of whom must be a registrant. The registrants must not outnumber the lay members by more than one.[74] A member who has sat on the Committee when granting an interim order may not sit in subsequent proceedings in the case.[75] Usually, hearings (other than case management meetings) are conducted by a committee comprising a legally qualified chair, a registrant member and a lay member.

The Committee may seek advice from a clinical adviser on a health-related issue or any other specialist adviser on issues within their speciality.[76] The Committee may be expected to rely on the specialist knowledge of registrant members, but with the following in mind:[77]

> the rules of natural justice preclude expert members from giving evidence to themselves which the parties have no opportunity to challenge and . . . where a specialist tribunal drawing on its own knowledge and experience independently identified an important fact or matter which may influence its decision but which has not been the subject of evidence adduced by the parties, it should state this openly and give the parties an opportunity to seek to adduce evidence and/or make submissions on it.

Indeed, a decision of the former Statutory Committee was quashed because, when its members deliberated in private, they consulted *Martindale* without reference to the parties on a point that was not covered by the professional knowledge of the pharmacists on the Committee.[78]

Procedure prior to hearings

As soon as reasonably practicable after an allegation has been referred by the Investigating Committee or the Registrar, the Council must serve on the registrant finalised particulars of the allegation, sufficiently particularised to enable him/her to understand the allegation, together with any witness statements, expert reports or other documents relied on by the Council, and any evidence or documents in the Council's possession that may assist the registrant in the preparation of his/her defence. As soon as reasonably practicable after service by the Council, the registrant must serve on the Council any witness statements, expert reports and other documents the registrant relies on.[79]

---

[74]Regulation 18 of the General Pharmaceutical Council (Statutory Committees and their Advisers) Rules 2010
[75]Rule 19 of the Statutory Committee Rules
[76]Rule 23 of the FTP Rules
[77]*Lawrence v GMC* [2012] EWHC 464 (Admin)
[78]*Fletcher and Lucas v Pharmaceutical Society of Great Britain, Pharm J*, July 1978 p. 93
[79]Rule 14 of the FTP Rules

There are rules for case management and, if a direction is required, any party may request a management meeting, for example as to compliance with the rules, the disclosure of evidence, issues as to witnesses or to seek a ruling of law. At such meetings, the chair of the FTP Committee, sitting alone, may give directions in order to secure the just, expeditious and effective running of the proceedings before the Committee. Such hearings may take place by telephone conference, rather than personal attendance.[80]

Fitness to practise hearings

At fitness to practise hearings,[81] both the GPhC and the registrant may be represented by a solicitor or barrister or, in the case of the Council, by an employee.[82] A registrant may also be represented by a person from a defence organisation or trade union. Whilst registrants are not required to attend, not attending, especially when dishonesty has been alleged, virtually invites removal from the Register, if insight is not demonstrated.[83] At the start of any hearing to determine whether a registrant's fitness to practise is impaired (defined as a 'principal hearing'), the FTP Committee must determine any preliminary legal arguments. The chair will then establish whether the registrant makes any admissions and, if so, will announce that the facts admitted have been found proved. Where facts are in dispute, the case for the Council is then presented to the Committee and evidence will be given in support. A pharmacist, Noor Shaikh, was accused of operating a repeat dispensing service to which patients had not consented, with a view to dishonestly obtaining payment for dispensing. On the evidence of witnesses who did not attend the FTP hearing, the allegations were found proved. Mr Shaikh appealed to the High Court,[84] arguing that the FTP Committee was not entitled to take hearsay evidence into account. Mr Justice Supperstone rejected the appeal, holding that rule 24 of the FTP Rules allows the FTP Committee to receive any evidence so long as it is reasonable and fair.

After the GPhC's evidence is presented, the FTP Rules[85] permit a registrant to argue that there is no case to answer. Unless the case is dismissed because there is no case to answer, the registrant will then present his/her case and may call evidence. The burden of proving disputed facts is on the Council. The standard of proof is the civil one (see also chapter 1): facts must be proved on the balance of probabilities[86] even where a criminal

---

[80]Rule 20 of the FTP Rules
[81]Rule 35 of the FTP Rules
[82]Rule 43 of the FTP Rules
[83]*Burrows v General Pharmaceutical Council* [2016] EWHC 1050 (Admin)
[84]*Shaikh v General Pharmaceutical Council* [2013] EWHC 1844 (Admin)
[85]Rule 31(8) of the FTP Rules
[86]Rule 42 of the FTP Rules

offence is alleged. The FTP Rules do not mention that the parties may make submissions as to the findings the FTP Committee should make, but the making of such submissions is accepted practice. The Committee will then deliberate privately before announcing its findings of fact in public.

After announcing its findings of fact, the Committee must receive further evidence and hear any further submissions from the parties as to whether, on the basis of the facts found proved, the registrant's fitness to practise is impaired (see the section above on Grounds for finding impairment, as to the exclusive reasons that must be proved in order for fitness to practise to come under consideration). The Committee will then retire to deliberate in private before announcing in public its decision on the registrant's fitness to practise.

Fitness to practise criteria

When deciding whether the requirements as to fitness to practise are met in relation to the registrant, the FTP Committee must have regard[87] to whether or not the conduct or behaviour that has been found proved:

a presents an actual or potential risk to patients or to the public;
b has brought, or might bring, the profession of pharmacy into disrepute;
c has breached one of the fundamental principles of the profession of pharmacy; or
d shows that the integrity of the registrant can no longer be relied upon.

In cases where it is alleged that a registrant's fitness to practise may be impaired by health factors, the Committee must have regard to whether or not there is evidence of actual or potential self-harm, or harm to patients or to the public.

The determination of fitness to practise has been considered by the courts in a number of key cases.[88] The courts have held that the task of the Committee is to take account of any conviction or misconduct of the practitioner and to consider it in the light of all the other relevant factors known to them in answering whether, by reason of the registrant's misconduct, conviction, deficient professional performance and so on, his/her fitness to practise is impaired at the date of the hearing. This is a process of looking forward, as well as back, and taking into account the practitioner's

---

[87] Rule 5 of the FTP Rules
[88] *Meadow v General Medical Council* [2007] 2 W.L.R 286; *Cohen v General Medical Council* [2008] EWHC 581 (Admin); *Cheatle v General Medical Council* [2009] EWHC 645 (Admin); *Yeong v General Medical Council* [2009] EWHC 1923; *The Queen (on the Application of Zygmunt) v General Medical Council* [2008] EWHC 2643 (Admin); [2009] *LS Law Medical* 219; *Professional Standards Authority v General Medical Council and Uppal* [2015] EWHC 1304; *R. (on the application of Squier) v GMC* [2015] EWHC 299 (Admin); QBD (Admin); 13 February 2015; *R. (on the application of Alami) v Health and Care Professions Council* [2013] EWHC 1895 (Admin); Official Transcript; QBD (Admin); 10 July 2013

efforts to address his/her problems and reduce the risk of recurrence. Insight and remediation and the risk of repetition of offending behaviour are all relevant to the assessment and, in a case in which a GP was found to have lied about whether he had spoken to a baby's mother, the High Court ruled that 'not every act of dishonesty results in impairment'.[89] Even if an isolated dispensing error is found to be misconduct, the Committee may conclude that the chance of it being repeated in the future is so remote that a registrant's fitness to practise is not impaired.[90] In the case of a series of errors, such as that of Aukse Austinskaite (see above), the Committee noted that its 'task [was] to determine not whether at some time in the past the registrant's fitness to practise was impaired, but whether it was currently impaired'. The Committee took the view that the concept of 'remediability' is applicable to cases where impairment might arise from deficient professional performance caused by a consistent tendency to make dispensing errors. On the facts of that case, the Committee found that the registrant's fitness to practise was impaired.

In the case of a doctor who had falsified documents in support of an application that would qualify him for appointment as a consultant, Mrs Justice Lang held[91] that consideration should be given not only to whether the practitioner continues to present a risk to members of the public, but also to whether the need to uphold proper professional standards and public confidence in the profession would be undermined if a finding of impairment were not made in the particular circumstances.

The FTP Committee may find that the registrant's fitness to practise is not impaired but may nevertheless issue a warning or advice to them or any other involved person. If the FTP Committee decides that the registrant's fitness to practise is impaired, it must announce its finding in public and give reasons for that decision. The Committee may then receive further evidence and hear any further submissions as to the appropriate sanction, if any, to be imposed.

Sanctions

If a registrant's fitness to practise is found to be impaired, the FTP Committee will hear submissions as to what sanction may be appropriate. These are likely to include reference to the GPhC's Sanctions Guidance[92] and may include any mitigating circumstances and any relevant matters in the registrant's history,

---

[89] *Professional Standards Authority v General Medical Council and Uppal* [2015] EWHC 1304
[90] *Cohen v General Medical Council* [2008] EWHC 581 (Admin); [2008] *LS Law Medical* 246
[91] *Professional Standards Authority v General Medical Council and Igwilo* [2016] EWHC 524 (Admin)
[92] *Good decision making: fitness to practise hearings and sanctions guidance* published by the GPhC in July 2015

such as previous adverse findings. The Committee may receive submissions not only from the parties at this stage but also from any other person, perhaps a patient, who has a direct interest in the proceedings.

The Committee is required to have regard to the Sanctions Guidance.[93] This guidance emphasises that the purpose of sanctions is not to punish the registrant but to protect the public and maintain confidence in the profession of pharmacy and proper standards of behaviour. Aggravating features include dishonesty,[94] sexual misconduct in relation to professional duties and lack of insight. Mitigating features include repayment of any misappropriated funds, ill health at the time of misconduct or deficient professional performance, open and frank admissions at an early stage, demonstrating insight and the absence of actual or potential harm to patients or the public.

In reaching its decision, the Committee will attach greater weight to the interests of the public than the interests of the registrant.[95] The Committee will aim to apply sanctions proportionately. In other words, it will impose a sanction that is no more severe than necessary to achieve its purpose. The Committee will therefore usually consider its powers in ascending order of seriousness to determine whether, starting with a warning, this would be sufficient to address the impairment it has found.

Similar procedures will be followed where an allegation is made in respect of a body corporate that carries on a retail pharmacy business. If the body corporate or one of its officers or employees has been convicted of an offence or has been guilty of misconduct which would render the person concerned unfit to be a pharmacist, the FTP Committee may direct that the body corporate be disqualified from running a retail pharmacy business at all its premises or at specific premises.

Insight is a key factor in the choice of sanction. It involves 'a recognition and acceptance of what has been done wrong and the implications that flow from it'[96] or, as expressed in the Sanctions Guidance, it means a registrant 'can accept and understand that they should have acted differently and that

---

[93] Rule 31(14) of the General Pharmaceutical Council (Fitness to Practise and Disqualification) Rules

[94] In *Yusuf v Royal Pharmaceutical Society of Great Britain* [2009] EWHC 867 (Admin), Mr Justice Munby dismissed an appeal against removal from the Register, saying 'there may be cases of misconduct – even dishonesty – in a non-professional context where a disciplinary tribunal could, in appropriate circumstances, conclude that some penalty short of the ultimate penalty suffices. A trivial act of shoplifting in a "moment of madness" by a professional person of otherwise blameless character is very different indeed from the wholesale misconduct and dishonesty in a professional context of which the appellant was here found guilty'

[95] The consequences of suspension or removal from the Register will often be severe for the registrant and the registrant's family, but the courts have said, for example, in *George v General Medical Council* [2016] EWHC 1738 (Admin), that personal mitigation has a limited role in fitness to practise cases where the overriding concern is the public interest

[96] *PSA v GPhC and Onwughalu* [2014] EWHC 2521 (Admin)

they will take steps to prevent a reoccurrence'. Insight may be demonstrated by an admission of the allegations, but it is possible to maintain innocence and yet demonstrate insight.[97] A lack of insight may be taken to represent a risk that the wrongdoing may be repeated.

After deliberating in private, the Committee will announce its decision in public. The Committee may:[98]

a give a warning to the registrant;

b give advice to any other person or body involved on any issue related to the allegation;

c give a direction that the registrant's name be removed from the Register (except when impairment is only by reason of health);

d give a direction that the registrant's entry in the Register be suspended for a specific period up to a maximum of 12 months; or

e direct that the registrant's entry in the Register be conditional upon complying with such requirements as the Committee thinks fit, such conditions may run for up to 3 years; examples of conditions[99] include undertaking training, practising under supervision or not holding the position of superintendent pharmacist.

The outcome of hearings will often be case specific, depending on the Committee's view of the gravity of cases and the insight of the registrant, taking the Sanctions Guidance into account. Although dishonesty is often considered to be an aggravating factor, a registrant who has been found guilty of dishonesty will not necessarily be removed from the Register. The Sanctions Guidance states 'Some acts of dishonesty are so serious that the [FTP] Committee should consider removal as the only proportionate and appropriate sanction. This includes allegations that involve intentionally defrauding the NHS or an employer, [or] falsifying patient records'. In practice, while some registrants found to have acted dishonestly will be removed, others have received suspensions of varying lengths. The High Court appeal[100] by Elizabeth Burrows sheds further light on the expected approach. Mrs Burrows had been given a police caution for fraud. She had

---

[97] *Karwal v General Medical Council* [2011] EWHC 26 (Admin)

[98] Article 54 of the Pharmacy Order 2010

[99] The GPhC has published a 'bank' of standard conditions to help the FTP Committee in decision making. Examples relate to the registrant: putting him/herself under the supervision of a GP; undergoing testing for substance misuse; finding a workplace supervisor; naming a mentor; undertaking further training; not working alone; not working as a superintendent pharmacist; and having no involvement in the ordering or dispensing of controlled drugs or lifestyle drugs

[100] *Burrows v General Pharmaceutical Council* [2016] EWHC 1050

returned dresses to a department store after swapping cheaper price tickets for more expensive ones. The fraud involved less than £100. Mrs Burrows did not attend the FTP hearing, thus depriving herself of the opportunity to demonstrate insight. Mr Justice Kerr said 'not attending the hearing amounts virtually to courting removal . . . Cases of dishonesty are always likely to lead to removal. The fact that removal is not inevitable . . . does not mean it is necessarily too harsh for a first disciplinary offence'. It is interesting to note that the GPhC's representative had suggested that a suspension would be appropriate, and the FTP Committee's decision to impose a more severe sanction was upheld by the Court.

Warning

In a case in which a pharmacist became aware that an error had been made in the supply of warfarin, the FTP Committee held that the registrant had not taken urgent and effective steps to check the position because he was reluctant to believe that an error had occurred. The Committee decided to give him a warning, saying 'these events have had a profound and devastating effect upon him. In our view, there is nothing that needs to be brought home to [the registrant]. We do not consider that any sanction we impose could serve any useful purpose in that respect'.[101]

Amy Connelly was a pharmacy technician employed by Poole Hospital NHS Trust. She admitted repeatedly accessing patient records of people she knew personally. It was not alleged that she had shared with others any of the information she had inappropriately accessed. She had been dismissed from her post, and found new employment, having disclosed to her new employer the details of her dismissal from Poole Hospital. The Committee found[102] that Miss Connelly had shown sufficient insight and that there would be no repetition of misconduct. It gave her a warning that she should at all times in the future fulfil her personal responsibility to make herself fully aware of all of the provisions of the GPhC's Standards of Conduct, Ethics and Performance, and that she should at all times strictly maintain the boundary between personal and professional activities.

Mrs Elizabeth Nickels (whose case is also referred to above under the heading 'Misconduct') was given a warning, among other things, to ensure she applied the same high standards of patient care to the supply of medication via an internet pharmacy as to the supply of medication to a patient in a physical pharmacy.

---

[101] Manhar Prabhubhai Patel, 4 December 2013
[102] 18 March 2013

Conditions

Piotr Majchrowicz told a patient seeking emergency hormonal contraception that she was ending a life and it would be on her conscience. He did not direct the patient to another pharmacy or provide her with other options. The FTP Committee[103] imposed conditions that included notifying all employers or prospective employers of the allegations that had been found proved, not engaging in the provision of emergency hormonal contraception, and refraining from providing advice or information to patients based on his personal, moral or religious beliefs.

Suspension

In the case of a pharmacy technician who had received police cautions for drug offences many years before, the FTP Committee considered that these could not give rise to current impairment, but the failure to declare the cautions when he must have realised that they were required to be disclosed led to a 3-month suspension.[104] (It should be noted that there is now a 6-year time limit after which cautions no longer need to be declared, and that the FTP Committee has not found impairment in cases where a registrant believed he had received a warning from the police, not a formal caution, and the failure to declare was not alleged to have been dishonest.[105])

Aukse Austinskaite (referred to above) had made dispensing errors that were 'comparatively large in number... and included serious errors in the form of exposure of the patients to risk...'. However, the Committee considered removal, which not only carries a lasting stigma but would also prevent the registrant from practising for at least 5 years, would be too severe and a disproportionate sanction. The Committee considered that the registrant should be given an opportunity to come back to pharmacy and 'learn to do the job properly'. The Committee directed a suspension for a period of 12 months, saying that in view of her good testimonials she did not deserve to have her name removed, and that the public interest did not demand the removal of her name.

The case of Glackin sheds light on the approach to drug misuse.[106] The registrant's fitness to practise was found to be impaired because of cocaine use. The chair of the Committee said, 'Regular, even if infrequent misuse of drugs, presents a risk to health and might therefore prejudice patients. It is bound to undermine public confidence in the profession, it breaches a fundamental tenet of the profession and it is contrary to the Code of Ethics'.

---

[103] 18 July 2013
[104] Jacob Kaufman (*Pharm J*, 21 September 2013 p. 293)
[105] For example, Tavankar, 13 November 2016
[106] Brendan Ambrose Glackin (*Pharm J*, 30 June 2012 p. 795)

Ordering a 12-month suspension, the Committee said that, when a review took place, the registrant would need to provide evidence that he had kept his knowledge up to date and complied with CPD requirements; proof of attendance at a return to practise course; reports concerning any work he had carried out; and a report from his GP concerning his health, insofar as it might affect his fitness to practise, with particular reference to drug abuse.

Mr Vijay Mistry[107] had been convicted of an act intended to pervert the course of justice. He had 'doctored' evidence to show that a car caught on a police speed camera was not his. He was convicted after a trial at which he had pleaded not guilty. The Crown Court imposed a suspended prison sentence. The FTP Committee found that Mr Mistry had 'at least partial insight' and suspended him from practice for 12 months.

Mrs Folake Idowu[108] had pleaded guilty to dishonestly claiming almost £5000 in local authority housing payments to which she was not entitled. The dishonest conduct was over a period of time, but it was limited to one particular set of circumstances unrelated to work and there had been no previous or subsequent dishonesty. A 12-month suspension was imposed.

Mohammed Zahirulhasan[109] had been given a police caution for stealing aftershave, headphones and skin cream to the value of £79.98 from his employer. Mitigation included the isolated nature of the incident, his previous good record, the repayment to his employer of the value of the goods, and the absence of harm to patients or the public. He had made frank admissions to his employer and the police, and referred himself to the GPhC. The FTP Committee found that he had only limited insight and imposed a 9-month suspension.

Asif Alam[110] dishonestly enrolled ineligible patients for the Scottish Minor Ailments Scheme (MAS). The Committee was satisfied that his prime motivation was to enhance his reputation at work and to relieve the considerable pressure he was under. He had not set out to defraud the NHS. Mr Alam was suspended for 9 months.

It is extremely rare for fitness to practise cases to reach the Supreme Court. In an appeal against a striking off after a pharmacist had been convicted of serious and repeated acts of violence towards his wife and her family, the Supreme Court[111] held that, because the conduct did not relate to professional performance and no patient had been, or was likely to be, put at risk, striking off was disproportionate. The Court held that the sanction proportionate to the disrepute into which the pharmacist's conduct had brought the profession was a suspension for 12 months.

[107] 14 February 2012
[108] 22 May 2013
[109] 5 November 2014
[110] 8 June 2016
[111] *Habib Khan v General Pharmaceutical Council* [2016] UKSC 64

Effect of suspension and review hearings

If the FTP Committee imposes a suspension, it will usually conduct a review hearing before the expiry of the extension. At the review hearing, the Committee may decide to remove the registrant's name from the Register or extend the suspension by up to 12 months; if the registrant has already been suspended for at least 2 years, the Committee may suspend the registrant indefinitely. At the end of any period of suspension, the Committee may impose conditions of practice. In the Austinskaite case, referred to above, the Committee said that if, when her suspension was reviewed, there was no evidence that the registrant had any intention of learning to practise to an accepted level of competence, it may be that the Committee would decide to remove her name at the review hearing. If she were able to provide the Committee with evidence of competence, it would probably permit her to return to practice.

At a review hearing, there is, in practical terms, a persuasive burden on the pharmacist or pharmacy technician to demonstrate that s/he has fully acknowledged why the past offending behaviour was deficient, and through insight, application, education, supervision or other achievement, has addressed the past impairment.[112] The review committee asks: does the registrant's fitness to practise *remain* impaired?[113]

It has been argued that since a suspended pharmacist must be treated as not being entered in the Register (Art.19(8)) the effect of suspension is to prevent a pharmacist who owns an NHS pharmacy in his/her own name from providing services and thus put him/her at risk of removal from the pharmaceutical list (in other words, losing his/her NHS 'contract').[114] However, it is thought that the better view is that a suspended pharmacist may continue to own an NHS pharmacy but may not personally provide NHS services during the period of suspension. This view would be consistent with section 132(8) of the National Health Service Act 2006.

Removal from the Register

Neelu Sharma[115] was accused of selecting a pair of shoes in a store and, pretending she had paid for them, exchanged them for a cardigan worth about £10 or £12. The FTP Committee found she was guilty of a 'dishonest scam'. Her persistence in denying the allegation was regarded as a lack of remorse and insight that led to her removal from the Register.

Neil Brown was a pharmacy technician employed by the Royal Air Force. He was convicted of stealing equipment which he ordered. The FTP

---

[112] *Abrahaem v General Medical Council* [2008] EWHC 183 (Admin)

[113] *Habib Khan v General Pharmaceutical Council* [2016] UKSC 64

[114] Regulation 74(1)(b) of the National Health Service (Pharmaceutical and Local Pharmaceutical Services) Regulations 2013 (SI 2012 No. 349)

[115] 11 July 2013

Committee[116] said that dishonesty 'lies at the top end of the spectrum of gravity of misconduct'. The Committee noted the severity of the impact on the registrant and his family of removal, but removal from the Register was required. Unusually, the Committee expressed the view that removal need not be the end of Mr Brown's career and that, after a period of reflection, he might apply for restoration to the Register.

Sanjeev Patel was instrumental in submitting to GlaxoSmithKline 92 apparently valid prescriptions for large quantities of drugs that were extremely expensive and in short supply. The drugs thus obtained were then sold on at a profit. The FTP Committee[117] said that, whatever Mr Patel's personal qualities as a pharmacist, the sustained dishonesty meant that a suspension could not possibly meet the seriousness of what he did.

Iestyn Evans reported himself to the GPhC because of drug dependency. This did not impair his fitness to practise, but he was found to have stolen drugs over a sustained period from the pharmacy where he worked. Removal from the Register was considered necessary to meet the public interest.[118]

Interim suspension following a decision to suspend or remove from the Register

A suspension or a direction to remove a registrant's name from the Register will not normally take effect until the 28-day period for appealing has expired. The Committee may order the suspension or removal to have immediate effect if it is satisfied that this is necessary for the protection of members of the public or is otherwise in the public interest or in the interests of the registrant (Art.60). If the FTP Committee has decided that the appropriate sanction is a period of suspension, an immediate suspension to prevent the registrant practising during the appeal period will not count towards the period of suspension imposed as the sanction. Although there appears to be a tendency for the FTP Committee to decide that, if it has found that suspension or removal from the Register is appropriate, there should be an immediate suspension, this must be *necessary* to protect the public or there must be a genuine public interest in immediate suspension. In many cases, the upholding of proper standards of conduct and behaviour may reasonably be said to have been achieved by the sanction the Committee has already imposed.[119] In the case of Kiran Mehta,[120] for example, he was suspended for 4 months because he had made a dispensing error and then

[116] 3 May 2013
[117] 29 April 2013
[118] 19 November 2012
[119] *Ashton v General Medical Council* [2013] EWHC 943 (Admin); *Davey v General Dental Council* 2015 WL 6757832
[120] 23 August 2013

dishonestly tried to conceal what had happened. The FTP Committee held there was no additional public interest that made it appropriate to impose an immediate period of suspension and that, to the contrary, on the basis that Mr Mehta's business provided a service to his community, the public interest was served by enabling him to arrange for the smooth transition of his business to enable it to operate during the period of suspension.

Costs

Before a principal hearing or a restoration hearing (see below) takes place, a party may serve the other party and the secretary to the committee a schedule of costs and expenses related to or connected with the hearing. This must be done no less than 24 hours before the date of the hearing. After announcing the Committee's decision, the chair may invite representations as to whether costs or expenses should be assessed against either party.

In practice, the Committee does not routinely award costs and there is no principle that costs are paid by the 'loser' to the 'winner'. Costs will usually be awarded only because of the way one of the parties has conducted itself. For example, costs have been awarded against the RPS (when it was the regulator) because a case ought not to have been brought against two out of three registrants who were partners in a pharmacy business but who were not alleged to have been involved in the misconduct by a third partner.[121] In another case,[122] a registrant had made false expense claims to an employer. He made admissions of dishonesty when interviewed by the police. When fitness to practise proceeding were brought, he contested the allegations and a hearing was listed for 2 days. On the first day of the hearing, the registrant accepted that the account he had given to the police was correct and the hearing was completed that day. The expense of arranging the second day was, therefore, wasted. The Committee held that it was unreasonable to have contested the allegations up to the morning of the first day of the hearing, and ordered the registrant to pay the wasted costs.

Where the Committee orders a party to pay costs or expenses, the chair may summarily assess the costs or expenses or require the parties to agree a figure or have them assessed by a person appointed by the secretary.

Appeals

There is a right of appeal (Art.58) to the High Court against decisions to direct removal from the Register, suspension and the imposition of conditions of practice. A notice of appeal must be lodged at the High Court within 28 days, beginning with the date on which written notice of the reasons

---

[121] Tanna (*Pharm J*, 1 March 2008 p. 235)
[122] Shiraz Mughal, 12 September 2011

for the decision was sent to the appellant. There is no power to extend this period.

Appeals to the High Court take the form of a re-hearing,[123] although it is not usual for the court to hear witness evidence. Fresh evidence is not normally admitted, and the court will usually deal with appeals by reference to a transcript of the fitness to practise proceedings. An appeal is only allowed where the decision is plainly wrong or unjust because of a serious procedural error or other irregularity. Appropriate deference is given to the FTP Committee in view of its special expertise, especially in cases regarding professional practice. As regards sanction, the court will not conduct a re-sentencing exercise, substituting its view for that of the FTP Committee.[124]

Professional Standards Authority for Health and Social Care

The fitness to practise role of the GPhC is overseen by the PSA. If the PSA considers that a fitness to practise decision (including a decision not to take a disciplinary measure) is not sufficient for the protection of the public for the PSA to do so, the PSA may appeal against the decision to the High Court.[125] The question for consideration in such an appeal is whether the GPhC's decision was sufficient:

a to protect the health, safety and well-being of the public;
b to maintain public confidence in the profession; and
c to maintain proper professional standards and conduct for members of that profession.

In *Professional Standards Authority v General Pharmaceutical Council and Onwughalu*,[126] Mrs Onwughalu had been convicted of two counts of cruelty to a child under 16. She received prison sentences for each offence. The FTP Committee decided to suspend her for 12 months. Mrs Justice Cox noted that there were serious aggravating factors and that the applicant had not demonstrated 'true insight'. The judge held that the Committee had not explained how suspending the registrant would be sufficient to maintain professional standards and to maintain public confidence in the pharmacy profession. She held that the FTP Committee's decision was plainly wrong in view of the registrant's lack of insight, and the offences were directly related to clinical practice and to standards of professionalism. The suspension was quashed and replaced with an order for removal from the Register.

---

[123] Paragraph 22.3(2) of the Practice Direction of Part 52 of the Civil Procedure Rules
[124] *Abdul-Razzak v General Pharmaceutical Council* [2016] EWHC 1204 (Admin) and *Burrows v General Pharmaceutical Council* [2016] EWHC 1050 (Admin)
[125] Section 29 of the National Health Service Reform and Health Care Professions Act 2002
[126] [2014] EWHC 2521 (Admin)

Restoration to the Register and registration following removal

In the case of a person whose name has been removed from the Register at the direction of the FTP Committee, no application for restoration may be made before the expiration of 5 years from the date of removal or within 12 months from the date of an earlier application.[127] The Registrar will refer any application for restoration to the FTP Committee. The burden of proof in a restoration application is on the applicant, who must prove that s/he is entitled to be registered.

A person whose name was removed from the Register before the GPhC became the regulator will not have been on the Council's Register. As such, an application for restoration cannot be made, and such a person would have to apply for registration to the Registrar. There is no time restriction of the kind that applies to applications for restoration. Initially, the Registrar usually determines such applications without a hearing. If an application is refused, there is a right of appeal to the Appeals Committee (see also chapter 20). The procedures that have to be followed in order to appeal are set out in the Regulations.[128] Appeals take the form of a re-hearing, which may be on paper. The appellant may request a hearing and may give oral evidence. The appellant bears the burden of establishing that the Registrar's decision should be overturned, and the standard of proof is the civil one, i.e. the balance of probabilities.[129]

Summary

- The GPhC will consider fitness to practise on an application for first registration and when it receives information or an allegation that fitness to practise may be impaired.
- Allegations of impairment are usually based on a conviction, misconduct, deficient professional performance or health.
- Dispensing errors may be misconduct or deficient professional performance, but single errors are not usually referred for fitness to practise proceedings unless very serious.
- Allegations are usually passed by the GPhC's Registrar to the Investigating Committee, which will decide whether to refer the case to the FTP Committee.
- The FTP Committee may impose an interim suspension while awaiting a full hearing if it considers this necessary for the protection of the public or is otherwise in the public interest.

[127] Article 57(2) of the Pharmacy Order 2010
[128] The General Pharmaceutical Council (Appeals Committee) Rules (SI 2010 No. 1614)
[129] Rule 10 of the Appeals Committee Rules

- At a full (or 'principal') hearing, the FTP Committee will decide the facts and whether a registrant's fitness to practise is impaired.
- If a registrant's fitness to practise is found to be impaired, the FTP Committee can give advice, a warning, impose conditions of practice, suspend for up to 12 months or direct the registrant's removal from the GPhC's Register.
- In deciding on the appropriate and proportionate sanction, the FTP Committee will have regard to published guidance ('Indicative Sanctions').
- The FTP Committee has power to order the GPhC or a registrant to pay costs.
- A registrant has a right of appeal to a court against a decision to suspend or to remove from the Register.
- Following removal from the Register, an application for restoration cannot be made before 5 years have elapsed.

Further reading

Glynn J, Gomez D (2012). *Regulation of Healthcare Professionals*. London: Sweet & Maxwell.
Charles Russell Speechlys LLP (February 2016). *A guide to GPhC investigations and fitness to practise proceedings*.
GPhC (November 2011). *Prosecution policy*.
GPhC (undated). *The Threshold Criteria* (relating to referral to the Investigating Committee).
GPhC (13 February 2015). *Guidance on the GPhC's Threshold Criteria Policy*.
GPhC (July 2015). *Good decision making: fitness to practise hearings and sanctions guidance*.
GPhC (February 2016). *Good decision making: investigating committee meetings and outcomes guidance*.
GPhC (January 2016). *Good decision making: conditions bank*.
GPhC (September 2010). *Code of Conduct for Pharmacy Students*.
Hamer K (2015). *Professional Conduct Casebook*. Oxford: Oxford University Press.

Websites

Chemist and Druggist (a weekly publication for community pharmacy but also publishes short reports of some fitness to practise cases and has links to transcripts on the GPhC website): http://www.chemistanddruggist.co.uk
Crown Prosecution Service: http://www.cps.gov.uk
Crown Prosecution Service (guidance on prosecution policy): http://www.cps.gov.uk/legal/l_to_o/medicines_act_1968/
General Pharmaceutical Council: http://www.pharmacyregulation.org
General Pharmaceutical Council (details of pharmacy standards): http://www.pharmacyregulation.org
The GPhC also publishes an annual Fitness to Practise report which is available on its website.
The GPhC carries an online register which contains details of any publicly available fitness to practise hearings and their outcomes. To find a case, go to the home page and enter the name (or the registration number if known and still valid) into the Register search function. A link to the fitness to practise case will appear against the registrant's name if available. The GPhC also publishes every 2 months *Regula+e*; this carries updates on the Council's activities as well as lessons to be learned from selected fitness to practise cases.
Legislation: http://www.legislation.gov.uk

Royal Pharmaceutical Society: http://www.rpharms.org

- fitness to practise procedures: http://www.pharmacyregulation.org/raising-concerns/hearings/committees/fitness-practise-committee
- fitness to practise cases: http://www.pharmacyregulation.org/search/search_decisions

The RPS is a membership organisation for pharmacists and the *Pharmaceutical Journal* is provided free to its members. Fitness to practise cases are often the subject of short reports in the *Pharmaceutical Journal*. The RPS also issues annually the *Medicines, Ethics and Practice Guide*, which is intended to assist members in interpretation of the law and standards of practice in real-life situations.

23

Regulation of health professions

Gordon Hockey

Medical scandals and convergence of regulation

During the 1990s and into the first years of the 21st century, a series of scandals, mostly involving doctors (although a nurse, Beverley Allit, in 1993, is a notable exception), led to a radical overhaul of the regulation of all health professions, including pharmacy. Space does not permit a full account here but the following overview is well supported by website resources (see end of chapter) covering the detailed inquiries that followed the scandals. One of the first inquiries, in 2001, was the Kennedy Inquiry,[1] which investigated a flawed system at an NHS hospital, which 'led to around one-third of all the children who underwent open-heart surgery receiving less than adequate care. More children died than might have been expected in a typical (comparative) unit'. The inquiry criticised in particular the presence of a 'club culture' and the absence of any agreed means of assessing the quality of care, of standards for evaluating performance or of clarity as to who in the NHS was responsible for monitoring the quality of care. This last finding led to the development of clinical governance within the NHS (now termed quality and performance; chapter 24) and then in private healthcare. The inquiry also led the following year to the establishment of what is now the Professional Standards Authority for Health and Social Care (PSA),[2] a super-regulator, which has provided increasing oversight of the regulators of health professionals.

[1] Kennedy 2001, *The Report of the Public Inquiry into Children's Heart Surgery at the Bristol Royal Infirmary 1984–1995: Learning from Bristol*
[2] The Professional Standards Authority for Health and Social Care. This was established as the Council for the Regulation of Health Care Professionals under the National Health Service Reform and Health Care Professions Act 2002, and renamed the Council for Healthcare Regulatory Excellence by the Health and Social Care Act 2008, before being renamed again as the Professional Standards Authority for Health and Social Care by section 222 of the Health and Social Care Act 2012

A second inquiry, at Alder Hey Hospital in Liverpool,[3] set out to inquire into the removal, retention and disposal of human tissue and organs following coroners' and hospital postmortem examinations, and the extent to which the Human Tissue Act 1961 had been complied with. In this Inquiry, it was found that the doctors and staff at Alder Hey had failed to provide suitable advice, counselling and support necessary to affected families and showed a lamentable grasp of the modern concepts of consent and involvement of patients, parents and relatives in medical care. Following both inquiries, individual doctors were subject to General Medical Council (GMC) disciplinary procedures.

To some extent, the above two inquiries pale into insignificance beside a third, the Shipman Inquiry,[4] at least in relation to the harm caused. Dr Harold Shipman, by all accounts a benign and caring GP with a single-handed practice in Hyde, a small town in a pleasant part of northwest England, was eventually proven to have murdered at least 200 of his patients and more were suspected. When he was eventually imprisoned for life after nearly 30 years of practice, he hanged himself, thus taking any further information about numbers or his motives to his grave. Two of the key outcomes of the Shipman Inquiry were a series of recommendations to modify the legislation regarding Controlled Drugs to limit the likelihood of such unnoticed diversion occurring again, and a series of changes to the regulation of doctors and subsequently all the health professions. The role of the PSA was also strengthened to ensure regulation works in the public interest. A further series of inquiries were published into the conduct of Clifford Ayling,[5] Richard Neale[6] and, jointly, William Kerr and Michael Haslam.[7] These revealed both appalling flaws in the professional behaviour of a few doctors and the failure of those in positions of authority or the regulator (the GMC) to detect signs of this behaviour and to take timely and effective action to protect patients from harm.

The most recent inquiry, by Robert Francis QC, considered the appalling care Mid Staffordshire NHS Foundation Trust provided to its patients between 2005 and 2008.[8] The Francis Inquiry concluded that the suffering of patients was due to a 'serious failure on the part of the Trust Board ... to tackle an insidious negative culture involving a tolerance of poor standards and a disengagement from managerial and leadership responsibilities', which

[3] Redfern et al. 2001, *The Royal Liverpool Children's Inquiry Report*

[4] Smith J 2002–2005, *The Shipman Inquiry* (six individual reports)

[5] Department of Health 2004, *Committee of Inquiry: Independent Investigation into how the NHS Handled Allegations about the Conduct of Clifford Ayling*

[6] Department of Health 2004, *Committee of Inquiry to Investigate how the NHS Handled Allegations about the Performance and Conduct of Richard Neale*

[7] Department of Health 2005, *The Kerr/Haslam Inquiry, Full Report*

[8] Independent report of the Mid Staffordshire NHS Foundation Trust Public Inquiry 6 February 2013 (The Francis Inquiry)

was compounded by a failure of the various NHS checks and balances, and of regulators to do something effective to remedy the situation. The report indicated that the Trust's care of patients was compromised by a desire to meet various targets; one of the key recommendations was to ensure a common culture shared by all in the NHS of putting the patient first, and that compliance with standards should be professionally led.

A further factor in the convergence of regulation of health professions has been the use of 'section 60' orders,[9] which, since 1999, have provided a relatively swift mechanism to change the primary legislation governing the individual regulators. In the absence of these orders, securing the necessary time and political support for changes in primary legislation is very difficult.

Professional Standards Authority for Health and Social Care

The PSA was established due to political concern about the unsatisfactory nature of self-regulation of doctors,[10] and is now charged with providing assurances to Parliament that the regulatory bodies of health and social care professionals are carrying out their legal functions and protecting the public. The PSA oversees the bodies regulating the medical, dental, nursing, optical, chiropractic, osteopathic, pharmacy, and health and care professions.[11] Its role is to review and scrutinise their regulatory systems and drive up standards, and to foster harmonisation of regulatory practice and outcomes. The PSA may investigate and report on the performance of each regulatory body, and may recommend changes to the way in which the body performs its functions. It reviews every final decision made by the regulators' fitness to practise committees, and may refer to the High Court a case that appears to be too lenient on the individual professional, and therefore does not adequately protect the public.

The PSA also advises the Secretary of State and health ministers in Scotland, Wales and Northern Ireland on regulatory policy, and from time to time carries out special reviews. These have included a report of the General Dental Council's whistleblower's complaint (2015) and a strategic review of the Nursing and Midwifery Council (2012). The report into the General Social Care Council (2009) was followed 2 years later by its closure.[12]

In recent years, the PSA has increasingly taken on the lead role in the regulation of health professionals, steadily addressing issues common to

[9]Health Act 1999

[10]Including the Kennedy Inquiry in 2001

[11]General Medical Council, General Dental Council, Nursing and Midwifery Council, General Optical Council, General Chiropractic Council, General Osteopathic Council, General Pharmaceutical Council, Pharmaceutical Society of Northern Ireland and the Health and Care Professions Council

[12]Health and Social Care Act 2012; on 1 August 2012, when the Health Professions Council took over responsibility for the regulation of social workers in England it was renamed as the Health and Care Professions Council

regulators, undertaking research and policy development, and encouraging and cajoling the regulators to develop.

Section 60 Orders

Section 60 of the Health Act 1999[13] provides powers to change the regulation of the health professions by Order in Council. This has accelerated the pace of legislative change because it avoids the need for new primary legislation. Such Orders in Council may:

a modify the regulation of any profession, so far as appears to be necessary or expedient for the purpose of securing or improving the regulation of the profession or the services which the profession provides or to which it contributes; and

b regulate any other profession which appears to be concerned (wholly or partly) with the physical or mental health of individuals and to require regulation.

Many changes have since been made to the statutory regulations of the health regulators, including, for example, the establishment of the GPhC by the Pharmacy Order 2010.[14]

Law Commission proposals on regulation

In 2012, the Law Commission undertook a review of the regulation of health (in the UK) and social care professionals (in England) and consulted on proposals to introduce a single Act of Parliament to provide the legal framework to replace all the individual governing statutes and orders.[15] The intention was to simplify and modernise the current complex arrangements for professional regulation and impose consistency across the regulators by giving Government the power to make regulations for any of the regulators or merge or abolish existing regulators or establish a new regulator. The report and draft bill were published on 2 April 2014 and early in 2015 the Government accepted the majority of the recommendations. However, for whatever reason, the bill has not progressed and it remains to be seen whether the delay is temporary or permanent.

[13] As amended by the Health and Social Care Act 2008 and the Health and Social Care Act 2012

[14] Pharmacy Order SI 2010 No. 231

[15] Law Commission, Scottish Law Commission and the Northern Ireland Law Commission 2012, *Regulation of Health Care Professionals: Regulation of Social Care Professionals in England*

Development of regulation

As might be expected, following the scandals, inquiries and increasing public and media interest in the issues, the regulation of health professionals has developed significantly over the last 15 years. A milestone in this journey was the White Paper 'Trust, Assurance and Safety – The Regulation of Health Professionals in the 21st Century', published in 2007. This is referred to subsequently as 'the 2007 White Paper'. It followed two reports in 2006, Sir Liam Donaldson's (Chief Medical Officer's) report 'Good doctors, safer patients' and the Department of Health report 'The regulation of non-medical healthcare professions' (Andrew Foster from the department led the report), which both indicated the need for fundamental changes to regulation.

The 2007 White Paper drew a metaphorical line in the sand, assuring the various professions of their independence to regulate, provided that they reformed. Broadly, this reform was, first, to move from self-regulation to shared regulation (with the public), second, to move from simply dealing with problems after the event to seeking to avoid them in the first place (revalidation), and, third, to ensure that the investigation of complaints was fairer to the public and the professions. In doing so, the 2007 White Paper clarified a number of issues, which had been the subject of discussion and some progress up to that time, as follows.

Context and purpose

In the early 2000s, as the scandals were exposed, there was a temptation to forget that each was an exception. The 2007 White Paper was a timely reminder that the vast majority of professionals are skilled, dedicated and trustworthy, and that the purpose of regulation was as much to support safe and effective clinical practice and maintain the justified confidence of patients, as to deal with those who did not maintain the necessary standards.

Governance and accountability

Pre-2000, the governing councils of the regulators often had large numbers of council members, with a significant majority of them elected by the profession. Small numbers of lay members were also appointed. A majority of professional council members was seen as appropriate given that they were there to 'self-regulate' and representation should match taxation or, in this case, the funding through annual registration fees. This gradually started to change as the public interest in the role of regulation was increasingly acknowledged and, also, that the cost of regulation was ultimately borne by the public.

The 2007 White Paper indicated that, for patients and the public to have confidence in the regulators, they should be, and be seen to be, independent and impartial. To achieve this, they needed to have smaller, more board-like governing councils with equal numbers of lay and professional appointed members. This approach both allows and demands the appointment of those with the right skills mix to do the job (rather than election of the most popular). In time, the GMC has moved to 12 members of whom 6 are lay,[16] and the GPhC to 14, of whom 7 are lay.[17] The 2007 White Paper also indicated that governing councils' roles should be more consistent and clearly in the public interest, and that they should be independent of the profession's various interest groups and those who employ them, including the NHS. The Royal Pharmaceutical Society of Great Britain's combined representative and regulatory function was confirmed as no longer sustainable, which paved the way for its split and the creation of the GPhC in 2010; no merger of regulators was proposed.

The changes in governance over the last 15 years have undoubtedly changed the regulatory landscape. The club-like feel of regulators of health professionals, which involved members, membership and prestige, has largely gone, giving way to registrants, registration and greater public involvement and accountability.

Principles of regulation

Pre-2000, regulators sometimes saw themselves as being there to adjudicate between the two parties, and not there to investigate allegations or, put another way, not there to make a case against the individual professional if a complainant could not do so. In addition, those adjudicating on complaints and hearings were sometimes also involved elsewhere in the complaints processes, which raised issues under Human Rights legislation.[18] This failure to carry out their role and lack of transparency started to change during the 2000s.

The 2007 White Paper stated that, to be effective, regulators must be seen to be independent, transparent, accountable, ethical, dispassionate and just. This was similar to the five principles of better regulation set out in the early 2000s by the Better Regulation Task Force (which in 2006 become the Better Regulation Commission) of proportionality, accountability, consistency, transparency and targeting. To these, the PSA has since added a fresh approach to governance and an additional principle.

The fresh approach to governance, which the PSA indicates is evidenced by the Francis Inquiry, is the need 'to focus on the personal qualities and

[16]The General Medical Council (Constitution) (Amendment) Order 2012 (SI 2012/1654)
[17]The General Pharmaceutical Council (Constitution) Order 2010 (SI 2010/300)
[18]*Preiss v GMC Privy Council* Appeal No. 63 of 2000

attributes that are required to ensure that the practice of governance is informed by resilience, diligence, courage and care'. The PSA argues that 'the technical competence to serve on a board is as nothing without personal commitment to the public interest. Accountability is meaningless when it only means describing what has been done, rather than taking responsibility for its consequences'. The additional (sixth) principle of better regulation is 'agility'. The PSA argues that regulators should anticipate change by assessing risks based on evidence and respond accordingly, rather than reacting to problems after the event. The PSA describes this as 'right touch' regulation and it is similar to the 2007 White Paper's principle that regulation should not create unnecessary burdens, but be proportionate to the risk it addresses and the benefit it brings. However, the perennial difficulty for regulators is the absence of virtually any objective measure of the risks or how regulation reduces those risks.

Revalidation and ensuring continuing fitness to practise

Pre-2000, continuing professional development (CPD) was either strongly encouraged or a professional requirement, but during the 2000s there were increasing efforts by regulators, including those outside health regulation, to strengthen the requirements and enforce them. In due course, some have made annual renewal of registration dependent on completion of enough CPD. However, the perennial problems with CPD have been, first, ensuring its quality, second, whether it has any impact on the individual's fitness to practice (i.e. is it practical and effective and not simply academic study?), and, third, whether it has been done. Some regulators have sought to accredit CPD courses to ensure quality; others have been tougher on audit and enforcement. In some cases, the latter approach has resulted in numerous disciplinary hearings, which are costly and burdensome to the regulator and the profession concerned. But the key question is whether the individual professional remains fit to practise – up to date, with the safety and quality of his/her practice maintained.

The 2007 White Paper sought to address continuing fitness to practise, and indicated that doctors would be subject to revalidation every 5 years. It was proposed that this would comprise a genuine evaluation of an individual doctor's fitness to practise, a recommendation which can be found in the Shipman Inquiry, Fifth Report.[19] In the end, it is generally accepted that the costs of revalidation were prohibitively high and the full proposals were watered down: the NHS appraisal process that was intended to support revalidation effectively became the process itself. Although this may not be ideal, it was a cost-effective and pragmatic answer that provides some assurances that an individual doctor is practising safely.

[19]Recommendation 103 of the Shipman Report

The 2007 White Paper indicated that other professionals should demonstrate their continuing fitness to practise through appropriate revalidation arrangements. The GPhC describes revalidation as 'the process by which assurance of continuing fitness to practise of registrants is provided and in a way which is aimed primarily at supporting and enhancing professional practice', and indicates on its website that the arguments for introducing it remain compelling. But will it be introduced? What happened with the dentists would suggest it won't be. In 2010, the General Dental Council (GDC) consulted on revalidation but, 6 years later, it has not been implemented. The GDC says that it is still considering the issue and whether its introduction will be proportionate and cost-effective. The difficulty for small businesses or self-employed professionals is that, although they are part of the wider NHS, generally they are not part of the NHS appraisal system.

Complaints procedures and disciplinary hearings (fitness to practise)

These include the assessment, investigation and screening of complaints and, if required, formal, court-like hearings to determine whether a professional remains fit to practise. Procedures have changed markedly over the last 15 years and three general themes are discussed below.

A conduct jurisdiction alone is insufficient to address the problems

In the early 2000s, there was increasing recognition that conduct procedures alone either did not cover, or were not appropriate to deal with, the myriad of issues in practice and could not ensure the safe practice of doctors. Health problems could not be addressed directly, only the manifestation of those problems as misconduct. The position was similar for performance; very poor practice was apparently not misconduct but, if a conduct issue was involved, such as recklessness, it might be. Some smaller regulators did not accept these restrictions and perhaps were less susceptible to appeals and judicial review, but, nevertheless, the extent to which health issues affecting practice and poor clinical practice could be addressed was limited by a 'conduct' jurisdiction. In the late 1990s, the GMC, the leader in the regulatory field, had added separate fledgling health and performance procedures to seek to address these issues, but this was not enough. There needed to be one process that dealt with all the issues concerning a professional at one time to address the central questions: is s/he fit to practise? Therefore, in 2004, the GMC introduced fitness to practise procedures dealing with conduct, health and performance (and more) in one system. The GMC's move in 2004 was a game changer and in due course each regulator developed along similar lines. The fitness to practise procedures for the GPhC are described in chapter 22.

Typically, health cases involve addiction to either alcohol or drugs. Drug addiction is broadly accepted as a medical problem, but unfortunately alcohol addiction less so. This is odd given that, as far back as 1951, the World Health Organization recognised alcoholism as a serious medical condition, requiring medical treatment rather than moral censorship.[20] The breakthrough for regulators came in the 2000s when they accepted this wholeheartedly and started to adopt procedures that allowed the underlying medical problem to be addressed. This was and is permissible, provided that public protection was maintained, for example through supervised practice, conditions of practice and regular testing, and, if it cannot be, the individual professional is removed from the Register.

A health-focused approach is generally less expensive, more effective and kinder to the individual professional than formal disciplinary hearings, and works best if those with health problems receive some kind of additional support. Discipline and support are different sides of the same coin, and support is just as important as discipline if a good outcome is to be achieved. It is suggested that this is the underlying message of the report by the GMC into the number of suicides of doctors under investigation.[21] Such support is usually provided by the voluntary or charity sector and, arguably, it would be inappropriate for a regulator to provide it. However, if regulators are outcomes focused, there is a strong argument that they should help to fund this support that is so vital to their work. It is to be hoped that this will be a future development.

Fitness to practise procedures have allowed cases to conclude, determinations to be made and action to be taken, without necessarily identifying any form of evil intent or recklessness on the part of the individual professional, and this has been a significant factor in protecting the public.

Complaints are not simply a matter for the regulator, but a legal process

Pre-2000, referral of a case to a disciplinary hearing was to some extent considered to be at the discretion of the regulator. This was firmly put to one side in the early 2000s with a number of judicial reviews which clarified and confirmed that the process was determined by the provisions of the legislation, and complainants could expect serious cases to progress to hearings, or they could expect to receive a proper explanation as to why the case was not serious.[22] This had the effect of ensuring that complaints could be closed only after sufficient investigation when a good explanation (or at least one that could withstand judicial review) could be provided. They were

---

[20] Report of the first session of the alcoholism subcommittee, http://apps.who.int/iris/bitstream/10665/40164/1/WHO_TRS_42.pdf

[21] Doctors who commit suicide while under GMC fitness to practise investigation, Internal review, Sarndrah Horsfall, Independent Consultant, 14 December 2014

[22] *R v The General Medical Council, ex parte Arpad Toth, Dr David Jarman Interested Party* [2000] EWHC Admin 361, [2000] 1 W.L.R. 2209 and *R v General Medical Council, ex parte Richards* QBD [2001] Lloyds Med. Rep. 47

seemingly innocuous judicial reviews involving the GMC, but they had a profound effect on regulators and significantly increased their workload and the costs of regulation.

Hearings panels required trained members with published procedural guidance

During the 2000s, the regulators started to provide comprehensive training and guidance for those involved in fitness to practise procedures, accepting that what was a complex and difficult process, with the potential for judicial scrutiny, needed careful management. An early example of such guidance emerged in the case of Wood.[23] In his judgment, the judge set out and approved the guidance followed by GMC screeners indicating that it had been developed by the GMC following the case of Toth (see footnote 22). Guidance documents are now published on the regulators' websites and the GMC Sanctions Guidance indicates that it: 'provides guidance to tribunals on imposing sanctions on a doctor's registration, including why a tribunal should impose a sanction and what factors it should consider. It provides a crucial link between two key regulatory roles: setting standards for the medical profession, and taking action when a doctor's fitness to practise is called into question because they have not met those standards.'

Against this backdrop, the 2007 White Paper recommended that all regulators should use the civil standard of proof on the balance of probabilities. Disciplinary proceedings are civil and not criminal in nature, but, despite this, some used the criminal standard of proof, beyond all reasonable doubt or so that you are sure. The recommendation was subsequently implemented by those regulators it affected, including the GMC. This was controversial around the time, with some fearing that professionals would be found guilty too easily, but those fears have not materialised and, broadly, the change has been accepted. The 2007 White Paper also recommended the separation of investigation and adjudication functions, the argument being that the investigators, the equivalent of the police, and panel members, the equivalent of the judiciary, should not be part of the same organisation: you should not be judge in your own court. Whilst many regulators have taken steps to seek to ensure that these two aspects of their work are separate and insulated from one another, the perception of fairness can still be compromised. As a consequence, an independent body to adjudicate on GMC hearings and potentially other health regulators' hearings (the Office of Health Professions Adjudicator) was proposed. It was almost introduced, but in 2012, when it was still being set up, it was culled in the 'burning of the quangos' that year. Following its demise, the GMC came up with an ingenious method of seeking to ensure the independence of hearings by creating the Medical

---

[23] *Christine Wood v GMC* [2002] EWHC 1484 (Admin)

Practitioners Tribunal Service (MPTS), a quasi-independent body managed by a committee of the GMC. This has largely been accepted as providing the necessary independence and impartiality.

The 2007 White Paper also proposed local resolution of complaints against doctors. The intention was to facilitate a proportionate, local response for less serious complaints, but also allow any patterns of misconduct or behaviour to be tracked and assessed. This was implemented with legislation that came into force in 2011, which set out a framework for responsible (medical) officers to be appointed by healthcare organisations and some other bodies, who would be responsible for evaluating the fitness to practise of doctors employed by the organisation.

Education

The 2007 White Paper had less to say on education, but approved a three-fold approach: undergraduate development, postgraduate education and CPD. The need for professionals to have an appropriate level of English language was also recognised. However, there was a long-standing view that the European rules on the free movement of workers prevented such language testing. After a tragedy in 2010, there was renewed impetus to resolve the issue, and in 2015, legislation started to be introduced that allows language testing of EU health professionals.

Registration

Pre-2000, the Register tended to be simply a list of members, with, for example, the individual's qualifications and address, and often whether s/he was practising or non-practising. The 2007 White Paper indicated that registers should be much more: an authoritative source of information on individual professionals, including disciplinary matters and alert notices for the public and patients. It also indicated that registers should include only those practising the profession, and that there should be greater information sharing between regulators and employers, including soft intelligence, given that, when scandals were exposed, it often became apparent that problems were known locally but no action had been taken. The proposals were directed at the GMC and doctors, but, broadly, have been taken up by other regulators.

New roles and emerging professions

The 2007 White Paper considered how best to regulate the various emerging professional groups and proposed either separate regulation or regulation by the lead health profession. The result has been that some health professions have increasingly taken on responsibility for the regulation of other members of their teams. In the case of pharmacy, this means pharmacy technicians; for dentists, this means six additional groups, including clinical dental technicians. The 2007 White Paper also proposed that regulatory practice and legislative provisions should be harmonised, but, as seen with the Law Commission's proposals, this is one recommendation that has not, or not yet, been implemented.

Right-touch regulation

More recently, the PSA has recommended 'right-touch' regulation,[24] after having indicated there is a need to rethink regulation.[25] Whether right-touch regulation is truly new is questionable, but it is a useful statement of how regulation should be undertaken and, given the PSA's pre-eminence in the regulatory arena, is likely to be the way regulators regulate for the foreseeable future. Right-touch regulation embraces the five principles of better regulation and adds a sixth, 'agility', and suggests that regulators should apply the right 'regulatory force' to reduce the relevant risks. Not too much, otherwise effort is wasted; not too little, otherwise the regulation is ineffective. It promotes the use of more options than simply regulation, for example strengthening employment practices, or promoting good practice, arguing that the outcome is more important than the regulatory approach. It also recognises that it must be cost-effective.

The PSA has identified eight elements that comprise right-touch regulation:

1 Identify the problem before the solution.
   The PSA indicates that regulatory change often comes before the problem is identified, which means that there is insufficient thought given to other non-regulatory answers, such as strengthening employment practices.
2 Quantify and qualify the risks.
   This is a twofold approach to assessing risk, which is perhaps more commonly expressed as the likelihood and significance of the risk. The likelihood is about how often it will occur; the significance is how serious it will be if it occurs. The PSA also goes further to ask whether the risk is new or currently managed in some way. Without this assessment, based on evidence, the PSA argues cogently that it will be difficult to choose the right response to reducing the risk.
3 Get as close to the problem as possible.
   The PSA makes the point that regulation is distant (usually national) and regulators should look for a solution that is as close to the problem as

---

[24] Right-touch regulation, October 2015 policy report, PSAHSC
[25] Rethinking regulation, PSA

possible. This means understanding the context in which the problem arises and the different tools that may be available to tackle the issues. There may be a need to work with other organisations and individuals who are closer to the problem than the regulator.

4 Focus on the outcome.
A right-touch approach should stay focused on the outcome, rather than the process or outcomes other than patient safety. The PSA also emphasises that outcomes should be tangible and measurable.

5 Use regulation only when necessary.
The PSA indicates that doing nothing may sometimes be appropriate and, if applying new measures, the principles of better regulation should guide those measures.

6 Keep it simple.
The PSA indicates that, to be effective, regulations and guidance should be easily understood and followed. If you cannot explain the purpose of any new regulation and why it will work, it should not be introduced.

7 Check for unintended consequences.
The PSA comments that, in a complex and interconnected healthcare environment, there will be consequences associated with new regulatory measures and it is important to check the risk is not simply transferred elsewhere.

8 Review and respond to change.
This is in effect recognition that a regulator needs to be agile and respond to evidence of new risks. The PSA suggests a system of regular reviews and post-implementation evaluations.

The GMC's priorities for 2016[26] demonstrate right-touch regulation in practice. Its emphasis is on raising standards and supporting safe practice, dealing fairly with complaints, and using better 'intelligence' about doctors, as well as working with patients and others to improve its overall effectiveness.

The Cavendish report,[27] which considered healthcare assistants and support workers in the NHS and social care settings in the wake of the Francis Inquiry, is another good example of right-touch regulation in practice. The easy answer would have been to propose statutory regulation, but its recommendations are more subtle and more numerous, although in essence they were to use the current oversight systems better. The PSA gives it a qualified endorsement, but perhaps most interesting of all is its recommendation that there needs to be 'time to care'. With the NHS under

[26] GMC, Our priorities for 2016, http://www.gmc-uk.org/publications/28694.asp
[27] An Independent Review into Healthcare Assistants and Support Workers in the NHS and social care settings, https://www.gov.uk/government/uploads/system/uploads/attachment_data/file/236212/Cavendish_Review.pdf

such financial pressure at the current time, it is to be hoped that health professionals continue to be given time to care.

Summary

- The history of professional regulation suggests that it might have had greater emphasis on self-protection than self-regulation.
- The introduction of the PSA, a super-regulator, has brought greater consistency and accountability to the healthcare regulators.
- A simplified mechanism to introduce new primary legislation, the Section 60 Orders, has seen a rapid change in the legal framework for regulators.
- There were moves (through the Law Commission) to introduce a single Act of Parliament to govern the regulation of health professionals, but this has stalled.
- The 2007 White Paper consolidated the expectations of modern regulation and set the direction of regulatory development to date.
- The governance and accountability of regulators has improved to give patients and the public greater assurance that they act in the public interest.
- Ensuring professionals stay up to date in the profession, and being safe to practise, is essential and underpins requirements for CPD and revalidation.
- Fitness to practise should be fair and just, minimise harm to patients, and seek to change the behaviour of individuals and organisations.
- The health professions should take responsibility for the regulation of other members of the team.
- Right-touch regulation is the current regulatory approach.

Further reading

Glynn J, Gomez D (2012). *Regulation of Healthcare Professionals*. London: Sweet & Maxwell.

Websites

General Dental Council: http://www.gdc-uk.org/
General Medical Council: http://www.gmc-uk.org/
General Optical Council: http://www.optical.org/
General Pharmaceutical Council: http://pharmacyregulation.org/
Health and Care Professions Council: http://www.hpc-uk.org/
Law Commission: http://www.lawcom.gov.uk/
Nursing and Midwifery Council: http://www.gnmc-uk.org/nmc/main/home.html
Pharmaceutical Society of Northern Ireland: http://www.psni.org.uk/
Professional Standards Authority for Health and Social Care: http://www.chre.org.uk/

24

NHS law and organisation

Sarah ME Cockbill, Stephen Lutener, Edward Mallinson and Joy Wingfield

Legislative framework for the NHS

The National Health Service (NHS) Act 1946 made it the duty of the Minister of Health (now the Secretary of State for Health) in England, and later the Secretary of State for Wales, to:

- promote the establishment in England and Wales of a comprehensive health service designed to secure improvement in the physical and mental health of the people of England and Wales and the prevention, diagnosis and treatment of illness;
- provide or secure the provision of services to do this; and
- provide these services free of charge unless otherwise expressly provided in any other Act.

In Scotland, a similar health service was established by the NHS (Scotland) Act 1947, the minister responsible being the Secretary of State for Scotland. The service was reorganised into a single management structure in England and Wales by the NHS Reorganisation Act 1973 and in Scotland by the NHS (Scotland) Act 1978. The 1978 Act for Scotland is still the basis for the NHS in Scotland although there have been a number of later amendments (notably the NHS Reform (Scotland) Act 2004). For England and Wales, the provisions of the 1946 Act and most of the provisions of the 1973 Act, including those affecting pharmaceutical services, were consolidated into the NHS Act 1977. The 1977 Act has been effectively replaced by the consolidated NHS Act 2006 (for England) and the NHS (Wales) Act 2006. All three Acts (for England, Scotland and Wales) retain broadly the same duty upon the relevant government minister as set out in 1946, but in England the Health and Social Care Act 2012 (see below) introduced significant changes to the way the NHS and public health are organised.

NHS Act 2006

In Part 1 of the NHS Act 2006, the Secretary of State must promote in England a comprehensive health service designed to secure improvement in the physical and mental health of the people of England, and in the prevention, diagnosis and treatment of physical and mental[1] illness. The Secretary of State's duties also extend to providing:

- hospital accommodation;
- other accommodation for the purpose of any service provided under the Act;
- medical, dental, ophthalmic, nursing and ambulance services;
- facilities for the care of expectant and nursing mothers and young children;
- facilities for the prevention of illness, the care of persons suffering from illness and the aftercare of persons who have suffered from illness; and
- services for the diagnosis and treatment of illness.

Under the NHS Act 2006, the Secretary of State may direct that any of his/her functions be carried out by a strategic health authority, a primary care trust (PCT, now abolished), an NHS trust or a special health authority by way of statutory 'Directions' (see below). Broadly, the NHS is operated under NHS contracts between one health service body 'the commissioner' and another 'the provider'. These contracts are not generally enforceable at law but only through appeal to the Secretary of State. In April 2013, strategic health authorities and PCTs were abolished by sections 33 and 34, respectively, of the Health and Social Care Act 2012, when the NHS Commissioning Board (NHSCB; now known as NHS England) took over the commissioning of the four primary care services: GPs, pharmacies, opticians and dentists.

Arrangements for the NHS contractual framework (henceforward called a contract) for community pharmacy service and local pharmaceutical service (LPS) appear in Part 7 of the NHS Act 2006 and are dealt with in more detail later in this chapter (but note that, whilst the contractual framework for community pharmacy services is not a contract in law, the LPS is a legal contract). From April 2013, the main responsibility for commissioning of community pharmacy services rests with NHS England, administered through its regional teams.

Part 8, section 169 of the 2006 Act continued the arrangements for appeals, and the Secretary of State directs the NHS Litigation Authority to exercise any of his/her functions relating to the determination of appeals. Secretary of State Directions require the NHS Litigation Authority to determine appeals concerning applications for entry onto pharmaceutical lists,

---

[1] The phrase 'physical and mental' has been added by the Health and Social Care Act 2012

and in relation to appeals against determinations over the hours of opening of NHS community pharmacies.[2] The Authority also considered appeals concerning performers' lists and decisions made by PCT disciplinary committees but this has now transferred to the first-tier tribunal within the Ministry of Justice.[3] Part 9 contains the provisions for prescription charges to be paid by certain people presenting NHS prescriptions in the community. Part 10 makes a series of requirements concerning the protection of the NHS from fraud, such as compulsory disclosure of documents and information. Part 12 includes details of how the public and patients will have an input into NHS planning and operation and Part 13 contains provisions enforcing controls on the maximum price of medicines (the Pharmaceutical Price Regulation Scheme) and other medical supplies to the NHS. The Department of Health negotiates the Pharmaceutical Price Regulation Scheme on behalf of the whole of the UK. Part 14 contains sections covering interpretation and defined expressions and brought the Act into force on 1 March 2007.

Earlier legislation relevant to pharmacy

Health Act 1999

Although the provisions of the Health Act 1999 which are directly related to the management of the NHS are now incorporated into the NHS Act 2006, there remain some other sections of the 1999 Act that are relevant to pharmacy. These include the statutory duty of quality on NHS bodies and services (termed *quality and performance* or *clinical governance*) and enabling powers to regulate healthcare professions, including pharmacy. Section 60 of the Health Act 1999 in particular provided power to change the regulatory and disciplinary powers of the RPSGB. The section 60 and 62 order making powers were later used to make the Pharmacy Order 2010, which transferred the regulatory and disciplinary powers of the RPSGB to the GPhC in September 2010 (chapters 20, 21 and 22).

Health and Social Care Act 2001

Again, most of the NHS provisions in the Health and Social Care Act 2001 have been subsumed into the NHS Act 2006, but section 63 amends the Medicines Act and adds pharmacists to the groups of health practitioners who are able to authorise a prescription for a POM (see independent and supplementary prescribing in chapters 8 and 9).

[2] The National Health Service Litigation Authority (Functions relating to Pharmaceutical Services and Local Pharmaceutical Services) (England) Directions 2012
[3] Under the Transfer of Tribunals Order SI 2010 No. 22

National Health Service Reform and Health Care Professions Act 2002

The NHS reforms in the National Health Service Reform and Health Care Professions Act 2002 are now in the NHS Act 2006, but the 2002 Act also provided for the establishment of an over-arching body to regulate and discipline healthcare professionals, which under the 2012 Act is now the Professional Standards Authority for Health and Social Care (usually abbreviated to PSA).

Health Act 2006

The Health Act 2006 became rather famous for introducing a ban on smoking in public premises but it also contained a wide range of provisions affecting the NHS and other matters. For pharmacists, the most important provisions are in Part 3, which contained powers to change the Regulations under the Misuse of Drugs Act (chapter 16) following the Shipman scandal (chapter 23). Section 30 inserted a new section into the Medicines Act 1968 to change the requirement for a pharmacist to be in 'personal control' of a pharmacy to there being a 'Responsible Pharmacist' for each pharmacy (chapter 5). Moreover, section 26 of the Health Act 2006 inserts further sections into the Medicines Act 1968 to change the interpretation of 'supervision' in sections 10 and 52 of the 1968 Act. Consultation was expected on these changes in 2008 and 2009, but no real progress had been made by September 2016.

Other amendments to the 2006 Act may change the way future pharmacy services are commissioned locally. Regulations[4] to permit more flexibility around 'pooled' NHS and social services budgets came into force in April 2016, as did the 'Devolution Act'[5] which enables, by way of secondary legislation, any public authority function such as the NHS to be conferred on a county, district or combined council.

Health and Social Care Act 2008

The Health and Social Care Act 2008 introduced changes in two areas affecting pharmacy. First, it established the GPhC (chapters 20, 21 and 22). Second, in 2014, this Act was used to introduce mandatory indemnity arrangements[6] as a condition of registration for all healthcare professionals (see also chapters 19, 20 and 23).

---

[4] The NHS Bodies and Local Authorities Partnership Arrangements (Amendment) Regulations SI 2015 No. 1940

[5] Cities and Local Government Devolution Act 2016, s.19, sch.4

[6] The Health and Social Care Act 2008 (Regulated Activities) Regulations SI 2014 No. 2936

Health Act 2009

The Health Act 2009 brought in the NHS Constitution (s.1) and quality accounts (s.8) (to report on the quality of NHS services provided by an NHS body). Quality accounts are published annually by each provider, including the private sector, and are available to the public. They do not yet (September 2016) have to be prepared by primary care providers.

Health and Social Care Act 2012

The most fundamental change to the NHS in England since its inception was introduced by the Health and Social Care Act 2012.[7] This section looks at the layout and content of the Act, where relevant to pharmacy; later, policy directions implicit in the Act are considered and then the structure of the NHS in England. Much of the Act substitutes for, amends or replaces existing provisions in the 2006 NHS Act. Part 1 of the 2012 Act is concerned with the health service in England and sets out the duties of the Secretary of State, the role and duties of NHS England, of Clinical Commissioning Groups (CCGs) and roles for local authorities such as county and metropolitan councils to undertake the provision of public health services. A small but significant change in Part 2 (s.59) is the repeal of the 1987 AIDS (Control) Act and its Regulations, which prohibited the marketing of diagnostic tests for the human immunodeficiency disease.

In Part 3, Monitor (a body corporate originally concerned with the authorisation of foundation trusts; see below) acquired new duties to promote the provision of a healthcare service which 'is economic, efficient and effective and maintains and improves quality . . . ' and to promote competition between providers of healthcare services where this is in the interest of the patient. In Part 3 too are provisions for registration of most healthcare providers with the Care Quality Commission (CQC). Part 4 proposed the eventual abolition of all NHS trusts as they were all expected to reach foundation trust status by April 2013; this has not been achieved.

Part 5 established a Committee of the CQC called Healthwatch England, whose role is to provide the Secretary of State, NHS England, Monitor and English local authorities with advice, information and assistance on the views of local healthwatch organisations and people who use health or social care services. In addition, local authorities had to establish health and wellbeing boards (HWBs), which, together with local healthwatch, inform their 'joint strategic needs assessment'[8] and develop the local health and wellbeing strategy for the locality. Changes to the

---

[7] The Health and Social Care Act (Commencement No. 1 and Transitory Provision) Order SI 2012 No. 1319

[8] Section 116 of the Local Government and Public Involvement in Health Act 2007

arrangements for the award of contracts for pharmaceutical services appear in Part 6, and the establishment of the National Institute for Health and Care Excellence (NICE) as a corporate body, together with a formalised role in developing quality standards for healthcare, appears in Part 8. Part 10 lists certain public bodies that are to be abolished (most notably the National Patient Safety Agency, although its functions have been transferred to NHS England) and Part 11 includes a duty of co-operation between Monitor and the CQC in their respective functions. Some 23 schedules then cover the detail of these provisions.

Despite these major changes in the structure of the health service, the Secretary of State continues to be required to exercise the functions conferred by the Act so as to secure that services are provided in accordance with the Act, and the Secretary of State retains ministerial responsibility to parliament for the provision of the health service in England. Since the 2012 Act, no over-arching primary legislation has been passed and the NHS structures, as legally constituted, broadly remain the same. However, in October 2014, under a strategic plan called the *Five Year Forward View*, a number of informal localised initiatives to vary the commissioning and delivery of services have been encouraged and secondary legislation has been necessary to facilitate this.

In December 2015, the NHS shared planning guidance for the next 5 years required every health and care system in England to produce a multi-year Sustainability and Transformation Plan (STP),[9] showing how local services will evolve and become sustainable over the next 5 years – ultimately delivering the Five Year Forward View vision. By January 2016, plans evolved to form 44 STP 'footprints' for new ways of working. STP footprints are not statutory bodies, but collective discussion forums which aim to bring together health and care leaders to support the delivery of improved health and care based on the needs of local populations. They do not replace existing local bodies or change local accountabilities, but will start to deliver new models of care from Autumn 2016.

These models include the integration of health and social care budgets[10] and provision[11] locally (most notably in Greater Manchester), co-commissioning[12] and delegated commissioning models for CCGs, pooled budgets across CCGs and merging of Commissioning Support Units (CSUs)

[9]See NHS England website https://www.england.nhs.uk/ourwork/futurenhs/deliver-forward-view/stp

[10]Facilitated by amendments to NHS Bodies and Local Authorities Partnership Arrangements Regulations SI 2000 No. 617

[11]The Health and Social Care (Safety and Quality) Act 2015 facilitates integration and sharing of information relating to users of health and social care services

[12]The Legislative Reform (Clinical Commissioning Groups) Order SI 2014 No. 2436 made under Legislative Reform Act 2006

(see below). Some 50 'vanguard sites' also aim to trial integrated primary and acute care commissioning, multispecialty community providers and enhanced healthcare in care homes. Other novel models have been developed such as the management of GP practices by NHS hospital trusts, merging of CCGs, integration of CCGs, social services commissioners and metropolitan council into one body, and turning a CSU into a company owned by a number of its client CCGs. Some of these may blur the long-standing separation of roles between commissioner and provider and create new possibilities for conflicts of interest. It is therefore likely that, to ensure adequate governance and accountability, some of these models will need to be underpinned by legislation under the 'Devolution Act' (see above).

NHS directions and policy statements

In addition to the statute law set out above, power is also given to the Secretary of State for Health (or equivalent ministers in Wales and Scotland) to make additional 'directions' written by senior civil servants acting under the authority of the relevant minister. Policy statements and guidelines, all of which describe the standards to which the public sector is expected to work, supplement the legal framework further (see under the managed service later in this chapter and also chapter 1).

NHS policy and planning

Government ministers and health departments continually issue large quantities of strategic and planning documents, supplemented with guidance and procedures as to how policy should be implemented. Where changes to legislation are required, the government will issue a white paper (in England, chapter 1) or similar blueprints in Scotland and Wales setting out how policy goals will be secured. A constant feature of reforms of the NHS in England since the 1980s has been the management of the relationship between commissioners and providers of healthcare. In essence, commissioners buy healthcare and providers provide it. The process of commissioning involves identifying health need, researching how it can be addressed, setting specifications for the services then needed, contracting with providers to provide them and reassessing performance in addressing the identified need. Pharmacists are mainly engaged in provision of pharmacy services within hospitals or community pharmacies, but many are also involved in the commissioning side, particularly in relation to the management of drug budgets and optimal use of medicines.

As described above, since the 2012 Act for England, many models of care are being introduced and the functions of commissioning and provision of NHS services are increasingly likely to be managed by a single body or collaboration of bodies, as local structures proliferate.

The NHS Constitution

First published in January 2009 and revised in March 2010, the NHS Constitution established the principles and values of the NHS in England. It sets out patient and staff rights and responsibilities and is intended to ensure that it delivers high-quality healthcare that is free for everyone. The Constitution was updated in 2012 and again in July 2015 to highlight the importance of 'whistleblowing' (raising concerns about aspects of the service which may endanger patient care or safety) and the duty of candour (see also chapters 19 and 20). There are seven key principles to the NHS Constitution:

1 the NHS provides a comprehensive service, available to all irrespective of gender, race, disability, age, sexual orientation, religion or belief;
2 access to NHS services is based on clinical need, not an individual's ability to pay;
3 the NHS aspires to the highest standards of excellence and professionalism;
4 NHS services must reflect the needs and preferences of patients, their families and their carers;
5 the NHS works across organisational boundaries and in partnership with other organisations in the interest of patients, local communities and the wider population;
6 the NHS is committed to providing best value for taxpayers' money and the most effective, fair and sustainable use of finite resources; and
7 the NHS is accountable to the public, communities and patients that it serves.

All people who work in the NHS or who deliver NHS services are expected to observe and implement the principles set out in the NHS Constitution.

NHS structure in Great Britain

Like the legislation that underpins it, the structure of the NHS undergoes constant change. Although the structures and titles vary significantly in England, Wales and Scotland, all have organisations that plan and commission local health services and deliver family health practitioner services, plus organisations that provide secondary (mostly hospital) care. Reference should be made to websites at the end of the chapter for the latest information on NHS developments in each home country.

NHS structure in England

The Department of Health

The Department of Health has five ministers (the most senior is called the Secretary of State for Health) who work with the Departmental Board consisting of the Permanent Secretary and the department's policy advisers together with non-executive members to form the strategic and operational leadership of the Department. An Executive Board, consisting of the civil servants who sit on the Departmental Board, supports the Permanent Secretary.

The Board is responsible for advice to ministers, setting Department of Health standards and establishing governance frameworks. The Department has four directorates; pharmacy falls into the community care directorate.[13] The Department of Health works with a wide range of 'arms-length bodies' (also called non-departmental public bodies or more often, quasi-autonomous non-governmental organisations – QUANGOs) to deliver its objectives, principal among these being NHS England (see below). Others include the MHRA, the Care Quality Commission, Public Health England and tribunals such as the NHS Litigation Authority. These 'arms-length bodies' are constantly evolving.

The Department of Health oversees three distinct services: the NHS, the Public Health Service and the Social Care Services. Pharmacists can expect to be involved professionally in the first two of these.

Figure 24.1 gives an overview of the main health service structures in England from April 2013.

NHS England

NHS England (legally constituted as the NHS Commissioning Board) took on its statutory responsibilities from April 2013.[14] NHS England has a duty concurrently with the Secretary of State to promote a comprehensive health service designed to secure improvement in the physical and mental health of the people of England, and in the prevention, diagnosis and treatment of physical and mental illness. The duty does not extend into public health functions (which remain with Public Health England and at local level with the local authorities).

Each year, after public consultation, the Department of Health publishes a mandate[15] setting out objectives and a budget for NHS England. This helps ensure that the NHS remains accountable to Parliament and the public.

NHS England is required to arrange for the provision of services in accordance with the 2012 Act and must exercise its functions relating to CCGs so as to secure the provision of those services provided by CCGs. The Board must exercise its functions so as to ensure that each provider of primary medical services (a GP) is a member of a CCG and that all areas of England are covered by CCGs whose areas do not overlap.

NHS England has a chair, appointed by the Secretary of State, and at least five other appointees of the Secretary of State. These are non-executive

---

[13] As at July 2016. The directorates change quite regularly

[14] NHS Commissioning Board Authority (Establishment and Constitution) Order 2011 SI No. 2237, NHS Commission Board Authority Regulations 2011 SI No. 2250

[15] A command or instruction

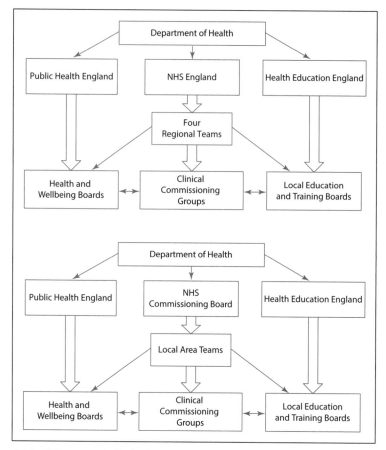

Figure 24.1 NHS structure in England.

members. These non-executive members appoint a Chief Executive together with other executive members, such that the total number of these executive members is less than the number of non-executive members. The Chief Executive's appointment is subject to the consent of the Secretary of State, and the first Chief Executive Officer was required to be appointed by the Secretary of State. NHS England must publish guidance for CCGs on the discharge of their commissioning functions. Before it publishes guidance on commissioning, it must consult the Healthwatch England committee of the CQC. The Chief Pharmaceutical Officer sits within the medical directorate of NHS England. The NHS England Board also comprises a varying number of National Clinical Directors to focus on particular clinical areas across England, such as cancer, dementia, heart disease and end of life care.

Clinical networks, senates and academic health networks

NHS England hosts clinical networks, which advise on distinct areas of care, such as cardiovascular, maternity, mental health and cancer care. NHS England also hosts 12 clinical senates which provide multidisciplinary input to strategic clinical decision making to support commissioners, and embed clinical expertise at the heart of NHS England. The purpose of these groups is to ensure that CCGs and NHS England itself have access to a broad range of expert clinical input to support and inform their commissioning decisions. This work is supported by 15 academic health science networks (AHSNs), which are based in universities to promote research and collaboration to improve health and generate economic growth in their areas.

Regional and area teams

The intermediate structures between NHS England and CCGs have evolved, from April 2013, into four regional teams[16] which have commissioning responsibilities for GP services, dental services, pharmacy and certain aspects of optical services as well as commissioning of specialised services and for military and prison health. The regional teams also provide a focus for local professional networks and for varying numbers of area teams. These bring together clinicians and members of local representative committees, most notably local pharmaceutical committees (LPCs; see below). Local professional networks for pharmacy provide clinical leadership in medicines optimisation to the regional teams and help to develop the role of local community pharmacy.

Clinical commissioning groups

A CCG is responsible for providing services for the purposes of the health service in its area.[17] It is essentially a group of primary medical services providers. When a group of providers of primary medical services is ready to form a CCG, it must apply to NHS England, providing a copy of the CCG's constitution. Its constitution must specify the name of the CCG, the members of the group and the area of the group. It must specify the arrangements made by the CCG for the discharge of its functions. The constitution must also specify the procedure to be followed by the CCG in making decisions, and the arrangements it makes to ensure that there is transparency about its decisions and the manner in which they are made. The board of the CCG must appoint an accountable officer who is responsible for ensuring that the CCG complies with its statutory obligations, complies with any provisions

[16]North of England, Midlands and East of England, London and South of England
[17]NHS (Clinical Commissioning Groups) Regulations 2012 SI No. 1631

published by NHS England relevant to the CCG and exercises its functions in a way which provides good value for money.

The CCG is required to exercise its functions in a way that promotes the NHS Constitution, and it must promote awareness of the NHS Constitution among patients, staff and members of the public. It must exercise its functions with a view to securing continuous improvement in the quality of services provided, and in particular secure continuous improvement in the effectiveness, safety and quality of patient experience that are achieved from the provision of the services. CCGs must also promote the involvement of patients and their carers in decisions relating to the prevention or diagnosis of illness in the patients, or the care or treatment of patients as well as enabling patients to make choices about their treatment. CCGs must obtain appropriate advice from persons who (taken together) have a broad range of professional expertise in the prevention, diagnosis or treatment of illness, and the protection or improvement of public health. Although there is no formal requirement to include a pharmacist on the CCG board, a pharmaceutical input is likely to be necessary to ensure a proper range of professional expertise.

In relation to any health services which are provided under arrangements made by a CCG, the CCG must ensure public involvement in the planning of the commissioning arrangements, in the development and consideration of proposals by the CCG for changes in the commissioning arrangements (if these are going to affect the public), and in decisions of the CCG affecting the operation of the commissioning arrangements where the implementation of the decisions would have an impact on the public. A CCG must prepare and publish an annual commissioning plan setting out how it proposes to exercise its functions, providing a copy to NHS England and to any relevant HWB. In preparing a commissioning plan, the CCG must consult individuals for whom it has responsibility and any relevant HWBs. The CCG must also publish an annual report on how it has discharged its functions in the previous financial year and send a copy to NHS England. NHS England will conduct a performance assessment of each CCG, each financial year. At the time of writing, there were 211 CCGs in England. Since 2015, a number of differing local models for CCG commissioning have developed such as 'vanguard sites' (see also under the 2012 Act above). Following a National Audit Office report in September 2015[18] which noted the potential for conflicts of interest[19] in these models, statutory guidance[20]

[18] National Audit Office, Managing conflicts of interest in NHS clinical commissioning groups (2015) HC419

[19] A conflict of interest occurs where an individual's ability to exercise judgement, or act in a role, is or could be impaired or otherwise influenced by his/her involvement in another role or relationship

[20] NHS England Managing Conflicts of Interest: Revised Statutory Guidance for CCGs (2016)

to CCGs was issued by NHS England requiring, among other measures, the appointment of a 'conflicts of interest guardian' in each CCG, and drawing attention to the legal and professional sanctions for failure to manage such conflicts.

Commissioning support units

CSUs were established after the 2012 Act to support CCGs by providing business intelligence, health and clinical procurement services and other back-office administrative functions, including contract management. From an original 25 regional units, many have now been amalgamated or taken in-house by local CCGs. Remaining CSUs are currently governed by NHS England, but are gradually becoming private organisations since 2016 in order to operate independently in a competitive market for commissioning support.

NHS trusts

A trust is an NHS body which is permitted, by individual Orders under the NHS Acts, to assume responsibility for the ownership and management of a health service body. Its most familiar form is the NHS hospital. A trust is run by a board, which may engage staff and set rates of pay and may borrow capital and dispose of assets. However, this freedom is constrained in that the staff remain NHS employees and the premises remain NHS property. Secondary care trusts are essentially providers of healthcare and their services are commissioned mainly by CCGs.

There are several types of trust, taking legal responsibility for providing particular health services in particular localities. The most familiar perhaps are acute trusts, which manage hospitals delivering secondary healthcare. Some acute trusts are regional or national centres for more specialised (tertiary) care or are attached to universities and train health professionals (teaching trusts). There are also ambulance trusts, providing emergency access to healthcare, and mental health trusts, often working closely with local authority social services to provide health and social care for people with mental health problems. A small number of care trusts have also been established to deliver social care, mental healthcare and primary healthcare in a given locality.

Foundation trusts

Foundation trusts are non-profit-making, public benefit corporations which were created to devolve decision making to local organisations and communities. Foundation trusts are subject to NHS standards, but because they are not directed by Government, they have greater freedom to decide their own strategy, and are accountable to their local communities and their commissioners through their board of governors. Successive governments have determined that all hospital NHS trusts should become NHS foundation trusts, and this was again the aim of the Health and Social Care Act 2012, but this objective has not been achieved. Some 200 foundation trusts now exist, registered by the CQC and licensed by Monitor, of which the majority were acute trusts, plus around 40 mental health trusts. The remainder are supported by the Trust Development Authority (TDA). Both organisations are now part of NHS Improvement (see below).

Health services in prisons and the armed forces

NHS England is directly responsible, through some of its area teams, for commissioning all health services (except emergency care) for people in prisons. Similarly, NHS England commissions health services for members of the armed forces and their families and reservists who require NHS services while mobilised. These arrangements are in line with commitments made by the Government under the Armed Forces Covenant.

Special health authorities

Special health authorities are health authorities that provide a health service to the whole of England not just to a local community. These form, merge or are abolished regularly but in 2016 they were listed as:

- Health and Social Care Information Centre
- Health Education England
- Health Research Authority
- National Institute for Health and Clinical Excellence
- National Patient Safety Agency
- National Treatment Agency
- NHS Blood and Transplant
- NHS Business Services Authority
- NHS Commissioning Board Authority
- NHS Litigation Authority
- NHS Improvement.

NHS 111

NHS 111 is a telephone service designed to improve access to NHS urgent care services. It is intended that this service is used by patients for medical advice where the health concern is not sufficiently serious or urgent to use the 999 service. NHS 111 is accountable to the relevant local CCGs.

Walk-in centres

NHS walk-in centres are managed by local CCGs usually using nurses and intend to improve access to primary healthcare services. Legally they are equivalent to NHS hospital outpatient units, so supplies of medicines and collection of prescription charges may be made on the spot to patients who use the centres. If appropriately trained, nurse prescribers in walk-in centres may also issue NHS prescriptions. Most NHS walk-in centres also supply a range of medicines under Patient Group Directions (PGDs) (chapters 8 and 9).

NHS Choices

NHS Choices is an online collection of information about the NHS. It contains a directory of pharmacies, GPs, NHS trusts, and so on. It allows users to quickly locate health services in their area. The website also contains healthy living advice.

Public Health England

Public Health England is an executive agency of the Department of Health and will 'provide strategic leadership and vision for the protection and improvement of the nation's health'. It works with NHS England, local authorities and local HWBs to develop national priorities in public health. It appoints Directors of Public Health (jointly with local authorities), who are responsible for the health of the population of the local authority.

Health and wellbeing boards

Each local authority must establish an HWB for its area. The HWB consists of the director of adult social services, director of children's services, a representative of the local Healthwatch organisation, a representative of each relevant CCG, at least one councillor of the local authority and other persons whom the local authority thinks appropriate. These boards are intended to encourage local authorities to integrate health and local government services. The responsibility for preparing a 'pharmaceutical needs assessment' (PNA) as a basis for awarding community pharmacy contracts (see below) now sits with the HWB and is a major influence on the commissioning of public health services locally. Local authorities also work with their HWB to commission local public health services such as smoking cessation or anti-obesity schemes from community pharmacies.

Health Education England

Bodies and processes to manage the postgraduate training and numbers in the medical and nursing workforce have been part of NHS planning for some time through medical deaneries and university contracts for training. The 2012 Act establishes Health Education England,[21] a national leadership organisation responsible for ensuring that education, training and workforce development drives the highest quality public health and patient outcomes.

Local education and training boards

Local education and training boards (LETBs) are responsible for the education and training of health and public health workers at a regional level. All such providers and professionals should be members of, or represented on, the LETBs, which work to improve the quality of local education and training outcomes to meet the needs of service providers, patients and the public.

NHS England and Public Health England work together at national level with Health Education England to ensure that there is an adequately trained workforce available to deliver health and public health services. At local level the CCG, the local authority planners (health and wellbeing boards informed by Healthwatch) and the local education and training boards are required to co-operate to support national strategic plans.

Managed health services and the private sector

The term 'managed service' generally implies services paid for 'out of the public purse', that is through the payment of taxes to the state. In that sense, pharmacists who work within CCGs, NHS trusts (mostly hospitals but see above), most prison health services and health services for the armed forces are working in the managed sector. Increasingly, pharmacists working for GP practices are subject to NHS management. By contrast, pharmacists in community practice are employed privately but their NHS services are subject to NHS management arrangements. The private sector (such as private hospitals run by a range of insurers and provident societies or care homes providing nursing care run by commercial agencies) is financed by shareholders and by direct payments from the service users.

Boundaries between these sectors, at least in the provision of health services, have become increasingly blurred, and management and measurement of the quality of these services are converging. Since April 1991 (removal of Crown immunity), the major statutes concerning medicines (including Controlled Drugs) and related matters have applied to NHS hospitals as well as to hospitals and care homes providing nursing care which are privately owned. Prison services, whether state or privately run, are expected to comply with UK law as far as is practicable, as are military health services, even

---

[21] Established in June 2012 under the Health Education England (Establishment and Constitution) Order SI 2012 No. 1273

when operating overseas. In addition, it is now relatively common for an NHS trust to register the hospital dispensary or pharmacy department with the GPhC as a Registered Pharmacy (chapter 5), thus enabling it to engage in over-the-counter sales to patients, relatives and staff.

Trusts and other public bodies are legally responsible for the services they provide. Litigation against them is increasing and it is important that pharmacists employed in these sectors of pharmacy understand not only the legislation but also the criteria against which accepted standards of care may be judged. The common law principles of negligence (chapter 21) and professional responsibility apply to pharmacists in the managed sector and professional obligations to safeguard patient care and safety should take precedence over managerial obligations.

Quality and performance in the NHS

There are three main mechanisms intended to assure the quality of NHS and public healthcare: the development of outcome frameworks, the work of independent regulators and the involvement of patients and the public. Outcomes frameworks have developed from the concept of clinical governance, which was introduced by the Health Act 1999 and strengthened by subsequent NHS Acts. The concept of clinical governance is now embedded in a wide range of mechanisms for maintaining the competence of health professionals and ensuring the quality of health services provided both within the NHS and in the private sector.

Outcomes frameworks

The Department of Health sets out an annual NHS Outcomes Framework that is used by the Secretary of State for Health to hold NHS England to account for improvements in health outcomes. The Framework covers five domains of health for which specific outcomes are expected from commissioners and providers:

Domain 1: preventing people from dying prematurely
Domain 2: enhancing quality of life for people with long-term conditions
Domain 3: helping people to recover from episodes of ill-health or following injury
Domain 4: ensuring people have a positive experience of care
Domain 5: treating and caring for people in a safe environment and protecting them from avoidable harm.

A similar framework sets the outcomes expected of Public Health England. Although not strictly relevant to pharmacists, an Adult Social Care Outcomes Framework also represents agreed outcome measures across the Department of Health, the Association of Directors of Adult Social Services and the Local Government Association.

Quality and Outcomes Frameworks have been in place since 2004 as measures of the performance of GPs offering general medical services in the community; many have suggested that the Quality and Outcomes Frameworks should be developed to reflect and promote the involvement of community pharmacists in the delivery of such outcomes but no change has yet taken place. CCGs may now develop their own alternative frameworks but very few have done so.

National Institute for Health and Care Excellence

The original version of NICE was set up in 1999 to reduce variation in the availability and quality of NHS treatments and care: the so-called 'postcode lottery'. Its role has changed in subsequent years to include health guidance but it retains the same acronym. NICE produces evidence-based guidance on which medicines, treatments, procedures and devices represent the best quality care value for the NHS. It also produces public health guidance recommending best ways to encourage healthy living, promote wellbeing and prevent disease. It is developing a library of 150 quality standards, which will be reflected in new Commissioning Outcomes Frameworks, in Quality and Outcomes Frameworks and in the Commissioning for Quality and Innovation Payment Framework. NICE manages NHS Evidence, a web-based service that provides access to authoritative clinical and non-clinical evidence and examples of best practice in healthcare. CCGs are expected to have regard to relevant NICE guidelines in their commissioning decisions. In April 2014, a court found that Thanet CCG had unlawfully denied a NICE-recommended treatment to one of its patients because it gave no grounds for exceptional circumstances to support the decision.[22]

Regulators

The Care Quality Commission

The CQC regulates, inspects and reviews all adult social care services in the public, private and voluntary sectors in England. Under the Health and Social Care Act 2008, the CQC also has powers to register providers of NHS care and has a wide range of enforcement powers to achieve compliance with registration requirements; it may require a ward or service to be closed until safety requirements are met as well as being able to suspend or de-register services where absolutely necessary. The inclusion of the functions of the Mental Health Act Commission in the remit of the CQC strengthens the oversight of patients subject to compulsory detention for mental health reasons. At the end of 2014, the CQC added the 'fit and proper person' test[23]

---

[22] *R (on the application of Elizabeth Rose) v Thanet Clinical Commissioning Group* [2014] EWHC 1182 (Admin)
[23] The Health and Social Care Act 2008 (Regulated Activities) Regulations SI 2014 No. 2936

for directors of NHS care to its inspection regime for hospitals and other CQC-registered providers, along with a responsibility to promote a duty of candour by the provider and its staff (see chapter 19). Under the Health and Social Care Act 2012, the CQC and Monitor (see below) operate a joint licensing regime for providers of NHS services. Community pharmacies will not have to register with the CQC provided that they are engaged only in 'dispensing and associated activities', nor will registration be required for 'diagnostic testing of the simplest kind'. However, prescribing, clinical services or services designed to promote health and wellbeing may become subject to registration requirements. Registration of GP practices opened in July 2012 and inspection began in 2015.

NHS Improvement

NHS Improvement was established in April 2016 to bring together Monitor, NHS Trust Development Authority and Patient Safety, including the National Reporting and Learning System, to provide support, oversight and governance for all NHS trusts and independent providers that provide NHS-funded care. Directions also set up the Healthcare Safety Investigation Branch within the Trust Development Authority to examine clinical errors in the NHS.[24]

Special measures

In serious cases where a trust or a CCG is not providing good and safe care to patients, and the management cannot fix the problems by themselves, it may be put into 'special measures'. This usually happens after an inspection by the CQC (see above) and involves action by Monitor or the Trust Development Authority. Special measures are of five types:

- Partnering a high-performing trust or CCG with the underperforming trust to help the trust improve.
- Designing and implementing an action plan to address improvements needed and progress made.
- Appointing an improvement director at the failing trust or CCG to monitor progress.
- Removing some of the freedoms that operate for NHS foundation trusts.
- Reviewing the management of the trust or CCG and replacing members.

Whistleblowing

Following an extensive inquiry into failings at Mid Staffordshire NHS Foundation Trust, Robert Francis QC published his final report[25] in February

[24] *The National Health Service Trust Development Authority (Healthcare Safety Investigation Branch) Directions 2016*

[25] The Stationery Office, Report of the Mid Staffordshire NHS Foundation Trust Public Inquiry, (February 2013) HC 947 'The Francis Report' followed by DH response Hard Truths: The journey to putting patients first (January 2014) Cm 8777-1 in two volumes

2013. One of the key findings concerned the difficulties associated with staff raising concerns – 'whistleblowing' – about standards of patient care or patient safety within the NHS. A review of progress in addressing these difficulties resulted in a policy[26] to be adopted by all NHS organisations as a minimum standard for raising concerns and to the appointment within the CQC of a national guardian for NHS whistleblowers. Regulations to ban the 'blacklisting' of whistleblowers were expected at the time of going to press.

Patient and public involvement

The 2012 Act established Healthwatch England as a committee of CQC and it was launched in 2012[27] to advise the Secretary of State, NHS England, Monitor and local authority HWBs. It has the power to recommend that the CQC takes action where there are concerns about health or social care. Since 2012, Healthwatch bodies have also been set up at local level. Providers of health services, including trusts and community pharmacies, are expected to allow reasonable access to members of Healthwatch teams to 'enter and view and observe the carrying-on of activities' and to respond to reports issued by the local Healthwatch.

Patient complaints

In relation to complaints (and general advice), each trust has been required since September 2003 to set up a 'patients advice and liaison service' (PALS) to provide information, advice and support to help patients, families and their carers to get the most out of the NHS. This may include giving advice and support on the making of complaints and referral to the Independent Complaints Advocacy Service; this service aims to secure consistent national standards and performance indicators for the handling of complaints. Since 1993, there has been a Health Service Commissioner (Ombudsman) to consider complaints about clinical matters and complaints involving practitioners. The Ombudsman can only consider complaints related to NHS care in England which have had a response from the practitioner. There are separate Ombudsmen for Scotland and Wales.

In December 2008, the Department of Health announced plans for a single complaints system to cover all health and adult social care services in

[26]NHS Improvement and NHS England, Freedom to Speak Up: raising concerns (whistleblowing) policy for the NHS (April 2016)

[27]The CQC (Healthwatch England Committee) Regulations SI 2012 No. 1640

England. This is now enshrined in statute.[28] The arrangements required of pharmacies (and other providers of health and social care) must ensure that:

- complaints are dealt with efficiently;
- complaints are properly investigated;
- complainants are treated with respect and courtesy;
- complainants receive, so far as is reasonably practical:
  - assistance to enable them to understand the procedure in relation to complaints, or
  - advice on where they may obtain such assistance;
- complainants receive a timely and appropriate response;
- complainants are told the outcome of the investigation of their complaint; and
- action is taken if necessary in the light of the outcome of a complaint.

The arrangements for PALS were not changed by the 2012 Act but they now work with Health Watch England and local units of Health Watch to improve complaints handling and responses across the NHS in England.

Pharmaceutical Price Regulation Scheme

A voluntary regulatory scheme to allow the NHS to have access to good quality, proprietary medicines at reasonable prices while allowing a fair return for the pharmaceutical industry has been in place since 1957. The current scheme applies to the whole of the UK. It is underpinned by sections 260–266 of the NHS Act 2006 (see above) and Regulations.[29] Whilst the bulk of the industry participates in the voluntary scheme, those that do not are subject to statutory controls.[30] The legislation allows the NHS to control the prices it will pay to any company which chooses not to sign up to the voluntary agreement or fails to reach agreement. The implementing Regulations should be renewed annually to comply with the requirements of Council Directive 89/105/EEC. There is a current loophole in the regulations: if a company is in the voluntary scheme, the Government cannot control the prices of any generic medicines that the company also manufactures. The Health Service Medical Supplies (Costs) Bill seeks to close this loophole and

---

[28] The Local Authority Social Services and National Health Service Complaints (England) Regulations SI 2009 No. 309

[29] Health Service Branded Medicines (Control of Prices and Supply of Information) Regulations SI 2008 No. 1938, Health Service Medicines (Information Relating to Sales of Branded Medicines, etc.) Regulations SI 2007 No. 1320 (as amended)

[30] Health Service Branded Medicines (Control of Prices and Supply of Information) (No. 2) Regulations SI 2008 No. 3258

provides powers for the Government to obtain almost any information it requires from those in the supply chain about the costs of medicines supplied to the NHS and the supplier's profits.

The pharmacy contractual framework in England

Made initially under Part III of the National Health Service Act 1977, later replaced by Part 7 of the National Health Service Act 2006, the principal regulations covering the provision of pharmaceutical services in England are the National Health Service (Pharmaceutical and Local Pharmaceutical Services) Regulations 2013.[31] These replaced earlier regulations of 2012,[32] primarily to reflect the structural reforms of the NHS. The changes saw local authority HWBs take over responsibility for preparing the pharmaceutical needs assessment (PNA) and the National Health Service Commissioning Board (NHSCB, but more commonly known as 'NHS England') assuming from PCTs responsibility for commissioning community pharmacy (and other primary care) services.

The 2012 Regulations replaced the 'necessary or expedient' test for applications to open new pharmacies by requiring most new pharmacy applications to be assessed against the PNA. The 2012 regulations retained an exception from this test for distance-selling pharmacies (i.e. those operating wholly by mail order or internet) but removed three of the former exemptions (for pharmacies undertaking to open for the provision of pharmaceutical services for at least 100 hours per week; for pharmacies in large out of town retail developments; and for pharmacies in new one-stop primary care centres). Those exemptions from the test for new applications had been introduced in 2005,[33] substantially changing the arrangements which had been in place since 1987.

The 2013 Regulations incorporate, among other things, provisions to enable any person to receive such drugs, medicines and appliances as are ordered and include the 'Terms of Service' for pharmacy 'contractors'.

The commissioning arrangements made between NHS England and primary care providers are normally through contracts whose substantive terms are specified in regulations, but pharmacy contractors are not formally contracted – instead, pharmacy owners are entitled to apply to have their pharmacy premises included in a pharmaceutical list (see below) and, once so included, they may provide pharmaceutical services in accordance with these Terms of Service. These terms and adherence to them is similar to

---

[31] SI 2013 No. 349 ('the 2013 Regulations')

[32] The NHS (Pharmaceutical Services) Regulations SI 2012 No. 1909 ('the 2012 Regulations')

[33] The National Health Service (Pharmaceutical Services) Regulations SI 2005 No. 641 ('the 2005 Regulations')

holding a contract but differing in enforcement provisions – nevertheless, pharmacy owners whose pharmacies are included in a pharmaceutical list are commonly known as and are referred to in this text as pharmacy contractors.

NHS England is required to prepare two pharmaceutical lists for each HWB area: firstly of the names and addresses of all those persons who have undertaken to provide pharmaceutical services in particular by way of the provision of drugs; and secondly those who have undertaken to provide pharmaceutical services only by way of the provision of appliances (appliance contractors).

Any pharmacy contractor who wishes to be included in a list must apply to NHS England in the prescribed form.

Pharmaceutical needs assessments

The pharmaceutical needs assessments (PNAs) were introduced in 2004 when PCTs were advised to develop a PNA as part of their preparation for the revised control of entry arrangements that were to be adopted from 2005. The PNA was to be a key part of the Joint Strategic Needs Assessment (JSNA) developed in partnership with the local authority, identifying the health and wellbeing needs of the local population. The PNA would be used by PCTs in commissioning pharmaceutical services by identifying the needs of the local population.

Prior to the 2012 regulations, an application (other than 'minor' relocations, changes of ownership or one which fell into the four exemptions listed above) would be granted for a pharmacy only if the PCT was satisfied that it is necessary or expedient to grant the application in order to secure, in the neighbourhood in which the applicant's premises are to be located, the adequate provision of pharmaceutical services specified in the application. Proposals to modify these exemptions were included in the Pharmacy in England White Paper[34] published in 2008, and the Health Act 2009 amended the National Health Service Act 2006 to require PCTs to prepare PNAs, with the first PNAs to be published by 1 February 2011. From April 2013, the duty to prepare and publish PNAs transferred[35] to the HWBs of the local authorities. The Health Act 2009 also provided that these PNAs would, when the legislation is brought fully into force, form the basis for the determination of pharmacy applications carried out by PCTs.

The 2013 Regulations transferred these responsibilities relating to the preparation and publication of the PNA to the HWBs. The HWBs had until 1 April 2015 to prepare and publish their own PNAs, the former PNAs published by PCTs remaining in force until then.

[34]Pharmacy in England: Building on strengths – delivering the future. Cm 7341
[35]Health and Social Care Act 2012, section 206

Health and Social Care Act 2012

As part of the implementation of the major reforms of the NHS in 2013, the Health and Social Care Act 2012 made provision for both the duties of the PCT – to maintain pharmaceutical lists – and the determination of new pharmacy applications to be transferred to NHS England. The Act also made provision to modify the PNA-based test, once the responsibility for determining applications rested with NHS England and the development of the PNA became the responsibility of the local authority.

The effect of the changes was to allow (but not compel) NHS England to grant an application that proposes to meet a current or future need only if it is satisfied that it is necessary to do so, whereas, under the former test, an application that proposed to meet a need identified in a PNA was required to be granted.

The 2013 Regulations

The 2013 Regulations set out the framework for the development and publication of the PNA, the maintenance of the pharmaceutical lists, the process for applying to be included in a pharmaceutical list, arrangements for dispensing by doctors, fitness to practise and performance sanctions as well as the 'Terms of Service'.

Part 2 sets out the requirements for the production of PNAs. The first PNAs to be produced by HWBs were required by 1 April 2015.

Part 3 contains the requirement for maintenance of, and applications for inclusion in, pharmaceutical lists. 'Routine' applications (defined in Reg.12) are assessed against the PNA with applications undertaking to meet current or future needs being assessed under Regulations 13–16. Applications that seek to secure improvements or better access are dealt with under Regulations 17 and 19, and applications that offer improvements or better access to pharmaceutical services that were not foreseen when the PNA was published are dealt with in Regulations 18 and 19.

Part 4 sets out the 'excepted' applications. These include relocation applications that do not result in significant change to pharmaceutical services provision (Reg.24), distance-selling pharmacies (Reg.25) and change of ownership applications (Reg.26). A new provision (Reg.26A) added in October 2016 provides for applications for consolidation of the business of two or more pharmacy premises onto one site.

Part 5 contains grounds for refusing some types of application, for example where there are already pharmacy premises on the same or an adjacent site, or to defer applications if the area has been designated for the purpose of developing an LPS arrangement.

Part 6 provides for refusal, deferral or authority to impose conditions on applications on fitness to practise grounds.

Part 7 covers determinations as to whether or not an area is a controlled locality (a rural area) in which a patient may request that his/her doctor provides a dispensing service. In these areas, applications from pharmacies (other than those in 'reserved locations', see Reg. 41) or doctors are granted only if to do so would not prejudice the provision of pharmaceutical services, LPS or primary medical services (Regs.44 and 48).

Part 8 sets out the arrangements for doctors to dispense.

Part 9 sets out conditions that apply in special cases for a pharmacy to continue to be included in a pharmaceutical list, for example the ongoing conditions for a distance-selling pharmacy to remain in the pharmaceutical list.

Part 10 contains performance-related sanctions and market exit provisions; there are arrangements for local dispute resolution, formal breach notices and financial withholding.

Part 11 deals with enforcement, review and appeals relating to fitness to practise matters.

Part 12 brings together the remuneration, charges and refunds arrangements and sets out the arrangements for publication of the Drug Tariff (on the authority of the Secretary of State), provides for the withholding of remuneration where an overpayment has been made, and includes the reward scheme (a reward is available when forged prescriptions have been identified at the pharmacy).

Part 13 contains the arrangements for LPS.

Part 14 of the Regulations contains miscellaneous provisions.

There are 10 Schedules to the Regulations, but the main ones of relevance to NHS community pharmacy are: Schedule 1 (contents of PNAs); Schedule 2 (procedures for applications for inclusion in the pharmaceutical list); Schedule 3 (appeal processes); and Schedule 4 (Terms of Service).

The Terms of Service in Schedule 4 include obligations to provide the 'essential services' that must be available at each pharmacy. The essential services consist of: dispensing and repeat dispensing services; disposal of unwanted drugs; signposting to other providers where necessary; providing support for self-care; provision of public health advice; and promotion of healthy lifestyles. As well as providing these essential services, a retail pharmacy business must also have an acceptable system of clinical governance and notify NHS England should any fitness matters arise.

Terms of Service for pharmacy contractors

Essential services

Part 2 of Schedule 4 of the 2013 Regulations sets out the terms for the essential services which must be provided by every pharmacy contractor. This includes the dispensing of prescriptions and repeat dispensing.

Dispensing may be against a paper prescription or an electronically transferred prescription bearing the prescriber's advanced electronic signature. The pharmacy contractor must supply any drugs except those called 'scheduled drugs'[36] (popularly known as the Black List, which comprises medicines in certain categories that cannot be prescribed for supply at NHS expense). The categories were originally indigestion remedies, laxatives, analgesics for mild to moderate pain, bitters and tonics, vitamins and the benzodiazepine tranquillisers and sedatives. The list now includes many other medicines.[37] Some medicines may be prescribed only in specified circumstances.[38]

All supplies of medicines (and appliances where relevant) must be made with 'reasonable promptness'. The pharmacy contractor is expected to give an estimate of the time when drugs or appliances will be ready, if asked.

In a case of urgency, a pharmacy contractor may (but is not compelled to) dispense a medicine (other than a Controlled Drug) requested by a doctor who is unable to issue a prescription without delay provided that the doctor undertakes to supply a signed prescription or transmit an electronic prescription within 72 hours.

Prescription charges

All prescriptions dispensed attract an NHS prescription charge which must be paid to the pharmacy contractor, unless an exemption applies.[39] Where an exemption has been claimed other than on age grounds, pharmacy staff are required to check at the point of dispensing whether the patient has evidence of entitlement to exemption. Where the patient cannot produce satisfactory evidence, an 'evidence not seen' box on the reverse of the prescription form must be marked with an X, but the prescription need not be refused. Where a patient does not provide, where required, evidence of entitlement to exemption the pharmacy must advise that checks are routinely undertaken to ascertain entitlement to exemption.[40] Any charges collected by the pharmacy contractor are later offset against the payments due to the pharmacy contractor from the pricing authorities. The exemption categories fall into four types (full details are to be found in Part XVI of the Drug Tariff):

- persons who are exempt on age grounds;
- holders of a range of exemption certificates;
- persons who receive, or are partners of someone receiving, state benefits; and
- persons receiving no-charge contraceptives.

[36] See Schedule 1 of National Health Service (General Medical Services Contracts) (Prescription of Drugs etc.) Regulations SI 2004 No. 629
[37] See Drug Tariff Part XVIIIA
[38] See Drug Tariff Part XVIIIB
[39] The National Health Service (Charges for Drugs and Appliances) Regulations SI 2015 No. 570
[40] Paragraph 7(3A) of the Terms of Service

Providing ordered drugs or appliances

The pharmacy contractor must only supply the drugs or appliances as ordered on the prescription (para. 8) but, provided that they are not Controlled Drugs (other than those specified in Schedule 4 or 5 of the Misuse of Drugs Regulations 2001),[41] a pharmacist may exercise his/her professional skill and knowledge to remedy deficiencies on the prescription in dosage or strength or, where quantity is not stated, to supply treatment for up to 5 days.

The pharmacy contractor must supply in manufacturer's original packs where the amount specified on the prescription corresponds to an original pack. Where the amount prescribed differs from an original pack, the pharmacy contractor must dispense the amount ordered unless the product is available only in a special container (any container with an integral means of application or from which it is not practicable to dispense an exact quantity) or where the drug is sterile, effervescent or hygroscopic, a liquid preparation for addition to bath water, a coal tar preparation or a viscous preparation. In these cases, the pharmacy may round the quantity dispensed to the nearest container quantity (unless it is a Controlled Drug). All supplies of a manufactured medicine must be made with a patient information leaflet.

A pharmacist may refuse to provide the items prescribed (para. 9):

- where the pharmacist reasonably believes that the prescription is forged;
- where to supply would be contrary to the pharmacist's clinical judgement;
- where the pharmacist or others on the premises are subject to or threatened with violence;
- where the person presenting the prescription commits or threatens to commit a criminal offence; or
- where there are irregularities or there are other circumstances in a repeat dispensing service which mean that a repeat supply is not appropriate (in this case, the pharmacist must refuse to dispense).

The pharmacy contractor must ensure that appropriate advice on use and information is given to patients about their drugs or appliances supplied (para. 10) to enable them to use them appropriately. This may include advice on safe keeping and safe destruction, providing guidance about only requesting repeats of items that are actually needed, and details of any items or part items that are owed.

Patients who have a long-term stable medical condition and require regular medicine must be given appropriate advice about the benefits of repeat dispensing.

Records must be kept of supplies made and of any clinically significant advice, interventions or referrals made. If the supply of an item on a

[41] SI 2001 No. 3998

repeatable prescription is refused by the pharmacist on the grounds that the patient is no longer taking the medicine appropriately, or is suffering side effects that make refusal appropriate, or there have been changes to the patient's health that make it desirable to review the treatment, the prescriber must be informed. Where a patient is refused drugs or appliances, other than where the pharmacist believes it to have been stolen or forged, the patient must be referred back to the prescriber for further advice.

Electronic prescription service

Introduced in two phases, Release 1 and Release 2, the electronic prescription service (EPS) enables pharmacies to receive prescriptions electronically from any GP who has been authorised to issue these. In Release 1, the electronic message was received after scanning a bar-coded paper prescription (the paper prescription was required as this was the legally valid prescription). Under Release 2, the electronic prescription message itself is the legal prescription, and this is sent to the pharmacy 'nominated' by the patient. In August 2016, just over 80% of GPs were authorised to send electronic prescriptions, and virtually all pharmacies were capable of receiving them.

The EPS is accessible only by an individual holding an NHS smartcard. The smartcard may be issued only to individuals who are directly involved in patient care and who have a legitimate reason to access the information. The smartcard is issued based on the individual's role (which limits the degree of access to information) and normally based on the premises at which the individual works. A locum pharmacist who might be called upon to work in more than five pharmacies at short notice may obtain a smartcard that will work in any EPS-enabled pharmacy.

Paragraph 11 of the Terms of Service requires the pharmacy contractor to inform patients about the EPS whether or not the pharmacy is participating in the service and, if not participating, to inform the patient of at least two other pharmacies in the area who are participating (if known). The Terms of Service also requires the pharmacy contractor to record in the Patient Demographics Service[42] (PDS) the name of the pharmacy nominated by the patient to receive his/her electronic prescription, where the patient wishes to use that service and the pharmacy is enabled for 'Release 2' of EPS.

Supply of 'specified' appliances

Where a 'specified appliance' is supplied, there are additional requirements. A 'specified appliance' means:

a   any of the following appliances listed in Part IXA of the Drug Tariff:
  i   a catheter appliance (including a catheter accessory and maintenance solution),

---

[42] The Patient Demographics Service is managed by NHS Digital (until July 2016 NHS Digital was called the 'Health and Social Care Information Centre', which was established under section 252 of the Health and Social Care Act 2012)

ii   a laryngectomy or tracheostomy appliance,

iii   an anal irrigation system,

iv   a vacuum pump or constrictor ring for erectile dysfunction, or

v   a drainage wound pouch;

b   an incontinence appliance listed in Part IXB of the Drug Tariff; or

c   a stoma appliance listed in Part IXC of the Drug Tariff.

Where a pharmacy contractor supplies these products, a home delivery service must be available. The pharmacy contractor must offer to deliver the specified appliance to the patient's home and, if that offer is accepted, the delivery must be made with reasonable promptness and at an agreed time. The delivery must be in a package which displays no writing or other markings which could indicate its content, and the manner of delivery (e.g. the delivery van) must not convey the type of appliance being delivered.

When a specified appliance is provided, the pharmacy contractor must also provide a reasonable supply of appropriate supplementary items (such as disposable wipes and disposal bags).

The pharmacy contractor must also ensure that there are facilities for a patient receiving specified appliances to obtain expert clinical advice regarding the appliance. In appropriate circumstances the pharmacy contractor must refer the patient who seeks advice to a prescriber or must offer the patient an 'appliance use review' (see below). If the pharmacy contractor cannot provide specified appliances or an appliance use review, the patient can be referred or signposted to another provider who can.

Summary Care Record

The Summary Care Record (SCR) is available to authorised pharmacists, and contains details from the GP's electronic records, including medicines prescribed, allergies and adverse reactions. Each pharmacy from which the SCR is accessed must have at least one person who has attended a face-to-face implementation briefing. Every organisation, e.g. pharmacy owner, that accesses the SCR must nominate a privacy officer responsible for monitoring access.

Where a pharmacy has access to the SCR, it must, when dispensing prescriptions, access the SCR if it is in the best interests of the patient to do so,[43] and in doing so, the pharmacist must act in accordance with the 'NHS Care Record Guarantee'.[44]

Other essential services

Paragraphs 13, 14 and 15 of the Terms of Service require that a pharmacy contractor shall accept and dispose of unwanted drugs (returned from households) in the appropriate manner. NHS England has contracts with

---

[43] Paragraph 29A Schedule 4 of the 2013 Regulations

[44] 'The Care Record Guarantee – Our Guarantee for NHS Care Records in England' published by the National Information Governance Board for Health and Social Care in January 2011.

waste disposal contractors, and arranges for appropriate bins to be made available in pharmacies and for collection and disposal of any unwanted drugs collected at the pharmacy.

The pharmacy contractor must comply with the legislation applicable to waste (chapter 19). The pharmacy contractor must segregate hazardous from non-hazardous waste and, if requested by the waste contractor or NHS England, must also segregate the different wastes (solids, liquids and aerosols). The pharmacy also has an obligation under the waste legislation to segregate waste that can be recycled, for example paper and cardboard. Before collecting waste from a pharmacy, the waste contractor may require the pharmacy to produce details of a pre-acceptance waste audit (an audit of the types of waste produced at the pharmacy) carried out at the pharmacy.

The pharmacy contractor is responsible for the accurate completion of consignment notes for any hazardous waste, and for waste transfer notes for any other type of waste handed to the waste contractor.

The pharmacy contractor must ensure staff handling waste are appropriately trained and must provide equipment close by the waste storage to deal with spills.

The pharmacy contractor may accept for disposal, under an NHS-funded service, waste medicines from households which includes residential care homes (but not homes providing nursing which must make their own arrangements) and may also dispose of outdated or obsolete stock which was held for the purpose of dispensing as part of the NHS-funded arrangements.[45]

Further guidance on waste is available in 'Safe management of healthcare waste' published by the Department of Health.[46]

Paragraphs 16 to 18 of the Terms of Service require the pharmacy contractor to promote public health messages to the public and to undertake prescription-linked interventions, backed up by leaflets and referral if necessary for patients who have diabetes, are at risk of coronary heart disease, smoke or are overweight. Records of any clinically significant advice must be made in a form that facilitates audit and follow-up care. This service involves both opportunistic interventions as well as participating in up to six public health campaigns a year as specified by NHS England.

Paragraphs 19 and 20 of the Terms of Service set out the duty to provide information to users of the pharmacy about other health and social care providers and organisations ('signposting') where advice is requested which cannot be provided at the pharmacy.

[45] See service specification, at http://psnc.org.uk/services-commissioning/essential-services/disposal-of-unwanted-medicines/

[46] A link is available on http://webarchive.nationalarchives.gov.uk/+/www.dh.gov.uk/prod_consum_dh/groups/dh_digitalassets/documents/digitalasset/dh_126348.pdf

Paragraphs 21 and 22 of the Terms of Service set out how the pharmacy contractor shall also provide advice and support to people caring for themselves or their families. This includes providing advice on the purchase of appropriate over-the-counter medicines.

Hours of opening

Pharmacies are required[47] to be open for the provision of pharmaceutical services for at least 40 core hours per week unless NHS England allows a lower number. Change to the number or distribution of core hours requires a successful application to NHS England.

Pharmacies that had their applications for inclusion in the pharmaceutical list granted under the former exemption for those pharmacies undertaking to provide pharmaceutical services for at least 100 hours per week may not reduce their hours below 100.

A pharmacy can open additional hours (called 'supplementary hours'). These hours can be changed by giving at least 3 months' notice to NHS England.

Unless the pharmacy is a distance-selling (internet or mail order) pharmacy, a notice showing the hours when the pharmacy is open for the provision of pharmaceutical services must be exhibited.

At times when the pharmacy is closed, a notice must be displayed which lists the addresses of other pharmacies and their opening hours from which drugs and appliances may be obtained.

A pharmacy is not normally required to open on Good Friday, Easter Sunday, Christmas day or on bank holidays, but NHS England has powers to direct a pharmacy to open on these days or indeed any other date or time where the needs of the people in the area are not being adequately met (subject to a right of appeal).

Clinical governance

Paragraph 28 of the Terms of Service requires that the pharmacy contractor shall 'participate in an acceptable system of clinical governance', which must comprise:

A patient and public involvement programme. This is met by means of a practice leaflet for the public giving information about the pharmacy services available from each premises, a requirement to promote the NHS services provided, the undertaking of an approved survey of users of the NHS services of the pharmacy using a 'community pharmacy patient questionnaire', having arrangements for monitoring drugs or appliances that are out of stock, adopting monitoring arrangements to ensure compliance with the Equality Act 2010, and co-operating with any statutory inspection or review.

[47]See paragraph 23 of Terms of Service

A clinical audit programme. The pharmacy contractor must implement each year at least one pharmacy-based clinical audit and one clinical or policy-based audit chosen by NHS England.

A risk management programme. This includes the appointment of a clinical governance lead, arrangements to manage the quality of stock and maintenance of equipment, appropriate standard operating procedures for dispensing prescriptions and repeatable prescriptions, and providing advice and support for self-care, appropriate safeguarding procedures for service users, an approved incident reporting system together with arrangements for analysing and responding to critical incidents, arrangements for dealing with communications concerning patient safety such as MHRA drug alerts, waste disposal arrangements for confidential waste, and monitoring of compliance with health and safety legislation (chapter 19).

A clinical effectiveness programme. The programme would include having arrangements to ensure appropriate advice is given in respect of repeat dispensing and to people caring for themselves or their families.

A staffing and staff management programme. This includes induction and training, checking of qualifications and references, addressing poor performance for all staff, identifying and supporting development needs of staff, and whistle-blowing procedures.

An information governance programme. This provides for compliance with approved procedures for information management and security, and submission of an annual self-assessment of compliance via approved data submission arrangements.

A premises standards programme. This includes a system for maintaining cleanliness at the pharmacy which is designed to ensure that the risk to people at the pharmacy of healthcare-acquired infection is minimised, and arrangements for compliance in the areas of the pharmacy in which patients receive NHS services with any approved particulars that are designed to ensure that those areas are an appropriate environment in which to receive healthcare.

Professional standards

The pharmacy contractor must provide pharmaceutical services and exercise professional judgement in conformity with the standards accepted in the pharmaceutical profession.[48] Effectively, this means that a pharmacy contractor will need to adhere to the GPhC Standards of Conduct, Ethics and Performance as part of the NHS arrangements.[49] By way of example, because the GPhC includes in Standard 7.9 a requirement that pharmacists make sure that their work, or work that they are responsible for, is

---

[48]See paragraph 29 of the Terms of Service
[49]Under review at the time of going to press

covered by appropriate professional indemnity cover, an NHS pharmacy providing pharmaceutical services must operate with appropriate indemnity arrangements.

Inducements

A pharmacy contractor must not give, promise or offer any person any gift or reward (whether by way of a share of or dividend on the profits of the business, or by way of discount, rebate or otherwise) as an inducement for any kind of prescriptions to be presented to a particular pharmacy.[50] The staff must also not give, promise or offer to any 'relevant person' (e.g. a GP or a member of the GP's staff) any gift or reward (including by way of a share of, or dividend on, the profits of the pharmacy contractor's business, or by way of discount or rebate) as an inducement to the person recommending to any person, that they present a prescription to the pharmacy, nominate the pharmacy for the purposes of the EPS or request that the pharmacy provides them with any directed service (see below for details of 'directed services').

Direction of prescriptions

Closely related to inducements is the practice of direction of prescriptions. This involves the forwarding of prescriptions by a medical practice to a pharmacy without the consent of the patient or, in some cases, influencing of a patient by the GP or practice staff to use a particular pharmacy. The EPS can be misused to direct prescriptions by setting the EPS nomination for the patient to a particular pharmacy without patient consent. The motive for this conduct could be the presence of a commercial interest in the pharmacy by the medical practitioners and/or the staff of the medical practice. There are no regulatory provisions explicitly prohibiting this (although Principle 4 of the NHS Constitution[51] does give patients the right to be involved in all decisions about their care and treatment, and therefore decisions about where a prescription will be dispensed should be made by or in consultation with the patient).

NHS England, the British Medical Association's General Practitioners Committee (GPC) and the Pharmaceutical Services Negotiating Committee (PSNC) have agreed to address this inappropriate conduct, with the GPC, PSNC and Pharmacy Voice issuing joint guidance to medical practices and pharmacies reminding the practitioners of good practice. NHS England has issued a poster to be displayed in all NHS pharmacies and medical practices to remind patients that the decision about which pharmacy their prescriptions are to go to is their choice.[52]

[50] See paragraph 30 of Terms of Service
[51] https://www.gov.uk/government/publications/the-nhs-constitution-for-england/the-nhs-constitution-for-england
[52] See link for NHS England poster, and GPC/PSNC/PV guidance on http://psnc.org.uk/contract-it/pharmacy-regulation/direction-of-prescriptions/

Fitness to practise

The pharmacist (including the superintendent pharmacist and other pharmacists who are directors of a pharmacy body corporate) must notify NHS England about any convictions or adverse fitness to practise incidents as they arise.[53]

Health Education England

A pharmacy contractor must co-operate with Health Education England in the discharge of its duty as to education and training.[54]

Complaints

A pharmacy contractor is required by paragraph 34 of the Terms of Service to have in place arrangements which comply with the requirements of the Local Authority Social Services and National Health Service Complaints (England) Regulations 2009 No. 309, for the handling and consideration of any complaints about the provision of pharmaceutical services.

Inspection and access to information

Paragraph 35 of the Terms of Service requires pharmacy contractors to allow persons authorised in writing by NHS England to enter and inspect the pharmacy at any reasonable time for the purpose of ensuring compliance with the Terms of Service, and for the purposes of auditing, monitoring and analysing the provision of pharmaceutical services and the management by the pharmacy contractor of the pharmaceutical services provided. This authority to enter the premises does not extend to entry to parts of the premises used solely for residential purposes. During such an inspection, the confidentiality of patient information should be protected.

Directed services

Regulation 11 of the 2013 Regulations sets out the general provisions relating to the Terms of Service, and these apply to any 'directed services' that the pharmacy undertakes to provide. Directed services are those provided in accordance with the Secretary of State Directions issued in the exercise of powers conferred by sections 127, 128, 272(7), (8) and 273(1) of the National Health Service Act.[55] These may be for advanced services (for which a national tariff has been set) which may be provided by any pharmacy contractor that wishes to (on condition it meets the eligibility criteria) or for enhanced services (where the fee is agreed between NHS England as the commissioner and the pharmacy contractor), which will be provided only if

[53] See paragraph 31 of Terms of Service
[54] See paragraph 33 of Terms of Service
[55] These include the Pharmaceutical Services (Advanced and Enhanced Services) (England) Directions 2013 published in the Drug Tariff

NHS England and one or more pharmacy contractors agree that the services will be provided.

These Directions set out the conditions that apply to the advanced services, namely the Medicines Use Review (MUR) (or a prescription intervention that leads to an MUR), the New Medicine Service (NMS), the Appliance Use Review Service (AUR) and the Stoma Appliance Customisation Service. In 2015, the Directions were amended to include a new advanced service – the National Influenza Adult Vaccination Service. This was time limited to run until 29 February 2016. The service was again commissioned for the 2016–17 flu season, with vaccinations for at-risk groups authorised via a national patient group direction until 31 March 2017.

The Medicines Use Review service. This was the first of the advanced services which can be provided by accredited pharmacists from premises that meet accreditation requirements for confidential consultation areas. The service includes reviews undertaken periodically (usually no more frequently than annually) as well as those arising in response to significant prescription intervention during the dispensing process. The MUR is intended to help patients to use their medicines more effectively. This is achieved by improving patient knowledge, concordance and use of medicines by establishing the patient's actual use, understanding and experience of taking his/her medicines, identifying, discussing and assisting in resolving poor or ineffective use of his/her medicines, identifying side effects and drug interactions that may affect patient compliance, and improving the clinical and cost-effectiveness of prescribed medicines and reducing medicine wastage. At least 70% of all MUR consultations each year are to be carried out on agreed target groups: (a) patients taking 'high risk' medicines (specified in the Directions as being an NSAID, an anticoagulant (including low-molecular-weight heparin) antiplatelets or diuretics; (b) patients discharged from hospital in the previous 8 weeks who had changes made to the drugs they are taking; (c) patients with respiratory conditions who are prescribed a respiratory drug included in the BNF subsections adrenoceptor agonists, antimuscarinic bronchodilators, theophylline, compound bronchodilator preparations, corticosteroids or cromoglicate and related therapy, leukotriene receptor agonists and phosphodiesterase type-4 inhibitors; and (d) patients who are at risk of or diagnosed with cardiovascular disease and are regularly being prescribed four or more medicines, at least one of which is a medicine included in the BNF for the cardiovascular system, drugs used in diabetes, or thyroid and anti-thyroid drugs.

The New Medicine Service. This service was introduced in 2011 to provide support for people with long-term conditions who are newly prescribed a medicine in order to improve medicines adherence. The service includes the provision of advice when providing for the first time a specified medicine for one of the specified conditions listed below, the making of an arrangement for a further discussion about 2 weeks later, and a final discussion at about 4 weeks from the initial supply.

The specified conditions are asthma and chronic obstructive pulmonary disease, type 2 diabetes, antiplatelet/anticoagulant therapy and hypertension. The Directions specify the BNF subsections in which the prescribed drugs must be listed.

Community Pharmacy Seasonal Influenza Vaccination. The seasonal influenza vaccination service has been commissioned on an annual basis during 2015–16 and 2016–17. For the 2016–17 season, the Directions enable pharmacy contractors to participate in arrangements for the administration of inactivated influenza vaccine to patients in accordance with a national PGD, as part of the NHS England/Public Health England (PHE) and Department of Health (DH) annual flu programme.[56]

The service specification allows the pharmacy contractor to provide the service at the pharmacy premises or at a care home (for which prior approval by NHS England is required). Pharmacists who are to administer the vaccine and other staff who may perform any role in providing the service must be appropriately trained. All staff who may be involved in the service are required to be advised in respect of vaccination against hepatitis B.

Full details are provided in the Directions as set out in the Drug Tariff and the service specification. Note that, as the seasonal influenza vaccination service has been commissioned on two consecutive time-limited periods, both of which expired before this book went to print, details of any service commissioned will need to be identified for future years.

Appliances advanced services. There are two appliance-based services: an Appliance Use Review service, which is similar to the Medicines Use Review service above, and the Stoma Appliance Customisation service for patients who require stoma appliances to be customised to ensure a better fit. These services are provided mainly by Dispensing Appliance Contractors.

Enhanced services

The 2013 Directions list 21 services that may be the subject of arrangements for enhanced services.

The enhanced services specified in the 2013 Directions may be commissioned only by NHS England. Similar services may, however, be commissioned by a local authority or CCG (see below), but these are not described as enhanced services within the community pharmacy contractual framework.

The enhanced services include:

- monitoring and screening for patients taking anticoagulants
- advice and support for patients in care homes

[56]www.gov.uk/government/collections/annual-flu-programme

- smoking cessation services
- services to school staff and children
- home delivery of medicines
- needle and syringe exchange schemes
- services using PGD authorisation (chapters 8 and 9)
- full medication reviews
- minor ailment services
- emergency supply service.

Locally commissioned services

Some of the services listed above may also be commissioned locally by a CCG or local authority or by other commissioners.

One of the public health services which may be commissioned by local authorities is the NHS Health check which was introduced in 2009.

The NHS Health check is a risk assessment for diseases affecting the vascular system including diabetes and chronic kidney disease. It may be offered to persons between 40 and 74 years old and is intended to reduce premature death from vascular conditions.

Other public health services which local authorities may commission include smoking cessation, sharps disposal, needle exchange schemes, emergency contraception, chlamydia screening and treatment, and weight management.

CCGs may also commission services locally through pharmacies, including services such as minor ailments and emergency supply, which can make better use of the resources that are funded through CCGs.

Local pharmaceutical services

NHS England may commission any other services (LPS schemes) from pharmacies, usually services not traditionally associated with pharmacy, to address local needs. These are most commonly contracts for small pharmacies that are provided with additional support where the pharmacy would otherwise be unviable. These pharmacies must provide the services determined to be required by NHS England and usually follow public consultation. All LPS pharmacies must be contracted individually and there are mandatory terms specified in Schedule 7 of the 2013 Regulations that must be included in their contracts.

Local pharmaceutical committees

Local pharmaceutical committees (LPCs) are recognised by NHS England under section 167 of the NHS Act 2006 as representative of the persons providing pharmaceutical services in the area for which it is formed.

Those LPCs which have adopted the model constitution promulgated by the PSNC in 2014 usually comprise 13 members (although it is for each LPC to determine the optimum number). Some LPCs have adopted a constitution that allows for both pharmacist and non-pharmacist members, elected or appointed by contractors in accordance with the model constitution. The number of members representing independently owned or multiple-owned pharmacies should be proportional to the number of pharmacies owned within each sector.

Each LPC appoints its own secretary or chief officer and the appointment should be notified to NHS England and to PSNC. The LPC also appoints a chair, a vice-chair and a treasurer. These officers need not be members of the LPC. The term of office for members of the LPC is 4 years and the LPC has power to appoint members in the event of casual vacancies. A person ceases to be a member of the LPC if s/he is no longer a pharmacy contractor, a representative of a pharmacy contractor, or his/her appointment is withdrawn by one of the appointing bodies (e.g. the Company Chemists Association).

The LPC seat must be declared vacant if the member has been absent without reasonable cause from three consecutive meetings of the LPC, or for more than 50% of the ordinary meetings of the LPC.

The duties of an LPC include governance and finance, representation of pharmacy contractors, support for pharmacy contractors, and relationships with other bodies, in the interests of pharmacy contractors, and it shall adopt a 'fit and proper person' provision for its members.

Governance and finance

The LPC is required to conduct its affairs in accordance with accepted principles of good governance (e.g. in accordance with the Nolan principles), ensuring that the appropriate structures and resources are in place to discharge its duties in a proper manner: it must maintain appropriate management and administrative structures to ensure that the LPC's business is carried out efficiently and effectively (the LPC is able to pool resources with other LPCs); it should respond to any request for an inquiry by a contractor who believes that the LPC or an officer of the committee has acted unconstitutionally; and it will request NHS England to allot to the LPC such sums as are required to defray the Committee's administrative expenses.

Representation of pharmacy contractors

The LPC will receive, and where appropriate should respond to, national or local consultations which are relevant to the pharmacy contractors in its area. It should appoint or nominate representatives to any committee, subcommittee, working group or other body on which representation of pharmacy contractors is required, and should make representations to the commissioners and to the PSNC on matters of importance to pharmacy contractors.

Support for pharmacy contractors

The LPC should ensure transparency and equality of information and opportunity for all pharmacy contractors in matters relating to the local purchasing of pharmaceutical services, ensure appropriate arrangements are in place to advise any pharmacy contractor who needs help or assistance on NHS matters, provide appropriate levels of guidance and support to pharmacy contractors or groups of pharmacy contractors in the formulation of bids for funds held at any level, advise on submissions for LPS and local commissioning, and consider any complaint made by any pharmacy contractor against another pharmacy contractor involving any question of the efficiency of the pharmaceutical services. If agreed by two-thirds of members voting, it may establish or assist in the establishment of a body corporate formed for the sole purpose of supporting the interests of pharmacy contractors (many commissioners prefer to contract with a limited number of providers – using an intermediate body corporate reduces the administration for the commissioner).

Relationships with other bodies, in the interests of pharmacy contractors

The LPC should aim to establish effective liaison with other bodies concerned with the health service in its area, collaborate as appropriate with PSNC on all matters relating to the provision of LPS and aim to collaborate with other pharmaceutical bodies including other LPCs and other non-pharmaceutical bodies to the benefit of pharmacy contractors. The LPC must prepare an annual report and accounts and must circulate them to the pharmacy contractors in the area and to PSNC. Once agreed by the pharmacy contractors in the area, the Annual Report is sent to NHS England.

Fit and proper person

Members and officers are expected to be a 'fit and proper person' and to act in a way that preserves and protects the reputation of the LPC. The LPC has power to suspend or remove a member or officer who has been suspended or removed (for a fitness to practise reason) from a pharmaceutical list, or has been suspended or removed from a professional register by a professional regulator, or has been convicted of a criminal offence for which a term of imprisonment may be imposed. Before taking action to suspend or remove members, the LPC must seek an explanation from the member and periods of suspension must be kept under review. Members removed under these provisions are ineligible for election or appointment to the LPC for 12 months.

Pharmaceutical Services Negotiating Committee

The PSNC is recognised by the Secretary of State as being representative of pharmacy contractors in England on NHS matters. It negotiates terms and conditions of service for pharmacy contractors. The PSNC has 31 members: 13 independent contractor members elected on a regional basis from England, 1 member from Wales, 2 independent members appointed by the National Pharmacy Association, 12 members appointed by the Company Chemists Association, and 3 non-Company Chemists Association multiple pharmacy members elected by owners of multiple pharmacy businesses who are not members of the Company Chemists Association. The PSNC has five subcommittees, concerned with funding and contract, service development, LPC and implementation support, health policy and regulation, and resource development and finance. The PSNC has also set up the Pricing Audit Centre, which carries out both random and routine checking and special checks at the request of a contractor of the pricing of prescriptions by NHS Business Services Authority Prescription Services.

NHS law and organisation in Wales

The NHS (Wales) Act 2006 and subordinate legislation governs the operation of the NHS in Wales. The Act defines the duty of Welsh ministers to promote the effective, efficient and economical provision of certain administrative, professional and technical services (called the shared services) and a general power to provide these services. The Act allows Welsh ministers to give directions to NHS bodies on their establishment, regulation and operation. These directions may be by way of Statutory Instruments (i.e. regulations, orders, etc.), by Ministerial Letter (previously through a series of Welsh Health Circulars) or other form of written instruction, or may be issued as guidance. Any instruction or guidance issued has the same legal standing as a Direction, and must therefore be treated as mandatory by NHS bodies who have a legal duty to comply. In addition, the Welsh Health Specialised Services Committee and the Emergency Ambulance Services Committee are joint committees of each Health Board (HB) in Wales.[57]

The Directions define the terms of NHS Contracts and make provision for the constitution and membership of NHS bodies in Wales. They also set out more detailed procedures and administrative arrangements for these bodies, forming the basis on which they determine their Standing Orders and other operating arrangements. In this way, organisational roles and responsibilities are defined within and between NHS bodies and between NHS bodies and any community partners.

[57]Established under the Welsh Health Specialised Services Committee (Wales) Directions 2009/35 and 2014/9 (w.9) (the WHSSC Directions) and the Emergency Ambulance Services Committee (Wales) Directions 2014/8 (w.8) (the EASC Directions)

The NHS Act 2006 contains some legislation that applies to both England and Wales. This includes section 72 which places a duty on NHS bodies to co-operate with each other in exercising their functions and section 82 which places a duty on NHS bodies and local authorities to co-operate with one another in order to secure and advance the health and welfare of the people of England and Wales and to take cognisance of any wider, relevant, legislative framework. The current NHS Wales came into being on 1 October 2009 and covers seven HBs: Abertawe Bro Morgannwg University HB, Aneurin Bevan HB, Betsi Cadwaladr University HB, Cardiff and Vale University HB, Cwm taf HB, Hywell Dda HB and Powys Teaching HB. Three further NHS trusts provide services on an all-Wales basis: Public Health Wales NHS Trust, Velindre NHS Trust and Welsh Ambulance Services Trust. There are no longer any regional offices within the NHS Wales structure. The structure of relevant bodies in NHS Wales is depicted in figure 24.2.

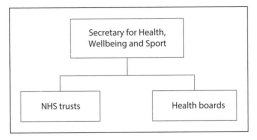

Figure 24.2   NHS structure in Wales.

Shared service provision and pharmacy in Wales

The NHS Wales Shared Services Partnership is hosted and governed by the Velindre Trust[58] and provides a comprehensive range of services to support the Statutory bodies of NHS Wales. This includes audit and assurance, e-business, contractor employment, facilities, legal and risk, prescribing services unit, procurement and Welsh Risk Pool. Welsh HBs and NHS trusts have agreed the terms of a co-operation agreement for implementation of these services setting out how they will work together to ensure that the arrangements are introduced and operate effectively by collective decision making.

The Prescribing Services Unit is responsible for reimbursement services to pharmacies, GPs and appliance contractors for the medicines and devices they provide on NHS prescriptions, and for the provision of prescribing and dispensing information to NHS staff delivering medicines management services.

---

[58] Velindre NHS Trust Shared Services Regulations 2012 (2012/1261 (w.156)) and the Shared Services Partnership Committee (SSPC)

Community pharmacy contract in Wales

An NHS community pharmacy contract will be awarded after application to and consideration by the HB[59] in which it is proposed to establish the pharmacy. Negotiations on reimbursement and national service payments are undertaken by *Community Pharmacy Wales* (CPW). CPW was legally established in April 2004; full details of its constitution and activities are available on the relevant website. Wales has adopted a community pharmacy contractual framework that is similar to that in England, particularly with regard to essential, advanced and enhanced service levels.[60] However, the detailed arrangements, especially fees and some services, diverge from those in England. For example, Wales no longer charges for NHS prescriptions and has not adopted either LPS or NMS schemes or the exemptions to control of entry that currently apply only in England, whereas Wales has a discharge medicine review service but England does not. These differences are current at the time of going to press but other differences in the provision of services will emerge and readers are advised to check the websites for CPW and NHS Wales for current information.

NHS law and organisation in Scotland

Scotland has had its own Parliament since July 1999 and it has powers to make primary legislation on healthcare. The NHS in Scotland has always operated separately from the service in England and Wales. Although the principal Act remains the NHS (Scotland) Act 1978, this has now been modified by the NHS Reform (Scotland) Act 2004. NHS Scotland policy is developed and administered through the Scottish Government Health Department via 14 territorial 'unified' NHS boards. Primary and secondary care are separate divisions within the unified NHS boards, with representation from each local authority to improve management of health and social care. In addition, there is oversight of the board's activities by NHS Healthcare Improvement Scotland. This was established by the Public Services Reform (Scotland) Act 2010 and brings together NHS Quality Improvement Scotland and the Scottish Health Council, the latter becoming a committee of NHS Healthcare Improvement Scotland.

The functions of the NHS boards include the planning and provision of healthcare services and the management of pharmacy contracts. The Scottish Health Council monitors the performance of the NHS boards and promotes public involvement in healthcare. Each board also supports community health partnerships, which are co-terminous with local authority boundaries and which focus on planning and provision of local health services. Each

[59]The NHS (Pharmaceutical Services) (Wales) Regulations SI 2013 No. 898 (w.102)
[60]The Pharmaceutical Services (Advanced and Enhanced Services) (Wales) (Amendment) Directions 2011

community health partnership has on its committee a place for a registered pharmacist whose name is included in, or who is fully or substantially employed by a person or body whose name is included in, a pharmaceutical list prepared by an NHS board. Most NHS boards have the services of a pharmacist, called variously a 'consultant' or 'specialist' in pharmaceutical public health and who provides strategic pharmacy advice to the NHS board. The overall control of pharmaceutical services within each NHS board lies with the board's director of pharmacy. In addition, all NHS boards have an area pharmaceutical committee. These committees comprise pharmacists who work in both the hospital and community sectors and are representative of the professionals working, or living, in the area.

The Practitioner Services Division of NHS National Services Scotland manages payments for pharmacy contractors. Responsibility for inspection and audit of healthcare lies with the NHS Healthcare Improvement Scotland. The Scottish Health Council represents the patient's voice in healthcare and may inspect both primary and secondary care establishments. Figure 24.3 outlines the NHS structure in Scotland.

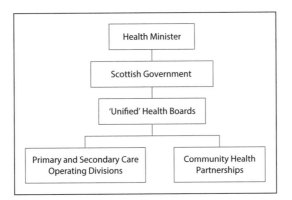

Figure 24.3 NHS structure in Scotland.

Pharmacy organisation in Scotland

Negotiation on remuneration and reimbursement on behalf of Scotland's community pharmacy contractors is carried out by *Community Pharmacy Scotland* (previously known as the Scottish Pharmaceutical General Council). This body negotiates nationally on behalf of 14 area pharmacy contractor committees, one for each NHS board. The Community Pharmacy Contract in Scotland is radically different from that in either England or Wales and its scope is to be found in the Smoking, Health and Social Care (Scotland) Act 2005 (asp.13). The Scottish contract comprises services in four areas:

Minor Ailment Service. This is a scheme whereby patients who are registered with a Scottish GP and who are exempt from prescription charges (with some exceptions) may register with a community pharmacy and receive over-the-counter medicines within a formulary, free of charge, following consultation with the pharmacist.

Public Health Service. This involves community pharmacists and staff in national programmes to promote healthy lifestyles and public health interventions such as smoking cessation, chlamydia screening and supply of emergency hormonal contraception.

Acute Medication Service. This essentially is the dispensing of acute prescriptions.

Chronic Medication Service. This covers the dispensing of repeat prescriptions and the management of patients' medication in conjunction with their GP.

Gluten Free Food Service. This service was introduced on a trial basis between 1 April 2014 and 31 March 2015. Patients with coeliac disease can obtain from their local community pharmacy gluten-free products from a national prescribable list without the need to obtain prescriptions from their GP. Following a review published in September 2015[61] and the response to its recommendations,[62] the service was included in the core services of the contract.

The Terms of Service for chemists in Scotland are laid down in the NHS (Pharmaceutical Services) (Scotland) Regulations,[63] as amended.[64] Amendments include arrangements for the provision of the Chronic Medication Service element of the contract and changes to the handling of applications for Pharmacy Contracts. Arrangements for disciplinary service committees and tribunals are covered by the National Health Service (Tribunal) (Scotland) Regulations 2004 (SI 2004 No. 38).

Control of entry to pharmaceutical lists in Scotland differs from that in England and Wales. There is no provision for 100-hour pharmacies under the Regulations and all applications are considered under the terms of paragraph 5(10) of the 2009 Regulations, as amended,[65] by the NHS

---

[61] http://www.gov.scot/Publications/2015/09/4234

[62] http://www.gov.scot/Resource/0048/00485204.pdf

[63] NHS (Pharmaceutical Services) (Scotland) Regulations SI 2009 No. 183

[64] NHS (Pharmaceutical Services) (Scotland) Amendment Regulations SI 2009 No. 209, NHS (Pharmaceutical Services) (Scotland) Amendment Regulations SI 2011 No. 32

[65] An application made in any case other than one to which paragraph (3) or (4) applies shall be granted by the board after the procedures set out in Schedule 3 have been followed, only if it is satisfied that the provision of pharmaceutical services at the premises named in the application is necessary or desirable in order to secure adequate provision of pharmaceutical services in the neighbourhood in which the premises are located by persons whose names are included in the pharmaceutical list

Board Pharmacy Practices Committee. The Regulations were again amended in 2014 with the introduction of requirements pertaining to applications within areas served by dispensing doctors and the requirement for wider public consultation.[66] Whilst there are three pharmacists on the committee (two contractor representatives and one who is neither a contractor nor an employee thereof), nominated by the area pharmaceutical committee, none has a vote on the final outcome.[67] Appeals on the decisions of the Pharmacy Practices Committee are made to the National Appeal Panel, which comprises a legally qualified chair (appointed by Scottish Ministers),[68] one pharmacist[69] and one lay member[70] nominated by the health boards. Here, however, the pharmacist is a voting member of the panel.

Summary

- The statutory framework for NHS services differs across England, Scotland and Wales, although the objectives are similar.
- The NHS is a mixed market of commissioning and provision of services by a range of health service bodies, overseen by civil service departments reporting to governments.
- NHS trusts, mostly hospitals, provide NHS secondary care in England and Wales; in Scotland, the provision of secondary care comes under the acute operational divisions of the NHS boards.
- NHS England and CCGs in England and local health boards in Wales secure the provision of primary care, including pharmaceutical services, through 'contracts' with local owners of pharmacies. In Scotland and Wales, this activity has passed to NHS boards.
- HWBs appointed within local authorities now prepare PNAs, which are used in the determination of pharmacy applications, and they are also responsible for local public health commissioning.
- CCGs (groups of providers of primary medical services) will commission many services locally for the populations for whom they are responsible.
- There are controls over the granting of rights to provide NHS pharmaceutical services, mainly based on the need to secure adequate provision of those services, as identified in the PNA for the area.

[66] NHS (Pharmaceutical Services) (Scotland) Amendment Regulations SI 2014 No. 148
[67] NHS (Pharmaceutical Services) (Scotland) Regulations SI 2009 No. 183, Sch. 4, Art.7(2)
[68] NHS (Pharmaceutical Services) (Scotland) Regulations SI 2009 No. 183, Sch. 4, Art.10(1) and (2)
[69] NHS (Pharmaceutical Services) (Scotland) Regulations SI 2009 No. 183, Sch. 4, Art.11(b)
[70] NHS (Pharmaceutical Services) (Scotland) Regulations SI 2009 No. 183, Sch. 4, Art.11(c)

- Persons providing NHS pharmacy services must comply with conditions set out in the NHS chemists' Terms of Service.
- Specifications for the amount and conditions which apply to payments under the NHS chemists' Terms of Service are set out in the Drug Tariff.
- Negotiations for payments take place nationally through the PSNC, Community Pharmacy Wales or Community Pharmacy Scotland, and locally through LPCs or their Welsh or Scottish equivalents.
- The public interest in the NHS is represented by Local Healthwatch works and the PALS in England, community health councils in Wales and local health councils in Scotland.

Further reading

Community Pharmacy Five Year Forward View http//:psnc.org.uk/wp-content/uploads/2016/08/CPFV-Aug-2016.pdf (accessed 9 October 2016).

NHS England Five Year Forward View https//:www.england.nhs.uk/wp-content/uploads/2014/10/5yfv-web.pdf (accessed 9 October 2016).

NHS England Five Year Forward View – Time to deliver https//:www.england.nhs.uk/wp-content/uploads/2015/06/5yfv-time-to-deliver-25-06.pdf (accessed 9 October 2016).

Scottish Executive (2002). *The Right Medicine: A Strategy for Pharmaceutical Care in Scotland*. Edinburgh: Scottish Executive.

Welsh Assembly Government (2002). *Remedies for Success: A Strategy for Pharmacy in Wales*. Cardiff: Welsh Assembly Government.

Websites

Care Quality Commission: http://www.cqc.org.uk

Community Pharmacy Scotland: http://www.communitypharmacyscotland.org.uk

Community Pharmacy Wales: http://www.cpwales.org.uk

Department of Health (England): http://www.dh.gov.uk/en/Healthcare/Medicinespharmacy andindustry/index.htm

General Pharmaceutical Council: http://www.pharmacyRegulation.org

Health Education England: http://www.hee.nhs.uk

Health Inspectorate Wales: http://www.hiw.org.uk

Monitor: http://www.monitor-nhsft.gov.uk

National Institute for Clinical Excellence: http://www.nice.org.uk

National Patient Safety Agency: http://www.npsa.nhs.uk

NHS 24: http://www.nhs24.com

NHS Choices: http://www.nhs.uk/Pages/HomePage.aspx

NHS Constitution: http://www.dh.gov.uk/en/Publicationsandstatistics/Publications/PublicationsPolicyAndGuidance/DH_132961

NHS Direct Wales: http://www.nhsdirect.wales.nhs.uk

NHS Direct: http://www.nhsdirect.nhs.uk

NHS England: https//:www.england.nhs.uk; for pharmacy: https//:www.england.nhs.uk/commissioning/primary-care-comm/pharmacy (accessed 9 October 2016)

NHS Prescription Service (England): http://www.nhsbsa.nhs.uk/prescriptionservices.aspx
NHS Primary Care Commissioning: http://www.pcc.nhs.uk
NHS Scotland: http://www.scotland.gov.uk/Topics/Health/NHS-Scotland
NHS Wales: http://www.nhswalesgovernance.com; http://www.wales.nhs.uk
Parliamentary and Health Service Ombudsman (England): http://www.ombudsman.org.uk
Patient Advice and Liaison Services: http://www.pals.nhs.uk
Pharmaceutical Services Negotiating Committee: http://www.psnc.org.uk
Public Services Ombudsman for Wales: http://www.ombudsman-wales.org.uk
Scottish Public Services Ombudsman: http://www.spso.org.uk

Appendix 1

Supplementary prescribing: clinical management plan

Meaning of clinical management plan (HMRs Reg.215)

A clinical management plan means a written plan (which may be amended from time to time) relating to the treatment of an individual patient, agreed by the patient to whom the plan relates, the doctor or dentist who is a party to the plan and any supplementary prescriber who is to prescribe, give directions for administration or administer under the plan.

Particulars to be included in a clinical management plan (HMRs Sch. 14)

A clinical management plan must contain the following particulars:

a the name of the patient to whom the plan relates;
b the illnesses or conditions which may be treated by the supplementary prescriber;
c the date on which the plan is to take effect and when it is to be reviewed by the doctor or dentist who is a party to the plan;
d reference to the class or description of medicinal product which may be prescribed or administered under the plan;
e any restrictions or limitations as to the strength or dose of any product which may be prescribed or administered under the plan, and any period of administration or use of any medicinal product which may be prescribed or administered under the plan;
f relevant warnings about the known sensitivities of the patient to, or known difficulties of the patient with, particular medicinal products;

g the arrangements for notification of:
   i suspected or known adverse reactions to any medicinal product which may be prescribed or administered under the plan, and
   ii suspected or known adverse reactions to any other medicinal product taken at the same time as any medicinal product prescribed or administered under the plan; and
h the circumstances in which the supplementary prescriber should refer to, or seek the advice of, the doctor or dentist who is a party to the plan.

Appendix 2

Patient Group Directions

Taken from the Human Medicines Regulations 2012 No. 1916 (Regs.229, 230, 231, 232, 233 and 234, and Sch. 16)

Particulars to be included in a Patient Group Direction (PGD)

The following particulars are to be included:

1 the period during which the Direction is to have effect;
2 the description or class of medicinal product to which the Direction relates;
3 the clinical situations which medicinal products of that description or class may be used to treat or manage in any form;
4 whether there are any restrictions on the quantity of medicinal product that may be sold or supplied on any one occasion and, if so, what restrictions (but see note, below);
5 the clinical criteria under which a person is to be eligible for treatment;
6 whether any class of person is excluded from treatment under the Direction and, if so, what class of person;
7 whether there are circumstances in which further advice should be sought from a doctor or dentist and, if so, what circumstances;
8 the pharmaceutical form or forms in which medicinal products of that description or class are to be administered;
9 the strength, or maximum strength, at which medicinal products of that description or class are to be administered;
10 the applicable dosage or maximum dosage;
11 the route of administration;
12 the frequency of administration;
13 any minimum or maximum period of administration applicable to medicinal products of that description or class;

14 whether there are any relevant warnings to note and, if so, what warnings;

15 whether there is any follow-up action to be taken in any circumstances and, if so, what action and in what circumstances;

16 arrangements for referral for medical advice; and

17 details of the records to be kept of the supply, or the administration, of products under the Direction.

Note that the particulars specified in point 4 may be omitted in the case of a PGD relating to administration only, for PGDs constituted under the following Regulations:

- HMRs Reg. 230 – Exemption for supply etc under a PGD to assist doctors or dentists;
- HMRs Reg. 231 – Exemption for supply etc under a PGD by independent hospitals etc.;
- HMRs Reg. 232 – Exemption for supply etc under a PGD by dental practices and clinics: England and Wales;
- HMRs Reg. 233 – Exemption for supply etc under a PGD by persons conducting a retail pharmacy business;
- HMRs Reg. 234 – Exemption for supply etc of products under a PGD to assist the police etc.

Classes of individuals by whom supplies may be made

The following groups may make supplies under a PGD:

- pharmacists
- registered chiropodists and podiatrists
- registered dental hygienists
- registered dental therapists
- registered dietitians
- registered midwives
- registered nurses
- registered occupational therapists
- registered optometrists
- registered orthoptists
- registered orthotists and prosthetists
- registered paramedics
- registered physiotherapists
- registered radiographers
- registered speech and language therapists.

Persons on whose behalf a PGD must be signed, for supply by NHS bodies and local authorities (HMRs Sch. 16, Part 2 and Part 3, as amended)[1,2]

Class of person or force or service by whom or on whose behalf the healthcare is provided or the product is supplied	Person by whom or on whose behalf the Direction must be signed
Common Services Agency	The Agency
Health authority	The health authority
Special health authority	The special health authority
NHS trust or NHS foundation trust	The trust
Local authority	The Chief Executive or Director of Public Health of the local authority
Public Health England	The Chief Executive of Public Health England
Public Health Agency	The Public Health Agency
A person who supplies medicinal products pursuant to an arrangement made with a the Common Services Agency b a health authority c a special health authority d an NHS trust e a clinical commissioning group f the National Health Service Commissioning Board g a local authority h Public Health England i Public Health Agency, or j an NHS foundation trust	The Common Services Agency (where the arrangement has been made with the Agency); otherwise the a health authority b special health authority c NHS trust d a clinical commissioning group e the National Health Service Commissioning Board f a local authority g Chief Executive of Public Health England h Public Health Agency, or i NHS foundation trust, with which the arrangement has been made
A police force in England and Wales	The chief officer of police for that police force (within the meaning of the Police Act 1996)
A police force in Scotland	The chief constable of that police force (within the meaning of the Police (Scotland) Act 1967)
The Police Service of Northern Ireland	The Chief Constable of the Police Service of Northern Ireland

(continued overleaf)

[1] Amended by the National Treatment Agency (Abolition) and the Health and Social Care Act 2012 (Consequential, Transitional and Saving Provisions) Order SI 2013 No. 235
[2] Amended by the Human Medicines (Amendment) Regulations SI 2015 No. 323

Class of person or force or service by whom or on whose behalf the healthcare is provided or the product is supplied	Person by whom or on whose behalf the Direction must be signed
The prison service in England and Wales	The governor of the prison in relation to which the healthcare in question is being provided
The prison service in Scotland	The Scottish Prison Service Management Board
The prison service in Northern Ireland	The Northern Ireland Prison Service Management Board
Her Majesty's Forces	a the Surgeon General b a Medical Director General or c a chief executive of an executive agency of the Ministry of Defence
Contractor carrying out helicopter search and rescue operations on behalf of the Maritime and Coastguard Agency	Medical Director of the contractor carrying out search and rescue operations on behalf of the Maritime and Coastguard Agency

Appendix 3

Schedule 1A to the Poisons Act: Regulated and Reportable Substances

Schedule 1A to the Poisons Act lists regulated and reportable substances. Part 1 lists regulated explosives precursors and Part 2 regulated poisons. Members of the general public require a licence in order to lawfully import, acquire, possess or use one of these regulated substances. Details of the transaction must be entered on to the licence and the item must bear a warning label (see chapter 18). Part 3 lists reportable explosives precursors and Part 4 reportable poisons. No licence is required to possess these substances, but a supplier must report any transaction, involving the supply, or proposed supply, of a regulated or reportable substance to a customer if the supplier has reasonable grounds for believing the transaction to be suspicious.

Part 1 Regulated explosive precursors

Substance	In concentrations (weight in weight) over (%)
Hydrogen peroxide	12
Nitromethane	30
Nitric acid	3
Potassium chlorate	40
Potassium perchlorate	40
Sodium chlorate	40
Sodium perchlorate	40

Part 2 Regulated poisons

Aluminium phosphide

Arsenic; its compounds other than calcium arsenites, copper acetoarsenite, copper arsenates, copper arsenites and lead arsenates

Barium, salts of, other than barium sulfate: barium carbonate and barium silicofluoride

Bromomethane

Chloropicrin

Fluoroacetic acid; its salts; fluoroacetamide

Hydrogen cyanide; metal cyanides, other than ferrocyanides and ferricyanides

Lead acetates; compounds of lead with acids from fixed oils

Magnesium phosphide

Mercury, compounds of: nitrates of mercury, oxides of mercury, mercuric cyanide oxides, mercuric thiocyanate, ammonium mercuric chlorides, potassium mercuric iodides, organic compounds of mercury that contain a methyl (CH_3) group directly linked to the mercury atom

Oxalic acid in concentrations over 10% weight in weight

Phenols (phenol; phenolic isomers of cresols, xylenols, monoethylphenols); compounds of phenols with a metal in concentrations over 60% weight in weight of phenols or, for compounds of phenols with a metal, the equivalent of 60% weight in weight of phenols

Phosphorus, yellow

Strychnine; its salts; its quaternary compounds

Thallium, salts of

Part 3 Reportable explosives precursors

Hexamine

Sulfuric acid

Acetone

Potassium nitrate

Sodium nitrate

Calcium nitrate

Calcium ammonium nitrate

Ammonium nitrate in concentration of 16% by weight of nitrogen in relation to ammonium nitrate or higher

Part 4 Reportable poisons

For circumstances where requirements of the Act do not apply to a specified substance or mixture, see regulations made under section 9B of the amended Act.

Aldicarb

Alpha-chloralose

Ammonia in concentrations greater than 10% w/w

Arsenic, compounds of: calcium arsenites; copper acetoarsenite; copper arsenates; copper arsenites; lead arsenates

Barium, salts of: barium carbonate; barium silicofluoride

Carbofuran

Cycloheximide

Dinitrocresols (DNOC); their compounds with a metal or a base

Dinoseb; its compounds with a metal or a base

Dinoterb

Drazoxolon; its salts

Endosulfan

Endothal; its salts

Endrin

Fentin, compounds of

Formaldehyde, in concentrations greater than 5% weight in weight

Formic acid, in concentrations greater than 25% weight in weight

Hydrochloric acid, in concentrations greater than 10% weight in weight

Hydrofluoric acid; alkali metal bifluorides; ammonium bifluoride; alkali metal fluorides; ammonium fluoride; sodium silicofluoride

Mercuric chloride; mercuric iodide; organic compounds of mercury except compounds that contain a methyl (CH_3) group directly linked to the mercury atom

Metallic oxalates

Methomyl

Nicotine; its salts; its quaternary compounds

Nitrobenzene, in concentrations greater than 0.1% weight in weight

Oxamyl

Paraquat, salts of

Phenols (as defined in Part 2 of Schedule 1A) in substances containing no more than 60% weight in weight of phenols; compounds of phenols with a metal in substances containing no more than the equivalent of 60% weight in weight of phenols

Phosphoric acid

Phosphorus compounds: azinphos-methyl, chlorfenvinphos, demephion, demeton-*S*-methyl, demeton-*S*-methyl sulfone, dialifos, dichlorvos, dioxathion, disulfoton, fonofos, mecarbam, mephosfolan, methidathion, mevinphos, omethoate, oxydemeton-methyl, parathion, phenkapton, phorate, phosphamidon, pirimiphos-ethyl, quinalphos, thiometon, thionazin, triazophos, vamidothion

Potassium hydroxide, greater than 17% of total caustic alkalinity

Sodium hydroxide, greater than 12% of total caustic alkalinity

Sodium nitrite

Thiofanox

Zinc phosphide

Appendix 4

Summary of standards of conduct, ethics and performance (until 1 May 2017)

This document sets out the standards of conduct, ethics and performance that pharmacy professionals must follow. The Council uses the term 'pharmacy professionals' for pharmacists and pharmacy technicians registered with them.

It is important that pharmacy professionals meet the standards and are able to practise safely and effectively. Their conduct will be judged against the standards, and failure to comply could put registration at risk. When the Council receives complaints or concerns against a pharmacy professional it is these standards that are considered when deciding whether or not any action against that individual is necessary. The Council stresses that these standards apply in whichever sector of the profession a pharmacist or technician practises and so they also apply in education, research and other settings, even if the professional is not involved in interacting directly with patients or the public.

There are seven standards and pharmacy professionals must comply with each. Within each standard there are a number of components (number in parentheses).

1 Make patients your first concern (10).
2 Use your professional judgement in the interests of patients and the public (5).
3 Show respect for others (9).
4 Encourage patients and the public to participate in decisions about their care (7).
5 Develop your professional knowledge and competence (5).

6 Be honest and trustworthy (9).

7 Take responsibility for your working practices (12).

Included within the document the Council states:

We do not dictate how you should meet our standards. Each standard can normally be met in more than one way and the way in which you meet our standards may change over time. The standards are of equal importance.

You are professionally accountable for your practice. This means that you are responsible for what you do or do not do, no matter what advice or direction your manager or another professional gives you. You must use your professional judgement when deciding on a course of action and you should use our standards as a basis when making those decisions.

You may be faced with conflicting professional or legal responsibilities. In these circumstances, you must consider all possible courses of action, and the risks and benefits associated with each one, to decide what is in the best interests of patients and the public.

Index

Note: Page references in axx refer to appendices; bxx refer to boxes; fxx refer to Figures; and those in txx refer to Tables